Y0-CPE-456

Sustainable Development

Bridging the Research/Policy Gaps in
Southern Contexts

Sustainable Development

Bridging the Research/Policy Gaps in Southern Contexts

VOL. 2: SOCIAL POLICY

OXFORD

UNIVERSITY PRESS

Great Clarendon Street, Oxford OX2 6DP

Oxford University Press is a department of the University of Oxford.
It furthers the University's objective of excellence in research, scholarship,
and education by publishing worldwide in

Oxford New York

Auckland Cape Town Dar es Salaam Hong Kong Karachi
Kuala Lumpur Madrid Melbourne Mexico City Nairobi
New Delhi Shanghai Taipei Toronto

with offices in

Argentina Austria Brazil Chile Czech Republic France Greece
Guatemala Hungary Italy Japan Poland Portugal Singapore
South Korea Switzerland Turkey Ukraine Vietnam

Oxford is a registered trade mark of Oxford University Press
in the UK and in certain other countries

© Oxford University Press 2005

The moral rights of the authors have been asserted

First published 2005

All rights reserved. No part of this publication may be reproduced, translated,
stored in a retrieval system, or transmitted, in any form or by any means,
without the prior permission in writing of Oxford University Press.
Enquiries concerning reproduction should be sent to
Oxford University Press at the address below.

This book is sold subject to the condition that it shall not, by way
of trade or otherwise, be lent, re-sold, hired out or otherwise circulated
without the publisher's prior consent in any form of binding or cover
other than that in which it is published and without a similar condition
including this condition being imposed on the subsequent purchaser.

ISBN 978-0-19-597998-5

Disclaimer: The findings, interpretations, and conclusions expressed in this study are
entirely those of the authors and should not be attributed in any manner to the
Sustainable Development Policy Institute and the Oxford University Press.

Poster design by Nigar Nazar

Second Impression 2007

Typeset in Times
Printed in Pakistan by
Kagzi Printers, Karachi.
Published by
Sustainable Development Policy Institute
3, UN, Boulevard, Diplomatic Enclave I, Islamabad.
and
Ameena Saiyid, Oxford University Press
No. 38, Sector 15, Korangi Industrial Area, PO Box 8214
Karachi-74900, Pakistan.

CONTENTS

Alternative Realities: The Voice and Role of Fiction Writers

Mass Media, Civil Society and Advocacy

Population, Health and Poverty

PREFACE

This book results from our concern for translating specialized multi and transdisciplinary research into effective policy measures in the global South. For this purpose, SDPI organized a conference entitled, 'Sustainable Development: Bridging the research/policy gaps in Southern Contexts,' where researchers, academicians, creative writers, theorists, activists and policy-makers came together to debate and discuss issues such as: How can the research we produce in third world contexts be translated into effective policy for sustainable development? Is sustainable development only a question of reorienting the research/policy connections? Or, is it about claiming and putting value into the fragmented and disparate work that speaks to and about the third world? These themes can be seen in almost all the sections of this two-volume effort.

Both volumes highlight the crosscutting linkages between the environment and social sectors and the increasingly complex demands upon the policy arena to respond to these issues quickly and effectively. The first volume addresses the broad theme of the environment and its interface with governance and globalization; the second volume addresses the issue of sustainable development *vis-a-vis* the social sectors.

The contributors to the two volumes investigate critical policy issues about knowledge production and its appropriate utilization. The first volume examines these issues in the context of the natural environment and its impact upon human life. Specifically, the first section in this volume looks at the environmental dimensions of human security and livelihoods, at natural resource management and its interface with governance issues, at the design and enforcement of environmental quality standards in South Asia, and renewable energy. The second section addresses trade and sustainable development, globalization and the WTO in the context of people's livelihoods, and governance issues.

Contributors to the second volume examine the complex interlinkages between gender issues and labor policy, peace and conflict, migration, education, language and identity, mass media and its control, population policy and the pressures to conform to global agendas. Most interestingly, this volume also contains a section on the voices and role of fiction writers in the production of alternative realities. The different thematic subsections in this volume consistently highlight the relevance of knowledge production in the South and their relationship with the dominant discourses of power.

Although there are no definitive answers, we have raised important issues and debates in these two volumes that are challenging and will continue to occupy central position in many people's thought and work in the third and first worlds. Finally, on a note of caution, the authors have attempted to focus on the conceptual issues involved in the different debates; they might be relying on data from late 2003 or early 2004. For us, the important issue is to outline the trends and patterns with regard to sustainable development in South Asia.

Saba Gul Khattak
Executive Director
SDPI

ACKNOWLEDGEMENTS

This anthology comes out of the papers presented at the Sustainable Development Policy Institute's (SDPI) Sixth Sustainable Development Conference (SDC) held from 11-13 December 2003 in Islamabad, Pakistan. The overarching theme of the Conference was 'Sustainable Development: Bridging the Research/Policy Gaps in Southern Contexts'. The anthology consists of research papers, thought pieces, essays, perspectives and literary writings contributed by researchers, scholars, journalists, academics and fiction writers from across different regions of the world—Pakistan, India, Bangladesh, Nepal, Latin America, USA, Canada and Europe.

The SDPI acknowledges the financial support provided by the following institutions for the Sixth Sustainable Development Conference: Norwegian Development Agency (NORAD); Swiss Agency for Development and Cooperation (SDC); Heinrich Boll Foundation (HBL); Friedrich Ebert Stiftung (FES); The Asia Foundation (TAF); South Asia Watch on Trade, Economics and Environment (SAWTEE); International Institute for Environment and Development (IIED); National Institute for Competence in Research (NCCR); the British Council; and the Gender Equality Project (GEP) managed by the British Council and funded by the Department for International Development (DFID).

The SDPI is grateful to the entire staff who extended their full support for the Conference in various ways right from the conceptualization of the overarching theme of the Conference to organizing the numerous panels, to getting the posters designed and printed and to ensuring that the event went on smoothly at the venue and that the guests were looked after.

Finally, a special note of appreciation goes to Shafqat Shehzad, Research Fellow; Kiran Ahmed, Research Associate; Sarah Siddiq, PEP Coordinator, and Huma A. Waheed, SDC intern, who assisted the SDC Coordinator in text editing, in standardizing the bibliography/ reference style of the final papers and in proofreading of the final copy printed in this anthology.

Uzma T. Haroon
SDC Coordinator
Sustainable Development Policy Institute
3, UN Boulevard, Diplomatic Enclave I
Islamabad
Phone: (92-51) 2278-146, 2278-134, 2278-136
Fax: (92-51) 2278-135
URL: www.sdpi.org
Email: main@sdpi.org

Note of appreciation

The SDPI is grateful for technical and editorial advice on the papers from the following colleagues and friends:

Ratnakar Adhikari, South Asia Watch on Trade, Economics & Environment, Kathmandu, Nepal.
Kiran Ahmed, Sustainable Development Policy Institute, Islamabad, Pakistan.
Karamat Ali, Pakistan Institute of Labour Education and Research, Karachi, Pakistan.
Farzana Bari, Quaid-e-Azam University, Islamabad, Pakistan.
Lubna Chaudhry, State University at Binghampton University, New York, USA.
Mita Ditta, Consumer Unity and Trust Society, Calcutta, India.
Lars Dyrud, Quaid-e-Azam University, Islamabad, Pakistan.
Ali Ercelawn, Pakistan Institute of Labour Education and Research, Karachi, Pakistan.
Kiran Habib, Sustainable Development Policy Institute, Islamabad, Pakistan.
Saiful Islam, University of Rajshahi, Rajshahi, Bangladesh.
A. R. Kamal, PIDE, Quaid-e-Azam Unviersity, Islamabad, Pakistan.
Aliya Khan, Quaid-e-Azam University, Islamabad, Pakistan.
Shaheen Rafi Khan, Sustainable Development Policy Institute, Islamabad, Pakistan.
Foqia Sadiq Khan, Sustainable Development Policy Institute, Islamabad, Pakistan.
Saba Gul Khattak, Sustainable Development Policy Institute, Islamabad, Pakistan.
Mahmood A. Khwaja, Sustainable Development Policy Institute, Islamabad, Pakistan.
Sajid Kazmi, Sustainable Development Policy Institute, Islamabad, Pakistan.
Khawar Mumtaz, Shirkat Gah, Lahore, Pakistan.
Shafqat Munir, ActionAid, Islamabad, Pakistan.
Yameema Mitha, Mazmoon-e-Shauq, Islamabad, Pakistan.
Maniza Naqvi, Fiction Writer, Washington DC, USA.
Rita Pandey, National Institute of Public Finance and Policy, New Delhi, India.
Ali Abbas Qazilbash, Trust for Voluntary Organizations, Islamabad, Pakistan.
Tariq Rehman, Quaid-e-Azam University, Islamabad, Pakistan.
Ram Charitra Sah, Forum for Protection of Public Interest, Kathmandu, Nepal.
Rubina Saigol, SAHE, Lahore, Pakistan.
Ameena Saiyid, Oxford University Press, Karachi, Pakistan.
Ahmad Salim, Sustainable Development Policy Institute, Islamabad, Pakistan.
Karin A. Siegmann, Sustainable Development Policy Institute, Islamabad, Pakistan.
Faisal Shaheen, Sustainable Development Policy Institute, Islamabad, Pakistan.
Shafqat Shehzad, Sustainable Development Policy Institute, Islamabad, Pakistan.
Farhat Sheikh, The Asia Foundation, Islamabad, Pakistan.
Abid Suleri, OXFAM GB, Islamabad, Pakistan.
Eaisha Tareen, Psychologist and Sociologist, Colchester, England.
S. Akbar Zaidi, Economist, Karachi, Pakistan.

1
LABOR POLICY IN PAKISTAN

*Karamat Ali**

ABSTRACT

This paper looks at the formulation of Labor Policy in South Asia, with a specific focus on Pakistan. In the era of globalization, basic labor rights, especially the right of association and collective bargaining are being severely curtailed in South Asian countries.

This situation can be traced back to colonial times, when granting unconditional rights to workers in the colonies was opposed. This resulted in 50 per cent of Pakistan's labor force, engaged in agriculture, not being recognized as workers under the labor law. This labor force also had a dismally low level (3 per cent) of unionization. In 1959, under Ayub Khan's government, a new labor policy was announced.

As a result, until 1969, Pakistan did not have a basic trade union law and the labor policy was characterized by arbitrariness. The Industrial Relations Ordinance (IRO) promulgated in 1969, did not address the basic problems of workers' rights. Due to its long list of exclusions and the lack of coverage of the agricultural labor force, it applied only to around 10 per cent of the labor force in Pakistan. This did not change with the new IRO implemented in 2002.

The paper stresses that the attitudes of the ruling elites are important in determining what happens to the rights of the workers, since they do not allow the passage of any law that will harm their self-interests.

*Karamat Ali is the Executive Director of Pakistan Institute of Labor Education & Research (PILER), Karachi.

The last eight or nine years of the twentieth century marked the advent of globalization in the form of liberalization of the economy and de-regulation of labor markets. This has happened, either as a result of imposition of structural adjustment programs, or due to the imperatives of the new global capitalist trade and investment regimes under the WTO. The de-regulation of markets demands dilution or complete withdrawal of most or all legal protections for labor. They are seen as labor market distortions and irritants. Thus, we observe a process in all South Asian countries where the basic labor rights, especially the right of association and collective bargaining is being severely curtailed. This is a blatant violation of their constitutions that guarantee these rights. Additionally all South Asian countries are signatories to the ILO Conventions, especially conventions 87 and 98, which pertain respectively, to the right of association and collective bargaining. These measures are also in violation of the Universal Declaration of Human Rights to which these governments are signatories.

This has been happening despite the fact that in 1995, just before the Marrakech Declaration, at a meeting of non-aligned and developing countries, held in Delhi, the labor ministers unanimously agreed and signed a declaration committing themselves to recognize and respect all basic rights as guaranteed by the ILO Conventions. They took the position that labor rights should not be linked to trade in the new WTO arrangement. However, they have failed to fulfill that commitment. This commitment was reiterated in Seattle at the WTO ministerial meeting and various other meetings of the WTO. In South Asia, there is no country that has a level of unionization beyond five to ten percent. So, a vast majority of labor in South Asia is unorganized, insecure and lacks basic legal protection. This is a deplorable state of affairs.

A common feature of labor policies and laws in this region has been that at the time of independence, it inherited a common set of laws and policies formulated by the British administration in India, beginning from the 1920s. These policies and laws were common to Pakistan, India, Sri Lanka and Bangladesh. Nepal however, did not have any labor laws at that juncture. The basic principles of the labor policy were enunciated by the then British secretary of Colonies, Lord Passfield, a renowned sociologist and a distinguished member of the British labor party, in the famous, Passfield Memorandum of 1929. He and his wife had written various books on trade unions and labor rights before he became the secretary. The Passfield Memorandum discusses how and to what extent, labor rights should be accorded to workers in the colonies. He opposed the granting of unconditional rights for workers in colonies and argued:

> Without sympathetic supervision and guidance, organizations of laborers without experience of combination for any social and economic progress may fall under the domination of the disaffected persons by which their activities may be diverted to improper and mischievous ends.[1]

In 1929, such thinking lay behind the labor policy that was being formulated in the sub-continent. Again in 1943, the then Governor General of India was asked whether the right to strike should be accorded to workers in India. He said, "Not at all, as at this stage in the evolution of trade unions it will be pre-mature, indeed dangerous".[2]

If one looks at the present situation in 2003, in most South Asian countries and specifically in Pakistan, it seems that the ghost of Lord Passfield decisively influenced the process of formulation of labor policies and laws. When the Trade Union Act of 1926, the basic law governing the formation and administration of trade unions in the Indian sub-continent, came for discussion in 1925, in the imperial legislative council, there were two members who consistently argued for basic labor rights and fought for unconditional rights of association for all workers, except the uniformed employees of the armed forces. Even the non-uniformed civilian employees of the armed forces had the right to form unions under this Act. Who were these two? They were Mr. P.C. Joshi and Mr. Mohammad Ali Jinnah, both well-known social reformers from Bombay. It should be mandatory for labor policy makers in South Asia, especially those in Pakistan, to have a close look at that debate. It shows the commitment that Mr. Jinnah, the founder of Pakistan, had to the basic democratic rights of all people, including labor. But soon after the creation of Pakistan, the state started curtailing the rights that were already available to workers under the 1926 Trade Union Act. Today, agriculture workers are not considered as workers under the labor law. No labor law is applicable to labor in agriculture that accounts for close to 50 percent of the entire labor force.

In the early years of Pakistan, most unions existed in the service sector, as there were very few industries. However, the level of unionization was relatively high at over 30 per cent. Today, as stated earlier, the level of unionization in South Asia is below 10 per cent, but in Pakistan, it is dismally low at less than 3 per cent. Over 97 per cent of labor in Pakistan is unorganized and denied of their basic rights through a cynical manipulation of various legal instruments. Workers' rights are curtailed by differentiating workers on the basis of number of workers employed in an organization, and by not allowing the formation of industrial trade unions. In Pakistan, only plant-based or enterprise based unions are permitted—again a curtailment of rights that existed under the Act of 1926, whereby the workers could freely form unions of their own choice. There was no state intervention as to what kind of union would be formed. Consequently, in the early 1950s, unions such as the tonga drivers union, bidi-makers union, shoemakers union, and transport workers unions, etc., existed. Today, this is not possible. In 1959, Ayub Khan's government, tampered with the 1926 act. A new labor policy was announced, whereby, the Trade Union Act 1926 and the Industrial Disputes Act of 1947 were scrapped. This ended the possibility of forming industrial unions. For the next ten years, Pakistan did not have a trade union law and the labor policy was characterized by blatant arbitrariness. The bureaucracy and the employers did whatever they felt like, making this a very dark period in Pakistan's labor history. This finally led to the emergence of a tremendous countrywide mobilization of labor in 1968. These mobilizations contributed considerably to the downfall of Ayub Khan's dictatorship.

The 1969 labor policy announced by Mr. Noor Khan was an extremely interesting document. The Industrial Relations Ordinance (IRO) candidly recognized the negative attitudes towards labor rights associations prevalent among the government and the employers. It was noted that:

...the employers have looked upon trade unions as instruments rather than an institution through which mutual give and take can lead to peaceful resolution of conflict... They have therefore used all sort of unfair means to inhibit the growth of trade unions.[3]

The document goes on to describe the government's attitude. It says:

the government itself is too conscious of the need to keep the production going regardless of the human and social costs involved and in many cases prohibited the expression of industrial conflict rather than trying to resolve it. It is obvious that just as in national life, the government failed to appreciate the importance of political process. So also in industrial relations it has not realized that conflicts cannot be resolved by their suppression; they can only be resolved through a process of mutual give and take which is only possible through strong trade union institution particularly in labor surplus economies where otherwise the individual worker is in a weak bargaining position in relation to the employers.[4]

After admitting all this, when the new law, the Industrial Relations Ordinance (IRO) 1969 was promulgated, it did not address the basic problems so vividly described in the policy document. For example, it did not apply to labor in agriculture. It had a long list of exclusions, and in the end, as the ILO asserted, the Industrial Relations Ordinance 1969, applied only to around 25 percent of the labor force in Pakistan. However, in practice it was made even more restrictive when the Rules were framed for its operationalization. In our current system, the officers of the labor ministry frame Rules exclusively, after the promulgation of a Law. Whereas, the laws should at least be discussed at a tripartite level among representatives of the workers, employers and the government, but here, rule-making is the exclusive preserve of the bureaucrats. This is a regressive process as compared to the practice under the colonial rule. If one examines the Trade Union Act 1926, the rules were framed along with the law and were passed by the then parliament, or rather, the legislative council, there was thus no possibility for a bureaucrat to curtail basic rights by forming distorted rules. In Pakistan, however, this has changed and thus what the workers are allowed in a particular law can be taken away when the rules are formed. The real applicability of the basic labor laws, such as the IRO, is thus brought down to merely 10 per cent of the work force.

What are the reasons for such developments? Both the kind of economic development policies that have been adopted, as well as the attitudes that the employers and the governments have had towards the working people, have to be considered. The social and political attitudes of the ruling elites are equally important in determining what happens to the rights of the workers. Pakistan inherited many colonial legacies, including a huge absentee, feudal landlord class. Mr. Mohammad Ali Jinnah defined this class very succinctly in 1943, while addressing the Muslim League Council Session in Delhi. He spelt out his future policy for the new state and made the following statement:

> Here I should like to give a warning to the landlords and capitalists who have flourished at our expense by a system which is so vicious, which is so wicked and which makes them so selfish that it is difficult to reason with them. The exploitation of the masses has got into their blood. They have forgotten the lessons of Islam. Greed and selfishness have made these people subordinate to the interests of others in order to fatten themselves. I have visited villages. There are millions and millions of our peoples who hardly get one meal a day. Is this civilization? Is this the aim of Pakistan? Do you visualize millions have been exploited and cannot get one meal a day. If that is the idea of Pakistan I would not have it. If they are wise they will have to adjust themselves to the new modern conditions of life. If they do not, God help them, we shall not help them.[5]

So, here he was basically saying the new state would not help the oppressive and exploitative feudal lords. The new state would instead, help those who had been exploited by them, but unfortunately, soon after the creation of Pakistan, Jinnah died. Soon afterwards, the same landlords took over the reins of the state and decided there would be no land reforms. Jinnah had set up a committee to look into the question of land tenures. Its report was released in 1948 and is a very illuminating document. An unusual bureaucrat, Mr. Masood Khadarposh, wrote a note of dissent. It suggested that the first step to democratize this country is to do away with the sharecropping system. Radical land reforms were needed and by principle, land must be distributed to the actual tillers. His advice was completely ignored. Since then, the landlord class has further expanded in numbers, as well as increased its influence considerably. One reason for the development and persistence of the present retrogressive labor policy and laws is that in Pakistan, landlords dominate the parliament, the bureaucracy, and the upper layers of the leadership in the armed forces. They will not allow any law that will hit at their interests. The second reason is the attitude of the state functionaries towards the people. In an interview, the Director General of the Barani Areas Development Program in the Punjab in 1984, a serving Army General, made this shocking observation, when asked about the prospects of agricultural development. He said:

> The 245,000 villages of Pakistan are economically redundant. What can we do with these people? The best thing is to get them as soon as possible out of the country. So they help the country, which they kept hitherto in a state of backwardness, by their remittances. We better demolish the old villages and build one modern township for every ten of them.[6]

What kind of a labor policy can be expected, when people who are running the state have these kinds of attitudes towards the working people? In 1946, when the Pakistan resolution was slightly amended in the General Council of the Muslim League in Delhi, the preamble of the resolution reiterated the reasons for the creation of Pakistan. One of the main given reasons was that Hinduism, due to the caste system, is an obstacle to equality in human development. It clearly implied that the new state would do away with the caste system. However, after the creation of Pakistan this hideous social system has been reinforced. Thus, the concept of human equality is absent at all levels and the working people in our society are known as 'kammees'—the lowest on the earth. This too is reflected in labor policies. The Pakistani establishment has been devising policies and making laws for those kammees, not for the citizens of an independent state. That is the major reason why even in year 2002, when the new Industrial Relation Ordinance (IRO 2002) was promulgated, its authors maintained the old practices and perspectives. Section 4 of the IRO reads as follows:

> It shall apply to all persons employed in any establishment or group of establishments or industry except those employed;(a) in the police or any of the defense services of Pakistan; (b) in any installation or services exclusively connected with the armed forces of Pakistan including ministry of defense lines of the railways; (c) by the Pakistan Security Printing Corporation or the security papers limited or Pakistan mint; (d) in the administration of state other than those employed as workmen by the railways, post telegraph and telephone department; (e) by an establishment or institution maintained for the treatment or care of sick, infirms, destitutes and mentally unfit persons excluding those run on commercial basis; (f) by an institution established for payment of employees' old age pensions or for workers welfare; (g) as a member of watch and ward, Security or Fire Service staff of an oil refinery or of an establishment engaged in the production, transmission or distribution of natural gas or liquefied petroleum gas or petroleum products or of a seaport or an airport.
> Provided that the Federal Government may suspend, in the public interest, by an order published in the official Gazette; the application of this Ordinance to any establishment or industry for a period specified in the order but not exceeding six months at a time.[7]

Agriculture labor is not covered by the Ordinance. Due to these exceptions and exclusions, the new Ordinance covers only a tiny fraction of the work force. It is even more regrettable because, for the first time in the history of Pakistan, there was a bilateral consensus between employers' organizations and workers' organizations, as well as tripartite consensus at the level of workers, employees and the government achieved at the Pakistan Tripartite Labor Conference (PTCL), held in July 2001.

Pakistan is under obligation to respect such a consensus as it has ratified the ILO convention on tripartism. It must also honour the recommendations of the tripartite labor conference. The late minister for labor, Omar Asghar Khan had worked hard to create such a precious consensus. It is worthwhile to have a look at the recommendations of the tripartite labor conference as it created agreement on two very important issues: the right of association should be accorded to all workers except armed forces and the police; all basic laws will be extended to agriculture and the informal sector. This was a major step forward recorded in the files of labor ministry.

When the Ministry of Labor drafted the new law after the 2001 tripartite conference called 'Draft IRO 2001', it was sent to PILER for comments. In PILER's five-page comment, we drew attention to the fact that the drafters had completely ignored and failed to incorporate the basic consensus and other recommendations of the tripartite conference in the draft. The minister for labor agreed with the observations and instructed the Secretary of the ministry to revise the draft accordingly. He wrote:

> I have reviewed the detailed comments of the Pakistan Institute of Labor Education and Research on the draft IRO-2001. I endorse these comments and would like the Ministry of Labor, Manpower and Overseas Pakistanis to now revise the draft IRO-2001 in the light of these comments so that the spirit of the discussions held in the Labor Advisory Council, WEBCOP and the PTCL held in July 2001, are reflected in the IRO-2001.[8]

Unfortunately, the revision that followed after the resignation of Omar Asghar Khan in December 2001, reflected an even more blatant disregard of the consensus, as well as the instructions of the Minister, and further curtailed the basic rights of labor. Today, the implementation of labor laws stands totally suspended as all the provincial governments have decided to suspend inspection of factories and other work places, ostensibly as a measure to restore investors' confidence. Most labor courts in the country are lying empty, as there are no judges. Who, even when they are there, are not known for dispensing justice.

All institutions created for the welfare of labor need urgent reforms as currently they cover less than 10 percent of workers. Yet, the three recent reports (done between 2000–2001) lying with the ministry relating to the reform/ restructuring of the Employee's Old Age Benefits Institution (EOBI), of the Employees Social Security Schemes (ESSIs) and of the Workers Welfare Fund (WWF) scheme. Also there seems to be no serious discussion on their implementation.

Today, a very disturbing situation prevails in Pakistan, wherein labor has its hands tied, as legal rights are not protected. A similar situation exists elsewhere in South Asia. History states that there are big upheavals in South Asian countries after every 10 to 15 years' of total neglect of labor interests. Most economic gains made by our countries under authoritarian labor control regimes are nullified by such upheavals. Pakistan is rapidly heading once again in that direction, whether we have a military government or a civilian one. It is, therefore, imperative to take a fresh look at the policy formulation not only in the context of a single country but also in the wider context of the SAARC region. For example, there are around three million South Asian workers in Pakistan. We must also legislate for them to protect their basic human and labor rights. If we really wish to make SAARC a regional economic cooperation organization, we will have to recognize the rights of all South Asians to be able to come and work in each other's country with equal rights as workers, if not as citizens. We will have to ensure protection of core labor rights in the region to collectively face the challenge of the ever-increasing domination of the global economy by the advanced industrialized countries. Otherwise, this overwhelming thrust of globalization is going to throw our societies back into the 19th century where slave drivers will control labor and democracy will become a thing of the past.

Notes

1. H. Jeffrey, Trade Union Foreign Policy: A study of British and American Trade Union Activities in Jamaica, Macmillan, 1972, p. 208.
2. Op. cit.
3. Government of Pakistan, Labor Policy 1969, p. 3.
4. Op. cit.
5. Jinnah, Mohammad, Presidential address at the 30th Session of All-India Muslim League, Delhi, 24 April 1943.
6. Director General Barani Areas Development Program, in interview by Joost Kuitenbrouwer, in 'Rural politics and contradictions in Pakistan in the Seventies and their implications for the Eighties,' I.S.S. Working Paper no. 20, The Hague, 1984.
7. Government of Paksitan, The Industrial Relations Ordinance 2002, Karachi: The Ideal Labor Laws, Karachi, 2003.
8. Official note from the Minister's Desk, addressed to Secretary (LMOP), 17 September 2001 in the Labor Laws file of the Ministry at Islamabad.

2

WOMEN AT WORK IN BONDAGE: UNFREE LABOR IN PAKISTAN

*A. Ercelan**

ABSTRACT

This note draws attention to the economic, social and political arrangements which restrict income opportunities by compelling labor supply for nominal or nil compensation, or which tie labor services to a specific employer. Women are focused upon for the obvious reason that they remain excluded from much advocacy and most policy interventions even though they form a large part of unfree labor, and bear additional burdens of bondage in South Asia.

Sharecropping agriculture remains the major sector for unfree labor. However, recent research shows an increasing presence of forced labor in industry, driven by a similar need to intensify labor services, in order to procure high returns on capital. An attempt is made to contrast situations according to the degree of effective and substantive bondage.

The issue is not a market or non-market economy, but rather a developmental versus predatory state, that supports a humane or oppressive society. The note illustrates that *mitigation* and *relief* from oppressive working conditions is a feasible objective for both activists and the government. This objective must be achieved in a society and state where women and migrants are classed as second rate citizens. Naturally, *eradication* of forced labor depends upon the broader political struggles for realising fundamental economic and social *rights for all* through a vigorously participatory democracy.

Exploitation, including sexual harassment, prevails upon the labor force. Also, *bonded* labor is an extreme combination of the many dimensions of exploitation—where socially imposed circumstances of the weak force them into bondage with the powerful, because of an unjust and uncaring state.

---

*The author is Senior Research Fellow at the Pakistan Institute of Labor Education & Research (PILER), Karachi, Pakistan.

INTRODUCTION

The paper supports a debate on public action towards realisation of women's rights to fuller lives and prosperous livelihoods. It focuses on both rights to work and at work that are grossly violated in situations of unfree labor, and specially of debt bondage in Pakistan. Observations are drawn primarily from PILER's recent report on the brick kiln industry through field assessments in and around six cities (across all provinces except Balochistan), and an earlier PILER report on Sindh agriculture.[1] These observations are supplemented from studies in other sectors.[2]

The article begins with an outline of unfree labor and its various aspects. It concludes with an exploration of public action towards redress of inequities for women as unfree labor.

UNFREE LABOR

Two circumstances may be distinguished.[3] One is a general situation of *forced labor* regardless of the size of debt. This subsumes situations of *debt bondage* when additional or more onerous obligations are imposed upon indebted labor through advances or subsequent loans. Since the *quit option* is unavailable or quite expensive to avail for debt-bonded labor, their obligations become more substantive and effective.

Labor becomes unfree when forced to provide services for nominal or nil compensation (or uncertain future compensation that remains very much at the employer's discretion, traditions notwithstanding)—through explicit or implicit threats of physical or *economic violence* such as deprivation of job, land or housing.

Such indentured services can be unrelated to the production process. Typically, families of sharecroppers and permanent labor are required to provide domestic services to landlords in return for meals and the like, or sometimes as implicit rent for housing. As women are made more insecure than men, by family, society and state they are therefore, more intensively affected by unfree labor e.g. through type, duration and timing of required services. Another source of inequity arises when men are spared additional tasks in order to intensify their labor in production. Some times the managers and employers may demand sexual services from women as a personal privilege, or as a price for escaping labor services.

Forced labor can be required in the production process itself. Sharecropper families are required to work for nominal or no wage at farming tasks on 'self-cultivated' parcels of the landlord (or neighbouring landlord). All costs and no (or very uncertain) benefits as the lot of labor is obvious in this case. Forced labor also arises when labor is intensified on sharecropped land and the burden of this intensification falls largely or wholly on the sharecropper family. It is assumed that fairness requires at least equal shares in all costs. Since specific tasks are the responsibility of the sharecropper, the implicit costs of using family labor fall upon the sharecropper. However, this is not reflected in output receipts, specially when gross output does not increase in proportion to labor input. Particularly stark is the inequity resulting from forced labor for long-term improvements on the farm that may or may not be available to the same sharecropper in the future. Again, the situation of women may be more inequitable through type, duration and timing of their contributions (even ignoring the implications of double burdens for women).

Forced labor through the family is inevitable for household survival at low output levels, low (explicit or implicit) output share rates and high shares of purchased inputs for the tenant—when all labor is properly accounted for, then average earnings per labor unit are even lower than the prevailing dismal wage rates. Though such intensification of labor input is apparent in agriculture, the situation also prevails in industry e.g. in brick kilns where entire families of *Patheras* prepare clay bricks. A family could barely survive at prevailing low piece rates unless adult male labor was supplemented by labor of women and children. However, since compensation for the resulting additional output of bricks does not fully account for supplemental labor, such labor should be considered as forced labor. In the event, such labor is extracted from women. Another method to extract such labor is by imposing otherwise unachievable output levels on adult males—specially when debt servicing threatens bare subsistence.

It is not just the landlord/employer, but also adult men in the household who collaborate in imposing unfree labor upon women. Frequently restricted to family labor by social norms, women cannot choose alternative employment—that could yield higher incomes for the same labor effort, both to them personally and to the family. Ease of child care at family work site also biases women towards family labor. Migrant families, so common among *Patheras*, will generally have women working at most tasks related to making bricks. Locals, however, will often work only as all-male labor units at the kiln, with women working as casual farm labor.

A landlord or an employer cannot intensify labor services if family members were let free to work elsewhere at their own discretion. Family as 'tied' labor is another instance of unfree labor common to both sharecropping agriculture and industry such as brick kilns.[4] Since non-farm work opportunities are specially restricted to them, women become particularly constrained even if some adult males are permitted to work elsewhere. Whatever the nature of labor services provided in the production process, women do so as family labor where men deal with other men as regards tasks, output and earnings. This means that women are denied direct compensation, and hence payment for their contribution—however meagre that may be. Such women workers therefore become a specially exploited category of forced labor.

DEBT BONDAGE

When advances and loans result in *substantive and effective* obligations upon labor, such labor is said to be in debt bondage. The neoliberal position of a 'voluntary' contract must be as forcefully rejected as one would reject the 'free trade' involved in 'your money or your life' imposed by a dacoit robber.

As implied by the term, labor becomes bound to the employer or labor for services in special ways. Bondage requires labor to provide services entirely at the discretion of the landlord or employer. Inevitably, labor and their families become more vulnerable to various forms of forced labor. Women, in particular, become more subject to abuse in the production process as well as in predatory behaviour.

Locked into debt bondage, labor is not free to work elsewhere until the debt is redeemed. This constraint extends even to slack periods in farming, or when a brick kiln is closed for the season. Since intensification of labor is the objective, all adults are bound in this fashion if they have been part of the labor pool. For young women, there is an option of marriage that takes them away from the farm or kiln. Unfortunately, marriages often keep them in the same class of labor. Since (potential and open-ended) labor services is the primary, and sometimes the only, collateral for debts, it is inevitable that the landlord or employer attempts to place the entire family in debt bondage by threats—explicit or implicit. These are threats of physical and economic violence upon labor and family. Invariably labor is landless, and hence a potent threat is eviction from the residence provided by the landlord or employer. Women are naturally made to feel more insecure through this threat. A specific situation of bondage may be ended by transfer of the labor pool to some other landlord or employer who redeems the existing debt through a new advance to labor. Hence labor continues in bondage, where the new creditor may want to extract more forced labor.

Flight from bondage may occur in particularly intolerable situations. But this is made more difficult by insisiting that women and children stay behind when men take leave, i.e. holding women as hostage. Another instrument of effective restraint is the *jamadar*: the labor contractor in kilns, with advances and loans going through the jamadar as collateral to labor. The jamadar acts as the enforcer in debt bondage by threats and promises of more loans, and keeping a watch on labor and family. Jamadars are usually effective in recovering labor that has 'gone astray.' No less importantly, police can be 'persuaded' to act as agents of the landlord or employer. Bonded labor can benefit from judicial intervention—but only when exploitation becomes particularly oppressive. Unfortunately, those unambiguously guilty of imposing abusive bondage are rarely penalised despite provisions in law due to their personal links within the legal system supporters.

Employers believe that they de serve appreciation for extending help to poor households who need shelter, credit and regular employment. The employer needs cheap labor and low turnover. Both labor and employer are therefore better off tying shelter and credit to labor i.e. debt bondage. Given market and government 'imperfections', kiln owners feel that they are justified in imposing bonded labor as they are the last hope for those in dire need. Advances serve to ensure security of work, earnings and shelter for their families. Agreeing to pledge family labor is then merely a premium for such insurance. Since the contract is voluntary, why the fuss?[5]

Neo-liberals would also frame the supply of advances as incentives to induce a stable, disciplined, productive labor force to work under probably hazardous, certainly unpleasant conditions. Perhaps implicit, advances are also seen as an appropriate response to the needs of labor for lumpy expenditures which cannot be delayed—treatment for unexpected illness; young persons who want to and should get married young. Clearly, neither owners nor labor expect these lumpy expenditures to be financed by savings due to admittedly low earnings. Hence, advances are a (devious) way to lock in labor supply.

Excessive debts can never be repaid at usual earnings from prevalent piece rates. Coercion occurs because indebted labor is lazy, i.e. does not produce the number of bricks that were agreed upon when the advance was given. Or labor tries to run off without honoring its debt. Violence is rare, and claims of physical abuse, specially of women, are trumped up (since well-off owners can afford better services). Employers feel that such people must be brought to justice that may be private if necessary because property has the *first* right to state protection, and so on.

The growing mass poverty in Pakistan has afflicted less than a fifth of the population in the 80s, but presently, well over a third of the population. Since advances provide a sense of security in earnings and shelter, it is no surprise that some labor considers bondage as a route to alleviate, if not escape, deprivation. Moreover, bondage offers an employment opportunity where more work is rewarded proportionately and hence debts, it is so perceived, can be repaid with less difficulty than otherwise. The 'peshgi system' allows for additional loans over time to 'generously' respond to specific and unforeseen needs for large cash outflows. In these explanations—which focus on compelling needs but lack alternatives—one must therefore also allude to the role of *social* structures in fostering seemingly private bondage.[6] Most labor consider it dishonorable to walk away from a 'fair' debt (an amazing but perhaps not atypical illustration of the effectiveness of internalisation as social disciplining).[7] When kilns close down for extended periods, employment becomes restricted and though, it means adding to debts, currently, few explore some other opportunity to repay their debts by higher incomes elsewhere.

In order to attract and retain labor, the owners prefer to give large and continuing advances to giving a much higher piece rate or regular wage, providing treatment and compensation for illness and injury. This is however a mere speculation. The advantage of an advance is that it is directly recoverable, and an implicit return may be earned through speeding up production via piece rates. For labor, larger production gives higher labor income, and allows swifter repayment of debt that enables future additional debt or an earlier release from bondage. Debt accounts can be fiddled with by employers. Furthermore, advances give more flexibility of 'rewarding' particular workers through size and frequency of 'peshgi' and debt servicing.

Labor must complete enough daily work to attain subsistence earnings. The lower the piece rate the more bricks must be produced by a household. Furthermore, higher rates can lead to larger labor incomes, hence lower working hours and lower output. To owners, the disadvantage of higher rates is that once given they cannot be taken back, and rate discrimination can lead to a 'price war' that goes out of control, and would endanger employer relations with other rural employers, in particular landlords who remain part of the local social and state alliances. Higher rates are seen as a hinderance to higher labor productivity, thus involving more risk and supervision than larger advances.

Previously, many kiln workers were employed in agriculture; it remains an obvious employment alternative; and the sector is itself pervaded by forced labor and debt bondage. These factors indicate a comparison between brick kilns and agriculture. A rapid assessment suggests that conditions of forced labor and debt bondage in brick kilns are much less severe as compared to oppression of landless farm labor and small sharecroppers. Factors explaining the differing conditions would include the following: Oppression and resistance both need social support. As compared to kiln owners who are mostly non-local land leasers, agricultural landlords are much more of a 'community' and hence more prone to collude in oppression. Landlords are also able to call upon the 'assistance' of the local administration more easily. Some labor may be able to call upon a countervailing (and competitive) source of power through a land owner to dilute the power of the kiln owner. In some kilns—in and around large cities such as Lahore and Peshawar but also in Haripur—general trade unions and specific bonded labor associations provide a degree of countervailing power against the worst abuses: mediating with the owner, or assisting in court cases and providing refuge to runaway labor.

LABOR IN KILNS

A description of the main components of the production process is a good beginning towards understanding the working lives of women, and of their men and children who labor at brick kilns (or 'brickfields'). From early morning to late evening of Saturday through Wednesday, mud bricks are prepared and sun-dried by a hundred or more, site-based or local, *Patheras* or *Thaperas* in a large area spread out in the vicinity of the kiln itself. On Thursday, the work stops at mid-day, to begin later on Friday. One, and sometime two, senior, adult males from among the *Patheras* will be their male *Jamadar*—who arranges for labor and distributes advances; distributes earnings after debt servicing deductions of debt; guarantees repayment of debts; and supervises work. Dried bricks are loaded from the adjacent brick field and transported to the kiln in through the afternoon—by half a dozen or more local male *Kharkars* with donkeys. These bricks are then handed over inside the kiln to a couple of male *Bharai walas* for stacking up under the supervision of a male *Mistri*. Usually the *Kharkars* and *Bharai walas* belong to a common piece-work labor team. Sometimes the *Bharai walas* working inside the kiln can be salaried employees. When a stock is to be built up to ensure uninterrupted kiln operation, additional bricks will also be stacked up on the site.

Inside the kiln, bricks are covered by a mixture of mud and baked brick dust by one or two site-based salaried, male *Keri walas*, and then baked for some days. The kiln is usually fired by coal brought mainly from Quetta and Hyderabad, but also from a few places in Punjab. Baking is done by a team of 4–5 site-based, salaried, male *Jalai walas*, working in six-hour shifts of 2 persons throughout the week. This team is headed by a skilled, male *Mistri* who usually recruits other team members. Amongst kiln tasks *Jalai* is the most obviously hazardous because of work with open fires.

Baked bricks are removed—six days a week—from the kiln by half a dozen or so male *Nikasi walas*, sorted for quality and then stacked up nearby. Customers cart away the bricks by bullock cart, tractor trolley or trucks. Usually transporters have their own labor, but *Patheras* and other males can join in for extra income. *Nikasis* finish work quite early in the day so as to allow transport of bricks to nearby markets.

At most times, a kiln will have a week's sale ready to be unloaded from the kiln. A kiln will close when unseasonal weather does not permit preparation of unbaked bricks and the stock of unbaked brick is inadequate. In some areas kilns close for a fortnight or more after every 3-4 months — apparently to ensure a stable sale price, but closing down can also serve to offset pressures for higher piece rates by labor as well as for prices of other input suppliers. During such closures, labor ask for subsistence advances which increase their indebtedness.

CHILD LABOR IN KILNS

Children are conservatively defined here to be around the ages of 10–14. Everywhere, children participate in the work of *Pathera*, *Bharai*, and *Nikasi*. Both male and female children will be found working as *Patheras*. Only male children are seen amongst *Bharai* and *Nikasi walas*. They will help load or unload bricks but more often will only be involved in carriage. No children were ever found working as *Jalai walas*—certainly because this is more skilled labor, most hazardous, requires constant alertness; and quite tiring work. Juvenile males are frequent as *Jalai walas*, most likely because these are not considered (by owners and officials) to be embraced by protective legislation.

FOOTLOOSE LABOR IN KILNS

A broad definition of migration includes most who reside on the kiln site. This covers both seasonal and permanent migrants, as well as situations of migration within and between tehsils rather than across districts or provinces. All (self-declared) Afghans are taken to be migrants. The typical kiln description has been one where almost all labor are from migrant families. However, now a kiln site even in the Punjab will often employ a combination of migrants and locals—both family and only male migrants; and migrants as well as locals working at the same site. Virtually everywhere, *Bharai* and *Nikasi* are done by locals. At most kilns, migrants dominate *Patheras* and *Jalai walas*. Among migrant *Pathera* families, the most common are 'classic' brick makers—both Muslim and Christians—from Central and

Southern Punjab. The entire family can spend many years at one kiln and then move to another kiln, sometimes hundreds of miles away.

Family migration is not common among the 'new' brick labor, and generally not so in the NWFP. In these cases, only adult and juvenile males migrate for some months, though not necessarily across short distances. Afghan Pathan labor remains widespread in the NWFP. It is also found in Punjab though less so in places close to Islamabad. Hardly any is to be found now in Sindh. These are almost always male adults and juveniles, coming to work from a nearby Afghan settlement (official or informal).

EARNINGS IN KILNS

The security of a fixed salary extends only to a dozen or so male kiln workers—Munshi(s), Chowkidar(s), 4–5 Jalai walas, a couple of Keri walas, and sometimes a Bharai Mistri or two. A couple of Nikasis can also be regular employees. A driver for the tractor and trolley will be seen at the larger kilns. The most numerous jobs are for piece rate workers: a dozen or so in Bharai; a half dozen for Nikasi; and scores of Patheras. In most brick kilns, active Patheras will be more than 50 men, women and children. Except for the Munshi, salaried workers live on site. Also living on-site are migrant Patheras: as 20 or more households consisting of 100 or more men, women and children. In the NWFP but also elsewhere, migrants will largely consist of males. Jalai walas also live as entirely male households.

For Bharai the observed range of piece rates varies, from Rs 28 to 80 but mostly under Rs 50 for every (undamaged) 1,000 bricks. As compared to Bharai, Nikasi is paid a lower rate since cartage is to a much shorter distance of a few yards. Rates ranged from Rs 12 to 30 per 1,000. Patheras can be paid a very wide range of rates per 1,000 bricks since they make both bricks and tiles, and each has a range of sizes and quality. Across sites, the extremes for bricks were Rs 90 and 160, and for most tiles the range was from Rs 140 to 300. A team of 4–5 Jalai walas gets a monthly total sum of Rs 15-20,000, with higher wages going to the more skilled Mistri, and to more skilled teams. In poorer areas, wages can drop for the group to Rs 10,000. A Keri wala is paid around Rs 1,500 per month, or may sometimes be paid on a piece rate. At rates of Rs 130–150 per 1,000 bricks, production of 600 – 1000 bricks daily would translate into Rs 80 – 150 per adult Pathera worker. When even lower rates prevail, such as in the NWFP generally, and for Afghans as a rule, daily earnings would range between Rs 60 – 120. For Patheras, the usual deduction for debt servicing is Rs 40 to Rs 50 per 1,000 bricks. Those with particularly large debts had a deduction closer to Rs 100 but then gross family income was also much higher. At the end of each month, labor is verbally informed of the size of outstanding debt.

INDEBTEDNESS IN KILNS

All categories of kiln labor can and do take advances—at the time of joining a kiln as well as subsequently. Those taking advances include both salaried workers such as Jalai walas and piece rate labor. Since repayment is through labor, advances are based largely upon the size and quality of labor being offered by a household.

After the initial advance, owners prefer to term subsequent advances as 'friendly loans,' probably to avoid being held in violation of bonded labor law (with higher penalties than usual civil law), and to retain the right of recovery, in the infrequent case of being taken to court by rebellious labor. Equally likely, owners want to reduce the risk of losing funds in the event that government or courts give a general public proclamation of cancellation of *Peshgis*, as they did in the late 80s. But labor, too, differentiates between subsequent, small subsistence advances and *Peshgi* as the large sum that can be demanded at the beginning of every season if past debts have been cleared.

As an average for kiln labor across the country, the size of *Peshgi* and accumulated advances per family could be less than Rs 5,000. The classic *Pathera* family—large family and large labor pool from Central and Southern Panjab—continues to have large and continuing debts of around Rs 10,000 per adult worker, and hence totalling Rs 50,000 and more for the family. When a new kiln starts up, these families and even some of the new migrants will negotiate large advances to move to the new kiln. If labor migrates under pressure, it may have to accept work from a creditor-owner who pays lower rates.

Among the reasons often cited for large debts were 'lumpy' expenditures such as a major illness or marriage of children. Some labor expressed marriage of young unmarried daughters as a compelling demand of *ghairat*—a matter of honour to provide protection (or respectability) to females—in the kiln environment of numerous young males. Afghans in particular and new labor in general is willing to work with smaller advances than the traditional migrant labor— they had low debts of around Rs 3,000 or less, which they felt would be repaid in a short time. One reason for accepting smaller advances would be their greater poverty, including fewer alternative opportunities for work specially for 'illegal' Afghans. But there were also indications that some needed smaller advances because of other sources of income, wealth or credit—e.g. rations and shelter in Afghan refugee camps; farm labor and homestead for locals.

If the person has a separate *khata*, the exit option can be exercised if the debt is accepted by other family members and they appear capable of redeeming the debt through their own labor. In this regard, a probably atypical case was narrated by a mother who had to absorb the debt of a young son who ran away 'because of a clever wife' and the father was incapacitated.

Debts are generally not forgiven upon incapacitation or death. A father or brother must accept the debt of a son or brother; a woman must assume the debt of a husband; and a male child must accept the debt of a father. We did not inquire about the obligations of female children towards debts acquired by their fathers or brothers. Measured as the intensity and frequency of violence, *explicit* severity of bondage was clearly observed to be low. One may speculate that the risk of court action in a high profile sector is a deterrent. It is more likely that violence is seen by owners as counter productive when labor is easily available in times of widespread unemployment and a stagnant construction sector. Owners may also realise that the costs of slacking by demoralised labor can be very high. No doubt, even a few well advertised cases of violence do suffice to keep most labor in line.

Of grave concern should be the recent and continuing cases of kiln labor selling a kidney to redeem large debts. These cases were encountered in Northern Punjab (but news reports indicate that they also occur in other places in Punjab). In one family, it was a middle-aged man (as the single male adult labor); in another, it was a juvenile daughter-in-law (orphaned, but married into a large family) who had used a local hospital. In a third family, a juvenile daughter (from a family that had adult brothers in kiln labor) had gone to Lahore for arranging the sale of her kidney. Clearly, debt bondage can impose immense psychological burdens on labor that remain veiled in the easier focus on physical violence. As compared to reports from sharecroppers in (particularly that were Sindh) agriculture, reports of sexual abuse were very rare in the sites we studied. But it must be pointed out that female team members sometimes felt that women were reluctant to speak out on such sensitive subjects. Perhaps their reticence was in fear of retaliation by *Munshis* or owners since strangers cannot be obviously trusted at a first (and last) meeting to keep names and information in confidence.

RELIEF AND REMEDY

The findings on debt bondage suggest obvious measures for relief and remedy. These are discussed briefly.[8]

Increasing income is the obvious route to at least preventing growth of debt or reducing occurrence, and hence against increasing severity of bondage. *Piece rates* in all provinces remain below the equivalent of national minimum wage (Rs 2,500 per month); shortfalls are more severe once we account for family labor by women or for the official poverty line income. In Sindh and NWFP, official piece rates are much lower than those required by the national minimum wage. A few activists (including lawyers) even mentioned collective action on minimum income. This may reflect the perceived distinction between poverty and bondage which is usually checked only when accompanied by overtly extreme violence.

Low wages are linked to credit and shelter. Workers agree to low wages when owners provide credit and shelter. The threat of homelessness serves to reduce effective threats of higher wages in some other employment, or quitting.[9] Hence the linkages between 'markets' need to be countered by government action.[10]

As long as incomes remain inadequate, alternative sources of *credit* shall be needed to complement increases in income. Extension of micro credit schemes to support subsistence and health can be of obvious importance as investments in human capital. If one's 'own' shelter is assured then micro credit for direct income generation can be relevant to all labor rather than just the locals who already live off-site. Income generation requires adult labor, and would therefore be possible only when some adults can be freed from kiln work through higher piece rates and lower debt.

The threat of women and children being rendered homeless is enormous, and hence bondage is most severe for families that must live on kiln site because they have no alternative shelter and can afford none because of low incomes and high debts. The government should make arrangements for alternative affordable *shelter*. The Khuda-ki-Basti scheme (implemented by Tasneem Siddiqi, earlier, in Hyderabad and now in Karachi) is an obvious model of an effective shelter policy for the poor.

The sluggish pace of implementation of the National Policy and Plan of Action (prepared under the tenure of Omar Asghar Khan) provides no room for being optimistic about any serious action taken by the government generally, and by senior labor officials in particular. There are no obvious reasons why even simple steps remain apparently daunting for government, whose inaction leads to evasion, and even contempt, of whatever little legislation is in existence.

More than two decades ago, kilns were declared by the Punjab government to be factories and all labor was considered to be workers. Yet, kiln registration *remains* grossly incomplete even in Punjab. For the small number of registered kilns, government has *yet* to ensure coverage under Social Security for even their very limited labor that owners have declared to be industrial workers.

Education is frequently declared a priority in various official pronouncements. But the government is *yet* to mobilise resources for kiln workers through the Workers Welfare Fund. Perhaps most tragic is that government has *yet* to provide relief and rehabilitation to bonded labor through the special fund of Rs 100 million created by Chief Executive General

Musharraf. Now the Baitul Maal has asked the Ministry to return the fund, presumably reflecting incompetence of the Ministry of Labor and the specially cavalier denial of the Sindh government *vis a vis* the masses of bonded *haris* in the province.

Child health and safety require special attention and action. But government and judiciary do not interpret the Employment of Children Act to include brick kilns within the 'building and construction industry' specified in the federal list of prohibited child labor. Government may even disagree with the obvious since the National List of Hazardous Forms of Child Labor (September 2002) does not explicitly include brick kilns. When children are not held to have rights independent of family, then exclusion of family enterprises remains another loophole for evading action.

Reducing deprivation and exclusions is the primary goal of development. Expanding opportunities for *decent work* follows as a priority objective of social policy. This, in turn, requires strategies to implement labor standards as a focus on realising *core labor rights*. Such concerns escape the attention of national (such as the Ministry of Agriculture and SMEDA) and international (e.g. ADB) policy makers in formulating strategies for accelerating employment growth through agriculture and small industrial enterprises. Their focus on capital—ignoring that both labor and capital form an enterprise—leads to unacceptable analysis: such as completely ignoring the widespread and increasing use of child and bonded labor. Their emphasis upon expansion evades the recognition that larger enterprises do not necessarily provide better working conditions, as illustrated by large brick kilns. Irresponsible recommendations follow—such as exemption from primary labor legislation even of working hours and minimum wages—rather than seeking verifiable compliance with labor standards in return for financial assistance to accelerate enterprise growth.

Whether sectoral or economy-wide, *growth with equity* has to remain the goal of sustainable development. Much political action therefore remains necessary to move South Asian states to act seriously against oppressive exercise of unequal social power, and hence also to eliminate the immense inequity of wealth that underpins the power to amplify exploitation into oppression.[11] Collective bargaining by labor has become even more urgent as government retreats from protection of labor. Yet legal action is even more difficult after the promulgation of the new Industrial Relations Ordinance—what one General (Yahya) giveth is for another General (Musharaff) to take back.

GLOSSARY

Baitul Maal	government foundation for assisting the poor and needy.
Begar	compulsory unpaid or nominally paid work.
Biradri	sub-caste or sub-tribe.
Bharai	task of stacking unbaked bricks in the kiln, usually including loading and cartage from brick field by a group.
Bharai wala	man who does Bharai.
Bhatta	kiln.
Chakkar	a completed baking cycle, usually requiring one month.
Chowkidar	watchman or guard.
Ghairat	self-respect; honour.
Gharain	group of related households.
Izzat	honour.
Jalai	task of firing the kiln and baking the bricks.

Jalai wala	man who does Jalai.
Jamadar	man who oversees labor, often to include hiring, distribution of advances and of compensation, and guarantees repayment.
Katoti	deduction from output of *pathera*, usually for rain damage.
Keri wala	man who spreads a mixture of clay and cinders on a set of stacked bricks in preparation of firing and baking.
Kharkar	man who carries bricks usually on a donkey from brick field to kiln or from kiln to stacks, usually combined with *bharai* or *nikasi*.
Khata	named account of advance and output of a worker/labor unit maintained by *munshi*.
Mazdoor	laborer; worker.
Mistri	skilled male leader of a labor group; always in *jalai* and sometimes in *bharai*.
Munshi	male manager-cum-accountant.
Nikasi	task of unloading baked bricks from the kiln, usually including cartage and stacking nearby by a group.
Nikasi wala	man who does *nikasi*.
Pawa	large stack of bricks, sometimes used as unit of work in *bharai* or *nikasi*.
Pathera	man, woman or child who prepares unbaked bricks, including preparation of clay.
Pera	lump of clay prepared for mould.
Peshgi	advance to labor.
Qalib	wood and metal mould used for making 4–5 bricks.
Quom	tribe or caste.
Sancha	metal mould for making a single brick.
Thapera	alternative term for *pathera*.
Zaat	caste.
Zina	fornication, or adultery.
Watta-satta	marriage arrangement under which the husband is obliged to give his own sister in marriage to his wife's brother.

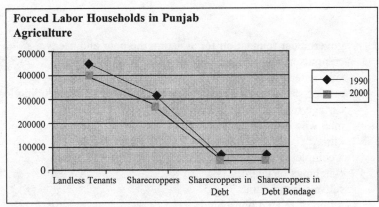

Source: Ercelan and Sohnia Ali, 2003.

FIG. 1: FORCED LABOR IN PUNJAB

Table 1: Rapid Assessment of Sample Brick Kilns in Pakistan

Characteristics	Range of Observations
Locations (in & around city & district)	Panjab: Multan, Lahore, Rawalpindi; NWFP: Peshawar, Haripur; Sindh: Hyderabad
Kiln Land	Often leased; seldom owned
Kiln Size	400,000 – 1,100,000 baked bricks in chakkar of around a month
Sale Price of Bricks and Tiles	Rs 700 – 2,400 per 1,000
On-site housing	Mostly migrant Patheras; single males only – mainly families
Jalai Labor children	4–5; usually migrant adult and juvenile males; never females or
Nikasi	3–10; local adult and juvenile males; rare females; children rare
Bharai	5–25; local adult and juvenile males on piece rates; never females; children rare
Pathera	30–150; only locals—mainly migrants. Only male adults, juveniles and children (10–14)—mainly families
Migrants	From same tehsil—different province
Afghans	None—mainly
Jalai Jobs	All salaried; Rs 1500-4000 per month
Nikasi	One or two salaried—all piece rate; Rs 12–30 per 1,000 bricks/tiles
Bharai	One or two salaried—all piece rate; Rs 28–80 per 1,000 bricks/tiles
Pathera	All at piece rate: Rs 90–160 per 1,000 bricks; Rs 140–500 per 1,000 special bricks and tiles
Nikasi Earnings	15–40,000 bricks through afternoon
Bharai	20–50,000 bricks in day
Pathera	600–4,000 bricks by adult males in day; 1–4,000 bricks by family in day tile preparation is 70–80% of brick output by given labor
Katoti on Pathera for Damaged Bricks	0–20 per 1000 bricks upon Pathera
Debt Servicing Charge	Rs 20–80 per 1,000 bricks; Rs 60–400 per week; 20–50% of gross earnings
on Pathera Jamadar Commission by Pathera	Rs 0–20 per 1,000 bricks
Advances from Owner	Bharai: Rs 0–20,000; Patheras: 0–100,000

Source: Ercelan 2004.

Table 2: Sample Sites for Rapid Assessments of Brick Kilns, 2002

South Panjab Multan	Central Punjab Lahore	North Punjab Rawalpindi	NWFP Peshawar	NWFP Haripur	Sindh Hyderabad
City, Kabirwala, Muzaffargarh, Bahawalpur, Shujabad, Jalalpur, Vehari	Multan Road, Jallo Mor, Bedian Road, Wagah Road, Kala Khata, Cantt, Kasur, Sheikhupura	City, Khanna, Taxila,Tarnol, Rawat, Gujar Khan, Tarlai, Fatehjang, Chakwal	City; Charsadda, Kohat Road, Canal Road, Nowshera-Mardan Road, Bara Road, Canal Road, Jalozai Road, Inqilab Road, Takht Bhai, Jalala	Khanpur Road, Hattar Road, Kangra Colony, GT Road	City, Hala, Shadadpur, Bhit Shah, Shaikh Birkhio, Tando Allah Yar Khan
October, November	October, November	November	November	November	December

Source: Ercelan 2004.

Table 3: Major Types of Labor

	Multan	Lahore	Rawalpindi	Peshawar	Haripur	Hyderabad
Number of Workers in Kiln						
Jalai (usually migrant male; always employees)	4–5	5	5	5	4–5	4–5
Nikasi (usually local men)	4–10	3–10	4–5	5–6	4–5	4–9
Bharai (usually local men)	5–25	8–17	10–20	8–10	10–15	8–12
Pathera (local & migrant: men, women & children)	30–100	35–75	50–100	30–60	30–60	100–150
All	70–200	50–250	250	100–150	100	
Families Living On-Site (usually Patheras)	0–25	20–60	15–50	0–50	None or few	Some

Note: Jalai is always done by employees; Patheras always, and Nikasi, Bharai mostly, work on piece rates. Small numbers in Bharai labor can reflect only stacking labor in the kiln, with a different group responsible for carriage from the brickfield

Source: Ercelan 2004.

Table 4: Women & Children as Pathera Labor

	Multan	Lahore	Rawalpindi	Peshawar	Haripur	Hyderabad
Women & Juveniles (15+)	Seldom	Regular	Regular	Seldom	Seldom	Often
Children 10–14	Regular Often only male	Regular	Regular	Often Usually male Regularly with Afghans	Usually male	Regular
Younger Children	Rare	Rare	Rare	Rare	Seldom	Rare

Source: Ercelan 2004.

Table 5: Locals & Migrants in Pathera Labor

	Multan	Lahore	Rawalpindi	Peshawar	Haripur	Hyderabad
Source of Pathera Labor						
Local Males	Often	Seldom	Often	Often	Often	Often
Local Families	Often	Often	Often	Seldom	Seldom	Often
Migrant Males from	'Nearby'	Bahawalpur, Chistian	Bahawalpur, Nowshera, Mardan Afghans	Afghans, Afridis, Mardan, Nowshera, Swat	Mostly Afghan: Peshawar; Malakand, NWFP, Sahiwal	Larkana, Khairpur, Badin Sukkur, Thar, Afghans from Quetta Punjab replacing Afghans
Migrant Families from	'Nearby' Sindh, Chistian, Bahawal nagar Minawali, Nawabpur	South/Central Punjab Depalpur, Muultan, Sahiwal, Kasur Mian Chunnu, Vehari, Bahawalpur 'adjoining districts'	Mandi Bahuddin, Jhelum; Gujrat; Charsadda, Bajaur, Hyderabad, Bahawalpur, Afghans, Gujrat, Sargodha, Peshawar, NWFP	Afghans, Charsadda, FATA, Najaur, Mohmand Agency, Sargodha, Gujrat, Bahawalpur	Afghans, NWFP, Pindi	Sukkur, Tando Mohammad Khan, Jacobabad, Toba Tek Singh, Rahim Yar Khna, Multan, Faisalabad, Okara Odes Afghan Tajiks & Uzbeks

Source: Ercelawn 2004.

Table 6: Piece Rates for Labor

	Multan	Lahore	Rawalpindi	Peshawar	Haripur	Hyderabad
Piece Rates (Rs per 1,000 bricks)						
Nikasi	12–30	16–30	24	19–25	23	20–30
Bharai	28–80	40–50	40–50	32–65	40–50	35–70
Patherra	110–160	100–150	110–160	90–140	120–150	120–150
	Special /tiles 140–500	Special/tiles 250–300	Special/tiles 200, 220	Special/tiles 150–200		Special/tiles 200–350
Damage Deduction from Pathera (briccks per 1000 bricks)	0–20	0–20	0–20		0–20	0–20
Deduction for Debt Servicing from Patherra (Rs per 000 bricks)	20–40 (50–200 per week)	30–80 (20–50% of earning)	(300–500 per week)	60–500 per week)		20 (30–50% of earning)
Daily Wages in Area (Rs)	100		80–150	50–100	100–120 factory: 1500–1800 2000 monthly	100–150

Note: Higher piece rates can include commission to jamadar; lower rates can reflect higher commission deducted for larger debts. Low Bharai rates can reflect payments to one group when work is split between stacking and carriage.

Source: Ercelan 2004.

Table 7: Labor Productivity

	Multan	Lahore	Rawalpindi	Peshawar	Haripur	Hyderabad
Daily Output (000 bricks) /Labor (adults, children)						
Nikasi	15–30/ 4–10 men	25–40/ 3–10 men	20–30/ 4–5 men	15–30/ 5–6 men	20–25/ 4–6 men	15–30/ 4–9 men
Bharai	20–25–40/ 5–25 men	30–35–50 8–17 men	25–35 10–20 men	20–40/ 8–10 men	25–35 8–10–15 men	20–40/ 8–12 men
Pathera	1/ 1 man 1 – 1.5 – 2 / 2 men 2 / man+woman 2–2.5 / 3 men+1 child 2–3 / 4 men+children Special/tiles 0.2–0.4–0.6 / 2 men 0.8 – 1 / 3 men 1 / man+woman 1 / 2 men	1–1.2/ man+woman 1.5–2/ man+woman+ children 3 / 3–4 men+ women+children	0.8–1/ man 1 – 1.3 – 1.5 / man + child 1.2 / man+woman 1.5 / man+2 women+1 child 2 / 3 men+2 women 2.5 / 2 men+2 women 4–5 / 3 young men 4 / 4 men+woman 5 / 3 men+3child special/tiles 0.8 / man+woman+ child 2.5 / 4 men	0.6–1/ man 1 – 1.3 – 1.5 / man+children 1.2–1.8 / 2 men 1.5–2–3 / 2 men+children 2 / 3 men 2,5 / some men + children 3 / man+woman+ child 3.5–4 / 4 men special/tiles 0.7–0.8 / familyu 3 / 2 men+6 children	1–1.2–1.5/ man 1.2 – 1.5 / per adult in 2.5 / 2 men+woman 1.2–1.5 / man+woman+ child 2–2.5 / 3 men 2–3 / men + children 3 / 2 men+children 3 / man+woman+3 children	0.5–0.9/ man+child 1.4–2 / man+woman 1.4 / 2 adults + 2 children 2–2.5 / 3 men special/tiles 0.8 / man + child 1 / 2 male 2 / 6 males

Note: children appeared to have an age around 10-14 years; men and women include juveniles.
Source: Ercelawn 2004.

Table 8: Size and Duration of Debt by Sharecroppers to Landlord, Sindh 2000

Period of Debt (years)	Respondents	Size of Debt (Rs 000)	Respondents
Upto 1	81	Upto 10	35
1–2	233	10–20	57
2–3	185	20–30	94
3–5	237	30–50	215
5–7	71	50–70	116
7–10	57	70–100	202
More than 10	76	More than 100	250
All	940	All	969

Note: debt is the amount that tenants recall as claimed by landlords but almost always denied by tenants. period of debt accumulation is understated because it refers to last tenancy whereas debt claimed by last landlord includes payments made to previous landlords when tenants are 'acquired.'
Source: Ercelawn and Nauman, 2000.

Table 9: Tenant Complaints of Compulsory Labor (Begar), Sindh 2000

	Respondents
Children	406
Women	824
Men	877

Note: Compulsory labor is taken by landlord for nominal or no payment from tenants and family members on self-cultivated land or house of landlord etc in addition to tenant labor on sharecropped land. Such labor excludes work done on sharecropped land by family members, including child labor, at the insistence of landlord.
Source: Ercelawn and Nauman, 2000.

Table 10: Abuse of Tenants and Duration of Abuse, Sindh 2000

	Men Jailed	Women Jailed	Children Jailed	Men Chained	Women Chained	Women Abused
Duration (months)						
Upto 3	127	108	94	71	36	84
4 – 6	216	201	134	98	52	125
7 – 12	222	205	165	84	51	134
13 – 24	130	123	99	68	51	94
25 – 36	61	55	43	25	14	45
More than 36	89	82	72	37	21	54
All	845	774	607	383	225	536

Note: jail refers to any open or closed enclosure designated by the landlord as the boundary of mobility, usually enforced by armed guards. Abused women abused to sexual assaults by landlord, relatives, friends, or employees. Incidence of abuse is computed conservatively by counting no response as no incident.
Source: Ercelawn and Nauman, 2000.

Table 11: Relief, Rehabilitation, Mitigation & Abolition of Bonded Labor

Measures	Action	Relief of Freed Labor	Rehabilitation of Freed Labor	Mitigation & Abolition of Bonded Labor
National Identity Cards	Mobile Teams	P		
Voter Registration	Mobile Teams	P		
Resident Registration in Camps	District Certification	P		
Re-settlement in Camps	Transport & Funds	P		
Secure Land for Camps	Site Allocation	P *N*		
Water & Sanitation for Camps	Funds & Facilities	P N		
School for Camps	Funds & Facilities	P N		
Health for Camps	Mobile Teams	P N		
Consumption Grant	Funds	P N		
Micro Finance	Funds		P N	P *N*
Skill Development	Technical Assistance		P N	P
Tenant/Worker Registration	Mobile Teams			P
Debt Registration	Mobile Teams			P
Debt Redemption	Funds & Legal Assistance			P
Legal Assistance	Funds	P N	P *N*	P *N*
Minimum Wages	Enforce, Extend			P
Social Security	Enforce, Extend			P *N*
Bonded Labor Act	Enforce, Amend			P N
Tenancy Act	Enforce, Amend			P
Collective Bargaining	Enforce, Extend			P *N*
Tenancy Tribunals	Amend, Enforce			P
District Vigilance Committees	Amend, Activate	P	P N	P
Land for Housing	Sites & Funds		P *N*	P
Land for Cooperatives	Sites & Funds		P	P
Surveys of Bonded Labor	Funds & Collaboration		P N	P N

Note: P denotes measure proposed by PILER; N denotes measure present in the official National Policy and Plan of Action; *N* denotes ambiguity in the official Plan.

Source: Ercelan, Karamat and Nauman, 2002.

References

AWAN, Zahoor, *Bonded Brick Kiln Workers: 1989 Supreme Court judgement and after*, Rawalpindi: APFOL, 1998.

BALES, Kevin, *Disposable People: New Slavery in the Global Economy,* London, 1999.

BARDHAN, Pranab, *The Economic Theory of Agrarian Institutions*, London, 1989.

BRASS, Tom, *Towards a Comparative Political Economy of Unfree labor*, London, 1999.

BRASS, Tom, *Unfree labor & capitalist restrictions in the agricultural sector*, *Journal of Peasant Studies*, Vol. 14, 1986.

CHANG, Ha-Joon, 'Breaking the Mould: An Institutionalist Political Economy Alternative to the Neo-Liberal Theory of the Market and the State,' *Cambridge Journal of Economics,* Vol. 26, 2002.

ERCELAN, A. and M. Nauman, '*Unfree Labor in South Asia: Debt Bondage at Brick kilns in Pakistan,*' *Economic and Political Weekly*, Mumbai, Vol. 39, 2004.

ERCELAN, A. *Labor, Debt and Bondage in Brick Kilns*, Islamabad: Ministry of Labor, Government of Pakistan, 2004.

ERCELAN, A. and Karamat, Ali, *Mitigation and Abolition of Bonded Labor: Policy, Law and Economy in Pakistan*, Karachi: PILER, 2001.

ERCELAN, A. and M. Nauman 'Bonded labor in Pakistan: Directions for National Policy and Action,' *Asia-Pacific Journal*, Vol. 7, Manila, 2002.

ERCELAN, A. and M. Nauman, *'Bonded labor in Pakistan,'* Working Paper 1, Geneva: ILO, Infocus Programme on Promoting the Declaration, 2001.

ERCELAN, A. and M. Nauman, *Bonded labor in Pakistan: An overview*, Karachi: PILER, 2000.

ERCELAN, A. and Sohnia, Ali, 'Forced Labor in Punjab Agriculture,' *The Journal*, Vol. 8, Karachi: NIPA, 2003.

GIDWANI, Vinay, 'The Cultural Logic of Work: Explaining Labor Deployment and Piece-rate Contracts,' *Journal of Development Studies*, Vol. 38, 2001

Government of Pakistan, *Rapid Assessment Studies of Bonded Labor in Different Sectors in Pakistan*, Islamabad: Ministry of Labor, 2004.

GRANOVETTER, Mark, 'Economic Action and Social Structure: The Problem of Embeddedness,' *American Journal of Sociology*, Vol. 91, 1985.

MITHA, Yameema and Karamat, Ali, *Women in the Brick Kiln Industry*, Lahore: ASR, 1989.

MITHA, Yameema and Nighat Said Khan, *Patterns of Female Employment in Mining and Construction Industries*, Lahore: Systems Ltd., 1981.

PILER, *Unfree Labor in Pakistan—work, debt and bondage in brick kilns in Pakistan*, Working Paper 24, Geneva: ILO, Infocus Programme on Promoting the Declaration, 2004.

Notes

1. This paper draws much from a paper, Ercelan and Nauman, 2004. See also Ercelan 2004 for details on sites and methods of assessment. Complementary research at PILER is taken from Ercelan and Karamat 2001; and from Ercelan and Nauman 2001, which includes a survey of formerly debt-bonded haris in lower Sindh.

2. These notably include Mitha and Karamat 1981 and Mitha and Nighat 1989. More recent assessments are by Awan 1998. Other research which informs our paper includes various sector studies in the series on forced labor prepared for the Research Forum on Forced Labor; see Government of Pakistan 2004, or the Working Papers published in 2004 by the ILO at the InFocus Programme on Promoting the Declaration.

3. The discussion has benefited much from a reading of ILO conventions and its publications on 'decent work.' Two recent books are essential reading for an understanding of unfree labor: Bales 1999 and Brass 1999.

4. Mainstream economics interprets tied labor as the 'double coincidence of wants;' e.g. Bardhan 1989. A trenchant critique of such attempts to give a social efficiency gloss to exploitation is given in Brass 1999, specially chapter 7.

5. 'If we want to decide whether a particular market is free or not, we need to take a position on the legitimacy of the underlying rights-obligations structure for the participants in the relevant market (and, indeed, certain non-participants too),' as expressed by Chang 2002.

6. If we grant that an employer exercises no individual coercion in *offering* advances and shelter in return for labor to a worker seeking them, social coercion is evident in the fact of dismal alternatives made available to the worker.

7. Brass 1986 draws attention to how debt provides a political/social legitimacy for tied labor and consequent exploitation: there is an 'ideological decommoditisation of the wage from itself, a process whereby labor-power is separated from the value it produces... a bonded labor works to pay off a debt rather than for a wage.' That the social construction of bondage may even lead to a 'cultural preference' for the debt-labor relationship over an explicit employer-employee relationship, specially since women and children are part of the family labor; is an important insight provided by Gidwani 2001.

8. A more detailed review is given in Ercelan, Karamat and Nauman 2002.

9. Low wages are with reference to a social wage since prevailing wage rates in alternative employment are usually themselves depressed by the availability of large numbers of unfree labor.

10. Some would point to efficiency losses, specially in the all-or-nothing monopsony scenarios, where debt for labor at low wages or piece rates is the labor market counterpart of two-part tariffs in monopolistic commodity markets. We consider such efficiency losses to be irrelevant in a framework of citizen rights to be free of oppression. One just cannot ignore the macro distribution of power and wealth that keeps wages, productivity

and opportunities to so low as to engender the so-called efficiency gains of bondage. For a broad critique, see Brass 1999.

11. 'Any attempt to problematise the connection between unfreedom, the law, and the state must begin by addressing the issue of class power;' (Brass 1999). Work by Mark Granovetter is an earlier, renowned exposition of the thesis that behavior and institutions cannot be understood without reference to social relations; see Granovetter 1985.

3

DEVELOPMENT—AT WHAT PRICE FOR WOMEN?

*Gloria de Silva**

ABSTRACT

In this paper, I have attempted to present an overview of the current demographics regarding women in Sri Lanka; the economic background since independence and its impact on women; women's education in the post-independence period; current and future trends in the labor market; and some serious issues being consistently ignored by international financial institutions (IFIs).

In conclusion, I have made some recommendations based on my view that development is proceeding with a reckless disregard for long-term social impact and human cost, and concentrating purely on short-term profit.

---

*The author is presently the Director of the Centre for Family Services, Colombo, Sri Lanka, where she works on the holistic development of disadvantaged women and children.

DEMOGRAPHIC AND ECONOMIC BACKGROUND

Sri Lanka is a small island, approximately 25,000 square miles in area, situated off the southern-most tip of the Indian sub-continent. It has a population of over 19 million. At the last official census conducted in 2001, approximately 52 per cent of the total population in the south were women. (Here, the south is identified as being different from the north and east, where an armed conflict has been raging for almost 20 years). The census could not be conducted in the north and east due to the armed conflict in those areas. Another significant fact is that almost 20 per cent of current households in Sri Lanka are female headed.[1]

In the decade following political independence from the British Empire in 1948, the colonial economy remained unchanged. It was heavily dependent on the export-oriented plantation sector, comprising tea, rubber and coconut, had a relatively stagnant agriculture sector and an extremely limited industrial sector.

By the late 1950's, however, deteriorating terms of trade, the fall of commodity prices in the international market and consequent slow economic growth created resource constraints for the Sri Lankan economy, and stimulated the introduction of import substitution policies. In agriculture, irrigation-based land settlement schemes were opened up in the dry zone— areas neglected by the British colonists. The Gal-Oya scheme was opened in the 1950s, the Uda Walawe scheme in the 1960s, and the Mahaweli scheme in the 1970s. The industrial sector saw the emergence of large, state-organized, capital-intensive ventures such as paper, salt, steel, and cement. This period also saw a proliferation of small and medium-scale, labor intensive industries, both in the public and private sectors. Chief among these were handloom fabrics and handicrafts. However, the plantation-dominated agrarian economy continued and the share of the manufacturing sector in GDP had increased only marginally from 11.6 per cent in 1966, to 12.5 per cent in 1977[2]. These closed and controlled economic policies resulted in a virtually stagnant economy, which in turn impacted adversely on employment opportunities. This was probably one of the main reasons for the youth uprising in 1971.

All of the above, and the rapid economic expansion and growth of south-east Asian countries such as Singapore, Malaysia and Thailand influenced the thinking of the United National Party (UNP), voted into power with an overwhelming majority in 1977. The UNP quickly introduced sweeping macro-economic reforms which reflected a radical shift from the previous import-substitution-oriented industrialization to export-led industrial development, with a strong emphasis on industrial export promotion and reliance on direct foreign investment.[3] These macro-economic reforms were implemented in Sri Lanka over two main phases, the first phase introduced in 1978, and the second phase in 1989. These broadly encompassed: liberalization of trade, devaluation of the rupee, reduction in public expenditure, export promotion, elimination of consumer and producer subsidies and privatization of public enterprises. These macro-economic reforms were linked on one hand, to the rapid process of globalization and trade liberalization, dominated by the Structural Adjustment Programmes (SAPs) promoted by the International Monetary Fund (IMF) and the World Bank (WB), and subsequently by the World Trade Organization (WTO). These macro-economic reforms have had a tremendous impact on the welfare, livelihoods and life-styles of the general population, and on women in particular.

THE IMPACT OF POST-INDEPENDENCE ECONOMIC POLICIES

Before undertaking an analysis of any kind, it is necessary to look at whether and how, the economic policies since post-independence affected women. Despite the domesticating colonial influence on women in the upper and middle classes in Sri Lanka, rural women have traditionally been economic producers, working side by side with men in the area of agriculture. Chief among these activities were the cultivation of paddy land, the slash and burn system of chena cultivation and the maintenance of home gardens. These economic activities were traditionally viewed as unpaid partnerships.

With the introduction of the large-scale agricultural development schemes in the dry zone, women lost their traditional land inheritance rights as a result of the practice of primogeniture under the Land Development Ordinance of 1935.[4] Under these schemes, women were perceived to be 'farmers' wives' and not 'women farmers'. Therefore, land was allocated only to male heads of household. In the continuing paradox of Sri Lankan society and its politics, recent land distribution in the 'wanni' area, (within the conflict zone), also adhered to the above policy—title deeds for land were only invested in male heads of household, and it was only where a male head of household was reported or presumed dead, that the title deed was invested in the woman. Women whose husbands had left them or whose whereabouts could not be ascertained were not deemed eligible for land grants. This was in spite of the fact that almost 20 per cent of current Sri Lankan households were headed by females. (The Land Reform Acts of 1972 and 1974 had little positive impact on women, since they did not increase either women's ownership of land, or their participation in related economic activities.)

Among plantation workers, more than half of the labor force comprised of women, who continued to receive unequal wages for equal work with men. This situation was rectified in 1984, as a result of the political clout of the main plantation-sector Trade Union. However, this policy was not extended to other 'informal sectors' such as fisheries, agriculture and daily-paid contract labor. Even today, women outside the plantation sector work for less pay, even though their work output equals, and sometimes, exceeds that of men.

The Department of Rural Industries initiated the establishment of village-based Women's Societies from 1954 onwards. In accordance with the gender-role assumptions of the policy makers, the main activities of these Societies were home-based commercial projects, requiring a low level of skill and generating only a modest income. One of the more popular projects was the coir industry (products and by-products of coconut cultivation) in the Southern coastal area. However, the handloom fabrics industry was a major exception to the general requirement of low levels of skill. Though requiring more capital investment and much higher skill, it was nevertheless a 'Feminized' industry, considered suitable for women.

But, as a result of the open economic policies and macro-economic reforms introduced after 1977, almost 40,000 women lost their livelihoods in the handloom industry between 1977 and 1980[5]. Women whose traditional livelihoods were weaving, lace-making, pottery and other handicrafts, also faced severe economic constraints with the abrupt market liberalization policies introduced in the late 1970s. The reason was that rapid mechanization of much of this work, the high price and diminishing availability of raw materials, withdrawal of governmental subsidies and protective quotas, and the import of cheaper competing goods from neighboring countries, changed the economic equation against them.

The change in macro-economic policies also opened up spaces in the labor market for women. A great number of young women between the ages of 18 and 30 are employed in the export-oriented, industrial sector, chief among them being the garment industry. The middle-east market for domestic labor is another major employment avenue, while the out-sourcing industry which has grown rapidly, is also a feminized one.

However, all of the above employment opportunities are dominated and characterized by the following limitations:

- Increased emphasis on acquiring profits which has resulted in deteriorating quality of employment—women work longer hours for lower wages
- No opportunities to acquire new skills and thereby achieve upward job mobility
- Diminishing employment stability and security
- Diminishing protective labor legislation
- Diminishing concern for the social well-being of employees

Macro economic reforms introduced through the SAPs which have resulted in the withdrawal of fertilizer and agro-chemical subsidies, rising production costs brought about by 'Green Revolution' technologies, and trade policies which are skewed in favor of rich and influential countries have resulted in women's labor being used to adjust to the above constraints.

Another significant fact is that as a result of the employment opportunities currently available due to the open economic policies, the number of women in the agriculture work force, has declined. More women have given up working alongside their menfolk in their fields and have migrated to the cities and towns or to the Middle East, in search of employment. This has created a serious lacuna in food security, both at domestic and national levels, and Sri Lanka's rising malnutrition rate bears ample testimony to this problem.

EDUCATION IN POST-INDEPENDENCE SRI LANKA

Education has also played a major role in influencing changes in the labor market. Government policies and programs have shaped and influenced education and it is necessary to look at its history and current status, especially with regard to women.

In the decade following independence, state policies and programs reflected a socialist perspective. As a result of the above, state infrastructure expanded, a lot of attention was paid to the extension of health and education services and there was state control of the economy. Therefore, Sri Lanka enjoyed a relatively high Physical Quality of Life Index (PQLI) in the 1970s and a high ranking Human Development Index (HDI) in the 1990s[6].

Given below is a table from the book 'Women in Post-Independence Sri Lanka', edited by Prof. Swarna Jayaweera. The data are compounded from tables published by the Department of Census and Statistics of the Central Bank of Sri Lanka[7].

With the government's commitment to providing free education, literacy levels in all sectors (other than the plantation sector) showed rapid improvement between 1946 and 1981. Although there has been a slight decrease in the literacy levels between 1981 and 1985/86, it has improved again in the period 1991–1994.

Literacy by Sector and Sex (%)

		1946	1953	1963	1971	1981	1985/6	*1991	*1994
All Island									
	Average	62.8	69.0	76.8	78.5	86.5	84.2	86.9	90.1
	Male	76.5	80.7	85.6	85.6	90.5	88.6	90.0	92.5
	Female	46.2	55.5	67.1	70.9	82.8	80.0	83.8	87.9
Urban									
	Average	76.2	82.6	87.7	86.2	93.3	89.1	93.2	93.2
	Male	84.5	88.5	91.8	90.3	95.3	92.4	94.0	94.8
	Female	65.7	74.1	82.7	81.5	91.0	86.1	84.3	91.8
Rural									
	Average	60.1	66.4	70.1	76.2	84.5	84.6	87.1	89.5
	Male	74.7	79.0	83.9	84.1	89.0	88.5	89.9	92.1
	Female	43.0	52.4	63.6	67.9	79.9	80.7	84.3	87.1
Estate									
	Average						59.4		66.1
	Male						74.5		79.0
	Female						45.9		52.8

Sources: Census of Sri Lanka, 1946, 1953,1963, 1971, 1981; Labor Force and Socio-Economic Survey, 1985/86; Household Income and Expenditure Survey, 1991; and Demographic Survey, 1994, Department of Census and Statistics, Government of Sri Lanka, Colombo.
* Excludes north and east.

Another significant fact was that even though free education had been extended through state policies and programs, it had a minimal impact, since entry into universities and secondary schools was confined to a limited number from the English-speaking elite. It was the introduction of the use of Tamil and Sinhala as the medium of instruction in senior and secondary grades in the late 1950s, that transformed this elitist situation. Two new universities were established to meet the increasing demand and the per centage of women students entering university increased from 18.7 per cent in 1950 to 44.4 per cent in 1970[8].

The immediate impact of this was the entry of women in large numbers to professional and middle-level jobs in the service sector. It must be noted that given the government's socialist policies in the three decades following independence, state infrastructure, especially in the social and economic sectors, had expanded. In the space created, educated women from upper and middle classes, with families who had economic resources, 'escaped' from the limitations imposed by their conventional lives and found urban-based employment. Women in rural, less-affluent families, who also emerged from universities and secondary schools in the 1960s, gained upward social and economic mobility, through professional and middle-level employment.

Women also began to enter into the clerical, sales and travel services by the 1970s, and to seek entry into high-level public employment; the prestigious Foreign Service was opened to women in 1950, while the elite Administrative Service, so long a male bastion, was opened to women in 1963. By the 1960s, the universities were admitting women into law, engineering, veterinary science, dental and agriculture faculties.

By the late 1960s, policy priorities regarding education shifted from providing education opportunities to diversifying education. This had become imperative since the sluggish economy had been unable to absorb the outputs of the education system. The vocational education sector was expanded from 1970 onwards. However, the internalization of gender roles led to a stereotyping of the courses offered, and led to wide gender imbalances in the enrollment in programs. For example, secretarial, dress-making, home-science and beauty culture courses were designed and offered for females, while technical skills development was not a priority.

Another significant, negative decision taken by the state in the period 1965–1975 was to freeze university admissions, in order to deal with the problem of unemployed, educated youth. As a result of this decision, universities lost their autonomy as regards admissions and the per centage of women entering universities declined from 44 per cent of the total enrolment in 1970, to 40 per cent in 1975. A major positive development in the education field in the period between the mid 1970s and 1980s was international donor-supported programs that focused on raising the literacy level in the plantation sector. As a result of these interventions, the percentage of females in the plantation sector schools increased to almost 46 per cent of the total enrolment by 1984.

Both the qualitative and quantitative development of education was adversely affected after the introduction of economic liberalization policies in the late 1970s. These policies, instigated by the IMF and WB, resulted in a massive and abrupt reduction in public service expenditure. In the case of education, the allocation for education in the national budget was reduced from 20 per cent in the 1970s to eight per cent in the 1980s. This led to a stagnation, both in enrolment rates and literacy levels.

Concern for extending educational opportunities resurfaced in the 1990s, since Sri Lanka has always enjoyed a high quality of literacy and related prestige in this regard. Income disparities and increasing rate of poverty and the political unrest in the mid and late 1980s, compelled the government to implement special poverty alleviation programs. They included allowances for meals to school children, distribution of free materials for school uniforms and free distribution of text books. The UN Conference on Education for All in 1990, the ratification by Sri Lanka of the UN Convention on the 'Rights of the Child' in 1991 and its sequel, the 'Children's Charter' in 1992, also gave momentum to this concern. This in turn, resulted in the reintroduction of the Education Ordinance of 1939, that makes education compulsory for children between the ages of 5 and 14, after a lapse of almost sixty years.

However, with the accelerated implementation of SAPs, now called Poverty Reduction Strategy Papers (PRSPs), under the UNP government, voted into power in 2001, access to quality education for the poor and disadvantaged groups in Sri Lanka has once again been threatened. Allocations for education in the national budgets have been lowered to a minimum (approximately 4 per cent in the 2003 budget). The rapid privatization of the education sector is the alternative being promoted by both the government and IFIs; more than 400 village-level schools have been closed down between 2002 and 2003. Rules and procedures that make the distribution of free material for school uniforms extremely complicated and bureaucratic have been introduced.

Since the 1980s, another vulnerable group has emerged—the children caught up in the war in the north and east. They are traumatized, displaced and excluded from the school system. The state has not been sensitive to their needs and even currently, no policies or programs exist in the education field that address, or even attempt to identify the complex issues and deprivations engendered by this environment.

However, a new, educated elite is emerging in Sri Lanka, and the situation is similar to the one that existed before the late 1950s – i.e. those with access to resources such as funding and knowledge of the English language are able to use the many opportunities available, to obtain basic and higher education. These are being offered through elite private schools and institutes and colleges with affiliations to foreign universities.

ECONOMY, EDUCATION AND WOMEN'S LABOR MARKET

I shall now attempt to show some links between economic policies and programs, and the role of education, in accordance with the facts presented earlier, in order to try and establish their relationship to current labor market trends among women.

Rural women in Sri Lanka have traditionally worked as partners in the field of agriculture. However, the large-scale land settlement schemes in the dry zone served to disempower women by depriving them of their land inheritance rights, while market liberalization and the implementation of the SAPs served to exploit women's labor. Both these resulted in women being forced out of the agriculture sector. Currently, women represent approximately 40 per cent of the total agriculture work force.

The sweeping macro-economic reforms introduced abruptly in the late 1970s led to the collapse of many traditional livelihoods, chiefly among women. Women in the coir, handloom and handicraft industries found themselves bereft of income sources. However, many poor, young, rural women found employment in the burgeoning garment industry, established in Sri Lanka in the late 1970s. Currently, there are three Export Processing Zones (EPZs) in Sri Lanka, and approximately 90 per cent of the labor force of the garment industries comprises of young women. Dennis Ramanayake (1984) writes:

> The educational qualifications of production workers in the zone is high and corresponds closely to the general pattern in Sri Lanka. As many as 23 per cent have passed the GCE O-level with six subjects, while 6 per cent have even higher qualifications. Only two per cent have qualifications below the fifth standard.[9]

Another great attraction for poor, rural women is the Middle-East domestic job market. This was created with the oil boom in the OPEC countries in the late 1970s. Many women who have quit the agriculture sector are now employed either as garment factory workers in one of the EPZs, or as domestic workers in one of the Middle East countries. Migrant, female, domestic workers jumped from 0.4 per cent in 1976 to 78.9 per cent of the unskilled female workers in 1994[10]. Currently, these domestic workers are the second-largest source of foreign exchange revenues for Sri Lanka, having overtaken tea, rubber and coconut, our traditional main exports for years. It is also interesting to note that women have been seeking employment in the Maldives, Cyprus, Greece and Italy, since the early 1980s.

Leelangi Wanasundera (2001) writes

> ...as a total per centage the number of workers hosted by these countries is less than two per cent of the total migrant domestic workers. But their earning capacity is substantially higher than that of women who migrate to the Middle East... Almost all had a primary school education, a substantial number had passed GCE O-Level and higher exams, a few even had a university degree.[11]

The 'comparative advantage' of low-cost, female labor and the incentives being offered by the government to attract foreign investors has resulted in a proliferation of subcontracting industries. Chief among these are the assembling of electronic parts, embroidery, making artificial flowers, coir, growing tobacco and construction. Women figure prominently in these subcontracting industries, since it offers the opportunity of working from their own home, thereby making easier, the multiple responsibilities of supplementing/providing the family income, taking care of the household chores and caring for children and the elderly. However, they also face the burden of being paid extremely low rates for labor-intensive work, with no protective legislation, employment security or bargaining power.

Self-employment projects among women have increased. Women displaced from traditional or local industries, confined to the home because of child-care responsibilities, displaced by the armed conflict, in impoverished families or without access to formal sector or overseas employment, are often engaged in these activities. These types of programs are highly visible in Women in Development programs, Change-Agent Programmes, Credit and Savings Programmes based on the 'Grameen Bank' model and most recently, the Poverty Alleviation Self-Employment Programmes.

When considering the middle and upper level job markets, there is a direct correlation between gender and job position/remuneration; while at the same time, socio-economic disparities rather than gender determine access to educational facilities in Sri Lanka. By the mid 1980s, almost 50 per cent of the professional and semi-professional work force in the service sector were women, while approximately 42 per cent in clerical related occupations in the mid 1990s too were women. However, at the highest administrative and managerial positions, both in the public and private sectors, there has been minimal movement towards recruiting women. There has been a high visibility for the few women who have been able to bypass the 'glass ceiling', but women's representation at management and key decision-making levels remains abysmally low. There are many women teachers, lawyers, accountants, secretaries, lecturers and managers, but few principals, judges, financial managers, vice-chancellors and managing directors. This is in spite of comparable educational qualifications, social status and work experience.

SOME REFLECTIONS

Dr A.T.P.L. Abeykoon writes:

> The female labor force can be defined as that part of the female population which contributes and is willing to contribute to the production of economic goods and services. Thus the female labor force includes both the employed and unemployed females in the population[12] (Abeykoon, 2000, p. 151)

The female labor force, according to a Census of Population and Labor Force Survey conducted in 1990, was 2.5 million. Another survey by the same source shows that females employed between 1963 and 1998 reflect the following—in the primary sector comprising agriculture, forestry, hunting and fishing, it is 43.1 per cent of the total working population; in the secondary sector which includes mining, quarrying, manufacture and construction, it is 24.8 per cent; in the tertiary sector comprising utilities, commerce, trade, transport, storage, communications and other services, it is 30.1 per cent.

A survey to ascertain the percentage of employed/unemployed females between 1963 and 1998 shows that proportion of females in the employee category has declined from 82.2 per cent in 1963 to 57.3 in 1998, while the proportion of unpaid family workers has increased to 24.8 per cent (from 6.6 per cent) in the same period. The proportion of self-employed has also increased from 8.9 per cent to 17.2. per cent. And a survey conducted to ascertain the percentage of employed females has shown that female unemployment has remained consistently higher than the overall unemployment rate.

Taking all of the above data into consideration, it is evident that in spite of the much vaunted statistics and rhetoric, the labor market for most women is getting progressively narrower and 'unhealthier'. Women are being forced out of situations where they have direct control over, and access to, resources. This is apparent in the mechanization and rationalization of the agriculture sector. Women have lost their land inheritance rights and their control over food security in the increasingly technological innovations brought about by the 'Green Revolution' and liberal market policies. They have been forced to become hired laborers, instead of land owners and partners in agriculture production.

In spite of achieving GCE O-level or higher educational qualifications, an increasing number of women are getting trapped in low-paying, labor intensive, monotonous and repetitive work. A case in point is the garment industry, where young women work in assembly lines that require no major skills other than nimble fingers, manual dexterity and a docile disposition. However, recent studies have shown that their working conditions, which are so often of secondary consideration in work places hell-bent on making profits, have had serious long term impacts on their physical and mental health and well-being. Having to stand for long hours, sometimes almost 12–14 hours a day or sit in one position for the same time period, use the toilet only at approved times, being exposed to hazardous waste, etc. has resulted in extremely serious physical ailments, while the lack of freedom to socialize, even at the work-place, the loss of family relationships and the mental apathy brought about by working long hours at extremely unrewarding and repetitive tasks has long-term negative psychological effects.

The Middle East job market is another case in point. Very little attention is paid by national policy makers to either the appalling conditions or human rights violations faced by migrant women domestic workers. To become the main wage earner for the family and to be able to increase their land and housing assets, educate their children and improve their physical quality of life, they pay a high price: they have been the victims of rape, sexual harassment and/or abuse, physical violence and even death. The latest reported atrocity is the murder of women for their body parts. Many women have become disabled in trying to escape from harrowing work conditions, while others have become psychologically disturbed either as a result of the above or by the experience of having to languish for months in jail, while either being subjected to more abuse or indifference by both the Sri Lankan and Middle East governments. The Foreign Employment Bureau, established in 1985, has belatedly tried to implement certain programs to raise awareness among women seeking employment in the Middle East, but the atrocities continue.

Another area of concern as regards the female labor market is the integration of women who were affected by the armed conflict. These women have had to face severe economic hardship, physical insecurity, unequal access to resources and increased vulnerability brought about by displacement and conflict situation. Many of these women have become heads of household, and it is essential that their situation be sensitively analysed using gender-disaggregated statistics and community-based participation. Reintegration and reconstruction programs should use this data in program design and the formulation of national policies. It is also essential to look at the question of Sri Lanka's continuing gender disparities in the middle and upper-level job market.

Last but not least, it is essential to look at the current development programs being promoted by the Sri Lankan government and objectively assess their impact on women, both in the short and long term. In the main development document put out by the Sri Lankan government in May 2003, 'Regaining Sri Lanka: Vision and Strategy for Accelerated Development', it is stated that the government is committed to creating two million new jobs[13]. Yes, but what kind of jobs? In order to overcome the public debt crisis that they themselves have created in the post independence period, the government (there being very little to choose between the economic policies promoted by the two main political parties, the UNP and the People's Alliance (PA)), all governments voted into power since 1977 have been trying to shift the debt burden onto the people. Currently, every Sri Lankan, man, woman and child, is paying off a public debt that translates to Rs 77,000 per individual. This is before the much publicized 'aid' pledged at the Tokyo summit is added to the total, since it too is a loan, not a grant. Currently Sri Lanka's national debt exceeds her Gross Domestic Product (GDP). Successive governments since 1977, have not only increased the public debt through corruption and mismanagement which has led to further borrowing, but have also come up with the novel concept of handing the running of the country over to the private sector and quietly retiring into the background. This is in keeping with the dictates of the IFIs, who themselves are the lackeys of transnational corporations and the governments of the developed or G7 countries.

How does this specifically affect and impact on women? My recommendations are linked to this crucial question.

RECOMMENDATIONS

Employment stability, protective labor legislation and the social well-being of employees are not issues that get addressed by proponents of SAPs. However, it should be the primary concern of a democratically elected government, which is the representative of the people. The government is bound by the Constitution to protect and ensure the rights and well-being of all citizens. Therefore, the government cannot summarily abdicate and transfer its responsibilities to the private sector. Since it is the politicians who will have to come before the people during election time, I suggest that they take a long, hard look at the Regaining Sri Lanka document. If government ministers are unable to understand the content, they must get professional and unbiased help, since they have a duty towards their constituents to protect their interests and rights. I say this in all seriousness, backing up my recommendation with a quote from the Daily Mirror newspaper of 15 July 2003:

> World Bank laments the role of MPs: In a hard hitting speech, the World Bank Country Director in Sri Lanka said yesterday he was sad to say he did not know how much Sri Lanka's MPs knew or how much they were involved in the formulation of projects such as Regaining Sri Lanka.

The International Labor Organization (ILO) should play a bigger role in ensuring that Sri Lanka, which has ratified thirty ILO conventions to date, adheres to following the dictates and conditions of these conventions in the formulation and implementation of its policies and related legislature. The ILO should insist that the Sri Lankan government conduct an extensive gender-disaggregated study to ascertain whether core-labor standards are being maintained in the current context. The ILO should also more effectively monitor the current development programs and see whether they satisfy both core labor standards and are geared towards achieving the Millennium Development Goals.

Academicians and professionals should get more involved in lobbying and advocacy work. Unfortunately, many of them are now being bank-rolled by the IFIs which make unbiased and objective analysis difficult, if not impossible. However, there are still many progressive and enlightened academicians and professionals who should be concerned not only with the snowballing public debt, but also with the proposals to turn water into a commodity, thereby making access to water impossible for a majority of Sri Lankans, the privatization of health, transport and education services, which will again affect millions, and lead to a deterioration of the high Human Development Index maintained so far. This should be a concern of the ILO and some of the UN bodies as well—UNDP, UNESCO, UNICEF, UNIFEM, etc. The World Health Organization (WHO) too should be taking a greater interest in the development programs taking place in developing countries and their short and long-term impacts on both the physical and mental health of their citizens.

Civil society groups should mobilize themselves to study all the relevant documents and take a greater role in raising public awareness, meeting and lobbying parliamentarians and strengthening networks to undertake joint action and launch campaigns. They should also try to translate or document some of the relevant information in the national languages, in an easily understandable form.

Women's organizations should study all existing documents and educate women on the long and short-term impacts of accelerated development programs. Special emphasis must be paid to the following concerns:

- that the government should bring in protective legislation to ensure that basic labor standards are maintained, and that the quality and nature of employment contributes to human resource development
- that where women employees face retrenchment, there is policy intervention that ensures that they are retrained in modern skills, at the employers' expense
- that since most women workers perform multiple roles, and are seen as major contributors to the economy, an expansion, instead of a reduction in state sponsored social welfare programs is made mandatory
- that state-sponsored awareness-raising and protection programs around the issues of social diseases such as HIV/AIDS be made mandatory, and that these programs be presented using the popular media. Otherwise, there is the very real danger that Sri Lanka will end up like sub-Saharan Africa, with its AIDS epidemic overshadowing everything else
- that as a result of public expenditure being cut under the SAPs, the related implications for women, such as declining birth weights, high malnutrition levels, high morbidity levels, should be addressed in government policies and programs
- that an urgent effort be made to create the state infrastructure and services to deal with the negative impacts of current development policies and programs, such as the increasing rates of incest, substance abuse, suicide and violence

CONCLUSION

We have seen the overall situation with regard to the current female labor market in Sri Lanka, and hopefully established the links between economic policies and education in relation to the above. We have also seen how this has changed in the post-independence period. I have analyzed, in a very broad sense, the implications for women, if the current labor market trends were to continue. Finally, I have tried to make some concrete and objective recommendations, bringing in most of the players in the arena.

If the women in Sri Lanka are to enjoy a better overall quality of life, merely proposing development programs which are based totally on export-promotion and privatization strategies, is very short-sighted and callous, to say the least, and possibly downright dangerous or disastrous.

Export-promotion oriented strategies are focused on profits, not on long-term sustainable development, either of the individual or the community. However, women are co-creators and main care-givers of the next generation. If women do not enjoy and are not ensured good physical and mental health, future generations will be adversely affected. Excluding women from decision making processes and from access and control to fair and healthy working conditions, will have long-term negative repercussions that our myopic political leaders will do well to recognize and acknowledge. This then, may be the first step towards putting right, a process and situation that is both unjust and dangerous, violating both human rights and the principles of sustainable development.

Bibliography

ABEYKOON, A.T.P.L., 'The Changing Pattern of Female Labor Force Participation in Sri Lanka,' Sri Lanka Labor Gazette: The National Journal of Labor Affairs Millennium Issue, 2000, pp. 151–165.

JAYAWEERA, Swarna, 'Women in Education and Employment,' Women in Post Independence Sri Lanka, 2002, pp. 103–127.

RAMANAYAKE, Dennis, 'Sri Lanka: The Katunayake Investment Promotion Zone,' Export Processing Zones and Industrial Employment in Asia, 1984, pp. 183–235.

Sri Lanka Government, Regaining Sri Lanka: Vision and Strategy for Accelerated Development, May 2003, p. 4.

TAMBIAH, Yasmin, Women and Governance in South Asia: Re-imagining the State, Sri Lanka International Centre for Ethnic Studies, 2002, pp. 421–497.

UNDP (*United Nations Development Programme*), 'Trends in Growth and Human Development,' Human Development Report, 1996.

WANASUNDERA, Leelangi, 'Conclusion,' Migrant Women Domestic Workers: Cypress, Greece and Italy, Cenwor Study Series No. 23, 2001, pp. 220–232.

Notes

1. Tambiah, 2002, p. 425.
2. Ramanayake, 1984, p. 184.
3. Ramanayake, 1984. p. 184.
4. Jayaweera, 2002, p. 108.
5. Jayaweera, 2002, p. 120.
6. UNDP, 1996, p. 29.
7. Jayaweera, 2002, p. 103.
8. Jayaweera, 2002, p. 104.
9. Ramanayake, 1984, p. 232.
10. Jayaweera, 2002, p. 124.
11. Wanasundera, 2001, p. 221.
12. Abeykoon, 2000, p. 151.
13. Sri Lanka Government, 2003, p. 4.

4
FORCED MIGRATION AND HUMAN TRAFFICKING

*Salma Ali**

ABSTRACT

In this age of globalization, migration is a common phenomenon. Millions of lives in the world are shaped by migration and 2.5 percent of the world's population is migrant. Many factors may cause migration but the most unexpected one is forced migration and it is least accepted in society.

Migration and trafficking are two distinct but inter-related phenomena. Migration is a broad general concept and trafficking is only a subset or category of the broader concept. Forced migration in some cases should be considered as trafficking, as both the cases occur without the concern of the person trafficked and migrated forcefully. Political change, natural calamities, famine, development programs and opportunities of employment are although the major reasons of migration—these should not take place if the persons involved are not willing.

This paper explores the point of demarcation and similarities between forced migration and trafficking and portrays the scenario of trafficking in women and children in this region. The socio-economic perspective of trafficking and forced migration is another focus of the paper, which ends with some recommendations for combating incidences related to trafficking and forced migration.

---

*The author is an Ashoka Fellow, Human Rights Activists & Executive Director, Bangladesh National Woman Lawyers' Association (BNWLA), Dhaka, Bangladesh.

INTRODUCTION

Today, networks for producing and exchanging goods, services and information stretch across the world. Growing hand in hand with these global networks is the international movement of people. Whether of temporary or permanent nature, international migration is more and more an integral component of contemporary life. Globalization, together with trade liberalization and global economic integration, encourages mobility of labor force, but also appears to increase the gap in the standard of living between the developing and the developed worlds. In the light of the changing nature of migration, new methods are needed to achieve and maintain an orderly movement of persons in the midst of a global society that is more and more committed to mobility.

Despite the lack of hard data, a complex set of factors can be identified that contribute to the persistence of human trafficking. These factors are the product of evidence based on years of working with trafficked persons and survivors, tracking the prosecution of perpetrators, and following other sources of information. In order to explore these complex factors, it is useful to consider factors that push the vulnerable into situations of high risk to be recruited by traffickers. There are also pull factors that encourage young people or those already living in dangerous circumstances, to seek out more glamorous or sustaining life options than they feel are available in their own communities. Once mobile, some of these migrants are more vulnerable to being coerced by traffickers, for example, children (particularly girls) and women who have less exposure to the world outside their villages, and know of few survival skills in new circumstances.

For women, the casualization of female labor increases vulnerability to trafficking. Landlessness is also increasing for varied reasons—pressure from increasing population density, environmental erosion, and natural disasters—without corresponding increases in employment opportunities in other sectors. There have been substantial livelihood losses in areas where the demand for traditional skills is declining. These conditions lead to increasing numbers of women and men, moving in order to seek alternative livelihood options—and hence become more vulnerable to being trafficked.

Despite these complexities, this paper analyses the links between trafficking and migration, factors related to the encouragement of trafficking, as well as supply and demand, distinction between migration and trafficking, impacts of forced migration, as well as trafficking and finally, highlights some of the recommendations for combating incidences related to trafficking and forced migration.

LINKS BETWEEN TRAFFICKING AND MIGRATION

Links between trafficking and migration are clearly evident in most accounts of trafficked persons. Some argue that, while trafficking involves human rights abuses, it fundamentally involves movement of people and should perhaps be better understood by using the migration theory. The fact that trafficking episodes start mostly after migration or movement from one place to another has already begun, validates the need to look at what causes people to move and why they are vulnerable to being trafficked during movement. This is a starting point to understanding the factors contributing to human trafficking.

In Bangladesh, a stakeholder-led Thematic Group on Counter Trafficking (coordinated through International Organization of Migration [IOM]) has been meeting regularly, seeking to clarify various aspects of human trafficking. This group identified the following needs or motivations that compel a person or an agent of a person to move them from one situation to another, i.e., migrate. These factors do not apply only to Bangladesh, but to migration in general:

- To meet basic needs, e.g. food, shelter, clothing, health, etc.;
- To increase security to ensure sustainability of basic needs over time;
- To increase status and /or income;
- To escape stigmatization from incidents such as incest, rape, former sex workers, divorced and widowed;
- To respond to or avoid social considerations, e.g. marriage without dowry, elements of society that limit women's personal development, political oppression, etc.;
- To take up adventure based on a desire to experience life and explore the world; and,
- To obtain emotional stability for many reasons such as dysfunctional family situation or need for emotional support system.

(Bangladesh Thematic Group on counter trafficking matrix, September 2003)
The motivation and/or needs are influenced by a series of agents, including other family members, recruiters, smugglers, traffickers, returnees or other migrants, community leaders and neighbours. A series of factors also hinder or facilitate a person through a migratory process that can result in either a positive outcome (where needs are met or motivations achieved) or a negative outcome (such as the consequences of being trafficked). Examining the needs and motivations that initiate the migratory process and the factors that influence the outcomes can help to identify activities to reduce the vulnerability of those most at risk of being trafficked. Figure-1 illustrates the broad categories of these actors and how they may be linked together.

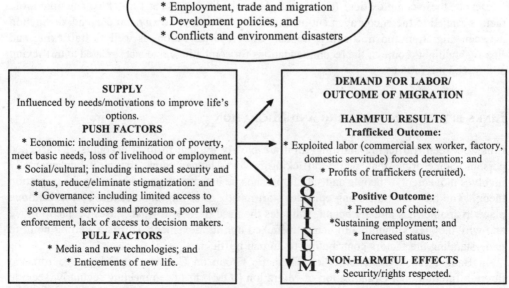

MACRO LEVEL INDICATORS
* Impacts of globalization
* Employment, trade and migration
* Development policies, and
* Conflicts and environment disasters

SUPPLY
Influenced by needs/motivations to improve life's options.
PUSH FACTORS
* Economic: including feminization of poverty, meet basic needs, loss of livelihood or employment.
* Social/cultural; including increased security and status, reduce/eliminate stigmatization: and
* Governance: including limited access to government services and programs, poor law enforcement, lack of access to decision makers.
PULL FACTORS
* Media and new technologies; and
* Enticements of new life.

DEMAND FOR LABOR/ OUTCOME OF MIGRATION

HARMFUL RESULTS
Trafficked Outcome:
* Exploited labor (commercial sex worker, factory, domestic servitude) forced detention; and
* Profits of traffickers (recruited).

CONTINUUM

Positive Outcome:
* Freedom of choice.
*Sustaining employment; and
* Increased status.

NON-HARMFUL EFFECTS
* Security/rights respected.

Fɪɢ. 1: Dʏɴᴀᴍɪᴄs ᴏꜰ Hᴜᴍᴀɴ Tʀᴀꜰꜰɪᴄᴋɪɴɢ

CROSS BORDER/INTERNAL FACTORS RELATED TO TRAFFICKING AND MIGRATION

Trafficking in women and children within the country is increasing at an alarming rate. Because of its illusive nature, authentic statistics regarding the magnitude of the problem are not available. Throughout South Asia, men, women, boys and girls are trafficked within their own countries and across international borders against their will, in what is essentially, a clandestine slave trade. The number of trafficked persons is difficult to determine as the bribery and corruption surrounding the practice renders an estimate of its magnitude virtually impossible. Estimation of the spread of the problem is further complicated by the fact that the crime so often goes unreported, even if reported, there is lack of follow up data regarding recovery and sometimes the incidents of missing children are not taken into account while dealing with trafficking.

In Bangladesh, children fall victims to trafficking due to different reasons. The organized gang of traffickers usually target the poorest of the poor and disadvantaged children and women and traffick them from Bangladesh to India, Pakistan and the Middle East for engaging in forced prostitution and various kinds of bonded labor such as slavery, sex slavery, etc. Most of the Bangladeshi women and children victims of cross border trafficking are sold in the brothels or forcibly engaged in prostitution in cage brothels in the receiving countries like India, Pakistan and different Middle Eastern countries.

Although there has been increasing anxiety and worry among the concerned groups, both at government and NGO levels, concerning the pervasive nature of trafficking, unfortunately, extensive effort from the concerned groups has not been made except a few ones in this regard. Bangladesh could not formulate an anti-human trafficking policy or plan of action as yet, to operationalise the initiatives at various levels.

As the status of implementation of the existing laws relating to trafficking in women and children is very dismal, it is difficult to combat trafficking in terms of ensuring prevention, protection, recovery, rehabilitation and reintegration of the survivors of internal and cross border trafficking. Moreover, the relevant Government departments do not have the necessary data and information about the trafficking scenario in the country. As a result, comprehensive action programs with full geographical coverage have not been possible, on the part of any party including government, and non-government to undertake.

Bangladesh has available statutes with direct implication to prostitution, trafficking in women and children. These are: The Penal Code, 1860, The Children (Pledging of labor) Act 1993, The suppression of Immoral Traffic Act 1933, The Children Act 1974, and the Women and Children Repression Prevention Act 2000.

Facts and figures show that the minor problem of trafficking has assumed a monstrous shape. This is a very complex problem. Due to that, there is an urgent need to analyze such responsible factors at micro and macro level.

Bangladesh National Women's Lawyers' Association (BNWLA) is sheltering the trafficked victims at its own premises and providing all types of basic need support including food, clothing, education, medical and psychological treatment. BNWLA is also imparting skills related to training computers, garments and handicrafts and finally, rehabilitating and reintegrating them into the family as well as in the society. BNWLA is relentlessly carrying out its different projects addressing trafficking since its inception in 1979 and providing legal assistance both to the survivors and to the community, when needed in an emergency. Along with the above works of BNWLA, long-term prevention action, especially awareness raising in trafficking prone areas, has been taking place during the last 10 years. It should be noted here that BNWLA has identified 14 focal trafficking prone areas within the country and is providing area-based support to the desired one.

A strong database has already been developed under the trafficking cell of BNWLA, disseminating relevant information to the different quarters of the society and indirectly pressuring the policy makers to form effective laws for addressing these issues.

The most commonly identified push factors that start the trafficking process is poverty. The necessity to meet basic needs, in combination with other factors is the most commonly identified motivation to migrate or to encourage a family member to leave. However, a simplistic view of poverty based on low-income levels or livelihood options does not assist in understanding why it is that women and children appear to be the most vulnerable to negative outcomes from migration such as trafficking. An understanding of non-economic elements of poverty like lack of human and social capital, gender discrimination also helps identify the most vulnerable to marginalization from the development process and simultaneously, to trafficking.

Despite Bangladesh's low human development index, which is lower than most South Asian countries, there has been a decline in those living below the poverty line from 47% in 1996, to current level 45%. Some key social development indicators have improved, for example, the education gap between male and female primary school enrollment, which stood at 22% in 1985, declined to 3% over the past 15 years. While women in Bangladesh have much lower skills than men, their contribution to the economy is largely unrecognized. Women are still primarily involved in the nonmonetized sector and subsistence activities and hence tend not to be reported in macro statistics. When women do receive wages in the informal sector, there are wide gender differences. Women's participation in the formal work force has increased, as the demand for low cost, unskilled labor has grown in the urban areas, particularly, in the garments' section.

Extensive persistent poverty remains in South Asia, and there is evidence that women are disproportionately excluded from development opportunities through deep-rooted gender-based discrimination. Table 1 provides some basic indicators drawn from the gender related development index in the United Nations:

The United Nations Development Programme (UNDP) Human Development Report 2001 for the three countries compared to the Philippines, demonstrates the greater gaps in development achievements between women and men in South Asia.

Table 1: Indicators Comparing Gender Gaps for the Philippines, Nepal, India and Bangladesh

Indicator	Philippines		Nepal		India		Bangladesh	
GDI ranking	62		120		105		121	
	Women	Men	Women	Men	Women	Men	Women	Men
Estimated earned income (PPP US$)	2,684	4,190	849	1604	1195	3236	1076	1866
Combined enrollment in 3 levels of education (%)	84	80	49	76	49	62	33	41
Adult Literacy	94.9%	95.3 %	21.7%	56.9%	43.5%	67.1 %	28.6%	51.1 %
Maternal Morality Per 100,000		170		540	410		440	

Source: UNDP, Human Development Report 2001.
* All data provided is from 1999.

Based on UNDP definition of three indicators, given the statistics, it would appear that there is considerable feminization of poverty in South Asia. It can also be argued that the feminization of poverty in South Asia is accompanied by the feminization of survival strategies.

A range of policies and environmental circumstances also influence the incidence of poverty and vulnerability to risks for migrants being trafficked. For example:

- Impacts of globalization have included the spread of modernization with greater access to transport, media, etc., but also for many, the disappearances of traditional income sources and rural employment, pushing the poor and unskilled to migrate to survive
- Conflicts and natural disasters that force communities to move often en masse to meet their basic needs. When individuals within those communities have no skills or education, are exposed to health risks, their capacities to secure sustainable livelihoods is limited and their risk to trafficking is heightened
- External migration policies that exclude many unskilled people, particularly women, from legal migration and are therefore forced to seek alternative livelihood options through illegal means
- Internal Displaced Persons (IDPs) are also highly vulnerable to being trafficked. Conditions such as violence, human rights violations, environmental disaster, natural calamities, political unrest and loss of land and property all displace families forcing them to search for places of refuge. As IDPs are generally without resources and without official residence or government recognition, their status makes them more susceptible to adverse situations such as trafficking
- The overwhelming majority of children vulnerable to trafficking are those belonging to poor families with few or no skills or assets, often working as seasonal laborers or in factories or construction sites

Those most at risk are:

- Children separated from their families or with disrupted family backgrounds, (e.g. orphans, victim of abuse, children from single parent families, etc.)
- Economically and socially deprived children
- Children from other marginalized groups (e.g. certain minorities, IDPs)
- Children from the conflict areas

Some stakeholders also argue that the demand for child labor is increasing. Employers prefer children because they are naïve, uncomplaining, easily controlled, vulnerable, desperate and dispensable. Many children are moving around alone in the most vulnerable conditions to being trafficked. Even when children arrive with their parent(s), the pressure of urban life on new migrants can overcome their tenuous family ties and these children end up alone on the street. There have been few studies of those children most at risk in Bangladesh. A research and service NGO in Bangladesh (INCIDIN) has carried out two recent studies: one in 1997 for Red Barnet/Danish Save the Children and the second one in 2001 for ILO and the IPEC, rapid assessment on child trafficking in children for exploitative employment in Bangladesh. The former focused on urban street children and identified that from the study sample, almost 70 per cent of those already involved in commercial sexual exploitation migrated into Dhaka from rural areas, but about 57 per cent of these arrived with either one or both of their parents. It was found that almost all the children who were interviewed stated that they moved in search of jobs, triggered in 40 per cent of the case, by sudden disasters such as loss of land, death of parents or divorce of parents. Children without birth certificates are also vulnerable to trafficking. Traffickers find many of their victims in remote areas where poverty is high and registration rates are low, knowing that girls without papers are less likely to run away from their perpetrators. UNICEF states that birth certificates provide recognition of a child's existence, to secure his/her access in all State facilities.

Poor people are more vulnerable to weak governance and increased risks of being trafficked. Contributing factors in this respect include absence of effective legislation, policies and institutional structures in addressing human trafficking; poor law enforcement combined with corruption and exclusion of poor and vulnerable groups from basic social and economic services.

DISTINCTION BETWEEN MIGRATION AND TRAFFICKING

Migration is linked with trafficking in several ways. People may voluntarily choose to migrate, but may be deceived about the kind of work they are subsequently expected to do. In this case, what started as migration has become trafficking. Or, a person may willingly migrate for employment but may be trafficked from the initial employment site.

The initial process was not trafficking and no crime was committed until the second phase of migration occurred. Hence while trafficking normally involves migration, migration does not always involve trafficking. This distinction is significant for potential anti-trafficking interventions. Given that trafficking may occur either in a person's original home base or at a subsequent work site, intervention to combat trafficking should also recognize that for each individual case, the factors that create the need or desire to migrate and the vulnerability to being exploited by traffickers during migration might be quite different.

Likewise, it is important that anti-trafficking interventions consider the direct or indirect impact on a person's right to mobility. Yet, it is difficult to distinguish voluntary migration from trafficking at the departure point since the deception. It is only after arrival at an unexpected and exploitative outcome that the crime of trafficking is apparent.

Another distinction arises with respect to legal and illegal or irregular migration. Where legal migration across boarders is not possible (e.g. because people lack the relevant documents or where the process of obtaining these is inaccessible to the poor and illiterate), people may migrate illegally. If this person is trafficked and subsequently intercepted by State authorities, the focus is usually upon his/her status as illegal migrants (and therefore criminals) rather than as trafficked persons, and the crimes committed against them go without redress.

IMPACTS OF TRAFFICKING AND MIGRATION

The impact of trafficking is another area where little or no research or data collection has been undertaken. The following are general areas suggested for further queries:

Social Impacts

There are conflicting aspects. Since for many trafficked women, trafficking episodes, while causing harm, also provide opportunities to remove themselves from otherwise oppressive circumstances. As stated in a USAID report of April 2002 titled 'Beyond Boundaries (A critical look at women labor migration)' by Therese Blacnchet, women who have returned remained silent about their experiences, especially concerning commercial sexual exploitation and brought home with them, not only some savings, but also more experience of the world. Some of these women have managed to turn these experiences into personal empowerment within their communities. In many other cases, however, the return home has proved to be too restrictive and they return once more to a migrant life. These experiences point out that migration experiences can be safe and empowering for women, calling for more understanding of how trafficking can be curbed, while the positive elements of migration are enhanced.

Economic Impacts

Economic losses to communities and governments are enormous, if considered in terms of lost returns on home or social capital investments. The cost of countering criminal trafficking activities puts additional strain on already limited government resources for law enforcement. Vast amounts of potential income from trafficked labor are lost in hidden sectors or is expropriated by criminal traffickers and diverted out of the formal economy.

Health impacts

Trafficked persons have often faced extreme psychological stress that in turn leads to trauma, depression and in some cases, suicide. A trafficked woman or child may have been exposed to isolation, fear, sexual abuse, rape and other forms of physical and mental violence. Emotional stress is usually compounded by constant fear of arrest and public stigmatization, making the thought of returning home, fearful. These harmful effects are both short and long term. Women and children in commercial sex sectors, either trafficked or otherwise, face higher risk of contracting sexually transmitted diseases, tuberculosis and other diseases. The following BNWLA case study portrays a clear scenario regarding the impact of trafficking:

Amina's Story: Melancholy tale of a trafficked victim

For Amina, Dubai was the land of dreams come true. Amina was the daughter of Karim Mian and widow of late Amir Ali. Unfortunately, Dubai could not give her anything but a dreadful memory of agony and pain.

Amina, a 25-year old woman, hailed from Narayanganj district. She lost her husband at an early age and became distressed with her two children due to pervasive poverty. At that time, one of her brothers-in-law (cousin's husband), Abu Taleb, convinced her to go to Dubai and lured her with false promises of good employment and good earning. She was tempted with the jugglery of words that her brother-in-law used in favour of going abroad. Abu Taleb also convinced Amina's father to send her to Dubai. Subsequently, Karim Mian managed Tk. 80,000 by selling and mortgaging land and taking a loan and sent his daughter Amina to Dubai to earn a huge amount of money. Amina went to Dubai in January 2001.

On arrival in Dubai, UAE, Amina got work in the household of an Arabian family as maidservant from where she did not receive any money. After two months she was provided with a job by her Bangladeshi agent, Karim, at a Srilankan agency where she was confined in a room and was brutally tortured. In a bid to escape from sexual assault she fell from the rooftop of a two-storied building and broke her back and legs. She was taken to a hospital at Dubai and received treatment but there was no improvement. BNWLA in collaboration with the Labor and Employment Ministry of the Government of Bangladesh repatriated Amina from UAE on 26 June 2001. On arrival at Zia International Airport, representatives of BNWLA received her and took her to the Holy Family Red Crescent Hospital where she was initially provided with treatment. After that, BNWLA sent her to the Centre for the Rehabilitation of the Paralysed (CRP) at Savar for treatment and rehabilitation support on 2 July 2001. She received specialised treatment at CRP for seven months under the supervision of BNWLA and slowly got better and finally stands on her feet, which seemed impossible at the time she was repatriated from UAE.

In recognition of CRP's service for Amina, BNWLA provided CRP with monetary support. Besides, the organisation kept constant contact with CRP during the period Amina received treatment there. During the whole period, the lawyers and counsellors of BNWLA provided Amina and her family with psychosocial counselling. After she fully recovered from her injury, BNWLA reintegrated her into her family on 20 February 2002. BNWLA is communicating with her regularly and recently BNWLA gave her one cow for income generating purposes. In fact Amina is now living a happy life.

(All the names used in the aforementioned case study are fictitious but the story is true)

RECOMMENDATIONS

Traditionally, countries receiving migrants have tried to reduce irregular migration by strengthening control or enforcement procedures. What is needed today, is a more systemic approach. To address the issue of irregular migration effectively, one must recognize the links between the movement of people and the economic, social, political, trade, labor, health, cultural, security and foreign and development policy spheres. What must be avoided is having two types of migration; one that is managed by governments and another parallel irregular information flow that feeds on policy inconsistencies (e.g. between migration and employment), facilitated by smuggling networks taking advantage of loopholes within the government approach. One of the big challenges for governments in this area is to establish credibility, best achieved by providing legitimate channels of entry while deterring irregular movement. One thing needs to be focused here that, BNWLA does not believe that in the name of trafficking, brain drain is happening and the country is facing several problems. As in the case of Bangladesh, targeted people are mostly the illiterate and living below the poverty line. Following are some policy recommendations:

- A collective response and attention should be devoted to understanding and responding to the factors that force people to leave their communities and countries
- A regional database should be developed to trace the incidents related to migration and trafficking
- Regional bodies such as the SAARC, ASEAN should include root causes of migration in their study processes
- In particular, the impact of international economic, trade, aid, development, environmental, and defense assistance on migration flows should be examined
- International organizations, including UNHCR, the International Organization for Migration, NGOs and others should adopt a rights-based approach to migration A rights-based approach—in contrast to the prevailing border control approach—would put the rights of migrants, asylum seekers, and refugees at the center of the discussion
- Governments must protect the basic human rights of all migrants in compliance with their existing treaty obligations and regional commitments
- States should sign and ratify the 1990 Convention on the Protection of the Rights of all Migrant Workers and Members of their Families
- The Global Consultations should address the need for an effective international agency and regime to protect the rights of migrants
- Every country should have self-migration policy based on transparent and coherent assessments of labor and demographic needs
- Opening legal migration channels will protect the rights of migrants to freedom of movement and lessen the possibility that migrants will resort to dangerous means of migration
- Governments should support the principle that migration plays a positive role in the economic, political, social and cultural development of countries and should develop policies in that framework
- The link between deterrence policies and the increase in illegal human trafficking and smuggling rings should be seriously examined in the context of global consultations
- Particular attention should be paid to the gender dimensions of human trafficking and smuggling

Governmental, regional and international measures to combat trafficking and smuggling should not focus exclusively on crime control measures. They should also ensure that the fundamental human rights of trafficked and smuggled persons are upheld, including the right to seek and enjoy asylum.

In fact, combating forced migration, as well as trafficking in Bangladesh, requires major political will by governments and the civil society groups.

Materials/documents consulted:

1. Bangladesh Thematic Group on counter trafficking matrix, Sept. 2003.
2. ADB, 2003, Country Strategy and Program Update, Bangladesh.
3. ADB, 2001, Women in Bangladesh.

5

TRAFFICKING OF WOMEN AND CHILDREN: CHANGING SCENARIO AND POLICY IMPLICATIONS IN SOUTH ASIA

Prof. Ishrat Shamim*

ABSTRACT

This paper examines the issues of human trafficking in South Asia. Trafficking mainly affects women and children. They are most frequently trafficked for sexual abuse or/and labor exploitation, though they sometimes end up falling into begging, delinquency, adoptions, false marriage or trade of human organs. Victims of trafficking are exposed to physical and psychological violence and abuse, denied labor rights, are illegal before the law and are often found in forced and unwanted relationships of dependency with their traffickers. Among the South Asian countries, Bangladesh, Nepal and Sri Lanka are the major countries of origin, while India and Pakistan are countries of destination or transit to other regions, especially the Middle East. In the countries of South Asia, traffickers work through several networks operating from both within the national boundaries as well as the neighboring countries and beyond. It is reported that young girls and women are being trafficked across well-beaten paths within South Asia and further beyond.

*Ms Ishrat Shamim is President, Centre for Women and Children Studies, Bangladesh.

INTRODUCTION

Millions of human beings are trafficked throughout the world. The growing phenomenon is due to several factors: globalization of international economies, an increase of international organized crime syndicates with transnational and trans-criminal links, rising unemployment for women in developing countries, an increased demand for services in developed countries, exposure to the internet, racism, poverty, war and a need to survive. Human beings are trafficked, moved, used and reused for a variety of different reasons—migrant workers, domestic slaves, sex slaves, indentured servants, prostitution, sweatshop workers, garment dungeon workers, begging slaves, and even mail-order brides, who are sometimes exploited by their own husbands. Today, human beings are looked upon as just another commodity for trade by the predators and traffickers.

The highly complex nature of human trafficking affects various different actors in the trafficking chain: trafficked persons, their families and community, and those who recruit, transport and use trafficked labor. It is difficult to measure the magnitude of the problem because of its illegal and clandestine nature. Moreover, the mechanisms, routes and *modus operandi* of traffickers change rapidly according to economic conditions based on supply and demand.

The defining variable of trafficking in persons is the violation of the migrant's human rights. Trafficking mainly, affects, women and children. They are most frequently trafficked for sexual abuse and/or labor exploitation, though sometimes, they end up falling into begging, delinquency, adoptions, false marriage or trade of human organs. Victims of trafficking are exposed to physical and psychological violence and abuse, denied labor rights, are criminals before the law and are often forced into an unwanted relationship of dependency with their traffickers (International Organization for Migration, 2003. p. 61). Radhika Coomaraswamy points out, 'traffickers fish in the stream of migration' and can easily identify those who are most easily deceived or coerced (Coomaraswamy, 2001. Cited in Asian Development Bank, 2003. p. 39).

In South Asia, it appears that the 'worst forms' of trafficking relate to the illegal movement of women and children for the purposes of exploitation, mainly commercial sex work, forced servitude and child labor (Asian Development Bank, 2003). Trafficking is contemporary slavery. Its bonds are not shackles of iron, but poverty; the inferior status of girls and women; the sexual abuse of girls, often by members of their own families or close relations; and the willingness of families and guardians of poor families to send their daughters to urban centers and even leave the country for their own material gain, without knowing the grave consequences (Shamim and Kabir, 1998. p. 1). But when the women and girls return to their homes, they suffer stigmatization and are unacceptable, thus, pushing them into more harmful situations and further exploitation.

Women and children are exposed to the scourge of poverty and deprivation. The combination of unacceptable health, nutrition, education and social conditions, exposure to abuse and violence produces a relatively large number of women and children living in very difficult circumstances. In addition, periodic natural disasters such as cyclones, floods, river erosions, drought and earthquakes, result in a large number of homeless and destitute women with children. For example, in Southern India, trafficking is more common in areas that are prone to natural disasters, situated in less productive agro-climatic zones and where large number of families live below the poverty line (Mukherjee, 1997. Cited in Asian Development Bank, 2003. p. 45).

The effects of increasing landlessness, poverty and male migration in search of employment are fast changing the traditional roles of women. The burden of endemic poverty, widespread malnutrition, illiteracy and socio-economic inequities are falling heavily on the shoulders of women. Deep-rooted patriarchal gender-bias and discriminatory and negative social attitudes perceive women and liabilities. The social unit of the family, however, provides a way for most women to fit into the social system. But shelter-less, abandoned, divorced and widowed women, may find themselves outside the normal social support system. The situation of economic hardship contributes to the crisis within the family, which turns women and children out into the streets and into a life of hunger, disease, violence, fear and exploitation.

These factors, together with the help of unscrupulous pimps, procurers, brothel owners, traffickers and agents, trap young girls and women into sexual exploitation. Too often, there might be information about a trafficker that cannot be traced, as the crime is committed in one country, whereas the trafficked victims are in a vulnerable situation in another country. Unfortunately, the laws do not permit extraterritorial prosecutions (Shamim and Kabir, 1998. p. 3). Moreover, absence of effective legislation and poor law enforcement combined with corruption are important factors that further accelerate the process of trafficking in women and children.

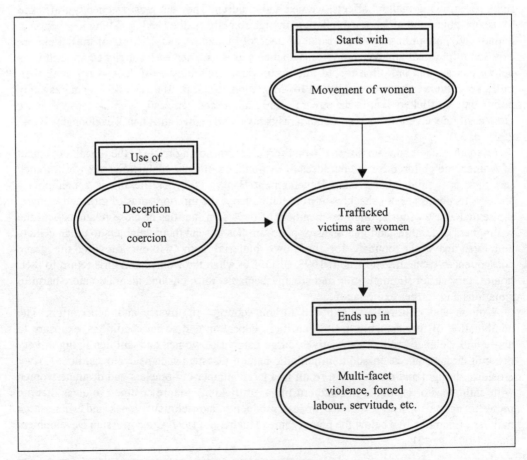

FIG. 1: TRAFFICKING HAS MAINLY THREE CORE ELEMENTS

The underlying cause range from the expansion of global market forces and a growing materialism perpetuated by the media, to rapid social transformation and the erosion of social values. Moreover, the problem of unemployment, under-employment and abject poverty has led to the growing international trafficking and labor migration of women and children in recent years (Shamim and Kabir, 1998. p. 2).

CORE ELEMENTS OF TRAFFICKING

Many times, women voluntarily migrate but end up being trafficked. Migration with consent does not mean trafficking with consent. 'Trafficking with consent' is a contradiction in terms, as no one ever consents to slavery like servitude or forced labor conditions. There is 'deception', where trafficked women are tricked into a vulnerable situation. Women may be offered well-paid jobs or marriage, but end up in forced labor or forced marriage. However, if a woman is trafficked into prostitution, she may know she is going to work in the sex industry, but does not know that she is going to be deprived of her liberty or her earnings. This is still trafficking. In most cases, traffickers deceive trafficked women about the conditions under which they will be forced to live or work and will be deprived of the amount of money they would earn. Some agents may use force to abduct a victim and other use violence or blackmail to keep trafficked women under their control. Trafficked victims are dependent upon the traffickers for food, clothing and housing. Traffickers usually restrict a victim's freedom of movement, and if at all allowed, victims cannot leave the premises without their escort (Global Alliance Against Trafficking in Women, 2001. p. 34–39).

Women and girls are more vulnerable to being trafficked because of factors contributing to the following demand and supply:

FACTORS CONTRIBUTING TO DEMAND	FACTORS CONTRIBUTING TO SUPPLY
• Women's perceived suitability for work in labor-intensive production and the growing informal sector which is characterized by low wages, casual employment, hazardous work conditions and the absence of collective bargaining mechanisms. • The increasing demand for foreign workers for domestic and care-giving roles, and lack of adequate regulatory frameworks to support this. • The growth of the billion-dollar sex and entertainment industry, tolerated as a 'necessary evil' while women in prostitution are criminalized and discriminated against. • The low risk, high profit nature of trafficking encouraged by a lack of will on the part of enforcement agencies to prosecute traffickers (which includes owners/managers of institutions into which persons are trafficked). • The ease in controlling and manipulating vulnerable women. • Lack of access to legal redress or remedies, for victims of traffickers. • Devaluation of women and children's human rights.	• Unequal access to education that limits women's opportunities to increase their earnings in more skilled occupations. • Lack of legitimate and fulfilling employment opportunities particularly in rural communities. • Sex-selective migration policies and restrictive emigration policies/laws, instituted often as a 'protective' measure, limit women's legitimate migration. Most legal channels of migration offer opportunities in typically male-dominated sectors (construction and agriculture work). • Less access to information on migration/job opportunities, recruitment channels, and a greater lack of awareness of the risks of migration compared to men. • Disruption of support systems due to natural and human created catastrophes. • Traditional community attitudes and practices, which tolerate violence against women.

GLOBALIZATION AND ITS IMPACT ON WOMEN IN SOUTH ASIA

The new market tools and rules of this global era have failed to alleviate the poverty of most of South Asia's women. Globalization has moved us towards a free and worldwide economy. Simultaneously, with the unprecedented wealth and progress in the developed world and the elite sectors of developing countries, the economic opportunities available to the majority of South Asian women are extremely limited. The average earned income share of women in South Asia is 24.7 per cent, far below the developing country average of 32.4 per cent (UNDP, 1999). While globalization encompasses more than simply economic changes, it is the economic impact of globalization on women that is important. One effect is increasing unemployment. Conversely, poor, less educated and credit constrained women, especially those who work in the urban and rural informal sectors, may not see many of the benefits of globalization at all. It has caused a rapid growth of the informal labor sector such as street vending and of unregulated work in factories, particularly in the garment industry in Bangladesh. Female workers have become more vulnerable and subject to abusive working conditions, because these marginalized and unregulated areas of work are not visible, and thus not subject to labor laws and regulation. Moreover, recent trends in globalization have broken down the traditional family structure for many rural households. Each member of the family has become 'a separate and independent unit of labor' to be plugged into the modern labor market.

Increasingly, more women are heading households and bearing the financial burden of raising children. In rural households, where husbands often go to work in the urban centers and mostly do not send money to their families back home, women have to manage on their own. Consequently, they have to seek livelihood activities to support their children and sometimes have to migrate for mere survival.

Most women are unlikely to benefit from such liberalization policies because these programs do not take account of gender-specific impacts. It is true that significant opportunities are available in low-tech manufacturing industries (i.e. garments), for women who have not so far been employed in the industrial sector. Nevertheless, it is likely that the victims of cost-cutting initiatives will outnumber those who are being hired in new factories. Most of those losing their jobs are unskilled, while those keeping their jobs or being hired are highly skilled. The outcomes of downsizing initiatives include an increase in low-paying home-based, sub-contracting work, most of it done by women. As a matter of fact, globalization tends to increase income inequality between different sectors and groups, which, if not countered through re-distributive fiscal and employment policies, will further marginalize vulnerable groups. Women form a vast majority of these in South Asia.

Women in the smaller countries of South Asia have made more progress than women in the larger countries—the earned income shares of women in Nepal, Bhutan and the Maldives has increased. However, in all these countries, there are still wide wage differentials between men and women and fewer opportunities for women to apply new technologies. Globalization has also failed to address the issue of economic and environmental sustainability, particularly in the agricultural and informal sectors. Globalization has put poor and uneducated women in a more acute situation of need than ever before. Gains have been limited and even where they have been more extensive, such as in industries in India, Sri Lanka and Bangladesh; there is much that remains to be done. As far as the Bangladesh experience is concerned, there is definitely something that other South Asian countries can learn, at least in terms of how to begin the process of pro-poor growth in the global era. However, to a large degree, South

Asian women have suffered the brunt of negative effects of globalization; adjustment policies in particular, lead to an intensification of women's domestic and market work, interruption of girls' education, and an increase in the amount of time women spend to obtain basic services or to self provide them (Beneria, 1995).

Countries in the South Asian region are experiencing rapid change in economic, political, demographic and labor trends. The wide diversity of labor and population profiles in the region encourages migration, either legal or illegal. Such migration is in response to the dynamics of supply and demand. Usually, women from poorer countries like Bangladesh and Nepal are thus most at risk for exploitation and trafficking to neighboring countries in India and Pakistan.

It is reported that young girls and women are being trafficked across well-beaten paths within South Asia and beyond. From just two routes (Nepal to India and Bangladesh to Pakistan) involve an estimated of 9,000 girls and women trafficked in a year (Giri, 1999). They are most often trafficked from countries or regions suffering from poor economies and environmental stress, which force families into urban areas and generate the feminization of poverty. On the whole, it may be said that the number of girl children and women who are trafficked and are in prostitution, is the highest in Asia and Central/South America. More than one million children, the majority of whom are female, are forced into prostitution every year. In the wake of the HIV/AIDS epidemic, younger children are being sought, in the belief that they are less likely to be infected (Bunch, 1997).

FEMINIZATION OF MIGRATION TO TRAFFICKING

Women have been out numbering men in the migrant labor market in the last decade. Nowhere is the feminization of labor migration more felt, than in the Asian region. But the demand for Asian women's labor is severely gender-tracked with low status. This prevails, usually in the domestic and entertainment spheres. Many end up in prostitution. State policies and programs, and the international demand for cheap labor abroad have facilitated the present massive migration of women for work. It is legitimizing a system that involves government and private sector recruiters and marketers.

International crime syndicates are prone to be involved because of the high profit potential with least fear of detection and if detected, undergoing comparatively low penalties. Aside from passport fraud and visa offence, multi-million dollar profits are untaxed, moving offshore for money laundering purposes and use of large-scale fraudulent documents. These activities fall upon the responsibilities of government agencies, both in the receiving country and in the sending country. As a consequence of restrictive migration policies in many countries, regular migration has declined and illegal migration has increased. This trend has also affected expanded trafficking in women. Trafficking for commercial sexual services is the most common form of exploitation in both Asia and Europe, although trafficking for other purposes like domestic labor, work in factories, construction or agriculture, marriage, mail-order bride services, begging, adoption and drug trafficking, may be more common in Asia.

Women become helpless victims of violence when they are trapped in situations from where they cannot escape. They are victims of trafficking, abduction and prostitution. Trafficking primarily for purposes of prostitution is today, a phenomenon of global magnitude, that violates the human rights of millions of women and girls all over the world. Trafficking in women and prostitution are situated in a continuum of sexual exploitation that perpetuates and continually reinforces the subordinate status of women. The prostitute is treated as the personal property of the pimp or trafficker and is therefore, a saleable and negotiable item. Sexual exploitation also takes many forms such as pornography, sex tourism, bride-trade and temporary marriages, and sexual violence such as rape, incest and sexual harassment. As the sex industry grows, so does the market for trafficking. The increase in tourism is also linked to the escalating demand for entertainment and sex services, also fuelling the sex market and thus feeding the trafficking business. Furthermore, the myths in certain cultures regarding rejuvenating the power of sex with virgins and young girls, and the wish to avoid AIDS, may lead men to seek younger and virgin partners.

Trafficking takes place by a variety of means such as promises of jobs or marriages, and at times, even by physical violence and abduction. Where there is massive poverty, promises of jobs hold new hopes for a better life for the whole family. Also, the early involvement of girl children of acutely poor families, in economic activities for quick and easy money leads to trafficking. But the employment is usually not of the kind that they had anticipated. It is also reported that some of them have been sold to brokers by their own parents, guardians and husbands, to evade poverty and hunger. They often become unwittingly and unwillingly, victims of sexual exploitation and prostitution. Once the young girls and women are in the hands of procurers, through whatever means, they are virtually controlled through threats of violence and total confinement. Girls and women who try to escape are severely beaten or tortured. Even those who escape have nowhere to go. They find it hard to go back to their place of origin, because of non-acceptance and social stigma attached, especially to young girls and women. Moreover, young women who have worked as prostitutes may face legal and moral isolation. Too often, they even do not want their families to know what has happened to them (Shamim and Kabir, 1998. p. 3).

Trafficked women are vulnerable to arrest, detention and deportation, because destination countries are unwilling to recognize them as victims of crimes. Destination countries view trafficked women as undocumented migrants who entered illegally and/or worked illegally. As such, women are particularly subject to arrest, detention and deportation if they were trafficked into the sex industry. They often do not have the chance to lodge complaints, seek damages, assessment whether it is safe to return home, collect their belongings or apply for asylum. Many laws and police officials fail to distinguish between prostitutes and victims of forced trafficking, treating the latter as criminals rather than those who deserve temporary care [and protection] (Shamim, 2002. p. 8).

Fear and shame lead many girls and women to remain silent about their experiences of abuse and thus they fail to warn others who might be vulnerable. Exploitation disturbs the natural development process, impairs self-esteem and relationship, and causes failure in friendships. Victims may display highly sexualized or highly aggressive behavior, depression, or disassociation to relieve anxiety. Exploitation destroys a girl's trust in others and makes her vulnerable to further exploitation or becoming an exploiter herself. Many are at risk of suicide (CEDPA, 1997). The consequences of trafficking for sexual exploitation are disastrous, and strong emphasis is to the plight of girls who have returned to Nepal, for example with possible exposure to HIV/AIDS.

COUNTRIES OF ORIGIN, TRANSIT AND DESTINATION IN SOUTH ASIA

Among the countries of South Asia, Bangladesh, Nepal and Sri Lanka are the major countries of origin, while India and Pakistan are countries of destination or transit to other regions, especially to the Middle East. In the countries of South Asia, traffickers work through several networks operating from both within the national boundaries, as well as the neighboring countries and beyond. Along the borders between Bangladesh and India, the check posts and border forces are widely dispersed and few in numbers, while Nepal and India have an open border. As a result, it is difficult to maintain strict vigilance, although border forces are knowledgeable about illegal crossing of borders by traffickers, along with their victims. Moreover, trafficked women and children do not know that they are being taken to be trapped in exploitive situations until they reach their destination. Moreover, traffickers make sure that trafficked victims do not disclose that they are going with agents because they will be detained and picked up by law enforcing agencies. The US State Department of Trafficking in Persons Report (2003) provided updated information about the following countries of origin, transit and destination in South Asia:

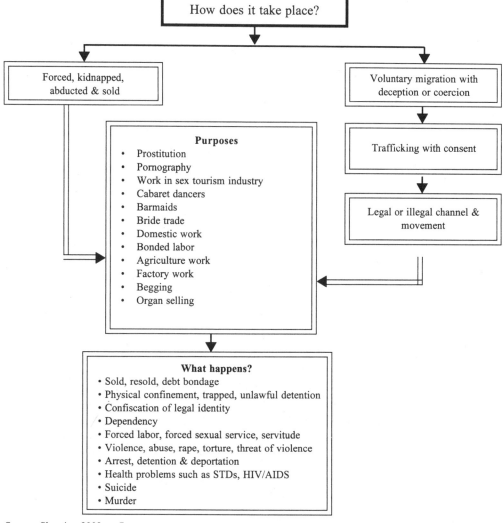

Source: Shamim, 2002. p. 7.

FIG. 2: MECHANISMS OF TRAFFICKING IN WOMEN

Bangladesh is a country of origin and transit for women and children trafficked for purposes of sexual exploitation, domestic servitude and bonded labor. Women and girls are trafficked to India, Pakistan, Bahrain, Kuwait, and the United Arab Emirates for commercial sexual exploitation and domestic work. A small number of women and girls are transited through Bangladesh from Burma to India. Boys are also trafficked to the United Arab Emirates and Qatar and forced to work as camel jockeys and beggars. Internal trafficking of women and children from rural areas to the larger cities for commercial sexual exploitation and domestic work also occurs (US State Department, June 2003. p. 28).

India is a country of origin, transit, and destination for thousands of trafficked persons. Internal trafficking of women, men, and children for purposes of sexual exploitation, domestic servitude, bonded labor, and indentured servitude is widespread. Indian men and women are also put into situations of coerced labor and sometimes slave-like conditions in countries in the Middle East and the West. India is a destination for sex tourists from Europe and the United States. Bangladeshi women and children are trafficked to India or transited through India enroute to Pakistan and the Middle East for purposes of sexual exploitation, domestic servitude, and forced labor. Nepalese women and girls are trafficked to India for commercial sexual exploitation (US State Department, June 2003. p. 79).

Nepal is a source country of women and girls trafficked primarily to India, for the purposes of commercial sexual exploitation and debt bondage. Nepali women traveling to the Middle East in search of work have been put into situations of coerced labor and other slave-like conditions. Internal trafficking also takes place in Nepal. Women are trafficked from rural areas to cities for commercial sexual exploitation and children are placed into debt bondage or other exploitative child labor by their impoverished parents. Human Rights Watch (1995) noted that Nepalese girls have been trafficked either directly or after spending time in India to places such as Hong Kong, China, Thailand and Gulf countries (US State Department, June 2003. p. 111).

Pakistan is a country of origin, transit, and destination for women and children trafficked for purposes of sexual exploitation and bonded labor. Internal trafficking of women and girls from rural areas to cities for purposes of sexual exploitation and labor also occurs. Pakistan is a source country for young boys who are trafficked to the United Arab Emirates, Kuwait, and Qatar as camel jockeys. Pakistani men and women travel to the Middle East in search of work and are put into situations of coerced labor, slave-like conditions, and physical abuse. Pakistan is a destination for women and children trafficked from Bangladesh, Afghanistan, Iran, and Central Asia for purposes of commercial sexual exploitation and labor. Women trafficked from East Asian countries and Bangladesh to the Middle East transit through Pakistan (US State Department, June 2003. p. 118).

Sri Lanka is a country of origin and destination for trafficked persons. Commercial sexual exploitation of children, especially of boys, occurs domestically, often in tourist areas. Many of these children, especially girls, are lured by promises of job opportunities or overseas travel, and family members or friends often introduce them into commercial sexual activity. Internal trafficking of persons for purposes of domestic servitude and combat also takes place in Sri Lanka. In many cases, Sri Lankan women go to the Middle East to countries such as Lebanon, Kuwait, Bahrain, United Arab Emirates, or Saudi Arabia in search of work, only to be put into situations of coerced labor, slave-like conditions, or sexual exploitation. A small number of Thai, Russian, and Chinese women have been trafficked to Sri Lanka for purposes of sexual exploitation (US State Department, June 2003. p. 140).

Prevention Efforts in South Asia

In Bangladesh, the Ministry of Women and Children Affairs is implementing a project, Child Development: Coordinated Programme to Combat Child Trafficking (CPCCT), since 2000, giving strong emphasis in the areas of capacity building, awareness raising, legal issues, rehabilitation, repatriation and reintegration through grassroots level NGOs. A special anti-child trafficking cell has been established in the Ministry of Home Affairs. Two other cells, one in Bangladesh Rifles and the other in CID Police have been formed under the same Ministry, whose functions are to identify those involved in trafficking and arrest them and promptly rescue the trafficked persons. The International Organization for Migration (IOM) has been conducting training courses for the law enforcement agencies since 2001 under the project, 'Capacity Building of Law Enforcement Officials to Prevent Trafficking of Women and Children', to improve the investigation and interview skills of officials, while dealing with trafficked persons.

In **Bangladesh**, the government adopted the National Plan of Action against the Sexual Abuse and Exploitation of Children including trafficking, which is a comprehensive plan to combat child sexual exploitation focusing on prevention, protection, recovery and reintegration, perpetrators, child participation, HIV/AIDS, STIs and substance abuse and coordination and monitoring (Ministry of Women and Children Affairs, May 2002).

In **India**, the Indian central government and an international organization signed a $400 million agreement for a five-year program to prevent trafficking and to assist at-risk children. The state of Goa, together with NGOs, is supporting public awareness campaigns about pedophilia and sex tourism on the beaches. The State Transport Network in the state of Maharashtra conducts training programs for drivers and bus conductors to spot girls in distress and has prominently displayed anti-trafficking help line numbers at major bus stations. The state of Tamil Nadu established village level 'watchdog' committees to prevent trafficking in women and children. These committees include representatives from the village council, school officials, representatives from police stations, and members of NGOs. The Chennai Central Railway Station set up a 'Childline' to rescue and keep a record of children being taken out of the state for labor and to watch for runaways and other at-risk children. In Bihar and West Bengal, NGOs and representatives from village governments and police have developed community-level watch groups to monitor the movements of women and children from, to and through the area (US State Department, 2003. pp. 79–80).

In **Nepal**, the Ministry of Women and Children and Social Welfare of Nepal developed a comprehensive 13-point strategy for the prevention of trafficking in 1998. The Ministry has hosted meetings on trafficking and provided a forum for NGOs, government organizations, CBOs, policymakers, women's groups, international agencies and members of the civil society. Various anti-trafficking IEC materials were developed to raise greater awareness among the public. Nepal police have also been vigorously involved in the campaign against girl trafficking (Asian Development Bank, 2003).

In **Pakistan**, the government does not support specific anti-trafficking prevention programs. The government supports targeted prevention programs such as poverty alleviation, the eradication of child labor, promotion of girls' education, and women's income generation projects, aimed at eradicating the root causes of trafficking. The Federal Investigative Agency (FIA) Academy in Islamabad provides trafficking awareness training (US State Department, 2003. p. 118).

In **Sri Lanka**, the government, together with NGOs, has conducted public awareness campaigns regarding child labor and created hotlines for reporting child labor abuse. Some

NGOs also work with the government in starting educational campaigns geared towards keeping mothers from working in the Middle East, where they often work without many civil protections. The government is working collaboratively with other governments in educating Sri Lankan women about their rights in destination countries (US State Department, 2003. p. 140).

Protection of Trafficked Victims

In **Bangladesh,** victims are not detained, jailed, or prosecuted for violations of immigration or prostitution laws. Once a victim files a civil suit or makes a criminal complaint against a trafficker, the government will prosecute the case at no cost to the victim. The government works closely with, and refers victims to NGOs that provide shelter and access to legal, medical and psychological services. The government provided specialized training to its officials in assisting victims, but has yet to provide training on protection and assistance to its embassies and consulates in foreign countries, that is, destination or transit countries for its citizens (US State of Department, 2003. p. 29).

In **India**, a recent Supreme Court of India decision held that victims of trafficking might testify in camera. The Department of Women and Child Development (DWCD) helps NGOs finance the repatriation of women and children trafficked to India from other countries. Over the past two years, state governments have established eighty Protective Homes that provide custodial care, education, vocational training, and rehabilitation. The DWCD and the Juvenile Justice Act sponsor a network of 350 short stay homes for the protection and rehabilitation of victims. The DWCD launched a project in 2001 called 'Swadahar', to provide services for women in difficult circumstances, including trafficking victims, that includes shelter, food, clothing, counseling, medical and legal assistance, vocational training, and education. The state government of Andhra Pradesh created a statewide rescue and rehabilitation policy, which requires every district to form anti-trafficking committees. Together with NGOs, the Calcutta City Police have opened support service centres in every police station that has a female police officer to help victims of trafficking or rape. Indian embassy officials in key destination countries help citizens trafficked into exploitative labor situations (US State of Department, 2003. p. 81).

In **Nepal**, the Government of Nepal provides limited resources to non-governmental organizations to provide victim assistance for rehabilitation, counseling, and medical care. Victims are not jailed, detained, or deported. Once a victim files a civil suit or makes a criminal complaint against a trafficker, the government will prosecute the case at no cost to the victim (US State of Department, 2003. p. 111).

In **Pakistan**, the government sponsors a variety of shelters and training programs throughout the country that provide medical treatment, limited legal representation, and vocational training. The government provides temporary residence status to foreign trafficking victims, as well as a lawyer on demand. Still, many victims languish in jail for months or years without having their cases heard. On the provincial and local level, the Punjab Ministry for Social Welfare collaborates with approximately 400 NGOs in providing women's shelters, orphanages, and rehabilitation programs for women and children. In destination countries for Pakistani laborers, embassy officials assist those who have been trafficked or placed in abusive working conditions (US State of Department, 2003. pp. 118–119).

In **Sri Lanka**, the Police Women's and Children's Bureau, the National Child Protection Authority (NCPA), and a police unit directly attached to the NCPA, work together to combat trafficking and protect victims. The government provides rehabilitation camps and other services for victims. The government's ability to provide long-term assistance to victims is limited; however, the NCPA provides medical and psychological assistance to Sri Lankan victims of trafficking and former child soldiers. The NCPA also coordinates the monitoring of the tourism industry and the commercial sexual exploitation of children. Sri Lanka shares information with foreign governments and law enforcement organizations about the identification of child abuse. The government has assigned welfare officers to its embassies to countries in the Middle East to assist women who may have been trafficked (US State of Department, 2003. p. 140).

Legal Framework and Prosecution of Traffickers

In **Bangladesh**, the Women and Children Repression Prevention Act, 2000 prohibits trafficking in women and children and provides penalties of 20 years of imprisonment, life imprisonment or death sentence (Women and Children Repression Prevention Act, 2000). The government does investigate trafficking cases; however, the court system is backlogged by approximately one million cases, severely hampering the ability to bring criminal cases to closure quickly. The government has arrested and prosecuted some traffickers, and courts have handed down tough sentences. During the year, the government arrested 60 alleged traffickers and convicted 30, an increase from four last years. For those convicted, the sentences ranged from 20 years to life. Police and government officials received specialized training from international organizations and NGOs in investigating and prosecuting trafficking cases. However, corruption is widespread at lower levels of the government; police, customs, immigration officials and border guards are reportedly susceptible to bribery (US State Department, 2003. p. 28).

In **India**, The Immoral Traffic (Prevention) Act (ITPA) of India prohibits trafficking in persons, criminalizes sexual exploitation, and provides enhanced penalties for offences involving minors. During investigations, police frequently do not utilize all provisions of the ITPA and, as a result, may minimize potential criminal penalties against traffickers and brothel owners for exploiting minors. Officials use numerous provisions of the Indian Penal Code and the Juvenile Justice Act to prosecute traffickers. Legislation also exists in numerous states to prohibit the dedication to religious shrines of girls for exploitation. In India, prosecution of traffickers, brothel owners, and others associated with trafficking, once rare, has increased significantly over the past year. Three special courts in New Delhi have been designated to hear trafficking cases. A total of 48 cases against traffickers and brothel owners are in the queue to be prosecuted and 14 people have been convicted and sentenced in New Delhi so far. In Mumbai, a Swiss couple was sentenced to seven years imprisonment for kidnapping and molesting a child, and making child pornography films for distribution on the Internet. Low-level border guards have taken bribes or turned a blind eye to trafficking across borders. In addition, some law enforcement officials have been implicated in 'tipping off' brothels to raids (US State Department, 2003. p. 80).

In **Nepal**, the Human Trafficking Control Act of 1986, prohibits selling persons and provides for penalties up to twenty years imprisonment for traffickers. Last year, 92 cases against traffickers were taken to court; prosecution and sentencing statistics are not yet available. Nepal's open land border with India does not allow for stringent monitoring. Border officials receive training from non-governmental and international organizations on how to recognize potential trafficking victims. Former trafficking victims patrol along side border officials and help them spot potential trafficking situations. The Governments of Nepal and India have agreed to form a Joint Cross Border Committee against Trafficking in order to collaborate on investigations and more efficiently share information about traffickers (US State Department, 2003. p. 111).

In **Pakistan**, the government passed a law in October 2002 that criminalizes all aspects of trafficking, from recruitment and transporting, to receiving a person. The Federal Investigative Agency (FIA) reports that 11 people have been arrested for trafficking under the new statute, and prosecutions of those individuals are pending. Backlogged courts slow legal proceedings. Pakistan and Iran signed an agreement to conduct joint investigations on trafficking in persons and narcotics. The country worked with Iranian authorities on cases involving the trafficking of camel jockeys. The government is improving its ability to patrol its borders through training and equipment, but large areas of uncontrollable borders allow traffickers to bring women and children into Pakistan. Despite the establishment of a National Accountability Bureau and some noteworthy prosecutions of corruption cases, corruption remains a problem throughout Pakistan (US State Department, 2003. p. 118).

The **Sri Lankan** Penal Code specifically criminalizes trafficking in persons, and law enforcement authorities have undertaken some investigations of traffickers. Sri Lanka has a labor mediation board and the government also helps in investigating fraudulent employment agencies and contracts. The government's Overseas Employment Bureau works with Sri Lankan embassies abroad to resolve problems that domestic workers encounter (US State Department, 2003. p. 140).

Policy gaps in Enforcement and Prosecution

Bangladesh needs to curb corruption among law enforcement officials, monitor its borders better, increase prosecutions of traffickers, and invest in more protection programs, such as, increasing the shelter capacity for victims. The Indian government should speed up the prosecution of trafficking cases, increase training on trafficking for low-level police officers throughout the country, and increase prosecutions of corrupt officials. A major concern is the high number of child victims forced into commercial sexual exploitation in the mega-cities of India. Prosecutions of those involved in perpetrating the commercial sexual exploitation of children should substantially increase over the next year to combat this dreadful scourge. In Nepal, stronger coordination of law enforcement efforts, and serious efforts to curb corruption will improve its anti-trafficking efforts. The government of Pakistan should increase training for low-level police officers, prosecutors and judges throughout the country. Prosecution and conviction of those involved in perpetrating trafficking should increase over the next year. Sri Lanka can improve its anti-trafficking performance by stepping up law enforcement efforts, particularly against sex tourists. The government needs to ensure that foreign women who are trafficked to Sri Lanka are not arrested.

Conclusion and Forward Looking Strategies

Women and child trafficking is now considered a serious crime by the governments of the South Asian region. In January 2002, representatives of the seven member states of SAARC expressed their commitment to combat trafficking in women and children at the Ninth SAARC Summit at Malee, Maldives. Convention on Preventing and Combating Trafficking in Women and Children for Prostitution was signed—which is the first sub-regional treaty, addressing trafficking in women and children. The convention includes specifications of criminal offenses for trafficking, provides for mutual legal assistance in conducting investigations, trials and other proceedings. With regard to prevention and interception of trafficking, the convention requires state parties to sensitize the law enforcement agencies and judiciaries about trafficking, and to exchange information on a regular basis.

Given the multi-dimension of the problem of trafficking in women, young girls and children, Shamim (1993) identified some pertinent issues to be considered as interrelated for effective future strategies:

- Invisibility of the problem of trafficking in women and children, owing to its illegal nature
- Powerlessness and vulnerability of the women and child victims, especially due to their gender and age
- Use of women and children as economic commodities to be exchanged or sold by strong trafficking syndicates
- Lack of proper and timely prosecution
- Lack of legislative measures addressing regional trafficking in women
- Societal attitudes condone trafficking in women and young girls and cause stigmatization

Trafficking is complex and has many harmful effects on trafficked women and children and therefore, action should be taken at many levels: local, regional and international. Moreover, various strategies are also needed to address the specific problems at the different stages of the trafficking continuum.

Policy and Strategies of the State and State Agencies

- Prioritizing trafficking of vulnerable women, young girls and children as a major human rights violation
- Developing national plans of action to combat trafficking and the process should be used to build links and partnership between relevant government department and agencies involved with the issue of trafficking
- Developing guidelines and procedures for relevant State agencies and officials such as police, border forces and immigration officials involved in the detection and accurate identification of trafficked women and children
- Sensitizing law enforcement authorities and officials by providing adequate training in the investigation and prosecution of cases of trafficking. It should be sensitive to the needs of trafficked women and children
- Ensuring proper implementation of the laws, as well as amending or adopting national legislation in accordance with international standards
- Establishing special anti-trafficking units comprising of both women and men from law enforcing authorities to work in partnership with NGOs, so that trafficked women and children receive the necessary support and assistance
- Strengthening the capacity of law enforcement agencies to arrest and prosecute those involved in trafficking as a preventive measure
- Offering technical and financial assistance to NGOs and local communities for the purpose of developing and implementing anti-trafficking strategies

- Monitoring and evaluating the impact of anti-trafficking laws, policies and interventions, to be able to make distinctions between measures that have been successful and those that have not
- Facilitating cooperation between NGOs and other civil society organizations in countries of origin, transit and destination. This is particularly important to ensure support and assistance to trafficked women and children who are repatriated
- Adopting bilateral agreements between 'sending' and 'receiving' countries to ensure that the victims are repatriated. Foreign missions abroad, both in the sending and receiving countries in South Asia, should also be involved in such efforts.
- Supporting NGOs in rescuing, recovering and rehabilitating victims of trafficking
- Addressing the corruption such as bribery, threats of violence and vested interests in the profits of trafficking at the local level
- Complying with the obligations under international treaties, to guarantee the fundamental human rights of women and girls, particularly under the CEDAW and the CRC.

Given below are more specific interventions and policy implications outlined in the UNIFEM Briefing Kit on Trafficking in Persons: A Gender Rights Perspective (undated) related to research and advocacy, prevention, protection, legal strategies, repatriation, return and reintegration:

Research and Advocacy

- Ensure data collected is disaggregated on the basis of age, sex and ethnicity
- Ensure that research is gender-sensitive
- Ensure governments and NGOs conduct periodic evaluations on policy and programme impacts to help enhance their efficacy
- Develop codes of ethics in data collection and research that respects the rights of trafficked persons
- Develop substantive data bases and information networking systems

Prevention

- Increase literacy, access to education and life skills training for sustainable livelihoods
- Enhance economic opportunities that are market responsive, innovative and sustainable
- Ensure access to information on risks of migration and avenues for assistance
- Ensure appropriate legal documentation for birth, citizenship and marriage
- Change community attitudes through targeted consciousness-raising and advocacy activities
- Create awareness of the links between violence against women and trafficking
- Incorporate gender sensitivity and human rights concerns into the school curriculum
- Facilitate community-based committees to catalyze local responses to combat trafficking
- Provide training to officials to respond sensitively to needs of vulnerable women and communities

Legal Strategies

- Amend and/or adopt national legislation in accordance with the UN Trafficking Protocol and other international standards

- Strengthen transnational cooperation to prosecute violators
- Make legislative provision for confiscation of assets of traffickers to support and compensate trafficked persons
- Establish mechanisms to monitor the human rights impact of anti-trafficking laws, policies, programs and interventions
- Adopt labor migration agreements in accordance with international standards
- Decriminalize trafficked persons, regardless of immigration status, recognizing them as victims and survivors
- Criminalize traffickers, and penalize public officials involved in trafficking and related activities
- Consult with trafficked persons in the formulation, implementation and monitoring of laws

Repatriation, Return And Reintegration

- Ensure safe, voluntary, timely repatriation
- Provide legal alternatives to repatriation, where necessary
- Provide integrated rehabilitation and re-integration facilitates
- Assist families and communities to respond to needs of returnees' protection
- Develop guidelines to facilitate the rapid identification of illegal migrants who are victims of trafficking
- Provide appropriate health care, shelter and counseling facilities
- Ensure legal and other assistance during criminal proceedings against traffickers
- Protect the identity and ensure safety of trafficked persons and witnesses in legal proceedings
- Ensure right of access to diplomatic representatives of the trafficked persons' country of origin
- Pay special attention to the needs and concerns of trafficked children

Protection

- Develop guidelines to facilitate the rapid identification of illegal migrants who are victims of trafficking.
- Provide appropriate health care, shelter and counseling facilities.
- Ensure legal and other assistance during criminal proceedings against traffickers.
- Protect the identity and ensure safety of trafficked persons and witnesses in legal proceedings.
- Ensure right of access to diplomatic representatives of the trafficked persons country of origin.
- Pay special attention to the needs and concerns of trafficked children.

References

Asian Development Bank, Combating Trafficking in Women and Children in South Asia, Manila, April 2003.
BENERIA, I., 'Towards a Greater Integration of Gender in Economics,' World Development, 23 (11), 1995, pp. 1839–1850.
BUNCH, Charlotte, 'The Intolerable Status Quo: Violence Against Women and Girls,' Progress of Nations, New York, 1997.

Centre for Development and Population Activities (CEDPA), Girls' Rights: Society's Responsibility, Taking Action Against Sexual Exploitation and Trafficking, Facts on Asia and Country Profiles, Washington, USA, 1997.

COOMARASWAMY, Radhika, Addendum Report to the Human Rights Commission regarding Mission to Bangladesh, Nepal and India on the issue of Trafficking of Women and Children October-November 2000, Asian Development Bank, 2001.

GIRI, V.M. Kanya: Exploitation on Little Angles, New Delhi: Gyan Publishing House, 1999.

Global Alliance Against Trafficking in Women, Human Rights and Trafficking in Persons: A Handbook, Bangkok, 2001, pp. 34–39.

Human Rights Watch, Rape for Profit, 1995, cited in Asian Development Bank, Combating Trafficking of Women and Children in South Asia, Manila, April 2003.

International Organization for Migration (IOM), World Migration 2003:Managing Migration Challenges and Responses for People on the Move, Geneva, 2003.

Ministry of Women and Children Affairs, National Plan of Action against the Sexual Abuse and Exploitation of Children including Trafficking, Government of the People's Republic of Bangladesh, May 2002.

MUKERJEE, K.K., 'Combating Trafficking of Women and Children in South Asia 2003,' Joint Women's Programme (JWP) Seminar, New Delhi, cited in Asian Development Bank, p. 45.

SHAMIM, I., Child Trafficking and Sale, Dhaka: Bangladesh Shishu Adhikar Forum, 1993.

SHAMIM, I. and F. Kabir, Child Trafficking: The Underlying Dynamics, Red Barnet, Dhaka, 1998.

SHAMIM, I., 'Strategizing to Combat Trafficking in Women and Children,' Proceedings of the International Seminar and Regional Workshops on Strategizing to Combat Trafficking in Women and Children, Dhaka: Centre for Women and Children Studies, June, 2002.

Unifem, Trafficking in Persons: A Gender Rights Perspective, Briefing Kit, New York, undated.

United Nations Development Programme, Human Development 1999, New York: Oxford University Press, 1999.

US State Department, Trafficking in Persons Report, Washington, June 2003.

6

CAN WOMEN BE PEACE BUILDERS?

*Gloria de Silva**

ABSTRACT

This paper attempts to present a broad overview of Sri Lanka's ethnic, religious, political, and social composition and background; the contradictions that exist regarding the status of women in Sri Lankan society, the reasons for those contradictions; the history of violence and conflicts in the last 25 years, the mobilization of women around these issues of violence and conflict; and the needs and gaps that must be addressed in mobilizing women in building sustainable security and peace at local and national levels.

I have tried to analyze the current situation that exists within Sri Lankan society, in order to emphasize pressing needs and concerns regarding policy and programme formulation. I have also attempted to highlight some of the misconceptions prevalent in the region regarding the status and mindset of Sri Lankan women, and to present the fact that the involving of women in security and peace-building is not an activity confined to post-conflict situations. In the prevailing climate of social and political violence, both in the private and pubic sphere, it has become essential that women, who are so often the victims and survivors of this violence, take a stand on bringing about a state of non-violence by becoming key players in building peace and security.

In conclusion, I have made some hopefully objective recommendations based on my experience and work with women during the past ten years, in an attempt to transcend traditional thinking in defining women's roles in security and peace building.

*The author is presently the Director of the Centre for Family Services Colombo, Sri Lanka, where she works on the holistic development of disadvantaged women and children.

Social, Political and Cultural Background

Sri Lanka is a small island, approximately 25,000 square miles in area, situated at the southernmost tip of the Indian sub-continent, and having a population of approximately 19 million. Seventy per cent of the majority race is Sinhalese. Plantation Tamils, whose forbears were shipped in by the former British colonial government, account for 5 per cent of the population, while Tamils with earlier Sri Lankan ancestry are 12 per cent. Malays and 'Moors' (who originally hailed from Arabic-speaking countries) are together classified as 'Muslims' and form 7 per cent of the population. 'Burghers' (descendants of Portuguese, Dutch and British colonials) and Chinese are the smallest ethnic groups. There is also a small indigenous population, the Veddhas (Samuel, 2001, p. 185). The Sinhalese and Tamils are the result of successive waves of migration from all parts of India, mixing in various degrees among themselves and with the island's aboriginal inhabitants. During later periods, Arab, Asian and European traders also established themselves in the island (Jayawardena, 2003, p. 110). The plantation Tamils are the descendants of conscripted labor from South India, introduced by the British in the 18th century, to work in the coffee and tea plantations.

Buddhism was introduced into Sri Lanka in the third century BC and quickly became the dominant religion. Islam, Hinduism and Christianity are the other major religions in Sri Lanka and have direct links to the various ethnic groups. Sinhalese are predominantly Buddhist, Tamils are predominantly Hindu, Muslims and Malays are predominantly followers of Islam, while a few Sinhalese and Tamils and almost all Burghers are Christians.

At the last official census conducted in 2001, approximately 52 per cent of the population in the south were women. Census could not be conducted in the north and east due to the armed conflict. Sri Lankan women gained adult franchise and the right to run for political office in 1931 (Jayawardena, 2003, p. 129) and have enjoyed a better quality of life than women in other Asian countries—a literacy rate of 83 per cent among women, a maternal mortality rate of 1.2 per 1,000 live births and a life expectancy of 67 years (Jayawardena, 2003, p. 109). Sri Lankan women also did not suffer from most of the social evils of their regional partners; practices such as *sati*, child marriage, genital mutilation, ban on widow remarriage and *purdah*. Sri Lanka also enjoys the distinction of having had the first woman Prime Minister—Sirimavo Dias Bandaranaike in 1960; and the first woman President—Chandrika Bandaranaike Kumaranatunge in 1994.

In spite of all of the above, Sri Lanka remains a classic example where women have enjoyed adult franchise, education, mobility, access to opportunities and freedom from most cultural taboos, yet has not been able to develop a movement for women's emancipation that transcends the existing social parameters of patriarchy and subordination. In order to understand this more fully, let us take a look at some of the contradictions that exist in Sri Lankan society.

Contradictions

Although women have enjoyed adult franchise since 1931, have a literacy rate of 83 per cent and have had a voter turnout of 80 per cent among women in all of the elections held so far, women's representation in formal politics at national, provincial and local government levels has never exceeded 4 per cent. There are only nine women parliamentarians out of a total of 225, 3.3 per cent representation in the provincial councils and 1.7 per cent in municipal/urban councils (Tambiah, 2002, p. 431). Although there have been three governments headed by women (Sirimavo Dias Bandaranaike 1960–1965 and 1970–1977 and Chandrika Bandaranaike Kumaranatunge 1994–2000), women's concerns have not been given much attention. This is especially true of the period between 1994 and 2000, where both the President and Prime Minister were women, with considerable executive and legislative powers at their disposal.

The Sri Lankan Constitution while recognizing that women should not be discriminated against on the basis of their sex, then goes on to lump them together with children and disabled persons, thus undermining a positive and vibrant image and portraying them as weak and vulnerable. Article 12 of the Constitution, under Chapter III, 'Fundamental Rights', states:

(1) All persons are equal before the law and are entitled to the equal protection of the law; (2) No citizen shall be discriminated against on the grounds of race, religion, language, caste, sex, political opinion, place of birth...

However, just two clauses down, one reads:

(4) Nothing in this Article shall prevent special provision being made, by law,... for the advancement of women, children or disabled persons.

The openly discriminatory laws that exist as regards land entitlement in the Mahaweli region, the citizenship law for Sri Lankan women who marry foreigners, laws regarding marital rape and the right of a woman to obtain an abortion in situations of rape, laws on incest or fetal abnormality, are other glaring contradictions that exist in the so-called progressiveness of Sri Lankan society and its policies, laws and practices.

There is also a surprisingly low level of gender-awareness among politicians, professional women, and civil society, in spite of the high literacy rate, access to information and mobility of Sri Lankan women. This can be best exemplified by some of the remarks in a speech made by Chandrika Bandaranaike Kumaranatunge (before she took up the presidency in 1994).

The Sri Lankan woman does not, unlike her counterparts in the western world, need to stridently fight for liberation... Where political leadership is concerned, the Sri Lankan man seems to have willingly abdicated. (Tambiah, 2002, p. 424).

Here, once again, President Kumaranatunge is legitimizing the myth of a politically empowered Sri Lankan woman and a liberal and progressive Sri Lankan man.

Out of a total strength of 49 judges, there is only one female judge in the Supreme Court, one in the Appeal Court and two in the High Court. In the lower judiciary there are 41 women out of a total of 185, a much better ratio. This dismal representation is in spite of equal educational qualifications, social status and professional experience for men and women. There have been a few positive indications; a few years ago, a woman was appointed as the Vice Chancellor of the Colombo University, and women have also been appointed to the posts of Post Master General, General Manager of the Bank of Ceylon, Commissioner General of Inland Revenue and Legal Draftsman. However, overall, there is a large vacuum with regard to women's representation in the management and policy making levels in judicial, public administration and financial sectors. There is only one woman sitting on the prestigious Parliamentary Select Committee which is the main decision-making body for all development policy and programs, and there have been no women involved at any level in the 6 rounds of peace talks held so far.

There is also an absence of leadership and articulation by women in the fight for their rights and responsibilities. As Yasmin Tambiah argues:

> With rare exceptions to this rule, women have been unable to venture out of a purely private, 'coping with the violence' mindframe to a sustained and powerful public articulation of their grievances ... This diminishes the individual and collective power that could otherwise have been wielded where such positive interventions are desperately needed (Tambiah, 2002, p. 425).

The willingness of women politicians to abdicate their hard-fought position to male kith and kin, to subjugate their identity and individuality and to wrap themselves in the mantle of wife and motherhood, immediately reinforces the gender stereotyping of a woman's primary role being that of a wife and mother. These are other examples of the Sri Lankan woman's contradictory behavior in spite of education, exposure and social mobility.

Another alarming contradiction has surfaced in recent years with women emerging as perpetrators of violence. This was seen in the increasingly vitriolic rhetoric of President Chandrika Bandaranaike Kumaranatunge. In one of her election campaign speeches in 2001, she exhorted her followers to meet violence with violence—even to kill if necessary. The violence unleashed at the North-Western provincial council elections in 1997, and again in the General Election of 2001, saw many women candidates justify the use of violence as a form of intimidation and defence.

REASONS FOR CONTRADICTIONS

It is now necessary to examine the reasons for the above contradictions in a society that prides itself on being both progressive and emancipated. The role of political parties is central to the issue of poor representation of women in the political arena. Political parties play a crucial role in determining who is nominated as a candidate for election. However, political parties have shown little commitment to fielding more women candidates for elections and grooming and supporting capable women candidates who can compete on their own merit. They have instead preferred to field less competent candidates who have links to political families or male patronage.

The system of Proportional Representation (PR), first introduced in 1989, also seems to have contributed to a drop in the number of women representatives, since there is no commitment on the part of the state or political party structures to implement this effectively. The PR system has also resulted in vicious in-fighting because of the preference vote, and many women have been further intimidated by threats and actual acts of violence in this regard.

Sri Lankan politics over the last 25 years has been marred by unprecedented levels of violence. Political thuggery, threats of violence and actual acts of violence resulting even in assassination, has contributed to the criminalisation of the entire political culture. This has led to the political arena becoming male dominated, with capable women refusing to enter the political arena for fear of the resulting violence and abuse.

The state has long been a complicit partner in the discriminatory practices against women's representation. Women's groups actively lobbied and were successful in getting a reservation for women at local government level included in the draft constitution for 1997. However, this was conspicuously absent when the draft was debated in Parliament in August 2000.

The Women's Bureau was set up in 1978 to look into the welfare of women, and the Ministry of Women's Affairs was set up in 1983 to coordinate the overall functions and financial management of all the agencies under it—Women's Bureau, National Committee on Women. It was charged with the task of mainstreaming gender, and formulating, implementing and monitoring policies and programs for the empowerment of women. However, the Women's Bureau has remained an agency primarily dealing with income generation projects for women, while the Ministry of Women's Affairs remains locked in its own institutional constraints and lack of vision or awareness of gender issues.

Another key factor is the inherent belief of most Sri Lankan women in the superiority of the male. In spite of education, skills and proven abilities, many women continue to operate within the parameters of powerful inhibitions brought about by generations of social conditioning. This has been the single, most-powerful factor in the non-representation of women in the political arena. This is reflected in the willingness of two women Chief Ministers to abdicate their posts in favor of their husbands, while another elected minister went so far as to allow her parliamentarian husband to make her acceptance speech on her behalf.

There is also a misplaced sense of complacency about the true status of women in Sri Lankan society. Many honestly believe that because a few women have attained high positions in the political and professional arenas, this reflects the status of most women. Coupled with this is the fact that in the post colonial period, Sri Lankan women enjoyed a quality of life index that far surpassed any of her regional neighbors. This too has led to complacency on the part of Sri Lankans as to the current status and situation of women in society. With the changing trends in education and the introduction of open market policies, many Sri Lankans have a chauvinistic or indifferent attitude to historical events, their place in shaping modern society and their impact on the lives of people. They are also intellectually and politically ignorant, unlike the liberal and progressive thinkers of the early and mid twentieth century. This has led to a situation where subjugation and oppression are accepted as the norm, although paradoxically, many of them are not even aware that they hold this extremely debilitating view.

Many women's decision, such on whom to vote for, continues to be heavily influenced by the family, i.e. male members. Again, female candidates are voted for on the basis of their acceptability and respectability, not on ability. Thus, a candidate perceived to be a good wife and mother will get more votes, than an unmarried or childless woman. Widows will have the sympathy vote, linked with the abilities and charisma of the deceased male relative—father, husband or son.

All of the above are contributory factors to the low representation of women in the political arena, and clearly reflect the contradictions that exist in Sri Lankan society. Women political leaders in South Asia have rarely been born great. They may have been born to great families, married eminent men, borne great sons, but they have rarely been considered great in their own right. As Darini Rajasingham-Senanyake writes:

> The phenomenon of women from powerful political dynasties becoming president or prime minister literally over the dead bodies of their husbands and fathers is a telling reflection and indictment of the gendered nature of political power and violence in the South Asian region. (Rajasingham-Senanayake, 2001, p. 102).

Also, these women have rarely succeeded in addressing or stemming the violent trends in politics. Nor do they seem to have an alternative vision or pragmatic plan for elevating the status of women in their country. They seem to be more interested in strengthening the family networks of power and influence, rather than work towards challenging the social structures and norms that deprive women of an equal status in society. Perhaps it is an unconscious or conscious negation or oversight on their part, since challenging the existing structures would undermine their position and influence as well.

In Sri Lanka, Sirimavo Dias Bandaranaike used state-sponsored violence and emergency law to crush the youth uprising of 1971, while Chandrika Bandaranaike Kumaranatunge has used Emergency Regulations and the draconian Prevention of Terrorism Act to deal with the war in the North and East, justifying the use of these measures in the name of national security. What is frightening is that the root causes of these uprisings remain unaddressed, even today. However, that is yet another discourse.

Chandrika Bandaranaike Kumaranatunge's political career and her attempt to distance herself from nationalistic and chauvinistic ideologies, has been hampered by the alliances she has been forced to make to retain power, specifically the Muslim and Tamil parties and more recently the Janatha Vimukthi Peramuna (JVP). However, the central problem remains the indifference, for whatever reason, on the part of women political leaders to address the issue of women's disempowerment within the existing political and policy-making frameworks.

Religion too has played a major role in reinforcing the gender stereotypes of 'a good wife and mother'. Although Buddhism opposed many of the teachings and rituals tied up with Hinduism, and even went as far as admitting women into the ranks of its clergy (which resulted in the founding of a nun's order), the social structures continued to remain patriarchal and gave women a subordinate role. Male monks, however junior, could speak in a gathering of nuns; but no nun, however senior, could speak in a gathering of monks.

Christianity and Islam have been used to reinforce the subordinate status of women in society. Many of the Christian missionary schools of the nineteenth and early twentieth century reinforced the Victorian paradigm of what a woman should be—chaste, modest, humble, a good housewife, and accomplished in the arts of housekeeping, needlework and music. Surprisingly, this view has changed very little over the past 50 years, and many of the advertisements on the mass media promote the concept of female subjugation; a primary role of the woman is supposed to be that of a good wife and mother.

Sri Lanka is not immune to the influences of the changes occurring in the Islamic world and in recent years has seen a resurgence of frightening radicalism which is forcing more and more women to wear the purdah, take a back seat in secular affairs, and reinforce the myth of male superiority.

The emergence of 'couple politics' (husband and wife teams, especially at provincial level), and 'proxy' women politicians, with no political will or vision of their own, has also led to a deterioration of the empowering of women and of the focus on women's issues within the political framework. These wives are very different to the political wives of the early twentieth century, who had definite views of their own, often contradicted their husbands when necessary in matters of policy, and actively campaigned and worked for women's rights and empowerment.

Before looking at the history of women's mobilization around the issue of violence and conflict, it is necessary to look at the instances of such conflict in the past 25 years.

HISTORY OF CONFLICT AND VIOLENCE

The traditional homeland of the Sri Lankan Tamils has been the north and east of Sri Lanka. However, a significant number have also settled in the south. The plantation Tamils live mainly in the central province, while a small percentage has moved to Colombo in search of employment.

Due to the present conflict, there are no Muslims residing in the North today. However, they make up about one-third of the population living in the eastern province, while the Sinhalese and Tamils make up the remaining two thirds. Muslims live in most other parts of the island as well.

Since independence, the primary conflict has been between the Sinhalese and the Sri Lankan Tamils, although the Muslims and Plantation Tamils have been drawn into the fray as well. The ethnic conflict encompasses many grievances, ranging from economic to socio-political discrimination and lack of recognition and identity. At the core of the problem is the inability and non-attention of the Sri Lankan state to establish a political framework that is able to reflect the ethnic plurality of Sri Lankan society and ensure the democratic rights of all citizens. I would like to present two examples of blatant discrimination in national policies that led to increasing tension between the Sinhala and Tamil peoples: 1) The 'Sinhala-only' language policy that was introduced by S.W.R.D. Bandaranaike (Chandrika Bandaranaike Kumaranatunge's father), in 1956; and 2) The 'standardization' examination policy, introduced in 1972, which restricted the entry of Tamil youth to the universities.

The post-independence governments were indifferent to the need to develop a sense of national identity that would ensure, protect and reflect the rights of a pluralistic society; and the growing chauvinistic rhetoric, and hastily-implemented national policies among the Sinhala politicians and leaders, led Tamil political parties to make demands for regional autonomy and power sharing. First, the demands for first a federal state, and later, an independent state, were completely ignored, and led to anti-Tamil riots in 1958, 1977 and 1983. These served to increase tension between the two ethnic groups and led to the formation of a Tamil militant movement which eschewed the more moderate demands for a political negotiation and launched an armed struggle for a separate state.

Although there were many such groups at the beginning (1986), the Liberation Tigers of Tamil Eelam (LTTE) emerged as the dominant military group by eliminating all other rival groups. The LTTE also assassinated all moderate politicians who attempted to bring about a negotiated settlement. This conflict, between the LTTE and state forces, that has spanned a twenty year period, has resulted in the deaths of more than 60,000 people, and the displacement of almost a million.

The period between 1987 and 1990 was marked by unprecedented violence between the Sinhala-chauvinistic JVP and the government in power at that time, the United National Party (UNP). Although the JVP has its roots in Marxist doctrine, it has been a party dominated by educated, unemployed or under-employed, rural youth from the south of Sri Lanka. The JVP has mobilized them with arguments about social injustice, and in the recent past, the JVP rhetoric has become increasingly chauvinistic along Sinhala, Buddhist lines. In 1985, they organized themselves into an extremist political group, violently opposed to the Indo-Sri Lankan Peace Accord, and launched a campaign of ruthless terror against the government in the form of forcible work stoppages and political assassinations. The UNP retaliated with equally ruthless counter-violence, and during this 4-year period, an estimated 60,000 persons were killed, abducted or simply 'disappeared'.

The past twenty-five years have seen the emergence of many gangs and underworld groups, many of which appear emboldened by surreptitious or ostentatious political patronage. It has also been a time of unprecedented political violence that has resulted in the assassination of many able and progressive leaders. Elections, too, have been marred by rigging, intimidation, public humiliation of women candidates, and threats and actual acts of violence, even murder.

These facts have led to the establishment of a culture of violence in Sri Lanka, which has in turn resulted in an escalation in the levels of violence, both in the public and private domain. Women, of course, have continued to be the most vulnerable group—being on one hand the victims of the above violence and on the other, the survivors who have had to take on increasingly complex and different roles in both the private and public spheres. Some 20 per cent of current households in Sri Lanka are female headed. (Tambiah, 2002, p. 425)

MOBILIZATION OF WOMEN

Many women's groups have mobilized around this issue. It is very important to examine these groups, their activities and their limitations, since most of them play a vital role in mitigating to some extent, the lack of attention and focus given by state and government to women's issues. Other groups have mobilized to transcend traditional norms and limitations regarding women's activities and roles, chief among them being the women cadres of both the Sri Lankan Army and the LTTE.

All political parties in Sri Lanka have a women's wing. However, the members are dominated by the party ideology and exist mainly to mobilize the female constituency at election time and to provide supportive services to the men. Very seldom does membership in these wings pave the way to political leadership. Therefore, one of the best resources to groom and nurture women to take on political leadership has been expeditiously used by men (and some influential women) to further their own ends and agendas.

The United Nations International Year for Women and the International Decade for Women in 1975, re-motivated the women's movement in Sri Lanka to look at the many questions facing women. A number of women's groups were formed to look at women's social, political, economic and civil rights. Some of these groups were research-based while others were activist-oriented. All of them were concerned with examining the causes for female subordination, exposing the male biases in society and mainstreaming gender concerns. These groups were also involved in raising people's consciousness of feminist issues, and educating people by disseminating information.

Most of the above groups came together to set up the Sri Lanka NGO Forum in 1993, in order to facilitate Sri Lankan women's participation at the Fourth World Conference on Women in Beijing in 1995. The Forum continues to function as a broad network and monitors the implementation of the Beijing Platform for Action in Sri Lanka.

The Women's Action Committee (WAC), established in 1982 and based in the south, was the first significant group to challenge the issue of human rights, ethnic politics, armed conflict and their impact on women (Samuel, 2001, p. 189). They were the first group to consistently and systematically call for political negotiation as opposed to military confrontation to the ethnic conflict. They also organized marches, demonstrations, pickets and public appeals. The WAC was also one of the first groups to build links with women's groups in the north and plantation workers in the hill country. The WAC also actively assisted in sheltering and succoring the thousands of Tamil civilians, displaced and traumatized by the ethnic conflict in the north and the anti-Tamil riots of 1983. Samuel writes:

> Throughout the 1980's the WAC continued its call for a solution to the ethnic conflict, joining with other women's groups ... It also linked the ethnic conflict and the politics of violence to the deterioration of democracy, with its consequences for all ethnic communities of Sri Lanka. (Samuel, 2001, p. 190)

In the mid 1980s, with an escalation of hostilities and war-mongering being the preferred policy of the state, the WAC joined forces with a group of women academics and professionals to call for peace. This was in the form of an appeal, published in the English, Sinhala and Tamil-language national newspapers. The appeal was issued in the name of a new alliance called 'Women for Peace'. The appeal called for an end to the war and the commencement of talks that could lead to a politically negotiated settlement to the ethnic conflict. However, when the first round of political negotiations began between the government and Tamil militants at the All Party Conference held in 1984, not one woman had been invited to participate. This group disbanded in 1987 as it succumbed, like so many others, to the difficulty of working across ethnic lines at a time when the state was waging a 'War for Peace'.

With the disbanding of the WAC, another coalition was formed which called themselves the 'Mothers and Daughters of Sri Lanka' (MDSL). This coalition was formed mainly in response to the terror, unleashed by both the JVP and state, during 1987–1990. This coalition went public with the slogan 'Stop to All Killings'. The most recent coalition of women's groups mobilized around the ethnic conflict has been the 'Women's Coalition for Peace', which came together in 1997. It comprises women of all ethnic groups, religions, social classes and political affiliations. The coalition's main objective is to ensure that women play a significant role in the peace process. The coalition has also repeatedly stressed the need for women's representation at all levels of government.

One of the most significant movements to emerge in the 1980s was the Mothers' Front of the North and South. Here, women used their role as mothers to politicize the disappearance and abduction of their men-folk and to seek redress for human rights violations. The Northern Mothers' Front was formed in 1984 to demand the release of over 500 men who had been detained by the Sri Lankan armed forces. This proved to be a very effective move and secured the release of most of the men. The women in the northern Mothers' Front continued to be active and took the hitherto unprecedented step of condemning human rights violations by both the armed forces and the LTTE. They were also vociferous in calling for a political settlement to the ethnic conflict. However, with the increasingly repressive actions of the LTTE, the northern Mothers' Front too disappeared from the public arena.

The southern Mothers' Front came together in the mid 1990s at the end of a period of terror unleashed by both the JVP and the state. At the height of its popularity, the Front had a membership of about 25,000 women, most of whom came from poor, rural backgrounds. The Front kept records of the 'disappeared' and visited police stations and camps in search of their missing men-folk. However, the southern Mothers' Front was convened by two opposition-party male parliamentarians. This ultimately led to the Front becoming dysfunctional; when the Peoples' Alliance was voted into power in 1994, and the above men became ministers in the new government, they lost any further interest in using the Front as a political tool.

In contrast to the mobilization of the women's groups mentioned above, around the issues of human rights, women's rights and the ethnic conflict, there have been other forms of women's mobilization which have taken more radical and revolutionary paths. When the Tamil militant struggle began in the north, many women were drawn into joining the Tamil nationalist organizations. They first served in the capacity of fund-raisers, service providers and propagandists. However, very soon afterwards, the LTTE began training women as fighters to be used in combat and as suicide bombers. In time, LTTE women cadres made up almost 50 per cent of its fighting force and have proven to be quite formidable. Their elite 'suicide battalion' has been singled out for particularly important assignments, such as the successful 1991 assassination of the Indian Prime Minister, Rajiv Gandhi (Tambiah, 2002, p. 435).

The Sri Lanka Army and Air Force have mobilized and trained women as well. However, they still form part of the non-combat force, and in most instances have been deployed at check points and to provide security.

Although many women and women's groups have mobilized around the issues of women's politicization and empowerment, the reality is that women are still outside the mainstream decision-making processes in the country. So far, in spite of all the efforts of women's groups, only two women have been directly involved in the negotiations dealing with the peace process: President Chandrika Bandaranaike Kumaranatunge, and Adele Ann Balasingham, the Australian-born wife of the LTTE's main negotiator, Anton Balasingham. It is also important to note that their role in the negotiations has not been gender-focused.

As a result, gender specific issues, such as rape and the fear of rape, body searches and the fear of sexual violence, the situation of women who are internally displaced, etc., have never been raised in any of the peace talks. All the social, political and institutional structures continue to be dominated by men, while even the few women who have the space and opportunity to address and change this situation, seem to remain either oblivious to the issue, or unable to do so. These issues must be addressed if women are to be included in the existing structures and processes in a tangible and productive way, instead of being confined to symbolic and exploited roles.

How then can this be achieved?

RECOMMENDATIONS

Women politicians must use the space they have to bring this issue to the forefront. They must have the courage and commitment to break the mould of 'accepted female behavior' as defined by a male dominated society. They must develop their own identity and individuality, without depending on either the physical presence or the memory of a charismatic male-figure as a prop. They must be ready to disturb and challenge traditional structures of gendered thought and behavior, without feeling guilty or ashamed.

In order to take on this formidable task, women politicians must broaden their knowledge base and understanding of political issues and concerns. Despite the much-vaunted statistics of national literacy levels, most women parliamentarians (and men too), lack awareness and understanding regarding the issues of governance, democracy, the role of the state, and gender. This must be addressed with a commitment to learning to use the electronic media to access current information, recruiting able and qualified staff and advisors instead of political stooges, and building links in order to gain exposure and information and to develop discourse with women academicians, activists and regional and international progressive women parliamentarians.

Women politicians must also develop a sense of vision and commitment to developing the women's wings of their political parties to become distinct entities and not just adjuncts to the main male-dominated parties. These wings must develop the integrity and commitment to groom and support women with charisma and ability to take on leadership roles within the political structure instead of continuing to support women coming from political dynasties and/or with powerful male patrons.

This is not as difficult as it seems, since there is a enormous human resource base that can be drawn on and mobilized, if consciousness regarding the true status of women and its gendered role within the existing structures and processes can be truly raised and women motivated in this regard.

Women's organizations and networks have a vital role to play in addressing the above identified gaps. The initiatives taken by women's groups have failed because often these actions are only symbolic and lack the depth and breadth necessary to look at this highly complex issue in a pro-active manner. Women's organizations must not only lobby to increase women's representation at all levels, but must also ensure that women entering the political arena are educated, sensitized and committed to changing the inequalities that exist within the current structures and processes. Women's groups must also lobby and be active in fostering the concept of a collective sense of 'women's power', which cuts across political party affiliations, ethnicity, religion and class. They must use the space available to foster dialogue between women politicians of different political parties.

Women's groups and organizations also have a vital role to play in educating Sri Lankan society, especially women, about the existing inequalities and constraints within current structures and processes. However, this must be done in a factual and culturally sensitive manner, so as not to alienate women who are conditioned by generations of socially learned behavior. This would also ensure that men are not able to exploit this process and undermine it by branding it as 'western feminism' or reinforcing the feelings of 'shame and guilt' connected with stepping out of the private sphere and into the public one.

So far, I have dealt primarily with the empowerment of women as a whole. However, women affected by conflict are a distinct and separate issue that merits special consideration. Rajini Thiranagama, a senior lecturer at the University of Jaffna, was killed by the LTTE in 1989 for her outspoken criticism of the LTTE and their history of human rights abuses. I quote:

> Women have come out strong during the war ... they have stood out as individuals or as small groups exposing the atrocities and violations of dignity ... women in the midst of war pleaded and argued with the militants for their families and the whole nation ... there is powerlessness, disappointment and disillusion, but also hope. We have done it, a little bit. (Rajasingham-Senanayake, 2001, p. 102)

Women affected by violence must be part of any and all security and peace building efforts. This has been the tragedy and history of all countries: war and peace have been played out in a male-dominated space, with long-term negative implications for all.

How is the situation of women affected by conflict and violence different? Although widows of politically powerful figures have succeeded in transcending the stigma attached to widowhood within the South Asian culture, this is not the reality for most women. Very often, young widows are expected to live chaste lives, bereft of social and sexual relationships.

However, in times of armed conflict, women have been forced to step out of the private sphere and into the public one, as they assume the role of head of household and main income generator. They also become the main negotiators when dealing with the armed forces, government officials, and those of humanitarian aid agencies. As a result of these activities, important changes have been wrought in the social and cultural fabric of conflict areas. Although conflict has placed a burden on many women, it has also opened up new spaces for social and cultural transformation.

One crucial fact that must be recognized and acknowledged is that a return to peace should not be a return to the traditional gender status quo. A return to peace should not mean a return to the kitchen, the portrayal of women as helpless victims and the social limitations and constraints placed on widows, especially within a traditional Hindu culture. In this formidable task, women must indeed take the lead and be educated and sensitized to do so. Otherwise, women's role within peace-building and security will once again become purely symbolic, if not non-existent.

A very important issue in creating this new space is to challenge the present land distribution schemes in the Vanni area. The title deeds for land in this area are still being invested in male heads of household. It is only where a male head of household is reported or presumed dead, that the title deed is invested in the woman. Women whose husbands have left them or whose whereabouts cannot be ascertained, are not deemed eligible for land grants.

CONCLUSION

These gaps and issues must be addressed and bridged, if women are to productively and meaningfully enter the process of peace-building and security. If women are not holistically empowered, they cannot enter into this process. They are once again pushed into roles and images, configured and delineated by the wider, traditional society.

In the efforts to build sustainable security and peace, the empowerment of women at all levels is vital. The lack of this empowerment is central to the fact of women's exclusion from the peace process and all other national decision-making processes. It has also been shown that education does not necessarily translate into affirmative action or a change in attitudes and perceptions. This too is a process that must be developed and fostered.

Women's groups must become sensitive to the fact that the issue of social transformation in conflict and peace building is a central one. Women who are affected by violence can never return to their 'old way of life'. They now have new responsibilities and roles.

Women must develop a pro-active vision for building peace and security that transcends mere symbolism and lip service. When Agnes de Silva, the leader of the group that lobbied for women's franchise in Sri Lanka in 1927, talks about her experiences in addressing and lobbying the Donoughmore Commission, she says, 'we went in the spirit of crusaders'. This should be the vision of Sri Lankan women in building bridges that foster peace and security— to go in the spirit of crusaders to challenge the existing power structures, to educate women about the existing imbalances in society, to work towards empowering them to challenge these imbalances, and to be aware that for many women who have been affected by the violence, there is no return to the status quo of the 'old way of life'. As Darini Rajasingham-Senananyake says:

A multi-ethnic women's politics that crosses ethnic lines might be the best and last bulwark against growing ethnic chauvinism that is being built up by democratic politicians, intent on shoring up vote banks and personal power at the cost of national peace. (Rajasingham-Senanayake, 2001, p. 128)

Peace building and security cannot be an isolated activity. It must be part of a greater process and movement. However, this greater process must identify the different links that are vital for holding it together and strengthening it. I have tried to develop this concept within this paper. Therefore, I have not focused on the process of peace-building and security within conflict or post-conflict situations. I have looked at conflict and violence and the disempowerment of women as related issues, just as much as the empowerment and participation of women at all levels is vital to the processes of building peace and security.

If this vital issue is not addressed and developed, women will continue to be pawns in the political game, caught up in the struggle of political survival and unable to transcend it. Women's initiatives within peace-building and security will continue to neglect the social transformations wrought for women within conflict situations and the cultural frameworks that denigrate women will continue to flourish.

A culturally appropriate language must also be found to articulate the experiences of women and the transformations it has wrought in their lives. In response to intense lobbying by women's groups, the Sri Lankan government very recently appointed four women from the south, while the LTTE appointed four women from the north to be part of the negotiations in the peace process. The women nominees from the south, reflect ethnic and religious diversity and have for years been active in the field of human rights and women's empowerment. On the other hand, the nominees by the LTTE are all LTTE cadres who can hardly be classified as reflecting the diversity and plurality of the civilian population in the north and east. However, with the break-down of the peace talks, none of these women has yet got the opportunity to participate. Although the appointment of these women is a giant step forward, it remains to be seen how much space they will be given and how much attention paid to their recommendations in the formulation of national policy.

I shall end with an excerpt from the Statement made by Women for Peace in October 1995:

> We need new strategies for creating consciousness, social spaces for those women in the margins, for voices to be heard and faces to be seen, for us to transcend barriers and shackles that patriarchy and the masculine state have imposed. (Tambiah, 2002, p. 453)

Bibliography

JAYAWARDENA, Kumari, 'Emancipation and Subordination of Women in Sri Lanka,' *Feminism and Nationalism in the Third World,* 2003, pp. 109–136.

RAJASINGHAM-SENANAYAKE, Darini, 'Ambivalent Empowerment: The Tragedy of Tamil Women in Conflict,' *Women, War and Peace in South Asia,* 2001, pp. 102–129.

SAMUEL, Kumudini, 'Gender Difference in Conflict Resolution: The Case of Sri Lanka,' *Gender, Peace and Conflict,* 2001, pp. 184–204.

TAMBIAH, Yasmin, 'Sri Lanka International Centre for Ethnic Studies,' *Women and Governance in South Asia: Re-imagining the State,* 2002, pp. 421–497.

7

RESEARCH, POLICY, REALITY: WOMEN, SECURITY, SOUTH ASIA

Swarna Rajagopalan[*]

ABSTRACT

The subject of this essay is a question about which I have been thinking for almost ten years. This essay is one moment's view in a long-term engagement, and I want to register that by dating this essay to November-December 2003, when it was written.

The theme for this conference posits a gap between what researchers study and what policy-makers consider important. This essay will show that when we discuss the security of women, the true disjuncture is between research and policy on the one hand and reality on the other.

At the root of this disjuncture is the understanding of 'security' that is common to both mainstream security studies research and the security policy establishment, and that does not reflect the real life experience of women. This becomes clear whether you adopt a feminist perspective, or the simple yardstick of relating policy and research to the lives of most women. From either standpoint, both research and policy are found wanting.

This essay will contrast the concerns of security policy-makers, the issues raised by feminist scholars and the reality of South Asian women's lives, both to illustrate this disjuncture as well as to seek remedies for it. It will do so by posing two questions in each instance:

1. What does security mean in this context?
2. Who or what are the chief referents of security?

The ultimate objective is to identify what both research and policy should be about, what we should raise as security policy concerns and how we should make the argument for their inclusion in security agendas.

[*]Dr. Swarna Rajagopalan is an independent Chennai-based analyst of South Asian politics and security issues. She is the author of 'State and Nation in South Asia' (Lynne Rienner, 2001) and other books. Her research interests lie at the intersection of security, governance and identity politics, in addition to women in politics and security.

SECURITY AND THE POLICY UNIVERSE IN SOUTH ASIA

The universe of policy-making and policy debates is a state-centered one, and the primary referent of security policy is the state.

The security of the state is the first concern of policy-makers. The threats to this security are variously identified. They come from other states, from challengers within the state to the state's legitimacy and continuance in a particular form, from challengers based in other states and from external forces like globalization that undermine the state's scope of action.

The state is also a provider of security, both externally and internally—in fact, some believe that the provision of security to its citizens is the first function and *raison d'être* of the state. In addition to securing the state, the policy establishment is also concerned with the security mandate of the state.[1] Since the state's ability to act on its security mandate depends on its own secure survival, the latter acquires priority over the former.

Mohammed Ayoob's definition of the Third World security predicament is easily illustrated by the security preoccupations of each South Asian state (Ayoob 1995). The primary insecurities of the larger states in our region are concomitants of the state-building process itself, reflecting the traumas of state foundation and consolidation *vis-à-vis* their neighborhood on the one hand and the consequences of state-building policies on the other. In addition, the insecurities and calculations predicted by classic realist and neorealist international realists are also displayed by the ruling elites, particularly in the larger states of the region. Thus, the phrase 'security issues' conjures up a laundry list of mutual problems: border disputes, arms races, insurgencies and counter-insurgency operations, mutual political interference and even textbook geopolitical problems like access to sea-routes.

Let's start with **India:** India's most intractable security problem, no matter what one's perspective or politics, is the dispute with Pakistan over the status of Kashmir. There are few better examples of state foundation-related conflicts. In addition, India has unresolved border disputes with China. India also expresses a sense of threat over the movement of any external armed forces into the Indian Ocean region and keeps a watching brief over Central and Southeast Asian affairs. The Indian security policy establishment considers the extended neighborhood to be critical to its own security and disapproves of its South Asian neighbors entering into treaty or contractual relationships with extra-regional partners. This applies also then to the unmonitored or hard-to-limit inflows of people, terror, weapons or drugs along its long land and coastal borders. India would attribute the insurgencies it faces to the aggravation and/or assistance rendered by these flows. Many of these result either from or in disputes, with or within countries, in the neighborhood.

Sharing a long border and ethno-cultural continuities with all its neighbors, it is also hard for the central government, in India, to ignore the press of regional public opinion in the face of crises elsewhere in the subcontinent. This has been an important factor in India's repeated involvement with other countries' problems. Indian interventions in Bangladesh and Sri Lanka, if given force by other temptations, were responses to the immediate pressures of refugees and concern about ethnic kin.

To some extent, the feeling in some sections of India's ruling elite of encirclement in a hostile neighborhood is not unjustified. India bears the cross of being a giant—in every sense—in a region of relatively smaller states, and its own dealings with its neighbors reinforce their suspicion that its every move or shift is calculated to do untold harm to them. Take the question of terrorism: like every other country that has the means, India has done its share to train and arm militants operating in other parts of its neighborhood. However, that does not alter the reality that most parts of India have seen rising levels of terrorist violence, killing hundreds and wounding many more. On either side of a conflict, no matter what the cause, that is an inexcusable waste of lives. Today, ordinary Indians live with an unexpressed anger and sense of victimhood that is real. What makes them insecure today, will spill over tomorrow to affect others as they express resentment and hostility. The Indian state in part reflects this feeling when it speaks belligerently.

Socio-economic change has come to India over the last five decades, but it has had uneven impact. Some parts of India like Punjab and Maharashtra have fared relatively well, while others remain mired in pre-industrial economies, suffering scarcity and starvation. The middle class has grown and prospered, especially recently, but things are not changing fast enough for the very, very poor. Some of these developments have exacerbated divisions of class, caste and ethnicity within different parts of India and led to the rise of insurgent movements. Declining institutions and perfidious political leaders have further contributed to India's 'million mutinies' which create—for both the state and its citizens who are caught in the crossfire between state and insurgents.

So, how must the term 'security' most be used by Indian policy-makers? I would say that 'security' is used in its most minimal sense in Indian security discourse—'safety' and by extension, 'defense' and 'protection.' This is neither to impute an innocence of motives nor a lack of offense in Indian security policy or action; it is merely intended to suggest that the Indian establishment does not think beyond this very narrow definition of security and insecurity.

How does **Pakistan** fare? Pakistan is sandwiched between two neighbors, engagement with both of whom is a drain on its economy, society and polity. With India, beyond Kashmir and the arms race, there is the problem of being the lower riparian in the Indus system. On the other border lies Afghanistan, whose endless political tribulations spill over into Pakistan in the form of refugee inflows, foreign military presences and alliances that become part of Pakistan's political fabric and arms and narcotics trafficking with their consequences for society. Pakistan is thus rather unfortunately located.

For the Pakistani state, insecurity first stems from the presence of India at their eastern threshold which they suspect has still not come to terms with their existence or its rationale and which has played a vital part in their loss of one wing. It is manifest in the complexities of the Kashmir issue, and in the way that has played out over five and a half decades. From India's looming presence comes a consciousness that Pakistan now needs allies to balance or check this neighbor. This has resulted in close relationships with China, the US and the community of Islamic states. In turn, the vagaries of the relationship with the US and the price Pakistan has paid for it are sources of insecurity to Pakistan. Pakistan's engagement with Afghanistan can also be described partly as an attempt to ensure a friendly western neighbor.

The Pakistani state has also been threatened, like the Indian one, by violence from within. While it has faced and been partitioned on account of one secessionist movement, others like the Pakhtoon and Sindhi ones have lost momentum as events have overtaken them. Instead it is the escalation of urban violence that has threatened Pakistan, with Karachi being the worst example. Escalating levels of violence are at some point beyond the capacity of the police and the paramilitary and army come to be deployed. This ratchets up the violence further, and also politicizes those institutions. In Pakistan, the army is already a political player. In that sense, the identification of the state with its security apparatus is near complete in this case. As a corollary, the line between regime and state security blurs.[2]

Escalating violence militarizes and brutalizes society. It also generates and fortifies alienation among those who find themselves on the margins and/or caught in the crossfire.

The growing popularity of *jehadi madrasas* in the last few years is testament to this. Militancy in the name of Islam threatens Pakistan as much as it threatens those that are the militants' better-known targets. It does so in three ways. Firstly, it legitimizes the use of violence as the language of dissidence. Secondly, it intensifies the identification of regime and state, and their security. Inasmuch as the regime in power is viewed as the last bastion against such militancy, its own inadequacies are overlooked and its security is seen as a precondition for state security. Finally, the militants redefine the political spectrum, making earlier conservatives look moderate and previously untenable political compromises more appealing. The result is a shift in the political discourse over time, and usually to the detriment of citizens' lives.

In Pakistan's policy universe, how is 'security' understood? In light of the above survey, I would answer, as 'survival.' The next question is, 'Survival of what?' The answer to this is classic realism again: the state and/or the regime in control of it. While the consequences of Afghanistan's problems and escalating violence are felt by society as a whole, it does not appear as if those concerns are perceived as 'security' problems.

Sri Lanka's ethnic conflict has obscured every other security issue the island-state faces. Looming presence of the Indian subcontinent, with expansionist Tamil kingdoms just across the Palk Straits that have been the most consistent threats to the survival of kingdoms on the island through history.

Like many of the security issues plaguing India and Pakistan, Sri Lanka's conflict can also be described as a consequence of particular aspects of the founding and consolidation of the state. A pattern of negotiations followed by one party reneging on the deal persists, with the government initially being the regular defector, and now the Liberation Tigers of Tamil Eelam taking their turn. From the point of view of the Sri Lankan state, the fundamental question is that of survival in its present form—that is, without a partition. Given the demographics of the country—that it has a majority Sinhalese population—the government largely represents and reflects their threat perceptions. For the majority community, the minority Tamil community is seen as acting not alone but with the backing of the Tamils across the Straits, thus vastly outnumbering the Sinhalese.

The Indian state has intervened variously in the conflict, initially arming and training Tamil militants, then mediating and finally, disastrously overseeing the demobilization of the militants and guaranteeing the peace. Since the 1990s, it has kept a distant, watching brief on the conflict, but Indian intervention is always a possibility—more welcome at some times than others.

To Sri Lanka, then, as to Pakistan, security is survival. Today, Sri Lanka faces the situation that Pakistan did in 1971, however, without the complications of physical separation, outside intervention at its expense and with the real prospect of resolution.

The most inescapable determinant of security and insecurity in **Nepal** is its location. 'The kingdom is like a *tarul* (fruit) between two stones. Great friendship should be maintained with the Chinese Emperor. Friendship should be maintained with the Emperor of the Southern Seas' (Baral 1988: 15). Nepal can take neither India nor China for granted. After India let the trade and transit arrangements with Nepal lapse in 1989, sealing 13 out of 15 of its transit points to Nepal, that landlocked state cannot be sanguine about its only easy access to the sea. China's annexation of Tibet on the other hand, does not make Nepal secure in that relationship either.

The most pressing security issue faced by the Nepalese state today, however, is the Maoist insurrection that directly challenges the bases of the state. The Maoists challenge both the social and the political order, pointing to the neglect of certain regions and the failures of

Nepal's democratization process. Thus, they threaten both state and society, but it is the state that is rendered most insecure by their actions. Because one of the demands of the Maoists is the abolition of the monarchy, in the counter-insurgency operations undertaken against them, state and regime security have nearly become identical. As Nepal has tried to cope with the rebellion, its democratically elected governments have floundered. This has left the army largely in charge of the situation and placed the monarch in a position of renewed significance.

In the Nepali context, security is again survival—between the two giant neighbors, away from the sea, against the Maoist threat and the line between state and regime security is thin.

For **Bhutan**, landlocked in the same way as Nepal, the solution has been to stay close to India and keep a low profile otherwise. Bhutan's most pressing concern has to do more with societal security than with state or regime security.

As a small country with more land to till than people to till it, Bhutan allowed migrant workers from densely populated Nepal to meet that need. The Nepalese-origin population in Bhutan has grown, and in fear of being swamped and losing their cultural distinctiveness, the Bhutanese government introduced new citizenship laws and a cultural policy that defined dress and behavior codes for 'Bhutanese' culture largely along the lines of the Drukpa culture. This has created a large refugee problem, spurred a Nepalese-led democratization movement and a law and order problem as people take advantage of the large numbers of displaced to loot and raid. Moreover, the forested plains in the southern reaches of Bhutan have become staging grounds for militant outfits in India's northeast. They take advantage of the area's contiguity with India and the poor enforcement capability of the Bhutanese state to hide out and regroup here. In December 2003, at great risk to itself, the kingdom of Bhutan undertook extensive operations to uproot the camps and drive out the militants.

Bhutan's insecurities thus stem from its smallness, in terms of population and resources, rather than the malevolent intentions of its neighbors. It fears being overrun by outsiders, be they migrant workers or militants. The primary referent for its fears is really the Drukpa community and its continued cultural survival.

For the **Maldives**, too, security is survival, but the most imminent threat is of a different kind. Maldives is most vulnerable to rising sea levels that can engulf its coral reef atolls. This is the international policy area on which the republic is most vocal and active. So the referent of security in this instance is the very physical existence of the state.

Realpolitik analyses would problematize the archipelagic nature of its geography, which leaves distant islands that are vulnerable to secessionism and occupation by pirates, seafaring powers or other armed actors, at a remove from the integrationist drives of the central islands. While these do pose problems for the Maldives as its history of attempted coups suggests, there is not to them the inevitability of the environmental threat. Furthermore, these are threats to the regime and not the state itself.

In addition to physical and regime security issues, Maldivian politics suggest an anxiety about societal security—as in the secure continuance of values and customs. The Maldives are South Asia's only more or less homogenous society even though the culture of the islands is a product of centuries of trade and travel contacts with the littoral cultures of the Indian Ocean. Apart from strictures on the identity of the President and the defining provisions of its constitution, one illustration of this anxiety are the restrictions that confine tourists to certain islands, not allowing them much access to the rest of the island.

Security here, then, is survival and survival at different levels of urgency. For both the Maldives and Bhutan, South Asia's smallest states, the primacy accorded by realist theorists and 'realistic' policy-makers to state security of a certain sort, make much less.

Both blessed and beleaguered by the outflow of two perennial rivers through its territory, **Bangladesh** has been instrumental in highlighting the interconnectedness of national policies on water. Too much or too little water, location in the river's course, river water usage and the consequences of flooding and flood erosion all raise survival issues for people.

India borders Bangladesh on three sides. Shifting river tides create and submerge islands along the southern reaches of the border, creating demarcation issues between the two states. However, with undocumented migration from Bangladesh into India, the fencing of the border has complicated and added urgency to the issue. Bangladesh faces its own inflow problems, having become the *entrepÙt* for narcotics traffickers and a safe haven for militant groups from both India and Myanmar. This is developing into a thorny issue in its relationship with both states. Moreover, affiliates of Al Qaeda have been active in Bangladesh targeting academics and others perceived as liberal. Bangladesh has also faced internal conflict as a consequence of state-building politics. Development and nation-building projects dispossessed and alienated the peoples of the Chittagong Hill Tracts, and led to a confrontation between them and the military forces. As in other South Asian states, the military in Bangladesh is used as the law enforcement and disaster management agency last resort.

How do we characterize the common usage of the term 'security' in Bangladesh? Security is used both in the sense of survival safety. In common with the Maldives, an important component of security involves coping with the hand dealt to the state by nature and geography. The other referents are the state and to some extent, the regime.

South Asian states for the most part understand security as either survival and/or safety. For India, it is safety. For the others, crowded by India's presence and preferences, it is survival. For Bangladesh, the Maldives and Bhutan, size, location and terrain, accentuate the urgency of survival concerns. State-building definitions contribute to the ease with which regime and state security are conflated in all these states.

There is some variation in the referent in the seven states. Other states, sub-state groups, cross-border movements, development projects with trans-state consequences, the vagaries of nature and environmental change define the range. The individual seldom features in this calculus and the female individual is altogether invisible.

To be fair, there is an element of circular reasoning in this account. Having attributed a certain point of view to states and international relations scholarship, I have listed examples that support my contention. However, the account broadly reflects the issues that make the headlines in each state, and any omissions are hardly as detrimental to the well being of millions as the states' own omissions are.

Who gets left out of this way of looking at security? People at large do. There are many moments when focusing on the security is tantamount to securing the people. However, in certain circumstances, as individuals and members of other collectivities, the security of the state can be inimical to that of ordinary people. Ethnicity, religion and class, all lend themselves to mass mobilization. Gender however does not. Women and men do not live in mutually exclusive communities, untouched by other affiliations or histories. Rather, all other politics are engendered, and reflect in their symbols, issues, inclusions and exclusions, the dominant pattern of gender relations.

FEMINIST CRITIQUES OF THE SECURITY DISCOURSE

This brings us to the second part of this essay. What does feminism lead us to expect of the security discourse?

First of all, I should clarify that I associate 'feminist' with three somewhat separate, though mutually identified, contexts. I grew up, in a family of feminists, with the first one, in early 1980s Bombay. It was the grounded activism of the anti-rape agitation following the Mathura case judgment.[3] My own feminism still stems from the values reinforced and lessons learned at this time. The second is the context of feminist theory, mostly emanating from Western academia with prominent non-western critiques. The third is writings by a subset of feminist scholars of international relations and security studies who have since the late 1980s built a corpus of writings and arguments critiquing mainstream scholarship in the field. In this section, it is the third I will draw upon.[4]

Feminist theory, like many contemporary theories, contends that people identify in more than one way and many of those identities are constructed. Allowing this reality to inform security analyses allows full play to the complexity of the subject matter (Elshtain 1995: 348). In addition to identity, the state and power (1995: 350, 354) and the dichotomized equation of 'peace-feminine' and 'war-masculine' are also to be deconstructed.

Conventional security studies evolved from the study of war. Women traditionally are invisible in such studies. In recent writings however, women are both agents and victims of war. They fight or manipulate (Fraser 1994; Addis, Russo and Sebesta 1994); they are raped, killed or objectified (Enloe 1989). However, theorists have paid most attention to women not as soldiers or victims, but as mothers. In their maternal role, they are supposed to be nurturing and naturally ill disposed to war and violence (Brock-Utne 1985, 1989). This essentialist view posits also that having very different experiences of security and insecurity, women would bring a distinctive viewpoint while identifying security issues.

The public-male/private-female dichotomy is also challenged by a number of writers including Grant (1991), Peterson (1992: 34), Tickner (1992) and Keohane (1998). By relegating women to the domestic sphere and men to the public, men get to dominate the means of coercion and the state's infrastructure while women perform service and voluntary tasks (Peterson 1992: 45). Going beyond the erasure of the internal-international distinction, the work of feminist scholars like Cynthia Enloe (1989) illustrates the linkages between domestic (household) relationships and international relations.

This dichotomy has dramatic consequences for women. Enforced as law, it places women at risk by excluding many of their experiences from its jurisdiction. Thus, the case has to be made for including issues like female infanticide, domestic violence and marital rape in its purview, even though they threaten women's lives and safety every day. Breaking down the private-public distinction reinforces the idea that domestic and international relations are closely interlinked. Essentially, this is also a critique of the levels of analysis approach to international relations and adopting this perspective allows us to admit to the scope of security studies internal, inter-state and trans-state problems. From the feminist point of view, this is useful for admitting issues like human trafficking to the field.

Keeping women confined to the private sphere deprives them of agency. They are objects of protection for men who will fight for their safety and honor in the streets, in the political arena and on the battlefield. Because men are chosen to bear arms and lay down their lives, women are chosen to be lesser members of the community. This sacrifice is the full measure of patriotism and citizenship, posing a structural impediment for women to whom this opportunity is usually denied in reality and whose presence in the public sphere is ignored by theory.

J. Ann Tickner's exposition[5] of how one might refine definitions of security based on women's and feminist ideas, is one of the clearest so far available (1992). Asking how women might define security, she culls historical instances that establish that there is no simple answer to this question (1992: 54-55). Security is defined in a wide range of terms—internationalism and disarmament, safe working conditions, freedom from the threat of war or unemployment, economic and social justice. Insecurity stems, among other things, from self-destructive nationalism, foreign debt and its economic consequences, structural violence nuclear war and the relationship between war and violence against women.

Piecing together from the literature feminist perspectives on security, Tickner shows that the neorealist idea of the state as an island of order and security in an environment of anarchy is inaccurate by citing examples of women's insecurities within the state. Some of the 'particular vulnerabilities of women within states' discussed here are the threat of rape, domestic violence, feeling unsafe in public places, the direct correlation between increasing economic troubles, militarisation and violence against women and the impact of (usually state-led) modernisation on such violence. One important difference between conventional and feminist perspectives would be that feminists do not view violence and insecurity at different levels of analysis as unrelated (Tickner 1992: 58). Further, women do not view security as a zero-sum game, where one person's security is enhanced in inverse proportion to another's insecurity (Tickner 1992: 55). Finally, based on her summary of feminist ideas, one might expect women's definitions of security to embrace many dimensions, diversity and co-operative action, as well as the ambiguities that must follow thence (Tickner 1992: 64-6).

Feminists thus argue for a more nuanced, less dichotomy-ridden approach to security studies and security policy. An erasure of categorical differences will yield a richer and more inclusive analytical reach. Security policy can then include inside-outside, internal and inter-state concerns that pertain equally to women and men. Accordingly, recent writing on security studies, whether written by feminists or not, has considered issues like declining sex ratios, trafficking of women and the problems of girl soldiers (for instance, Bertone 2000; Hudson and Den Boer 2002; Mazurana et al 2002; Ward and Vann 2002). What feminist theorists in IR and security studies have not done is attempt to answer the questions: what is security and what are the proper referents thereof? In fact, these questions are rendered irrelevant by the opening up of the field to all sorts of considerations. As the floodgates open, the question that becomes more pertinent is: what is NOT security? This is most easily answered looking at real South Asian women's lives.

REAL WOMEN, REAL LIVES, REAL INSECURITIES

My grandmother was 15 when she was married. Brilliant and musically gifted, she had already won gold medals in her studies and sung on the radio. Within a dozen years she endured several pregnancies, giving birth to six girls. She died giving birth to the seventh. Her husband, my grandfather, died in his late thirties, leaving six daughters behind, five to be raised and married in their turn. What to do with such a liability as five girls with no property to their names? The suggestions were many: Marry them off to widowers or childless men, separate them and raise them, leave some in an orphanage. My mother and her sisters were uniquely fortunate in their maternal great-grandparents. My retired great-grandfather went to work and his sons gave up their chance at higher education to support raising the girls. All five of them were educated and learned to support themselves.

In North Arcot, the Tamil Nadu district, from which both my parents' families come, the sex ratio has declined from 1013 in 1941, 998 in 1961, 988 in 1981, 962 in 1991 and 945 in 2001[6] (Chunkath and Athreya, 1997). The killing of female children is thus an issue that is very close to my heart; singular good fortune allows me to be alive and write this paper.

Conventional wisdom places great faith in the civilizing influence of modernity. However, over fifty years of planned development in India have seen a decline in sex ratios. Further, it has accompanied an improvement in other social indicators. In fact, technological advance has been an accomplice in these murders; even as pre-natal diagnosticians have been legally proscribed from determining the sex of a child or informing the parents or their relatives, mobile ultrasound units ply the Indian countryside and illegal sex-selective abortions continue to be performed.

A surviving fetus still faces the threat of infanticide. No matter what the rationale or the explanations for the practice of feticide and infanticide, one thing is certain—it is women who are most often involved, usually the paternal grandmother or the midwife, in the actual killing. (To say this is not to suggest that the women are acting in isolation of structures, customs and power relationships in society or to place blame solely upon individual women. However, there is some irony and tragedy in the fact that women end up killing women.) According to one report, 35 midwives in one North Indian village claimed to each have killed 3–4 babies in one month and to another 10 midwives claimed to have killed 1–2 babies a month. With approximately 500,000 midwives in that state, the possible total number of girl babies killed boggles the mind (Bahukhandi 2001).

> I grew up in Bombay, as I proudly and frequently inform people. I would go out with my cousin sisters from other cities and notice how much more hesitant their steps were. I strode like I owned the world and had no time for anyone's objections to that; they walked like they had permission for a finite number of steps. Some of the Bombay girls' confidence came from the safety of Bombay streets—we used to say. The Bombayite would stay out of your business, but heed your cry for help, and so why worry?
> On Bombay's crowded suburban trains, two or three bogeys are designated 'Ladies' compartments,' usually one each in the second and first class categories. At rush hour, both are packed to bursting point. Other than baby boys coming with their mothers, any male straying into the compartment faces summary eviction. Women travel in other compartments too, particularly when they travel with male companions or in a large, mixed group. Vendors and beggars, usually women and children, go in and out of every compartment on the train. Unlike other cities where women return like homing pigeons at sundown, Bombay girls grow up knowing they can be out on the trains and buses as late as they need.
> On 14 August 2002, a drunken man raped a 12-year-old girl in front of five men who looked away. There were five men in that compartment who saw him rape her. They looked away. One of them was a reporter; he wrote that they were afraid.

Sexual violence knows no limits—really, not even gender. As a form of brutal domination, it is indiscriminate in its victims. In this section, although the victims of violent sexual abuse are both male and female, I want to focus on girls and women without denying that horrors are inflicted on young boys and men in similar situations.

In relatively conservative South Asia, the specter of rape and sexual violence fills every girl's life with strictures, taboos and warnings: 'Don't stay out late, don't wear this or that, don't talk to so and so, don't play there, don't go alone.' These stem partly from an anxiety to protect the child from violence, but also from the high value placed on chastity and virginity in the patriarchal societies of the region. A girl is property to be transferred at some point to her rightful owners (*paraaya dhan*) and as such must be preserved unsullied. As she enters adulthood, the consequences of this fear multiply.

It makes silence about abuse imperative. When abuse occurs, the girl or woman must face it alone. It makes the abuse of boys, whose virginity is not priced in the same way, palatable.

It transforms the victimhood of the girl or woman into culpability of sorts. Precautions following from the fear of rape limit the girl or woman's horizons and opportunities. They deprive her of a chance to be educated; she gets married off early; she cannot leave the house to earn a livelihood and must therefore depend on others for survival; and she internalizes these limitations as affirmations of her weakness and incompetence. This in turn increases her dependence on the very structures and relationships that made her vulnerable in the first place.

Childhood sexual abuse, rape and domestic violence are three of the most common threats faced by women.

For those who would abuse children, opportunities abound in South Asia. Joint and large extended families where age hierarchy and patriarchy forge a climate of silence, extreme poverty that feeds into sexual tourism and trafficking, relationships of faith and surrender that places certain contexts beyond question, and most recently, with more and more women leaving their families behind in order to earn a livelihood—there is little a child can say or do to counter the overwhelming press of circumstance. A survey by an Indian NGO of 348 girl students yielded some horrific statistics: 83 per cent had experienced physical eve teasing; 47 per cent had been molested or had experienced sexual overtures; 15 per cent had experienced serious forms of sexual abuse including rape. If these were not bad enough statistics, 10–15 per cent of those in the first two categories were younger than 10 when they had these experiences and 31 per cent of those who experienced serious abuse were less than 10 years old.[7] A national security system or a regional security discourse that leaves the truly defenseless vulnerable does not appear to serve any useful purpose.

Rape is not the consequence of uncontrolled passion. It is, in all circumstances, an act of violence and of the coercive assertion of power. South Asian women, like other women and like men in certain circumstances, are vulnerable to rape in a variety of situations. Rape is possible within the household, whether as incestuous rape, marital rape or sexual assault by someone outside the family. Public spaces have to be neither secluded nor dark for the threat of rape to be real, as the incident on the Bombay train shows (Sharma 2002), and the victim does not have to be poor or disabled, as the recent incidents of rape in New Delhi of a college student and a Swiss diplomat have shown (Vetticad and Subramanyam 2003). Rape is also an instrument of choice in inter-caste, inter-ethnic and inter-communal conflict, serving as an assault not on a particular woman's body, but that of her community as a whole.

The Zina Ordinance in Pakistan illustrates how law and custom connive to exacerbate this situation. Where people are predisposed to look at a rape victim as being responsible through careless or immorality for her experience of violence, this law makes it possible for a rape case to be tried as a case of extra-marital sexual relations, an offence for which both men and women may be tried. The burden of proof with the woman, who is obliged by evidentiary requirements to produce four adult eyewitnesses who have to be Muslim and male. The Human Development in South Asia report Mahbub-ul-Haq Human Development Centre, 2000, from which I draw this example says, 'Ö it is virtually impossible that a woman could get raped in front of four adult males of good character' (2000: 99). However, the Bombay train example belies this optimism. Further, if families are willing to use this ordinance as an excuse to control their own daughters and imprison them for their own reasons, then a raped woman has even less chance of finding four people who were eye-witnesses to speak for her.

Domestic violence is underreported in every society and consequently statistics are hard to come by. The idea that spousal abuse is part of the married woman's lot and that the virtue of a woman is measured by her capacity to bear with it, remains ingrained in most South Asian households and where it was fraying, it is being reinforced by a majority of the family dramas that have a stranglehold on our television sets—in any language.[8] In September 2000, the United Nations Population Fund reported that 47 per cent of Bangladeshi women faced assault by men, giving them the dubious distinction of topping 'world charts when it comes to violence committed against its women' (Dawn 9-21-00). This was reported in several South Asian papers, along with the fact that India followed soon thereafter with 40 per cent. High female literacy is usually considered a precursor to better status of women, but even in Sri Lanka, the Human Development Report, 2000, tells us that 60 per cent of Sri Lankan women suffer domestic violence (2000: 93). Laws in South Asian states inadequately address this problem.

Even as we try and grapple with documenting and then analytically weaving the insecurities faced by women into a policy-oriented research-informed agenda, new forms of violence against women emerge to supplement the old ones. Where *karo-kari* and *sati* (or at least, *sati* worship) continue, we also now have acid attacks.

> My need to work on women-security issues stems from my discomfort at many levels with my profession. Security studies is a male dominated field and as such, one is often the only woman in a seminar room or one of a very few women. Men gossip and trade jokes as if they were in a locker room, use sexist metaphors or in my book, worst of all, mistake suggestive lewdness for insight. Sometimes women speak up; sometimes we are silenced. One has moments when one is suddenly as ill at ease as if one were locked in a confined space with menacing strangers.
>
> And then there was the Rupan Deol Bajaj versus KPS Gill case, in which a senior Indian Administrative Services officer accused a prominent police officer of fondling her inappropriately in a social situation.
>
> By any definition, academics and bureacrats occupy the more privileged echelons of the workforce. It is not unreasonable to assume that domestic workers, caregivers for children and construction workers are more vulnerable than Ms Bajaj and I are. So, the question is: where is the line drawn between those colleagues and work relationships in which you are secure, and those in which you are not? And the answer: in the sand, amid a blowing gale.

The Sri Lankan government set up a Bureau of Foreign Employment because so many hundreds of Sri Lankans were going abroad to work. Many of those going are women who would work as housemaids. Year after year, it is reported that large numbers of these women are returning abused—ill treated, raped, beaten. In the meanwhile, at home, the incidence of incestuous abuse is on the rise and the children left behind by these working mothers are the victims. Nepal and Bangladesh have responded to this threat by prohibiting their women from going abroad to work. Where does this leave the women? It leaves them unable to support themselves and their families, trapped in poverty and in dependence on more or less reliable family support. Protection of women, yet again, takes the form of treating them like children, making decisions for them and placing restrictions on their mobility rather than curtailing those who would threaten the women in the first place.

Thus limited, women in extremely poor settings become all the more susceptible to the promises held out by dream-spinners who turn out to be traffickers. Bangladeshi NGOs estimate that 10,000–15,000 women and girls are trafficked to India every year and Nepali NGOs place their estimate at 5,000–10,000 (E/CN.4/2001/73/Add.2: 8). Most of them end up as sex workers. In the case of girls who are trafficked thus, it seems as if everyone who should be caring for them and protecting them is complicit in their suffering—parents, police, border agents and local officials. Again, the solution sought is restricting their movement or summarily putting them on buses and trains to head home. However, the high likelihood that they have contracted HIV/AIDS or some STD means that the return home is not simple.

2 p.m. My sister, who works in a newspaper office, just called to say that reports of communal clashes were coming in from different parts of the city. Buses were being stopped and passengers beaten. My daughter usually leaves college at 1:30 and should be on her way. I hope she got past the violence.

3 p.m. She still has not come home. She normally gets here around 2:45. I hope she is alright. 3:15. 'Has she reached? Some women were stripped and molested in that area. There are all sorts of rumors.' Oh, God, where will she call from in these circumstances? Bring my daughter back safely, please. 3:30 p.m. 'What bus does she take? Does she take a ladies' special? They are being targeted.' Yes, she does. Why did we allow her to study so far away? Girls are not safe in such times.

4 p.m. 'Has she reached?' No. 'Has she reached?' No. 'Look, don't panic prematurely, but things are really bad. You know they were saying some women had been molested? We don't know which community they were from but now there are rumors of reprisals everywhere.' Please, bring my daughter back safe and sound.

5 p.m. No, she has not come.

6 p.m. I would be worried anyway because it is now pitch dark outside. What-what you hear. Women are stripped, beaten, raped, gang-raped. Just bring her back in one piece. I will not let her out of my sight. 6:15. A doorbell. Relief?

6:30. Just wanted to let you know she is here. She is okay. But very shaken. The bus right behind hers was stopped, evacuated and burned. By the time they reached the big junction, there were roadblocks and the buses were being searched. She saw them pull the women aside. Some were taken around the corner. She managed to walk really fast and walk past before anyone noticed, but when she looked back, she saw the police feeling some of the girls up as if they were carrying concealed weapons. She is very shaken. And she had to walk almost one-third of the way home. She has been walking since 3. Just wanted to let you know.[9]

This is an incomplete litany, both in terms of what threatens women and what threatens women in each of the seven countries. Constraints of space limit this to an indicative discussion. Women are insecure in many spheres—in the home, in public spaces, in the workspace, and in their capacity as individuals and as members of particular groups. Their class, caste, and communal identity, inheritance rights, family laws and limitations on political participation also compound their vulnerability.

In the last book of the Ramayana (1981), which was added later on and describes the post-coronation life of Rama and his family, there is a wonderful description of *Ramarajya*, which is one South Asian vision of utopia, where the perfection of Rama's governance is established by the absence of pain during childbirth (see Subramaniam 1981). We have come a long way from there, and as we theorize and mobilize around specific gender-related questions, we still stop short of making women's lives painless in every way. To raise questions about women's welfare in the context of security or any other 'national' policy, we have to first justify why this is an issue that should concern everyone. But I want to ask: who is secure when almost half the population is not?

To describe the vulnerabilities of women is not to deny either their culpability in making others (even other women) insecure or their agency in securing their lives. It is not to erase the presence of those women who record and report, who narrate and remember and who interpret, advocate and analyze. It is simply to try and answer the two questions posed at the beginning: what does security mean in this context and who or what is the chief referent of security here?

The experiences of women suggest a range of meanings, equally urgent, for the term 'security.' The first is survival—in the womb, as an infant and thereafter. The second is safety—against violence (both physical and structural), abduction and torture. The last is a minimum physical quality of life, which depends on equity. This provides some insurance to her against threats to her survival and safety, but more important allows her to get past survival crises and build a more positive security for herself. Given the immediacy of each of these, the most practical referent is the woman herself and possibly people around her. The survival struggles of women are so dramatic as to make it hard to imagine that for most of them, wishing to secure a glacier, oil wells, the stock exchange or even government buildings would have the same sense of urgency.

> A few weeks ago, I sat through a seminar where we were told it was really important to address the threat of nuclear terrorism. No one would deny that nuclear weapons are harmful and that nuclear terrorism sounds scary, but as I listened to the discussion, I thought of the woman who works in our house and another. She is a widow raising her two daughters alone, with her mother living there for support. She feeds four mouths on a salary, which however generous we might deem it, is less than what she needs. Her dwellings are in a shanty and have burned down, leaving them homeless, more than once. She gets water once every few days and every wind that blows her way is an ill wind. I thought about her and how I would explain the urgency of the nuclear threat to her.
>
> To bring the countless women in her position and the state of the security discourse in South Asia to the same place should be the objective we pursue.

A COMPARISON OF THE THREE PERSPECTIVES: A NEW AGENDA FOR RESEARCH AND POLICY?

Let us now juxtapose the three perspectives—that of the policy establishment, that of feminist scholarship on security and that of ordinary South Asian women—by juxtaposing the answers to the two questions posed in each instance.

What is security and to whom does the term refer? To South Asian policy-makers it is either the safety and/or survival of the state, and in some instances, this is read as being coterminous with the regime. To feminist scholars of security studies, these are irrelevant questions as they push for a non-zero sum, non-dichotomous, nuanced understanding of politics itself that is inclusive in terms of issues and identities. In practical terms, that leaves us with a field of unmanageable scope for both research and policy. In the previous section, I concluded that for most ordinary women, security is survival, safety and a minimum physical quality of life. In this one, I would put that down to survival and safety—for each woman, her survival and safety and that of her immediate relations. As we expand the focus of our research and policy-oriented advocacy, this lends our efforts an even greater urgency.

When we contrast the perspectives of policy establishment and feminist security scholarship, they seem diametrically different. Feminist scholars would deconstruct the very state that policy-makers are engaged in securing. To policy-makers, even those who are feminists, what scholars would push for in their critiques, would not leave them much which is feasible to work with. On the other hand, while the issues that concern policy makers do affect women as much as men, the threats that are particular to them by virtue of gender seldom make it to the attention of those in the security policy establishment—which is ultimately what we are concerned about. We are concerned about bringing closer the content and politics of the three perspectives discussed here. Finally, contrasting scholarship and the lives of real women, it would appear that while the recommendations of feminist scholars are to the point and would create a paradigm shift that would benefit women and others who are marginalized, there is still a gap between the two. That is a gap between the abstract, theoretical and general on the one hand and the very concrete, tangible and specific things that threaten women on the other.

Recent empirical scholarship does begin to bridge that gap, but the field itself is too new to provide ready answers.

So how do we forge a research-driven, policy-oriented work agenda that reflects the inescapable everyday threats faced by women? To put it another way, how do we give their concerns the leverage that is gained by labeling something a 'security' concern? To take issues like feticide and infanticide out of the ghetto of women's studies or better prenatal care out of the slow-cooker called development projects, and accord to them the urgency with which their consequences are played out, should be our primary motivation. Let us screen and filter the other two perspectives, focusing on the lives of real women. This provides us with two parameters.

The first is to focus urgently on the concrete and the tangible. In facing all the threats listed and not listed in this short essay, time is of the essence. To policy-makers, this means prioritizing the 'who is safe and who is now hurt or homeless' question over stands that reflect abstract ideals or distant legal principles. So what is happening in Kashmir is not 'the problem of Kashmir' but the problem of making life safer and better for Kashmiris. In the context of our paper, to illustrate, it means fighting as hard for the girl children who are going missing as for soldiers lost at war and it means fortifying border patrols to secure girls, boys and women who are being trafficked as much as it does fortifying them against smugglers of arms or drugs. Above all, it means acknowledging that for each person who is insecure, urgency is required—by the time policy-makers finish their white papers and academics finish their literature reviews, it will be too late for the bride who is burnt, the female fetus who is aborted, the woman who is beaten, the girl or boy who are smuggled across to a strange country and sold. When you look at security through the lens of each person's life, there is no time to be lost.

This brings us to the second parametric shift—a shift in the referent from the state to the individual. Of course, these are not mutually exclusive. Securing the state is often tantamount to securing the individual, but securing the state alone simply reinforces a legal-ideational edifice. Therefore, national security policies—as they stand by and large—only do part of the job. To simply append to this existing view, a rag-tag collection of concerns about women would not be effective. It still keeps state and individuals separate rather than seeing them as being organically related.

A state cannot exist without people. Therefore, it may be seen as a set of people, marginally more than its parts so far as it serves their ends. Seen thus, a threat to the parts is a threat to the whole. The whole has no independent existence and if almost fifty per cent of it is under threat, then that becomes a more pressing concern than any faced by descriptive abstractions adopted by the whole. In other words, a state is little more than the people who make it up, and if almost half of those people are threatened on a daily basis, then that is a more real threat than any other. Such a view brings to the mind things that threaten the survival and safety of women, and also for instance, things that cause large-scale death like famine or human rights issues that place individuals at risk from the agents of an abstract extension or whole of a community.

The threats faced by women are manifold. However, policy-making is about establishing priorities and each threat must be weighted against the other. Therefore; in all urgency, some threats much be selected randomly and the measure of physical survival and safety from violence should be adopted here. Threats effecting the lives and physical safety of women should be prioritized over those effecting their livelihood and self-esteem. An unhappy compromise allows us to save people's lives in peacetime and at war. Thus, childhood sexual abuse, sati, honor killings, acid attacks and rape may be categorized as security threats, while eve-teasing, poverty, poor prenatal care and lack of education do not—although in their own way they could affect a woman's ability to survive. Just as in the present dispensation, prioritizing territorial security does not mean that we do not fund irrigation, it is to be hoped that categorizing physical survival and safety from violence as security matters, does not preclude our commitment to the structural changes that are required anyway.

Where do the old issues that each state faces go when you do this? Some of them lose importance while some gain it. Placing people at the center makes it easier to think of ways to resolve long-standing disputes because you save and lose face for different reasons. You lose face when something you say results in large-scale loss of life or displacement; you gain when you prevent that from happening. Battles of attrition that are costly when they are fought over territorial or ideological issues are completely counter-productive to some of the problems discussed in our last section. Many of the states in the region face security problems that stem from particular state-building programs or policies. If the state is only a little bit more as a whole than its parts, then there is no rationale for pursuing or continuing to defend those policies that ultimately pose a threat to those parts. On the other hand, for those states whose security concerns have to do with natural resources or natural disasters, this approach reinforces those concerns. For example, where Maldivians will go if their atolls are submerged, is an urgent question for them as individuals and as members of a collective society.

To regard individuals and their survival and safety as the centre of security thinking, is not however to regard them in isolation of their relationships. Feminist scholarship asks us to redefine categories and this must include the individual or the individual woman. In our quest to reframe security thinking, we should recognize the multiple relationships and affinities that colour each woman's experience or view. Does this mean one security policy per woman? No. It means a security policy that acknowledges that women don't automatically share interests—so protecting the female infant may mean arresting female midwives and grandmothers. It may mean revoking the license of female health care professionals and placing their livelihood (ergo survival) in jeopardy. In the choices we make, all this must be considered. This is where research can help.

Feminist scholarship also asks us to abandon dichotomies, which also means we should not frame individual security as precluding the consideration of all other categories. States, communities, cultures, institutions and property need protection as well, but not at the expense of individual safety. The one need not exclude the possibility of the other.
To summarize:

1. Security questions require urgent consideration and action, not years of arcane debate.
2. Individuals are the proper primary referent of security, not states and other collectives.
3. Security means first, physical survival and second, safety from violence.
4. We cannot essentialize the referent and must remain cognizant of complexities and contradictions in the identities and interests of referents.
5. Security is indivisible. That which we wish to secure exists in relation to other referents and the one cannot be secured in isolation of the other.

With these building blocks, what is the research or policy agenda that we can design?
If this is to be the new security agenda then what is the role of research and what is the role of the policy community? The theme for the SDC conference posits a symbiotic relationship between research and policy. Research is meant to inform policy, and policy is supposed to take cognizance of current research. What must people research and what kinds of advocacy might we need?

From the point of those real women whose lives we took as our third perspective, security research should question their lives and the things that render them secure or insecure. Why is the practice of dowry spreading? Why has public health remained a low priority in developing countries? What are the problems faced by women displaced because of conflict? Research like this is now being undertaken, and we need to see more of it in the South Asian context. Further, such research needs to build a case for intervention by the security policy establishment in these areas that hitherto have been sealed as 'private' or 'domestic.' It also needs to do so in concrete legal and practical terms rather than in broad brush general moral prescriptions like those in this paper. But academic research is not enough.

Those who conduct the research should work witrh those who are engaged in advocacy to get these issues in the public eye. In this region, scholars regularly contribute to the various mass media, and media persons undertake their own research and analysis. A concerted effort to make scholarly work on questions related to women's security more accessible to the public and to strengthen the analytical content of media interventions on the same subject is required. Other emerging media than print, radio and television may also be used. The Internet is a great resource as several advocacy groups have shown over the last ten years. To use email and the web to disseminate and make available in usable modules the information that we generate through research is extremely important in this age of marketing and consumption.

Researchers manage to work with media in South Asia, but their access to governmental circles where they could advise or lobby remains limited. Rather than the American model of acting through pressure groups and lobbies, South Asian scholars tend to hope for government patronage as a path to engagement. What we need to get recognition for the threats women face as security threats is an active interest group in each country and region-wide that will frame and articulate issues rather than respond to events and policy statements. We need such groups to seek out and lobby legislators and bureaucrats in relevant departments and to create in them an interest in our interests.

Will South Asian scholars like me and others who read what I have written have what it takes to initiate these actions? That remains to be seen—the subject of another person's paper ten years from now, I hope.

Bibliography

ADDIS, Elisabetta, Valeria E. Russo and Lorenza Sebesta, *Women Soldiers: Images and Realities,* New York: St. Martin's Press, 1994.

AHMED, Kiran, *'Urban Women Rebels: Voices of Dissent in Urdu Popular Fiction,'* Islamabad: Sustainable Development Conference, 2003.

AYOOB, Mohammed, *The Third World Security Predicament: State Making, Regional Conflict, and the International System,* Boulder: Lynne Rienner Publishers, 1995.

BAHUKHANDI, Manushri, Female Infanticide in India, *War Room: http://www.warroom.com.femalinfancide.htm,* Accessed 4 April 2001.

'Bangladesh tops world in violence against women, says UN,' *Dawn,* the Intrnet edition, 21 September 2000. *wysiwing://7/http://www.dawn.com/2000/09/21/top16.htm,* Accessed 7 February 2001.

BARAL, Lok Raj, *The Politics of Balanced Interdependence: Nepal and SAARC,* New Delhi: Sterling Publishers, 1988.

BERTONE, Andrea Marie, 'Sexual Trafficking in Women: International Political Economy and the Politics of Sex,' *Gender Issues,* Vol. 18, no. 1, Winter 2000, pp. 4–22.

BROCK-UTNE, Birgit, *Educating for Peace,* New York: Pergamon Press, 1985.

BROCK-UTNE, Birgit, *Feminist Perspectives on Peace and Peace Education,* New York: Pergamon Press, 1989.

Census 2001 figures for Tamil Nadu. http://gisd.tn.nic.in/census-paper2/Oldfiles/PAPER-2%20TABLEs.xls, Accessed 23 November 2003.

CHUNKATH, Sheela Rani and Athreya V. B., 'Female Infanticide in Tamil Nadu Some Evidence,' *Economic and Political Weekly*, Vol. 32, no. 17, April 1997.

Htt://www.hsph.harvard.edu/Organizations/healthnet/Sasia/suchana/1210chunkath.html, Accessed 13 April 2002 Tables linked separately.

ELSHTAIN, Jean Bethke, 'Feminist Themes and International Relations,' *International Theory: Critical Investigation*, New York: New York University Press, 1995

ENLOE, Cynthia, *Bananas, Beaches and Bases: Making Feminist Sense of International Politics*, Berkeley: University of California Press, 1989.

FRASER, Antonia, *The Warrior Queens*, New York: Vintage, 1994.

GRANT, Rebecca, 'The Sources of Gender bias in International Relations Theory,' *Gender And International Relations*, Bloomington: Indiana University Press, 1991.

HUDSON, Valerie M. and Den Boer, Andrea, 'A Surplus of Men, A Deficit of Peace,' *International Security*, Vol. 26, no. 4, Spring 2002, pp. 5–38

HUNTINGTON, Samuel P., *Political Order in Changing Societies*, New Haven: Yale University Press, 1968.

KEOHANE, Robert O., 'Beyond Dichotomy: Conversations Between International Relations and Feminist Theory,' *International Studies Quarterly*, Vol. 42, no. 1, 1998, pp. 193–8.

Mahbub ul-Haq Human Development Centre, *The Gender Question: Human Development in South Asia 2000*, Oxford: Oxford University Press, 2000.

MAZURANA, Dyan E., Susan A. Mckay, Khristopher C. Carlson, and Janel C. Kasper, 'Girls in Fighting Forces and Groups: Their Recruitment, Participation, Demobilization, and Reintegration,' *Peace and Conflict*, vol. 8, no. 2, September 2002, pp. 97–124.

PETERSON, V. Spike, (ed.) *Gendered States: Feminist (Re) Visions of International Relations Theory*, Boulder: Lynne Rienner Publishers, 1992.

PETERSON, V. Spike, 'Security and Sovereign States: What is at Stake in Taking Feminism Seriously?' *Gendered States: Feminist (Re)Visions of International Relations Theory*, Boulder: Lynne Rienner Publishers, 1992.

RAMAN, Surekha, 'Violation of Innocence: Child Sexual Abuse and the Law,' *The Lawyers Collective*, Vol. 10, nos. 10-11, October-November 1995, pp. 4–7.

http://www.hsph.harvard.edu/Organizaitions/healthnet/Sasia/forums/girlchild/articles/violation.himl, Accessed 16 December 2003.

RAMAYANA, translated by Subramaniam Kamala, 1st edition, Bharatiya Vidya Bhavan, Bombay, 1981

SHARMA, Kalpana, 'Mumbai's 'lifeline' under a cloud,' *India Together*, September 2002. *http://indiatogether.org/opinions/kalpana/ks0902-1.htm*, Accessed 24 November 2003.

TICKNER, J. Ann, *Gender in International Relations*, New York: Columbia University Press, 1992.

United Nations, Economic And Social Council, Commission on Human Rights. 2001, *Integration of the Human Rights of Women and the Gender Perspective: Violence Against Women*. Report of the Special Rapporteur on violence against women, its causes and consequences, Radhika Coomaraswamy, submitted in accordance with Commission on Human Rights resolution 2000/45. *Addendum: Mission to Bangladesh, Nepal and India on the issue of trafficking of women and girls (28 October–15 November 2000)*. E/CN.4/2001/73/Add.2. February 6.

VETTICAD, Anna M.M. And Chitra Subramanyam, 'Terror in Sin City,' *The Indian Express*, October 19, 2003.

WARD, Jeanne And Beth Vann, 'Gender-based Violence in Refugee Settings,' *The Lancet Supplement*, Vol. 360, December, 2002.

Notes

1. Thus, we might define the 'security policy establishment' as comprising those laws, offices and agencies that are concerned with the security of the state and the security mandate of the state. The extended 'security policy community' includes, along with this, the epistemic community of scholars, media persons and activists who seek to participate in the policy process with regard to both sets of security questions.

2. Early writers on political development feared revolutionary activity and dramatic change and the academic literature reflected their concerns (see Huntington 1968 for a classic statement of this view). Stability became a desirable political attribute and lasting institutions—regimes—something to which to aspire. In itself, this is not an objectionable goal; however, to the extent that a regime is not representative or accountable to its citizens and to the extent that it is not marked by rule of law, those of us that value civil and political rights may object to this identification of regime and state. The security apparatus of the state and its monopoly over legitimate means of coercion are placed at the disposal of whoever controls the government.

The state is hardly a monolithic black box, being better described in any or all of the following ways. First, the 'state' is a legal-institutional complex that is actually run by human agents who bring to their actions and interactions the whole range of values, interests and temperaments. Thus, to speak of the state in a fashion that obscures the push and pull of this plurality is to simplify what it is. Second, the state does not operate in a vacuum but in a social and cultural setting that is both more unchanging and more dynamic than the state itself, and whose hierarchies and internal boundaries are played out in the state arena also. Neither does the state exist in a moment without past or future. In other words, the state is embedded both in a socio-cultural and a historical context. Finally, inasmuch as the state's agents act in its name, it follows that those who dominate the political process determine the actions that the state takes. A given intersection of gender, class, ethnicity and generation characterize the group(s) that is/are most influential in a particular polity at a particular historical moment. Every state, every South Asian state, manifests this oligarchic tendency.

3. In 1980, two policemen raped a young tribal woman called Mathura. The lower courts acquitted the policemen on the grounds that the woman had a prior sexual history. The Bombay High Court found the policement guilty and the Supreme Court reversed that judgment on the grounds that Mathura had not raised an alarm and there were no marks of injury on her body. This case was the catalyst for a nationwide campaign against existing rape laws and this in turn, provided just the spur for a radicalized, renewed women's movement.

4. This theoretical discussion is drawn from the one written for 'Women, Security, South Asia: An Exploratory Essay' in *Women, Security, South Asia: A Clearing in the Thicket* (forthcoming) co-edited with Farah Faizal, and is substantially very similar.

5. This and the next paragraph are drawn verbatim from Swarna Rajagopalan, Women, Security, South Asia: An Exploratory Essay, in Farah Faizal and Swarna Rajagopalan, eds. *Women, Security, South Asia: A Clearing in the Thicket* (forthcoming).

6. North Arcot district was bifurcated in 1989 into Vellore and Thiruvannamalai. The child sex ratio (sex ratio for population 0-6) for Vellore is 937 and for Thiruvannamalai 952, making the average 945. Interestingly, the average sex ratio for the entire population is 997, showing that more and more female children have been killed in recent years than were in previous decades. (Source: Census 2001 figures for Tamil Nadu)

7. The NGO is Samvad and the survey is cited in Raman (1995).

8. Kiran Ahmed points out rightly, feelingly and with a great deal of evidentiary support that there are dissenting voices in the mainstream media. She uses short stories in Urdu women's magazines to illustrate this point. As she says, these are completely ignored by those, like this author, who use generalizations to underscore the inherent conservatism of the mainstream. Kiran Ahmed, Urban Women Rebels: Voices of Dissent in Urdu Popular Fiction, paper presented at the Sustainable Development Conference, Islamabad, December 2003.

9. This is a fictional anecdote I have written for the purposes of this paper.

8

DECONSTRUCTING THE HUMAN RIGHTS DISCOURSE: RELEVANCE FOR AFGHAN WOMEN

*Dr. Huma Ahmed-Ghosh**

ABSTRACT

This paper discusses the current socio-economic and political situation in Afghanistan and draws attention to the complexities of an ongoing discourse on human rights in the country. Since 2001, the invasion and control of the region has been legitimized through a discussion of Afghan women's status and rights. The international community observes the denial of universal human rights to Afghan women as the major reason for the country's backwardness, and hindrance to development. As attempt to compare the western hegemonic discourse of human rights in Muslim states, with the colonial justification of foreign rule in third world countries, is made in this paper. Once again, women's bodies are being inscribed with a post-colonial script to gain social, political and economic control over Muslims by undermining their faith and culture.

Muslims are caught between the intransigence of Muslim culture on the one hand, and the imperialism of western secular culture on the other hand. (Riffat Hassan, www.religiousconsultation.org/hassan2.htm)

*The author teaches at the Department of Women's Studies, San Diego State University, San Diego, CA, USA.

INTRODUCTION

This paper lays out the current socio-economic and political scenario in Afghanistan and draws attention to the complexities of an ongoing discourse on human rights in the country. Since 2001, invasion and control of the region has been legitimized through a discussion of Afghan women's status and rights. The international community views the denial of universal human rights to Afghan women as the major reason for the country's backwardness, and a major stumbling block to its development. Experience and observation had shown that while such rhetoric may have some truth to it, its overemphasis has led to a problematic discourse expense of human rights at the expense of economic development in the country. Afghanistan today, is one of the poorest nations in the world and unless the focus is shifted to the economic empowerment of people, especially women, in Afghanistan, women will continue to be dependent on the men in the family and community. Due to their economic bankrupt situation, the men will continue to exercise power over their women through conservative and oppressive, social and cultural institutions. This paper also attempts to compare the western hegemonic discourse of human rights in Muslim states, with the colonial justification of foreign rule in third world countries a century ago. Once again, women's bodies are being inscribed with a post-colonial script to gain social, political and economic control over Muslims by undermining their faith and culture.

METHODOLOGY

The discussion on the legitimacy, political manipulation, and simultaneously, the importance of women's human rights is based on my recent visits to Afghanistan in the summer (July-August) and winter (December) of 2003. I visited Kabul and Jalalabad, and interviewed women managing non-government organizations, the minister for Women's Affairs, housewives, students, and some working women. In Kabul, I had the opportunity to attend a workshop conducted by the Afghan Women's Human Rights Commission (AWHRC). My impressions are based on these interviews and observations. The AWHRC, while conscious about women's rights and being motivated to empower them, had a couple of observations. Firstly, it was noted that the security situation in the country was too precarious for women to step out of the house. Secondly, it was observed that the focus of the AWHRC while aimed at protection of women and a call for punishment for crimes committed against them, did not include a dialogue on structural changes in the family or social institutions, for their empowerment. At this juncture in Afghan history, perhaps they were being politically astute by not disturbing the status quo.

An attempt to highlight the immediate problems and needs of women in Afghanistan, as well as the political rhetoric of a human rights discourse, has been made by giving a brief backdrop of the history, politics and cultural institutions in the country. This will be followed by an analysis of women's rights in various Afghan Constitutions. This background will describe the socio-economic situation of Afghan women to emphasize the urgency for women's economic empowerment before their engagement with issues of human rights. Secondly, the politicized discourse on human rights within the framework of neo-colonial parameters will also be highlighted.

Brief Historical and Political Background

Afghanistan is a landlocked country, now left with few economic resources. It is mountainous with rough terrains and has been suffering a drought for almost a decade. The single largest crop in Afghanistan is poppy, with other food crops trailing behind it. The economy is also dependent on cattle raising since most of the land is pastoral. Only 12 per cent of the land is arable. Poppy/opium continues to be the staple crop.[1] According to a recent report (*Los Angeles Times*, 2–9–04), 'Opium output hit a record high in Afghanistan in 2003, with another increase expected this year in the war-torn country that does not have any other real exports.' Many accounts of human trafficking, especially of women and young boys and girls have been given.

Afghanistan had been engaged in conflict for the last twenty five years, first at the hands of the Soviet Union who occupied Afghanistan from 1979 to 1989, and then the civil war of the 1990s under the Mujahideen (1992–1996) and the Taliban (1996–2001). Since 2002, President Hamid Karzai had formed a transitional government in the country. In January 2004, another Constitution was signed with the hope, in the hopes of bringing about a democratically elected government that would rapidly put Afghanistan on the path of development and reconstruction.

Historically, Afghanistan has never been 'united' nation. The central government has mainly been based in Kabul and has run the country through a loose administration, mostly headed by royalty. for centuries, tribal leaders have been seen as main social, economic, and political controllers of their regions. Thus, Afghanistan has always had a two-tiered political system. Today, many tribal leaders (alternately referred to as warlords) are gaining legitimate power by being included in the present central government. Ethnic diversity and tribal interplays have been the hallmarks of Afghanistan politics. Rough estimates put the Pashtuns at 40 per cent, Tajiks at 25 per cent, Hazaras at 10 per cent, Uzbeks at 8 per cent, and other minority ethnic groups (Aimaks, Turkmen, Baloch, etc.) at 13 per cent. Sunnis are the majority at 84 per cent; Shias are 15 per cent and others 1 per cent. Pashtu and Dari are the official languages, with the recent Constitution also recognizing the Turkic languages (Uzbeki, and Turkmen) as official languages in Provinces where they are spoken. (http://afghansite.com)

HISTORICAL ATTEMPTS AT GAINING WOMEN'S RIGHTS

Rights for women and their economic empowerment are not modern concepts or new ways of thinking for the Afghans. In the early 1900s, Amir Habibullah Khan (1901–1919) and King Amanullah (1919–1929) experimented with laws granting rights to women in marriage and divorce, education and employment, and laws prohibiting bride price etc., but never succeeded in 'modernizing' the nation due to persistent opposition from the tribal leaders. In fact, King Amanullah's reign was the most modern period of Afghan history, outside of the Soviet occupation. With support from his wife Queen Soraya, and with the secular and modern ideas of his father-in-law Mahmud Beg Tarzi, King Amanullah opened schools for girls, hospitals, introduced industrialization, traveled to the West, received an honorary degree from Oxford and tried to put Afghanistan on a path of development and modernization (Ahmed-Ghosh, 2003). But these efforts were seen as heretical and led to his exile to Italy in 1929. In ensuing decades, sporadic efforts were made to introduce rights for women in the Constitutions and in society but did not materialize in a concrete manner till the Constitution, which of 1964.

Elections were held after the promulgation of 1964 under the auspices of the PDPA, (People's Democratic Party of Afghanistan), a Soviet aligned political party (Ahmed-Ghosh, 2001).

The 1964 Constitution is touted as the most liberal Constitution to date. The Constitution of 1964 formed the basis of organizing the Bonn Talks in 2002 and was supposed to be the blue print for the 2004 Constitution. Though it did not specifically mention women, the Constitution did contain 'equality clauses' for the people of Afghanistan. Mariam Nawabi (2003), in her article on Afghan Constitutions, clearly lays out clauses in different Constitutions that pertain to women's issues. Nawabi points out that:

> Although the 1964 Constitution has been widely cited as guaranteeing equal rights for women, its provisions did not expressly do so. The use of the word 'people,' however, was interpreted as including women and thus has been utilized as the basis of equal rights for Afghan women (2003, p. 20).

After the adoption of the Constitution, women participated in large numbers in the country's government, the civil service, and according to many reports, started flooding the professions of teaching, medicine and business companies. According to Nawabi, the 1976–1977 Constitution specified, 'all the people of Afghanistan, both men and women, without discrimination and privilege, have equal rights and obligations before the law' (2003, p. 20). In the year 1977, there was an increase in women in the Afghan legislature, bringing it up to 15 per cent.

The 1987 Constitution, passed during the Soviet Occupation in Article 28, was most inclusive of women stating,

> Citizens of the Republic of Afghanistan, both men and women, have equal rights and duties before the law, irrespective of their national, racial, linguistic, tribal, educational and social status, religious creed, political conviction, occupation, wealth, and residence. Designation of any illegal privilege or discrimination against rights and duties of citizens are forbidden.

Law, as mentioned in these Constitutions, did not refer to Islamic law, but secular laws. As pointed out by Nawabi (2003) and Khattak (2002), it was during the 1980s and early 1990s that to margin 70 per cent of teachers, 50 per cent of government workers and University students, and 40 per cent of doctors were women. This was the decade when Afghanistan was recruiting and losing thousands of men to war against the Soviets. Though the 1987 Constitution has been the most secular and inclusive of women and minority rights, it has not been touted as a model Constitution due to its close association with Soviet occupiers (1979–1989).

The 2004 Constitution of Afghanistan is reflective of the shifting dynamics between nation states and a changing world order. This Constitution is a product of global politics, where since the 1970s, Islamic states have emerged to claim autonomy and legitimacy against a perceived western dominance. To understand and justify the rise of fundamentalism in Muslim states, many theories have emerged, ranging from failed attempts by secular states to modernize the nation, to increasing poverty and unemployment among the citizens, and international interference and control of economic resources and political leadership in these states. Given the complexities of reasons for such an emerging world system, the Afghan Constitution stands today as a document whose ideology and philosophy are based on a global politics of dominance by the West and defensive politics of the East (Muslim states).

The recent constitution of the Islamic Republic of Afghanistan was announced with much fanfare heralding a 'new era of democracy'. Ironically, even though the Constitution finally passed because of intense pressure from the US and UN, mentions of women's rights and human rights remain somewhat invisible in the document. Although the current Constitution does not claim to be based on the Shariah, it states that no Afghan law can be contrary to the beliefs and provisions of Islam. The head of the Supreme Court continues to be a religiously trained *Mullah* with fundamentalist beliefs. While the Constitution states, 'the citizens of Afghanistan whether man or woman have equal rights and duties before the law', the law is determined by Islam, the current government and the Supreme Court and, 'When there is no provision in the Constitution of other laws regarding ruling on an issue, the courts' decisions shall be within the limits of this Constitution in accord with Hanafi jurisprudence.' (http://www.afghangovernment.com/2004constitution.htm. Ch. 7. Art. 15). There could be contradictions in the formulation of rights in the Constitution, which also does not address issues of past war crimes or issues of human and specifically trafficking of women and children. Given the current Constitution, little is expected from the government to bring about changes in Afghan society, social and political institutions, and more importantly in the lives of Afghan women.

Despite these drawbacks, the implementation of the Constitution still rests on elections that according to experts can be moved from June 2004 to September 2004 (though in some quarters there is talk of elections not occurring till the Spring of 2005) due to security issues. Implementation will be difficult because of the lack of security, rampant lawlessness, control of regions by warlords, the widespread cultivation of opium, and no military or international control of areas outside of Kabul.

Women's Economic Conditions In Afghanistan

A wide chasm exists between the urban and rural populations of Afghanistan. Historically, the rural areas, or any area outside of Kabul and other major cities, have usually been in the grip of tribal leaders/warlords (Ahmed-Ghosh 2003). In rural Afghanistan, tribal and Islamic laws govern the people, especially women (Moghadam 1997). These hybridized tribal laws have led to the secondary and oppressed status of women in Afghanistan. Strict interpretations of the Quran by the *Mujahideen* and a stricter one by the Taliban have rendered most women with no will, mobility or opportunities to claim human rights. Women were confined to the house, not allowed to attend schools or seek employment, thus rendering them totally dependent on the men in the family, leading to further impoverishment of women. The first step towards development is to change the economic and social environment of women in the country, especially in rural Afghanistan.

Numerous reports continue to highlight burning of girls' schools outside of Kabul, forced marriages, child marriages, suicides, trafficking of women and children, and the abysmal socio-economic situation of women in the countryside. A recent report on rural women claimed that, 'they [rural men] will let them [rural women] die rather than take them to a male doctor' (Irin, 2004, p. 1). According to Ocha Irin, an Afghan lady doctor, 'high levels of illiteracy, the complexities of traditional culture, and a lack of female doctors meant that Paktika was experiencing high rates of maternal mortality, with over 50 per cent deaths among expectant mothers' (Irin, 2004). The Author's visit to the villages in the outskirts of Jalalabad to evaluate an NGO's literacy, health, and irrigation projects reinforced the relative neglect of rural Afghanistan. Besides, the apparent poverty in these areas, the hold of very conservative social norms was very visible. Almost all women wore the burqa (head-to-toe garment covering the face),[2] few were visible on the streets, Nangarhar University had a very small number of female students (unlike Kabul University, where almost 40 per cent students were female), and most resisted being photographed claiming that it was un-Islamic or that they needed their fathers' or husbands' permission. There were no local schools for girls, though a few did exist for boys. Where girls were attending schools, it was due to international or Afghan NGO efforts with close monitoring by these agencies.

An added economic pressure in the rural areas is the return of Afghan refugees from neighboring countries. The refugee problem of Afghanistan has been the largest in the world. At its peak, there were six million Afghan refugees worldwide, with most in Pakistan and Iran. The last few years have seen the return of half of these refugees. Seventy-five percent of all refugees are women and children. Due to the long period of war and ensuing poverty, many families are female-headed because of a high incidence of deaths of men in war and through out-migration of men for economic reasons. This has led to a feminization of poverty resulting in a life expectancy of 45 years for women. Women's deaths due to childbirth and incidences of mental ill health and suicide continue to rise. Literacy rates for women range from 11–20 per cent, and only 3 per cent of girls are currently enrolled in school. Rural areas are seeing the highest return of refugees. This has added to the already impoverished conditions of the countryside.

On the other hand, Kabul has always been the centre of change and modernity. In the last decade, there has been a decline in women's status, uniformly in rural and urban areas in all social and economic institutions. But over the last three years, Kabul continues to be the only city in Afghanistan where some change has taken place. In Kabul, while the burqa is visible, an overwhelming number of women are walking around with long coats and headscarves, their faces uncovered.[3] Women are often seen in the streets, in marketplaces, and in places of employment. I also saw a few women driving cars. Schools for girls are mushrooming all over town, as are skill training and adult literacy centres for women. While some of the physical changes in women's lives in Kabul may be superficial, they contrast with women's lives in rural areas. This rural/urban divide has always been the intersection of conflict for the country. Even today, the international community is concentrated in the urban areas, very much to the neglect of rural Afghanistan where traditional politics of tribal leaders/warlords continues to exist and hamper any attempts at improving the lives of all Afghans, especially women.

While discussing the development of the country, it is pertinent to focus on the livelihood and rights of the women in Afghanistan. Meena Nanji, a filmmaker who visited Afghanistan and made a film on Afghan women (2004), in her article, succinctly lists reasons for why nothing changes for women in Afghanistan. She claims that the Ministry of Women's Affairs in Afghanistan is a figurehead to keep the international donors happy, and has no legal jurisdiction or implementation power. The present government has brought back the dreaded *Department of Vice and Virtue*, renamed, the Ministry of Religious Affairs. Co-education has been banned and President Karzai has upheld the 1970s law prohibiting married women from attending High School classes that in the recent year has resulted in the expulsion of 2,000 3,000 women from local schools. The present situation in Afghanistan continues to be harsh for both women and men, and unless further international intervention starts a process of economic reconstruction, security and poverty will continue to dictate fundamentalism and a conservative social order. Hence, one can claim that while human rights for women are a serious concern, their implementation is definitely curtailed by the current socio-economic order.

Neo-Imperialism/Mayo's Ghost Haunts Afghanistan

Dut to the neglect of women's (and men's) economic status by the international community, the overemphasis on a human rights discourse seems politically charged. The tussle to define women's status in Afghanistan in either Islamic or western terms does not only negate Afghan women's voices, but continues to thrive on international politics of polarized dichotomies where patriarchal institutions in the West and Afghanistan will continue to wrestle their differences by using women, their bodies, and their lives to play out masculinized power struggles.

As mentioned earlier (Ahmed-Ghosh 2001, 2003), foreign dominance in Afghanistan has historically played a central role in the country's economic and political development. Vested interests and the Cold War hostilities have prevailed in the country for decades. In recent years, war in Afghanistan has further justified foreign dominance; by using the status of women in Afghanistan as a matter of foreign concern. This has led to a highly politicized discourse on human rights as being the legitimizing institution for creating global friction and justifying policing of non-western countries by the West. Women's rights as human rights have thus become the battle cry for the West, and yardstick to measure civilization of non-western nations.

What becomes apparent is the impotence of a human rights discourse at this juncture in Afghan history. In Afghanistan, the shrill cry for the creation and implementation of human rights without adequate attention to the economic section in the country resonates with a colonial ring. It was to save women's human rights that a war was waged in Afghanistan. Afghans, the Taliban in particular, were blamed for the low status and mistreatment of women, which in turn was seen as an important cause for the 'backwardness' of Afghan society. Thus, making the urgent call to impose universal human rights in the country to ensure development for all. Such thinking is reminiscent of precolonial justifications of foreign rule in the name of 'local men's inability to rule' because of the low status they ascribe to their women. It is suggestive of an Eurocentric standpoint of yesteryears. In the name of civilizing or modernizing local populations in colonies, colonizers often resorted to social and political imperialism. This was done by belittling local cultures, emasculating local men, and by referring to cultural norms pertaining to women as barbaric or backward. On the global stage, Afghanistan is well positioned to endorse a neo-colonial ideology of this kind.

The push for human rights in the above stated impoverished situation is reminiscent of British justifications for rule in India. British policies in India were influenced by, and influenced, a much controversial text titled Mother India written by an American, Katherine Mayo. Mrinalini Sinha (1998) does an incisive analysis of the text and points out that the 'central argument explaining the root of all of India's problems lay in the sexual organizing of Hindu society'. Sinha (1998) continues that according to Mayo, the book 'contained a strong indictment of the demands for India self-rule and an argument in favor of continued British rule over India, due to the deplorable treatment of women, untouchables and animals'. Such sentiments seem to reverberate in Afghanistan and other Muslim nations, where Islam is projected as being backward, and now symbolizing a new movement, that of terrorism. A conflation of Islam and regional culture by the West results in a condemnation of all Muslim nations and thus, creates the space for western intervention. Similar to colonial India, women's 'deplorable' status in Afghanistan is once again projected as requiring liberation and rights based on western models of human rights. Matters become complicated when foreign intervention inadvertently lowers women's status, as Khattak points out, 'Although progress on women's rights in Afghanistan was undeniably slow, it was reversed when the US-backed *mujahideen* took over in April 1992' (2002, p. 19).

Sinha points out that, 'Her [Mayo's] argument that the backwardness of India stemmed not from political or economic causes but from religious and cultural ones served two important purposes: it countered nationalist Indian claims of Indian superiority in the realm of culture and spirituality over the materialist west; and it exempted colonial rule from any respect for the backwardness of India, eliciting instead sympathy for the reform work of the countless British men and women who laboured selflessly against such odds' (1998, p. 4). This argument succinctly describes the relationship between Muslim nations and the West today, almost eight decades after the publication of Mother India in 1927. Whilst the Islamic elite tries to ascertain their moral superiority through the rejection of the 'corrupt' western value system, the crass materialism of the West, lack of family values, and the licensee allowed to women, the western discussion on human rights tries to establish its primacy over Islamic laws by highlighting the inequality between genders as expressed in Islamic texts. Correspondingly, American military and the young soldiers in Afghanistan (and now also Iraq) are congratulated for saving the world from terrorists and complimented and rewarded for their patriotism and courage.

Another area of dissent between the West and the Muslim East is the politicization of masculinity in terms of military might, self-righteousness, and protection of the fairer sex. None of which the Afghan/Muslim man is capable of due to non-compliance of a universal human rights code. Thus, the Afghan man stands emasculated and his need to root his masculinity through the oppression of women becomes the neo-colonial trope. This struggle over Western and Afghan masculinity is expressed through control over Afghan women, who remain silent throughout such patriarchal wrangling. Such a perspective has been explored by Lata Mani in her seminal work on *sati* (widow self-immolation) in India where she points out that,

> although *sati* became an alibi for the colonial civilizing mission on the one hand, and on the other hand, a significant occasion for the indigenous autocritique, the women who burned were neither subjects nor even the primary objects of concern in the debate on its prohibition' (1998, p. 2).

Likewise, veiling, bride price and child marriages, and lack of mobility for Afghan women continue to be symbols of Islamic purity by the Afghan patriarchy and of Islamic oppression by Westerners. Simultaneously, these issues continue to be protested by western human rights activists. While these institutions are definitely repressive and detrimental to women's status, the international focus on these issues is based on the absence of such institutions in the West and hence, a sense of moral righteousness on their part to impose a cultural hegemonic ideology while laying claims to economic resources. Once again, women's voices and lived experiences are not part of this hyper-masculinized neo-imperialist agenda.

Khattak (2002) claims that 'Afghan patriarchal culture was the convenient scapegoat', even for foreign donors, who 'buttressed this culture', by turning a blind eye to the oppressive institutions it supported (2002, p. 20). She continues that, even though women were the majority of the refugees, not a single job was earmarked for women in the $87 million 10-year income generating project for refugees areas (IGPRA) by the UN High Commissioner for Refugees and World Bank.

Thus, while political dominance of Islamic states by the West is based in their economic need for oil, the 'clash of civilizations' is often debated upon. Such projections involve a condemnation and denigration of Muslim societies, which in turn lead further to the need by the elite in Muslim states to engage in a more rigid political process, resulting in the drawing of cultural battle lines. Irrespective of the critiques put forth by thinkers in perpetuating what may or may not be an historical and political conflictual situation, the reality today is definitely one of conflict where modernization is defined and redefined in terms of women's rights in the West and in the Islamic East. The sequence drawn out by westerners is: anti-West means anti-modern, which in turn is expressed through women's oppression by non-western states. But it is a myth (especially in the eyes of westerners) that modern can only mean western. Islamic and non-western history is rife with examples of modernity occurring or modernists existing in those nations, who have succeeded in or have pushed for women's rights in their societies. Therefore, the question that follows is: can there be a Muslim modernity similar to Christian modernity in the US and Europe and communist modernity in Russia, and China? The myth of modernity as the brainchild of the West and based only on western social and political principles has been further perpetuated by the constant presentation of non-western states as the 'other'. This legitimizes the West as modern and Muslim states as anti-modern. It is in this definition that political battle lines are drawn and an insistence on promoting universal human rights becomes the reason to pressurize the non-conforming nations.

CONCLUSION

A change in language may be the first step to diffuse these political tensions. By disassociating the concept of being modern from being Western, one can redefine modernity through a local cultural lens. Without engaging in the complex discussion on modernity, this is a culture-specific process. Polarized conceptualizations of dichotomies, especially the modern west and primitive 'others' alienate societies that otherwise want to engage in a global debate. An attempt should be made to de-center the debate on women's rights in Afghanistan from the West and west-based perceptions of women's rights, and to look at the needs and desires of women in Afghanistan in relation to their reality.

Literacy, education and empowerment are key issues for the claiming of rights for women. Right to literacy or education is also of importance to raise women's political consciousness but can only succeed when girls and women are literate and educated. For Afghan women, conflict and dilemmas will always exist as how to reconcile the political and economic responsibilities with family obligations. This dilemma becomes particularly acute when ideology and laws that are in contradistinction with the public life, dictate the private sphere of women's lives.

Documents such as the Universal Declaration of Human Rights should not be seen as ends in themselves trying to impose rigid guidelines for all. These documents while providing models on which to build, as drafts to incorporate national discourses, and guidelines to ensure rights to all citizens in a nation-state, have to incorporate a cultural specificity that along with international pressure and resource allocation for development, can provide alternative frameworks for women's rights. Human rights are not only about securing political and economic liberty and freedoms for the individual, but today, involves the freedom to one's culture, religion and community. The issue is, given the current sociopolitical and economic situation in Afghanistan, can there be a meeting of individual and group rights. Identities, status, and cultures are constantly shifting. Claiming of rights is also fluid with individuals moving within the collective, the group and as individuals. Hence conceptualizing human rights universal dictate always creates problems.

There were many complexities and contradictions in the new government in Afghanistan. However, it was apparent that economic sustainability needs to be prioritized over human rights. In instances of women's extreme dependency on men, abuse was not something reported or dealt with. The collective defines the women; economic and social security is tied to their group identity. Whilst realizing the importance of human rights for women in Afghanistan, one needs to focus on their economic status to facilitate better implementation of those rights. Given the current culture of dependencies, it is impossible for women to claim those rights in the face of opposition from the family, kin group and larger community. Where her entire being and her welfare is defined by the patriarchy and current poverty, she needs to tread gently on the tightrope of survival and dignity.

References

AHMED-GHOSH, Huma, 'A History of Women in Afghanistan: Lessons Learnt for the Future,' *Journal of International Women's Studies*, vol. 4, no. 3, May 2003, pp. 1–14.

AHMED-GHOSH, Huma, Lemar-Aftab, 'Feminist Perspective: September 11th and Afghan Women,' December, 2001: *www.afgahnmagazine.com.*

KHATTAK, Saba Gul, 'Afghan Women Bombed to be Liberated?' *Middle East Report*, Spring 2002, pp. 18–23

MANI, Lata, *Contentious Traditions: The Debate on Sati in Colonial India,* Berkeley: University of California Press, 1998

MOGHADAM, Valerie, 'Nationalist Agendas and Women's Rights: Conflicts in Afghanistan in the Twentieth Century,' *Feminist Nationalism*, ed. West, Lois A., New York: Routledge, 1997, pp. 75–100

NANJI, Meena, *Afghan Women after 'Liberation':* W4WAfghan@yahoogroups.com

NAWABI, Mariam, 'Women's Rights in the New Constitution of Afghanistan.' 2003: *www.nyu.edu/pages/cic/pdf/ E13WomensRights.Nawabi.pdf*

SINHA, Mrinalini. (ed.), *Selections from Mother India: Katherine Mayo*, New Delhi: Kali Press for Women, 1998 *http://www.afghansite.com. http://www.afghangovernment.com/2004constitution.htm.*

Notes

1. According to some reports in Kabul, poppy cultivation was used as a strategy to finance the Afghan Jihad against the Soviets. Many assert that it was a CIA brainchild, which has now come home to roost.

2. I do want to point out that the wearing of the burqa itself does not signify oppression, but in comparison to Kabul, these women stood out because of the pervasiveness. Second, many women did claim that before 1992 (the Mujahideen regime) they had not worn the burqa.

3. Again, preferring a headscarf to a burqa does not necessarily signify gender parity, but definitely is an expression of choice and a certain level of tolerance on the part of the urban community.

Doing Peace

Women Resist Daily Battle In South Asia

Ritu Menon

* Ritu Menon is a publisher and writer. She is co-author of *Borders & Boundaries*.

9

DOING PEACE: WOMEN RESIST DAILY BATTLE IN SOUTH ASIA

*Ritu Menon**

ABSTRACT

Any discussion of security from a gender perspective must address the question of armed violence against women in conjunction with ordinary, everyday violence against them. This paper examines both aspects in the context of four moments of armed conflict as experienced in South Asia:

1. The period before armed conflict breaks out, which is often characterized by economic stress and impoverishment, militarization, and the presence of increased arms dealing—the marketization of violence—and identity politics.
2. The period of war and repression itself; the entry of armed forces, the escalation of communal conflict, the disruption of everyday life, and the brutalization of the body, male and female.
3. The period of peace-making or refusing the logic of violence.
4. The post-war or post-conflict period, in which displacement and return, rehabilitation, and sometimes reconstruction and reconciliation, take place.

It then analyses responses to these by women and peace activists in the region, and strategies that they have evolved for working towards a just, secure and enduring future in their countries.

*Ritu Menon is a publisher and writer. She is co-author of *Borders & Boundaries: Women in India's Partition*, and of *Unequal citizens: A Study of Muslim Women in India*; and editor, *No Woman's Land: Women from Pakistan, India and Bangladesh Write on the Partition of India*.

1

The distinguishing feature of conflicts in South Asia over the last 50 years (barring peasant and other struggles for social and economic justice) is that they have been a) predominantly ethnic or communal, and b) protracted and increasingly violent. The most persistent of these have been the armed struggles for self-determination by the LTTE in Sri Lanka and by separatist groups in Kashmir; but others like the Chakma uprising in Bangladesh; the hostilities between the Bodos and recent immigrants in Assam; the Nagas and Kukis in Nagaland; the Muhajirs in Sind; the Nepalis and 'Bhutanese' refugees in Nepal; and the earlier Baloch and Khalsa 'nationalisms' in Pakistan and India have more or less established identity politics as an undeniable, lingering reality in the region.

The ethnic or communal dimension of South Asian conflicts has had all the well-known, and relatively more closely observed and analyzed, consequences on society and polity. Rada Ivekovic and other political philosophers, speaking of the 'majority-minority syndrome' have posited that the very categories are dictated by a communalist principle. Ivekovic says, 'Different from society which presupposes, among other things, the social link between individuals and a shared public space, communities do not themselves recognize either social link or public space in their constitution.'[1] Each community, thus, is organized around a paternal pattern. Religious or ethnic communities are, almost by definition, paternalistic and patriarchal; they are therefore rarely emancipatory for women, because they are rarely democratic. And they are not democratic, because the basic requirement of democracy, the individual, is generally subordinated in such collectivities.

Women are the first Other within a community because, as Ivekovic says, they embody the very principle of mixture which is the basis of life in biological terms.[2] They thus represent a dangerous potential for a dilution of the 'pure'—ethnic purity is an article of faith for the communalist—which is why, both, their appropriation by the Other and their control by their own community, are a particular characteristic of inter-ethnic violence.

Further, religious communities are 'brotherhoods', affirming what Benedict Anderson calls the 'deep comradeship' of men. These brotherhoods are articulated, and group identity constructed, by excluding the Other—the Enemy or the Outside Other and Women, or the Inside Other. 'Brothers,' elaborates Ivekovic 'only get a sense of identity through belonging to the group and developing an image of exclusion and domination of the Other.'[3] It is these antagonistic brotherhoods that operate in nationalist conflicts, especially those of the cultural or ethnic nationalist variety.

Two examples from India may serve to further elaborate this point; the first concerns the decade-long conflict in Kashmir, the second, the burst of brutal violence against Muslims in Gujarat in 2002.

Kashmir is the only Muslim majority state in the Indian union, and it has been the site of extreme militancy for more than a dozen years now. Targeted violence against Kashmiri Hindus in the state has led to mass migration by them to other parts of the country, thus exacerbating the communal divide and increasing violence. Kashmiri Hindu women who were vulnerable at the hands of extremists, find their counterparts in the mass of Kashmiri Muslim women who live with the potential of violent reprisal both from suspicious militants as well as the forces of the state: border security, the local police, and a heavily deployed army. It bears repeating that prolonged conflict heightens, and further entrenches, the communalization of all parties to the conflict, whether state, civil or militant; and that the impact of this on women is simultaneously dispersed and specific.[4]

Kashmiri Muslim women, for instance, have been told to veil themselves both by fundamentalist women's organizations like the Dukhtaran-e-Millat and Khawateen Markaz[5], and militant outfits like the Allah Tigers and Hizbul Mujahideen. Refusal to abide by these restrictions has resulted in disfiguring violence and driven many women into their homes. Visibilising difference through dress codes for women is a swift and simple way of marking off one community from another; ironically, however, making women thus 'visible' also means they are easily identifiable targets of violence by the Other.

Deliberate violence against women by state agents in the form of intimidation, the threat of assault, actual rape or physical abuse has been documented in much recent conflict across South Asia, as it has in Kashmir. The full force of how communalized these perpetrators can become was evident in the Gujarat carnage of February–March 2003. What Anuradha Chenoy has called 'the politics of gender in the politics of (communal) hate'[6] was seen in brazen and hideous play here.[7] The significant, disturbing difference in the Gujarat violence was that non-Muslim women who defended or protected Muslims were targeted almost in the same way as Muslim women; and peace activists were under constant threat by the administration and assorted lumpens to disband and discontinue their work. Organizations like SEWA (Self-Employed Women's Association, which has consistently organized women across community boundaries and has an almost equal representation of Muslim and Hindu women), Gandhians, a range of NGOs and women's organizations who mobilize around civil liberties and democratic and human rights, have all been working under duress and against terrible odds.[8] The implications of this for women's peace activism are sobering.

2

In her analysis of recent conflicts, especially in Ireland and Bosnia- Herzegovina, Cynthia Cockburn has developed a succinct and useful classification of gendered power relations in what she calls four moments of armed conflict. They are:

1. The period before armed conflict breaks out, which is often characterized by economic stress and impoverishment; militarization and the presence of increased arms dealing—the marketization of violence; and identity politics.
2. The period of war and repression itself; the entry of armed forces; the escalation of communal conflict; the disruption of everyday life, and the brutalization of the body, male and female.
3. The period of peace-making or refusing the logic of violence.
4. The post-war or post-conflict period, in which displacement and return, rehabilitation and sometimes reconstruction and reconciliation take place.[9]

I will attempt a brief examination of three of these moments—namely, two, three and four—and suggest that, far from being distinct periods with defined before and after chronologies, in South Asia, at least they have tended to overlap. One reason for this may well be that armed conflict in the region has usually been very protracted thus blurring the lines between phases; and the other that we are never really in a decisive 'post-conflict' or conflict-free situation for very long. A gendered analysis of the long duration of such conflicts, then, may enable some fresh insights to emerge.

Because the issue of violence against women, and targeted violence against them in times of war and armed conflict has been such a crucial one in feminist analysis, let me take this up first.

In India, as in many other parts of the world, our early exposure and resistance to violence against women was on the issue of rape, on which we mobilized, campaigned and lobbied with modest success, to have the laws changed and made more gender-sensitive. So—custodial rape was made a criminal offence, the onus of proof for all rape was now transferred to the assailant or rapist, and cognizance taken (but no legal amendment made yet) on the necessity of separating rape against minor children from adult rape. But just as this demand has not been accommodated, so too, marital rape has not been recognized as either rape or, obviously then, as a cognizable offence.

The struggle against rape was paralleled by mobilization against dowry deaths, a sustained, widespread and highly visible mobilization; and I would argue that it was this struggle—and all the analysis and painstaking documentation, together with rescue work, counseling and legal action by women's groups and activists—that not only introduced new laws and forced institutional changes in the police and judiciary, but made for a very important transition in our understanding of violence against women. It underscored the pervasive, insidious and deeply entrenched presence of domestic violence, of which bride burning was the most dramatic and shocking manifestation. We began to recognize that, in addition to being entrenched and widespread, domestic violence was structural and systemic.

If dowry deaths were shocking and dramatic then *sati* or widow immolation was, frankly, unconscionable. Not pervasive in the way domestic violence is, not on the rise in the way bride burning may be, perhaps, but the very fact that it happened, and in the recent past, galvanized the women's movement into, of course, protesting and campaigning, but also probing and unraveling the context—political, social, economic, cultural—in which it takes place.

In the 1980s and '90s India, again like much of South Asia, was engulfed by wave after wave of ethnic, communal, sectarian, fundamentalist and extremist violence, with all our societies entering a period of protracted and increasingly violent civil strife. Old and new forms of violence against women, and sometimes violence by women, resurfaced. Combat, conflict, militancy, dislocation, forced migration, homelessness together with rape, murder, and widowhood—the violence reverberated and rippled out in apparently endless circles. We were forced to consider those age-old borders and boundaries: nation, religion, community, gender, and those ancient myths about shame and honor, blood and belonging.

Rada Ivekovic, quoted earlier, who has written with great clarity and insight on the Bosnian tragedy, says that the global patriarchal consensus regarding the subordination of *all* women to *all* men is the first of all globalizations.[10] But there is another patriarchal consensus, in my view—and it proceeds from my understanding of all the forms of violence against women that I have mentioned—and that is the consensus around the very question of violence against women. Neither absolute nor monolithic, this consensus is nevertheless at once deep and wide-ranging, and encompasses almost all forms of violence, including child-abuse and almost all violence against women, *as women*, is sexual. It has two critical and distinguishing features: it sanctions the violent 'resolution' (so to speak) of the troublesome question of women's sexuality and sexual status—chaste, polluted, impure—and simultaneously insists on women's silence regarding it through the attachment of shame and stigma to this very profound violation of self. Thus, the woman raped; the woman who may be raped; the raped child; the young widow whose sexuality can no longer be channelised; the wife raped by kinsmen or others; the women who must be killed so that their sexuality is not misappropriated; the wives, daughters and sisters who must be recovered so that sexual transgression is reversed—are all compelled into acquiescing. The consensus is most successful when women 'voluntarily' participate in the violence that is done to them, and ensuring their silence is a necessary part of the consensus.[11]

It was while we were researching women's experience of the partition of India in 1947, that we came across almost the entire spectrum of violence against women, which enabled this insight. Gradually we realized that this violent 'resolution' was part of a *continuum of violence* that had death at the hands of one's own kinsmen at one end, and rape and brutalisation by men of the other community at the other. In between lay taking your own life, sublimating your vulnerability and making something heroic of it; also in between, and governed by the same logic, was the covert violence of the state exercised through the implementation of its recovery program, a program which forcibly recovered women abducted by men of the 'other' community.[12]

The business of reproducing the clan, the community, the nation, the species, rests on the principle of mixture— the dilution of purity—which women's bodies signify. And so, though the 'nation' is the woman, and 'race' is the woman, men's lineage, their purity, is guaranteed only through controlling women. In times of conflict, especially communal or ethnic conflict, women become special targets for all the reasons we are familiar with; what is less obvious— and perhaps not even acknowledged generally—is the link between the overt and dramatic violence against women during armed conflict, and the everyday violence against them which is assumed to be of a different order. I suggest that both are part of that continuum of violence that, for women, the weapons of war are not very different from weapons in peace.

So, moments of rupture and extreme dislocation, extraordinary as they are, underscore the more daily doses of violence against women and enable us to see them as part of the continuum—and, despite the shudder of horror, part of the consensus. One could even say that for women, violence means that they remain strapped to their sexuality, making violence endemic or intrinsic, a fact of their lives, in the home, on the streets, when there is armed conflict and even when there isn't. And so, its corollary, what is *non*-violence must mean, first and foremost, the dismantling of patriarchal control over their sexuality, breaking the cycle of violence that originates in the everyday and ordinary, but explodes into the extraordinary.

The protracted nature of contemporary South Asian conflicts has had significant and far-reaching repercussions for all our countries—most evident in sharply escalating military activity and a crackdown by national governments on civilians as well as 'terrorists'—but also on everyday life and work which have experienced a kind of disruption that has not yet been adequately understood or analysed. 'War and terror have the effect, sometimes deliberate, sometimes incidental,' says Cockburn, 'of rending the fine fabric of everyday life, its interlaced economies, its material systems of support and care, its social networks, the roofs that shelter it.'[13] Existing scattered studies note their specific impact on women: the high number of civilian casualties and the very large numbers of refugees and female-headed households; a serious dislocation of social and economic life and a much higher incidence of daily violence. According to preliminary findings in the northeast of India, for instance, the long period of violence has had an adverse impact on the sex ratio, not in favor of women (as one might expect) but against them. Paula Banerjee, working on Manipur, reports a decline from 1,015 women to 1,000 men in 1961 to 961 in the 1990s, and in Nagaland, it is down from 933: 1000 to 890.[14]

But it is also the case that protracted conflict has made women more visible and active in conflict, both as victims and agents. In between these two extremes lie a host of actors and I will draw upon Roshmi Goswami's classification (for the North-east) for a simple enumeration of who they are and where they are located on the scale, so that we are better able to evaluate the degrees by which men and women are affected by the same violence. Roshmi Goswami has identified six categories of women in conflict situations;[15] they are:

1) *Women relatives of armed activists*, the mothers, wives, sisters, daughters and partners of armed activists who are in the struggle, either by choice or compulsion, and targeted by the state or the opposing side. These women are the focus of retaliatory or terrorizing violence by both state and opponent, often subjected to extreme forms of sexual violence, physical abuse and intimidation.

2) *Women relatives of state armed forces and state officials,* who have no choice in the matter, who remain invisible and forgotten, ignored both by human rights activists and by the state. Theirs is a very specific and traumatic location, especially in the absence of their men.

3) *Women militants or combatants.* These are women who are actively involved in the struggle, either by choice or coercion, or who are participating because of force of circumstance. Rita Manchanda has noted that women are believed to comprise one-sixth of the LTTE force in Sri Lanka; one-third of the Maoists in Nepal; and are very active in the fighting ranks of the Shanti Bahini of the Chittagong Hill Tracts (CHT), the NSCN in Nagaland and the ULFA in Assam.[16] Although far fewer, there is also a sizeable number of women militants in Kashmir. The increasing presence of militant women, especially in the case of the LTTE, is a direct consequence of active recruiting by the Tigers to compensate for the huge casualties in the 16-year war—there are very few able-bodied men left in the required age group. Here is one very clear example of protracted warfare's impact on women.

4) The fourth category is *women as shelter providers*. These are women who provide shelter (and labor) to the combatants, either as sympathizers or through coercion, and either way, are extremely vulnerable. On the one hand they are hounded by the state for being sympathizers, and on the other, dare not refuse shelter for fear of being branded as informants or collaborators by militants.

5) *Women as victims of sexual and physical abuse.* These could be innocent, uninvolved civilians, and belong to any age group, caught in the crossfire between armed militants and armed forces.

One particularly vexed question for feminists has been: how do we deal with the now more commonly occurring, actively violent, role played *by* women in such conflicts? The woman as communal subject, as feminist researchers have pointed out, is one who exercises her agency on behalf of aggressively exclusionist ethnic or communal politics, often engaging in violence herself. Women militants and combatants have received much more attention than most of the other categories in Goswami's classification (other than women victims, of course), and the general understanding seems to be as follows. Tanika Sarkar, Paola Bacchetta and Neloufer de Mel's detailed studies of women in the Rashtriya Sevika Samiti (RSS) in India, and the female suicide squad of the LTTE, conclude that women's involvement is initially liberating it; frees them from the traditional constraints of marriage and domesticity, and enables an acceptable and legitimate entry into male-dominated public spaces, whether social, political or military.[17] This entry and presence, however, are regulated by rigid conformity to the overarching patriarchal and masculinist ideology of these organizations which are also, and always, highly gendered and hierarchical; consequently power relations between the sexes remain congealed in all the old hierarchies—with the exception, perhaps, of training and recruitment—and women are rarely equal or genuinely emancipated. The power reposed in men in such organizations is a moral, political, military and sometimes even intellectual, power, translating into the power to attack and kill. We should remember that war is essentially a contract between men in power—they decide when and how to wage it; the rules by which it is governed; when it should cease; and what it is supposed to accomplish. Consequently, even when women are conscripted either into armies (we may recall that more than 40,000 U.S. women were deployed in the Middle East during the Gulf War) or into ethnic and communal violence—as 'agents' rather than 'victims'—they are bereft of these powers in themselves. I would suggest, then, that even though subjects now, they remain female in all crucial respects. Moreover, the presence of some women actors in conflict does not suddenly or dramatically change the general picture of violence as male-dominated; just as the fact of some pacifist, feminist and non-violent men does not destabilize patriarchal power relations as a whole.

6) Finally, there are *women as peace negotiators*. These are women who take the initiative in violence-prone and actively violent conflicts, who may or may not be supported by the community or their men-folk, and are viewed with suspicion by all. As Roshmi Goswami says, 'Women's vulnerability increases depending on the kind of role they choose to play in the peace process. Women are accepted as 'healers' and 'pacifists ' but not when they attempt to play a more decisive role and raise questions of peace, linking it with basic concepts of democracy. Women who protest against state oppression are seen as the 'over-ground agents' of the 'underground non-state actors', while women who raise their voices against non-state oppression are branded as 'state agents' and silenced.

This brings me to the third phase or moment in armed conflict, that of refusing the logic of violence or 'doing peace'.

3

The tradition of the oppressed teaches us that the 'state of emergency' in which we live is not the exception but the rule.

— Walter Benjamin

The general failure of states across our region to reach politically negotiated, peaceful resolutions of the conflicts in their countries has had one unexpected outcome. It has propelled NGOs, civil society groups (including businessmen and industrialists), professionals, academics, women's organizations and sundry peace activists into being more proactive on peace. Together they have initiated a range of activities, both within their countries and across borders that include everything from research and dialogue to track- two diplomacy and actual relief work.

Men make war and women make peace; this has the kind of clichéd associations that are difficult to shake off, perhaps because there is a kernel of truth in the statement. Women are generally supposed to be nurturing and caring, naturally maternal and therefore predisposed towards peace, just as men are supposed to be the opposite. Women are more open to mediation, to negotiation and compromise because, it has been suggested, they are obliged to carry on the business of survival and sustenance when all social and economic supports have broken down, and they are often obliged to do so in the absence of their menfolk. And so they are more likely to be found caring for the sick or wounded, in relief and rehabilitation and in rebuilding communities, than carrying guns and going into combat. Because they are also among the worst sufferers in any situation of conflict, armed or otherwise, they are believed to be more inclined towards peace.

Feminist analysis has tried to move away from biological, essentialist and culturalist arguments in favor of women's tolerance and non-violence, and suggested instead, that 'if women have a distinctive angle in peace it is not due to their being 'nurturing' but more to do perhaps, with knowing oppression'.[18] Their historical exclusion from structures of power, both in the private and public domains, as well as their experience of subjugation gives them a stake in working for *peace and justice*—or a just peace—as well as in keeping democracy alive, for it is only through social justice and democracy that they will be able to realize their right to equality. According to this logic, a feminist culture of peace fundamentally critiques unequal structures of domination and is built on learning to live with difference, without aggression.[19]

I would like to suggest an additional factor that may be at work in women's peace activism, and this is their particular, gendered experience of violence, in war as well as in supposed 'peace'. As recent empirical work the world over has shown, for women, weapons of war are much the same as weapons of peace; those who wield them in the battlefield or on the front often return home and turn the violence inwards. Women have first-hand knowledge of the connected forms of domestic, communal and political violence that stretches from the home to the street and into the battlefield.[20]

I have already spoken of this with regard to Partition violence in India in 1947. Similarly, studies of post-Yugoslavia Bosnia, Israel-Palestine, Ireland and, closer home, Kashmir, Jaffna, Karachi, Dhaka and northeast India, demonstrate the links between militarization, misogyny and domestic violence. Rita Manchanda quotes Palestinian MP Dalal Salmeh as saying, 'The violence used against Palestinian men has made them violent at home, in the work place and in their free time.'[21] A number of testimonies by women from Kashmir and the North-east echo this observation,[22] as do those of women living in the crossfire of the MQM (Muhajir Qaumi Movement) conflict in Karachi.

It is the combined experience of oppression and violence, plus the responsibility for survival and sustenance during and in the aftermath of conflict that, I believe, provides the strongest impetus to women's peace making. Parveena Ahangar's search for her missing son in Kashmir eventually led to the formation of the Association of the Parents of Disappeared Persons (APDP) and to a cry for collective justice. The refusal of the women of Kunan-Poshpora to remain silent about their rapes by the Indian security forces led to the highlighting of military atrocities; the public cursing of the Mothers' Front in Sri Lanka forced the government into acknowledging its role in the disappearance of thousands of young JVPers; the Women in Black, the Madres of the Plaza de Mayo, the Jaffna Mothers' Front take their private sorrow and make it public, thus not only radicalizing the personal, radicalizing even motherhood, but shaming the institutional and authoritarian. As Rita Manchanda says, 'Women's construction of the legitimacy or illegitimacy of conflict is a critical factor in women turning their backs on it. In Kashmir, a turning point in the armed struggle came when Kashmiri women began to shut the door on militants.'[23]

But is there such a thing as women's practice of peace activism? Do we 'do peace' differently from other peace activists, and if so, are these alternative practices effective in the long run? Can they, for instance, work across borders, national as well as regional?

As with economic activity in South Asia, in peace work too, women belong in the informal sector, the informal spaces of politics, which by its very nature affects our practice. The ritualized cursing of the Mothers' Front or the sustained protest by the Mothers of the Plaza de Mayo, indeed the public mobilization of motherhood in the cause of peace and as a direct challenge to the state, are quintessentially 'womanist' forms of peace activism. Bearing witness, as happens in the World Courts on Violence Against Women and in various tribunals on violence or other crimes, is not womanist in the same way but has radicalised the hitherto marginal and powerless, and forced public and institutional notice outside the traditional arenas of such activity—the court, the police station, the executive or the bureaucracy.

Dialogue and networking have been among the most effective strategies used by the global women's movement, in working for social change, as well as in raising awareness. Dialogue that bridges difference and is predicated on respecting that difference is at the other end of the spectrum from what Ranabir Samaddar calls 'maximalist friendship'.[24] Such a friendship, he says, 'like cold war friendship depends on maximum enmity, and then, maximum hostility'. Far from being conducive to peace, it kills understanding; the alternative to this is accommodating difference, which, more than solidarity, requires a *politics of understanding*. And it is this politics of understanding that I believe, women in the region are trying to forge.

Cynthia Cockburn, describing a few notable examples of cross-border peace initiatives by women in Ireland, Israel and Bosnia-Herzegovina, identifies six characteristics that she believes made the difference between the women's efforts, and others.[25] They are: 1) affirming difference; 2) non-closure of identity; 3) reducing polarization by emphasizing other differences; 4) an acknowledgement of injustice; 5) defining the agenda; and 6) group process. Again, these may not be essentially womanist ways of doing peace, but they have been worked at successfully by the three groups she studied, and they are clearly different from conventional CBMs, two-tracks, and other people-to-people dialogues. Cockburn also draws attention to the importance of recognizing what she calls 'the space between us' in peace work—that social and political space in which we separately live and work—in order to craft a politics of understanding.

It is not easy to do.

In Sri Lanka, e.g., the Jaffna Mothers' Front and the Sinhala Mothers' Front were unable to cross the ethnic divide; nor could the Naga Mothers Association make common cause with the Watsu Mongdung in northeastern India. Occasionally, groups may come together on specific issues, as national women's groups did in Bangladesh with the Hill Women's Federation, but they parted company on issues of national identity. One instance of successful bridge building, however, is that of the MQM and the Women's Action Forum in Karachi.

But the crucial point is that women's fledgling attempts at making peace have highlighted the necessity of transparency and democratic process in any peace accord or negotiation *that will endure*. The inclusion of 'marginal' and hitherto unheard voices in this process, painstaking and protracted though it may be, may actually have a better chance of succeeding than that reached through force or subjugation. It may be, as Rita Manchanda says what, 'makes the difference between the survival or collapse of otherwise binary and closeted peace processes between armed groups and the state'.[26]

4

Dubravka Ugresic, a feminist in exile from the former Yugoslavia, writes:

I come from a Land of Blood Groups, from Croatia. There the dedicated blood-cell counters noted each of my blood cells. As a result I became... no one. Write *no one* I say to the officials in the booths each time they ask me my nationality, and they ask me often. Hurry up, they say, tell us what it is. Nationality: *no one*. Citizenship: *Croatian*, I repeat. We don't have that *no one* of yours in the computer, they say. The right to be *no one* is guaranteed by the Constitution; citizens are not obliged to declare their nationality if they don't want to, I say. In real life it's different, they say, everybody is obliged to be *someone*. That's just why we have wars, I say, because everyone agreed to belong to their own blood group. That's why we had wars, they say, because people like you wanted us all to be *no one*.

In the computers of Croatian officialdom, my name is entered in the category: *others*. I insisted on my position. They insisted on theirs: I no longer exist there. It's quite understandable, I myself insisted that I was no one. Now I live *outside*. Now, outside, I am what I no longer am *at home*: a *Croatian* writer. The representative of a country in which I barely exist, a country from which I ran away into exile on the assumption that exile meant freedom from enforced identification.

Here, alongside my occupation, *writer*, they never fail to put that designation, *Croatian*. So along the way they learn the name of a new European statelet, stumbling over it, *Cro-Cro, Cro-a-tian*. That gives them some satisfaction. People respect ethno-identities. I understand that, they don't wish to offend, I must be extra sensitive about these things, that's just why there's a war in my country, after all. And so: me Tarzan, you Jane... The more politically aware will add: *former Yugoslav*. The more culturally conditioned will add: *East European*. The politically sensitive will add: *post-communist*. The gender-aware will add: *woman*. The best-read will add: *Central European*. (For heaven's sake, Croatia was always Central Europe, wasn't it? What do they mean, Balkans? What nonsense!) And it seems I have no way of taking off the labels they have so kindly stuck on to me. Because it is only with those labels that they can recognize me, place me, communicate with me, it is only with those labels, they believe, that they can read and understand me *properly*. I understand them, it is only through my otherness that they can realize their specialness.

And I, a *voluntary* exile with a Croatian passport in my hand, am obliged to show reciprocal kindness: they expect me to accept my identities as though they were real.[27]

In this fourth and last phase of armed conflict in which displacement and return, reconstruction and rehabilitation are supposed to take place, I would like to focus on an aspect that has received relatively less attention than the more immediate and urgent ones mentioned earlier. This is the issue of belonging, of identity, of how people are named and either included or excluded from nations and societies, especially when a transition is made either from state-socialism to ethnic nationalism, as in the case of the former Yugoslavia, or when nations are partitioned or divided as a consequence of linguistic, ethnic or religious separatism.

As with the previous three categories, my concern here is primarily with women. I quote again from Rada Ivekovic:

> The nation gets embodied at several levels. In war, it is embodied on the front-line, and in peace it may also appear, among other things, in extremist or terrorist groups, in extreme-right parties. In a primary sense, the nation has nothing to do with the borders of the country, with the type of state construction, with so-called nationality: this concept denotes a completely determinate kind of male community, the one for which it has 'craved' since a long time, which appears at the 'call' of blood (...). When they join a community, women cannot belong in the same way as men, because they have a different genealogy.[28]

So women don't belong to the nation or to the race in the same way because they are not its bearers. The nation doesn't trust its women, in the same way that it doesn't trust its masses. As we know, today's wars are fought by non-combatants (in the conventional meaning) that is, not by soldiers or militants alone. In every disturbed area of the world civilians are in conflict with each other over religion, ethnicity, resources, livelihood, life itself. Five per cent of the first World War's casualties were non-combatants; in contemporary wars, 95 per cent are. As a result, there are millions of refugees, political fugitives, voluntary exiles, asylum-seekers, those on the run; they are to be found mostly in the developing world, and a very large proportion of them are women and children.

The designation 'stateless' is now so commonplace that it excites little comment, even as governments grapple with another category of people called 'permanent liabilities'. The repatriated Tamils of Jaffna and the Eastern Provinces, for instance, have no place to call their own in either India or Sri Lanka; 'displaced persons' of erstwhile East Pakistan are still in a kind of limbo in India and live under the threat of being declared 'infiltrators' or 'illegal immigrants' any time. Any number of second-class citizens are to be found in every country of South Asia and, everywhere, those in a minority whether linguistic, ethnic or religious, are vulnerable.

Hindu, Muslim, Sikh, Tamil, Sinhala; India, Pakistan, Khalistan, Bangladesh, Eelam— redrawn borders, newfound countries and old communities forming and reforming each other through bitter contest. The play of identity politics in South Asia has become so volatile over the last few decades (almost since independence, in fact) that it begs the question: is there a stable national or regional identity in the subcontinent today? The definition of nationality has changed to the extent that it defies any 'lowest common denominator' basis.

How and when women enter this redefinition is, often, a question of religious, ethnic or linguistic affiliation but, as we have seen, it is also contingent on their status *within* religious and ethnic communities and their relationship with national processes. 'Belonging' for women is also—and uniquely—linked to sexuality, honor, chastity; family, community and country must agree on both their acceptability and legitimacy, and on their membership within the fold.

The question: do women have a country? is often followed by: are they full-fledged citizens of their countries? Recent feminist research has demonstrated how 'citizen' and 'state subject' are gendered categories, by examining how men and women are treated unequally by most states—but especially post-colonial states—despite constitutional guarantees of equality. 'The integration of women into modern 'nationhood',' says Deniz Kandiyoti, 'epitomized by citizenship in a sovereign nation-state somehow follows a different trajectory from that of men.'[29] The sources of this difference, she continues, are various and may have to do with the representation of nation-as-woman or nation-as-mother (*Bharat Mata*, for example) to be protected by her male citizens; they may have to do with the separation of the public civil sphere (usually male) from the private-conjugal one (usually female); or with women as symbols of community/ male honor and upholders of 'cultural values'; and most crucially, with their role as biological reproducers of religious and ethnic groups. Nira Yuval-Davis and Floya Anthias identify three other ways in which women's relationship to state and ethnicity can be seen as different from men's: as reproducers of the boundaries of ethnic or national groups; as participating in the ideological reproduction of the community; and as signifiers of ethnic or national difference.[30]

When the question of ethnic or communal identity arises, women are often the first to be targeted; the regulation of their sexuality is critical to establishing difference and claiming distinction on that basis. Then the question of where women 'belong', of whether they emerge as full-fledged citizens or remain 'wards of their immediate communities' is contingent upon how the politics of identity are played out, and how their resolution takes place between community and state.

With depressing, and predictable, regularity we see how the post-conflict resolution— not reconciliation—of identities does precisely the opposite of what I outlined earlier as the difference between women's peace activism and the more conventional variety. Instead of non-closure it insists on maintaining a primordial identity; instead of affirming difference it introduces implacable hostility; instead of reducing polarization, it exacerbates it; it refuses to acknowledge mutual injustice; it rejects group process; and finally, its agenda usually reinscribes women's subordination.

This is what makes women suspicious of this spurious 'peace', makes of it as Vasuki says so eloquently says, a 'filth' word, because it is seldom free from further violence. More importantly, however, it usually re-establishes the domination of a militaristic, usually aggressively masculinist mindset that has thus far defined both insider and outsider; nationalist and traitor; those who belong and those who can't; and ultimately, the nation and nationality. There are not many like Dubravka Ugresic who will refuse to identify with a nation whose very foundation is repugnant to them. Yet even she, in the end, could not keep identity tags from sticking to her. Her resistance to 'belonging' to such a reconstituted, ethnically 'pure' nation which repudiates or subordinates all her other identities—political, social and gender, for instance—is a predicament for many women and men in so-called post-conflict situations. The impossibility of fixing or freezing identities—and, hence, settling the question of who belongs where on a map of continually redrawn borders—makes 'peace' a potentially messy (even violent) business unless, as discussed earlier, it is based on transparency and democratic processes that recognize and protect the presence of many identities and plural selves.

Notes

1. Rada Ivekovic, 'The Bosnian Pardigm', *Dialogue*.
2. Ibid.
3. Ibid.
4. A variety of accounts are to be found in Urvashi Butalia (ed.), *Speaking Peace: Women's Voices from Kashmir* (Delhi: Kali for Women, 2002. See especially, essays by Kshma Kaul, Hameeda Bano and Farida Abdullah.
5. Committee for Initiative on Kashmir, 'Kashmir Imprisoned: A Report', in Butalia, op. cit., pp. 56–61.
6. Anuradha Chenoy, 'The Politics of Gender in the Politics of Hate', in Ammu Joseph & Kalpana Sharma, *Terror, Counter-Terror: Women Speak Out* (Delhi: Kali for Women, 2003), pp. 173–184.
7. See sundry reports by citizens' and women's groups on the Gujarat violence, especially, *The Survivors Speak: Fact-finding by a Women's Panel* (Ahmedabad, April 2002); *Gujarat Carnage 2002: A Report to the Nation* (Delhi: 2002); International Initiative for Justice in Gujarat, *A Report* (Mumbai: 2002).
8. Self-Employed Women's Association, *Shantipath: Our Road to Restoring Peace* (Ahmedabad: 2002); People's Union for Democratic Rights, *Act Two: Six Months Later* (Delhi: 2002).
9. Cynthia Cockburn, 'The Gendered Dynamics of Armed Conflict and Political Violence,' in Caroline O.N. Moser & Fiona C. Clark, *Victims, Perpetrators or Actors? Gender, Armed Conflict and Political Violence* (Delhi: Kali for Women, 2001), pp. 13–28.
10. Rada Ivekovic, op. cit.
11. For a detailed discussion of this aspect see Ritu Menon & Kamla Bhasin, *Borders & Boundaries: Women in India's Partition* (Delhi: Kali for Women, 1998).
12. Ibid.
13. Cynthia Cockburn, op. cit.
14. Quoted in Rita Manchanda, 'Gendering Peace Processes,' paper presented at the WISCOMP summer symposium on 'Human Security in the New Millennium', Delhi, August 2000.
15. Roshmi Goswami, 'Women and Armed Conflict: Ground Realities in the North-East,' paper presented at the WISCOMP Symposuim 'Human Security in the New Millennium', August 2000.
16. Rita Manchanda, op. cit.
17. Tanika Sarkar, 'The Woman as Communal Subject: Rashtra Sevika Samiti and Ramjanmabhoomi Movement,' in *Economic & Political Weekly*, 31 August 1991; Paola Bacchetta, 'All Our Goddesses Are Armed: Religion, Resistance and Revenge in the Life of a Hindu Nationalist Woman,' in Kamla Bhasin, Ritu Menon & Nighat Said Khan (eds.) *Against All Odds: Essays on Women, Religion and Development from India and Pakistan* (Delhi: Kali for Women, 1994), pp. 133–156; and Neloufer de Mel, *Women and the Nation's Narrative: Gender and Nationalism in Twentieth Century Sri Lanka* (Delhi: Kali for Women, 2001).

18. Cynthia Cockburn, *The Space Between Us:* Negotiating Gender and National Identities in Conflict (London: Zed Books, 1998).
19. Ibid.
20. See especially Anuradha Chenoy, *Militarism and Women in South Asia* (Delhi: Kali for Women, 2001), and Indai Lourdes Sajor (ed*.), Common Grounds: Violence Against Women in War and Armed Conflict Situations* (Philippines: ASCENT, 1998).   .
21. Rita Manchanda, op. cit.
22. Urvashi Butalia (ed.), op. cit., and several statements by the Naga Mothers' Front and others.
23. Rita Manchanda, op. cit.
24. Ranabir Samaddar, 'Friends, Foes and Understanding', forthcoming in Ritu Menon (ed.) *Unmaking the Nation: A Three Country Perspective on the Partition of India.*
25. Cynthia Cockburn, *The Space Between Us*, op. cit.
26. Rita Manchanda, op. cit.
27. Dubravka Ugresic, 'Nice People Don't Mention Such Things,' in Nadezhda Azhgikhina & Meredith Tax (eds.), *Women's Voices and the New European Order* (New York: Women's WORLD, 2000), pp. 53–54.
28. Rada Ivekovic, op. cit..
29. Deniz Kandiyoti, 'Identity and Its Discontents: Women and the Nation', in *Millennium*, Journal of International Studies, Vol. 20, No. 3, 1991.
30. Nira Yuval-Davis and Floya Anthias (eds*.) Woman-Nation-State* (London: Macmillan, 1989), p. 7.

10
IMPLICATIONS OF IMMIGRATION ON PAKISTANI IDENTITIES[1]

Rukhsana Qamber[*]

ABSTRACT

Movement of people to and from Pakistan is the central theme of the paper. It draws generalizations from two groups of migrants: those who have left Pakistan to settle in Barcelona, Spain and those who made a conscious decision to come to, or remain in the areas comprising Pakistan during the independence period.

*The author is an Associate Professor in Latin American Studies, Area Study Centre for Africa, North & South America, Quaid-i-Azam University, Islamabad, Pakistan.

The great demographic upheaval at the end of British colonialism in South Asia profoundly marked the persons and the states involved. Large numbers of people left their homes during the independence period and even today are compelled to move in search of greener pastures. This study examines some of the implications for the people of Pakistan by their displacement across state frontiers. Physical movement profoundly affected Pakistanis at independence and standard reasoning for this displacement has formed the basis of the national ethos. However, few of us inquire the real motives for movement across political frontiers. This study attempts to explore the enormous space created by displacement that causes the persons involved to formulate complex identities.

One measure of the complexity of the displacement/immigration is the variety of terms that are employed to describe the phenomenon.[2] A list of the terms is presented below in alphabetical order to delineate displaced persons:

ABCD (American Born Confused Desi)[3]
Alien
Angrez (originally English person or other white person and its opposite, desi)
Colonist
Conquistador
Desi (home-grown, as both noun and adjective)
Diaspora (stateless people)
Evacuee
Exile
Expatriate
Farangi (foreigner, in the conquistador sense)
Foreigner
FOB (Fresh Off The Boat)
Gora/gori (white man/woman)
Guest Worker[4]
Immigrant[5]
Internally Displaced Person
Migrant
Mohajir (migrant)
Overseas Pakistani
Paki[6]
Pardesi (literally, from another land, i.e., friendly foreigner)
Permanent (Indian) Resident Abroad
Political Asylee
Refugee
Settler
Tourist
Traveler
Visitor
Wetback

These terms clearly show that they are region-specific, for instance, 'wetback' being an illegal Mexican entering the U.S. It is noteworthy that while most European and American countries have government departments to administer immigration issues, Pakistan is more concerned with emigration. It has an official 'Bureau of Emigration and Overseas Employment' and the 'Overseas Pakistanis Foundation,' better known by its acronym, OPF. People coming to live in Pakistan are dealt with by the Ministry of Interior and are, generally speaking, refugees from neighboring countries. Other immigrants, mostly foreign women married to Pakistanis, also fall under the administrative ambit of the Ministry of Interior.

There are two categories of immigrants or displaced persons: 1) Refugees (political and economic) who are forced to flee their homeland and who do not have time to plan their journey. 2) Others, such as people who are predetermined to live in another state, such as immigrants, guest workers, and so forth. The present work does not deal with refugees as a central issue.

Yet refugee status is exactly the central trope for the 1947 experience in South Asia, particularly as regards the creation of the state of Pakistan. The official story is that the Hindus had repressed the Muslims, did not want to grant them autonomy, wreaked terrible violence upon them, forced them to flee India and made them suffer intolerable atrocities *en route* to refuge in Pakistan. Thus, Pakistani society obtained a common basis, i.e., patriotism to the newly formed state based on the displacement/migrant imperative. For instance, one hit song had the following key verse:

Aoo bachoy sair karayian tum ko Pakistan ki
Jis ki khatir hum ney dei kurbani lakoon jan ki

(Come children, let's take you to see Pakistan
For whose sake we sacrificed hundreds of thousand people)

This nationalist theme founded on the imperative to find refuge in Pakistan is repeated vociferously during most public gatherings, including Friday sermons.[7] Textbooks and the media, in both Pakistan and India, have propagated this ethnocentric vision of the national identity, with India comprising 'the other' for Pakistan and vice versa.[8] At best, the belief is perpetuated that all Muslims faced second class status in post colonial India. However, not everyone agreed with the official story and this study presents some samples of unofficial narratives, including first hand experiences of 1947 displacement among Pakistanis.

Voices critical of the monolithic statist view were heard mainly in the field of literature. Sadaat Hasan Manto stands tall in his humanistic view of the freedom process in stories such as the exquisite madness of 'Toba Tek Singh,' and during his lifetime, suffered state sanction on numerous occasions.[9] One aspect of this paper is to explore the 1947 experience from the perspective of people who took a calculated decision to become Pakistani at that juncture. Was immigration/displacement a studied choice for such people?

Another central question addressed at the outset of this study concerns the definition of the term immigrant/migrant/displaced person. Most people who leave their place of origin are faced with a sense of alienation in the new environs and nostalgia for home. These feelings are exacerbated when the movement is involuntary or undertaken under compulsion. However, the term for forced emigration is reserved by the Pakistani state for only one group of people, i.e., Kashmiri refugees. People forced to leave Pakistan during the independence era are referred to by the state as 'evacuees.' An official Evacuee Trust (with a counterpart in India) deals with the vast property abandoned by the displaced Sikhs, Hindus and others.

Other people displaced from British India who settled in Pakistan are even today identified, many times gloriously, as migrants, or in Urdu as *mohajirs*. The term migrant signifies that during the period following the establishment of independent Pakistan and India, both states utilized the word in the informal sense to refer to a person who moves temporarily and within the borders of the home country. This would contrast with the term immigrant, i.e., one who requires a passport, and many times a visa, to traverse the boundaries of political states. Granting immigrant status to the millions of displaced persons who crossed the borders of present day Pakistan, Bangladesh and India would have been impossible in 1947. Initially, movement took place freely and people continued to 'migrate' up until the early 1960s. Many, if not most, people made the decision to be geographically close to their extended family. Therefore, instead of 'refugee' or 'migrant', the present study utilizes the more neutral term 'displaced person' interchangeably with 'immigrant' to describe the movement phenomenon during 1947, as well as during the twenty-first century.

If many people decided their citizenship on the basis of family affiliation, and therefore, were in a position to choose their nationality, did the persons displaced to Pakistan during the independence period fit into the classic mould of immigrant people? Some of the other queries addressed in this study are as follows: What are the push and pull factors for displacement in general? Can the 1947 experience be viewed in the context of general and timeless reasons for the urge to move across political borders? Were persons coming to Pakistan free agents in choosing their national identity? (It is recognized that each person continuously reconstructs/reinvents her/his own identities). What were their primary motives to move or to remain in present-day Pakistan? Did religious considerations play a major role in their decision making process? Did politics, and the figure of Jinnah, inspire them to create a new state? Have specific Pakistanis forged new identities?

This paper is divided into two parts. Firstly, it explores major criteria that generally affect displacement of persons across state borders. Secondly, it summarizes a cluster of interviews centered around two persons who made calculated decisions to leave or remain in Pakistan in 1947. The conclusion finds common trends in the two sections. For the first part, an extended study of immigrants in general and Pakistani living in Barcelona during 1999–2002 in particular, led to formulation of criteria to study the global phenomenon of geographic displacement. The city of Barcelona was chosen not only because of first hand experience, but also because it contains the largest number of Pakistani immigrants in Spain, approximately 12,000 during the period of investigation. Nevertheless, despite the numerical justification, the Barcelona experience of Pakistani immigrants does not presume to represent the experience of Pakistanis in other parts of Spain, or that of immigrants from other countries to Barcelona, such as Moroccan immigrants alluded to in the study. The key issues explored include the reasons why the immigrant/displacement project is undertaken at the individual level, the preparation involved, dealing with the new reality, the process of dismantling the previous identity/identities and the manner in which new identities are constructed.

PRINCIPLE REASONS TO MOVE

At the individual level, some of the main reasons why a person decides to cross political frontiers are as follows:
To improve oneself, economically, that in turn means achieving a position where one could help one's family and community. It may also include improved education, learning of new skills and technology and becoming more cosmopolitan. The most important secondary goals of Pakistanis abroad are:

- To have the capacity to eat and entertain well
- To indulge in elite leisure activities (such as to play cricket)

- To be able to speak English (mainly because it is a marker of social class among Pakistanis)
- To earn respect in the new community/environs
- To live at a good address

A central issue is the need to 'get out of a rut' for which the concept of *hijrat* is often quoted. Among the youth, *hijrat* may be interpreted as wanderlust.

Construct new identities: Most immigrants and/or migrants wish to leave behind the negative aspects of their society and culture, as it functions at the level of the family, region, state, religion, etc. They wish to obtain respect[10] among their family, in the community where they live and in their social circle in their home country.

Possess liberty/the right to work with dignity and to travel. This goal generally applies to citizens of developing countries who must undergo the tedious and frequently frustrating experience of seeking visas from foreign embassies. Immigrants sometimes quote the criterion of lesser professional exploitation than in their home country, mainly by obtaining a fixed salary, adequate fringe benefits and so forth.

To integrate: Integration means assimilation in the global context of immigration or geographic displacement.[11] Pakistanis abroad wish to have local (i.e., foreign/'gora' friends; enjoy the frequent public festivals and be able to communicate and negotiate with the local state authorities, specially on behalf of fellow Pakistanis in the community where they reside. Thus, in their own perception, they gain authoritative status and consequent 'respect.'

Return home: For first generation of immigrants, a primary goal is to return home after having 'made it' abroad,[12] right after the necessity to possess 'respect.' For most Pakistanis, home is usually where one's mother lives. Thus, generally speaking, Pakistanis, especially men, compete to have their parents live with them, whether in Pakistan or abroad. The presence of a parent in one's home automatically provides 'respect.' The desperate need of exiles to return home is well recognized.[13] Other involuntarily displaced persons, such as the descendants of slaves, not only have gone in search of their roots but also partook in the Back-to-Africa movement.

PREPARING TO IMMIGRATE

Contacts: The majority of people who move to a new geographic location—many times simply by traveling as tourists—go to where they have family and friends, be they German, French, American or any other nationality. Pakistanis tend to do the same in Barcelona and live in areas where they and their families would have the support of other people who speak their mother tongue. This is especially true for Pakistanis in Barcelona who encounter the double Catalan-Spanish language barrier. Whereas people of other nationalities grouped together are considered normal, Pakistanis in Barcelona are sometimes accused of constituting 'mafias' and of living in 'ghettos.'

Informants about the new environment: People may also decide upon their destination for residence by basing their choice on verbal stories, letters from relatives or friends,[14] television, cinema, newspapers and magazines.

Economic: Loans, given as a form of investment by relatives, friends, etc. Almost all of the nearly 200 Pakistanis approached in Barcelona during the years 1999 to 2002 stated that they had received such loans from relatives and friends mainly in and from Pakistan but also sometimes in Barcelona. No Pakistani in Barcelona was found to be a beggar (like some Moroccans). Young geographically displaced men mostly aim to become 'heroes' by being socio-economically successful. This 'baggage' weighs a lot with the Moroccans living in Spain. They do not give up a series of 'pains' at the moment of bidding farewell to their family and community. Equally, they carry with them the collective expectations of their cultural group and if they fail, they have to pay dearly. They suffer from depression and even impotence.[15] They know fully well that their way of life is not liked or wanted and this is especially true for the Moroccan immigrants. Many years may pass without seeing their family again and this represents an acute disruption of family ties. They are not in a position to repeat the experience of going away and returning without having obtained legalization, i.e., the status of resident. Preparation for the geographic movement mostly co-relates with the level of education of the displaced person/traveler.

THE NEW REALITY

Difficulties of living together or *convivencia: Convivencia* is a Spanish term that does not have a direct equivalent in the English language. It may be roughly translated as harmonious living together of different kinds of people. The difficulties of *convivencia* are mostly based upon differences of attitudes to life and/or of ethnicity, language, culture, religion and so forth. There are always difficulties of harmonious living together, be they that the new resident is a displaced person, an immigrant or a migrant from another part of the same country or had been there before as a tourist, student, for business, etc.

Professional Competition: The 'host' society only wants immigrants and other displaced persons to perform work for low pay, fewer benefits and of low status—unless they perform much needed and high profile tasks such as in the arts, in the technical field, etc. The term 'host' is controversial, as seldom is 'hospitality' shown to the new settlers from developing countries. An alternative term is 'receiving' country but again the 'reception' may not be welcoming but rather xenophobic. Job competition results many times when the displaced person wants to scale the social ladder. Mostly newcomers feel embarrassed with the first job obtained in the new environment. However, they have the intelligence to know that the position is temporary. When success results, at enormous cost and sacrifice, discrimination is faced almost invariably. Immigrants often justify their work, and/or residence in low-income areas, for being better than what was available to them in the country of origin. The word 'better' is a term preferred by the immigrants themselves.

Housing: Both persons displaced from other countries (immigrants) and migrants to Barcelona from other parts of the country, often face the twin problems of high cost for flats and discrimination by landlords. For instance, some stereotypes perpetuated by landlords are that single immigrant women are prostitutes; foreign men 'come alone and then amass a dozen others in the flat,' and so forth. This discrimination often compels the Pakistanis to concentrate in the Old City of Barcelona that, in turn, opens them to the charge of constituting ghettos.

New languages: For many foreign residents, like the Pakistanis, there are additional and severe linguistic problems: in their native village, they usually speak Punjabi and can communicate in Urdu, the national language of Pakistan. They know a smattering of the English language and wish to know it well in order to scale the social ladder in Pakistan. However, upon arrival in Barcelona, they have to learn Spanish and Catalan. All children attending free and quite good public schools must learn these two languages on a compulsory basis. The only other choice is private schools, which extremely few Pakistanis parents can afford. Society and law enforcement personnel ensure that all children attend school, regardless of their parents' legal status.

Food: Almost all immigrants/displaced persons, in whichever part of the world, have problems in adapting to the local food. Pakistanis, speaking very generally, do not like seafood, fish, cheese, black coffee, bitter chocolate or pork, including in the form of lard. For instance, children of Pakistani parents in Barcelona are unable to unthinkingly exchange food with their local friends, Pakistani adults place culinary conditions on their hosts, they cannot eat in just any bar or restaurant for fear of the use of lard, etc. Social and cultural negotiation becomes handicapped and this places limits on their 'integration,' which is a politically charged term.[16]

Children: Offspring of immigrant parents or grandparents find themselves located astride two cultures of the home and 'host' societies. They require, and many times manage, to create new space that allows them to express themselves freely. Most children learn languages very easily and in Barcelona schools, the Spanish and Catalan languages are taught compulsorily. Therefore, in terms of language, Pakistani children possess much authority over their parents. This means an exchange of roles normally performed by parent and child as many times the children have to interpret for their parents and also to explain their society through its culture, customs, etc., for doctors, nurses, teachers, and so forth. They use this authority to creatively interpret their culture for their interlocutors.

Another phenomenon observable in Barcelona is that when the parents make the decision for geographic displacement, the children often stop going to school in the home country. The time lag between the moment when the decision is made to move and the actual movement may last several months or even years and children's education takes a heavy toll. In other words, 'they are stuck in time', awaiting the legal process known as 'family reunion.' It will be seen that joining one's family was precisely a key motive for displacement across the political frontiers of the states of Pakistan and India in 1947.

Problems and pressures within the community: Amongst displaced persons/immigrants of a given country, great differences exist in terms of family customs, languages and regional cultures/societies. For example, some Pakistanis have more in common with Indians (due to the movies) than with their compatriots, state politics (Kashmir), religious identities (pre-Islamic and non-Arab customs) and so forth. It is often forgotten that those who leave, are looked upon by their compatriots at home as isolated and lost, neither situated in time nor in space.

Violence or shock: All immigrants encounter a hierarchy of values and powers that represent 'ridiculization' of their foreigner ways, be it simply for their pronunciation in the common language such as Spanish or English.[17] In the same manner, displaced persons often endure labeling and compartmentalization as 'immigrants.' They are assigned second-class status in the new environs, which, in most cases, they try desperately to overcome.[18] The displaced person is, therefore, compelled to deconstruct her or his previous identity/identities.

DISMANTLING PREVIOUS IDENTITIES

Self defense on the part of the displaced person, because of the ridicule suffered and other obstacles encountered in the new surroundings, results in the construction of a new set of identities. A first step in this permutation of identities is the recuperation of the memory of the country/culture/society by the displaced person. This memory depends on her/his level of education, personal attitude and socio-economic situation in the home state. For example, an educated person, one who is not just literate, recalls her/his multiple identities in terms of language, cultural, etc. It may be recalled that identities are multiple and that each person, no matter where she/he is located, continously reinvents her/his own identities. In other words, one's open and/or positive attitude affects one's 'integration' in the new society. This acceptance is also influenced by the reception that one encounters in the new state. The alternative to openness is normally to fall victim to fanatism and rigidity.

In the second place, the (re)constructed memory depends on the place(s) visited when the geographically displaced person revisits the home state, that is in turn influenced by factors such as with whom one interacts, the kind of treatment received, etc. In the third place, one must be very clear that the memory/recuperation of identity/culture/country depends, many times entirely, on a subjectivity frozen at the time when the person left or last visited the home state. The home - and 'host' - country/society changes constantly: for example, one encounters many changes in Pakistan during the absence of a period of only six months or less. This process of the recuperation of the 'original' set of identities of the displaced persons is still more complex for their children and grandchildren.

The reconstruction of identities among immigrant Pakistanis is, furthermore, deeply effected by the number of people in the group and also by the number and kind of Pakistanis they encounter in the new environ. For instance, a single person or a nuclear family would, perforce, have to 'adapt', as well as be 'received' and helped in the new society. Extended immigrant families have not 'integrated' to the same extent as nuclear families. In fact, it is in the case of extended families and/or groups of Pakistanis that the 'frozen in time' phenomenon is most observable. The extended family or other group displacement serves as a further shock-absorber of the cultural and other differences encountered. Juxtaposed with the 'ridiculization' effect, displaced/immigrant people tend to further 'cling' to their own identity.

However, a caveat always exists: Pakistani immigrants/persons displaced abroad as individuals or a nuclear family may 'integrate' more when dealing with the new society encountered while, simultaneously, assert their social (elite) status in Pakistan. Class bonding brings with it the advantage of social networking, bonding and support among the group. It may be held therefore, that displaced people may adapt to the new environs more easily than with their own extended immigrant group.

It was found that, in general terms, Pakistanis in Barcelona take a second look at their stated goals, justify their current status abroad, recollect an imagined past and reinvent their identities according to the circumstances in which they find themselves. Social memory thus reflects adaptibility, rather than validation/triangulation against political or other aspects of history. Viewed from this perspective, retrospective recollections assume pivotal significance, making a virtue of its normally percieved 'sin,' of changeability.[19]

Specifically, the goal of immigrants to earn a lot of money is perceived as fulfiled by counting one's income in Rupees and not Euros in order to make it appear large. Similarly, immigrants also tend to look at their expenses in terms of rupees rather than the local currency. For instance, newcomers especially engage in the practice of gauging that a 'naan' which cost Rs. 4 in Pakistan, cost them Rs. 40 in Europe. The context of this would usually be the 'missing home' conversations. Tips in restaurants are, many times, miserly because the calculations are made in rupees.

Pakistanis abroad are eager to help the family and community but, finding themselves unable to do so, they refrain from returning home for many years. Generally speaking, they do eat well but this is mostly mutton and chicken-based food rather than a balanced diet with plentiful fish that is available in Spain and especially in the Mediterranean port city of

Barcelona. They play cricket but seldom find a regular pitch upon which to practice the sport. They do speak English but it is a smattering; enough to impress the local non-English speakers but not their own 'English-medium' compatriots. They are extremely keen to have 'respect', and therefore, attempt to outdo each other in demonstrating their 'contacts' with municipal government officials.

In other words, the reinvented identities of Pakistani residents in Barcelona may be viewed as 'lies' because in the home state they seldom fulfill their stated goals for geographic displacement. For instance, one Pakistani university student in Barcelona wrote her doctoral thesis in English on the elites of Lahore. However, the work contained numerous factual and grammatical errors that were difficult to detect by teachers whose native languages, cultures and societies were quite different. Thus, in the new surroundings foreign residents are in a position to construct a false image of superiority, 'respect' and security. Very similar identities were imagined by the Spaniards who immigrated to America more than five hundred years ago.

> The conquistadores were reconstructing their memory, in some cases invented anew, in order to re-acquire dignity that had been denied to them since the conquest.[20]

The above criteria formulated for studying the phenomenon of displacement at the end of the twentieth century may be applied to the case of Pakistan at the time of its independence. Of particular significance are the discussions on memory in the preceding section that obviate employing quantitative methods to add to variations of the displacement experience during 1947 for approximately 10 million people.

The following section of this study deals with the reasons why people came to, or decided to remain in, the area now know as Pakistan. The narratives produced below are based upon several interviews. The central protagonists are two sisters, Asghari Sultan and Khurshid Begum. The other people interviewed are some their relatives who contribute additional dimensions to their testimonies. The informal interviews were guided by some of the following questions:

- What is your full name and profession?
- How old were you in 1947 and were you married?
- Many people had a choice to make in 1947. What decision did you take then and why?
- People changed identities during the independence period. They chose to own, discard or reinvent affiliations. Do you have any stories to tell?
- What is your eyewitness account of Partition? (The term 'independence' is preferable when referring to 1947. However, the trauma of the era may be considered in terms of 'Partition.')
- Which politician or what considerations of religion, ethnicity, etc. influenced your decision to be Pakistani?
- How many brothers and sisters do you have, where did they live after 1947 and where do they live now?
- Is anyone in your extended family in politics?
- It is said that displaced persons become rootless. Why did you settle in Pakistan?
- Did you/people possess clearly differentiated identities before 1947? How were the lines drawn: by religion, language, ethnicity or social class?

Asghari Sultan was a tenth class student in 1947. She lived with her parents and younger sister in the city of Lahore, in a house loaned by a relative. Three older siblings, the elder brother and two sisters, were married and lived in Delhi and Kashmir. Asghari appeared for her matriculation examination in Lahore in early 1947. After giving her exams in April, her brother asked the family to join him in Delhi as more riots and unrest were expected in Lahore than in Delhi, the capital. The brother just wanted the family to be together. The family, headed by the father, Muhammed Bakar, packed the household effects, locked up the house and took the train to Delhi, where it arrived without any untoward incident.

However, when the Partition Plan was made public and rioting erupted even in Delhi, the whole family decided to return to Pakistan in the company of its two state employees: Asghari's brother Raheem and an uncle, Muhammed Iqbal who was her *chacha*, or father's younger brother. For these men, the displacement to Pakistan, though a real option to choose citizenship, was officially considered transfer orders from Delhi to Karachi once the decision had been made. Iqbal, a senior bureaucrat, was allocated a whole train bogey and journeyed to the new state of Pakistan on 3 August 1947. Asghari accompanied her uncle Iqbal and his family because her older married sister, Khurshid, was residing in Karachi. Her own family came a few days later by government airplane and necessarily had to travel light.

Neither Asghari nor the other members of Bakar's family or her uncle Iqbal's witnessed any violence or had to go to the refugee camps. In fact, during an interview, another relative Syeda, younger daughter of Iqbal, who was in Class 8 at the time, recalled the journey by train quite happily.[21] According to her, the travel was luxurious, her family being in a position to pack the household goods at leisure. They brought with them everything, including, she still recalls, even their *tava* (griddle to make *chappatis*). On the train, Syeda immensely enjoyed the *palau* and *zarda* that they were served. She also remembered, however, that her father Iqbal was worried about his brother Muhammed Bakar and nephew Raheem's families in Delhi. When they all arrived safely, though with empty hands, he embraced them tearfully.

Returning to the narrative of Asghari Sultan, she merely accompanied her family. It was basically her brother Raheem and father Bakar, who decided to opt for Pakistan. This option to become Indian or Pakistan was given to all state employees in written form and the reply was accordingly documented. Why did they choose Pakistan? Asghari does not recall any discussion on the subject in the home, and therefore, had no information about the choices discussed. She went to Pakistan with the family and her personal goal was to be near one married sister who was residing in Karachi. Asghari later returned to Lahore with her brother Raheem to appear for the *Alim Fazil* examination in Urdu. They then packed up the necessary household items and transported them to the family in Karachi.

Asghari also had an older sister Zubeida, who was married and resided in Jammu. Zubeida became an authentic refugee, having to flee by foot to Sialkot with her husband and young children, including an infant. Other people, including relatives accompanied them. Zubeida's husband, Mannan, had an older brother, who was a state employee and *Masjid imam* in Jammu. While fleeing the city, he and his family of four daughters and wife were caught by hooligans. In another interview, his wife Ayesha recalled that his Quran was torn and thrown on the ground and when he tried to defend himself, the man, who was armed with a sword, killed him. Ayesha went to rescue her husband but she too was slashed on the shoulder by a sword and the infant daughter that she was carrying was killed. Their three daughters were also attacked. One was injured, and died later in Sialkot. The two oldest daughters, about 14 and 10 years old, were abducted. Ayesha came to Rawalpindi with some relatives and lived with them until her recent death.

An aftermath of this tale is that many years later Zubeida's family immigrated to Canada. One day one of her daughters-in-law was purchasing cloth in a Sikh shop where she found a woman narrating a fascinating story. She said that though she now belonged to the Sikh religion, she was born Muslim. She had lost her family during 1947, her father, a *maulvi*, having died before her eyes while they were fleeing from Jammu to Sialkot. The listener inquired if she remembered the names of any of her relatives and the Sikh woman recognized many of the names mentioned by Zubeida's daughter-in-law. The two women promised to meet again in the same shop but the Sikh woman 'disappeared'.

Other cousins[22] of Asghari also suffered atrocities during the independence period. There were two sisters, Jameela and Shakila who were also abducted by Hindus from Jammu. The story is known about only one girl, Jameela. The Hindu family that took her away raised her and later engaged her to marry their son. Four years after independence, 'lost' people were being announced on the radio who could be reached in the camps. Asghari's brother Raheem heard mention of Jameela in a radio bulletin and told the girl's father about her whereabouts. The father went to the refugee camp indicated and found his daughter. Upon seeing her parent, she decided to leave her adoptive family and accompanied her biological father. She later told her family that the Hindus had been very kind to her and that her adoptive mother had been brokenhearted at her departure.

Another story that runs in this family is about Nargis, a daughter of the older sister Zubeida. Nargis was born in Srinagar a few years before Independence. When she was an adolescent, she set her heart upon becoming a doctor. However, her grades were not high enough to pass the tough entrance test for medical college and she applied for the reserved seats for Kashmiri refugees. She was denied that seat because another girl had secured it. That girl was their neighbor's daughter and was not a Kashmiri. This news was such a shock for Nargis that she had a severe nervous breakdown and never recovered from it.

However, there are several other dimensions to these searing tales of atrocities and injustice for Kashmiris and other 1947 displaced persons. One aspect of this displacement phenomenon is that of the '*mohajirs*,' the people who voluntarily undertake displacement or *hijrat*. The original concept of *hijrat* derives from the Prophet's leaving Mecca for Medina, where he was warmly received. This is a crucial episode in Muslim history and marks the beginning of the Islamic calendar. Thus, *hijrat* is recommended for people who encounter acute problems in life. In Urdu, the term *mohajir* used to refer to all the persons displaced during the independence period, including the refugees. However, during the 1980s, the term was appropriated solely for use by the Urdu-speaking people who speak Urdu as their mother tongue. These *mohajirs* mostly concentrated in the port city of Karachi. For the *mohajirs,* the term also has ethnic and cultural connotations and became a political identity marker. Displacement became a central theme, with claim[23] to the primary reason for the creation of Pakistan and for special status for the *mohajirs*.

On a lighter note, these claims to importance have long been the butt of popular jokes. For instance, many people claimed rights to the properties abandoned by the departing Sikhs and Hindus on the basis of the properties that they supposedly owned, and were forced to abandon, in India. The joke made the rounds (specially during the pre-1980 period), that these *mohajirs* were merely owners of '*pudinay kay baagh*' or plantations of the tiny mint plant. Puns were also coined on the dual meanings of '*muraboan kay malik*' or owners of large acreage/ pickles, for those displaced persons who spoke of their families' extensive lands, properties or aristocratic lineage.

We return briefly to the interview with Asghari Sultan to recount an anecdote that she proudly mentioned about her family while still in Jammu. Asghari narrated that there was a

Hindu maharaja whose wife had a child but she did not have much milk to feed the infant. Consequently, a search was undertaken to find another woman who would have sufficient milk for both the aristocratic baby and her own. Asghari's grandmother was among the women interviewed and her milk was taken to see whether the Hindu child would like it. She fulfilled both criteria of sufficient quantity and quality of milk. However, Asghari's grandmother refused to oblige the maharani, even though she was offered much prestige and monetary benefit. She just did not want to nourish a Hindu child. What is fascinating about the anecdote is that Asghari mentioned it with great pride, whereas her older sister Khurshid Begum, also interviewed for this study, did not recall the incident and even now, more than sixty years later, did not give it much importance. In fact, Khurshid's memory is of much religious harmony and great neighborly empathy before and during the terrible days of Partition.

Khurshid Begum is the sister of Asghari Sultan who was living in Karachi. The years 1946–47 were eventful for her. In 1946, Khurshid's first born child, a son, had an accident at the age of three and died under tragic circumstances in Srinagar. Khurshid was residing there because her husband was posted in that city as a Lieutenant in the British Army. A few months after the child's death the Lieutenant was transferred to Karachi. The decision to become Pakistani was a really hard one for this couple. The husband was torn between loyalty to a brother and two sisters who had chosen to become Indian, mainly because they were married to people from that area. The rest of his family was in Pakistan. Also, there were professional choices to be made. In India, he would face stiff job competition but would be recompensed by the prestige of belonging to a very large country. In Pakistan, it would be easier to scale the socio-economic ladder, but Pakistan was much smaller and a far less developed state than India. The couple had a serious decision to make about their citizenship in 1947.

Khurshid Begum was quite firm in her decision: she would be Pakistani, come what may. She is now surprised at her own clear decision because she said that though she loved her husband so much that she was 'willing to die for him,' she would have left him if he had opted for India. Her reasoning was based on the fact that her immediate family was from this side of the border and would remain in Pakistan. If need be, she could support herself economically as she had held a job before her marriage and could return to it.

Khurshid recalls how a neighbor helped the couple to make up their mind. They were living in a posh flat and were close to these neighbors. One of the neighbors was a socially prominent Sindhi Hindu. One day the Hindu lady asked Khurshid about her decision and Khurshid told her that she would be Pakistani, even if it meant that she would have to leave her beloved husband. The neighbor fully understood her dilemma and talked with Khurshid Begum's husband. She told him that he really should not give even a single thought to his option to go to India. Interestingly, the neighbor herself also had her decision clearly chalked out with her family: they would all go to India. Khurshid remembers how she was 'of the standard of Indira Gandhi', and therefore, would be successful in the greater state of India. Her religion would be useful to her there as well. Interestingly, Khurshid did not mention religion as a factor for her own decision.

Did Khurshid Begum witness any violence? Not at all, as she traveled before the rioting began and remained in Karachi's cantonment area during the crucial period of upheaval.

During the course of the interview, Khurshid Begum mentioned the issue of claims to refugee status and to rights for the property abandoned by the evacuees, the people who fled Pakistan. She mentioned how some family members received some grants while other did not. In fact, she stated that her husband was offered a house by a departing Sikh. 'Well,' she said casually, 'he was sort of grateful to my husband.' She had to be prompted to relate the story that follows:

> During 1947, my husband had a close Sikh colleague who lived with his family in the outlying Malir area of Karachi. One day his wife called up frantically to say that some hooligans had entered the house and had told her to leave, along with her two small children. Panicked, she called her husband and luckily got through on the telephone. The husband turned for help to his nearest and trusted colleague, my husband. The 'hero' of this story, my husband, immediately sent over an army vehicle with some soldiers who arrived in time to rescue the family and their urgently required belongings. My husband had also apprised me of the situation and I prepared my home to receive the family.
>
> The young woman, I recall, was very beautiful. She told me that she was not afraid to lose her jewelry or even of violence to herself. She was petrified to think that her children may have been kidnapped. She was so shaken up that all she wanted to do was to flee Karachi and go to India. Her husband agreed with her.
>
> At that time, there were many ships taking people to and from India and Pakistan. My husband did his best and devoted all his time to make the right connections to see our Sikh friends' wish fulfilled. It did not take long, and I do not remember too clearly how long exactly they stayed with us, but within two or three days, we were able to see them off safely from Karachi port.
>
> Before leaving, the man, whose name was Ajab Singh Sohni, told my husband that he would like to gift him a house that he owned in the Samanabad area of Lahore. We could have it as long as Ajab Singh was away but in case he might not be able to return, he also wanted to legally gift us the house. However, he mentioned that he had a brother who was living in Lahore. So, my husband told Ajab Singh that it was better that he left the house to his own family. Later we learnt that the brother managed to successfully sell off the property and he too migrated to India.'

It is noteworthy how the term 'migrated' is used here as it supports the contention about terminology made earlier in this study.

When Khurshid's late husband finally announced his decision to remain in Pakistan, the deciding factors were that he did not want to be a second class citizen any more, like he had been under the British, and was sure he would be in India as a Muslim. Also, his chances of promotion would be far superior in Pakistan than in India.

Did any politician or political issue influence their decision? 'No,' came the swift answer. However, Khurshid Begum did recall the enormous impact that Gandhi had on the people during the anti-colonial movement. The most vivid memory was of his call to burn British fabrics and to boycott all imported goods. 'Every big cloth store participated,' she said 'and they were mainly owned by the Hindus. There was no hesitation or regret, but rather a great sense of solidarity, pride and unity among people of all faiths, classes, age and gender.'

Also, Khurshid Begum recalls that Subhas Chander Bose was assassinated and it was widely talked about but she does not know why or even who did it: the Hindus or the British? 'And why was Gandhi imprisoned?' she asks today. She did not even know of Jinnah until she got married. Her only recollection of political education was through her young cousin Saleem. He had joined the Red Shirt party and carried around a shovel. Khurshid remembers how Saleem showed her family the multiple uses of the shovel: for digging, filling in holes, for frying and egg and so forth. Also, Saleem had heard and read Iqbal in school and college and passed on that knowledge to his doting cousins.

Khurshid recalls very friendly relations with the Hindus and Sikhs. The only 'difference' that she experienced was that once,—and she stressed only once—while in Kashmir she came across a high caste Hindu in the street who shunned her for fear of her supposedly unclean shadow polluting him. She was emphatic in stating that no such discrimination existed amongst her multi religious classmates at school. Also, no sense of religious or political enmity was felt in her house. Her family happily accepted food from the kitchens of Hindus and Sikhs when they celebrated their festivals and in turn, during Muslim festivals they reciprocated, but with uncooked food.

An epilogue exists to the interviews with Khurshid. Her 50 year old son, i.e., a Pakistani by birth, walked into the interview and blithely announced that he was 'a *mohajir*, a Kashmiri *mohajir* as I trace my roots through my mother.' Given the political connotations of the term *mohajir* and the fact that he chose matriarchal lineage, it is clear that some people possess enormous space to claim their multiple identities. Geographic movement, nevertheless, is a central trope for most Pakistanis.

CONCLUSION

The key issues explored in this paper included the reasons why the immigrant/displacement project is undertaken at the individual level. Two disparate phenomena of displacement were examined, Pakistanis in Barcelona and Pakistanis displaced during 1947. In neither case refugee status was applicable, the aim of the investigation being to add to the narratives of displaced people who were not under immediate threat. Basically, migrant/displaced people wanted to improve their living conditions. In such cases, the answer is 'yes' to the question posed at the beginning of this paper, was displacement a studied choice for some people, especially during 1947?

Word of mouth and perhaps the media played crucial roles in the decision-making process to proceed to or from Pakistan. The most effective word was that of close relatives and included forming opinions about politics, religion and other affiliations. As such, religion and politics, or specifically the figure of Muhammed Ali Jinnah, were seldom the primary motives for displacement. Social class played a crucial role in the Partition experience, even if denied by the protagonists. For instance, people seldom witnessed the atrocities if they resided in the 'better areas.' Similarly, Pakistanis in Barcelona in general do not belong to the elite class and tend to live in the cheaper areas, underlining the fact that social class is a crucial criterion for the immigration/displacement process.

Preparation, for migration to Pakistan in 1947 existed for the privileged few mainly because the movement was not considered to be permanent. However, systematic preparation did occur for those officials whose displacement was deemed by the two states to be transfer of duty station. Despite the category of 'transfer of duty station,' people had a genuine choice to make about citizenship. Real brothers and sisters chose either Pakistan or India for a variety of reasons. Consequently, one of the most traumatic aspects of the new reality was the placing of severe impediments to movement across the political boundaries. As a result of state creation in 1947, identities were sometimes completely permutated and for very concrete reasons, as was amply demonstrated in the story of Nargis, the Kashmiri refugee. For Pakistanis in Barcelona, little preparation was made, given their social class.

Memory, and generally historic memory of displaced people, adds to the complexity of identity formation and articulation. Pakistanis displaced to Barcelona were found to have the leeway, the enormous space, to recreate a fictitious past and an euphemistically grand present for themselves. One must hasten to add that these reconstructed identities are not invariable or immutable—identities are seldom static in any case—in the presence of other Pakistanis. In fact, in such situations, displaced persons tend to become hostage to their reinvented persona(s). In the case of non-refugee Pakistanis displaced during 1947, displacement also afforded space to imagine details of the past in distinct ways. The issue was highlighted in the interviews of the sisters, one recalling communal antipathy and the other inter-religious tolerance (if not understanding) in pre-1947 South Asia.[24] Why one sister recalls and another erases from her memory past events is clearly indicative of their present identities. The human mind appears to see logic, continuity and justification in historic 'facts' for the existence of a particular identity. Political events and leaders were known vaguely, and appear to have had little influence on either the decision to displace or on identity construction.

Identities became blurred at the end of the Raj in South Asia and during displacement abroad, especially in the context of endowing 'displacement' with neutral qualities, in contrast with the numerous other terms applicable and listed earlier. The question about whether specific Pakistanis have forged new identities is also answerable with reference to the same list of terms for displacement, in particular, 'American Born Confused Desi' and its various modifications that are popular among adolescent and young people.

The motives for the demographic movements, the push and pull factors, were, and continue to be, varied. In 1947, people fled across borders, many becoming refugees. People left their residences to be with relatives and/or as a better job transfer to the new states of Pakistan and India. In 1947, as at the end of the twentieth century, people left for greener pastures across state borders. People remained and continue to remain where they were/are as a studied choice or simply because the great upheaval/movement did/does not affect them. Affiliations change, identities permute, and new identities spring forth both at the individual and group levels. Displacement of people did not end at the end of the British Empire but the new generations continue to move across borders, both in terms of politics and identity. It can be safely stated that every Pakistani has been affected by migration phenomenon, if not personally, certainly through a close family member.

Notes

1. The basic outline for the Barcelona section of this article were written in Spanish for the Institute Català per el Mediterania (The Catalan Institute for the Mediterranean) and was included in the publication *Gestionar la diversitat: Reflexions I experiències sobre les polítiques d'immigració a Catalunya* (Barcelona: IEM, 2003), 'Inventing Immigrant Identities: Pakistanis in Barcelona', *Report of the National Seminar on The State of Migration and Multiculturalism* (Islamabad: UNESCO and IPRI, 16–18 June 2003 and forthcoming in Imtiaz Ahmad, State, Society And Displacement: Displaced People In South Asia (Dakka).

2. I am grateful to my students in my M.Phil. class on 'Ethnicity and Migration in the Americas' at the Area Study Centre for Africa, North and South America, Quaid-i-Azam University, for contributing some of these terms during the Spring 2003 semester.

3. This term has become enormously popular and has been taken over by other Pakistanis abroad, for instance, BBCD (British Born Confused Desi) and even PBCD (Pakistan Born Confused Desi), as my seventeen year old niece says, 'I don't have to be foreign born to be confused!' For BBCDs, a recent article is Fareeha Altaf, 'From home to home, and back,' Encore, *The News* (Islamabad), 14 March 2004.

4. A term used for legal immigrant workers in Arab countries.

5. Argentina used to be one of the most immigrant-friendly countries in the world during the latter half of the nineteenth century and first quarter of the twentieth century and its capital, and main port, Buenos Aires, had a (rather euphemistically called) Immigrant Hotel.

6. A derogatory term in most of the English-speaking world, it assumes endearing qualities in Spain, where, it must be recalled, moro/mora (Muslim) and negro/negra (Black) are endowed with dual qualities in specific social contexts.

7. Pre-recorded *Khutba* delivered at the Jamia Mosque of Ayubia, 24 August 2003.

8. A.H. Nayyer and Ahmed Salim, *The Subtle Subversion* (Islamabad: SDPI).

9. Saadat Hassan Manto, *Mantoo kay behtareen afsanay*, (Lahore: Maktab-i-sahier-o-adab, n.d.), 213–220.

10. This is also often cited as the main goal by students seeking employment, higher education, etc. at the Career Counselling Centre at Quaid-i-Azam University, Islamabad. It basically means to possess authority.

11. One of the most comprehensive textbooks on the subject, including the theory, is S. Dale. McLemore, *Racial and Ethnic Relations in America.* Austin: University of Texas Press, 1983.

12. This phenomenon is known as 'hacer América' (to make America) when Spaniards went to their American colonies to make it rich.

13. Special issue of *Time* magazine, 18–25 August 2003.

14. This was a major inspiration to immigrate of the several young Pakistanis interviewed in Barcelona during the years 2001–2002.

15. Interviews with Dr. Josepa Axotegui, Dictor of SAPPIR, a psychological treatment centre for immigrants, 2001–2002.

16. Rosa Llopis i Llort, 'Políticas de inmigración. Entre la inclusión y la exclusión,' *Educación Social* 20, Barcelona: January-April 2002, 19–22.

17. This insight resulted from the long discussion held with Olga Uribe, a Colombian who had displaced to Barcelona more than thirty years ago.

18. Extended conversation with two Pakistani immigrants at the airport in Barcelona while we waited to register loss of our luggage, leading to the unanimous conclusion that the term immigrant today has derogatory connotations in the Spanish language, Barcelona, January 2004.

19. Labeling for the methodology has been avoided, such as 'purposive sample;' 'foreshadowed problem', etc. and continuous conclusions are discarded in favor of maintaining the integrity of the interviews, especially in the section that follows. Jack R. Fraenkel and Norman E. Wallen, *How to Design and Evaluate Research in Education,* Fourth Edition (Boston: McGraw Hill, 2000), 510 and 506.

20. My translation from the Spanish of Javier Laviña, 'Afromexicanos, curanderos heterodoxos y brujos,' *Boletín Americanista*, 49 (Universidad de Barcelona: 1999), 98.

21. Interview conducted on May 20, 2003, when she visited Islamabad from Multan.

22. Her khala's (aunt's) devar's (brother-in-law) daughters, who lost their mother at an early age and the father remarried and had additional children.

23. 'Claiming' identities is dealt with by Nell Bernstein, 'Goin' Gansta, Choosin 'Cholita.' Catholic University of America. Race & Ethnic Relations, 256–258.

24. I am wary of the term 'tolerance'—the avoidance of conflict—in the context of religion or culture as it may connote 'bearing for form's sake,' between neighboUrs of distinct religions or cultures without engendering real respect. It would be harmony as mere absence of conflict, participation as part of the Academic Team of the European Project for Interreligious Dialogue, 2002–2003.

11

Partition of India: The case of Sindh

*Ahmad Salim**

Migration, Violence And Peaceful Sindh

Abstract

The relative harmony among the Hindus and Muslims of Sindh, established over centuries became directly at risk due to many traditional and non-traditional factors. Traditional factors including the economic exploitation of the Sindhi Muslim at the hands of the Hindu moneylender arose after the British conquest and the resultant British Civil Code, which offered protection and prospects to the Hindu *bania* (money-lender). These factors jeopardized the possibilities of continuity of non-violent social infrastructure of Sindhi people. Related to these were non-traditional threats that directly devastated peoples' lives. They included social unrest flowing from communal hatreds; increasing poverty amongst the Muslims; as well as other immediate threats to human lives from disturbances and riots. It was demonstrated through incidents like riots of 1831, Larkana riots in 1928, Masjid Manzilgah issue and so on. Thus, it becomes far more imperative to consider these issues in detail for a true understanding of the constituents of the socio-political and economic fabric of Sindh.

Another important issue in the history of Sindh was its separation from Bombay presidency, which left the Sindh Hindus very bitter because they thought that their economic and political interests would be at stake in a government dominated by Muslims thus increasing communal bitterness. Partition of Sindh did not prove to be beneficial to the ordinary Sindhi, the status of *hari* (tenant) never changed. Although, he underwent a change of masters—from Hindu capitalists to Muslim w*aderas* (landlords).

This study first identifies the key factors that increased communal bitterness and then systematically explores how and why they directly affected the lives and social obligations of the individuals. Second, it assesses the communal atmosphere shortly after the Indo-Pak Partition of 1947. The absence of large-scale violence made the Sindhi experience different from that of the Punjabis and Bengalis. Among the Sindhi Hindus, there were fewer dispositions to panic because of violence; they panicked more because of measures adopted by the Sindhi Muslims wielding political power at the time shortly before and after the Partition. An assessment is also made about how with the influx of refugees in Sindh, Muhajir Nationalism was promulgated and Sindhi culture and its indigenous people became handicapped in the hands of people from Punjab and India.

*Ahmad Salim is a poet, journalist, keeper of public records and research worker. He works at the Sustainable Development Policy Institute as Director Urdu Publications and as Research Associate.

RELATIVE ISOLATION AND COMMUNAL FABRIC

Over a number of centuries, Sindh had enjoyed religious, cultural and social harmony where religions, castes and tribes evolved a common culture. Historically, Sindh acquired a rural character, but this did not prevent the establishment of important pockets of urban development, which grew up as administrative centres closely linked to trade. The River Indus led the outside world deep into the heartland of northern India and central Asia. First Daybul, and then Lahri Bandar and Karachi became the most important ports on the Indian Ocean. The importance of the Indus as a major channel of commerce through Sindh, in turn, encouraged towns and cities to establish themselves along the river.

Lines of communication in Sindh, like the Indus River, ran from east to west, linking the subcontinent with western Asia through the Bolan, Mula and Lak Phusu passes which led from Sindh into Baluchistan and beyond. Important caravan routes also crossed the Thar Desert to destinations in the Rajputana states and the coastal regions of Kacch, Kathiawar and Gujarat. The towns developed alongside them acting as trading centres as well as *'refuelling stations'* for traders.[1]

All the same, the ranges of Kohistan together with the eastern desert proved effective barriers, and Sindh was relatively isolated from events taking place elsewhere in northern India. Sindh was one of the first to be conquered by Arabs and somehow, always remained under the Muslim political hold. However, due to Sindh's isolation, it never fully drew into the wider political framework of northern India during the period of the Delhi Sultanates or the Mughals. Sindh was ruled either by local tribes such as the *Sumros* and the *Sammas*, who continually jostled with each other for local supremacy or by the semi-independent representatives of governments whose centres of power lay far away. To Kabul and Delhi, Sindh was a distant frontier province. The preservation of 'stability' along its borders remained their main concern, and so they delegated authority to local holders of power in order to achieve their aim. This pattern of political control remained virtually unchanged right up to the time of the British arrival: the Talpur Mirs, who ruled Sindh at the time of the British conquest in 1843, were under the suzerainty of the Afghan kings, but in practice they, like their eighteenth century Kalhora predecessors, ruled as 'independent' chiefs.

As far the religious harmony in Sindh is concerned, Hindus and Muslims had co-existed in relative harmony for decades. Sindh's relative isolation was important from the religious point of view. As a 'marginal' region located away from the main centres of orthodox Hinduism, and influenced only indirectly by strongly centralised Muslim states, Sindh developed its own quite distinctive religious character. Before the advent of Islam, a mixture of Buddhism and Hinduism dominated religion in Sindh. Combined with the fact that the bulk of Muslim conversions were eventually performed by sufis, this meant that popular Islamic practice in Sindh came to display strongly mystical and syncretic trends. Sindhi Sufism was a harmonious blending of both Vedantic and Islamic cultures, and is exemplified in Sachal's axiom: *'I am neither a Hindu nor a Muslim.'* The evening prayer of a Sindhi was often: *'God's blessings be on Hindus, on Muslims and on the rest.'* Sindhi Hindus bowed without hesitation in *durgahs* and Sindhi Muslims spontaneously referred to God as *Varuna Zindah Pir*.

Therefore, even when the province became predominantly Muslim, Hindus and Muslims continued to share much of the same cultural framework and many of their religious practices overlapped. By the nineteenth century, Sindhi Muslims outnumbered Hindus by three to one. With the exception of local Ismaili and Memon groups, Hindus made up the bulk of the trading and commercial community and dominated the economic matrix. Although, economically, administratively and even politically, communities changed positions but Hindus, especially *banias* had a firm grip on the economy of the province. The social effects of rural debt were aggravated in Sindh because the creditors were almost all Hindu, the debtors almost all Muslim. The British rule initiated critical changes in the relationship between debtors and creditors, especially by conferring full property rights on landholders. This put them in possession of a valuable asset, which increased their creditworthiness. The catch was that creditors could seize their land to recover their money, a power that was unthinkable in pre-British times.[2] This gave creditors the opportunity to acquire land cheaply. *Waderas* did not generally have a strong business sense. They did not appreciate the commercial value their land had acquired. Expressing their status through the size of their estates rather than the efficiency of their husbandry, they often sacrificed profits to buy up additional tracts of unproductive land, mortgaging themselves in the process. According to British officials, this left them prey to predatory *banias*. Forbidden by their religion to lend money on interest, Muslims had traditionally left all financial affairs to the Hindu minority. The latter, like minorities elsewhere, had established a reputation as shrewd merchants and bankers, wealthy but disdained by the majority community.

Most of the Muslims lived in the rural areas, earned their livelihood from the land and were largely illiterate. Although many Sayyed families lived in towns, it was the countryside, which provided the basis of the power of Sindh's religious elite. *Pirs* belonging to important shrines wielded enormous social influence and people who did not have a *pir* as their *murshid* were considered non-believers. Thus, *pir* and the *dargah* provided the main transmission belt along which Islam reached the people of the region. This process of conversion made such a deep impact that intense devotion for *sufi* saints and their lines of descendants became the hallmarks of religious practice in Sindh.[3]

The resultant harmony of communal relations and the valuable economic service rendered by the different communities to the province as a whole held prospects of undisturbed continuity of the status quo. Regional attachment was considered more important than communal consciousness. Even during the British attack, the Hindu community joined hands with the ruling Muslims to offer a stern resistance. Although the history of Sindh marks relative communal harmony unrivalled in the northern part of the sub-continent, certain levels of ambivalence were also demonstrated in the Hindu-Muslim relationship through incidents like riots of 1831, Larkana riots in 1928, Masjid Manzilgah issue and so on. Thus, it becomes imperative to consider these issues in detail for a true understanding of the constituents of the socio-political and economic fabric of Sindh.

Hindu-Muslim Riots of 1831–1930

In 1831–32, Hindu-Muslim riots broke out in Nussarpur. Built in 989 by Nasir Muhana, about sixteen miles northeast of Hyderabad, the town was the residence of influential Lagari Nawabs.

These riots were caused over a Hindu boy who was badly treated by his teacher and the Muslims gave him refuge in a mosque. This infuriated the Hindu community and the Hindu shopkeepers of the town closed their shops against Muslims. This was the way the Hindus usually protested, as the population was dependent on them for their necessities. The Muslims retaliated by polluting the wells used by the Hindus. Seth Naomul Hotchuand states that the next day a man called Sayed Nooral Shah walked through the bazaar swearing at Hindus. Hotchand's younger brother, Parshram, protested and argued with Sayed against his uncitizen-like conduct. At this Nooral Shah charged Parshram with blasphemy—he held that Parshram had abused him and the Prophet (PBUH). He visited Tatta, Shah Bandar, Mathiari, Halla and Hyderabad, stirring Muslims and soliciting co-operation and aid from every true Muslim in the name of the *musaf* (Koran). This incited the religious sentiments in Muslims who consequently gathered against the Hindus. Hindus were also planning their moves. Hotchand's brother Parshram, by that time withdrew from Sindh to Jessulmere. The Muslims assembled in large numbers at Hyderabad, raised a clamor, and prevailed upon Mir Muradali to address a *firman* to Seth Hotchand to send his son Parshram to Hyderabad. Parshram was not in Karachi, therefore Seth Hotchand himself proceeded to Hyderabad accompanied by about two thousand Hindus in obedience to another *firman* from Muradali, directing his presence in the absence of his son. The Mir referred the case to the Pirs of Nussarpur. At Nussarpur the *qazi* doubting the Muslims' intentions refused to listen to the Muslims or to permit a discussion at his place. The Muslims, however, forcibly lifted away Seth Hotchand and went to Tatta and Bagani, a town in the Shah Bandar Division. At Bagani, the Muslims began to meditate upon his circumcision and conversion to Islam by force.

In the meantime, Mir Muradali was apprised of their intentions. He repented the step he had taken. Seth Hotchand was liberated at his intervention, thus, ending the episode of riots in Nussarpur.[4]

The colonial era, starting in 1850 in Sindh, no doubt changed the status of Hindu moneylenders in the social fabric as British law gave them protection and stability against the creditors, who were Muslim farmers. Hindus had filed a number of cases against Muslim debtors in the courts. The accusations and counter accusations in this regard were indicative of communal antagonisms, which sporadically erupted into violence. The occasional conversion of Hindus to Islam was a common trigger for public disturbances. It provoked angry claims from representatives of the Hindu community that force had been used. This was in itself a measure of their increased security since they would hardly have dared an open challenge on so sensitive an issue if the British had not been there to intervene. Muslim representatives would angrily refute the charges and the debate would be taken to the streets. Disputes over conversions provoked riots in Sukkur in 1872, in the Sehwan area in 1884, in Hyderabad bazaar, for no apparent reasons, while a dispute over the playing of music in a temple in Thattha provoked violence in 1891.[5] In 1893, a Moharram procession in Sukkur turned into an anti-Hindu riot during which the Town Inspector of Police, a Hindu was badly beaten.[6]

These constituted evidence of friction between the two communities, but there were no specifically anti-*bania* riots in Sindh along the lines of the riots, which took place in Deccan in 1875.

In March 1928, Hindu-Muslim riots broke out in Larkana. The riots had been caused by the activities of the Hindu fundamentalists of the Shuddhi, Arya Samaj and Hindu Mahasabha movements who were busy scouring the countryside at the time trying to find and *'reconvert'* or *shuddhi* (purify) any person they suspected had been converted from Hinduism. A Hindu convert woman who had been married to a small landowner in a village near Dokri in Larkana District for more than fifteen years and was mother of several children was reported to have been kidnapped by Arya Samajist workers. Her family requested the Collector to issue a warrant. The police had brought her to Larkana but the Collector was very indecisive and kept her as *amanat* (i.e. in trust) in the house of a local notable, Nawab Lahori. The Collector delayed taking action to diffuse the situation, but it soon escalated into a confrontation. The husband and the children of the woman came to complain and asked for her return, but the Larkana administration took no notice.

The incident caused a great deal of resentment in the villages around Larkana as the action of the police was considered an attack on the home and family of a respectable man. A number of villagers entered the town and caused a disturbance. They precipitated a minor riot. The extremist elements particularly the workers of Hindu Mahasabha, went around attacking any Muslim they found alone. In the melee about sixty-nine people were injured, eleven of whom were Muslims and the rest Hindus, but one Hindu died as a result of his injuries.[7] Under pressure from Hindu political workers, the police made a large number of indiscriminate arrests. The Muslims felt helpless and unprotected, as there was no voice of protest from their side. The most important Muslim leaders of the town, Sir Shahnawaz Bhutto and Nawab Lahori had refused to come out of their houses or show any interest or sympathy. However, Khuhro responded immediately. He protested to the magistrate about his extremely arbitrary actions, such as arresting Muslims without proof on the behest of their opponents and enemies. He immediately organized a relief committee.

The Defence Committee succeeded in getting most of the arrested people freed, except ten leading citizens who were committed to the Sessions Court.

The communal friction and extremist organizations like the Shuddhi and Mahasabha movements were bent upon stirring up communal trouble. This case was the beginning of the strife between Hindu and Muslim communities in Sindh. The incident was followed by trouble in other towns as both the communities organised themselves for confrontations with each other strictly on communal and religious lines. Hindu households were armed and young men were trained for combat and taught to use arms. The atmosphere was charged with hostility and the failure of the extremists in Larkana was regarded as a defeat which had to be avenged. The tactic of the communal organizations was to create tension with displays of arms and militancy. If this resulted in provoking communal incidents, there was vociferous newspaper propaganda depicting Hindus as victims of *jat* or 'uncouth' Muslims. Cases were then brought against the rioters. In this way, the majority Muslim population would remain involved and helpless, especially as the bureaucracy was Hindu and able to influence the higher levels of officialdom.

From 1929 to 1931 there were frequent incidents of violence particularly in Sukkur, one of the major commercial centres of Sindh. The Hindu community was in a majority in the town and much more aggressive in their proselytizing. In August 1930, an incident occurred in Sukkur in which Muslims were beaten and injured by Hindus. Muslims of surrounding villages poured into the city to avenge the outrage. This resulted in a riot and incidents of looting in the city. The administration, following the Larkana pattern, made mass arrests of the villagers and charged them with the most serious crimes. There was a public outcry about the use of intimidation and punishment by the police of the suspected people.

Another element, which contributed to the communal friction, was the Indian religious exclusivism, which restricted social relations between the communities and the practice of *chhoot* or *'untouchability.'* This was not confined to the lower castes of Hindus, but also forbade socializing and eating with non-Hindus. In a majority Muslim province like Sindh this was not a problem but during the British *'neutral'* rule, when they also had the economic upper hand, religious exclusivism came out into the open. The collapse of Non Co-operation and Khilafat movements had unleashed an intolerant mood in India, which can only be explained by the use of the religious idiom by the politicians.

Inter communal marriages were absolutely taboo. However, in the rural areas it was a fairly common practice that lower caste tribal girls were sold by their parents or by middlemen to well off villagers who converted and married them. The *shuddhi* movement, therefore, not only threatened such households (of which there would be at least half a dozen in a big village,) but also created communal hatred far greater than the actual number of affected people.[8]

The almost century old British rule had seen the erosion of the traditional social equations in Sindh and created raw edges in the relationship of the Hindu and Muslim communities. To a large extent this was the result of the new legal and taxation systems, which allowed the *haris* and small holders to fall into debt and what was worse, lose their land which was the sole source of their livelihood. Those suffering the hardships of the new system found a ready scapegoat in the *bania* and the urban businessmen. The growing power of the latter and their intrusion into agriculture, where they became owners of large tracts of land and orchards, led to resentments across the spectrum of the traditional rural society.

Economic Matrix and role of the Moneylender

The Sindhi Muslims trembled before the Hindu moneylender's reed-pen.[9] The Hindu *bania*, the trader and moneylender, was the creditor, who tyrannized over the debtor, imposing harsher and inequitable terms. The Muslim *zamindar* was the perennial debtor. Debt was an intolerable burden on Sindhi Muslims in general, and the *waderas* in particular.

After the conquest the Hindus took advantage of the protection provided by British rule. They started taking up land to establish themselves as landholders. Evidence was provided in 1896 by an investigation into six *'representative'* villages from each of the forty-seven irrigated *taluqas* in Sindh.[10] The Report estimated that Hindus held twenty-eight per cent of the occupied area in 1895–96. This represented a revolution in land ownership for, half a century before, they had held virtually nothing. Moreover, of the 30,839 acres which they had acquired in the selected villages between 1890-91 and 1895–96, only 7,683 acres, roughly a quarter, was new land taken up by them: the rest, 24,143 acres, they had taken from Muslims. They also enjoyed the produce of a further fifteen per cent of the land, which was mortgaged to them. Altogether, then, by 1896, Hindus had the benefit of forty-two per cent of the occupied area.[11]

In this context, the growth of indebtedness could have serious political consequences. People who lost their land or witnessed the suffering of indebted neighbors might lose faith in the British Raj. They might cease to cooperate over crime and taxation; they might even oppose the British authorities. British officers, therefore, developed a jaundiced view of *banias,* regarding them as a troublesome complication, bent on eroding the foundations of the British administration. The political sensitivity of debt increased with time. It became explosive in the twentieth century, when Muslim indebtedness fuelled resentment against Hindu *banias,* boosting the popularity of the Pakistan movement.

No doubt the significance of credit in economic development cannot be denied. Some moneylenders were rapacious, but money had to be lent if cultivation was to take place.[12] *Banias* were tradesmen. Their interest in land grew out of their trading activities. Some may, like *waderas,* have hoped to boost their *izzat* (respect) through large holdings, but they were more interested in land as an investment. It guaranteed access to raw materials. Hindu merchants were keen to start their own farms. Much of the profit they realized from the growth of Sindh's export trade, based on the produce of Sindhi farms, was invested in land. To keep their overheads down, they preferred smaller, more intensively cultivated holdings than Muslims.[13]

As merchants, Hindus were middlemen. They bought produce from the cultivators at the threshing floor. Some they kept for retailing locally, the rest they sold on to the dealers. As traders, they were a natural source of credit, providing among other things, the investments that enabled agriculture to develop. The system had evolved to suit those engaged in trade. It saved the great merchants from employing a large body of agents to go shopping round the farms, while it provided the *banias* with secure trading contacts. Naturally, this was less advantageous to the producers. But the agriculturists had little choice. They did not have connections among the large dealers. Secondly, they were not simply selling their produce; they were regulating their accounts at the same time. Before they could sell their produce on the open market, they had to pay off the season's debts. Many, though, found themselves as impoverished at the end of the season as the start, if not more so.

The problem lay in the mixture of transactions that took place when farmers sold their produce. First, their *banias* established the value of the crop, with reference to the price they expected to sell it for in the market. This they compared with the outstanding debts. The price credited to the agriculturist represented the difference between the value attributed to the crop and the owed debt. The calculations were complicated by fluctuations in price throughout the year. An agriculturist who borrowed seeds at the beginning of the season, when prices were high, would repay at harvest time, when prices were low. The *bania* had to maintain a record of the prices prevailing at the different times. As one can imagine, the arithmetic could be extremely confusing, *'even if the bania were honest and not addicted to taking unfair advantage of the complication.'*[14] With illiterate clients who were ignorant of business, the temptation was strong for *banias* to twist the record to their own advantage, and they sometimes succeeded in buying produce at excessively low rates, which bore little relation to those quoted on the markets.[15] Even if the client were literate, it made little difference since accounts were kept in a specialist *bania* Sindhi script, which was incomprehensible to most non-*banias*.

Hindus occupied an ambiguous place in Sindhi society. Evan James gave an interesting account of what the improved circumstances of Hindus meant in day-to-day terms. When he first served in Sindh in the 1870s, Hindus still had an inherent fear of Muslims, not even venturing to ride horses which, it was generally agreed, were noble animals fit only for the superior community. When he returned to Sindh as Commissioner in the 1890s, he noticed that the Hindus who two decades previously *'never dreamed of riding aught but a camel, now bestride good horses as their former Beluch masters, and never think of alighting to salam whoever it be that passes.'* Idols and religious pictures, he remarked, were now openly displayed in shops and temples, something that would have been unthinkable during his earlier time in Sindh.[16]

The old order was changing to the advantage of Hindus. Lewis Mountford, the Manager of Encumbered Estates, accused Hindus of deliberately enforcing their power, as a community, through the civil courts. Most of the subordinate judges were Hindus. Mountford claimed that, with *banias* as friends and relations, they took a warped view of what constituted reasonable interest charges, tending to be overly sympathetic towards the claims of creditors. In other words, Hindus ran the courts for Hindus.[17]

When it came to crimes against Hindus, there is little doubt that *waderas* were interested parties who were, at the very least, unwilling to assist the British authorities to enforce justice. Since British rule depended on the influence of the *waderas,* anything, which reduced their willingness to collaborate, was, potentially, a threat to that rule. The problem was most acute in the Hyderabad region but Evan James warned in the 1890s that good relations between Hindus and Muslims were beginning to break down all over the province. This was a result of the improved social position of Hindus and Muslim resentment at the working of the Civil Code.[18] In this context the Sindh government tackled the problem of indebtedness. At worst, it seemed that *banias* were depriving indebted *waderas* of their land and therefore of their power. At best, indebtedness created a bad feeling among *waderas* and a sense of disenchantment with British rule. The Sindh authorities accordingly devoted themselves to relieving the debts of the Muslim landed magnates, the *jagirdars* and great *zamindars*.

However, in some way the new circumstances also enhanced the deep roots of communal harmony. Sindhis jointly initiated a number of movements against the British during the second and third decades of the twentieth century. For instance, the movement for separation of Sindh from Bombay Presidency resulting in Sindh's achievement of provincial autonomy under the last Reforms Act of 1935.

Separation of Sindh from Bombay Presidency

The separation of Sindh from the Bombay Presidency was one of the major issues in the first few decades of wentieth century. Sindh was part of the Bombay Presidency with a large and populous region including Maharashtra and Gujarat and therefore with an overwhelmingly Hindu population. However, constituted as a separate province, Sindh had a Muslim population of over 75 per cent. Therefore, it was a question of Muslim rights. It was also an important issue for the bureaucracy of the Bombay Presidency, as they were not wiling to let go of such an administrative prize and related privileges. This debate was conducted not on the question of privilege but on the question of finance. The Bombay officials argued that Sindh would not be financially viable and self-supporting and it would not be able to pay back the debt incurred for the Lloyd Barrage at Sukkur, which was under construction at that time. This was a strong point with the opponents of the separation.

Although in the system of 'Dyarchy' introduced in the Reforms of 1919 Sindh got a larger representation in the Bombay Legislative Council, its constitutional position remained essentially unchanged. Accordingly, Sindh leaders continued their efforts for the achievement of autonomy. Apart from lobbying the government of Bombay, Rais Bhurgri and his friends came to the conclusion that the issue must be brought to all India political forums. All India National Congress had been made aware of the issue since 1913, now All India Muslim League must also be asked to play its part. In December 1925, in its seventeenth session, Muslim League passed the resolution that Sindh should be separated from Bombay and constituted into a separate province.[19]

The end of World War I was followed by a number of dramatic political events in India including Jallianwala Bagh incident and Khilafat and non-cooperation movements. The political atmosphere assumed communal spirit after the failure of Non-cooperation Movement. The Shudhi Sangathan movements were started. The communal bitterness and strife spread throughout India in 1920s and its effects were felt in the peaceful, tolerant atmosphere of Sindh as well. Local branches of Shudhi and other movements were organized and sporadic incidents of violence occurred in different places. This rise of communalism affected the demand for the separation of Sindh in a fundamental way. Hitherto, Hindu leaders had put their considerable weight behind the demand for separation. Seth Harchandrai Vishindas had been a close associate of Rais Ghulam Mohammad Bhurgri and their group had been the main protagonists of autonomy. On 9 March 1924, Rais Ghulam Mohammad Bhurgri died at the age of forty-five. He had always carried with himself the most important Hindu leadership. As one of the architects of the Lucknow Pact, he commanded respect both in Congress and

Muslim League ranks. His death left no one to fill the gap and the time was not propitious for the growth of leadership acceptable equally to both communities. Besides, there was the change in the attitude of Harchandrai Vishindas who now withdrew his support from the separation movement.

Hindus opposed separation because of their majority in Bombay Presidency, whereas in separated Sindh, they would be a small minority of about 15 per cent. The fact that they were a mainly urban, educated and wholly affluent community with practically a monopoly over government service by the Amil class and world wide trading connections of the *bhaiband* class and that they would be more than able to hold their own, appeared not to reassure them. The Sindhi Muslims were as backward in Sindh as Muslims were in the rest of India.

At this critical time, Muslims badly needed new dynamic leadership to champion their cause and work for autonomy. Fortunately for them such a leadership of men like Shaikh Abdul Majid Sindhi, Noor Mohammed Vakil, Abdullah Haroon, M. A. Khuhro, G. M. Sayed, Syed Miran Mohammed Shah, Allahbaksh Soomro and Ali Mohammed Rashdi became available.[20] These two generations of leaders made a strong case for the separation of Sindh both on financial and political grounds. The earlier protagonists raised the issue on both Congress and Muslim League platforms and the latter leadership took Sindh successfully through the last and crucial stage of the struggle for autonomy between the years 1928 and 1935.

In response to Delhi Muslim proposals of March 1927, advocating the separation of Sindh, the All India Congress Committee met in Bombay to consider among other things the important questions of Hindu Muslim unity. Pandit Moti Lal put the following resolution before the AICC:

> The proposals that Sindh should be separated from the Bombay Presidency and constituted into a separate province is one which has already been adopted in the constitution of the Congress on the principle of redistribution of provinces on a linguistic basis and the committee is of opinion that the proposal may be given effect to.

On objections put forward by the Hindus, Pandit Motilal pointed out, that the separation of Sindh would not in any way affect the Hindus adversely. On the other hand, distinguished leaders of Sindh had in the past expressed their disapproval of Sindh being tied to the chariot wheel of Bombay. As for the financial commitments of Bombay in Sindh, such projects as the Sukkur Barrage *'was only a matter of book entry'* and the Congress was not now concerned with it.[21]

Although, All India Congress had accepted and supported the separation movement more than once, not all-Hindu opinion concurred with Pandit Motilal's attitude on financial as well as communal grounds. Jayakar, the Mahasabha leader, insisted that the separation of Sindh be made part of a complete scheme, whereby the entire country would be redistributed on a linguistic basis.

Moreover, the resolution did not propose any comprehensive scheme for the whole of India. It was simply an answer to Muslim proposals. In spite of all counsels of moderation, the Jayakar amendment on Sindh, Balochistan and NWFP was carried in a slightly changed form. The amendment now read:

> in regard to the proposal that Sindh should be constituted into a separate province, the Committee is of the opinion that the time has arrived for redistribution of provinces on a linguistic basis, a principle that has already been adopted by the constitution of the Congress... The Committee is further of opinion that a beginning may be made by constituting Andhra and Sindh and Karnatak into separate provinces.

The proceedings of the conference gave a hint of some of the difficulties that would be encountered in the future negotiations between Hindus and Muslims.

N.C. Kelkar while presiding over the Annual Session of Hindu Mahasabha remarked: '*The majorities will hold the minorities as hostages and thus prevail tyranny of majority in any province.*'[22] The idea of holding a minority as hostages was for the first time implanted in the minds of the people by Kelkar and this word, later on led to severe bitterness.

The years between 1928 to 1935 was a period of hectic constitution making in India. This period saw the arrival of Sir John Simon with his British Parliamentary Commission in 1928 to assess the constitutional needs of India. The Indian politicians responded with a variety of proposals including the Delhi Muslim Proposals, the All Parties Conference, the Nehru Report, M.A. Jinnah's Fourteen Points and the Allahabad Muslim League session of 1930.

There was an intensification of the separation struggle in Sindh with its outpouring of literature, convening of conferences and building up of public opinion. By the beginning of 1930, the game was back in the hands of the Sindh players. This period was undoubtedly one of the most crucial in the history of the sub-continent of India and shaped the subsequent course of history till well after the achievement of independence. A significant result of the period was the achievement of provincial autonomy, the inauguration of fully elected legislatures and fully responsible ministries at the provincial level. The Act of 1935 constituted Sindh into a separate autonomous province. The struggle for autonomy had lasted over twenty years and was a brilliant example of unity of purpose and devotion to a cause by the Muslims of Sindh.

Change of Masters

The demand for separation of Sindh was strongly advanced by the All India Muslim League in an attempt to increase Muslim provinces in India. The Sindh Muslims, who expected a larger share of political and economic benefits from a separate province, took up the issue. Though the scheme was strongly opposed mostly by the Sindh Hindus, the British government found it practical politics to separate Sindh from Bombay Presidency mainly because Muslim cooperation was necessary to formulate a sound constitution of India and partly because it was thought the separation of Sindh would minimize further communal strife. Separation of Sindh left the Sindh Hindus very bitter because they thought that their economic and political interests would be at stake in a government dominated by Muslims.

As discussed earlier, Hindu community had enjoyed the privilege of protection provided by the British law as the most powerful and economically stable community in the province. The growing indebtness of Muslim *waderas* and *haris*, to the Hindu moneylenders, complicated the political circumstances. Muslims lost their lands to Hindu moneylenders and were losing their faith in the British Raj. But the partition of Sindh did not prove to be beneficial to the ordinary Sindhi, the status of *hari* never changed. Although, there was a change of masters—from Hindu capitalists to Muslim *waderas*.

Waderas did not have a sense of justice and equity and were mostly illiterate although they were moneyed and well connected. They treated *haris* like domestic animals, who enjoyed no privileges of rationality, no rights as human beings. Such was the condition of the poor *haris* of Sindh who formed the bulk of its population and tilled its land. Even to this day, the *haris* of Sindh are no better than serfs, they live in almost primitive conditions without any conception of social, political or economic rights; they have only one interest in life that is food, with which to keep body and soul together. No other interest of life attracts them because the fundamental problem of living remains unsolved for them.[23]

The *haris* had no organized life nor had the consciousness of organized living developed in them. They lived scattered, far from one another, in small hamlets consisting of thatched mud houses. Even the wives and daughters of *haris* were not safe from the *zamindars*.

> Fear reigned supreme in their lives—fear of imprisonment, fear of losing his child, wife or life. The zamindar might at any time get annoyed with him and oust him—he might have to leave his crop half ripe, his cattle might also be snatched and he might be beaten out of the village—he might suddenly find himself in the fetters of police under an enquiry for theft, robbery or murder or, more often, under Section 110 of the Criminal Procedure Code. He is frequently threatened by the zamindar with imprisonment, which he believes can be arranged by him through his official friends. He well remembers the fate of other haris who incurred the wrath of the zamindar and were wrongfully locked up in ill-ventilated, congested and suffocating sub-jails for very long periods where they suffered terms of imprisonment under-trial more than what they suffered on actual conviction.[24]

The *zamindar* could at any time send for the *hari* for *baigar* (forced labor) for the construction of his house or sinking of wells, or some other minor works. The *hari* could be called to come with his plough and bullocks to cultivate the private fields of the *zamindar* to spend a few days on shoot with him; or to render some domestic service. He was, thus, always at the beck and call of the *zamindar* and he dare not refuse, as annoyance of the *zamindar* would spell his doom.

Therefore, change of masters did not decrease the plight of the poor Sindhi and his circumstances never changed. However, the train of political events kept on going as the partition of 1947 came nearer.

The Masjid Manzilgah Issue, Sukkur

In the administrative setup of Sindh and Indian political front, there was a total cleavage of opinion between the Muslims and Hindus on the issue of Partition. The Muslims were demanding Pakistan while the Hindus were for a united India, thus supporting Muslim League and Congress respectively. The Sindh Ittehad Party (Sindh United Party), of all other provincial parties, was the strongest in Sindh, having Muslims as well as Hindus on its membership and was also the majority party in Sindh Assembly. Allah Bakhsh's Premiership depended on the support of this Party.

The strategy of the Muslim League High Command was to disintegrate the unity of such provincial political parties, which were based on collaboration between Hindus and Muslims especially in Muslim majority provinces. Thus, in the case of Sindh, Allah Bakhsh Soomro and his Sindh Ittehad Party was their main target. Muslim League needed an opportunity to challenge the Allah Bakhsh government. It came in 1939 during an agitation resulting from the disputed status of a domed building, Manzilgah in Sukkur.[25] The local leaders of Muslim League like G. M. Sayed and Khuhro were quite active against the Hindu community in this movement.

The Sukkur Muslims claimed the building was really a mosque and should be restored to the Muslim community. The dispute was essentially a matter between the government and the Muslim community, but the issue assumed a communal aspect when the Hindus became concerned with its settlement.[26] The Muslim demand for the Manzilgah attracted Hindu interest not simply because of its religious nature, but also because the claim bore some relation to the widely disparate socio-economic levels of the two communities in Sukkur.[27] The feelings of fear and insecurity aroused during the separation movement days had never entirely left Sindhi Hindus and they viewed the Muslim claim to the Manzilgah as a threat to •their position of dominance and control. Thus, they opposed the claim and declared that the building should remain under government control.

Earlier deputations and appeals to the government by Sukkur Muslims had failed but their hope was renewed by the government's successful settlement of the Om Mandli and Hanuman Mandir affairs in May 1939.[28] Anticipating the determined opposition of the Sukkur Hindus, the Muslims in Sukkur approached the Sindh Muslim League. Finding a universal positive response from the town's various Muslim *anjumans*, Abdullah Haroon publicly declared League support at a meeting in Sukkur on 19 May 1939.[29]

The matter attracted common attention in 1938, after the Sindh Provincial Muslim League passed a resolution demanding the government to handover the mosque to the Muslims. The dispute was taken over politically as well as religiously. The government's failure to undertake immediate steps for the Manzilgah's restoration prompted the League to appoint a restoration committee to bring still greater pressure on the government. The first meeting of the committee was held on 22 July and July 23.[30] During the meeting 18 August 1939, was declared as Manzilgah Day. It was also decided that if the Ministry did not accept the Muslim demand, All India Muslim League volunteers would be asked to start *satyagraha*[31] to have the Manzilgah on 1 October.

Abdullah Haroon stayed in Sukkur and led the agitation. When the agitation later gained strength, the Sindh Premier ordered Abdullah Haroon to leave Sukkur, and M.A. Khuhro was put under house arrest. Afterwards, G.M. Sayed started the agitation and arranged a hunger strike at the doorsteps of the ministers and their supporters. Groups were formed to assist the hunger strikers. It was the concern of the provincial Muslim League to get the mosque back, and, therefore, a Restoration Committee was formed under the chairmanship of Abdullah Haroon. This made the Muslim League a mass Muslim movement in Sindh. The Hindu Association of Sukkur, Hindu Mahasabha and Hindu Panchayat opposed the restoration of Manzilgah to Muslims.

In subsequent weeks, the League leadership continued its efforts, but the government failed to grant the Muslim demand; it adopted a policy of avoiding the issue and postponing its settlement. Allah Bakhsh felt unable to take a stand because his pre-eminent goal was to stay in office.[32] Therefore, he could not lose his Hindu supporters.

The inability of the moderates, Haroon and Khuhro, to persuade the government to grant the Manzilgah demand, gave ascendancy to the radical wing in the League. In order to retain their leadership in the League, Haroon and Khuhro were compelled to support the radical method of *satyagraha* though they hoped to obscure their action by maintaining a public front of issuing appeals and letter writing.[33] The emergence of the radical wing as the dominant group in the party was clearly reflected in the resolution passed at the next meeting of the restoration committee on 29 September 1939. The resolution called for the commencement of *satyagraha* within three days unless a settlement was reached.[34]

Haroon and Khuhro invited Allah Bakhsh to Sukkur in a final effort to persuade the government to concede the Muslims' demand. The chief minister arrived on October 1, the day *satyagraha* was scheduled to begin, and held talks with the League leaders. But once again, no agreement was reached and as a result *satyagraha* was begun.

Satyagrahis and volunteers had been streaming into Sukkur over the past several days at the urging of Wajid Ali, a local League leader and a barrister from nearby Shikarpur, who was given the title of *'Dictator'*.[35] By the second day of *satyagraha* about two thousand people had gathered, and on the morning of the third day, a group of them pushed past the police and occupied the building. G. M. Sayyed was at the forefront of this movement, he states: *'My days with the Congress had taught me that once it has started, it is extremely insulting and damaging to call off an agitation halfway through. Therefore, I took over the leadership of the movement and had the Masjid Manzilgah taken over by force.'*[36] Thus, for the time being, restoration of the Manzilgah was achieved.

The government reaction to the taking of the Manzilgah was one of shock and embarrassment but Allah Bakhsh, undaunted, adopted an unusual tactic that he hoped would return the situation to normal. He gave orders through the Sukkur District Magistrate that all Muslim *satyagrahis* were to be released and all police withdrawn.[37] He said he had taken this decision because the jails were full and there was no more food to feed the prisoners, but in reality he hoped to defuse the situation, reasoning the *satyagrahis* would lose their cause and disperse if the government demonstrated leniency.[38] But subsequent events proved Allah Bakhsh had misjudged the situation. The *satyagrahis* did not leave. They were overtaken by bitterness realizing the government had no intention of giving up the mosque and became even more determined in their claim.

On the morning of 19 November G.M. Sayed and the other leaders of the restoration committee were arrested in Sukkur, and at noon the police took possession of the Manzilgah, expelling the *satyagrahis* with tear gas. After forty-eight days of Muslim occupation, the Manzilgah was once again in the hands of the government.

The expulsion of the Muslims from the Manzilgah and its reoccupation by the government was followed by a wave of communal disturbance and rioting that began in Sukkur and spread into the surrounding district.[39] Both communities suffered comparative losses in the riots in terms of property, injuries and loss of life in Sukkur town, but the Hindus suffered most dramatically in Sukkur District as more of them were killed than were Muslims.[40]

The combined result of these events was the riots of 1939, which, eventually led to the fall of the Allah Bakhsh Ministry in Sindh. It also afforded an opportunity to the Muslim League to push through the resolution demanding a separate homeland for the Muslims, but at great cost to both the League's image and Sindh's communal peace; results that posed serious questions about the League's ability to govern should they now come to power.[41]

The Case of Hindu Muslim Harmony (August–December 1947)

Although communal rifts started once again in Sindh, now under the influence of the 1947 partition, the communal harmony remained undamaged. The province had inherited a tradition of religious tolerance from the Mirs (the Muslim rulers displaced by the British conquest). Thus, the separation from India engendered a sense of insecurity amongst the Hindus, but there was less general disposition to give way to panic or despair.

> '...the Sindh Hindu Mahasabha's membership consisted of Hindu zamindars who aligned with the Independent Muslim Party, which consisted of the Muslim landed gentry. Religion obviously played no divisive role here as they joined hands to protect their class interest. This was my first insight into upper class, Hindu-Muslim solidarity...'[42]

The long-lasting inter-communal harmony and absence of large-scale violence made the Sindhi experience of Partition different from that of the Punjabis and Bengalis.

This lack of violence could be attributed to the overarching Sindhi identity which transcended Hindu-Muslim differences, a shared language, script and literature, a deep rooted syncretic tradition with shared pirs and saints and even a similarity in food and dress. Added to this was the economic cement in a feudal society where Hindus were well off, owned land and controlled business...[43]

In this scenario, the Hindu immigrants to India took partition as a temporary inter-communal ill will and the apparent intention was soon to return to old houses and old lives. They attributed warmth and co-operation to the Sindhi Muslim neighbors and friends, who escorted many of them to the railway station or harbor. Almost unanimously the deteriorating situation was ascribed to the

arrival of Muslims from outside, that is, from Uttar Pradesh and Bihar... Another reason for the relatively smooth transition was that the bulk of them came by the sea route. Of the ones who came by train, only one respondent reported ransacking of luggage by Muslims before they crossed the border. One or two suggested that if at all Sindhi women experienced sexual violence, it was in the refugee camps where cramped quarters and lack of privacy contributed to such instances. But no one could give eyewitness or any other credible accounts of such instances.[44]

However, in the mean time the media and Muslim leaders launched an organized propaganda to shatter the balance of inter-communal harmony. Gopal Das Khosla states that the Muslim leaders had, for some time before the establishment of Pakistan, carried on a ruthless anti-Hindu propaganda and their utterances were not calculated to promote peace. Mr Ayub Khuhro during his election campaign for the Sindh Legislative Assembly in 1945–46, is reported to have said:

I am looking forward to the day when the Hindus in Sindh will be so impoverished or economically weakened that their women, even like poor Muslim women today, will be constrained to carry on their heads the midday food to their husbands, brothers and sons toiling in the fields and market places.[45]

Later, as Minister for Public Works, he declared, 'Let the Hindus of Sindh leave Sindh and go elsewhere. Let them go while the going is good and possible, else I warn that a time is fast coming when in their flight from Sindh, they may not be able to get a horse, or an ass, or a gari, or any other means of transport.'[46]

Khosla adds that Agha Badaruddin Ahmad, M.L.A., Deputy Speaker of the Sindh Legislative Assembly, in a letter, addressed to the Sukkur District Muslim League Conference, said: 'These Muslims are anxiously and restlessly straining their ears to hear the sound of the hooves of galloping horses, the rattling of the swords and the sky-rending slogans of 'Allah-o-Akbar' of Muslim crusaders.'[47] Whereas, in the words of Khosla, the Muslim Press in Sindh was equally violent. Dawn, the official organ of the Muslim League, in its issue of 13 September 1947, called upon the Muslim League National Guards to help in searching the baggage and persons of Hindu passengers, both male and female, who were leaving for India. The Hilal-e-Pakistan, a Sindhi daily of Hyderabad, published a fanatical article on 6 October 1947, and called upon the Muslim criminals and hooligans to devote their energies in victimizing Hindus:

You should neither kill nor rob Muslims. On the contrary, your full strength, valor and weapons should be used to wreak vengeance on those people with whom even today thousands of Muslim women are prisoners... Every Muslim who casts his eye on this article and happens to know any dacoit, thief, aggressor or a patharidar should carry our request to him and should instruct him to convey the exact sense of our appeal to members of his Jamiat... You should inform us about your Association or meet us so that we may give you requisite instructions and directions.

This was published after the partition of the country and shows the extent to which the emotions of the Muslim masses were being worked up. The lead given by the Muslim leaders was quickly followed by religious preceptors and the local *zamindars* saw in this anti-Hindu propaganda an opportunity-for the satisfaction of personal greed.[48]

The Refugee Issue

The issue of assimilation of refugees presented a totally different situation in Sindh as compared to West Punjab. The refugee influx in West Punjab, except for a tiny minority, consisted of Punjabis. They took very little time to assimilate in their new surroundings as they shared the language, customs and culture with the people of West Punjab. 'Even the Urdu-speaking refugees, who chose to make Punjab their home, soon assimilated themselves in their new surroundings, and their next generation become as Punjabi as any Punjabi, particularly if they were not-so-rich.'[49]

In Sindh, the refugees had distinctive characteristics. Bringing with them non-Sindhi language, customs and culture, they promulgated Muhajir Nationalism, which was soon established as a symbol of bureaucratic, educational and cultural dominance. Contrary to Punjab, the assimilation of refugees in Sindh seemed improbable because of a different language, culture, and system of land ownership.

The government took over administration of Karachi as the Federal capital on 22 May 1948. This 'brought in a massive influx of Muslim government personnel, largely of aggressive Punjabis, and entailed extensive requisition of Hindu residential and business premises in the metropolis which was the seat and centre of Hindu economic domination...'[50] The educated and wealthy 'Muslim refugees from all parts of India tended to make for the capital of Pakistan; and Sindh's commerce, industry, and administrative services seemed less handicapped by shortage of trained personnel than those in the other provinces.'[51] Thus, with a high hand in government, these newcomers captured the most profitable means of production and became the owners of the industries, trade and commerce and most of the urban property. They constituted the Urdu-speaking refugees; the Punjabi refugees—of which, many were given ownership on the basis of claims in East Punjab and several purchased land; and the civil and military officers who had been rewarded with large tracts of irrigated agricultural land. The number of Muslims coming into the West Punjab from East Punjab considerably exceeded the numbers of non-Muslims who departed. Eventually, about a million of them had been diverted to Sindh. But, it also appeared as a sophisticatedly fabricated scheme by the top-seat government officials to render the Sindhis without a homeland of their own and instead instead establish a constituency of their own.

One month prior to the Constituent Assembly's declaration of Karachi as a *'federal area'*, the ministry of Ayub Khuro was dismissed. Official sources said that he was deeply involved in corruption and misadministration. However, varied accounts existed about these charges. It was said that just before the dismissal, serious differences had arisen between Khuhro and the Governor of Sindh, Sir Ghulam Hussain Hidayatullah, because the latter had reallocated the portfolios without consulting or informing the former. His real 'crime', however, was intolerable. He had differed with the highest authorities on the issue of Karachi's separation from Sindh, and was therefore, thrown out.

The separation of Karachi from Sindh and its handing-over to the federal government was a great setback to the political and economic infrastructure of Sindh, particularly, as the benefits of the process of establishment of new industries did not trickle down the Sindhi people. Even the smallest of policies were formulated by the federal government, which, by that time had begun forming 'an invisible government.'[52] G.M. Sayed also fought against Karachi's separation from Sindh. Though, he had supported the separation of Sindh from Bombay in his early political career. After his successful struggle for the separation of Sindh from Bombay in 1937, he joined the Muslim League and became so active that he had the Pakistan Resolution passed in the Sindh Assembly—an act that he had been repenting throughout his life.

By the time Karachi was separated, some 25,000 Muslim employees of the Central Government had reached Karachi from Delhi and had nowhere to live. Moreover, despite being cold-shouldered by the Sindh government, about 150,000 refugees from East Punjab had arrived all over the province and spread communal tension of the worst kind. These refugees had neither any place to live nor any means of making a living for themselves. The Sindhis were apprehensive that if an end was not put to the ever-increasing influx of refugees, it might contribute to creating a majority of non-Sindhis in the province, and the avenues for the political, social and economic development of Sindhis would continue to remain closed.[53]

Immediately after independence, three ministers were toppled within two years. As discussed earlier, on 3 May 1948, Pir Ilahi Bakhsh replaced Ayub Khuhro as minister. In February 1949, Yusuf Haroon formed a new ministry. In the same year, a draft communication was forwarded to the Speaker Sindh Legislative Assembly by G. M. Sayed, leader of the Sindh People's Front Assembly to be submitted as communication from the Assembly under rule 115 to the Governor of Sindh.

G. M. Sayed concluded in his revealing and thought provoking draft communication that the province of Sindh, from historical, geographical, economic, linguistic and cultural viewpoint constituted a distinct nationality.[54]

Riots in Hyderabad and Karachi (January 1948)

As discussed earlier, the inter-communal harmony in Sindh was contrary to the situation in Punjab and the Hindus were not evacuating. But the pressure kept on increasing with the influx of migrants and more and more protest rose from Upper Sindh and week-by-week echoes of these protests mounted as the refugee mass moved southward. By December 1947, the volume of appeal from Sindh for protected mass evacuation of Hindus had become formidable,[55] as the government personnel imported *en masse* into Karachi. Hyderabad was engulfed by communal riots. Thirty people were killed and many wounded in the attacks on Hindus after which curfew was imposed. The violence was not merely materialistic in nature with the desire to grab Hindu property, but it was more spontaneous and was committed by refugees arriving from Ajmer, India, in retaliation for the riots at Ajmer on 6 and 14–15 December (believed to have been perpetrated by Sindhi Hindu refugees on the local Muslims).

The Chief Minister Khuhro had announced during a press conference on November 13 that he would '...soon associate representatives of the Hindus with the administration of Sindh, and exchange views with the Congress members of the provincial assembly about the problems of the minorities.' Then, addressing a dinner gathering in the Karachi Club on 17 November he said, 'I am sure that those who left us did so in a hurry and must be feeling the pain of exile and regretting their decision. Therefore, we must do all that we can to get them to come back... If these sons of Sindh can come back we shall celebrate the occasion.'[56]

That is why Grandma Leelan and many other Hindu families refused to go to India, although their homes were attacked in order to force them to migrate. In the words of Dadi Leelan,

> At that time I had just graduated and was a music teacher in the training college. We were quite happy at the creation of Pakistan. For me it was as if the Muslims were becoming rulers again after the end of the Mughals. That era had been very good for the non- Muslims, particularly for Hindus. As Pakistan was our home, the new era would be good for us too. We were now free. But very soon our optimism came to an end. Every evening the Muslim refugees would stone our houses and shout why we weren't leaving and vacating the place for them. We got frightened. My brothers left for India, but my father refused to go away, and I decided to stay on with him. During those times the refugees would often be seen standing outside our house armed with sticks. They knew I was all alone in the house with my old father. I would sometimes ask them what they wanted, and they would say we should run away. But I was determined to stay on. I continued to teach in college and serve my country.[57]

The inter-communal disturbance, which started with the import of refugees into Sindh, kept on mounting till it finally exploded in January 1948. The riots of 6 January were a first organized attempt of massacre and looting in the post-partition Sindh. Much has been said and written about it and quite naturally the details found variations in different accounts. In all these versions, two facts stand out. First, the attacks had come from just one group – the refugees, and that there had been no provocation of any kind from the Hindus and Nanak-Panthis (who, in the Punjab, are called Mona Sikhs, or beardless Sikhs). Second, the only reason for the attacks on non-Muslims was to create panic among the minorities, forcing them to flee from Sindh and in turn the perpetrators would grab their property.

There is some difference of opinion about how the riots started. For instance, Narayan Shahani says that before the attacks, the refugees among the government employees had resorted to a pen-down strike. There are two eyewitnesses to the assault cases of January 6 in and around Pakistan Chowk, Karachi. According to them the spirit of amity among Hindus and Muslims in Sindh was so strong that many Hindus had themselves circumcised. These attacks absolutely destroyed this atmosphere of amity and understanding and obliged the Hindus to think in terms of migration. Apart from the terrible happenings in Hyderabad and Karachi, there were no other reports of communal riots or killings on a large scale anywhere in Sindh, but the violence in the two cities was sufficient to force the Hindus to decide on migration.

Sobho Gianchandani, a member of the Communist Party of Pakistan, who was not only a witness to the events of January 6 in Karachi, but was also actively associated with the later efforts to restore peace and sanity, while narrating his story, said, 'The muhajirs thought the Sindhi Muslims were not good, and that they (the refugees) would have to take things in their own hands. Something must be done to make the Hindus run away.'[58] He asserts that when curfew was imposed from 2.00 p.m., some 300 people had been killed according to government estimates, and about 1,100 if one went by the figures computed by the community. The intention was not to inflict wounds, but to kill. Along with other workers of the Communist Party, Sobho went around the city the next day and made frantic appeals for bringing back normalcy.

Sobho Gianchandani adds:

'On the night of 5 January at 10 p.m. a tailor comrade told some of us trade union workers that in the Mauladino musafirkhana, a meeting of desperate maulvis was held and it was decided that an atmosphere of terror should be created so that the Hindus should leave and vacate their houses. They were of the view that Sindhi Muslims were not self-respecting enough to force the Hindus to flee.[59]

So they had to leave Sindh and escape to India. Narayan Shaham told me that the:

Hindus had to leave Karachi in ships of the Scindia Steam Navigation Company. Sadhu Vaswani came to Karachi from Hyderabad. My father (K.D. Shahani) said to him that even if he went away this would prompt all other Hindus to depart. But Sadhu Vaswani had come determined to leave and had also brought along many Hindu families with the same intention.[60]

In the words of Mohan Kalpana, the eminent Sindhi writer:

The immigrants from Bihar rioted and killed several people. Stray mobs headed towards Ratan Talao... Because of these riots perpetuated by the non-Sindhis there was great trepidation and alarm among the Hindus. And one day we also loaded our belongings on a camel and headed towards the Karachi Port... I wished to turn into a draught of wind and blow over the land, the houses, and the people of Sindh, kissing them; ... First I had the expectancy to go back. I don't know when this hope died. Now my only wish is to see Sindh...[61]

A great sense of longing and suffering is found in most of the accounts. Mohan Kalpana adds that he wrote a letter to Jay Ram Das:

You ask me to forget Sindh. During your governorship of Bihar, your ancestral ring fell in the pond while boating. On official expense you drained the pond to retrieve but a ring!—What had you lost? Just a ring – we have lost our homeland sain![62]

But the immigrants' accounts generally blackout the information. And if it is recorded, the incident is often depicted as a mischief of Hindus. In certain cases, the information is provided but it has been given a very mild treatment and riots are shown to be lasting just few hours. Even, Maulvi Abdul Haque, known as Baba-i-Urdu (the father of Urdu), misrepresented what actually happened in favor of *muhajirs*.[63]

On the evening of 6 January Muslim mobs carried out a thoroughly organized looting of Hindu property in Karachi.

Groups of thugs swooped simultaneously on Hindu neighborhoods... Accounts of the operation by numerous victims agreed that there was little physical maltreatment, but the threatening attitude and the hearty curses of the looters were enough to induce the numbness of terror in the victims.[64]

Quaid-e-Azam Mohammad Ali Jinnah was shocked at the turn of events. Addressing a gathering of Muslim refugees on 9 January he said:

I understand the sentiments of the Muslim refugees and all those who have suffered trials and tribulations and sympathise with them. But they must control themselves and learn to acquire the ways of a responsible people. They should not take undue advantage of the hospitality extended to them, nor should they ignore the steps taken to ameliorate their plight. Once again I warn all

Muslims against lawless elements and fifth columnists and urge them to protect their Hindu neighbors from the goondas responsible for the riots. They must create a sense of trust and security among the minorities.[65]

Literary Response

Hundreds of thousand people residing in Sindh were forced, through communal riots, to leave their homes, to wander across the barren lands in search of rehabilitation. Communal riots and disturbances erupted in some other regions also which resulted in migration of people *en masse*. In this political upheaval, Sindhi Hindus suffered a lot because, contrary to Punjab, they did not get any land compensation when they arrived in India. Whereas, the dreams of Sindhi Muslims, who had initiated and strongly pleaded for creation of Pakistan, were somewhat shattered into pieces immediately after independence. Mostly backward in the fields of education and technology, as compared to the increasing influx of Muslim immigrants, they could not gain much in terms of political power and employments in the administrative fields of Pakistan.

While Punjab and Bengal were given half of their states, the Sindhi community had to face the permanent scar of separation from their entire homeland. This suffering and deprivation, alienation and anguish, the sorrowful situation of Sindhis, who were deprived of their cultural, historical, geographical and sociological identity, became the subject matter of Sindhi poetry.[66] The 1947 partition issues have remained favorite themes for Sindhi writers in India and Pakistan. The main literary trends pertaining to partition problems revolve around the attainment of freedom along with communal holocaust, the migration of Hindus from Sindh, their plight in resettlement camps, and their socioeconomic and various other problems of rehabilitation.

Some of the important aspects of fictional writings pertaining to the theme of partition are: 1) sweet recollections of Sindh where the writer was born and he spent his childhood; 2) deep anguish due to loss of the native place; 3) the feeling of alienation and rootlessness in the new environments in India where the writer is resettled; 4) love for Sindhi heritage, culture and way of living; 5) strong efforts for preservation and development of Sindhi language, literature and culture in India; 6) sympathy for various movements of Sindhi Muslims in Sindh, who are fighting for their rights; and 7) humanitarian outlook, considering Sindhis as a single community.

Remarkably, the Sindhi writers rarely portrayed grim pictures of communal riots and disturbances; instead they have tried to establish communal harmony by portraying inter-communal marriages and sweet relations among Sindhis residing in India and Pakistan.

In a story entitled *Claim,* by Narayan Bharti, an old Sindhi man says, 'I am Sindhi. The Sindh region belongs to me. I have every right to register a claim for getting it back.' In another story 'Dastavez' (the property deed, 1952) he has reinforced the issue of Hindu-Muslim harmony and love of the homeland.[67]

The partition proved to back a double-edged sword—both those who left and those who stayed felt the pain of separation. Popati Hiranandani bitterly observed that, 'While Punjabi Hindus and Bengali Hindus received half of their land, Sindhi Hindus were rendered homeless...'

During the Indo-Pak war in 1965, the great Pakistani Sindhi poet Sheikh Ayaz was faced with a dilemma. He saw the Sindhi poet Narayan Shyam on the other side, and said:

Oh! this war...
In front of me I see Narayan Shyam!
We share the same hopes
and despairs,
The same speech and its lilt
How can 1 aim a gun at him?
How can I shoot him down?
That I should do this
Is something not possible?[68]

IMPACT

The absence of large-scale violence made the Sindhi experience of Partition different from that of the Punjabis and Bengalis. Among the Sindhi Hindus there was less disposition to panic because of violence, they panicked more because of measures adopted by the Sindhi Muslims wielding political power at the time shortly before and after the Partition. This anti-Hindu discrimination was perceived to be only a taste of the future. Many Hindus sent their families away, at least till the situation was resolved.

With the influx of refugees in Sindh, *Muhajir* Nationalism was promulgated and Sindhi culture and its indigenous people became handicapped in the hands of people from Punjab and India. *Muhajir* Nationalism was soon established as a symbol of bureaucratic, educational and cultural dominance. This initiated a cultural and political discrimination against Sindhis in Pakistan, which exists even to this day. However, it would have been a different story altogether if there had been unity amongst Sindhis themselves like, for instance, people of East Pakistan. Bengalis of all classes and backgrounds were united in their cause. If Sindhis were to unite like the Bengalis did, the nature and degree of the discrimination and problems that they face would change dramatically.

The other great setback Sindh received at the time was separation of Karachi from Sindh, when it was established as Federal capital on 22 May 1948. This was followed by another blow to Sindh when Sindh University was shifted from Karachi to Hyderabad, in other words, it was moved from the booming industrial centre to the old *chakra* (bull cart) culture. The next step was elimination of Sindhi language from Karachi schools.

The plight of minorities is a chronic issue in Pakistan. Sindh even today has a significant population of the Hindu community as compared to other provinces of the country. These are people who generally did not leave Sindh at the time of Partition due to economic compulsions. Amongst them the urban business class is in a far more miserable condition than the Bhils, Kolis, etc. of the Thar area. Their misery could be justifiable in terms that Sindhis in general are treated as second-class citizens, and as Sindhi Hindus, they are treated as third-class citizens. The bitter feelings of Sindhi Muslims towards the pre-partition *banias* add to the communal friction in the province.

In 1955, the One-Unit scheme ignited a wave of fury among the Sindhi population, particularly among the student, intellectual and peasant classes. They had staged province-wide agitations only to be met with merciless resistance by the authorities. The abolition of the provinces under the garb of so-called parity, was aimed at capturing the economic and political life of small provinces, Sindh being the most prosperous and holding an enormous promise for the future. During the agitation against One-Unit, countless Sindhis were detained and many were prosecuted. Unmoved by them, the Khuhro leadership implemented the most hated scheme on 14 October 1955.

However, the One-Unit scheme could not last long. In the wake of the dissolution of One Unit, demands for rectifying many of the wrongs of that era grew intense in the smaller provinces. One of these demands was the restoration of the status of Sindhi as the provincial language of Sindh. The language Sindhi had enjoyed this status since 1851, but it had been eroded by a series of government actions after the creation of Pakistan. The newly elected provincial government of Mumtaz Ali Bhutto moved a bill in the Sindh Assembly in July 1972 for the promotion of the Sindhi language, without prejudice to the status of the national language, Urdu. However, '..so much mistrust had already developed between the two communities in the previous two years over this question that leaders of the Urdu-speaking community were not willing to accept anything less than a 'bi-lingual' province.' [69] Riots broke out in the province even before the bill had actually passed. Although intervention by the then President Zulfikar Ali Bhutto and the passage of a supplement bill helped cool the passions momentarily, these riots did an irreparable damage to inter-community relations in Sindh and the basis of Pakistan's unity. July 1972 had essentially been the re-enactment of the language controversy scenario of 1952 in East Bengal.

During the Bhutto regime, Sindhis received compensation with an exception to Sindhi writers, intellectuals and political workers, who were harshly suppressed. However, for securing political legitimacy General Zia ul Haq added fuel to the fire of ethnic violence in Sindh. To this day, Sindh is suffering the aftermath of General Zia's regime.

In the conflict between Sindhis and Urdu-speakers, the latter must accept their new Sindhi identity in letter and in spirit. But if all that is taken too mechanically, if no allowance is made for the logistical difficulties and human failings, and if the resistance of a minority of diehard Urdu-bigots is answered by a particularism, which attempts to stem the logical growth of Urdu, then such a movement will, in the final analysis, prove to be utterly reactionary and self-defeating. If the Sindhi middle class fails to recognize the dialectics of the productive forces in society and opposes the development of Urdu as a threat to purity of Sindh, it would essentially be working for feudal restoration in Sindh. Consequently, tightening its chains. The trend of Sindhi nationalism, like that of any other nationalism, is class collaborationist. Because where it speaks against the injustices meted out to Sindhis as a whole, it conveniently overlooks the injustices and humiliation meted out every day to Sindhi peasants. Even on the cultural question, the Sindhi feudal politicians have betrayed the Sindhi masses again and again.

As regards resolving the fate of *Muhajir* separatism, MQM (Muhajir Qaumi Movement) had its susceptibilities, which called for the ability of the state to manipulate the political process, the attitude of other ethnic groups towards *Muhajir* nationalism and, above all, the capacity of the *Muhajir* community to eschew its sense of self-righteousness. However, the ice has started melting. Muhajir Qaumi Movement has changed its name to Muttahida Qaumi Movement. It will be too early to denounce it as 'just a change in name', without allotting some grace period to the organization to demonstrate its shift from self-righteousness. Muthida has recognized the reality of Sindh and is facilitating integration. The organization is doing some serious thinking to respect and acknowledge the historical rights of the Sindhis.

Notes

1. Huges, A. W., *A Gazetteer of the Province of Sind*, Karachi, 1876, p. 85.
2. Regulation V of 1827, Chapter V, Section 15, The Bombay Code, 7.
3. Ansari, Sarah F.D., *Sufi Saints: a State Power*, Vanguard, 1992, p. 13.
4. Bhojwani, Rao Bahadur Alumul Trikamdas (tr.), *Memoirs of Seth Naomul Hotchand*, Oxford 1982, pp. 64–67.
5. District Sup. Police, to Collr,. Hbad., 26 August 1882 (P.S.C., J.D., file 1, 1882, Vol. II. Pt. II, compn. 47, 78–84; Comm., Sindh, note, n.d. (As quoted by David Chessman, *Landlord Power and Rural Indebtness in Colonial Sindh 1865 – 1901*, Curzon, p. 185.
6. Cheesman, op.cit., p. 185.
7. Khuhro, Hamida, *Mohammad Ayub Khuhro – A Life of Courage in Politics*, Ferozsons, 1998, p. 73.
8. Khuhro, op. cit., p. 185.
9. Burton, Sir Richard, Sindh Revisted, Vol. 1, p. 299, cited in Cheesman, op. cit., p. 161.
10. Commr., Sindh, To Govt., Bombay, 12 August 1896, Note A (P.G.D., R.D.L., 1899, July – December, Confi. 798–9.
11. Cheesman, op.cit., p. 162.
12. Cheesman, op. cit., p.163.
13. Ibid. p. 164.
14. Settlt. Offr. 6 Jan, 1873 (B.N.S. 194), Kotri S.R., 38.
15. Depy. Collr., U.S.F., To Commr, Sindh, 18 July 1904, *cited in Cheesman*.
16. Commr. Sindh, Note, n.d., (B.S.C.) JD, File 1, 1894, Vol. II, pt. 1, compn. 23, para 3.
17. Cheesman, op. cit., p. 165.
18. Commr. Sindh, Note, n.d., (B.S.C.) JD, File 1, 1894, Vol. II, pt. 1, compn. 23, para 3.
19. Khuhro to Iqbal, 21 November 1952, Khuhro papers.
20. Khuhro, Hamida, *Documents on Separation of Sindh from the Bombay Presidency*, Islamabad 1982, p.xxvii.
21. *The Nehru Report*, 1975 edition, p. 49.
22. Pervez, Ikram ul Haque, *The Contribution of Sindhi Muslims in Pakistan Movement*, University of Sindh, 1984, p. 156.
23. Hyder Baksh Jatoi, Statement of the Accussed, Hyderabad, 1997, p. 87.
24. Minutes of Dissent by Mr. M. Masud Khadderposh.
25. Manzilgah building and its mosque and rest house built during Akbar's reign, was in the government's hands. See for details, Soomro, Mohammad Qasim, *Muslim Politics in Sindh 1938–47,* Jamshoro, 1989.
26. *Causes of Sukkur Disturbances*, Appendix B, pp. 46.
27. P & J 4889, 'Note on the Honourable Home Minister's Tour', by R. M. Maxwell, I.C.S., n.p.
28. Sayed, G. M., *Struggle for a new Sindh*, p. 31.
29. *Weston Report*, p. 8.
30. *Weston Report,* pp. 27.
31. Soomro, op. cit., p. 54.
32. Cheesman, op. cit., p. 135.
33. *Weston Report*, pp. 28–29.
34. Cheesman, op. cit., p. 135.
35. *Weston Report*, p. 28.
36. Sayed, G. M., *The Case of Sindh*, Karchi, 1995, p. 27.
37. Ior, *Linlithgow Papers*, MSS Eur F 125/96, Graham to Linlithgow, no. 1, 4 January 1940, p. 1.
38. Sayed, G. M., *Struggle for a new Sindh*, p. 34.
39. Ior, *Linlithgow Papers*, MSS Eur F 125/95, Graham to Linlithgow, no. 124, 22 December 1939, p. 163
40. Cheesman, op. cit., p. 139.
41. Cheesman, op. cit., p. 140.
42. Suchitra, *The Sindhi Experience of Partition*, CSDS Archives, Ahmadabad, p. 5.
43. Ibid. p. 3.
44. Ibid. p. 3.
45. Quoted by Parsram V. Tahilramani in *Why the Exodus from Sind?*
46. Ibid.
47. *Alwahid,* Karachi, April 9, 1947
48. Khosla, G.D., *Stern Reckonings,* New Delhi: OUP, 1989, pp. 244–245.
49. Extracts from *Proltari*
50. *The Sindhi Exodus*, p. 355.

51. Salim, Ahmad, Pakistan aur Aqliattain, Karachi, 2000.
52. Salim, Ahmad, 'The Separation of Karachi from Sindh,' *Pakistan of Jinnah, The Hidden Face,* Lahore: Brother Publishers, 1993, p. 85.
53. Salim, Ahmad, op. cit., Pakistan aur Aqliattain, p. 136.
54. Salim, Ahmad, *'Sindh's Turmoil – A Document that was Ignored,'* Pakistan of Jinnah, The Hidden Face, Lahore: Brother Publishers, p. 89.
55. *The Sindhi Exodus,* p. 356.
56. Salim, Ahmad, op. cit., *Pakistan aur Aqliattain*, p. 136.
57. Ibid., p. 137.
58. Sobho Gianchandani, interview with the author
59. Salim, op. cit., *Pakistan aur Aqliattain*, p. 139.
60. Ibid. p. 139.
61. Farooqi, Musharaf (tr.), Mohan Kalpana, *Excerpts from Ishq*, Bhukh ain, Adab. p. 22.
62. Ibid. p. 25.
63. Haque, Maulvi Abdul, *Taqseem-e-Hind ke Fasadaat aur Anjuman ki Hijrat*, p. 187.
64. *The Sindhi Exodus,* p. 356.
65. Salim, op. cit., *Pakistan aur Aqliattain*, p. 139.
66. Makhija, Menka Shivdasani, Arjan Shad Mirchandani, (ed.), *Freedom and Fissures*, New Delhi
67. Jetley, M.K., *Partition of India as portrayed in Sindhi Literature*, p. 104.
68. Jotwani, Motilal, *Of Grass and Roots: An Indianist's Writings*, New Delhi: Sampark Prakashan, pp. 204–205
69. Ahmad, Feroz, 'The Language Question in Sindh,' *Regional Imbalances and the National Question in Pakistan*, Vanguard, 1992, p. 139.

ACKNOWLEDGEMENTS

Appreciation is expressed to Mohi ud Din Hashmi, Research Associate, for his assistance and contributions to all phases of this study. Appreciation is also expressed to Nandita Bhavnani for her critique and review, which enabled the author to correct conceptual mistakes in this study. Finally, Karamat Ali's suggestions and advice changed the shape of this paper.

12

THE PROBLEMATIC OF IDENTITY IN THE EDUCATIONAL DISCOURSE OF PAKISTAN: A HISTORICAL APPRAISAL

*Tahir Kamran**

ABSTRACT

The main theme of the article is premised on the problem of identity as it is being constructed in Pakistani textbooks, covering social sciences and humanities. Not only has the centrist discourse consigned the dissident voices to the epistemic marginality, it also has given rise to utter confusion while addressing the question of identity in textbooks. In those textbooks, no differentiation has ever been made between traditionalists like Ahmad Sihindi and Shah Walliullah and modernists like Syed Ahmed Khan, Iqbal and Jinnah. Pakistan which is undoubtedly a modern nation state, emerges as a state having its basis in Islamic tradition that is the anti thesis of modernity. So far as Pakistani identity is concerned, it is rooted in exclusivity of the Muslims from the Hindus. So the whole thrust is on the antipathy for the Hindus of India only. Such are the main points that have been elucidated in the article.

*Dr. Tahir Kamran is the Chairman, Department of History, Government College University (GCU), Lahore. He is the author of 'Idea of History through Ages' and Founder Editor of 'The Historian' a bi-annual history journal that comes regularly from the Department of History GCU.

Pakistan is a conglomeration of multiple social, cultural and ethnic identities with a few commonalities and myriad disparities. Particularly till 1971, Pakistan had a diversity of any conceivable form, encompassed in a centralized state structure, unmatched by any other precedence in the contemporary world, i.e. one province of the country existed more than a thousand miles apart from the rest of the country. All the federating units have diverse languages, cultural patterns and historical experiences. Therefore, each of these units constituting Pakistan can easily pass for the Western definition of a nationality, having only one commonality, the religion. This commonality failed to offer any solid ground for the edifice of a cohesive nation state. This is because the concepts of nation and nationalism[1] stem out of a particularized political discourse have their epistemic wellspring in modernity rooted in Western rationality.[2] Nevertheless, in the educational discourse a singular identity for diverse segments of peoples has been emphatically prescribed and professed. The first educational conference, held under the auspices of the Government of Pakistan in 1947, prioritized Islamic ideology as a postulate for forming the basis of education system.[3] However, Mubarak Ali opines that the problematic of Pakistani identity came into sharp focus during Ayub Khan's reign, particularly after the war of 1965.[4] The search for Muslim Heroes and symbols emerged that represented South Asian Muslims as a distinct and homogenous collectivity of people. In a bid to conjure homogenous Pakistani identity having its essence in Islamic tradition, the course of South Asian history was reinterpreted and new meanings were ascribed to it. Concepts like the 'Two Nation Theory' and 'Ideology Of Pakistan' were recurrently projected in textbooks and media as prime identity markers. Sheikh Rafique, a well-known textbook writer of History and Pakistan Studies has dedicated one of his books to 'those fearless and dedicated scions of Islam who have thwarted all sorts of conspiracies, hatched against Ideology of Pakistan...'[5]. In the present study, these identity markers as projected in the textbooks of History and Pakistan Studies will be historically apprised.

It is interesting to note that, text and reference books used in the academic institutions of Pakistan present contrasting and at times confusing images, made of both 'tradition' and 'modernity'. The struggle for Pakistan was conceived and launched by Muhammad Iqbal and Muhammad Ali Jinnah respectively. Both of them alongwith Sir Syed Ahmed Khan[6] (1817–1898) as their progenitor were thoroughly influenced by modern thoughts that had their basis in Western rationality. Contrarily, the heroes from Pre-Modern History like Sheikh Ahmed Sirhindi,[7] Aurangzeb[8] and Shah Walliullah,[9] were great exponents of 'Tradition'. Hence, 'Tradition' and 'Modernity' seem entwined into an epistemic complex, which circumvents common comprehension. Muslim tradition and Modernity had absolutely diverse cultural antecedents. This difference is overlooked while addressing the question of ideology as the basis of singular Pakistani identity.

1

The conceptual foundation of Pakistani nationhood described in the Pakistani textbooks of History and Pakistan Studies in the 'tradition' existed in the seventh century Islam in Saudi Arabia. That contradiction resonates in the Pakistani educational discourse curriculum and textbooks seem to endlessly propagate the notion of 'The Two Nation Theory' as the ideological foundation for the distinct and cohesive identity for a Muslim state (Pakistan). 'The Two Nation Theory' with its emphasis on separate nationhood is a modern category with its antecedents in nineteenth century Europe of Post Napoleon era. Therefore, the concept of a nation or a *Qaum* does not go beyond Sir Syed Ahmed Khan who initiated that concept in the contemporary Muslim political discourse. The traditional category whereby Muslims as a distinct social and political entity become explicable is *Umma* or *Millat*[10], a concept radically different from 'Nation'. Unlike the concept of Nation; it transcends any geographical or cultural referent. Hence, Muslims of every hue, irrespective of their country, culture or community were part of *Umma*. The concept of Nation or (Muslim). Nationalism became popular among the educated Muslims of India, when Iqbal got into an inconclusive conceptual debate with Hussain Ahmed Madni on the issue of Nation/*Millat* in the 1930s.[11] Indian Muslims had been termed as a nation, Jinnah also approved it by acknowledging Muslims as a separate nation in his Presidential address in March 1940, at Lahore; by so doing legitimacy was accorded to that concept which subsequently flowered into the 'Two Nation Theory'. That the theory typifying Indian Muslims, as a separate nation is inevitably a modern construction, however, the agency underpins that it is tradition (religion).[12] So, tradition was to be preserved and promoted through the spokesperson of such concepts fully imbued in its binary opposite, 'modernity'.

This shows that 'tradition' was deeply entrenched in Semitic (monolithic and monotheistic) set of cultural traditions, and could not smoothly be transplanted in a milieu, which was socially and culturally disparate given the multiplicity of beliefs is the Indian social formation. The backdrop of heterogeneous cultural and religious forms, in the Subcontinent, only the mystic tradition of *wahadat ul wujud*[13]/*vedanta*[14] could provide a common ground for the people. Therefore, through the efforts of a long chain of mystic sufis, *Wahadat ul Wujud* permeated through the girdle of monolithic identities laid down in the foundation for communal mutuality and oneness. That thought gained wide currency in North India because 'the common ground between *Vedanta* and Sufism was provided by monism alone... without monism, the Bhakti saints and the Muslim sufis would find it difficult to speak a common language'. I.H. Qureshi comments: 'The doctrine of monism, had a great hold upon the mind of the people at that time. Through the Bhakti movement it had percolated into the consciousness of the masses. It was accepted both by the mystics and the philosophers. Some of the greatest mystics among the Muslims had declared the experience of monism as the *summum bonum* of their 'attainment.' He further comments, 'In the growth of heterodoxy, monism had played an important role.'[15]

Hence, as and when any monolithic mode of behavior was tried to be super-imposed from above, it caused social rupture of immense proportion. Sheikh Ahmed Sirhindi (1562–1624) figures quite prominently in the discourse of Muslim identity as the chief exponent of Muslim distinctness, having its source in orthodox Islamic tradition *vis-a-vis* Akbar's (1556–1605) bid to nestle and nurture syncretic cultural and religious tradition. Akbar's endeavor to carve out a polity where all sorts of religious persuasions could find their respective resonance in the affairs of the state. Therefore, the ideology that formed the basis of such a polity was the outcome of syncretism embodied in the Bhagti Movement. This seemed to be the prototype of Modern day secularism. Such syncretic thoughts, in circulation in fifteenth and sixteenth centuries, persuasively professed the outright negation of binary opposites of any sort. *Ram* and *Rahim* were different only in name, otherwise they denoted the same reality. The popular acclaim that Bhagti Movement acquired proved to be a challenge that Muslim orthodoxy responded to through the philosophy of *wahdat ul shahud*, Ahmad Sirhindi (Mujadid Alf Sani) being its leading proponent. Though the practical manifestation of Ahmed Sirhindi's views could not become a possibility before Aurangzeb Alamgir ascended the throne. However, preventing Khusru from succeeding his grandfather Akbar as the next Mughal King instead of his own father Jehangir, the inability of Dara Shikoh to seize power and the subsequent fifty-year rule of Aurangzeb proved to be important variables, resulting in the eventual defeat of heterodoxy based on monism, advocated by *Wujudis*. That puritanical brand of Islam eventually led to inter-communal as well as intra-communal fissures among the Muslims of South Asia. Ahmed Sirhindi not only condemned Hindus as *Kufar* (infidels), but also enunciated *Shias* as heretics. In his booklet *Rad-I-Ravafiz* (condemnation of *Rafzis* or *Shias*), he emphatically asserted that they be put to sword because in his opinion they were anything but Muslims.[16] With such a criterion for a true Muslim as adumbrated by Ahmed Sirhindi, even the founder of the 'Islamic Republic of Pakistan's belief in Islam would become at least questionable because Muhammad Ali Jinnah was born in an *Ismaeli* household and subsequently converted to the *Isna Ashri* (*Shia*) sect.[17] Despite such views, he is hailed as the chief architect of the two-nation theory as prescribed in the Pakistani textbooks of History, Political Science and Pakistan Studies and also the savior of Islam in the Indian Subcontinent, which was in jeopardy because of the religious policy of Akbar. In a book of Pakistan Studies meant for Intermediate students, Ahmed Sirhindi is quoted as saying, 'The honor and glory of Islam lies in humiliating the infidels and their false beliefs. One who holds any infidel dear humiliates the followers of Islam'.[18] Then in the same book, an anecdote has been quoted that is as follows;

> When he, in the company of his disciples, passed by river Yumna, he was told that the Hindus bathe in these waters of that river for cleansing themselves from the sins. After listening to that, he forbade his followers to use the water of Yumna for drinking purposes. It could only be used for cleaning yourself after defecation[19].

Those thoughts were put into effect by Aurangzeb (1658–1707), the last great Mughal Emperor and provided a plausible reason to the Marathas to rebel against the Mughal centre putting forward the King's religious bigotry as the main irritant in the smooth inter-communal relationship. Besides the imposition of *jazia* (the protection tax on the non-Muslims in an Islamic state) on Hindus and the demolition of some Hindu temples, Aurangzeb also chose to fight against the Deccan States ruled by *Shia* rulers. Many historians contend that the motive of Aurangzeb's policy of stretching out to the South was essentially economic. Even if that point is conceded, his orthodox views and some of the state policies based on *shariah*, not only encouraged the Muslim orthodox elements to reorganize in the form of institutions like *Madrissa-i-Rahimia*, set up by Abdul Rahim father of Shah Walliullah, but focus on reinterpretation of Islamic jurisprudence with the help of traditionalist *Ulema,* in the form of *Fatawa-i-Alamgiri*[20], yet another example that has paved the way for the construction of a monolithic Muslim identity. Such policy initiatives on the one hand alienated the Hindus, and on the other hand, made both the ideologue (Ahmed Sirhindi) and the practicioner (Aurangzeb), the Heroes and role models for Pakistani youth in textbooks. Sheikh Ahmed Sirhindi's contribution remained latent and his message could not get beyond his handful of *Mujadidi* disciples till Abdul Kalam Azad brought it into popular circulation through his book *Tazikra.*[21] In the1920s, when intern communal antipathy was rampant, such figures professing separatism on the basis of religion, gained extraordinary hype. History writing also fell prey to the communalist sensibility and a host of writers started constructing India's past on religious lines. When Jadu Nath Sarkar's Fall of the Mughal Empire, (Vol. 1) got published in 1932, an extraordinary furor erupted in its wake because he laid all the blame of Mughal decline at the doorstep of Aurangzeb Alamgir whose religious policy marked by prejudice and bigotry resulted in the ruthless oppression of his Non-Muslim (Hindus and Sikhs) subjects. Consequently, Aurangzeb lost favor of the Hindus and the Sikhs who had started working against the Mughals. Jadu Nath Sarkar's contention may just have a semblance of a truth but it had the profoundest bearing on the two communities' way of looking at each other. The

Muslim writers like Shibli Nomani[22] and Z.A. Farooqi, in response to the insinuating narrative of Jadu Nath Sarkar, hailed Aurangzeb as the hero of Muslims and the protector of Islam, branding Shiva Ji (a Maratha Leader and adversary to Aurangzeb) as a treacherous villain. Shibli's book '*Aurang Alamgir Par Aik Nazar*' published in 1909 is one such example. Shibli and the scholars of his ilk had a great influence on the practice of History writing in Pakistan, particularly on Ishtiaq Hussain Qureshi, Aziz Ahmed and S.M. Ikram who were mostly responsible for infusing all sorts of ideological peculiarities in the general discourse of History in which the magnified images of Ahmed Sirhindi, Aurangzeb and Shah Walli Ullah are highlighted, discarding the regional personalities like Shah Inayat, Khushal Khan Khattak, Dulla Bhatti and Ahmad Khan Kharral as historical non-entities.

Shah Walliullah Dehlvi (1703-1762) is another oft-mentioned personality in the nation wide curriculum and officially prepared textbooks for the students of all levels. He tried to forge unity among the ranks of the Muslim community against Marathas and Sikhs. In a bid to strike unity among Muslims he strived to bridge the existing sectarian gulf between the *Shias* and the *Sunnis*, the two leading sects in the Muslim community, through his scholarly work '*Azala tul Khafa*'. Similarly, he worked towards forging unity among the *Wujudis* and the *Shahudis* who had been at loggerheads, since long. All those efforts of Shah Walliullah were directed to infuse the sense of the 'Self' among the Muslims against the 'Other' that obviously were the Hindu. Though Shah Walliullah was not as rigid in his religious views as Ahmed Sirhindi had been, yet he hardly wanted to see Hindus as the part of Muslim 'Self'. He at the first instance, urged Nizam-ul-Mulk Asif Jah (Chin Qulich Khan) to assume the leadership of the Indian Muslims but he declined and preferred to invest all his efforts and energy in establishing his independent rule in Hyderabad, Deccan. Then after weighing all the available options, Shah Walliullah turned to Rohillas and Ahmed Shah Abadali (the ruler of Afghanistan) and pleaded them to come and rescue Muslims from the impending threat of their subjugation to Hindu Marathas and Sikhs. What he could not conceive, was the possibility of bringing into effect some amicable relationship between the communities living side by side in the Subcontinent for centuries. Another danger, the East India Company was in the process of digging deep in the Subcontinent, escaped his 'overarching' vision. Sahibzada Abdul Rasul pays tribute to Shah Walliullah in one of his books for the undergraduate students of History in these words: 'He was not merely a person but a movement that went from strength to strength with every passing day.'[23] Mazhar Jan-i-Janan,[24] on the contrary, argued in favor of the communal relationship based on mutual trust and understanding. Belonging to the same chain (*silsala i Naqshbandia*) of Sufism Jan-i-Janan could not secure any *niche* in the Pakistani curriculum.

In fact the foremost cause of Mughal/Muslim decline, to Shah Walliullah, was their indifference toward Islam. According to his prognosis, the strict adherence to the tenets of Islam was the only panacea, which could stem the decadence, set in among the Indian Muslims in the early 18th century. Shah Walliullah's endeavors to restore pristine purity to Indian Islam through his books like *Fayuz ul Harmain, Haja tullah el Baligha* and Persian translations of Quran and *Muwatla Imam Malik*, a renowned work of Islamic jurisprudence was an attempt to purge Islam from indigenous adulteration. All such actions aimed at inculcating the sense of distinct identity among the Muslims. Shah Walliullah's legacy sustained by his successors even after his death. His own son, Shah Abdul Aziz, close relative of Syed Ahmed (Shaheed) and Shah Ismael (Shaheed) launched *Jihad Tehrik* during 1830s against the Sikh ruler of the Punjab, Maharaja Ranjit Singh.[25] Those stalwarts had a cherished aim of setting up an Islamic State in the North Western part of the Subcontinent, which was located in close proximity to Afghanistan, Central Asia and Iran, so that the Islamic state could presumably have congenial environment to flourish in the midst of a Muslim country. That utopian state met its inevitable fate at the hands of the European General of the Sikh army at Balakot (presently in NWFP) in 1832.[26] *Mujahideen's* debacle was precipitated by their own misreading of the situation that had led to 'treachery' of the local Pathan population who was irate over puritanical religious practices, completely at odds with the local culture, imposed by the *Mujahideen* through coercive means.

Shah Walli Ullah remained within the sight of Muslim religious scholars but his contribution for the Muslims attained eminence when Obaid Ullah Sindhi, in his book *Shah Walli Ullah Ke Siasi Tehreek* reinterpreted his role as a Muslim reformer, whose ideas were absolutely in conjunction with the changing realities of time and space. Obaid Ullah Sindhi had visualized the impact that the Bolshevik Revolution could invoke in British India. So, he tried to trace all such revolutionary thoughts regarding politics and economy, epitomized in the Bolshevik ideology of the 20th century, in the works of Shah Walliullah. Therefore, he was made into a thinker who had already suggested almost the same prescription for the social and economic injustice that Marx and Engle could think of more than a hundred years later. That is how Shah Walli Ullah was made to resurface as a larger than life Muslim reformer who waged a holy war against the natural process of indigenization of Islam and that is the reason he found space in Pakistani textbooks. Again Aziz Ahmed, S.M. Ikram and I.H. Qureshi made him popular enough and Sheikh Rafique, Shahibzada Abdur Rasul, Riaz ul Huda and Ikram Rabbani successfully used him for the indoctrination of the youth, through their textbooks.

2

The same tradition manifested once again in the form of the *Deoband* movement in Uttar Pardesh (UP) in 19th century when Rashid Ahmed Gangohi and Qasim Nanotvi established *Dar Ul Ulum Deoband*[27] (in the year 1866) with an expressed purpose of rejuvenating the traditional religious instruction which had come close enough to the verge of complete extinction in the face of fast emerging modern institutions either set up by the Colonial State itself or sponsored a few to work as its agency like Muhammadan Anglo Oriental College Aligarh (established in 1877 by Sir Syed Ahmed Khan, MAO College Aligarh was awarded University status in 1920). *Dar ul Ulum Deoband* exhorted Muslims of India to revive the pristine traditions to influence Muslim renaissance so that the lost glory could be retrieved. Quite conversely, MAO College stood for inculcating loyalty among the Indian Muslims for the Colonial masters. Sir Syed Ahmed Khan had disdainfully condemned all those Muslims who fought against the British in the War of Independence (1857) and used the epithet of bastard (*Haramzada*)[28] for them. Because of his unflinching faith in the viability of the British system based on rationalism, he earned the title of *naturee*. Sir Syed Ahmed Khan staunchly believed in western education as the only way for the down and out Muslims to secure respectability. He envisioned the role of the Muslim elite as central to lead their co-religionists out of dire straits. He also stressed upon Muslims to abstain from joining any political party, particularly Indian National Congress (founded by British, member of bureaucracy A.O Hume in 1885) lest they should incur the wrath of British rulers. He stressed that instead of dabbling in politics, Muslims must concentrate on getting Modern education so that they could notch up Government jobs and by becoming a cog in the all-powerful imperial machine, they would be in a position to cancel out Hindu domination. In the following days, acquiring education for securing government job, became a passion with the Muslims, leading to the emergence of

Muslim *salariat* in North India which according to Hamza Alvi (1921–2003), acted as a catalyst in driving the wedge between Hindus and Muslims on the question of representation in public services and legislative bodies. Till the early 1940s, All India Muslim League represented Muslim salariat almost unequivocally, however, for political expediency it switched its policy in favor of landlords—the only factor that could ensure electoral success.

Sir Syed Ahmed Khan, galvanized Muslims to take a separatist course but unlike his predecessors (Ahmed Sirhindi, Aurangzeb and Shah Walliullah for whom the reference point was puritanical tradition rooted in Arabian Islam with its emphasis on *Shariah*), Sir Syed referred to the Muslim identity nurtured in Indo-Persian tradition which he further wanted to complement with the Western modernity set in motion by the British who, according to him, were closer to the Muslims as they too 'are the holders of the book'. The only commonality he had with the above-mentioned personalities was his construction of the Hindus as the 'Other'. However, Sir Syed's point of reference was culture, punctuated with Persian tradition rather than puritan Islam. Consequently, the process of the 'Othering' of the Hindus got under way, in Sir Syed's time, when Urdu-Hindi controversy was occasioned at Benaras in 1867. Urdu, afterwards, became the most significant symbol articulating the separatist Muslim identity viz-a-viz Hindus in particular and other communities in general. That was the reason Urdu was accorded the status of the national language of Pakistan after 1947, the fact resented by all the nationalities but the Punjabis, living in Pakistan. Moreover, it became one of the major causes for the Bengalis to opt out of Pakistan in 1971, in fact the apprehension about their culture being put at stake at the altar of Urdu began just after Pakistan came into being. Even to this day, the issue of Urdu as the National Language is quite problematic. The Sindhis, Baluchis, Pathans and even Saraikis perceive it as an instrument of cultural coercion employed by the centrist forces to enforce homogenized identity at the expense of their own languages. According to the Census Report 1998, the mother tongue of 7 per cent of Pakistan's population is Urdu[29]. Elevated to the status of a national language of the country or not, must not obscure from us an important point with respect to the waning practical value of it. Now the globalization is the buzzword that has given rise to the fear of cultural homogenization at the expense of local traditions. Consequently, a large number of people were getting ready for the impending challenge that globalization is expected to pose. In this context, they are led to believe that the key to success lies with the English language. This realization has struck at the very roots of local and National languages particularly in the third world and Urdu is no exception. So, the future of Urdu, once the symbol of singular identity, is very much in doldrums.[30]

Ironically, in the second decade of the 20th century, the Muslim *Ulema* who were staunch followers of Ahmed Sirhindi and Shah Walli Ullah's religious persuasion had become politically active in support of Indian National Congress against the British Colonial rulers. Separatist Muslim identity ceased to be their primary concern. That task was taken up by the 'not-so-religious' Muslim League, comprising mostly of Muslims, educated in Western institutions. Pakistan was the realization of endeavors of that moderate class of Muslims, bred and nurtured in the tradition of modernity and Islam was merely used as a slogan to achieve that end.

In the textbooks, Iqbal is mentioned as the major ideologue (*Mufakir*) who envisioned the creation of Pakistan, which was articulated in his Allahabad Address at the annual meeting of the All India Muslim League in 1930. However, if the full text of Iqbal's address is read, one does not find any such thing as a separate Islamic state for the Muslims of North West India[31]. Despite that Iqbal is designated as the redeemer of Muslims in the textbooks. 'Iqbal while presiding over the Muslim League meeting at Allahabad in 1930, not only elucidated the concept of an Islamic State but also made it the common objective of the whole Muslim *Umma*.'[32]

But the fact remains that in his letters to Jinnah during 1930s, he vehemently pleaded for a separate state for the Muslims because they were a different 'nation' *viz-a-viz* Hindus. But Iqbal's concept of a 'nation' was different from that prevailing in the West. Nevertheless, the ideas of Pan-Islamism and Nationalism seem ambiguously entwined. Iqbal on the one hand unleashes trenchant criticism against Western notions like democracy, nationalism, etc., but on the other hand advocates delegation of the power to do *ijtahad* to the elected parliament. All said and done, Iqbal seems to be groping for some alternative to modernity but ends up suggesting an obtuse system of thought which may pass for its modern content but he also wanted Islam's Renaissance.

Iqbal as a thinker was essentially modernist who tried to re-define Islam in the light of Western epistemology and ascribed new meaning to it in his book *Reconstruction of Religious Thought in Islam.* Unlike typical religious ulema, he was educated from the institutions like Government College Lahore, University of Cambridge and University of Munich (Germany). The people that he drew inspiration from were Rumi, Sanai, Hegel, Nietzsche, Bergson, Milton and Goethe. Obviously, none of them are known for their deep understanding of Islam. Besides, he thought of bringing about revival of Islam by infusing in them dynamism that would be achieved through *Mard-i-Momin* (Supreme Man, a category, many believe Iqbal has borrowed from Nietzsche) who would be endowed with an attribute of *Khudi,* (ego) another borrowed category from a Western thinker, Fichte. Conclusively speaking, Iqbal, like people mentioned above, was convinced that Islam and other faiths existing in India were mutually exclusive, therefore he treaded the separatist path upholding modernist thought, with the aid of tradition.

3

The fact that deserves special mention here is about the treatment of the British rulers in the textbooks of Pakistan Studies, History and Political Science. The colonial experience and its overall repercussions are conspicuously absent from the main educational discourse and the communalist angle seems to be overemphasized. Therefore, Pakistani Academia is mostly singled out in the international intellectual circuit where Post Colonial discourse is reigning supreme particularly in the realms of social science and humanities and concepts like the 'Two Nation Theory' and 'Ideology of Pakistan' are not taken very seriously. Quite conversely, in Pakistan the problems of the state or the society are addressed not with any reference to the Colonial legacy or still well entrenched colonial structures. Instead problems are understood and mostly their solution sought, with reference to the conveniently presumed 'conspiracy of the eternal foes, the Hindus' against Pakistan, whose existence they have not yet accepted. Similarly, a very important question as to the impact of Colonial/Oriental persuasion on the Muslims of India had hardly been brought to focus in Pakistani educational discourse. Such mindset does not allow the villains of Colonialism to be properly studied and analyzed.

In the early decades of the 19th century, the Indian past was constructed from the vantage point of the British colonial masters that, obviously had been an outsider's view. By then, the British paramountcy was firmly established. Therefore, the colonialists found themselves in an enviable position to reformulate Indian History that had a profound bearing on the epistemic collective self of the Muslims. James Mill in his two-volume book, 'The History of India' published in 1818, reformulated the periodisation of Indian past, dividing it into Hindu, Muslim and British periods. Most of the History books produced in Pakistan follow the same pattern, set by James Mill and his likes. Similarly Elliot and Dowson produced multi volume works of Indian History by the name of 'History of India as told by its own Historians', in which Muslims and Hindus are portrayed as two completely different people. Muslim rulers of medieval times are projected as bigoted tyrants with utter disregard for other religious persuasions. Such constructions not only cultivated communal dissensions between the two communities but also provided epistemic and ideological prop to the idea of monolithic Muslim identity subsequently championed by the centrist forces in Pakistan.

In the second half of the 19th century, modern methods like print, postal service, railways, and telegraph worked amazingly to generate cohesion among the people on religious grounds. Pamphlets, tracts and newspapers, despite their utility, fanned the feelings of being different, among the followers of different religions.[33] The localized responses started to turn out into issues of national significance. The onset of electoral process in India by the British in 1883, in the days of Lord Rippon provided further impetus to the formation of separatist Muslim identity.

The creation of Muslim League in 1906 and the emergence of Muhammad Ali Jinnah as its leader and eventually 'The Sole Spokesman' of the Indian Muslim, was in fact a response to the circumstance conjured into existence by modernity. Muslim League was a political party with a modernist agenda and aims and Jinnah always talked in modernist terms. However, tradition was used to muster support from the people, whose majority could only appreciate the traditional idiom. So, Islam came into play. One can quote his presidential address to the 27th annual meeting of All India Muslim League in which Pakistan Resolution was passed:

> The Hindus and the Muslims belong to two different religious philosophies, social customs, and literature. They neither marry, nor interdine together, and indeed they belong to two different civilizations which are based mainly on conflicting ideas and conceptions. Their aspects on life and of life are different.[34]

From above quoted excerpt, Jinnah, the ambassador of the Hindu-Muslim Unity of 1910s seems to have traveled quite a distance on the separatist path. At that juncture he wants a separate state for the Muslims because they are the 'Other' of the Hindu majority. Jinnah wanted a modern nation state for the Muslims of India as exemplified in his speech to the Constituent Assembly on 11 August 1947 that stands in utter contrast to his speech on 23 March 1947. While addressing the Constituent Assembly Jinnah said:

> You may belong to any religion or caste or creed—that has nothing to do with the business of the state...We are starting with this fundamental principle that we are all citizens and equal citizens of one state... Now, I think we should keep that in front of us as our ideal and you will find that in the course of time Hindus would cease to be Hindus and Muslims would cease to be Muslims, not in the religious sense, because that is the personal faith of each individual but in the political sense as citizens of the state[35].

Hence, one can safely conclude that Jinnah and League used Islam as a means to an end but it became an end in itself, the sole determinant of Pakistani identity, at least in textbooks and academic institutions.

Notes

1. Bill Ashcraft, Gareth Griffiths and Helen Tiffins, in key concepts in Post-Colonial Studies quote Timothy Brennan saying, 'As for the 'nation' it is both historically determined and general. As a term, it refers both to the modern nation-state and to something more ancient and nebulous-the 'natio'a local community, domicile, family, condition of belongs. The distinction is often obscured by nationalists who seek to place their own country in an immemorial past' where its arbitrariness cannot be questioned. And the French Orientalist Ernest Renan, in his lecture at the Sorboune, reminded his audience of the beginning of the idea of a nation: 'Nations... are something fairly new in history. Antiquity was unfamiliar with them; Egypt, China and Ancient Chaldea were in no way nations. They were flocks led by a Son of the Sun or by a Son of Heaven. Neither in Egypt nor in China were there citizens as such. Classical antiquity had republics and empires, yet it can hardly be said to have had nations in our understanding of the term.' (Routlege, London and New York; 1998, pp. 149–155.) For greater detail see Eric Hobsbawm, *Nations and Nationalism since 1780*, Cambridge University Press, 1997, pp. 9–13.
2. 'The term 'modern' derives from the last fifth century Latin term moderns which was used to distinguish an officially Christian present from a Roman, pagan. 'Modern' was used in the medieval period to distinguish the contemporary from the 'ancient' past. But 'modernity' has come to mean more than 'the here and now': it refers to modes of social organization that emerged in Europe from about the sixteenth century and extended their influence throughout the world in the wake of European exploration and colonization. Three momentous cultural shifts around the year 1500—the discovery of the 'new world', the Renaissance and the Reformation—had, by the eighteenth century, come to constitute 'the epochal threshold between modern times and the middle age', it is taken from J. Habermas, *Modernity versus Postmodernity*, New German Critique 22 quoted in Ashcroft, Gareth Griffiths and Helen Tiffens, pp. 144–147.
3. Nayyar, A.H. and Salim, Ahmad, *The Subtle Subversions, The State of Curricula of Textbooks in Pakistan*, Islamabad: Sdpi, p. 3.
4. Ali, Mubarak, 'Hero Prasti aur Muashra,'*Badalti Dunyan*, Karachi, March, 2004.
5. Rafique, Shaikh, *Mutaala-i-Pakistan for Intermediate*, Lahore: Fahad Publishing House
6. Sir Syed Ahmed Khan was the most important Muslim leader in the subcontinent in the second half of the nineteenth century. Born in a Syed family of Iranian origin, Sir Syed Ahmed Khan rose up as Muslim reformer and educationist. Muhammadan Anglo-Oriental College at Aligarh was his greatest contribution. For further details about him see, QURESHI, Ishtiaq Hussain (ed.), *A Short History of Pakistan*, University of Karachi, 1988, pp. 804-810.
7. His full name was Shaikh Ahmed Sarhindi of Faruqi al-Naqshbandi. He was born in 1562–63 (971 A.H.) His father, Shaikh Abdul ul Ahad, was a well-known scholar and theologian. In his early age he joined the *Qadiriyah Silsilah* under the discipleship of an accomplished mystic, Shah Kamal. His father taught him not only the subjects then included in the formal disciplines of education, but also trained him as a mystic in the *Chishtiyah Silsilah* and then gave him permission to accept others as his own disciples. At the age of 17, he had completed his education and made rapid strides in mystic attainments. Later, he joined the *Naqshbandi Silsilah* under the guidance of Kawajah Baqi-billah of Delhi, who thought highly of his spiritual capacities from the very beginning. Then he embarked upon his mission of bringing about a renaissance of Islam. The point he emphasized was the superiority of Shariah over tariqah. Because of his puritanical views, he was imprisoned by Jahangir in 1618 and released in the next year. He died on 29 November 1624 (1024 A.H.) and was buried in Sirhind. Qureshi, Ishtiaq Hussain, *The Muslim Community of the Indo-Pakistan*, Karachi: Ma'aref Limited, 1977, p. 167.
8. The sixth Mughal Emperor (1659–1707), third son of Shah Jahan (1627–59) and the last of the Greater Mughal Kings. Bhattacharya, Sachchidananda, *A Dictionary of Indian History*, New York: George Braziller, 1967, pp. 81–85.
9. Shah Waliullah was born in 1703. His father Shah Abdul Rahim was reputed theologian at Dehli. Shah Waliullah was trained and tutored by his own father. At a very tender age he visited Hejaz (1731–32). On his return, he found the Mughal Empire tottering in the face of Maratha power. He invited Ahmad Shah Abdali to come and crush Maratha power and stem the tide of the Marhathas. Afghan king came to India, and defeated Marahattas in Third battle of Panipat in 1761 but that battle could ward off the impending downfall of the Mughals. He bitterly lamented the negligence of the Muslims towards Jihad. He thought it Muslim's duty to revive the spirit of Jihad amongst the Muslim. Wasti, Razi, *Biographical Dictionary of South Asia*, Lahore: United Ltd., 1980, p. 495.
10. The word 'Umma' is derived from the Arabic word 'Umm', meaning mother. According to Hughes, Thomas Patrick, *A Dictionary of Islam*, Lahore: Premier Book House, p. 655, the word 'Umma' has been used for 'A people, a nation, a sect.' That word occurs about forty times in the Quran.

11. Madni, Hussain Ahmed and Iqbal, Illama, *Nazria-i-Qaumiat*, Dera Ghazi Khan: Kutab Khana Siddiqia, pp. 4 –31
12. Qureshi, Saleem (ed.), *Jinnah, The Founder of Pakistan*, Karachi: Oxford University Press, 1998, pp. 82–97.
13. Wahdatu-l-Wujud is a pantheistic sect of Sufis, who say that everything is God, and of the same essence. As Dara Shikoh used to interpret 'There is nothing but God' as against 'There is no god but God' as professed by Ahmed Sirhindi. Thomas Patrick, p. 659.
14. Vedenta is a collective designation for the philosophy of the Upanishads, which are an integral part of the Vedas. Literally the term means the end or goal of the Vedas. Chargya, Sachchidananda Bhatta, p. 833.
15. Qureshi, I. H., p. 175.
16. Javaid, Qazi, 'Baresaghir Mein Muslim Fikr ka Irteqa,' *Lahore Nigarshat*, 1986, p. 135.
17. Wolpert, Stanley, *Jinnah of Pakistan*, Karachi: Oxford University, 1993, p. 18 and Ahmad, Syed Nur, *Martial Law say Martial Law Tek*, Lahore: Darul Kitab, p. 53.
18. Wolpert, *Mutaal-i-Pakistan for Intermediate*, Lahore: Fahad Publishing House, 2003, p. 14.
19. Ibid.
20. *Fatawa-i-Alamgiri, A Book of Jurisprudence* composed at the will of Aurangzeb. Father of Shah Waliullah was among the group of those who put it together.
21. Azad, Maulana Abul Kalam, *Tazkera*, Lahore, reprinted 1999, pp. 37–42.
22. He was born in 1851. He taught Arabic at Aligarh 1882–98, wrote many books and was a prominent leader of Nadwat ul Ulema. He died in 1914. Razi Wasti, p. 35.
23. *Tehrik-i-Pakistan for Bachelors in History*, Lahore: M.R. Brothers Urdu Bazar, 1972, p. 62.
24. His real name was Shams ud Din Habibullah. He was Shah Walliullah's contemporary. Unlike other scholars from Naqshbandi order, he abstained from condemning Hindus as outright 'Kufar'. For more details, see Ikram, Sheikh Muhammad, *Rud-i-Kausar*, Lahore: Idara-i-Saqafat-i-Islamia, 1988, pp. 645–649.
25. Ranjit Singh (1780–1839) was the founder of a Sikh Kingdom in the Punjab. He ruled Punjab from 1778-1839. For details see SINGH, Khushwant, *Ranjit Singh- Maharaja of the Punjab*, London: George Allen and Union Ltd., 1962.
26. Sindhi, Obaid Ullah, *Shah Walliullah Aur Un Ki Siabi Tehrik*, Lahore: Sindh Sagar Academy, 2002, pp. 77-95.
27. Metcalf, Barbara Daly, *Islamic Revival in British India- Deoband 1860-1900*, New Delhi: Oxford University Press, 1982, pp. 87–136.
28. Qureshi, Muhammad Farooq, 'Jawab-e-Aan Ghazal Aqeeda Ya Siyasi Hikmat-e-Amli,' *Wali Khan aur Qarardad-e-Pakistan*, Lahore: Fiction House, 1997, p. 362.
29. Government Of Pakistan, *Census Report of Pakistan 1998*, Census Publication no. 160, Islamabad: Population Census Organization, Statistics Division, December 2001.
30. Rahman, Tariq, *Language and Politics in Pakistan*, Karachi: OUP, 1997, pp. 228–248.
31. The full text of Iqbal's Allahabad address can be read in Chaudhary, Zahid Chaudhary, *Pakistan Ki Syasi Tarikhn- Muslim Punjab Ka Syasi Irtika*, Hassan Jaffer Zaidi, (ed.), Lahore: Dara tul Mutalia-e-Tarikh, 1991, pp. 395–417.
32. Rafique, Sheikh, p. 41.
33. Robinson,Francis, 'Islam and the Impact of Print in South Asia,' *Islamabad Muslim History in South Asia*, New Delhi: Oxford University Press, 2000, pp. 66–104.
34. Pirzada, Sharifuddin, *Foundation of Pakistan*, Vol.11, Karachi: National Publishing House, 1970, p. 338.
35. Munir, Muhammad, *From Jinnah to Zia*, Lahore: Vanguard Books, 1979, pp. 29–30.

13

1971: HISTORICAL FALSEHOODS IN OUR TEXTBOOKS

*Ahmad Salim**

ABSTRACT

Pakistani textbooks either simply omit that period (1971), or foster the image of India as the main culprit. The ambiguous and vague term, 'political crisis', is used to describe the events of1971. The entire history of the treatment of East Pakistan as a colony, state oppression, exploitation and the role of the army is omitted. Some textbooks do try to explain it, however they shift the blame onto India. India is portrayed as the instigator of this 'rebellion'. Moreover, such explanations usually contain one or two lines about being vigilant and 'being ready to face the enemy by receiving military training'. Sheikh Mujib is mentioned in derogatory terms and he is generally portrayed as a conspirator.

The textbooks in Bangladesh, on the other hand, show the Awami League as struggling for freedom right from its inception. They portray Pakistan's central government as the villain. While this portrayal is closer to the truth, the fact nevertheless remains, that textbooks, in both the countries, tend to wipe out contradictions and present one-sided views.

*Ahmad Salim is a poet, journalist, keeper of public records and research worker. He works at the Sustainable Development Policy Institute as Director Urdu Publications and as Research Associate.

INTRODUCTION

Right from the realization of independence of Pakistan in August 1947, the state has failed to support the cause of a scientific and secular approach to history and the vision of a comprehensive people's past. The educational system could not hold a firm position on free enquiry, and suffered suppression. Consequently, the tendency towards introduction of unscientific and parochial concepts, along with the provision of inaccurate information and concealment of facts from people in text books and syllabi started taking root.

During the martial law of 1958, the government adopted controversial measures in an attempt to impose a disturbingly one-sided view of history about Pakistan's making. Other state governments have introduced similar changes in text books and syllabi, imposing their own versions of social cults and concepts, false ideas and historical inaccuracies through official fiats. In fact, numerous states benefit from the fact that education is a value-laden, moral activity because it provides a design for living.

State Dominant Ideologies—A Theoretical Framework

Formal education exists as both a process and a product. An important dimension of education includes an analysis of the way in which the educational process is influenced by the various social forces operating in civil society and its translation into policies, curricula, textbooks, school organization and school ideology. Educational aims do not exist in isolation, insulated from the domain of values and ideologies. Rather, certain values and ideologies historically become dominant, mature and develop as a current discourse, wherein education becomes an ideological apparatus for its dissemination.

In the context of the capitalist state, the various naturalizing mechanisms resorted to in order to establish the legitimacy of the capitalist logic are not unknown. Bowles and Gintis, Michael Apple, Bourdieu have discussed the manner in which the educational system provides an ideological basis for the sustenance of the political economy of capitalism. In 'Education and Power', Michael Apple argues that the way in which the form and content of education are instrumental in the continuous generation of the hegemonic ideology and creation of an active consensus constitutes an aspect of the state. 'Schools help maintain privilege in cultural ways by taking the form and content of the culture and knowledge of the powerful groups and defining it as legitimate knowledge to be preserved and passed on.'[1] Apple refers to three aspects of school as being instrumental in this process. Firstly, the day-to-day interactions and regularities of the hidden curriculum that tacitly teaches important norms and values, secondly, the overt curriculum itself and thirdly, the mediating role of teachers in its transmission and their perspectives.

The cultural mechanism of transmission of ruling class interest through education serves as a hegemonic device. Under the concept of 'culture capital', the worldview, languages, values, attitudes, socialisation patterns, behaviour patterns and the entire way of life of the middle class coincides with that of the school. Hence, the school reproduces the middle class culture and values and thus reinforces the habitués learnt at home. This further gets extended into the political and social life and a similar successful career follows.[2] The school system, thus, confirms and upholds one kind of knowledge and culture (of the dominant classes) as against the other (of the manual workers and lower classes) which subsequently is assigned an inferior status. Knowledge and culture are thereby rendered as tools for the exercise of power.

A number of dimensions of the educational process derive from the framework of social relations:

> The pupils are collected in classroom group so that they may be taught certain data. They are checked and corrected in ways to see that they have done the work and this is the manifest content of the classroom. Behind this obvious appearance, there is the routine of attendance, punctuality, self-submergence to authority, the silence of the class, the recognition of hierarchy, prefects, teachers and head teachers. These factors represent the latent content, the underlying effect of the organization of the school. Active learning represents the manifest content of schoolwork. The latent content is represented by passive learning, the habits, the data, attitudes picked up through constant, familiar steady contact with a state of affairs we do not have to think about.[3]

Thus, the political role of education that seeks to serve the interest of a particular section in society has been theoretically well established. The ideological function of education in the creation and establishment of a certain worldview that orients an individual towards pre-planned rationality becomes evident. Both the formal and informal mechanisms at the disposal of the school achieve this. However, there also exists a theoretical strand in parallel, which recognizes the autonomous individual space which could resist the imposition of a worldview, not coinciding with the habitués.

> Culture is, however, both subject and object of resistance; the driving force of culture is contained not only in how it functions to dominate subordinate groups, but also in the way in which oppressed groups draw from their own cultural capital and set of experiences to develop an oppositional logic.[4]

The resistance school of thought focuses on the role of the human agency as an active participant, in the process of acceptance or non-acceptance of all symbolic domination.

Evidently, the educational process, is created by both the exercised and the exercisers of power, and exists due to human effort at its social creation. State dominant ideologies are transmitted within educational process and they influence their subjects to a great extent. Hence, the process creates and recreates a particular form of social and cultural dynamics.

Pakistan, being a post-colonial state, presents an example of intensified dissemination of state dominant ideologies. The concept of irreligious, amoral, secular education was an artificial creation of the British colonialism for experimentation on the soil of the colonized, when their education had strong moral and religious undertones. In fact, an important fear was cultural hostility and reaction of the natives. Therefore, classical humanistic education was encouraged that required a strictly disciplinary approach to fields of knowledge. The suggested method of education was based more on memorization, rote learning i.e. sounds rather than meaning. The missionaries were critical of such pedagogical methods and curriculum content. They believed that education, without its moral content would be misleading.

> According to the missionary argument, to a man in a state of ignorance of moral law, literature was patently indifferent to virtue. Far from cultivating moral feelings, a wide reading was more likely to cause him to question moral law more closely and perhaps even encourage him to deviate from its dictates.[5]

There was an implicit nexus between the Christian missionaries and the colonial state. Both had an agenda which consisted of evangelistic ambitions, mutually harboured, though for different reasons. While the missionaries aspired for preaching and expanding the influence of the Gospel, the colonial state saw it as a hegemonizing mechanism that would secure English domination.

In fact, Pakistan could not be completely treated as a post-colonial state as the British colonialism translated into West Pakistan's colonialism over East Pakistan.

East Pakistan: A Colony of West Pakistan

The Pakistani leaders failed to frame a constitution and it was not before 1956 that a constitution was eventually framed only to be scrapped by the army which came to power in 1958. Interestingly, the politics centred around personalities in Pakistan and the importance of an office increased or decreased with the importance of the person who held it. Thus, after Jinnah's death, the office of Prime Minister became more important than that of the Governor-General. After the assassination of Prime Minister Liaqat Ali Khan, Khawaja Nazimuddin became Prime Minister of Pakistan and Ghulam Mohammad became the Governor-General. A man of boundless ambition, he began to work on Jinnah's precedent and taking advantage of Nazimuddin's weak personality, cleverly tried to build up his power. Since he did not have any political background, he leaned heavily on the civil services and the army dominated by the Punjabis. Politics in Pakistan had degenerated into intrigue. The ruling clique which was predominantly West Pakistani in composition, maintained itself in power by playing one group against the other, ('divide and rule') using the name of Islam for political purposes. Throughout this period East Pakistan was being exploited for the benefit of West Pakistan. A sense of deprivation and frustration began to develop among the Bengalis. It was out of this feeling that Bangladeshi nationalism was born. But there was a long period of groping before that phenomenon had taken shape. A new sense of awareness regarding East Bengal's separate political, economic, and cultural identity had begun to manifest itself at the time of the language controversy between 1948 and 1952. The break-up of the old Muslim league and the emergence of the Awami League signified a new development in the political life of Pakistan. The hold of religion on politics was weakening and politics leaned towards the secular. In 1949, the Awami Muslim League was founded and soon afterwards, secular organizations, such as Youth League and Ganatantri Dal were established. In 1955, the Awami Muslim League dropped the denomination 'Muslim' from its name. In the provincial elections of 1954 the Muslim League party suffered a humiliating defeat in East Pakistan. Besides the Awami League, two other secular political parties, viz. the Krishak Sramik Party and the National Awami Party made their appearance. The Communist Party though banned in Pakistan also increased its underground activities. The Pakistani ruling circles dominated by the army, the bureaucracy and big businesses were alarmed at these new developments. The dismissal of Fazlul Huq ministry in 1954, the establishment of One Unit in West Pakistan in 1956 and the imposition of martial law in 1958 were all parts of the same process to curb democratic and progressive forces in the country. In 1962, President Ayub Khan imposed an authoritarian constitution and instituted a system of so-called 'Basic Democracy'. Pakistan was virtually a dictatorship under a democratic garb. The National Assembly had little power, the independence of the judiciary was severely curtailed and the executive was made all-powerful. The Bengalis began to feel that only through a system of parliamentary democracy based on adult franchise and direct elections could they expect to get their due share in the administration of the country.[6]

By 1966, under the leadership of Sheikh Mujib-ur-Rehman, the Awami League had emerged as the national platform of the people of East Pakistan. The Six Points formulated by the

Awami League represented a program for political and economic development within a broad democratic framework.

The elections held in December 1970 demonstrated clearly that the people were overwhelmingly behind the secular political program of the Awami League. The Muslim League and the religious parties like the Jamaat-i-Islami were totally rejected by the electorate. The ruling military circles of Pakistan which had so long been exploiting the people by appealing to their religious sentiments got unnerved. They were unwilling to accept the reality of the situation. On 25 March 1971 the Pakistan army attacked the Bengali population. Gruesome genocide occurred, and it shocked the conscience of the world. Bengalis resisted the armed invasion. The war of national liberation had started which culminated in the creation of independent Bangladesh.[7]

All these socio-political developments in the region continued to be projected in the educational process. However, the situation intensified shortly after the tragedy of 1971, which was maliciously projected and propagated through the Pakistani educational system.

PAKISTANI TEXTBOOKS

The official textbooks of Pakistan present state-dominant ideologies and hegemonic views, with history rewritten to the point of complete distortion. The material in school textbooks is directly opposed to the goals and values of a 'progressive, moderate and democratic' Pakistan. The most significant problems in the current curriculum and textbooks include inaccuracies of facts and omissions that serve to substantially distort the nature and significance of actual events in the history of Pakistan. The curriculum could lead to incitement of militancy and violence, including encouragement of *jehadi* elements and perspectives that encourage prejudice, bigotry and discrimination towards fellow citizens, especially women, religious minorities and other nations.

In the textbooks of History, Social Studies and Pakistan Studies, students up to the matric level are not only fed on distorted versions of history, but also failed if they deviate from the textbooks. There is no attempt at self-criticism and no reference to the havoc caused by the military dictatorship. In the textbooks about the history of Pakistan, there is not a single paragraph that mentions the political developments in and around 1971 in a serious way. The Pakistan Studies for class IX-X states in this regard: 'After the elections the country faced a political crises which resulted in the separation of East Pakistan from the rest of the country.'[8] No wonder even educated adults do not know the truth behind the country's dismemberment in 1971 and are unable to diagnose correctly the sickness that has overtaken today's Pakistan. The same book on page 241, defines the relations of Pakistan with Bangladesh:

> Before December, 1971 Bangladesh was a part of Pakistan and was called East Pakistan. Pakistan recognised Bangladesh as an independent country in February, 1974 on the occasion of second Islamic Summit Conference.'

The emergence of Bangladesh as a sovereign, independent state represented the greatest tragedy that can befall any state. In our case the disaster of 1971 has persuaded us neither to examine our political ideals and practices nor to learn the obvious lessons. This is amply proved by, among other things, what Pakistani school children are told about the dismemberment of Pakistan. One of the textbooks in Punjab province says:

After the 1965 war, India, with the help of Hindus living in East Pakistan instigated the people living there against the people of West Pakistan and at last, in December 1971, herself invaded East Pakistan. The conspiracy resulted in the separation of East Pakistan from us. All of us should receive military training and be prepared to fight the enemy.

Pakistan Studies or civics is a subject our children study from class I to the highest course. In most institutions, children in classes I to IV are not told about the Pakistan that existed before December 1971. The books on Pakistan Studies prescribed by our textbook board for these classes contain no reference to East Bengal's separation. It is in the book for class five that we find a reference to the event in the following words:

> The war of 1971: After the 1965 war, Bharat, with the help of Hindus living in East Pakistan, invited the people of that province against the people of West Pakistan. Finally it (India) invaded East Pakistan in December 1971. The result of this conspiracy was that in December 1971 East Pakistan separated from us. All of us should be ready to face the enemy after receiving military training.[9]

This is how children are initiated into the conspiracy theory by an external enemy and subversion by Hindu citizens. And the remedy against political failure is to get military training. The impression created by the few half-truths reproduced above put a child on a path that leads him further and further away from a rational understanding of history and politics. The civics books for classes six and seven again ignore the separation of East Bengal. In the textbook for class eight we notice a passing reference to the event in the discussion on constitutional developments. This is what we find:

> After Ayub Khan, Yahya Khan assumed power. During his tenure the country had a general election. In East Pakistan (now Bangladesh) Awami League and in West Pakistan, Pakistan People's Party scored notable success. But before power could be transferred, East Pakistan fell a victim to Bharat's conspiracy and was separated form Pakistan.[10]

The matric textbook, which contains no index, makes no mention at all of Bangladesh. The events of 1971 are referred to in two sentences on pages 66 and 67 and the matter is referred to as a 'political crises' and a 'national catastrophe' which 'resulted in the separation of East Pakistan from the rest of the country.'[11]

Evidently, these books contain omissions related to events leading to the 1971 war and the systematic policy of keeping Bengalis out of power, which played a key role in the respective crises.[12]

The Pakistan Studies textbook for classes 9 and 10 states in the context of the separation of East Pakistan: 'In 1971 while Pakistan was facing political difficulties in East Pakistan, India helped anti-Pakistan elements and later on attacked Pakistan... As a result of this war in December 1971, the eastern wing of Pakistan separated and appeared as Bangladesh on the world map.'[13]

Similarly in the Social Studies for class six, page 40, the creation of East Pakistan is described in one paragraph and the causes are attributed to internal and external factors. The entire history of the treatment of East Pakistan as a colony, the state repression, the role of the army and exploitation is omitted.[14]

The textbook for Pakistan Studies for secondary classes while emphasizing the importance of 'national unity and integration', states: *Pakistanis are fully conscious of the importance of national unity and solidarity. The East Pakistan tragedy in 1970 only deepened these feelings.'*[15] The book proceeds to describe the essential elements of national unity in Pakistan as a separate national identity for Muslims, experiences of foreign rule and the desire to achieve a common goal. The separation of East Pakistan is regarded as a great setback for Pakistan. However, it is mentioned that: 'By 1970, only a few years after the birth of Pakistan, the sentiments for national unity had weakened so much in East Pakistan that it broke away from the mother country.' Among the important causes for this tragedy 'the role of the hostile element in East Pakistan,' and 'role of some foreign powers' is mentioned. The blame is then shifted to the Hindus living in East Pakistan, *'they had never really accepted Pakistan.'* The section is full of similar statements, few are as under:

- 'Some political leaders had deliberately encouraged provincialism for the selfish purpose of gaining power.'
- East Pakistan also had proportionately less representation in the civil and military services of Pakistan.'
- In the 1970 elections the Awami League fully exploited provincialism. It created hatred towards West Pakistan maintaining that all problems of East Pakistan will disappear once it broke away from Pakistan... These leaders had all the blessings of Bharat which hoped to either annex East Pakistan or make it a protégé of its own... Bharat actively supported the Awami League and the anti-Pakistan element. It not only launched an offensive through its press, radio and embassies, but also gave weapons to the anti-Pakistan elements, and later on its regular army attacked East Pakistan.'
- 'Separation of East Pakistan has been a great blow to the people of Pakistan yet it has shown them their weakness and made them conscious of the importance of national solidarity.'[16]

Sheikh Mujib-ur-Rehman is mentioned in derogatory terms in these books and his role is generally projected as that of a conspirator. 'The six points of Sheikh Mujibur Rehman, which envisaged that Pakistan, instead of being a State, should be a federation of States.'[17] The political uprising in East Pakistan is ironically represented in terms of a cyclone and the role of Awami League in helping the affected finds an interesting expression:

Elections were to be held according to schedule on October 5. But unfortunately, coastal areas of East Pakistan were hit by a severe cyclone... Five lac persons were killed and innumerable rendered homeless. The cyclone proved to be the best means for Sheikh Mujibur Rehman to achieve his political ends... Sheikh Mujibur Rehman condemned West Pakistan and tried to create hatred among Bengalis against West Pakistanis.[18]

The crises which preceded the elections of 1970 were totally attributed to Mujib-ur-Rehman and his stand on 'six points.'

On 20 December 1970, Sheikh Mujib-ur-Rehman declared that he would not budge an inch from his 'Six Point' Programme. It meant that the constitution to be framed by Sheikh Mujib-ur-Rehman's Party in the Constituent Assembly, would leave, only Defence and Foreign Affairs for the Federal Government... The two provinces will be regarded two separate 'states.' But West Pakistan was not at all prepared to accept such a constitution... on 1 March 1971, Sheikh Mujib-ur-Rehman issued a call for a general strike. Bloody riots broke out in East Pakistan that very day... On 30 March President Yahya Khan called a Round Table Conference of all political leaders, in which Sheikh Mujib-ur-Rehman refused to participate... he issued a call for Civil Disobedience Movement... As a result of the Civil Disobedience Movement, Awami League mischief mongers acquired control of the Government treasury and other government properties.[19]

One-sided and half hearted arguments on the arrest of Sheikh Mujib-ur-Rehman, the military operation and the consequent Dhaka fall sum up the story. India still dominates the scene.

Sheikh Mujib's arrest and military action in East Pakistan created a furore in the world. Some countries tried to incite the sucessionists. India was in the-vanguard of these countries. India not only aided and abetted the sucessionists, but also raised the bogey of countless refugees entering India for fear of military action, so that it could not stay away from the Bangladesh movement... Indian troops occupied East Pakistan on 16 December 1971 and captured over ninety thousand troops and civilians... Bangladesh (previously East Pakistan) emerged on the map of the world as an independent country.[20]

BANGLADESHI TEXTBOOKS

The Bangladeshi textbooks depict a very different picture regarding the East and West Pakistan crises. Within a year after the creation of Pakistan, *'first clash broke out between the two parts on the issue of language... From 1947 to 1971 East and West Pakistan were together. During these 24 years, the central government showed extreme discrimination towards East Pakistan. This discrimination was mainly demonstrated in the political, economic, military and cultural fields. '*[21] Likewise, the election of 1970 and post election scenario is represented in a very different manner. These books maintain that the Awami League contested the election on the Six-Point Program. The Awami League won absolute majority in the elections of 1970. *'The people of East Pakistan spontaneously voted for Awami League in the hope of the salvation and emancipation from the exploitation of the Pakistanis. '*[22] However, no political party emerged with a clear majority in both East and West Pakistan.

The results of the election considerably influenced the post-election political activities of Pakistan. *'Zulfikar Ali Bhutto, leader of Pakistan People's Party and General Yahya Khan prepared a blue print for not handing over power to Awami League. '*[23] After the election of 1970, the session of the National Assembly was convened on 3 March 1971 in Dhaka. But leader of the majority party in West Pakistan Zulfikar Ali Bhutto, demanded that the six-point program be changed and threatened to boycott the session. *'The ruling clique was indulged in a conspiracy to foil the result of the election i.e. to crush the victory of Bengali leadership. '*[24]

General Yahya Khan announced postponement of the National Assembly on March 1 for an indefinite period. The announcement of postponement of the National Assembly sparked off agitation in East Pakistan. The students and masses came out on to the streets demanding the handing over of power to the elected representatives.

In protest against the announcement Sheikh Mujib called to observe hartal in Dhaka city and throughout the country on 2 and 3 March respectively and the hartal was observed spontaneously... The government deployed military to break down the movement. A number of persons were shot dead by the Army at Joydebpur and the movement was geared up after the killing. To protest this killing Sheikh Mujib-ur-Rahman called for a non-violent civil disobedience movement from a rally held at Paltan Maidan on 3 March which paralysed the central government.[25]

Yahya Khan, at this stage convened a round table conference of the political leaders on March 10. But *Sheikh Mujibur Rahman rejected the invitation saying, 'I am the last person to attend such a conference over the blood of the martyr'*. Seeing the situation totally out of control, General Yahya Khan on March 6 summoned the session of the National Assembly on March 25th. On March 7, Sheikh Mujibur Rahman addressed a mass rally at the Race Course Maidan. He laid down his four preconditions for joining the National Assembly session. The preconditions included the lifting of Martial Law; immediate withdrawal of Army to barracks;

enquiry into the killing of innocent civilians; and transfer of Power to the elected representatives before the session started.

In reality, every chance of reconciliation with the Pakistani rulers became closed. So, Sheikh Mujib-ur-Rahman called upon the countrymen to be prepared for independence and said, 'Build up forts in every house and resist the enemies with whatever you possess.' This struggle is the struggle for emancipation, this struggle is the struggle for independence.

All the government, semi-government offices, courts, mill-factories, educational institutions remained closed at the call of Sheikh Mujib-ur-Rahman's non-cooperation movement creating a deadlock in the administration. The noncooperation movement turned into a violent one. Inspired by the struggle of independence the Bengalis came out in processions, rallies and chanted the slogan: 'Our destiny is Padma, Meghna, Jamuna.' Not Six-Point, but one Point i.e. independence.[26]

General Yahya Khan came to Dhaka on 15 March 1971 and asked Sheikh Mujib-ur-Rahman to sit for discussion. Discussions started on 16 March. The meeting was also attended by Zulfiqar Ali Bhutto and some other leaders from West Pakistan.

> But the chief motive of the leaders from West Pakistan was to kill time instead of negotiations and they utilised time, by bringing ammunition and Pakistani troops to crush the demand of independence of the Bengals as a whole... on the night of 25 March General Yahya Khan left Dhaka with his companions ordering the Pakistani army to attack and kill the unarmed civilians.[27]

The attack was made at different places and towns of the country including Dhaka city, killing hundreds of thousands of Bangalis. On 25 March in the dead of the night, the Pakistani army attacked Sheikh Mujib's house, arrested, and took him to Pakistan the following day. Even without him, the people of Bangladesh stood up stronger than ever. And that was when a new phase began. On 10 April 1971 at Mujibnagar, the elected representatives of Awami League issued the Declaration of Independence and also announced the formation of the Provisional Government.

> The Pakistani army started their attack, setting fire and opening fire indiscriminately in and around Dhaka City. They killed the innocent people and citizens of Dhaka at night when they were in deep sleep. They killed a number of people by attacking the residences of the teachers of Dhaka University and also Zahurul Haq Hall, Salimullah Muslim Hall, Jagannath Hall and the residential areas adjacent to the University campus. Lakhs of people crossed the border to take shelter in India. The youths, students and others taking training started guerrilla fighting from inside the country. In the frontal battle, they were able to bring about the collapse of the Pak army. The people of the country rendered all out help to the liberation forces by offering them food, clothing and shelter. The Pak army became devastated.[28]

The provisional government, after being sworn in, engaged in organizing the War of Independence.

> The freedom fighters joined the Liberation war for liberating the country from the clutches of enemies, even at the cost of their lives... In the beginning of 1971, the India-Bangladesh joint command was formed.[29] From 3-16 December the Pakistani army had to face the joint forces of the Mukti bahini and the Indian army until they became completely defenceless... At last on 16 December 1971 at Suhrawardy Uddyan (Race course Maidan) the Commander of the Pakistani Army General Niazi surrendered with 93 thousand enemy forces and huge quantities of arms and ammunitions. The name of Independent and Sovereign Bangladesh was at last written in the map of the world in letters of blood.[30]

An insight into Pakistani textbooks reveals that the omissions, misrepresentation of facts and promulgation of state-dominated ideologies has led to a complete distortion of historical facts. On the contrary, Bangladeshi textbooks project a comparatively close representation of facts. But, ironically, these facts are presented in a way that suits Bangladesh's state ideology. The question is, if textbooks of both the countries present different versions of the facts, then where is the truth? For instance, the Pakistani textbooks, in general, project that the 1971 war occurred because of India, which, after the 1965 war, with the help of Hindus living in East Pakistan, invited the people of that province against the people of West Pakistan. Finally India invaded East Pakistan in December 1971. The result of this 'conspiracy' was that in December 1971, East Pakistan separated from West Pakistan. However, the Bangladeshi textbooks maintain that General Yahya Khan's visit, along with leaders from West Pakistan, to Dhaka on 15 March 1971 and subsequent discussions with Sheikh Mujib-ur-Rahman were not aimed at resolving the crises. But the chief motive of the leaders from West Pakistan was to kill time instead, and they utilised this time by bringing ammunition and Pakistani troops to crush the civil rights of Bengalis. At his departure from Dhaka on the night of 25 March General Yahya Khan ordered the Pakistani army to attack and kill the unarmed civilians.

On the other hand, the areas where both the states are not in conflict, e.g. the past glory of Muslims and the Islamic invasions in the subcontinent, the facts are presented almost in similar perspective. But the conflicts in state ideologies e.g. Pakistan's regret over the loss of East Pakistan and the latter's resultant feelings of threat to their freedom and maltreatment of Bengalis by West Pakistanis, have a direct impact on the narration of history in the textbooks.

CONCLUSION

The general impression these books carry is the inability to deal with the contradictions. But these contradictions must be dealt with and history should be supplemented by historical evidence. History, being purely objective or scientific, is an ideal which should be properly pursued. However, history is almost always partisan and it depends on who tells the story and what is the evidence. In view of the complex nature of the issue and its direct interaction with such a great tragedy, it becomes necessary to analyse not only the various opinions about Dhaka Fall 1971, but also the very nature of the subject of history and the methods and ways used to 'arrive' at the truth.

History could not be Infallible

The events of history can define a period of time or can even define a nation. History is taking an in-depth look at the past that is still very relevant to life today. History is a happening in the past whose evidence and data has been analysed, scrutinized, and also interpreted until almost all facts are found to be correct. However, very often at times, these events in history are not recorded by a primary source and have been found to be inaccurate. History, will very seldom be recorded in a way that is infallible since facts can be misconstrued or distorted to the point that rumours of these events are created. Always in need of rewriting and re-examining, history should never be described as a 'closed case.' Since discovering what has occurred in the past can prevent or aid in the events to come, careful scrutiny of history is crucial to our future.

The criticism of historians who write 'present-minded' history lead one to wonder how history can be written without present day influences. Secondly, history of political views could be influenced by a historian's presently held political views and assumptions of the direction in which history goes. Historians would, at this point, acknowledge similarities between past events, and present events and also separate people from the past as good or bad, losers or winners.

Usually many of the historical accounts are seen from a partisan view and therefore some become inaccurate. However, while attempting to correct and rewrite them it is not surprising if one finds that history is constantly being re-examined and rewritten without anyone really knowing it. It is near impossible to tie together past events to events of the present as even after perfect attempts, there would still be missing pieces, such as events or conversations that prohibit accurate recording of the events. Some historians are blamed for not being objective; however, that is a trap we fall into. The so-called 'truths' that we grew up learning have turned out to be the candy covered versions of real history.

To stay objective is to have no opinions at all and be an independent thinker. With all of the outside influences and personal opinions, it is almost impossible to record history without some flash of one's own personality reflecting in it. History is only as important as the source that it comes from; be that primary, secondary or tertiary. Keeping in view the partisan nature of history, the provision of multiple and contradictory versions is very important, so as to facilitate the process of arriving at truth through alternatives and logical choices.

What should we tell our Children?

The fall of East Pakistan is a tragedy, but it has no redeeming feature of human greatness or a relieving end in catharsis, it is just a tale of shameful failure, an ignominious disaster. There were mainly two causes of this event. First, the policy of the Government of Pakistan which alienated the bigger part of the country from the idea of Pakistan itself. They were never allowed to feel that they were Pakistanis. Second, the way the protagonists tackled the developing crises.

> The Bengalis felt that they were being treated like a colony. And there were grounds for this feeling. They could sense a colonial snobbery in the general behaviour of the West Pakistanis which was the cause of their political and economic grievances. No one could have guessed that the country's first free elections of 1970 would end in the dismemberment of Pakistan. Neither of the two political champions were able to accept anything less than the supreme power. The Military Chief was not without ambitions of his own, a power rested in his hands... He provoked and aggravated the use of military power for solving the political crisis. He was outdone by the mass power of East Bengal and the superior, cleverer power of the Indian Military.[31]

We should tell our children the truth about the fall of Dhaka, but we should know the truth, first. In our part of Pakistan, it is generally believed that:

> Zulfikar Ali Bhutto alone was responsible for the break-up. The country could have been saved if he had accepted the Awami League's six point constitution because it had emerged as the majority party. In the former East Pakistan, Sheikh Mujib is blamed for the country's dismemberment because he was inflexible on constitutional issues. It was he who invited a ruthless army action which resulted in public massacres sealing the fate of a united Pakistan. The fundamentalist Jamaat-i-Islami, backed by the Beharis contributed to the holocaust, in the name of Islam and Urdu. This is

only partially true. The seeds of the break-up of Pakistan were sowed very early in the day. Feudal politicians of West Pakistan, their civil and military bureaucracy, and the newly emerging industrial class had monopolised state power. They were not ready to share it with the Bengalis. They were exploited and treated with contempt. They were culturally, politically and economically oppressed. The long years of Ayub Khan's military dictatorship frustrated the Bengalis, finally there was no hope for democracy and development for them. But they did no want separation. They stood for provincial autonomy, until the West Pakistani armed forces started their reign of terror.[32]

We should stop distorting history to suit the interest of the authoritarian rulers. Our children must face reality boldly, understand the compulsion and complexities of the 1960's and 1970's and also know the root cause of why the country was sundered apart. In the opinion of Shahnaz Wazir Ali, an ex-minister for education, East and West Pakistan were 1200 miles apart with a hostile country in between. The people of East Pakistan were weaker than those of West Pakistan in education, industry, trade and had little representation in civil and military services. Bengali language and literature had deep roots in the minds of the Bengalis, and they were not prepared to accept Urdu as their national language.

These factors had their impact right from 1947. The government of Pakistan was controlled by West Pakistanis even though East Pakistan had a larger population. Failure of the government of Pakistan to adopt effective measures to raise the status of the people of East Pakistan in education, industry, trade, representation in services naturally started generating discontent in the people of East Pakistan. Bengalis called the West Pakistani civil and military officers who controlled their administration as 'Brown Sahibs.' This discontent gave birth to several movements for political and economic autonomy.

These movements climaxed in the total victory of Awami League in the general elections held under General Yahya's Martial Law government in 1970. Awami League was now entitled to form the government of Pakistan. But General Yahya Khan, many West Pakistan politicians, the civil and military services, did not accept the democratic rights of East Pakistan's people.

The Awami League was prepared to formulate a confederal relationship between East and West Pakistan. But Yahya Khan and People's Party were not prepared to let the East Pakistanis decide the future shape of Pakistan and Yahya Khan refused to call the session of the National Assembly. The people of East Pakistan broke into confrontation with Yahya Khan's government. On 25 March 1971, Yahya Khan gave control of East Pakistan to the armed forces.

The warlike action of the armed forces against the revolting East Pakistanis drove millions of Bengalis to take refuge across the border in India. The accumulation of a vast number of refugees frightened India of the repercussions—on its administration and population. India also saw this as an opportunity for weakening Pakistan and proving the failure of the idea of Muslims of India being one nation.

India helped the militant Mukti Bahini of the revolting East Pakistanis, when it noticed the destructive operations of the Pakistan armed forces in East Pakistan. Indira Gandhi ordered the Indian troops to enter East Pakistan. West Pakistan finally surrendered to the Indian forces on 16 December 1971. From that moment, East Pakistan became Bangladesh.[33]

The experience of the transformation of East Pakistan into Bangladesh teaches humanity a fundamental truth: that people's aspirations for justice, freedom, quality and dignity have a stronger effect on human conduct than the sentiment of religion. However, the best explanation of the East Pakistan tragedy is that instead of mourning the past, we should learn from it.

Recommendations

1. Evaluating the veracity (truthfulness) of texts is very important. As state-dominant ideologies are promulgated through textbooks in both the countries, it becomes necessary to evaluate the texts keeping in mind that each country would neglect to mention its role in the atrocities or misgivings, and may in fact blame them on someone else. In this context for instance, West Pakistan neglects its role of keeping East Pakistan as a colony and shifts its blame on India.

2. Second comes the balance between credibility and reliability of historical texts.
Reliability refers to our ability to trust the consistency of the historian's account of the truth. A reliable text displays a pattern of *verifiable* truth-telling that tends to render the unverifiable parts of the text true. The textbooks of both Pakistan and Bangladesh may prove to be utterly reliable in detailing the campaigns during the 1971 war, as evidenced by corroborating records. The only gap in their reliability may be the omission of details about the real causes and their own mistakes.
Credibility refers to our ability to trust the historian's account of the truth on the basis of her or his tone and reliability. For instance, no where in the Pakistani textbooks is it mentioned that feudal politicians of West Pakistan, their civil and military bureaucracy, and the newly emerging industrial class had monopolised state power and were not ready to share it with the Bengalis which became a major cause of the dismemberment of Pakistan. A textbook that is inconsistently truthful loses credibility. There are many other ways these textbooks undermine their credibility. Most frequently, they convey in their tone that they are not neutral. For example, the books may intersperse throughout their reliable account of campaign details vehement and racist attacks of the Pakistan Army against Bengalis and vice versa. Such attacks signal to readers that these books may have an interest in not portraying the past accurately, and hence may undermine their credibility, regardless of their reliability.
A historical account which seems quite credible may be utterly unreliable. The textbook which takes a measured, reasoned tone and anticipates counter-arguments may seem to be very credible, when in fact it presents us with complete balderdash. Similarly, a reliable historical account may not always seem credible. It should also be clear that individual texts themselves may have portions that are more reliable and credible than others.

3. Excerpts from the textbooks of each country clearly establish that narrating history has an 'axe to grind' which renders the accounts unreliable.
Neutrality refers to the stake the historian has in a text. As, in our case, the state's view is predominant. There seems a considerable stake in the memoirs, which would expunge their own guilt. In an utterly neutral document, the creator is not aware that she or he has any special stake in the construction and content of the document. Very few texts are ever completely neutral. People generally do not go to the trouble to record their thoughts unless they have a purpose or design which renders them invested in the process of creating the text. Some historical texts, such as birth records, may appear to be more neutral than others, because their creators seem to have had less of a stake in creating them. (For instance, the county clerk who signed several thousand birth certificates had less of a stake in creating an individual birth certificate, than did a celebrity recording her life in a diary for future publication as a memoir.)
Objectivity refers to an author's ability to convey the truth free of underlying values, cultural presuppositions, and biases. Many scholars argue that no text is or ever can be completely objective, for all texts are the products of the culture in which their authors

lived. Many authors pretend to objectivity when they might better seek for neutrality. The author who claims to be free of bias and presupposition should be treated with suspicion: no one is free of their values. The credible author acknowledges and expresses those values so that they may be accounted for in the text where they appear. Therefore, *objectivity* is something which should be taken for granted.

4. Finally, the integrity of 'Epistemology' should be observed. Epistemology is the branch of philosophy that deals with the nature of knowledge. How do you know what you know? What is the truth, and how is it determined? While evaluating the causes and aftermath of Dhaka Fall-1971 and its projection in corresponding textbooks the important questions to reflect upon are: What could be known of the past based on this text? How sure could one be about it? How does one know these things?

This can be an extremely difficult question. Ultimately, we cannot know everything with complete assurance, because even our senses may fail us. Yet we can conclude, with reasonable accuracy, that some things are more likely to be true than others (for instance, it is more likely that the sun will rise tomorrow than that a human will learn to fly without wings or other support). The task of historians and students is to make and *justify* decisions about the relative veracity of historical texts, and portions of them. To do this, a solid command of the principles of sound reasoning are required.

ACKNOWLEDGEMENT NOTE

This brief study is a unique work as it is solely based on analyses of the misrepresentation of East Pakistan, events of 1971 and subsequent formation of Bangladesh. But, at the same time, it is a continuation of the earlier studies on the topic as the authors have touched upon this issue in addition to others. Rubina Saigol has presented the issue in her book *Knowledge, and Identity Articulation of Gender in Educational Discourse in Pakistan*. She maintains that, *'The curriculum is virtually silent about 1971, at best referring to the creation of Bangladesh as an Indian conspiracy.'* On this subject, she has written a paper as well, *'History, Social Studies and Civics and the Creation of Enemies'* published in Social Science in the 1990s by Akbar Zaidi (COSS 2003). Yvette Claire Rosser's paper, *'Hegemony and Historiography'* is quite valuable as she has done a comparative analysis of Indian, Pakistani and Bangladeshi textbooks.

Acknowledgements are due to all those who have taken part in earlier studies, as these studies have been an integral part of the research process. However, the findings that result from this research do not necessarily represent the opinions or policy positions of the other authors or institutions. I would also like to thank Mohi-ud-din Hashmi, who worked as Research Associate in completion of this study.

Notes

1. Apple, Michael, *Education and Power*, p. 41.
2. Bourdieu, P. and J.C. Passeron, *Reproduction in Education, Society and Culture*, Sage Publications, 1977.
3. Mannheim, Karl, *An Introduction to the Sociology of Education*, Routledge and Kegan Paul, p. 138.
4. Aronwitz, S and Giroux, A., *Education Under Siege*, Bergin and Garvey Pub, 1985, p. 95.
5. Vishwanathan, Gauri, *Masks of Conquest*, p. 47.

6. Akanda, Safar A., *'East Pakistan and the Politics of Regionalism'*, (unpublished Ph. D. thesis, University of Denver, 1970) p. 265 (Quoted by A.F. Salahuddin Ahmad, *'The Emergence of Bangladesh: Historical Background'*, Vol. I, New Delhi: South Asian Publishers, 1986.

7. Ahmad, A.F. Salahuddin, *'The Emergence of Bangladesh: Historical Background'*, Vol. I, New Delhi: South Asian Publishers, 1986, p. 144.

8. *Pakistan Studies for class IX-X*, Lahore: Punjab Textbook Board, 2002, pp. 66–67

9. *Civics for class V*, Punjab Textbook Board.

10. *Civics for class VIII.*

11. Khan, Farah, 'Diffrent Books, Different Education,' *Dawn*, 15 September 2003.

12. Hasnain, Khurshid and A.H. Nayyer, *Conflict and Violence in the Educational Process*, p. 4.

13. *The Pakistan Studies textbook for classes 9 and 10,* Punjab Textbook Board.

14. *Social Studies for class 6,* Punjab Textbook Board.

15. *Pakistan Studies for Secondary classes*, Lahore: Kamran Publishers for Punjab Textbook Board, March 1979, p. 38.

16. Ibid. pp. 40–43.

17. *History of Pakistan for class IX-X*, Lahore: Technical Publishers for Punjab Textbook Board, March 1977, p. 301.

18. Ibid. p. 301.

19. Ibid. p. 303.

20. Ibid. pp. 304–305.

21. *Social Science for Class VIII*, Dhaka: National Curriculum and Textbook Board, Revised Ed. 2002, pp. 75–77.

22. *Social Sciences for Class IX-X*, Dhaka: National Curriculum and Textbook Board, Revised Ed. 2002, p. 144.

23. *History of Bangladesh and Ancient World Civilizations fro Class IX-X,* Dhaka: National Curriculum and Textbook Board, p. 221.

24. *Secondary Civics,* Dhaka: National Curriculum and Textbook Board, Revised Ed. 2002, p. 130.

25. Ibid. p. 131.

26. Ibid. p. 132.

27. Ibid. p. 132.

28. Ibid. p. 134.

29. Op. cit., *Social Sciences for Class IX-X*, pp. 147, 150.

30. Op. cit., *Secondary Civics for IX-X*, p. 135.

31. 'What should we tell our children about East Pakistan', *The Frontier Post*, 13 December 1991.

32. Ibid.

33. Ibid.

14

LANGUAGE POLICY AND RESEARCH—FORCED IGNORANCE OF THE ROOT LANGUAGE

*Dr. Ahsan Wagha**

ABSTRACT

This paper examines the background of the problem of allotting some languages the status of language of media (including medium of instruction) and depriving other languages at two levels: 1) analysis of the actual linguistic dependence of modern Pakistani languages on Sanskrit which we see as the root language, and 2) reference to an identifiable mark of contemporary policy and research, the over projection of the Perso-Arabic linguistic feature of these languages aimed at undermining the Indo-Aryan (IA) root.

---

*Dr. Ahsan Wagha got his basic education in Perso-Arabic language and literature as a student of traditional madrasah at Taunsa, Pakistan. He got his Ph.D. in languages from the School of Oriental and African Studies, University of London, in 1997. He made his main career in broadcasting as producer/senior producer/program manager in Radio Pakistan. He is known as a language activist of Siraiki and has a few publications in Siraiki and English.

INTRODUCTION

Language development means developing a language for secondary uses such as writing, reading and syllabic learning. This requires developing a set of visual symbols, i.e. a script for a language compatible with its divisible sounds, preparing primers and textbooks for use as medium of instruction and compiling grammar to elaborate marked features of the language for non-native learners (Eastman, 1983). In this sense, not all, but some languages are developed.

Looking at the choice of language for development and instruction as a problem requires appreciation of '...the pragmatics of power manipulation in language. Language use has functions that go beyond the neutral conducting of messages in communication' (Sew, 1997).

Direct use of power is one, and the alternate means of achievement adopted by man also involve use of power—but delicate and subtle—such as communication through language. This was realized much earlier and is found relevant by contemporary writers:

> Aristotle ...recognized long time ago that facts and logic alone are often insufficient for persuasion. Facts and logic—the prescribed bases of persuasion—must be adapted to the situation, and it is language and language style that will bear the burden of this mission...(ibid.)

The most frequently occurring act of language communication is neither spontaneous nor voluntary. It is not spontaneous because it goes through a cognitive process of selection and omission before an utterance is made (Sperber and Wilson, 1987). And it is not voluntary because a speaker aims at achieving some results from his speech—at the minimum, expected implications and mutuality between the speaker and the hearer. Hence language communication in itself involves politics which is interest oriented:

> Our interaction is political, whether we intend it to be or not; everything we do in the course of a day communicates our relative power ... We may enter the transaction knowingly or not, we may function mainly as manipulator or manipulatee—but we are always involved in persuasion, in trying to get another person to see the world or some piece of it our way, and therefore to act as we would like them to act. If we succeed, we have power ... (Sew, 1997)

Use of this alternate means of power, i.e. language, in education is aimed at influencing the learner's mind to agreement to the teacher's syllabus so that they act accordingly. Development of a language for use as a medium of instruction etc. too is neither neutral nor voluntary. What requires to be worked out is a quest for policy.

This paper examines the background of the problem of allotting some languages the status of language of media (including medium of instruction) and depriving other languages at two levels: 1) analysis of the actual linguistic dependence of modern Pakistani languages on Sanskrit which we see as the root language, and 2) reference to an identifiable mark of contemporary policy and research, the over projection of the Perso-Arabic linguistic feature of these languages aimed at undermining the Indo-Aryan (IA) root, a politics of 'disappearance' (Shiva, 1993).

SANSKRIT AS ROOT LANGUAGE IN WORD FORMATION OF PAKISTANI LANGUAGES

In comparative linguistics, languages are seen as two types grammatically: 'analytic languages' also called 'isolating languages', and 'synthetic languages'. The isolating languages lack morphemic synthesis. Therefore, these depend on invariable words and word order to show syntactic relations. In simple words, having limited, or minus capacity for use of affixes and inflections, these languages rely grammatically on the combination of somewhat independent/ isolated morphemes for sentence construction. Chinese, Vietnamese and other South-East Asian languages are among known isolating languages (Crystal, 1997).

The synthetic languages, on the other hand, tend to rely on multi-morphemic type of words. Each word appears with various morphemes to adjust meaning change, and when in replicable order, this helps in word formation.

Synthetic languages are further divided in two categories: one that uses inflections to add, for instance, verb forms to the same morpheme, called 'inflectional languages, e.g. English/ *work*/+ inflection/*ed*/becomes (>)/*worked*/. Arabic and Latin are typical examples (ibid., p. 378). The second type is where flexible use of affixes helps in formation of new morphemes by combining various morpheme(s) in a linear sequence, for instance, English/*dis-establish-ment*/>/*disestablishment*/(ibid., p. 13, cf. Baart, 1999).

The modern Pakistani languages, most of them grouped with New Indo Aryan Languages (NIA) in historical linguistics, show at varying capacity, features of synthetic languages in their original lexicon (compared to loan words) based on the root language which being the same is recognized as Sanskrit, or Old Indo-Aryan Language (OIA). In the following, we test grammatical reliance of a few major Pakistani languages on Sanskrit mainly in their word formation, derivational or compositional. Word formation, in its general sense refers to the whole process of morphological variation in the constitution of words. The process of word formation includes two main divisions of languages: inflection which signals grammatical relationships, and derivation which shows lexical relationships (Crystal 1997).

HINDI (URDU) AND PUNJABI MARKED WITH SECONDARY DERIVATION FROM SANSKRIT

The stems in Hindi/Urdu tend to simplification of Sanskrit (Sk.) consonant clusters (e.g./*gn*/) which had changed into double consonants (/*gg*/) at Prakrit (Pk.) stage of historical linguistic development. At the New Indo Aryan (NIA) stage, some languages retained the Sk. consonant cluster, others opted for the Pk. double consonant, still others went through a phonetic process of retaining one Sk. consonant and compensating the omission of the other by lengthening the initial Sk. vowel as can be examined in the following;

Sanskrit	Prakrit	Punjabi	Hindi (Urdu)	
agni	*aggi*	*agg*	*aag*	(fire)
karman	*kamma*	*kamm*	*kaam*	(work)
hasta	*hattha*	*hatth*	*haath*	(hand)

(Shackle and Snell, 1990)

Variables of Sanskrit Root Word in Pashto, Urdu/Hindi, Punjabi, and Sindhi

Sanskrit	Pashto	Urdu/Hindi	Punjabi	Sindhi
varshati (to rain)	*varol/varval*	*barasana*	*varhana*	*vasaen* (to cause to rain)

(CDIAL, Entry No. 11394, Sindhi, 1992)

The Unique Variables of the Sanskrit Derivatives in Kashmiri

It appears as if Kashmiri, apparently a language with marginal mutual Indo-Aryan intelligibility, is but one of the languages consistently retaining its Indo Aryan vocabulary. Two main reasons behind the mismatch in the registers of vocabulary of these languages of the same origin are: first these retain derivatives from different root words of Sk., and second, as tested above, some of these languages consist of the secondary derivations of the Pk. stage while others, of the original Sk. root forms. Kashmiri, Siraiki and Sindhi seem to be the second type. For instance, a word for 'copper' in Kashmiri,/*tram*/, Siraiki,/*trama*/, Sindhi,/*tramo*/is derived from (<) Sk./*tamra*/as compared to Punjabi,/*tamba*/borrowed from Pk./*tanba*/ (CDIAL, Entry No. 5779, cf. Sindhi, ibid.).

Few derivatives of Kashmiri are tested below:

Sanskrit	>	Kashmiri	
nasa		*nass*	(nose)
aksi		*acchi*	(eye)
ostha		*vuth*	(lip)
durargha-		*drog*	(high priced, expensive)

(CDIAL, Entries 7089, 43, 2563, 6426; *Kashmiri-zaban*, pp. 30–7)

The Khowar Language of North, The Case Markers

A theory of linguistics, a common place now, claims sameness of grammar of the languages, the 'universal grammar' (Chomsky, 1980). In a major portion of their grammar, all the languages are common, different at various degrees in about 40 per cent of their grammatical features which apparently make them different to the level of mutual unintelligibility. These are called 'marked features'.

It puts additional burden on a learner's mind if a second language, especially when the medium of instruction at school level appears as having or lacking marked features in contrast to the learner's first language. A known example is the puzzling feature of the number and gender agreement of verb with subject in IA languages, e.g. Urdu for speakers of Pashto. The latter being gender neutral in verbs does not help its speakers comprehend the contrast in the first.

Khowar shows some case marker on its very IA syntactic forms which being non- existent in Urdu (and many other IA languages) require the student put extra labor in translating one into the other. Khowar adds relevant locative case suffix such as/-*ah*/,/-*i*/,/-*o*/, or/-*elto*/to a noun itself in 'objectival' position to indicates its location i.e. 'on', 'inside', 'beneath', 'attached to', respectively.

The Store of First Stage Sanskrit Derivatives in the Register of Siraiki and Sindhi

In contrast to Hindi (H.) and Punjabi (Pi.), Siraiki (Sr.) and Sindhi (S.) show interesting retention of the original morphemic characteristics of Sk. in their largely live IA register. As against H. where/-*b*-/,/-*v*-/, and/-*dv*-/of Sk. appear as/-*b*-/, the Sr. and S. languages retain Sk./ -*v*-/as it is, and show some rule pattern in derivation of their famous phonological set of implosives from specific Sk. phonemes. A few entries are reproduced here:

Sanskrit	>	Siraiki/Sindhi
prushita		*pru:tha* (rusted, sprinkled)
udva:syate		*ubassan* (to become musty)
bahu		*bahu:n* (much, enough)

(William, 1986, Entry of head-word/*pra*-/,p. 711; CDIAL, Entries 2084, 9187).

REFERENCE TO A PROMINENT FEATURE OF LANGUAGE POLICY, RESEARCH PLANNING AND DEVELOPMENT

Language planning, an organized and practical approach, results from formulated language policy adopted by a state usually, and by language-activist groups casually (cf. Eastman, Op. Cit., pp. 7, 33–4).

The One Language Policy

The British altered the rule of use of mother tongue in education with the inconsistent, selective and politically compromised notion of 'vernaculars' (Rahman, 1996). The concept was adapted for development of Hindi and Urdu to the status of national languages in India and Pakistan, but with a clear difference of policies.

The then contemporary Soviet model of dealing with the problem of linguistic heterogeneity, followed in India (Wagha, 1996) was also recommended but turned aside in Pakistan (Proceedings, 1947). Stalin, against the basic socialist theory of revolution that pressed compulsory annihilation of the 'super structure' together with its 'base structure' defended the Russian language by marking language beyond super structure. He was, however, careful in dealing with linguistic multiplicity of the Empire (Stalin, 1950). The same policy was followed with some twists by Nehru in India but forsaken in Pakistan which stuck between Soviet and Turkish experiments of opposite nature for obvious reasons, preferred casual attendance of the issues of languages. The reconciliatory language policy articulated during the Pakistan movement by not less then Maulavi Abdul Haq (Haq, 1951) had to be altered with a strong one-language-imposition policy immediately after independence. Even acceding from the recommendations made in basic document on education policy known as 'Sharif Commission Report', promotion of one national language was asserted through Constitutions (Constitution 1954, and 1968, Article 215 (1), 1973, Article 251).

Effects of the Language Policy on Research

There are volumes of works on languages and linguistics produced under sponsorship of various government organs directly, or under indirect influence of them in Pakistan. Except for a few, these works do not find a place in the shelves of contemporary works of grammar, or even historical linguistics. The most common feature of the pattern of language-research in

Pakistan has been the promotion of Arabic-Persian loans as the basic feature at the cost of the whole linguistic context of these languages.

Assessing the Nature of Arabic-Persian Loans in Indo-Aryan Languages

The term 'Arabic-Persian' (AP) stands for loans from Arabic (Ar.) and Persian (Per.) in New Indo-Aryan (NIA). Where Ar. loans remain isolated, Per. loans (for the shared origin of Indo-Iranian with Indo-Aryan) appear to be more assimilated, e.g. Per. stem *farma* 'give your command' > NIA verbal noun *farmävan/farmana* to be compared with Ar. *zikrun*, 'to remember' > NIA *zikr karan/karna* 'to mention' but not **zikran* i.e. Ar. loans are not accepted for assimilation in NIA.

NIA Morphemes with Confused Sanskrit-Arabic-Persian Origin

NIA word	{<*}	(i) AP root	<	(ii) IA root
nith (sit)		Per. *nashistan*		Sk. *nisïdati*
(7.1/180)				
dür (distant)		Per. *dür.*		Sk. *dürá-* (7.1/188)
subha, subhavelha (morning)		Ar. *subhun*		Sk. *subhavëlá*
(7.1/121)				

(Wagha, 1997).

Modern Indo-Aryan Compounds with Persian Prefixes

Per. prefix	NIA formation
be- (without)	*be-dard* (painless, insensitive)
—	*be-rïtaa* (non-customary)
dar- (in/inside)	*dar-parda* (secretly)
kär (use)	*kär-ämad* (useful)
sar-(head)	*sar-panch* (head of a community)

Arabic-Persian Loans Fully or Partly Assimilated into NIA

Unassimilated form	Assimilation in NIA
'*arz-däsht* (AP. compound, entreaty, written petition)	*ardäs*
gumnäm (unknown)	*gumnävän*
nä-muräd (unlucky)	*nä-muräd* m., *nä-muräden* f.

Glimpse From the Contemporary Research—Tendency to Link Original Indo-Aryan Register to Arabic-Persian Roots.

Study of Hindi (and Sanskrit) forsaken by the Muslims, has developed a fashion of linking origin of local Indo-Aryan words with Arabic and Persian roots.

Arabic-Persian Interpretation of Indo-Aryan Words, a Trend in Research

NIA Words		AP root assumed	plausible Sk. source
Sr. *ajäya* 'in vain',	<	Ar. *Zäi'* (waste)	< *jayá-* (victory)
zät (caste)	<	Ar. *zät(un)* (central Being)	< *játya-* (caste)

(CDIAL, Entries 151, 125, Cf. Wagha 1997)

Even the institutional research is marred with the above tendency as briefly examined in the two documents produced by the University of Punjab and the National Language Authority respectively, in the following; table.

An unsubstantiated philological work of Punjabi matching with the policy of the state.

Word of Punjabi	Ascribed Per. root	Original IA root	
va	*ba:d*	*va:yu-*	(air, wind)
vi:h	*bi:st*	*vimsha*	(twenty)
bhu:in	*bu:m*	*bhu:mi*	(earth, land)

(Husain and Rana,—, pp. 215, 217; CDIAL, Op. cit., 11544, 11615–16, 9557)

Ambiguous neologism from isolated Arabic-Persian roots by National Language Authority

the coinage	English term replaced	ambiguity
qismat	division	against popular use of word for 'luck/fate'
sighah	section	against popular use for 'word form' *naza:rat*
inspectorate	against popular use for 'scene'	

(*Mahkamu:n ke naam*, 1985, *paish-lafz*, intro.)

FINAL NOTE

Although language development is reductionist in nature, this proves counter productive by marking the enormous part of ungraspable vocabulary of a language as colloquial and slang and making it disappear, 'language choice' plays a pivotal role as far as development of modern knowledge and education systems is concerned. The hypothesis of language typology established above as analytic or synthetic type, actually does not count much in choice of language. A very common question, why speakers of the most demanding isolating languages such as Chinese, etc., cannot switch away, itself is the answer. No system can replace multiple codes of the first language of a learner. It is next to impossible, and accidental that people find a way out to shifting of any other language.

The language policy and the resulting research on languages which promoted Perso-Arabic linguistic abstracts entailed suppression of the real substance and power of languages and their knowledges, a naiveté justified in the name of construction of a cultural basis for the nation state.

Reference

BAART, Joan, *A Sketch of Kalam Kohistani Grammar*, manuscript, Islamabad, 1999.

CHOMSKY, Noam, *Rules and Representations*, Oxford, 1980.

CRYSTAL, David, *Dictionary of Linguistics and Phonetics,* London: Blackwell, 1997.

EASTMAN, Carol, M., *Language Planning: An Introduction,* San Francisco, 1983.

FARIDKOTI, Ainul Haq, *Urdu zaba:n ki qadi:m ta:ri:kh*, Lahore, 1972.

HAQ, Maulavi Abdul *Qawawaid-e Urdu*, Karachi: Anjuman-e Taraqqi-e Urdu, 1951.

HUSAN, Muhammad Bashir and RANA, Muhammad Aslam, 'Farsi aur Punjabi ke lisani rawabit', *Khoj,* Lahore: Punjab University, Oriental College, 1982.

Kashmiri zaba:n si:khane ke lie ba'z bunya:di usu:l, Markaz-e Adab-o Saqafat-e Kashmir, Rawlpindi, 1980.

Learn Telugu in 30 days, Balaji, Madras, 2000.

Mahkamu:n aur ida:ru:n ke na:m, Muqtadira Qaumi Zaba:n, Islamabad, 1985.

Proceedings of the Pakistan Educational Conference 1947, Karachi, 1948.

RAHMAN, Tariq, *Language and Politics in Pakistan*, Karachi: Oxford University Press, 1996.

Report of the Commission on National Education, Government of Pakistan, Karachi, 1959.

SEW, Wee Jyh, 'Power pragmatics in Asian languages', *Language series*, Great Britain, 1997, 19:4, pp. 357–67.

SHACKLE, C. and R. Snell, *Hindi and Urdu since 1800: A Common Reader*, London, 1990.

SHIVA, Vandana, *Monocultures of the Mind: Perspectives on Biodiversity and Biotechnology,* Delhi, 1993.

SPERBER, D. and D. Wilson, *Relevance- Communication and Cognition*, Oxford, 1987.

STALIN, Josef, 1950*: Marxism and Problems of Linguistics,* 1950, pp. 430–62, 2002:

TURNER, R., L. *A Comparative Dictionary of Indo-Aryan languages*, Oxford University Press, 1989.

WAGHA, Ahsan, 'The Language Policy of Pakistan- a review in South Asian context', *Pakistan Journal of History and Culture*, Islamabad, 1996, pp. 5–18.

WAGHA, Ahsan, 'The roots of conflict', *The Development of the Siraiki Language in Pakistan,* PhD thesis, SOAS Library, University of London, 1997.

WILLIAM, Monier, *Sanskrit-English Dictionary*, Marwah, New Delhi, 1986.

15

EDUCATION AND MEDIUM OF INSTRUCTION

Shafqat Tanveer Mirza[*]

ABSTRACT

No local or regional language was ever made the official language in the subcontinent before the British occupation. First it was Sanskrit followed by Pali, then Sanskrit again, Arabic (Indus Valley) and Persian. Same was the case in the united Punjab. The British had introduced local languages as the medium of instruction and second official language in all the provinces except the NWFP, Punjab, Kashmir, Balochistan and Bahawalpur. They were mostly Urdu- (or Purbi, Houdi) speaking who helped them to run the administration in Punjab. Therefore Urdu was made the medium of instruction and the second official language. Punjabi was given no share in power.

Urdu became the symbolic representative of the Muslim India before partition, when Bengal and Sindh were enjoying due status (educational and official) for their languages. The legacy of Urdu lingered on in other areas. No deviation was tolerated. It is mainly the Punjabi-dominated establishment which denies due status to the Punjabi language. Among other issues, this paper examines how the language of power was exclusively owned and used by power groups, races and communities.

---

*Mr. Shafqat Tanvir Mirza is a journalist. He retired as Editor from the now defunct daily newspaper, Imroze published from Lahore and Multan. He has written ten books and contributes columns to the daily Dawn, Lahore.

Three eminent educationists, Prof Siraj, former Principal of the Government College, Lahore, Dr Muhammad Ajmal, Head of Psychology Department, Government College, Lahore (and later on Vice Chancellor of the Punjab University and Federal Secretary, Education) and Dr Muhammad Baqir, Principal, University Oriental College, Lahore, have supported the move to introduce Punjabi language as a medium of instruction at primary level in the Punjab-speaking areas.[1] This support ensued after the Yahya Government presented an education policy in the same year.

Prominent writers and intellectuals from Punjab, in a joint appeal to President Yahya, urged the government that Punjabi be introduced as a medium of instruction at the primary level in Punjab with immediate effect. They included writers from all over Pakistan including Faiz Ahmad Faiz, Ahmad Nadeem Qasimi, Ashfaq Ahmad, Prof. Anwar Masud, Joshua Fazluddin, a former deputy minister of West Pakistan, Ahmad Rahi, Prof. Eric Cyprian, Malik Muhammad Jaffar, a former minister of state, Prof. Sharif Kunjahi, Lt.Gen. (Retd.) Bakhtiar Rana, N. M. Khan (retired ICS) and Ustad Daman.[2]

The UNESCO's position paper, '*Education in a Multilingual World, 2003*' clearly states:

1. Instruction in the mother tongue is essential for initial instruction and literacy, and should be extended to as late a stage in education as possible.
2. Communication, expression and the capacity to listen and dialogue should be encouraged, first of all in the mother tongue, then, if the mother tongue is official or the national language in the country, in one or more foreign languages.
3. Measures should be taken to eliminate discrimination in education at all levels on the basis of gender, race, language, religion, national origin, age or disability or any other form of discrimination.[3]

Dr Tariq Rehman (2003) narrates the situation prevailing in the country in the following words:

If one goes to an elitist English medium school and meets the principal one finds out that one's mother tongue—assuming one is a Pakistani—is had the right to be educated in Punjabi even in the junior most classes and he/she gave me the kind of look one reserves for the mentally handicapped.

About the violation of the UNESCO principles, Dr Rehman (2003) writes:

They force small children...children as young as three or four whose tongues can hardly lisp words of their own language...to speak English. They force their teachers, some of whom very wisely keep using Urdu, to put up the pretence of talking in the totally incomprehensible English to their tender pupils...and of course, these schools discriminate against children on the basis of wealth, urban culture and English.
Urdu-medium schools, the schools that most children attend...are less snobbish than their English medium counterparts. However, they too look down upon Punjabi and are completely ignorant of other minor or vernacular languages.

As far as tradition goes, the lands conquered and ruled by aliens never imparted education in the languages of the soil. During the Muslim rule the medium of education was either Arabic or Persian. The only difference was that local teachers while teaching frequently used the local languages about which there were no strong prejudices. The main reason was that the teachers and Sufis used the local languages to convey their message to the countrymen whose needs were quite different. Persian and Arabic were the court languages and it was not essential to learn these languages since there was no linguistic interference in day-to-day business. This was also the case in many of the European countries, particularly England, where English was not given the status of official language.

The ruling elite of all the countries preferred to keep the people at arm's length, socially and linguistically. That is what had happened in the subcontinent before the arrival of the Muslims. Sanskrit was the court language, therefore, it was also used for religious and educational purposes.

Language as such was not properly studied and the establishment was not responsible for the form in which people expressed themselves. Language of power was exclusively owned and used by power groups, races and communities. This is the reason why a language like Sanskrit disappeared with the change of the rulers who had come from other linguistic areas. Language and beliefs have always been used for the interests of the powerful and no power has ever shared these exclusive instruments, frequently used for suppressing the people or the rival claimants. Sometimes both the fields were taken as sacred and exclusive. The Hindu caste system is the best example of this concept.

Apart from the *sufis* and saints' involvement in people's languages and dialects, the Muslim rulers of the subcontinent never gave any importance to local languages. But in the middle of the Mughal rule, Hindus started using local languages for imparting their teaching, the Muslim rulers including Jahangir and Shahjehan were advised to let the scholars and teachers use the local dialects for Muslim teachings. It was then that the teachers mainly from the mosques wrote books on religious themes. In Punjab, Maulana Abdullah Abadi and Abdul Kareem from Jhang and Hafiz Barkhurdar from Gujranwala did the job. Waris Shah refers to some of these books that were taught in those days. Books like *Pacci Roti* were written and taught in those days. Nothing secular was taught in local languages by the Muslims except the poetry written by *sufi* poets which was free of religious dogma. The rulers never shared power with the people, therefore, their language was neither recognized nor mentioned in literary books of those days.

Only one Punjabi poet acknowledges the patronage of Jaffar Khan, a minister of Shahjehan. Hafiz Barkhurdar says that he was asked by Jaffar Khan to translate the story of Yusuf-Zulekha from Persian into Punjabi and he obliged the minister. Hafiz Barkhurdar refers to the co-education system in the Masjed School: *Sahiban likhdi phatian—Mirza parrhey Quran*. This, however, does not mean that the medium of instruction was the mother tongue of Mirza Sahiban, and the teaching of the Quran is a clear indication that it was religious teaching.

Language is one of the basic sources of power and the rulers never allowed the local languages to share power. Even during the Sikh rule in Punjab, they could not take the risk of introducing Punjabi as a state language or medium of instruction. It remained a medium of religious education in the Sikh religious institutions. The Sikh rulers followed the Mughals with respect to the official language. Persian was their court language. It was also the official language of Delhi, Kabul and the local princely states like Bahawalpur, Multan and Patiala etc.

The local languages were also divided on the basis of Muslims and non-Muslims. The former were written in Arabic script, while the latter were written in local scripts including Gurmukhi and Dev Nagari. In Punjab, there were three scripts for Punjabi: Arabic or Persian which was used by the Muslims, moreover it was the official script throughout the subcontinent; Gurmukhi was exclusively used by the Sikhs who contributed a lot to the language and literature; and Hindi or Devnagari was used by the Hindus whose contribution is comparatively less than the other two communities. The official script of the Sikh rule was

Persian and not Gurmuhki. Thus, the official script in Punjab was Persian throughout its 1000-year history.

No Punjabi writer or historian was engaged by the Sikh court for writing the history of their religion or their political development in Punjabi. This was also the case with the Muslim rulers of the semi-independent states in the northwestern part of India. About the local scripts Prof. Preetam Singh states that, since the time of Caliph Umar, the educational policy of the Muslims towards their conquered lands did not put any hurdles in the ways of Muslim settlers and converts using local or national languages, provided these were written in the Arabic script. Persian, Uzbek, Tajik, Turkish, Pashto, Baluchi, Sindhi, Western Punjabi (Lehnda), Kashmiri and Hindi were some of the languages that were extensively used by the Muslim writers. In fact, Muslim settlers were good pioneers in almost all these languages, but in each case Arabic or modified Arabic script was used. With the result that their original scripts along with the bulk of indigenous literary and cultural treasures preserved in these scripts were lost for good.[4]

The British overtook the Persian domination when they occupied the eastern parts of India including Bengal, Bihar and United Provinces (UP). They introduced English as the official language and encouraged the local languages at almost all levels as was done by the Muslim rulers against Sanskrit, the then official and religious language of the Hindu rulers. During the Muslim rule, Persian remained the official language in all parts of the subcontinent but a new language Urdu—a mixture of Arabic, Persian, Hindi, Punjabi and other local languages—was used as the cultural expression of the ruling elites. It was patronized by the Mughal rulers and it attained an important status which led the British rulers to develop it more and make it the second official language from Sutlej to Ganga in UP and Bihar. The locals, who accompanied the British invaders to Punjab, were well versed in this language, and at a lower level it was used for government functions and proceedings.

In Bengal, Bengali replaced the Persian language in 1837. The Muslim Ashrafia resisted this change. According to Dr Tariq Rehman (2003):

> Acceptance of Bengali as part of the Muslim Bengali identity...started as early as 1899 with the establishment of Nawab Ali Chaudhri's Muhammadan Society for Bengali Literature. In 1906, at the Muhammadan Educational Conference in Dhaka, Abdul Karim, a delegate of East Bengal pointed out that the Muslims of East Bengal couldn't do without Bengali...they could do without (Urdu and Persian).

Bengali and English were the official and educational language of East Bengal in 1947. In Sindh, Sindhi was the medium of instruction up to 10th grade level.

> In 1843, Sindh was annexed to the British Empire. For the first time in recorded history, Sindh was made the court language and medium of instruction in the educational institutions. Sir Bartle Frere, the British Commissioner in Sindh appointed a committee of experts who prepared the present Arabic-Sindhi script...eminent writers like Diwan Pribh Das and Mirza Sidique Ali were commissioned by the government to prepare textbooks.[5]

Contrary to that, the British rulers never favoured, rather opposed, the introduction of local languages in the conquered areas of Punjab, NWFP, Balochistan, Kashmir and states like Bahawalpur, and introduced Urdu as the second court and educational language. It helped them to rule these areas with the help of officials they had trained in Urdu-speaking areas of UP, Bihar, Delhi and adjoining areas. Almost all the religious communities of the Punjab i.e. the Muslims, the Hindus and the Sikhs willingly accepted Urdu in place of Persian. Had the

Sikh rulers of Lahore introduced Punjabi or Persian in stead the situation might have been different, and even the Gurmikhi script might have been acceptable to Muslims who had already accepted the non-Persian script for Bengali. One should remember the fact that the Muslim elite of Bengal had reluctantly accepted the Bengali language and its script. Bengali language shared the favour of the British, where as Punjabi did not, before or after the arrival of the British.

In the Punjab, Punjabi being the religious language of the Sikhs, was included in the curriculum with the Gurmukhi script, but not made the medium of instruction. The Maharaja of Patiala took this step in the first decade of the 20th century. Since Urdu was not held in great esteem during the British rule, the Punjabi Muslims preferred being taught in Urdu and English. Mainly the Muslim rulers evolved Urdu and it was a link language between all the Muslims of the subcontinent. With that background, the political aspirations of the Punjabi Muslims also preferred Urdu medium. They were never conscious of their Punjabi identity; instead it was the Urdu identity to which they associated. It was the Persian script that they considered sacred (after the British came into power). The script was a controversial issue and played an important role in the division of 1947. Urdu lost its political and cultural value among the Muslim Bengalis and they, according to Dr Tariq Rehman, opposed a Muslim League resolution in the annual session of 1937 which recommended Urdu as *lingua franca* of the Muslims all over India. The Bengali Muslims and the ones belonging to Gujarat and the southern part of India had no dispute over the script issue.

On the eve of partition, the overwhelming majority of Pakistanis had their local languages (Bengali and Sindhi) as mediums of instruction and the majority had script other than Persian. These two striking aspects were never considered seriously by the Urdu-speaking, Urdu oriented Punjabi, Pashto and Balochi speaking minority. That was denial of a democratic principle in the linguistic field because the majority had a very small share in power dominated by Urdu, Punjabi and Pashto-speaking communities.

The first language controversy started in Sindh where Karachi was made the temporary capital of the new country. Karachi, where the medium of instruction at the primary level was Sindhi, became the centre of the powerful Punjabi-Urdu ruling bureaucratic elite that was more urban than rural. Here Maulvi Abdul Haq, Baba-e-Urdu had declared that Urdu was the only Islamic language of the country while all other languages Punjabi, Bengali, Pashto, Balochi etc. were the languages of infidels.

The Bengali Muslims had disassociated with the non-Muslim Bengalis because they (majority from East Bengal) had no due share in power and they were sure that they would be compensated in the newly created country. But this never happened and their first confrontation was on the issue of national language. Urdu was declared the only national language of the country. This convinced the Bengalis that they would neither be able to become equals, nor major shareholders in the new power game. They feared that they would be deprived of their role in the newly created country and the national language would be used to reduce the importance of their region. This fear, on one hand, emerged in the complete annihilation of the centre-backed Muslim League in the first election (1954), and on the other, Urdu identity was asserted with more force by West Pakistan.

The national language controversy mildly affected the thinking of some of the Punjabi intellectuals, particularly the senior journalists like Hameed Nizami, Maulana Abdul Majeed Salik and Maulana Zafar Ali Khan who raised their voice in favor of the Punjabi language. Hameed Nizami in an article in the monthly *Punjabi* demanded that Punjabi be made the medium of instruction at the primary level in Punjab. Before that the progressive writers including Faiz Ahmad Faiz and Ahmad Nadeem Qasmi also supported the move to give due status to Punjabi in education institutions and that it be made the medium of instruction at the primary level.

The late Hameed Nizami of *Nawa-i-Waqt* through his paper was pleading the point of view of the Punjabi bureaucracy against the dominating Urdu-speaking bureaucrats who with the support of the Urdu-speaking prime minister of Punjabi origin were ruling supreme in the new capital, Karachi, where Sindhi politicians had also developed many complaints against the Urdu hegemony. The Punjabi bureaucracy never supported the cause of Punjabi language and literature because in that case the power was to be duly shared by Sindhis, Pakhtuns and Balochis. These languages were for a long time not included in the course for the Central Superior Services. It was this role of Punjabi bureaucracy and elite that was hated by the smaller provinces. The Urdu-speaking elite and bureaucracy also opposed the demand for due status to the regional languages and culture which was mainly rural, while the establishment was controlled by the urban elite.

Though the richest contribution to Punjabi literature was made by the Muslims mainly from west Punjab, in the western dialects, the impression was created that Punjabi was the religious language of the Sikhs with whom, the Muslims had developed a sort of enmity on the eve of independence. After Maulana Abdul Haq, Maulana Salahuddin Ahmad of *Adabi Duniya* outrightly condemned all moves favoring Punjabi. He spoke against Ayub's public speech in Hindko and declared it a sin committed against the solidarity and *Nazria-i-Pakistan*. Urdu had been introduced in Punjab colleges as the compulsory subject and that created a powerful anti-Punjabi group among the teachers, mainly headed by the late Dr Syed Abdullah and other Urdu-Punjabi teachers at the Oriental College of the Punjab University.

With the creation of the One Unit, Punjabi was introduced from class six, but no training for the teachers was ever arranged. Therefore, teaching Punjabi even at that level was made impossible. It was in the early seventies when the Bengalis had won overwhelming majority in the national elections and it was certain that Mujeeb-ur-Rehman, once a prominent student leader of Pakistan Movement, would form the government. All of a sudden, Punjabi prejudices nurtured by the top bureaucracy of West Pakistan thought of its identity and national news bulletins on Radio Pakistan were initiated. Masters in Punjabi was introduced at the Punjab University while the language was not being taught at any of the lower levels. This was a clear act of dishonesty and hypocrisy. With the passage of time the sudden favour extended in these emergency days lost its force. The logical steps to be followed, including introduction of Punjabi as medium of instruction at primary level and adopting it as a medium of instruction up to matric level, were never taken. With the fall of Dhaka, the fear of Bengalis also disappeared.

Before that the national election results from Punjab had shocked the traditional feudal elite of the other three provinces. It was the middle and lower middle class with leftist slogans that emerged from Punjab. This was also considered a great threat to the ruling junta including the feudal, tribal, and military and civil hierarchy. It was feared that if the lower and middle class Bengalis came into power, they would first eliminate the feudal political elite of West Pakistan who were considered responsible for the miseries of Bengali people. The Awami League, according to its manifesto, would introduce radical changes in the class-ridden socio-economic set up and if the feudal leadership of the Pakistan Peoples Party did not support the changes which were also included in its manifesto, many of the PPP Punjabi parliamentarians would take no time to extend their full support to Mujib-ur-Rehman and that would certainly topple the ruling elite of the West Pakistan. Had the lower and middle classes of Punjab and Bengal been allowed to implement their manifestos, the peoples' languages in West Pakistan would have earned their due social, cultural and educational status without much effort. The

Punjabis would have felt proud of their rich language and literature, in comparison with Bengalis and Sindhis and their assertion of Urdu identity would have gone. This would have been so in the light of the election results from Karachi from where religious leadership, the centralists by nature, had emerged with full force.

With the fall of Dhaka and the conditions prevailing in the rest of the country, the middle class and lower middle class of Punjab could not dare to play their progressive role in changing the socio-economic and cultural pattern. Punjab was given to feudals like Mustafa Khar, Nawab Sadiq Qureshi and Nawab Muhammad Ahmad Abbasi of Bahawalpur. The Peoples Party, which could not fulfill its commitment on the language issue in Punjab, embraced all the defeated feudal families of Punjab.

Before the 1970 elections, no serious effort for attaining an independent linguistic status for the dialects spoken in Punjab was seen. There were very feeble voices, mainly inspired by the late Dr Syed Abdullah, in favor of dialects. With the evaporation of feudal leadership in the elections, particularly in the central and some parts of northern and southern Punjab, the feudal belt of the South felt threatened by middle class Punjabis who stood for revolutionary agrarian reforms, tried to establish a new identity. They first opposed the introduction of Punjabi in the educational institutions. The elements which wanted to have a separate provincial status like the *Urdu Suba* also supported these anti-Punjabi moves and advocated for the further division of Punjab so that its strong hold on power could be weakened and feudal supremacy could be kept intact in their respective regions.

The prejudices based on dialects are mostly the results of uneven development and poor planning. The mass scale migration of 1947 and the colonization process also created problems.

Misunderstandings between the local landlords and the lower and middle class settlers from the upper and east Punjab, the speakers of two different dialects, had created a wedge which was further sharpened when the rural refugees from East Punjab replaced the non-Muslim population of these areas. There were many other factors also. For instance in the 1962 elections of the national assembly, Farooq A. Shaikh from Jhang district contested against Sajjad Husain Qureshi, Sajjada Nasheen of Bahauddin Zakariya. Farooq A. Shaikh was one of the owners of the Colony Textile Mills of Multan, while Sajjad Husain Qureshi was a *pir* and a landlord. Both of them belonged to the same linguistic group, that is Lehnda or Seraiki. But Farooq was dubbed as Punjabi and Sajjad as a Multani or Seraiki speaking local. The same logic was projected in the 1988 elections in Peshawar. Unhealthy political tactics have created bad blood amongst the people speaking the same language having different dialects. All this happened because the Punjabi language was never allowed entry into educational institutions where it could have ironed out its regional linguistic variations.

Bibliography

1. REHMAN, Tariq, 'The Right to Learn in Your Mother Tongue', *Daily Dawn*, 23 November 2003.
2. REHMAN, Tariq, *Language and Politics in Pakistan*, Karachi: Oxford University Press, 2003, p. 83.

Notes

1. *The Pakistan Times*, Rawalpindi, 2 August 1969.
2. *Monthly Punjabi Adab*, Lahore, September, 1696.
3. Rehman, Tariq, 'The Right to Learn in Your Mother Tongue', *Daily Dawn*, 23 November 2003.
4. Sekhon, Sant Singh and Kartar Singh, Duggal, *The History of Punjabi Literature*, Delhi, 1992, p. 6.
5. Rehman, Tariq, *Language and Politics in Pakistan*, Karachi: Oxford University Press, 2003, p. 83.

16

GENDER: IMPACT OF QUALITY EDUCATION AND EARLY CHILDHOOD EDUCATION

Shaheen Attiq ur Rehman[*]

ABSTRACT

Globally it is recognized that rural communities are more deprived than their city cousins, likewise their standard of life is not so 'comfortable', which results in mass migration to the city bringing on other problems. There is a need to facilitate rural communities, especially women, through learning to be able to earn more thus improving their standard of life. Education best manages to increase their income and make them aware of their livelihood assets. An illiterate is totally dependent on others. Unfortunately Pakistan has less than 35 per cent literate women.

Illiteracy results in ill health where the concept of safe motherhood is totally missing, desperately so in the rural areas where trained midwives are rare and the traditional birth attendants attend most births. It results in three women dying every hour and 20 more getting some birth related illness.

Illiteracy hampers the vision of families hence our women suffer from another problem, i.e. too many children. Officially our birth rate is said to be 2.1 per cent but ground reality shows a difference i.e. nearly seven to eight children in every family.

Mothers are also deprived of the best nutrition affecting the newborn resulting in stunting growth. With marginalized incomes and food security, the women eat less to give their men more to eat, though work-wise women often work more than the men.

Land holdings are depleting at a fast rate. One assessment says that 45 per cent of farmers hold less than five acres. With an increase in population at a rate of 3.1 million per year, land holdings will further deplete. Only if we manage our resources well, can we pull through. Attitudes have to be changed and there is no way better than with literacy particularly the neglected half, i.e. women.

It is essential to give rural communities, especially women, knowledge of issues most relevant to them, such as: how to increase their income, improve their health, make them aware of laws protecting them from domestic violence, custody of children, inheritance, land ownership; livestock and its ownership, child care, safe motherhood, etc.

---

*Ms Shaheen Attiqur Rahman, Director BUNYAD (NGO), received UNESCO'S Comminius Medal in 1998 in Paris for work in Literacy; was thrice Minister for Social Welfare and Women's Development, once of Literacy, and also remained Women Councillor of Lahore for two years.

GENDER: IMPACT OF QUALITY EDUCATION AND EARLY CHILDHOOD EDUCATION

By 2005, gender disparities in primary and secondary education should be eliminated. This is the commitment the international community made at the World Education Forum in Dakar in April 2000 when 57 percent of the 104 million children not in school were girls and two-thirds of the 860 million adults without literacy were women. The 2005 goal is just the first step.

By 2015, we are collectively committed to gender equality in education. So this is not just a matter of numbers. Parity is important, but it is not enough. Education is a right. This requires equal access to good-quality education for all; a learning process in which girls and boys, and women and men, have equal chances of fully developing their talents; and outcomes that bestow social and economic benefits on every citizen without discrimination. These benefits are immense. And they are attainable. As this report points out, there are policies and strategies which can put all societies on the educational path to gender equality, as those states which are well down this road can testify.

EFA GOALS AND STRATEGIES

WORLD EDUCATION FORUM (WEF) GOALS (DAKAR 2000)

1. Expanding and improving comprehensive early childhood care and education, especially for the most vulnerable and disadvantaged children.
2. Ensuring that by 2015 all children, particularly girls, children in difficult circumstances and those belonging to ethnic minorities, have access to and complete, free and compulsory primary education of good quality.
3. Ensuring that the learning needs of all young people and adults are met through equitable access to appropriate learning and life-skills programs.
4. Achieving a 50 percent improvement in levels of adult literacy by 2015, especially for women and equitable access to basic and continuing education for adults.
5. Eliminating gender disparities in primary and secondary education and achieving gender equality in education by 2015 with a focus on ensuring girl's full and equal access to and achievement in basic education of good quality.
6. Improving all aspects of the quality of education and ensuring excellence of all so that recognized and measurable learning outcomes are achieved by all, especially in literacy, numeracy and essential life skills.

THE COUNTRY SETTING

The Islamic Republic of Pakistan was formed on 14 August 1947. It has a geographical area of 79–61 million hectares. About 20 million hectares are under crop cultivation and approximately 3.5 million hectares is forest area. It is located in South Asia, bordering the Arabian Sea, between India on the east, Iran and Afghanistan on the west and China in the north. The Government is Parliamentary democracy. There are four provinces, 106 Districts, 397 Tehsils and two federally administered territories. Ethnic Groups in Pakistan are Punjabi, Sindhi, Pashtun (Pathan), Baloch and Muhajir (immigrants from India at the time of partition and their descendants) 97 per cent of the population is Muslim (Sunni 77 per cent Shi'a 20 per cent) while the remaining 3 per cent are Christian, Hindu, and others.

Indicators

Indicator	Estimate	Year	Source
Population (millions)	145	2001	UNFPA
Population Growth (1991 – 2001)	2.1	2001	Statistical Profile 2002
Population Density (per sq. km)	174.9	1999	WDI Database – 2000
Male / Female Ratio	51.9/48.1	2000-01	Economic Survey of Pakistan
Crude birth rate (per 1000 population)	30.2	1999	Pakistan Demographic Survey
Crude Death rate	8.3	1999	Pakistan Demographic Survey
Total Fertility rate	4.8	2000-01	Pakistan Reproductive Health & Family Planning Survey 2001–02
Infant Mortality rate (per 1000)	85	2000	Human development report 2002
Maternal Mortality rate	340	1997	Human development In South East Asia report
Literacy rate	45.0	1999	Pakistan demographic Survey
Literacy rate Females	32.0	1999	Pakistan Demographic Survey
Urban Rural Literacy ratio (%)	63/33.6	1999	Pakistan Demographic Survey
People below poverty line (%)	40	2000	Human Development Report 2002

FACTS AND FIGURES

A.	**Literacy Rate** (%)	49
	Male	61.3
	Female	36.8

B.	**Elementary Education**	
	Primary Education	
	Number of Primary Schools	
	Including 27,000 mosque schools	1,49,163
	Total Teachers	3,74,000
	Male	2,36,000
	Female	1,38,000
	Student Teacher Ratio	48:1
	Left out/ Out of school children	5.5 million
	Gross Participation Ration	83%
	Male	103%
	Female	64%
	Net Enrolment Rate	66%
	Male	82%
	Female	64%
	Dropout Rate	50%
	Male	44%
	Female	56%
	Middle Schools	24,877

C.	Secondary Education	
	Secondary Schools	8,509
	Secondary Vocational Institutions	580
	Higher Secondary Schools	682

D.	Technical Education	
	1. Number of Polytechnic Institutes/ colleges of Technology	
	Public sector	61
	Private Sector	47
	2. Vocational Institutions	310

E.	Colleges	
	Arts & Science Colleges	853
	Professional Colleges	308

Source: Education Sector Reforms Action Plan (2001–2004), Government of Pakistan, p. 90.
Note: Our social indicators are weaker than of Nepal or Bangladesh.

Table 1: Growth in Literacy Rate

Year	Male	Female	Total
1961	25.1	6.7	16.7
1972	30.2	11.6	21.7
1981	35.1	16.0	26.2
1998	56.5	32.6	45.0

Source: 1. Pakistan Economic Survey 1976–77.
  2. UNESCO, Literary Trends in Pakistan, Islamabad, 2002.

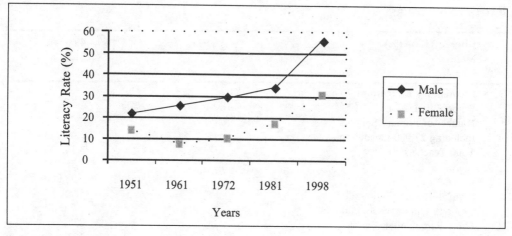

Source: Literacy Trends in Punjab, UNESCO Islamabad 2002.

FIG. 1: LITERACY RATE - MALE AND FEMALE

The overall male / female literacy rates are depicted in Figure I, figure highlights the gender divide The 'gap' between male and female can be seen as under; which is growing due to the rapid increase in population.

CURRENT EDUCATIONAL PRIORITIES AND CONCERNS

The National Education Policy (NEP) of 1998 reiterated Pakistan's firm resolve and determination to intensify its attempts to achieve universalization of primary education—a national goal that has been eluding the nation so far. The Policy lays down the following guiding principles to materialize the aims and objectives relating to the promotion of basic education thereby paving the way to achieve a gross participation rate of 105 per cent at the primary level by the year 2010:

- Universalizing primary education, eliminating drop-out, and fulfilling the basic learning needs by the year 2010
- Raising the literacy rate to 55 per cent by the year 2003, and to 70 per cent by the year 2010, through extensive adult education programs for functional literacy; the Prime Minister's Literacy Commission (PMLC) will prepare a plan of action in consultation with provinces for a co-ordinated effort within the framework of the National Literacy Movement
- Tackling women's education, and education of urban and rural poor through special programs for equal access to education and for bringing them within the realm of literate and productive citizens
- Improving the quality of education by reasserting the role of the teacher in the teaching-learning process, by modernizing curricula and textbooks, by improving physical facilities, and by introducing activity-oriented new sciences at all levels of school education
- Inviting the private sector for participation in educational programs and allowing progressive investment in educational institutions

- Giving teachers a prominent status in society, but at the same time subjecting them to accountability-based performance and evaluation
- Creating an overall operational framework which would enable the provinces to ensure effective translation of agreed policies into action, and in particular improve delivery services at the institutional level, thereby attaining the ultimate goal of enhanced quality

The goals of elementary education in Pakistan are to meet everyone's basic learning needs, to provide tools necessary for people to survive and improve the quality of their lives through continuous learning. Major **issues and challenges** of elementary education according to the 1998 NEP are as follows:

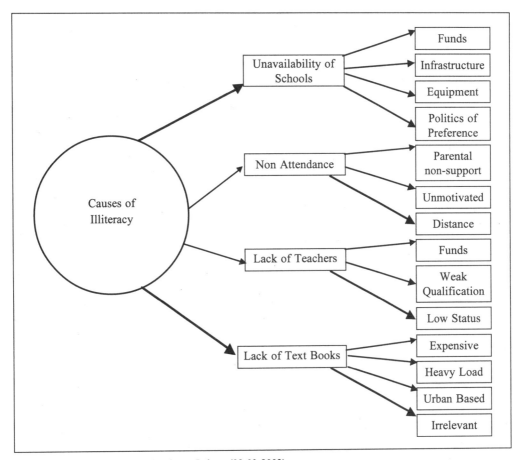

Source: UNDP + Civil Service Academy, Lahore (09-03-2003).

FIG. 2

Some important information on our state of illiteracy:

- More than 5.5 million primary school-age children (5–9) are left out
- Approximately 45 per cent of children drop-out of school without completing elementary education

- Teachers' absenteeism is common in schools especially in rural areas; teachers' commitment and motivation is lacking
- Instructional supervision is weak at elementary level
- About one-fourth of elementary school teachers are untrained and the present training infrastructure does not appear to improve the quality of instruction
- Learning materials are inadequate and of poor quality; teaching methods are harsh, they do not motivate pupils and they do not favour learning
- Above all, character building, which is the basic and fundamental objective of education and training, is neglected, creating serious problems both for the individual and the nation

CRITICAL ISSUES FOR WOMEN IN PAKISTAN

As shown in the table above, the literacy rate of women is very low in Pakistan, particularly in rural areas, it is therefore pertinent that some strategies be developed for an increase in the literacy rate that would ultimately lead to the transformation of the Rural scenario. Prior to that, we should look at the problems being faced by the women of Pakistan.

In Pakistan's economy, women play an active role. But their contribution has been grossly underreported in various census and surveys. The women in rural areas in particular work in the agricultural farms but their work is never accounted for. Even in the reports of Statistical Bureau of Pakistan, the work load of women farmers is never shown. Thus their share in the economy of the country is reported to be negligible. However the women are involved in farm work from sowing to harvesting as invisible and unpaid labour. Moreover, they are major contributors to household income. If women's contribution to economic production is assessed accurately, a conservative estimate of women's participation would be more than 40 per cent.

Education

In Pakistan, the educational process shows poor results. Particularly, the educational status of Pakistani women is among the lowest in the world. According to the UNESCO report on the literacy trends in Pakistan 2002, women have a literacy rate of 32.60 per cent, as against 56.50 per cent in men in 1998. Similarly, the literacy rate for the urban population of female is 55.60 per cent, whereas the literacy rate for the rural female population is 20.8 per cent. Moreover, this rural/urban differential is more pronounced in the case of women than in men. The literacy rate for urban men (72.60 per cent) is almost twice the rate of rural men (42.40 per cent). However the literacy arte for urban women is more than three times the rate for rural women.

In Punjab, according to the report on the literacy trends in Pakistan, women have a literacy rate of 35.10 per cent as compared to 57.20 per cent in men in 1998. Similarly the literacy rate for the urban population of females is 57.23 per cent, whereas the literacy rate for the rural female population is 24.78 per cent.

The chart below shows the huge gaps between out of school children and gender gaps.

School Children
(Government / Private and Other schools)
EMIS 2000–01 Punjab Scenario II*

	Total Population			Enrolled Children (000)			Out of School (000)			Gap Girls Enrolled
School Age Group	Total	Male	Female	Total	Male	Female	Total	Male	Female
5–9	11.23	5.82	5.41	9.19	5.26	3.93	2.04	0.56	1.48	-1.33
10–12	6.30	3.33	2.97	2.25	1.36	0.88	4.05	1.97	2.09	-0.48
13–14	3.30	1.70	1.60	0.93	0.58	0.35	2.37	1.12	1.25	-0.23
10–14	9.60	5.03	4.57	3.18	1.94	1.23	6.42	3.09	3.34	-0.71
15–16	2.93	1.50	1.43	0.42	0.20	0.22	2.51	1.30	1.21	+0.02

Source: EMIS Report (2002).

Another startling EMIS study shows that the ratio of drop-outs is very high, nearly 68.6 per cent primary girl-children do not complete class 5 and less then 10 per cent complete their 10th class.

Dropouts	Total	Female
Class 1–5	59.7 per cent	68.6 per cent
Class 1–8	75.9 per cent	80.9 per cent
Class 1–10	87.1 per cent	90 per cent

Source: EMIS Report (2002).

Above is another reflection on the 'poor quality' of Education, where families do not feel any 'relevance' of learning on their daughter's life. The 2 most striking reasons are—unwillingness of the parents to send their girls to school, parent and child unwilling to go, due to the inaccurate atmosphere of the school.

Reasons for Leaving School before Completing Primary (10–18 Years)
By Sex and Residence (%)(1998–99)

	Boys			Girls		
Reasons	Urban	Rural	Overall	Urban	Rural	Overall
Parents did not allow	3	3	3	20	19	19
Too Expensive	33	18	23	34	17	22
Too far	0	1	1	3	6	5
Education not useful	0	1	1	2	1	1
Had to help at work	8	8	8	1	2	2
Child not willing	41	45	44	21	27	25
Other	12	12	15	10	19	17
Completed desired Education	0	1	1	0	0	0

Source: Anonymous 2002.

Quality

In short—how much has the student learnt till the primary level, which should go beyond reading, writing and numeracy—it should make the child understand how to deal with lug dig life and to handle his/her daily problems.

BEST PRACTICES IN QUALITY BASIC/PRIMARY EDUCATION

There is no absolutely clear definition of quality. Quality has often been understood as being synonymous with effectiveness, efficiency and equity. It is the cumulative effect of a number of elements, which must work together to produce a generally acceptable level of efficiency that can be regarded as quality. It has been a multi-level concept and the following have been identified as the core elements of quality.

a) **Learning environment**: includes physical space, provision of (needed) facilities, school climate and ethos, and health services support.
b) **Learning process**: curriculum, philosophy and activities (holistic), relevance, methodology, materials, assessment procedures.
c) **Teacher** attitude, qualification, experience, flexible, caring.
d) **Teacher Development Programme**: relevance, content, methodology, frequency and follow-up.
e) **Support and Supervisory Mechanism**: Monitoring and Evaluation; and
f) **Parent/Community Involvement**.

The Expanded Commentary on the DFA (Para III/6/44) states:

> Successful (meaning quality) education programme requires: (1) healthy, and motivated students, (2) well-trained and committed teachers, (3) adequate facilities and learning materials, (4) a relevant curriculum, (5) a gender-sensitive and safe environment that encourages learning (6) a clear definition and accurate assessment of learning outcomes, including knowledge, skills, attitudes and values, (7) participatory governance and management, and (8) respect for and engagement with local communities and cultures (UNICEF, Florence, 2000).

UNICEF provides a synthesis of consensus around the basic dimensions of quality as below (UNICEF, 2000, Florence):

a) Healthy and well-nourished learners, supported in learning by their families and communities;
b) Healthy, safe, protective and gender-sensitive environments, providing adequate resources and facilities for quality education;
c) Relevant curricula and materials, which provide (appropriate) content for acquisition of basic skills, especially in literacy, numeracy and life skills, and knowledge in such areas as gender, health, nutrition, HIV/AIDS prevention and peace;
d) Trained teachers using child-centred teaching approaches in well-managed classrooms and schools and skillful assessment to facilitate learning and reduce disparities; and
e) Outcomes that encompass knowledge, skills and attitudes and are linked to national goals for education and positive participation in society.

It has been recognized that the quality assurance elements that are part of the internal efficiency and rooted in the external realities (home, immediate community and society/country) as enumerated in the three formulations of quality above.

In Bangladesh, quality is currently adjudged as mastery of the 53 terminal competencies, termed as Essential Learning Continua (ELC), at the end of five years of primary schooling. The present competency-based curriculum was introduced during 1992–1996; sequentially from grade I to grade V. Children are required to achieve another set of competencies in each of the subjects taught, by the end of the primary cycle.

Three formulations of Quality of UNESCO and UNICEF, are listed below:

1)   Elements of Quality

a) **Learners:** reasonably healthy, nourished and clean, motivated and supported by the family and the community.

b) LEARNING ENVIRONMENT: adequate physical space, clean and healthy surroundings, safe and secure, protective and gender-sensitive, good school climate and ethos (a culture of positive attitude), provides adequate facilities and access to health and nutrition services;

c) **Learning process:** relevant curriculum with adequate learning and supplementary materials, providing content that helps acquisition of basic skills in literacy, numeracy and life skills, knowledge relating to gender, health, nutrition, HIV/AIDS prevention, arsenic contamination and remedy.

d) **Teacher:** well qualified, appropriate attitude/aptitude, professionally trained, with opportunity for regular updating, and uses child-centered and interactive approaches in well-managed classrooms and schools, facilitates learning and helps reduce gender and other disparities; and makes skillful assessment of clearly defined learning outcomes;

e) **Support and supervisory mechanism:** provision of Academic Supervision of teachers, monitoring and evaluation of school performance with remedial action;

f) **Effective management of education:** participatory governance and involvement of parents and local community in the management and operation of the school; *and*

g) **Outcomes** that encompass knowledge, skills, attitudes and values, linked to national goals for education and development and positive participation in society.

All the quality elements may not come together in one best practice. Following Jomtien the rush was to open up the access, enhance retention and completion and decrease the dropout phenomenon. Intensive social mobilization and incentive programs were mounted to motivate, draw and retain children in schools, particularly girls, as they are much behind the boys. A good number of measures must also be taken to improve the quality of education and rate of children's achievement.

Quality in Basic/Primary Education:

1990 (Jomtien) Initiatives at improving quality following areas were identified:

(i)   School Management Committee:

The local people developed apathy towards the school since, in their view, the government took over the institution and it was for the government to manage it. As state employees, teachers felt relieved of local control and accountability to any local body; The recent devolution, it is hoped will have more local monitoring.

Urgency of community participation for effective operation of schools. As a measure involving the community the Government reorganized School Management Committees (SMC) with participation of local people for effective management of primary schools in the 1990s. The head Teacher of the Primary School acts as Member-Secretary. The section of local's include parents but most are non-functioning.

SMCs should serve as the bridge between the school and the community to ensure involvement and participation of community so as to turn the school into a community enterprise for effective functioning. It is recognized that appropriate training would help the SMC manage the school teacher by being more involved in making his/him better.

Teacher and Teacher Development

Teachers are at the core of education, at any level. Their commitment and quality of performance can make a major difference in attendance, retention and achievement of children, as well as the overall quality of primary education. The required qualification for appointment as Primary school teachers is now BA.

(ii) Improved Ways of Teaching and Learning

The basic core classroom innovation which uses the child-centered, participatory and group-orientated method of teaching, and learning, has recently been introduced in Teacher's trainings.

To provide academic support for the primary education system in the tehsil in order to:

- Improve classroom teaching-learning process;
- Improve teaching skills of the classroom teacher;
- Improve the quality of classroom and school management;
- Strengthen sub-cluster training by providing regular, professional and technical support services;
- Establish a data bank on quality indicators of primary education;
- Work as a demonstration center for educational technology and modern equipment.

(iii) Curriculum Review and Renewal

In Punjab, a strong emphasis put made on updating curricular on the same basis as that of South East Asia. The goal is achieved through interventions designed to enhance teaching-learning methods, school environment and children's learning achievement.

- Informing people about quality primary education
- Increasing community participation
- Changing the behaviour of teachers to make teaching and learning more participatory
- Maximizing the resources available for primary education

(iv) Management of Primary Education

One of the major problems of quality was associated with 'education and education management'. Good governance and management are among the major key factors that contribute to improving the quality of education. Often recruitment, transfers are biased due to political and 'influentials' manipulation.

(v) Capacity Building for Improved Management

Developing training materials and modules and conducting training workshops/ courses for the relevant officials.

- Trained, efficient and committed teachers guide the teaching-learning activities
- The child gets the opportunity to learn in a safe, healthy and joyful environment
- The children gain appropriate knowledge, skills and outlook about their future life through a (life-oriented) curriculum
- Local level planning, accountability and social ownership of the school gain acceptability at all levels (of society)

(vi) EMIS and Reliable Database

Reliable data in primary education has been a major problem. In the absence of birth registration, getting exact information on ages of children was indeed difficult. Enrollment of over-aged and under-aged children, dropouts, repetition, double or multiple enrollment (in government primary schools and/ or NGO learning centres) made the situation more difficult. EMIS and NEMIS is making an effort but their information is not too user friendly. In Punjab, there is no school mapping of education facilities.

(vii) Quality in Non-Formal Basic Education

To ensure quality of education, ensures that 66.67% operation and management standard in practice, the NFE, maintains a teacher/learner ratio of 1:30. per cent to 70 per cent of learners are girls; conducts class in a one-room facility (minimum 33.44 m²), where children sit in a U-shape arrangement; teacher follows a child-centred interactive approach to teaching-learning, gives very little homework. FEC meetings are held every month where the progress of children in the centre is discussed; it provides strong supervision of schools through program organizers.

RECOMMENDATIONS FOR QUALITY EDUCATION

a) Local government units at their respective levels can help energize the communities to ensure enrollment of all school-age children in primary schools, regular attendance, completion of cycle and reducing dropout or repetition; ensure regular attendance and improved classroom performance of teachers, availability of housing facilities, particularly for non-resident female teachers;

b) Modify the present system, which allows local governments to undertake education projects, among others, to encourage them to lend support to both government and non-government schools in their operation financially and in social mobilization and participation in local level planning and mobilization of local resources; to facilitate effective survey of school-age children and other target groups of basic education.

Coordination with civil society sector /public private partnership.
Another view of Quality is listed as under...

Pakistan
No of children (age 5–6)

Enrolled: 60 per cent	Never enrolled: 40 per cent
Completers: 33 per cent of enrolled	Non-Completers: 67 per cent of enrolled
20 per cent of total no. of Children	40 per cent of the total children
Achievers estimates: 50 per cent of completers	Non-Achievers: 50 per cent of completers
10 per cent of total children	10 per cent of total children
systems retering over all efficiency: 10 per cent	over all systems losses: 90 per cent

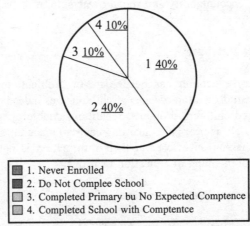

1. Never Enrolled
2. Do Not Comple School
3. Completed Primary bu No Expected Comptence
4. Completed School with Comptentce

Note: Pie chart above is based on the official figures presented in the country report and are drawn from 'Synthesis Report' EFA in south Asia and west Asia, (A decade after Jomtien, 2000.)

FIG. 3

Quality of education in the public sector is a large problem, as parents feel that it is not relevant that jobs are not reachable by their children, specially so in the rural areas. Often even after 5 years of schooling, the student 'learns' nothing. The chart above highlights the issue more clearly.

Teachers need constant training to up-date the knowledge of their subject while keeping the interest of their students alive. Curriculum must be made relevant and there are many problems faced by the urban rural divide; the gender gap, non-marketable topics; More dependence on languages rather than contents. Self expression is sadly missing. One main reason is that there are no clear defined benchmarks on having minimum standards of education, which can be identified as a comparison.

The basic criteria of 'Quality' is how much is learnt/absorbed by the learner, with only 10% achievements, we have a lot of catching up to do.

Bunyad Literacy Community Council (BLCC),

Lahore, Pakistan has been working in the rural communities of Punjab since 1992 and has implemented a large number of programs for supporting the marginalized,especially the women and children in the rural and peri-urban areas. Though the EFA goals were framed in 2000, Bunyad had already initiated the same work in 1995. In this connection it successfully implemented a project termed *Women's Empowerment for Poverty Alleviation,* which combined functional literacy, skill development and micro finance components to bear upon the social and economic situation of rural women.

Early Childhood Education

Bunyad has work experience in ECCWD, with 2 concepts: Spin –off, a UNICEF activity where we focused on giving some 'learning lessons or in-sights' to the siblings of our NFPE learners. This took place in Shujabad, but as support was for less than a year, sustainability could not be possible, though the interest of the child and parents was aroused.

Early Childhood Care and Education in Daska (Sialkot) targeted parents and communities who were captured by learning and by improving the special condition for this age group (3–5 years). Bunyad was one of the first NGO's to be in this sector i.e. focusing on this age group of the rural area. Urban areas have a large number of facilities for this age group like kindergartens, nurseries, day care centres but the concept is quite alien in the rural scene. Some areas of intervention are:

- Provide child-centered, family-focused, community-based holistic care and education to pre-school children: special focus on the disabled and the excluded
- Build capacity to improve quality of case and education
- Improve data gathering and analysis

E.C.C.D. (Early Childhood Care And Development)

Bunyad initiated a Pilot Project in one Union Council Gholatian Kalan Tehsil Daska of Sialkot district with the collaboration of Child Care Resource Centre of the College of Home Economics, Lahore, targeting 15 Locations of the Union Council and 2,854 community members of the 7 villages.

To develops village level model for Early Child Care and Development, the project components include social mobilization of communities, ECCD training material development, monitoring of ECCD activities and provision of funds.

Objectives of the project were:

- To sensitize the community on Early Childhood Care and Development concept
- To mobilize the community to adopt Early Childhood Care and Development practices
- To disseminate information to 100% households in the community

Strategy

The ECCD program highlights the importance of child development during his/her early years in the following three domains:

1. Physical Development
2. Mental Development
3. Social/Emotional Development.

Component

- Health and Care
- Nutrition
- Education (Non-Formal Education)

ECCD promotes a family approach up to grass-root level among communities and develops adopted skills with special emphasis on community based programs and caregivers' training. Target group included in ECCD is the caregiver of the children from 0 – 6 years.

Activities

1. The ECCD programs are designed to address:

- Children's health and care related issues
- Nutritional needs
- Development abilities (physical, moral, social emotional and cognitive)

2. The ECCD addresses the needs and the surroundings of young children (0–5 years) through:

- Families (Care givers)
- Institutional programs
- Communities

As these programs reflect cultural values, therefore, an understanding of traditional and existing child rearing practices are inevitable.

Universal Basic Education, in Murree and Sialkot was quite successful as in both Tehsils Bunyad achieved access to over 90 per cent of schools by involving VEC and parents—and motivating teachers and staff.

- Opportunity for All to receive a basic education of good quality
- Incorporate formal and non-formal approaches and programs within an integrated inclusive system of basic education
- Improve demand and increase supply through closer collaboration and partnership

Another project related to **Universal Primary Education (UPE)** is being implemented by Bunyad/BLCC in Sialkot. 97 per cent of the total children strength has been enrolled and as per third party evaluation dropout rate is below 0.7 per cent

Over 200,000 learners in Punjab are using curricula developed by Bunyad.

Suggestions

1. Stirring political will is needed, all political parties must have one voice for Basic Education, and move a bill that education is a fundamental Human Right.
2. The private school systems must get recognition for their contribution to the overall Quality in the Education sector, by incentives such as fewer taxes.
3. As nearly 50 per cent children dropout before completing their primary schooling NFPE (non- formal primary education) be strengthened as a safety net, that such children should not remain illiterate but have a second chance at learning.
4. AE—Adult Education, especially for women, must be encouraged as quality education cannot be achieved with an illiterate mother.
5. A learning society be made, where women are able to read and a culture of knowledge prevails, with CCL at the u.c level.
6. The gender gap must be narrowed as the dropout rate of girls is higher than that of boys.

Supportive Suggestions

- Involving teachers in development of curriculum
- Enhance public perception of teachers
- Incentives to attract and retain good teachers
- Strong on-going support and professional development support for teachers, supervisors and managers
- Adequate learning and reading materials
- Learning experiences and materials to ensure social and cultural relevance

Education Management Reform

- Accountability of school system to learners, parents and communities; ensuring strong and effective SMC's
- Development and monitoring of locally relevant indicators compatible with national standards and curriculum frameworks, identifying minimum achievement level indicators
- Increased emphasis on decentralization of management along with access to a strong EMIS, at tehsil level and union council

Integration of Development Activities

- Partnership between Govt., NGOs, donors in policy planning, implementation and monitoring: this means more than linking various components of EFA (ECCE, Literacy, Primary Education, Continuing Education)
- Formation of CLC—community learning centers, at UC level

Exchange of Information Experience and Innovations

- Use technology to promote equitable exchange of experiences and innovations
- Exchange to cover all dimensions of education: policy, curriculum, teacher education, and evaluation

References

1. Economic Survey of Pakistan, 2000.
2. Gender and Education for All: The leap to Equality, Summary Report, UNESCO Publishing
3. Literacy Trends in Pakistan, Islamabad: UNESCO, 2002.
4. Government Of Pakistan, National Plan of Action on Education for All 2001–2015, Islamabad: Ministry of Education, April 2003.
5. EMIS Data for Punjab, 2002.
6. Government Of Pakistan, Provincial Census Report of Punjab 1998, Islamabad: Population Census Organization, Statistics Division, January 2001.
7. UNICEF (2000b) defining quality, working groups on Education, Florence, June 2000.
8. Government Of Bangladesh, Report of the study on Best Practices, Ministry of Primary and Mass Education, 2003.

17

THE KNOWLEDGE PRODUCTION FUNCTION AND R&D SPILLOVERS

Prof. Dr David Audretsch and Dr Talat Mahmood

ABSTRACT

Innovative activity is linked to knowledge generating inputs through what has become known as the knowledge production function. While a long tradition of estimating the knowledge production function for firms has been established, or even for industries, most studies implicitly assumed that economic geography plays no role. Only recently has a wave of studies emerged, focusing on the extent of knowledge spillovers within geographically spatial units. This paper introduces a spatial model at the level of cities. Innovative activity, (measured as the number of patents issued to firms located within a city) is linked to knowledge producing inputs such as the R&D expenditures by private corporations, as well as research undertaken at university laboratories at the state level within which the city is located. In addition, several sources of knowledge specific to the city, such as the presence of a high degree of human capital and the number of research centers are linked to the innovative output of that city. We find that innovative activity tends to cluster spatially in those regions with a rich endowment in knowledge.

*Paper presented at the Sustainable Development Policy Institute (SDPI) conference on 12 December, 2003 in Islamabad. We wish to thank Dr Shafqat Shehzad, Research Fellow, at the Sustainable Development Policy Institute for her valuable comments.

Prof. Dr David Audretsch is the Director, Institute for Development Strategies, Indiana University .
Dr Talat Mahmood is the Senior Fellow, Social Science Research Center Berlin (WZB).
Correspondence to : Dr. (Econ.) Dr (Engr.) Talat Mahmood.
Research Unit: Competitiveness and Industrial Change, Social Science Research Center Berlin (WZB)
D-10785 Berlin, Germany.
Ph: ++ 49-30-25491-422 (sec: 407).
Fax: ++ 49-30-25491684.
Email: mahmood@medea.wz-berlin.de

INTRODUCTION

One of the most striking implications from the new economic growth theories is that increasing returns to knowledge within a spatially bounded region result in a divergence of growth rates.[1] Perhaps more than most other economic activities, innovation and technological change depend upon new economic knowledge. Thus, Romer (1986 and 1990), Krugman (1991a and 1991b), and Grossman and Helpman (1991), among others, have focused on the role that spillovers of economic knowledge across agents and firms play in generating increasing returns and ultimately economic growth. While the new endogenous growth theory models economic growth as a function of innovative activity, a different literature has tried to explain the level of innovative activity. In particular, Griliches (1979) introduced the model of the knowledge production function which explains innovative output on the basis of knowledge inputs.

Several studies have recently identified the extent to which knowledge spillovers take place. An important finding of Jaffe (1989), Acs, Audretsch and Feldman (1992 and 1994), and Feldman (1994a and 1994b) was that investment in research and development (R&D) made by private corporations and universities 'spills over' for economic exploitation by third-party firms. But all of these studies have imposed geographic boundaries at the spatial level of the state. The purpose of this paper is to shift the unit of observation from the state to the city, enabling some insight into the appropriate spatial dimension of knowledge spillovers.[2] In addition, we are able to link spillovers from new knowledge created by research and development (R&D) activities of private corporations, the research activities of university laboratories, embodied in high levels of human capital, and research centers to the innovative activity of firms within the framework of the knowledge production.

The second section of this paper presents, what has become known as the knowledge production function and how it has been applied to identify the extent of knowledge spillovers. In the third section, measurement issues are discussed and the data-base consisting of the patent activity of sixty US cities between 1988 and 1992 is presented. A knowledge production function, linking knowledge to inputs, is estimated in the fourth section. Finally, in the last section, a summary and conclusion are provided. There is strong evidence suggesting that both R&D expenditures from private corporations, as well as research undertaken in the laboratories of universities within a state provide important inputs generating innovative activity within the individual cities located within that state. At the same time, several knowledge producing inputs specific to the city, such as the presence of a high level of human capital and a large number of research centers, are found to be conducive to innovative activity within the city.

THE KNOWLEDGE PRODUCTION FUNCTION

As introduced by Zvi Griliches (1979), the knowledge production links inputs in the innovation process to innovative outputs. Arrow (1962) pointed out that the most decisive innovative input is new economic knowledge, and that the greatest source that generates new economic knowledge is generally considered to be R&D. While Scherer (1983) and Bound et al. (1984) estimated the knowledge production function in terms of R&D Inputs generating a type of intermediate innovative output,[3] Acs and Audretsch (1988 and 1990), Schwalbach and Zimmerman (1991), and Link and Bozeman (1991) estimated the knowledge production function in terms of R&D inputs generating a more direct measure of innovative output.

While the measure of innovative output varied across these studies, they had one common feature—the unit of observation was always in terms of product space, measured either by industries or firms. In this more traditional application of the knowledge production function, knowledge inputs were linked to innovative output within a unit of observation that was bounded in terms of the industry or, in several cases, even the firm, but were unbounded geographically in terms of the location of the innovating entities.

One of the more striking findings that emerge from studies focusing on the source of innovative activity is that small firms (generally considered to have fewer than 500 employees) are not only innovative, but in certain industries, more so than their larger counterparts. This result seemed to contradict the stylized fact that the bulk of R&D is undertaken by the largest corporations (Scherer, 1991 and 1992; Cohen and Klepper, 1991 and 1992). Since R&D inputs are presumably the key source for generating new economic knowledge in the knowledge production function, this finding raised the question, 'Where do small firms get the innovation producing knowledge inputs?'

One possible answer is that, while the model of the knowledge production function may be valid, the assumed unit of observation—at the level of the firm—may be less valid. Krugman (1991 and 1991b) extends the earlier thesis of Alfred Marshall (1920) by arguing that the relevant unit of observation may actually be a constellation of complementary firms within a geographic unit, so that knowledge can 'spill over' from one firm within the region to another. In fact, Marshall had summarized three types of forces that contribute to the localization of economic activity. The first of these forces involves the degree to which a pooled labour market exists.[4] Krugman (1991b) points out that it is actually the interaction of increasing returns and reduced uncertainty that bestows advantages in the pooling of labour markets associated with agglomeration. The second force that Marshall identified was a greater provision of non-traded inputs, or the development of specialized intermediate goods industries.[5] The third force emanates from economies in information flows or knowledge spillovers among the firms in an industry.

In what Glaeser, Kallal, Scheinkman, and Schleifer (1992, p. 1127) characterize as the 'Marshall-Arrow-Romer' model, new economic knowledge is viewed as spilling over firms within a given geographic space because, 'After all, intellectual breakthroughs must cross hallways and streets more easily than oceans and continents.' That is, location and proximity matter. While the cost of transmitting information may be virtually invariant to distance, presumably the cost of transmitting new economic knowledge, which is generally considered to be more of a tacit than an explicit nature, rises with distance.

In studying the networks in California's Silicon Valley, Saxenian (1990, pp. 96–97) emphasized that it is the communication between individuals that facilitates the transmission of knowledge across agents, firms, and even industries, and not just the high endowment of workers' knowledge, that has promoted the high degree of innovative activity:

'It is not simply the concentration of skilled labor, suppliers and information that distinguish the region. A variety of regional institutions—including Stanford University, several trade associations and local business organizations, and a myriad of specialized consulting, market research, public relations and venture capital firms—provide technical, financial, and networking services which the region's enterprises often cannot afford individually. These networks defy sectoral barriers: individuals move easily from semiconductor to disk drive firms or from Computer to network makers. They move from established firms to startups (or vice versa) and even to market research or consulting firms, and from consulting firms back into startups. And they continue to meet at trade shows, industry conferences, and the scores of seminars, talks, and social activities organized by local business organizations and trade associations. In these forums, relationships are easily formed and maintained, technical and market information is exchanged, business contacts are established, and new enterprises are conceived.... This decentralized and fluid environment also promotes the diffusion of intangible technological capabilities and understandings.[6]

An important finding of Jaffe (1986 and 1989) was that investment in R&D made by private corporations and universities 'spills over' for economic exploitation by third party firms. Jaffe modified the knowledge production function to include spatial boundaries, so that the patent activity within a geographical unit—a state—was related to the private corporate expenditures and R&D within that state, as well as the research expenditures undertaken at universities. Jaffe's (1989) statistical results provided evidence that corporate patent activity responds positively to commercial spillovers from university research. Not only does patent activity increase in the presence of high private corporate expenditures an R&D, but also as a result of research expenditures undertaken by universities within the states. Acs, Audretsch and Feldman (1992), Feldman (1994a and 1994b) confirmed that Jaffe's findings held when a direct measure of innovative activity was substituted for the measure of patented inventions. *In order to explicitly identify the recipients of R&D spillovers, Acs, Audretsch and Feldman (1993) modified the knowledge production for adaptation to a model specified to incorporate spillover effects within spatial units of observation:*

$$I = \alpha RD^{\beta_1} * UR^{\beta_2} * (UR * GC)^{\beta_3} * \varepsilon \qquad (1)$$

where I is innovative output, RD is the private corporate expenditures an R&D, UR the research expenditures undertaken at universities, GC measures the geographic coincidence of university and corporate research,[7] and represents stochastic disturbance. By estimating equation (1) for the innovative activity contributed by all firms separately from the innovative activity contributed by small firms, and then directly comparing the magnitude of the coefficients of RD and UR, Acs, Audretsch and Feldman (1993) were able to identify the relative importance of R&D spillovers from universities and corporate laboratories for large and small firms. In particular, their empirical results suggested that the innovative output of all firms rises along with an increase in the amount of R&D input, both in private corporations, as well as in university laboratories. However, R&D expenditures made by private companies play a particularly important role in providing Inputs to the innovative activity of large firms, while expenditures and research made by universities serve as an especially key Input for generating innovative activity in small enterprises. These results suggested that new economic knowledge created both in university laboratories, as well as in the R&D labs of private corporations spill over to generate innovative activity in third party firms.[8]

Other studies concur that knowledge spillovers tend to be geographically bounded within the region where new economic knowledge was created (Agrawal 2000, Anselin, Acs and Varga 1997; Orlando 2000, Autant-Bernard 2001a and b). Scholars have continued to work in this tradition, adding new measures of innovative output and refining the measures of innovative inputs and outputs. For example, Black (2002) developed a measure of innovation based on awards made in the United States Small Business Innovation Research (SBIR) Program. In estimating a knowledge production function along the lines of equation (1) for a variety of geographic units and using different measures of innovative output, the results concur that the logic of the knowledge production function is robust across geography. Autant-Bernard (2001a, 2001b) and Orlando (2000) model the interplay between geographic and technological proximity for inter-firm spillovers. Their results suggest that the importance of geographic proximity for spillovers is dependent on the propensity of similar industrial activity to agglomerate geographically.

Estimation of the knowledge production function has typically varied the spatial unit from relatively broad geographic units of observations, such as states, to much more focused geographic units of observations such as cities, counties or even zip codes. Most scholars concur that states are probably too broad to represent an appropriate geographic unit of observation. Some have tried to estimate the geographic extent of knowledge spillovers in miles using the concept of distance decay (Adams 2002; Wallsten 2001). Others contend that geography is more of a platform for organizing economic activity and that 'as the crow flies', measures of distance do not capture complex social relationships (Feldman 2002; Branstetter 2002).

MEASUREMENT

Krugman (1991a, p. 53), argues that economists should focus on the first two of Marshall's (1920) forces shaping the extent of geographic concentration, because '...knowledge flows are invisible; they leave no paper trail by which they may be measured and tracked, and there is nothing to prevent the theorist from assuming anything about them that she likes.' But Jaffe, Trajtenberg and Henderson (1993, p. 578) point out that 'knowledge flows do sometimes leave a paper trail'—in particular, in the form of patented inventions. We follow the example of Jaffe (1989) and Jaffe, Trajtenberg and Henderson (1993) by measuring innovative output in terms of the number of patents registered by firms within the relevant geographic area.

But what is the relevant geographic area? All of the studies identifying the extent of R&D spillovers, discussed in the previous section, implicitly assume that: state borders pose the relevant boundaries impeding the flow of knowledge between the source where it is produced and the enterprise which ends up transforming it into economic, knowledge, or innovative activity. This is a rather arbitrary assumption in which the obvious appeal is that it conforms to a number of data sources and is clearly a crude guess of the relevant economic market. As Krugman (1991 b, p. 57) emphasizes, 'states aren't really the right geographical units, because of the disparities in population size and the lack of concordance between economic markets and political units'. To assume that knowledge created in San Diego can spill all the way up to generate innovative activity by firms in the San Francisco Bay area, while new economic knowledge created in, say, Princeton, New Jersey cannot spill over to firms located in New York City is not accurate because borders cannot be marked.

Thus, in this study we adapt a more precise geographic unit of observation—the city, broadly defined. In particular, we try to link the innovative activity emanating from specific cities to knowledge generating inputs, not only contained within that city, but also within a broader geographic area, the state:

$$I = RD^{\beta_1} * UR^{\beta_2} * HK^{\beta_3} * RC^{\beta_4} * SRC^{\beta_5} * \varepsilon \qquad (2)$$

The measure of innovative output of each geographic unit, the city, is defined as the number of patents registered by firms located within the city between 1988 and 1992. RD is defined as the amount of 1989 private corporate R&D expenditures (millions of dollars) in the state within which the city is located (Source: National Science Board, Science & Engineering Indicators, Tenth Edition, 1991), UR is defined as the 1989 expenditures (millions of dollars) and research undertaken at universities located in the state within which the city is located (Source: National Science Board, Science & Engineering Indicators, Tenth Edition, 1991). An implicit assumption we make is that knowledge created beyond the city boundaries can spill over to influence the innovative activity generated within that city.

However, knowledge created within the city also directly influences the innovative Output of that city. HK refers to the level of human capital, or presence of workers more likely to be involved in the production of new economic knowledge, and is defined as the share of the 1992 labor force accounted for by workers who have graduated from a four year college (BA degree or higher). In addition, the number of research centers located in that city as of 1992 is represented by RC, while SRC represents the number of other (that is, located outside of the city) research centers located in the state within which the city is located (Source: *Fortune* survey, 15 November 1993). Including the number of research institutes located both within and outside the cities provides some insight as to the extent to which spillovers tend to be impeded as distance increases.

An important qualification concerning these last two measures is that, by measuring only the number of research centres, they remain un-weighted by importance. That is, some research centres are survey larger and generate more new economic knowledge than others. However, this same qualification applies to virtually all of the variables measured here. Just as some highly educated workers are more productive in generating new economic knowledge than others, some dollars of R&D are more productive than others. In fact, even the dependent variable is not particularly homogeneous. Some patents are clearly more important than others. Thus, an important measurement qualification concerns the obvious problem of heterogeneity of not just the explanatory variables but also the endogenous variable.

Table 1a indicates the patent activity between 1988 and 1992 of the sixty major US. cities. While the high number of patents issued to firms located in San Jose (10,138) and Los Angeles (9,598) are not particularly surprising, what is perhaps more striking is that the greatest number of patents, (11,793) were issued to firms located in Chicago. One explanation may be that Chicago accounts for a greater number of research centers than any other city, with the exceptions of New York and Boston. Of course, Chicago is also a much larger city than San Jose. When patent rates, or the number of patents per one hundred thousand residents, are compared in the second column, San Jose emerges as the most innovative city in the United States. San Jose, in fact, has the second highest education level (measured as the percentage of workers with a four-year college degree), where almost one-third of its workforce has a BA degree.

Table 1b reports the means and standard deviations of the explanatory variables. The sixty major US. cities are associated with 28 states. From the first three columns of the Table, a strong dispersion among the three variables can be observed, whereas the lowest deviation is found for the education level.

Table 1a: Patent Activity of Major U. S. Cities

City	Number of Patents	Patents/ Population	Number of Research Centers	Education Level (% of workforce with college degree)
Alban	3086	350.33	115	23.60
Atlanta	2776	86.80	205	26.10
Austin	2121	231.01	174	30.70
Baltimore	2400	98.14	225	23.10
Birmingham	223	25.81	72	19.70
Boston	9013	179.05	650	28.80
Buffalo	1498	124.98	23	18.80
Charlotte	953	77.13	25	19.60

Chicago	11793	154.92	516	24.50
Cincinnati	2353	149.73	141	19.90
Cleveland	3871	174.21	118	18.50
Columbus	1524	108.12	170	23.30
Dallas	4557	159.65	126	26.90
Dayton	1958	202.55	98	19.10
Denver	2097	121.34	302	29.10
Detroit	8652	200.46	361	17.70
Ft Lauderdale	1395	105.58	108	18.80
Ft Worth	1174	80.45	49	22.40
Grand Rapids	1301	132.78	26	17.80
Greensboro	1147	105.10	44	17.50
Hartford	1925	165.45	62	26.00
Honolulu	250	28.63	115	24.60
Houston	5765	163.00	199	25.00
Indianapolis	1818	126.30	69	20.00
Jacksonville	323	33.59	20	18.60
Kansas City	883	53.92	140	23.20
Las Vegas	273	27.26	27	13.30
Los Angeles	9598	104.99	515	22.30
Louisville	639	65.74	53	17.20
Memphis	473	45.19	85	18.70
Miami	1011	50:07	108	18.80
Milwaukee	2685	182,80	106	21.30
Minneapolis	7513	282.42	235	26.90
Nashville	417	40.18	117	21.40
New Orleans	647	49.69	73	19.30
New York	7482	43.92	788	25.40
Norfolk	689	45.74	67	19.80
Oakland	4445	205.66	283	29.90
Oklahoma	526	52.90	83	21.60
Orlando	957	71.56	33	20.40
Philadelphia	8565	171.95	469	22.60
Phoenix	3334	140.11	121	21.40
Pittsburgh	4367	182.22	220	18.70
Portland	1842	112.49	72	23.30
Raleigh-Durham	1745	188.55	248	31.70
Richmond	940	103.80	41	23.80
Rochester	7034	647.89	77	22.90
Sacramento	886	60.76	97	22.70
St. Louis	2473	97.57	136	17.70
Salt Lake City	1398	122.29	109	22.90
San Antonio	517	37.20	56	19.30
San Diego	4590	173.00	195	25.30
San Francisco	4233	259.04	345	34.90
San Jose	10138	665.14	91	32.60
Scranton	256	39.83	22	13.60
Seattle	3424	157.67	153	29.50
Tampa	1285	59.84	42	17.30
Tulsa	858	116.19	81	20.30
West Palm Beach	1460	157.73	25	22.10

Table 1b:

Total No. of States	Mean and standard deviation of the explanatory variables			
28	2907,72	138,99	158,06	22,41
	2880,16	118,56	156,76	4,49

Note: Means are in the first row and standard deviation in the second.

RESULTS

The number of patents issued to firms in each of the sixty cities listed in Table 1 is estimated in the knowledge production function represented by Equation (2), and the results from estimating the knowledge production function are reported in Table 2. The dependent variable is the natural log of patented inventions registered by legal entities located in the city. The natural log of each variable is taken to transform equation (2) into a tractable form for empirical estimation.

As the first column indicates, the positive and statistically significant coefficient of the industry R&D expenditures suggests that R&D inputs in the state within which a city is located, serves as an important source generating innovative output. Similarly, the positive and statistically significant coefficient of the expenditures on university research suggests that knowledge created in university laboratories serves as an important source for the innovative activity of private firms. While the coefficient of the number of research centres located within the city is positive and statistically significant, the coefficient of the number of other (outside of the city) research centres located within the state is negative and statistically insignificant. Taken together these results seem to suggest that the spillover of knowledge is more acute within a relatively narrow geographic area than within a broader one. That is, the new knowledge produced in research centers located in the city clearly contributes to the innovative activity of that city. However, there is no evidence that knowledge created in research centres located within the same state but in a different city spill over to contribute to the innovative activity of firms located within other cities.

While the coefficient of the share of the labor force accounted for by educated workers (in possession of the BA degree) is positive, it cannot be considered statistically significant in the first regression. However, when the 1993 population is included in the second and fourth regressions, not only is its coefficient positive and statistically significant, but the coefficient of the presence of educated workers also becomes statistically significant. Taken together, these results may suggest that human capital, or new knowledge produced and embodied in labour, contributes more to innovative activity in a more highly agglomerated environment. This is consistent with Marshall's 1920 theory and Krugman's (1991a and 1991b) more modern rendition of agglomeration economies arising from a pooled labor force.

Table 2: Regressions of (Log) Patents by City[a]

	(1)	(2)	(3)	(4)
Log Industry RD	0.369	0.310	0.342	0.301
	(3.53)a	(2.41)a	(2.96)a	(2.60)a
Log University Research	0.314	0.295	0.290	0.289
	(2.94)a	(2.30)a	(3.21)a	(2.92)a
Log Educated Workers	0.256	1.138	0.359	1.152
	(0.44)	(1.98)a	(0.64)	(2.13)a
Log Research Centers	0.610	0.160	0.629	0.161
	(4.91)a	(0.97)	(5.24)a	(0.98)
Log State Research Centers	-0.268	-0.003	–	–
	(-0.66)	(-0.07)		
Log Population	–	0.761	–	0.764
		(3.71)a		(3.82)a
Log-Likelihood results	-57.220	-50.412	-51.990	-50.415

[a] t-Statistics listed in parentheses. a denotes statistically significant at the 99 percent level.

CONCLUSIONS

While an established literature has identified a link between knowledge inputs and innovative output within a product dimension, that is, at the level of industries or firms, a recent series of studies have suggested that the knowledge production function also applies across firms and even industries within a spatial context. That is, new economic knowledge has been found to spill over from the source producing it to serve as an input for generating innovative activity by third party firms. Virtually, all of the studies identifying such knowledge spillovers have been undertaken at the level of the state, assuming that knowledge spills over freely within a state but cannot cross state borders.

In this paper, the unit of observation is shifted to a finer level, the city, and it has been discovered that the knowledge production function not only holds, but there is at least some indication that it holds more strongly in terms of linking knowledge inputs produced within the city to the innovative output of that city, than for knowledge inputs produced in a different city but within the same state. A very strong result, however, is that both private R&D, as well as university research undertaken in a state are found to be an important source of innovation generating inputs for cities located within that state.

While the knowledge production function apparently holds, its exact specification is clearly more complicated than may have originally been imagined. New knowledge can apparently be transmitted both across firms and even industries, as well as over space. At the same time, there are clearly costs of transmitting that new knowledge across enterprises, industries, and geographic space. Future research needs to focus more explicitly on how different types of new knowledge may incur differing costs of being transmitted across the various dimensions of product and geographic space.

Bibliography

ACS, Zoltan J. and David B. Audretsch (1988b), 'Innovation in Large and Small Firms: An Empirical Analysis,' *American Economic Review*, 78 (4), September 1988, pp. 678–690.

ACS, Zoltan J. and David B. Audretsch, *Innovation and Small Firms*, Cambridge: Mass: MIT Press, 1990.

ACS, Zoltan J., David B. Audretsch, and Maryann P. Feldman, 1992, 'Real Effects of Academic Research,' *American Economic Review*, 82 (1), March 1992, pp. 363–367.

ACS, Zoltan J., David B. Audretsch, and Maryann P. Feldman, 1994, 'R&D Spillovers and Recipient Firm Size,' *Review of Economics and Statistics Vol. 100 (2), May 1994.*

ADAMS, J.D., (2002). 'Comparative localization of academic and industrial spillovers,' *Journal of Economic Geography*, 2: 253–278.

ARROW, Kenneth J., 'Economic Welfare and the Allocation of Resources for Invention,' in R. Nelson, ed., *The Rate and Direction of Inventive Activity*, Princeton, NJ: Princeton University Press, 1962, pp. 609–626.

AGRAWAL, A. (2002). 'Innovation, growth theory and the role of knowledge spillovers,' *Innovation Analysis Bulletin*, 4(3): 3–6.

ANSELIN, L, Z. J. Acs, and A. Varga, (1997), 'Local geographic spillovers between University Research and High Technology Innovations,' *Journal of Urban Economics*, 42, 422–448.

AUDRETSCH, David B. and Marco Vivarelli, 1994, 'Small Firms and R&D Spillovers: Evidence from Italy,' CEPR Discussion Paper Number 927, forthcoming in *Revue d' Economie Industrielle.*

AUDRETSCH, David B., 1995, *Innovation arid Industry Evolution*, Cambridge, Mass.: MTI Press.

AUTANT-BERNARD, C. (2001a). 'Science and Knowledge Flows: Evidence from the French Case.' *Research Policy* 30, no. 7:1069–1078.

AUTANT-BERNARD, C. (2001b). 'The Geography of Knowledge Spillovers and Technological Proximity'. *Economics of Innovation and New Technology* 10, no. 4:237–254.

BOUND, John, Clint Cummins, Zvi Griliches, Bronwyn H. Hall and Adam Jaffe, 'Who Does R&D and Who Patents?' in Zvi Griliches, ed., *R&D, Patents, and Productivity*, Chicago, IL: University of Chicago, 1984, pp. 21–54.

BRANSTETTER, L., (2002) 'Measuring the Link between Academic Science and Innovation: The Case of California Research Universities,' mimeo, University of California, Davis.

COHEN, Wesley M. and Steven Klepper, 'Firm Size versus Diversity in the -Achievement of Technological Advance,' in Zoltan J. Acs and David B. Audretsch, eds., *Innovation and Technological Change. An International Comparison*, Ann Arbor: University of Michigan Press, 1991, pp. 183–203.

COHEN, Wesley M. and Steven Klepper, 'The Tradeoff between Firm Size and Diversity in the Pursuit of Technological Progress,' *Small Business Economics* 4 (1), March 1992, pp. 1–14.

FELDMAN, Maryann P., 1994a, *The Geography of Innovation*, Boston: Kluwer Academic Publishers.

FELDMAN, Maryann P., 1994b, 'Knowledge Complementarity and Innovation,' *Small Business Economics*, 6.

FELDMAN, M.P. (2002). 'The Internet Revolution and the Geography of Innovation.' *International Social Science Journal.* 54: 47–56.

GLAESER, Edward L., Hedi D. Kallal, Jose A. Scheinkman, and Andrei Shleifer, 1992, 'Growth of Cities,' *Journal of Political Economy*, 100, pp. 1126–1152.

GRILICHES, Zvi, 'Issues in Assessing the Contribution of R&D to Productivity Growth,' *Bell Journal of Economics* 10, Spring 1979, pp. 92–116.

GRILICHES, Zvi, 'Patent Statistics as Economic Indicators: A Survey,' *Journal of Economic Literature*, 28 (4), December 1990, pp. 1661–1707.

GROSSMAN, Gene and E. Helpman, 1991, *Innovation and Growth in the Global Economy*, Cambridge, Mass: MIT Press.

JAFFE, Adam B., 'Technological Opportunity and Spillovers of R&D: Evidence from Firms' Patents, Profits and Market Value,' *American Economic Review;* 76, December 1986, pp. 984–1001.

JAFFE, Adam B., Manuel Trajtenberg, and Rebecca Henderson, 1993, 'Geographic Localization of Knowledge Spillovers as Evidence by Patent Citations,' *Quarterly Journal of Economics*, 63 (3), August 1993, pp. 577–598.

JAFFE, Adam. B., 'Real Effects of Academic Research,' *American Economic Review*, 79 (5), December 1989, pp. 957–970.

KRUGMAN, Paul, 'Increasing Returns and Economic Geography,' *Journal of Political Economy,'* 99 (3), June 1991, pp. 483–499.

KRUGMAN, Paul, *Geography and Trade*, Cambridge, Mass.: MIT Press, 1991 b.

LINK, Albert N. and Barry Bozeman, 'Innovative Behavior in Small-Sized Firms,' *Small Business Economics,* 3 (3), September 1991, pp. 179–184.

LINK, Albert N. and John Rees, 'Firm Size, University Based Research and the Returns to R&D,' *Small Business Economics* 2 (1), 1^990, pp. 25–32.

MANSFIELD, Edwin, 'Comment an Using Linked Patent and R&D Data to Measure Inter-industry Technology Flows,' in Zvi Griliches, ed., *R&-D, Patents, and Productivity,* Chicago, IL: University of Chicago Press, 1984, pp. 462–464.

MARSHALL, Alfred, 1920, *Principles of Economics,* 8th edition, London: Macmillan.

ORLANDO, M. J. (2000). 'On the Importance of Geographic and Technological Proximity for R&D Spillovers: An Empirical Investigation', Federal Reserve Bank of Kansas City, Research working paper.

PAKES, Ariel and Zvi Griliches, 'Patents and R&D at the Firm Level: A First Report,' *Economics Letters,* 5, 1980, pp. 377–381.

ROMER, Paul, 1986, 'Increasing Returns and Long-Run Growth,' *Journal of Political Economy,* 64, pp. 100–237.

ROMER, Paul, 1990, 'Endogenous Technological Change,' *Journal of Political Economy,* 68, pp. 71–102.

SAXENIAN, AnnaLee, 1990, 'Regional Networks and the Resurgence of Silicon Valley,' *California Management Review,* Fall, 33 (1), pp. 89–112.

SCHERER, F. M. (1983 a), 'The Propensity to Patent, ' *International Journal* of *Industrial Organization,* 1, March 1983, pp. 107–128.

SCHERER, F. M., 'Changing Perspectives an the Firm Size Problem,' in Zoltan J. Acs and David B. Audretsch, eds., *Innovation and Technological Change. An International Comparison,* Ann Arbor: University of Michigan Press, 1991, pp. 24–38.

SCHERER, F. M., 1992, 'Schumpeter and Plausible Capitalism,' *Journal of Economic Literature,* 30 (3), September 1992, pp. 1416–1433.

SCHWALBACH, Joachim and Klaus F. Zimmerman, 'A Poison Model of Patenting and Firm Structure in Germany,' in Zoltan J. Acs and David B. Audretsch, eds., *Innovation and Technological Change: An International Comparison,* Ann Arbor: University of Michigan Press, 1991, pp. 109–120.

WALLSTEN, S.J., (2001), 'An Empirical Test of Geographic Knowledge Spillovers using geographic information systems and firm-level data,' *Regional Science and Urban Economics,* 31: 571–599.

Note

1. See for example Lucas (1993), Romer (1986 and 1990), and Grossman and Helpman (1991).
2. City size is incorporated into the analysis.
3. Scherer (1983), Mansfield (1984), and Griliches (1990) have all warned that measuring the number of patented inventions is not the equivalent of a direct measure of innovative output. For example, Pakes and Griliches (1980, p. 378) argue that 'patents are a flawed measure of innovative output; particularly since not all new innovations are patented and since patents differ greatly in their economic Impact.' In addressing the question, 'Patents as indicators of what?' Griliches (1990, p. 1669) concludes that 'Ideally, we might hope that patent statistics would provide a measure of the (innovative) output... The reality, however, is very far from it.'
4. According to Marshall (1920), 'Employers are apt to resort to any place where they are likely to find a good choice of workers with the special skill which they require: White men seeking employment naturally go to places where there are many employers who need such skills as theirs and where therefore it is likely to find a good market. The owner of an isolated factory, even if he has good access to a plentiful supply of general labor, is often put to great shifts for want of some special skilled labor and a skilled workman, when thrown out of employment in it, has no easy refuge.'
5. According to Marshall (1920), 'Subsidiary trades grow up in the neighborhood, supplying it with implements and materials, organizing its traffic...For subsidiary industries devoting themselves each to one small branch of the process of production, and working it for a great many of their neighbours, are able to keep in constant use machinery of the most highly specialized character, and to make it pay its expenses.'
6. Saxenian (1990, pp. 97–98 claims that even the language and vocabulary used by technical specialists is specific to a region: '...a distinct language has evolved in the region and certain technical terms used by semiconductor production engineers in Silicon Valley would not even be understood by their counterparts in Boston's Route 128.'
7. Jaffe (1989) argued that the proximity of university research to corporate laboratories should raise the potency of spillovers from the universities. While Jaffe was unable to substantiate this theory, Acs, Audretsch and Feldman (1992) found evidence linking the proximity of university research to corporate laboratories to innovative activity.
8. Audertsch and Vivarelli (1994) have confirmed that these results also hold for Italy.

18

BRIDGING THE IDEAL AND THE REAL IN SOCIAL SCIENCES: THE CASE FOR APPLYING CRITICAL DISCOURSE ANALYSIS IN EXAMINING ENVIRONMENTAL EDUCATION PRACTICES IN THE DEVELOPMENT CONTEXT OF PAKISTAN

*Kelly Teamey**
King's College London

ABSTRACT

With the underlying assumption that an ideal type of environmental education can improve peoples' lives and help to achieve various international and local policy objectives, the lack of opportunity provided for its use across a variety of development programs is relevant to its lack of legitimacy within the development field. This legitimacy deficiency is dependent upon a variety of factors relating to how power is circulated among different individuals, institutions and communities, whose knowledge is recognized as being legitimate, and the ways in which power and knowledge have constituted the truth. Within the context of Pakistan, the research represented in this paper focuses on the ways in which the Millennium Development Goals (specifically those concerning education and sustainable development) have been translated and mediated across different development-focused organizations to local practices. In particular, the ways in which these organizations (global, national and local) have interpreted policies and conceptualized education, development, poverty, sustainable development and environment, are examined and related to the space in which environmental education has been afforded.

*Ms Kelly Teamey is in the Ph.D. Education Research program at King's College London. She is presently working at the Sindh Education Foundation, in Karachi, as a research consultant as she completes her dissertation. She is from Oregon, USA. Prior to starting her Ph.D. course she was an environmental educator in New York City.

Introduction

Social science research has the power of being both highly relevant and irrelevant within a given context. The level of relevancy is dependent upon a variety of factors that relate to how power is circulated between different individuals, institutions and communities, which knowledge is recognized as being legitimate and the ways in which power and knowledge have constituted the truth. For instance, through selected socially-critical methods, social science research has shed light on how international development policies are interpreted into national policies and mediated through different genres by different development-focused organizations and put into practice. This research could be directly relevant both to policy makers and practitioners—to see how opportunities are being realized and missed. This research could also be indirectly relevant to those 'on the ground' that these policies are supposed to help if the knowledge gained through this type of research is able to change practices and forms of communication towards being more effective and socially just. However, on the same note, this research could be irrelevant to those on the ground if the knowledge gained is marginalized; particularly, if it counters more dominant notions and understandings of development as stated in international policies and is consequently, not recognized as legitimate knowledge.

The statement that social science research is inherently irrelevant has to do with the enormous complexities of our social world and the impossibility of being able to comprehend or retain a grasp on anything that even approaches holism. Despite any new relevant understandings or different perspectives that might better elucidate upon knowledge production and practices within social and development practices, only small fragments of social relations are able to be grabbed and explored, defying space and time. Only selected snapshots of social practices within some select contexts encompass what can be further scrutinized within social science research. There is the added irrelevancy of the inherent imposition in the role of the researcher, particularly one who is not from the context being investigated. My position as an outside researcher (within Pakistan) unintentionally brings in its own assumptions, regardless of any level of reflexivity to what is learned and experienced.[1]

'There is an intellectual bias inherent in the position of the social scientist who observes from the outside, a universe in which she is not immediately involved.' (Bourdieu 1992: 73)

Despite any limitations that social science research automatically brings in, there are methods and theories within social science research that have the potential to assist the society that is aiming to adjust power relations towards being more socially just and giving a larger space to typically marginalized and subdued voices, to be recognized.

For reasons no doubt relating to my own person and to the state of the world, I have come to believe that those who have the good fortune to be able to devote their lives to the study of the social world cannot stand aside, neutral and indifferent, from the struggles in which the future of the world is at stake. These struggles are, for an essential part, theoretical struggles in which the dominant can count on innumerable resources.' (Bourdieu 2003: 11)

This paper discusses how social science methods of policy and discourse analysis embedded within the post-structuralist branch of social science can be used to study how that, which is idealized in policies, is being translated into what is being practiced in reality. My research focuses on the ways in which the Millennium Development Goals (specifically those concerning education and sustainable development) have been translated and mediated across different development-focused organizations to local practices within the context of Pakistan. In particular, the ways in which these organizations (global, national and local) have interpreted policies and conceptualized education, development, poverty, sustainable development and environment, are examined.

The first section of this paper will briefly set the background of my research study; the research contract within the first year of my doctoral study that serendipitously brought me to Pakistan in the first place. A comprehensive list of how environmental education might be able to link with the Millennium Development Goals was created through an 'ideal type' of environmental education that was established as a result of this research and the issues and questions that were raised which led to my PhD research questions. The next section of the paper focuses on the key concepts and theories underpinning my positioning as a researcher; the lenses being used to frame my research questions and my analyses. In particular, social science theories and methods of critical discourse and policy analysis being employed are discussed alongside their values and limitations. In conclusion are some extracts of data and some brief analyses and discussions of what this might contribute to development policy-making, interpretation and practices.

BACKGROUND

Under the impetus of the Millennium Development Goals (MDGs), development organizations and institutions have created poverty reduction strategies to assist in attaining these policy targets. With this in mind, the Department for International Development (DFID) has been developing its own poverty reduction strategies and contracted research to outside agencies (academic and non-academic) with the attempt of locating new and innovative future poverty reduction strategies.

My research emerges from findings that were identified from research that was contracted by DFID in June 2000 to The Field Studies Council who subcontracted King's College London and the University of Bath, to carry out the majority of the work. As an academic team, we were engaged in carrying out research which had as its major outcome, the provision of advice and recommendations on the most appropriate ways by which DFID could mainstream environmental education into programs in developing countries and countries in transition with the underlying objectives of contributing to the attainment of the MDGs.

To achieve DFID's terms of reference, the research team looked at the extent, nature, effectiveness and impact of environmental education (EE) initiatives funded by development agencies and NGOs throughout the world, with one of the primary objectives being poverty reduction. The research provided examples of how EE has achieved wider impacts and benefits for curriculum development and implementation. In analyzing literature, the team identified the key institutional, legislative, policy and economic factors that might be critical to the sustainability of EE initiatives and some methods used to address wider opportunities and constraints. Discussions and formal interviews were carried out with academics, government officials, environmental education providers, project managers and other relevant people from a range of countries. Two field visits were undertaken in February 2001 to Pakistan—Karachi, Islamabad and Gilgit (by Justin Dillon and myself) and the Caribbean (by Dr Stephen Gough in Guyana, St. Lucia, Antigua, Trinidad & Tobago and Barbados). During these interviews (32 in Pakistan), discussions and observations were carried out to examine the possible linkages between EE and the MDGs (poverty reduction in general), how EE strategies are being implemented in practice and to see what lessons have been learned. In addition to the

Table 1: Possible links between the Millennium Development Goals and environmental education

Millennium Development Goals
Goals and targets

Goal 1   Eradicate extreme poverty and hunger
Halve, between 1990 and 2015, the proportion of people whose income is less than $1 a day and the proportion of people who suffer from hunger

Goal 2   Achieve universal primary education
Ensure that, by 2015, children everywhere, boys and girls alike, will be able to complete a full course of primary schooling

Goal 3   Promote gender equality and empower women
Eliminate gender disparity in primary and secondary education preferably by 2005 and in all levels of education no later than 2015

Goal 4   Reduce child mortality
Reduce by two-thirds, between 1990 and 2015, the under-five mortality rate

Goal 5   Improve maternal health
Reduce by three-quarters, between 1990 and 2015, the maternal mortality ratio

Goal 6   Combat diseases
Have halted by 2015, and begun to reverse the spread of HIV/AIDS. Have halted by 2015 and begun to reverse the incidence of malaria and other major diseases

Goal 7   Ensure environmental sustainability
Integrate the principles of sustainable development into country policies and program and reverse the loss of environmental resources. Halve, by 2015, the proportion of people without sustainable access to safe drinking water. Achieved, by 2020, a significant improvement in the lives of at least 100 million slum dwellers

Goal 7   Ensure environmental sustainability
Integrate the principles of sustainable development into country policies and program and reverse the loss of environmental resources. Halve, by 2015, the proportion of people without sustainable access to safe drinking water. Achieved, by 2020, a significant improvement in the lives of at least 100 million slum dwellers

Link to Environmental Education (EE)

- EE might help to provide a better sense of security by providing skills and knowledge for better management of local resources
- EE might provide opportunities for obtaining financial resources through the provision of alternative local resource management
- EE might provide more community and individual confidence for change and improvement
- EE might provide vocational skills
- EE might lessen local, regional or national environmental degradation
- EE might be linked to 'quality' education
- EE might have the potential in making the curriculum more relevant to the everyday lives and needs of students, teachers and the community
- EE could be a key tool for educational reform
- EE might provide a safe and secure school environment.
- EE may promote life-long learning
- EE might provide linkages between the school and the community
- EE might be best achieved through non-formal education that is linked to the formal curriculum
- EE has the potential of appealing to females to enroll and attend school
- EE may provide females with more effective household strategies for domestic chores
- EE might provide nutritional, hygienic and basic health skills
- EE may promote cultural reflection
- EE might provide different worldview perspectives.
- EE might provide greater political awareness
- EE might provide enquiry skills
- EE might provide advocacy/activism skills
- EE might provide the opportunity for developing reproductive health skills
- EE might provide the skills to better cope with environmentally-related diseases through better management of the local environment
- EE might provide the knowledge, confidence and empowerment to identify issues/problems and options towards solutions
- EE might provide community organizational skills
- EE may provide management skills
- EE might promote community ownership
- EE might promote advocacy/activism skills
- EE might promote self-reflection and a sense of place

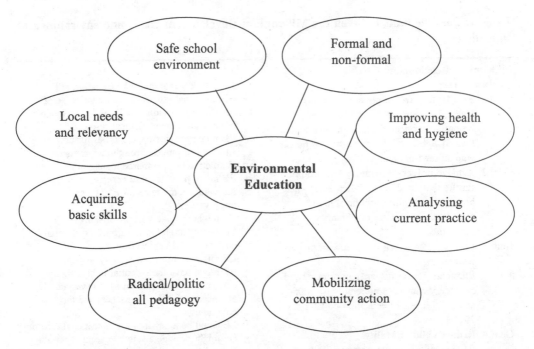

FIG. 1: IDEAL TYPE OF EE

report that was finished in June 2001 for DFID (Dillon, Gough, Scott, Teamey 2001), we wrote an additional report that was refined towards a Pakistan perspective (Dillon and Teamey 2001). Through the DFID research on mainstreaming environmental education, we located the emergence of patterns that signified a variety of ways in which environmental education *could* be related to the achievement of the Millennium Development Goals (MDGs) and EE in general, as the MDGs have been incorporated into national policies globally. We (Dillon and Teamey 2001) provided specific recommendations that might be useful for Pakistan to use EE as a tool to help in the achievement of the MDGs.[2]

We also developed an ideal type of what environmental education might best look like in practice (Teamey, Dillon, Scott and Gough 2003, p. 132). Weber uses the concept of ideal type as a construct that has been 'arrived at by the analytical accentuation of certain elements of reality' (Weber 1949, p. 89). An ideal type is an analytical construct that provides a thinking tool and basic method to conduct a comparative research study; it does not necessarily correspond to every detail of a given concrete reality but always moves at least one step away from it.

Although we uncovered some of the possible linkages between environmental education (EE) and poverty reduction, we discovered that EE was often not understood or utilized to assist in reducing poverty through these linkages. An immense variety of issues and research gaps emerged from the research upon analyzing the data. Three main issues surfaced across most agencies, with a large number of sub-issues related to each: conceptions and processes of empowerment, inadequate communication channels and segregation of formal/non-formal education (concepts and contexts of education). Each of these three issues were in some way related to the issue of the incredible diversity of understandings and perspectives of 'education', 'environment', 'development', 'poverty', and 'environmental education' that emerged through a vast literature review and interviews with a large variety of agencies (donor agencies, non-governmental agencies, community-based organizations, government ministries and academic institutions) doing some type of environmental education work in the development field. These issues matter because the different conceptualizations or discourses used by donors, government agencies, non-governmental organizations (NGOs) and academic institutions affect what they do and how they evaluate the effectiveness of their efforts.

One of the major issues that arose through the DFID research was that there were environmental education (EE) practices in formal education and non-formal education, but the two contexts were not integrated and therefore, could not complement each other. In formal education, the representation of EE was discursively constructed in some curriculum development space and school environmental events. EE was not seen as a tool for the improvement of the quality of education within the classroom, as a way to make learning in school more relevant for students. This was manifested through the practices of multi-lateral organizations focusing on the exterior environment of the school to encourage students to come and enroll in school.

This research does not further examine the possible links between the Millennium Development Goals/poverty reduction and environmental education (EE), as these links were already unearthed through the DFID mainstreaming environmental education research. Rather, the research is examining the reasons in which these links are not being realized, the constraints behind missed opportunities:

1. How much do international targets, serving as policies, reinforce different discourses, genres and styles of EE?
2. Why are different development-led organizations approaching EE so differently or not at all?
3. Why are different organizations using what I would call EE but not referring to it as such?
4. How much does question 1 help to explain questions 2 and 3?

These questions led me to ask further questions about power relations between the organizations I had interviewed, who was guiding their knowledge production and consumption, interpretations of policies and reasonings behind approaches and practices (amongst many others). These deeper questions guided me towards theories that are associated with the post-structuralist branch of social sciences. Post-structuralism holds the view that material objects (reality) are culturally and discursively structured, created in interaction as situated, symbolic beings (Philips and Jorgensen 2002). This view does not in any way discount the reality of dire situations that many people living within poverty find themselves in. Rather this view attempts to examine power structures in place that dominate ways of thinking and understanding social issues such as poverty. Concepts such as power, discourse, truth, knowledge, hegemony and doxa take precedence within a post-structuralist view. The next section provides a brief explanation of each concept as they are important towards understanding the relevance of the social science analytical and theoretical methods that have been used; particularly as contextualized within the development field. Though this next section moves toward being more abstract and theoretical, it is important to describe these concepts as it reinforces the relevancy of this type of research methodology within the social sciences.

KEY CONCEPTS GUIDING THE THEORETICAL POSITIONING

A preliminary definition of discourse is a particular way of talking about and understanding the world, or an aspect of the world (Phillips and Jorgensen 2003). Discourse constrains the possibility of thought. Each discourse establishes a different way of perceiving the world: altering and reproducing one's view of the world. Foucault (1972) claims that it is impossible to gain access to universal truth since it is impossible to talk from a position outside of discourse; there is no escape from representation.

> Discourses are practices that systematically form the objects of which they speak. Discourses are not about objects; they do not identify objects, they constitute them and in the practice of doing so conceal their invention. (Foucault 1972: 49)

Central to the understanding of discourse theory, is power. My interpretation of power is Foucauldian; power permeates all levels of society through every social practice. There is no single dominant power, but rather an intricate network of power relations, coursing above, below, through and between social practices. Power relations are embedded within social relations and are exercised through institutional relations that discipline our ways of thinking and acting through self-regulation (Foucault 1977). Power provides the conditions of possibility for the social world. It is in power that our social world is produced and objects are separated from one another and thus attain their individual characteristics and relationships to one another.

> Those endowed with capital are able to maintain their position in social space only at the cost of reconverting the forms of capital they hold into forms that are more profitable or more legitimate in the current state of the instruments or reproduction (Bourdieu 1996: 277).

Foucault developed a theory of power/knowledge; power does not belong to particular individuals, but is spread across different social practices (Phillips and Jorgensen 2002). Power is inextricably bound with knowledge and both are socially-constructed. Power and knowledge are not independent and are not linked by cause and effect, they pre-suppose each other. They manifest themselves within the space that a discourse occupies.

> We should admit rather that power produces knowledge; that power and knowledge directly imply one another; that there is no power relation without the correlative constitution of a field of knowledge, nor any knowledge that does not presuppose and constitute at the same time power relations (Foucault 1977: 27).

The concept of **truth** is also bound within the power-knowledge dependency and forms a sort of unbreakable triangle. All three are internalized through discourses and discursive practices.

> There cannot be possible exercises of power without a certain economy of discourses of truth which operates through and on the basis of this association. We are subjected to the production of truth through power and we cannot exercise power except through the production of truth (Foucault 1980: 93).

The theory of hegemony establishes a direct and intimate connection between power/knowledge and the subject to which it is addressed (Fontana 1993). The supremacy of a social group or class manifests itself in two different ways: through physical domination or coercion and 'intellectual and moral leadership' (Femia 1987: 24). Gramsci's notion of hegemony is that the prevailing commonsense (what is viewed as being 'normal') formed in culture is diffused by civic institutions that inform values, customs and spiritual ideals and induce 'spontaneous' consent to the status quo (Peet 2002).

Peet (2002) adds a Foucauldian-Gramscian notion of 'globally hegemonic discourse' referring to 'a system of political ideas derived from leading interpretations of regional experiences, elaborated in coherent, sequential theoretical statements as with policy formulations, within internationally recognized bodies of experts.' Peet (2002) established an AIM (Academic-Institutional-Media) complex theory to relate the power that development discourses hold within discursive practice. According to the AIM complex (Peet 2002), discourses become hegemonic by originating in theories elaborated by academics, often in elite institutions, usually leading universities with vast endowment funds (Harvard, Yale, Oxford, Cambridge, etc.). These theories are often sought by leading 'knowledge-based' institutions (think-tanks, research corporations) that most often lean in the conservative direction. Movement of personnel and ideas between these knowledge-based institutions, businesses and academic institutions are eventually integrated into government thinking and policy-making, particularly if they fit within the government administration's economic and political agendas. Eventually these theories are translated into languages that can be digested by the informational media—respectable newspapers (national and international), economic dailies or weeklies, popular magazines and news and commentary shows on TV and radio.

The New Capitalism

Since the 1980s, neo-liberalism discourses (neo-liberalism discourses is used as there is not just one neo-liberalism discourse—neo-liberalism manifests itself in different ways in different contexts—globally, nationally and locally) have moved from the periphery of development discourses to the center and have maintained the dominant end of development power relations. Neoliberalism discourses are arguably the dominant, hegemonic discourses within the field of development (Bourdieu 1998, Fairclough 2000, Bourdieu and Wacquant 2001, Peck and Tickell 2002, Peet 2002, Bourdieu 2003, Fairclough 2003). The neo-liberalist 'religion' has spread like a virus (Beck 2001). 'Neo-liberalism has pervaded every corner of the earth in some capacity' (Peck and Tickell 2002, p. 380). Neo-liberalism is the 'new planetary vulgate which is characterized by a 'Newspeak' English vocabulary including 'globalization and flexibility, governance and employability, underclass and exclusion, new market economy and zero tolerance, multiculturalism ... (with notable absence) of the terms 'capitalism', 'class', 'exploitation', 'domination', and 'inequality' ... having been pre-emptorily dismissed under the pretext that they are obsolete and non-pertinent—is the result of a new type of imperialism' (Bourdieu and Wacquant 2001). As all discourses, neo-liberalism discourses have not maintained the same characteristics since their conception. They have responded to external events and fields and alternative discourses to maintain a dominant status. The power of neo-liberalism discourses are that they have been able to represent the world of market rules as a state of nature, 'their prescriptions have a self-actualizing quality; (Peck and Tickell 2002, p. 382). Bourdieu (1998) describes neo-liberalism as a 'strong discourse'.

With the attempt of using the hegemonic AIM complex in a way that challenges the current neo-liberal order, a group of academics concerned with discourse analysis have devoted a web-site (http://www.cddc.vt.edu/host/lnc/lncarchive.html) to their study of language in the current age of capitalism. The term 'New Capitalism' has been formed to refer to the most recent of a historical series of radical social relation restructuring so that capitalism has reproduced and maintained the strength of its power. Within this network, Fairclough (2000a, 2000b, 2001, 2002) and Jessop (2000) describe contemporary society as having emerged toward a 'New Capitalism'. These transformations have 're-structured' and re-scaled relations between different domains or fields of social life—most obviously between the economic field and other fields, including a 'colonization' of other fields by the economic field. This is apparent through the changes in the global/local dialectic.

We have entered a 'knowledge-based' society, where knowledge and discourses have become commodities. The 'knowledge-based' and globalizing character of the new capitalist economy means that changes in social relations are increasingly 'discourse-led'. Powerful discourses, circulated through international communication networks, construct representations of change in activities, social relations etc., and these are 'operationalized' in new technologies (new ways of organizing workplaces, local government, education etc.), including new genres. Development agencies (such as the work we carried out for DFID) have spent millions of dollars conducting 'knowledge' research in order to help them better understand their programs' limitations. The major constraints of this type of research is that the development agencies contracting the research set their own boundaries about what they want to know and why. This research is therefore more aligned with evaluations rather than proper research. In addition, donor agencies such as DFID, want to acquire information from non-governmental organizations (NGOs) 'on the ground' but the dilemma here is that these NGOs are funded by donor agencies, so it is possible that they are often not as honest as they might like to be. This is one path in which power is reproduced within the development field.

The need for discourse analysis in social and educational research has increased substantially as a result of the 'New Capitalism'. There is a need to further analyze the power relations that influence the creation and dissemination of knowledge deemed as legitimate, thus occupying the greatest amount of space.

CRITICAL DISCOURSE ANALYSIS

Critical discourse analysis (CDA) is the study and critique of social inequality in which researchers must be activists (Van Dijk 1993b). Of particular interest in this study is the social inequality that exists within the field of development; how and why environmental education efforts that could assist in reducing social inequality and poverty are not being recognized.

> CDA is a type of discourse analytical research that primarily studies the way social power abuse, dominance and inequality are enacted, reproduced and resisted by text and talk in the social and political context. With such dissident research, critical discourse analysts take explicit position(s), and thus want to understand, expose and ultimately to resist social inequality (Van Dijk 2001, p. 352).

Though CDA has been criticized for bringing a strong political agenda in its wake (Caldas-Coulthard and Coulthard 1996), it does provide the opportunity to bracket the familiar discourses in order to analyze the theoretical and practice context with which it is associated (Foucault 1986: 3 cf. Escobar 1995: 6) and to locate the various agendas behind the players and try to perceive the power structures created within a particular space. What is distinctive about CDA is both that it intervenes on the side of dominated and oppressed groups and against dominating groups, and that it openly declares the emancipatory interests that motivate it. The political interests and uses of social scientific research are usually less explicit. This certainly does not imply that CDA is less scholarly than other research: standards of careful, rigorous and systematic analysis apply with equal force to CDA as to other approaches (Fairclough and Wodak 1997).

METHODS OF ANALYSIS

How critical is discourse analysis actually being employed? What tools are being used?

> The analyst has to work with what has actually been said or written, exploring patterns in and across the statements and identifying the social consequences of different discursive representations of reality (Phillips and Jorgensen 2002, p. 21).

To conduct critical discourse analysis, a range of tools were identified to help identify the development, education and environment discourses within interview transcriptions and policy documents of each examined organization. In addition, within my overall dissertation, an interpretation of the development field that I came into contact with has been sketched to further understand how power is reproduced between organizations—from the local to the global in order to map out how and where knowledge is legitimized. It is beyond the remit of this paper to provide further explanation of Bourdieu's field theory and power reproduction.

Fairclough (2003) combines a range of theories and tools in which to 'do' critical discourse analysis. These particular discourse analysis categories were chosen (and asking subsequent questions) during my analysis of interview transcripts and selected policy documents:

- Chain of social events that the text is apart of—genre chain: *Where did the text come from? What influenced it—from which organizations? Which genres have been sites of mediation (conferences, journalism sources, websites, policies, etc.)?*
- Network of social practices and social relations: *How have I had access to different organizations—what were the social relations involved? Which documents were provided to me?*
- Examples of how power is reproduced and maintained: *Are these directly stated or indirectly? How was power transferred and from what sources?*
- Development rhetoric ('Newspeak') used: *What rhetoric is used and how is it articulated? Within what discourses does this piece of rhetoric lie within?*
- Practices typical within different discourses: *Which social practices/events are included or excluded? What level of abstraction are they being represented?*
- Voices articulated (Laclau and Mouffe 1985)—included and excluded (Fairclough 2003): *What voices are being articulated? Who is included and excluded? Are they articulated specifically or non-specifically?*
- Difference tolerance: *How does the organization deal with difference or the possibility of difference? How does the person being interviewed value difference?*
- Assumptions—existential, propositional and value: *Which assumptions are made and how? Is the assumption stated as a fact, prediction, hypothetical, evaluation? What does the organization assume to be a problem or the method of solving it?*
- Ordering of different discourses: *What discourses are drawn upon in the text and how are they textured together? Is there a significant mixing of discourses? How are the discourses characterized?*

- Commitment level: *What do authors/interviewees commit themselves in terms of truth? Or in terms of obligation and necessity? What are their levels of commitment?*

It is with these categories that a space for relevant social science can be created. Texts and variances in language and discourse are capable of bringing about social change; either positive or negative. 'Most immediately, texts can bring about changes in our knowledge, our beliefs, our attitudes, values and so forth' (Fairclough 2003, p. 8). The main task of critical discourse analysis is to go beneath the surface and look for that which is assumed, that which is obvious and normalized (looking for the hegemonic depth that specific discourses such as neo-liberalisms have rooted themselves).

CRITICAL POLICY ANALYSIS

Critical policy analysis reflects the discourse analysis approach being utilised. This is due to my understanding and interpretation of what is meant by 'policy'. Following Stephen Ball, policy is an 'economy of power', a set of technologies and practices which are realized and struggled over in local settings. 'Policy is both text and action words and deeds, it is what is enacted, as well as what is intended' (Ball 1994, p. 10). Policies are both texts and discourses; they are implicit within each other. Ball (1994, p. 16) explains that 'policy is text in that policies are representations which are encoded in complex ways (via struggles, compromises, authoritative public interpretations and re-interpretations) and decoded in complex ways (via actors' interpretations and meanings in relation to their history, experiences, skills resources and context).' Policies shift and change their meaning in the arenas of politics; representations change, key interpreters change. They are represented by different actors and interests through real struggles, disputes, conflicts and adjustments that takes place over policies.

Ball (1994, p. 21) calls for the need for the appreciation in which policy 'ensembles, collections of related policies, exercise power through a production of truth and knowledge as discourses'

> We do not speak discourses, it speaks us. We are the subjectivities, the voices, the knowledge, the power relations that a discourse contstructs and allows. We do not know what we say, we are what we say and do. In these terms we are spoken by policies, we take up the positions constructed for us within policies (Ball 1994, p. 22)

International development policies such as the Millennium Development Goals (MDGs) are comprised of a hybridity of discourses that are primarily dictated by neo-liberalism discourses. Despite being rather vague and over-ambitious in their general form, once including the targets and methods of evaluating their levels of achievement, the MDGs become quite narrow and rigid. The textual genre of the MDGs have been translated and mediated through conferences, policy documents from a range of multi-lateral development organizations explaining the best ways in achieving these goals, national policies (the Education Sector Reform, Poverty Reduction Strategy Paper, National Conservation Strategy), through to practices including training workshops, documents in resource centers, etc. Though arguably well-intended, the MDGs marginalize many educational and environmental approaches through the rigidity of their discourses. For example, I was first struck in the marginalizing attribute of the title itself; these goals being 'Millennium'—how many millions of individuals in diverse cultures and countries in our world do not consider the year 2000 as that of the 'millennium?'

EDUCATION WITHIN DEVELOPMENT DISCOURSES

The educational objectives within development programs have predominantly been driven toward reaching the attainment of Education for All since 1990 and the subsequent establishment of the international development target of Universal Primary Education since 1996 and since modified in 2000 with the Millennium Development Goals. The measurement of these aims is through enrolment rates (in primary), attendance between years 1 and 5 and literacy rates among 15 – 24 year olds. This goal of Universal Primary Education (UPE) was agreed upon within the UN Millennium Declaration in 2000. The World Bank describes the necessity of UPE (World Bank group Millennium Development Goals website 2003):

> 'Education is seen as a powerful instrument for reducing poverty and inequality, improving health and social well-being, and laying the basis for sustained economic growth. It is essential for building democratic societies and dynamic, globally competitive economies.'

This understanding of education encompasses the rational educational discourse and the development discourses of neo-classical and neo-liberalism with a tinge of human development (health and social well-being). As the World Bank arguably drives the development agenda through its successful power reproduction strategies, it marginalizes alternative approaches. In the draft of the World Bank's 2004 World Development Report (which it posted on its website for public comment), there was a chapter devoted to education. This chapter was entitled 'Education Services'. The outline applauded the adoption of global standards in education that are based on competition and individual creativity. Teacher absenteeism was attributed as the most dominant reason for not reaching the UPE goal. Overall, the outline was shallow in its critical depth, overly strong in its economic discourse and fraught with assumptions that exuded linear, decontextualized, problem-solving without being thoroughly unpacked or demonstrative enough of ways forward.

ENVIRONMENT WITHIN DEVELOPMENT DISCOURSES

The understanding of 'environment' is currently attributed to the dominant understanding of sustainable development, linking the environment with social and economic stability. Sustainable development is based upon the utilitarian theory that was first written about and recognized in the 18th century by Jeremy Bentham (1789). Bentham formulated the principle of utility, which approves of an action in so far as it has an overall tendency to promote the greatest amount of happiness. Though based upon the utilitarian principle, the current mainstream 'normalized' use of sustainable development is mainly attributed to the 1987 Brundtland report. This report demonstrated the explicit reliance on technology, economic growth, the pool or resources provided by the environment during the process of achieving sustainable development, and matched neo-liberal, technical development as dependent on world order.

> In essence, sustainable development is a process of change in which the exploitation of resources, the direction of investments, the orientation of technological development and institutional change are all in harmony and enhance both current and future potential to meet human needs and aspirations.'
> (WCED 1987: 46)

POST-DEVELOPMENT AND OTHER DEVELOPMENT DISCOURSES

This section of the paper provides some discussion surrounding a post-structuralist view of development that centers it within discourse: post-development. Within a post-structuralist framework development is discourse, a story, a text, a narrative (Escobar 1995). Development is not simply a theory or policy but in either form is a discourse (Pieterse 2001, p. 13). To treat development as a discourse is to pay meticulous attention to development texts or utterances, not merely as ideology, but as knowledge.

Though there is an incredible array of different understandings of development, they have been united in their founding belief of the modern world; using Enlightenment notions of the scientific mind for improving existence through a complex maze of linked natural, economic, social, cultural and political conditions. The single humanitarian project of producing a far better world is the fundamental idea of development that is fused together primarily from modern advances in science, technology, political ideals and social organization (Peet and Hartwick 1999). The set of practices that constitute development are based upon a hybridity of theories from a variety of fields—economics, science and technology, sociology, anthropology, political science, social psychology and geography. Each development theory has, implicitly or explicitly, various layers of historical context and political circumstances that have guided their interpretation and use. Thus, understanding the values of different development theories, its uses (abstractly and tangibly) and implications are intensely complicated and complex.

> Understanding development theory in context means understanding it as a reaction to problems, perspectives and arguments at the time. Another dimension is explanation or assumptions about causal relationships. This implies epistemology or what constitutes knowledge. In addition, it involves methodology, or indicators and research methods. (Pieterse 2001, p. 8)

Bourdieu's conception of doxa also offers a useful heuristic with which to conceptualize development. Doxas are the taken-for-granted assumptions or orthodoxies of a particular time period which are deeper in the level of consciousness than mere ideologies, but are also productive of conscious struggles and new forms (Bourdieu 1977, p. 166). The concept of doxa is similar to Gramsci's notion of intellectual hegemony in that it is normalized and common sense. Doxa is that which is self-evident within the natural and social world (Bourdieu 1977). That development is essential is a doxa within modern society. Modern society (in the Western world) fundamentally believes that the world needs improvement, development, and progress. According to the development 'doxa,' as humans, we are continually evolving along a linear path and those within the 'developed world' are further along this evolutionary path than those from the 'developing world'. Thus, the assumption is that the developing world needs to be saved and guided along this evolutionary path.

Opposing the doxa of development, is the post-developmental stance on development. Post-development (Sachs 1992b; Escobar 1995; Crush 1995; Rahnema and Bawtree 1997; Pieterse 2001) takes a post-structuralist theoretical positioning by problematising poverty, equating development with Westernization, critiquing modernization and viewing development as discourse; imaginary myth. The idea that development has not worked catapulted the radical reaction of post-development into development discourses. Development is rejected as the 'new religion of the West' (Rist 1990), a 'ruin in the intellectual landscape' (Sachs 1992b, p. 1) and an 'alien model of exploitation' (Escobar 1992b, p. 419). Escobar argued that 'development proceeded by defining 'problems' (poverty, population growth, archaic agricultural practices) and identifying abnormalities' (the illiterate, the malnourished, small farmers to be clinically treated') (Peet and Hartwick 1999, p. 148). The result was the creation of a space of power relations struggling for knowledge that would be viewed as legitimate for solving these 'problems'.

> 'Development was—and continues to be for the most part—a top-down, ethnocentric, and technocratic approach, which treated people and cultures as abstract concepts, statistical figures to be moved up and down in the charts of 'progress' (Escobar 1995, p. 44).

There are several bases for criticisms against post-development. These have to do with issues inherent in discourse theory that don't recognize materialistic/tangible reality in a way that it deserves. Other criticisms are that there is a lack of deconstruction of the 'development discourse', a confused understanding of the evolution of development, an overly pessimistic view of development, complete dismissal of scientific practice and hypocritical usage of statistics in which to convey evidence. In response to these criticisms, I have separated development discourses into five categories. These discourses are based on development theories that have guided development actors in creating divergent development policies and carrying out corresponding development practices.

There is a continual struggle for space and power within the development field amongst many different discourses. The division and description of the different discourses that have historically, and are presently, struggling for space within the development field, tells a story of the evolution of development. Each discourse has a story of its own; the time and space of its emergence and its varied influence on more dominant discourses and development agents through time, including the present and future. Each of these discourses encompass a myriad of economic, scientific, political, cultural and social discourses which are themselves constructed within an incredible diversity of local, regional, national and international contexts that are all competing for legitimacy on the power relations highway system. Here, the complexity of the social world and its social practices become apparent very quickly. Though there are arguably more competing discourses within the development field (including different discourses represented within each of these), it was useful to classify the development discourses into these categories:

Neo-liberalism: The principle characteristics are free trade on a global scale, scientific and technological innovations for economic growth, restructuring of political, economic and social organization and a market-driven society.

Human development: Development must be sustained for the continued progress and satisfaction of human beings (Pieterse 2001). Human resource capacity development (productivity) is the means and ends of development. Human development approach has extended to gender, political rights and environmental concerns.

Alternative development: Focuses on local development and social agency, from grassroots groups and social movements to NGOs – local participation and strengthening of civil society (Pieterse 2001). Only a complete shift in social values and choices will permit the development of sustainable communities (Sauvé 1996).

Post-development: Development is a myth and is based on Western thinking, power relations and economic discourse (Escobar 1995 and Peet 1999).

Anti-development: Indigenous development—valued if it is rooted in cultural identity and if it preserves territorial integrity. It is based on a connective subsistence economy of solidarity and local autonomy (Pieterse 2001 and Sauvé 1996).

ENVIRONMENTAL AND EDUCATION DISCOURSES

In addition to the development discourses briefly listed above, discourses of education and environment are used through the data analysis. The section below identifies and succinctly explains these discourses. Each of these establish and provide a different way of viewing the world and knowledge that is legitimate within society.

Environment discourses: Sauvé (1996) describes several discourses of the environment that can be found in recent literature.

Environment as nature ... to be appreciated, respected, preserved: Dualistic, Cartesian interpretation, humans are removed from nature.

Environment as a resource ... to be managed: This is our collective biophysical heritage and we must sustain it as it is deteriorating and wasting away.

Environment as a problem ... to be solved: The biophysical environment, the life support system is threatened by pollution and degradation. We must learn to preserve its quality and restore it.

Environment as a place to live ... to know and learn about, to plan for, to take care of: Day to day environment—characterized by its human, socio-cultural, technological and historical components.

Environment as a community project ... in which to get involved.

Environment of a human collectivity, a shared living place, political concern, the focus of critical analysis: solidarity, democracy and personal and collective involvement in order to participate in the evolution of the community

Further discourses were added on the environment from Merchant (1992) and Grün (1996). Merchant (1992, p. 64) divides perspectives on the environment as grounds for establishing different environmental ethics, policies and practices into three main categories:

Ego-centric (self): Interest in maximization of individual self-interest: what is good for each individual will benefit society as a whole.

Homocentric (society): Utilitarian motive—greatest good for the greatest number of people where social justice and duty to other humans are priorities. Stewardship by humans as caretakers.

Eco-centric (cosmos): Faith that all living and nonliving things have value based upon unity, stability, diversity, interdependence and primacy of process over parts.

Grün (1996), using a Foucauldian archaeological analysis of environmental education, identifies two ecological discursive practices that are helpful in understanding hegemonic scientific epistemologies towards environmental and development decision-making:

Eco-mathematical—Defined by its classificatory, accounting and predictive character—mathematical accounting.

Eco-catastrophic—Owes its formation to relations between political, institutional, scientific discourses that recognized the possibility of total destruction of the human species – main issue is survival of man kind.

Education discourses: These education discourses were set out by Sauvé (1996) and translated from educational paradigms developed by Yves Bertrand and Paul Valois (1992). Their main interest was demonstrating the close and mutually reinforcing links between educational sociological paradigms.

Rational educational paradigm—industrial socio-cultural paradigm—importance attributed to objects of production, productivity, growth and competition. Society's relation to predetermined—mainly of a scientific or technological nature. Teaching strategies are typically formal presentations, demonstrations and task prescriptions.

Humanistic educational paradigm—linked to existential socio-cultural paradigm, emphasizes optimal personal potential and desires, the relationship to nature is one of respect and harmony. Humanistic approach focuses on the learner and the learning process and subjectivity is taken into account—goal is to develop many facets of a person.

Inventive educational paradigm—related to symbio-synergetic paradigm, focusing on the symbiotic relationship between humans, society and nature. Favors critical construction of knowledge (Freire) (implying a recognition of inter-subjectivity) and the development of relevant and useful actions. Vision calls for new educational practices such as making schools more open to the 'real world' co-operative learning, concrete problem-solving – making school more relevant to the real world. Fits with socially-critical paradigm (Robottom and Hart 1993).

In addition to this, is the *anti-education* discourse that education is a Western construct and the idea of education ought to be eliminated as a basic right and as 'essential for the survival and flourishing of every culture, past, present and future' (Prakash and Esteva 1998, p. 11).

SOME PRELIMINARY DATA ANALYSIS

Critical discourse analysis places the researcher inside the research; adding importance to the power dynamics that the researcher imposes on the retrieval and analysis of data. Therefore, reflexivity is integral to the entire research process. My identities as an 'outsider' researcher in Pakistan brings with it, obvious limitations, as I am inhabited by my own assumptions framed by the discourses which both affect and constitute my own views of the world and knowledge that I find legitimate. My identities (particularly as an American) have been challenged through my research as I have gained exposure to new places and new experiences (within Pakistan and also studying in the UK). My personal and professional relationships have also altered dramatically since my worldviews have been challenged by my experiences and have subsequently changed.

Similarly to using discourse theory, as a researcher I am unable to stand outside of the development, environmental or educational fields in which to observe the positioning of the various actors. As soon as I am describing a field, I am simultaneously entering that field and projecting my own assumptions. My positioning within these fields is dependent upon where I am. For instance, while in Pakistan, I have entered the power game through my interviews and observations being an 'outsider'. When in the UK I must re-imagine and remember my experience whilst in Pakistan to further explain and analyze my data.

> It is incumbent upon the researcher, according to Bourdieu, to not only objectify his or her relationship to the object of study, that is to cultivate awareness of the dispositions within the researcher's habitues as they may or may not affect observation, but further to objectify the act of objectification: to consider the position of the researcher within his or her own milieu alongside the field position of the object of research, and to comparatively reflect upon how positions within the field, both of the researcher and of the researched, might exert determinative influence upon the end product of social analysis. (Stepney 2003: 6)

The data analysis briefly set out in the next section includes data from my first and second visits to Pakistan. During my first visit, in 2001, an interview schedule was used to address the Terms of Reference set out by DFID. Thus, the data was not based entirely upon my own inquiries. The majority of the interviews were held with workers at the management level; thus the voices from the workers in the field were marginalized. The interview I found most interesting was the only one not scheduled for me. My second visit, that was postponed due to obvious security reasons, came in July and August of 2003. During those few weeks, I conducted a range of interviews with organizations that I met with in 2001 and other organizations that I had not met with previously. During the most recent stay my interviews brought me to Islamabad, Lahore, Peshawar and Karachi. Currently, I am completing the transcriptions from the interviews I recently held in Pakistan and also analyzing them.

Though over 30 organizations were interviewed, at this point in my data analysis 19 were chosen. Each of these agencies are typically categorized into different types of organizations within the development field: Multilateral agencies; Donor agencies; Government Ministries International Non-governmental Organizations (NGOs); National NGOs; and Community-based organizations.

A series of tables are explained below, representing each major organizational type. One or two examples from each type of stakeholder were chosen to demonstrate the differences across development, education and environment discourses compared with programs in practice and to provide some brief analytic commentary.

Table 2: Discourses represented by multi-lateral development agencies interviewed in Pakistan

Organization	Development discourses	Environment discourses	Education discourses	EE practices
Multi-lateral	Human with elements of neo-liberalism	As nature, as a problem, as a resource; Homo-centric; Eco-mathematical, Eco-Catastrophic	Rational and Humanistic	Focus on building 'child-friendly schools' to increase enrolment

The primary focus of this particular multi-lateral institution is on contributing toward the Universal Primary Education MDG of 100 per cent enrolment. Their involvement toward the achievement of this MDG has been fragmented i.e., instead of focusing upon the whole school there have been efforts on upgrading the environment and physical structure of the school and the provision of fresh water and toilets. This was explained through assumptions that were stated in a factual sense, i.e., improved exterior environment of the school will lead to higher enrolment rates. Curriculum and pedagogical improvements have been sporadic with no follow-through, thus representing both rational and humanistic educational discourses. Environment discourses are dualistic and any information about the environment was given in a statistical manner. That there were EE practices was simply my interpretation based on my ideal type of EE that includes the environment of the school and school infrastructure. EE is not a priority within this institution. During the interview (in which I was not allowed to tape record our discussion but took extensive notes) it was stated:

> EE is about survival skills—providing links that are real. Currently EE is not a priority. The priorities are on the real situation in schools—water and sanitation, health and hygiene (basic problems). The aim is to convince more girls to enroll and attend school.

Table 3: Discourses represented by donor development agencies interviewed in Pakistan

Organization	Development discourses	Environment discourses	Education discourses	EE practices
Donor 1	Human intertwined with Neoliberalism	As nature, as a problem, a resource, a place to live; Homo-centric; Eco mathematical, Eco-Catastrophic	Rational with elements of Humanistic	Very little and through NGO (with very little communication with NGO)
Donor 2	Human intertwined with Neoliberalism— though revered as being 'innovative' as a donor	As nature, as a problem, a resource, a place to live; Homo-centric; Eco-mathematical, Eco-Catastrophic	Rational with elements of Humanistic	Nothing because of development agenda
Donor 3	Human intertwined with Neoliberalism	As nature, as a problem, a resource, a place to live Homo-centric; Eco-mathematical, Eco-Catastrophic	Rational with elements of Humanistic	Nothing because of development agenda— not a priority, though funding for further knowledge about EE

Comparisons amongst donor agencies mirror comparisons with their corresponding foreign policies. However, similarities do exist in that the development discourses each donor agency espouses is a mix of neo-liberalism and human development discourses. These seem to manifest themselves differently within each institution as they arguably play off one another in the political and economic power struggle that continues. Donor 1 discussed some small EE programmes that were occurring though also admitting that they were not sure what exactly was going on as everything was handed to an NGO; this donor agency gives extensive autonomy to NGOs that are under contract. Environment discourses exuded those typically associated with neo-liberal development discourses; as a place for humans to live and in danger of disappearing (Eco-catastrophic and given in statistical terms—Eco-mathematical). Donor 2 is regarded as a better donor agency to work with by NGOs (this was anecdotally disclosed to me by many NGOs). Neo-liberalism discourses might not exist quite as strongly as other donor agencies, but it is still a strong discourse within all of their programmes. Donor agency 2 however does tend to give money to NGOs and CBOs that are doing more exciting and innovative programmes, more closely aligned with ground realities. Donor 3 exhibited the strongest presence of neo-liberalism discourses and when the enquiry was made about the possibility of EE, it was given low priority within their agenda in Pakistan. This might be due to the narrow view of the environment held by this donor agency and the lack of knowledge of the potential role that EE could play in helping to achieve the MDGs.

Table 4: Discourses represented by some Government Ministries interviewed in Pakistan

Organization	Development discourses	Environment discourses	Education discourses	EE practices
Government Ministry of Education 1	Human and neo-liberalism	As nature, as a resource, as a problem; Homo-centric; Eco-catastrophic	Mostly Rational (expressed desire to be Humanistic)	Nothing current—in 1997 population education curriculum developed through UNDP
Government Ministry of Education 2	Human and neo-liberalism	As nature, as a resource, as a place to live, as a problem; Homo-centric	Mostly Rational (working toward more Humanistic)	Curriculum development—infusion of EE, teacher-training and environmental events
Government Ministry of Education 3	Human and neo-liberalism	As nature, as a resource, as a place to live, as a problem; Homo-centric	Mostly Rational (working toward more Humanistic)	Public awareness campaigns

Interviews were held with both the Ministry of the Environment and the Ministry of Education—in different regions of Pakistan. Thus comparisons in this section can be made across the different Ministries and different geographical regions. Each Ministry expressed the importance of improving environmental awareness in Pakistan—though this was in a narrow sense and purely for human-centred needs and desires. Again there was information provided about the catastrophic state of the environment in Pakistan and the much-needed assistance that education could provide in remedying the situation. The Ministry of Education 1 discussed the need for curriculum innovation and showed us an initiative by the UNDP on population education that included elements of EE. This was pre-maturely scrapped due to political constraints and a lack of teacher training and follow-up. The Ministry of Education 2 exhibited their new curriculum for years 1 and 2 that included a great deal of environmental input. This input however was limited to the textbooks that contained drawings of local plant and animal species—the environment was displayed as separate from humans to be protected and nurtured for the betterment of humans. Planned teacher trainings associated with EE were described as being about environmental events sponsored by WWF. Thus there were no plans to incorporate any pedagogical innovations related to the new environmental inputs in the textbooks.

Table 5: Discourses represented by international and national NGOs interviewed in Pakistan

Organization	Development discourses	Environment discourses	Education discourses	EE practices
International NGO 1	Human (environment-centred) with elements of Neo-liberalism and Alternative development—thought apolitical in its approach	As nature, as a resource, as a place to live; Homo-centric and Eco-centric; Eco-mathematical, Eco-Catastrophic	Rational and Humanistic	Formal curriculum, environmental events, conservation management, small income generation projects (conserving the mangroves on the Arabian Sea)
International NGO 2	Human (environment-centred) with elements of Neo-liberalism and Alternative development	As nature, as a resource, as a place to live; Homo-centric and Eco-centric; Eco-mathematical, Eco-Catastrophic	Rational and Humanistic	Formal EE educational events, informal—community conservation efforts, trophy hunting (with IUCN), eco-tourism, information resource center
International NGO 3	Post-development and Anti-development some Alternative development—takes a political stance	As a place to live, as nature, as a community project, as a shared living place; Eco-centric	Inventive empowerment,	Community organization, literacy—individual and community identifying and solving everyday problems
International NGO 4	Human and Alternative development	As a place to live, as nature, as a problem, as a as a community project; Homo-centric	Humanistic	Nothing now—driven out due to development agenda in early 1990s formal education project work
National	Alternative development, with elements of anti development and post-development	As a place to live, as nature, as a community project; Homo-centric	Inventive	Publications distributed to villages to demonstrate links between women and sustainable development

Discerning different discourses and the spaces they occupy is more complicated within NGOs. This might be attributed to their reliance on donor funding and the competition they face amongst other NGOs to acquire funding; there is continual struggle for space and legitimacy within the development field. Though NGOs may have radical and alternative ideas about how they want to carry their programmes out in practice, they are most often constrained by donors and individuals within the organization itself and are therefore de-politicized. These 5 NGOs vary immensely in their development, education and environment discourses. One of the most striking characteristics of discourses located within the environment/conservation-focused NGOs was their limited view of the environment in comparison with non-environment centred NGOs, such as NGO 3. The international NGO 3 is not an environment-focused NGO yet they include the 'total environment' in their non-formal educational work. NGOs conducting the most exciting and innovative work are those that do not shy away from politicizing their work.

Legitimacy for political NGOs and CBOs that are doing perhaps the most valuable work is a constant struggle within the development field. This is most often due to the need for quick tangible results from funding agencies. International NGO 3 has had difficulties in proving its effectiveness to representatives of donor agencies. Individual and community growth is often not apparent. During the interview it was noted:

> A DFID project—a head in the British Head Commission. Last year, he toured all of Punjab and he went to our area. He asked why we aren't working on rights… people don't need too much services, because at the end they get nothing, it is never sustainable. They need educational rights. What is the difference here—he asked the community. The people told him about the process. He identified that nothing had changed—nothing to the community. So this is a negative element of our work—often people cannot perceive any type of change, the outsiders.'

Table 6: Discourses represented by CBOs interviewed in Pakistan

Organization	Development discourses	Environment discourses	Education discourses	EE practices
CBO 1	Post-development and anti-globalization	As nature, as a resource, as a community project, Homo-centric	Inventive and Anti-education	Political mobilization, against oppression
CBO 2	Post-development and alternative development	As a place to live, as nature, as a community project, Eco-entric	Inventive	Community work on livestock management, immediate income generation strategies from local community, local literacy and health and hygiene skills

Both CBOs espouse elements of post-development. The main differences between both CBOs is that CBO 1 refuses to accept funding from any institutions, particularly donor agencies. That CBO 1 is involved in EE practices is my own interpretation, based upon my own discourses and philosophical understandings of environment, education and development. This CBO is completely political with very strong notions about what development ought to entail and global influences causing high levels of inequality. CBO 2 is more closely aligned with alternative development discourses though both post-development and neo-liberalism discourses were located.

GENERAL FINDINGS AND CONCLUSION

The space for each discourse varied across each organization. The interviews analyzed for this paper represented all of the discourses except the Ego-centric discourse (environment). Most of the interviews conveyed a hybridity of discourses. Fairclough and Chouliaraki (1999) describe this as characteristic of late modernity.

> In late modernity, boundaries between social fields and therefore between language practices have been pervasively weakened and redrawn, so that the potential seems to be immense, and indeed hybridity has been widely seen as a characteristic of the 'postmodern' (Fairclough and Chouliaraki 1999, p. 13).

The main issue of hybrid discourses within the interviews was trying to discern between dichotomous expressions of personal thoughts and what an organization has to do in order to survive within the development game.

The donor agencies, multi-laterals, government ministries and international NGOs (except for one) interviewed in Pakistan have all been influenced by the neo-liberalism development discourses, through their orders of discourses being guided by rational educational discourses and emphasizing western-based ideals of personal growth and development of scientific, language and numeracy skills to successfully enter the societal job market. Only one of the international NGOs, 2 of the national NGOs and the CBOs, demonstrate radical moves away from a rational educational discourse. The development of the curricula within the educational institutions have all been guided from pre-partition during British colonization.

The discourses represented throughout many of the interviews echoed the Brundtland (1987) report. Even the environmentally-focused international NGOs who exist with environment as their very essence, resonate much of the rhetoric and discourses within the Brundtland report through their programs. The Brundtland report represents environment discourses as eco-catastrophic with environment as nature, as a resource and as a problem to be solved, heavily associated with a dualistic, Cartesian view that sees the environment as a global resource to be developed and managed for sustainable profit and as nature to be revered and respected for the enjoyment and survival of human beings. The environmental ethics in achieving a balance between continued development and having the environment as an adequate resource base is a combination of ego-centricism and homo-centricism. Recognizing an eco-centric, intrinsic value of the environment within the text is non-existent. The environmentally-focused international NGOs are primarily orientated toward the transmission of environmental knowledge within the classroom that rides upon the eco-catastrophic and eco-mathematical discourses to influence students to develop positive attitudes and behaviors toward the environment.

Sustainable development is a problem for people who are not comfortable with a utilitarian framework. The focus becomes centered on how to make development last rather than the non-human environment. 'Sustainable development calls for the conservation of development, not for the conservation of nature.' (Sachs 1990: 34) Only one of the international NGOs, 1 of the national NGOs and the CBOs were uncomfortable with the discourses sustaining sustainable development. Also their work arguably reached more marginalized members of communities than work from other agencies that were interviewed. It is interesting to note that these organizations did not define their programs as either 'educational' or encompassing 'environmental education.' However, their programs encompass what I envisage environmental education to be (my ideal type set out at the beginning of this paper).

How environmental education is being re-contextualized into practice is dependent upon the space of legitimacy that the particular organization is occupying at that particular moment within the development field. In many cases, the potential for EE is being missed entirely because of a lack of understanding or way of seeing beyond spaces that neo-liberalism discourses are retaining. EE has the potential for assisting with social change and providing more innovative and relevant means for improving peoples' livelihoods. Therefore, the marginalization of EE is a form of social injustice. Legitimizing knowledge that EE could provide through critical discourse and policy analysis is a relevant contribution that social science can provide.

254 SUSTAINABLE DEVELOPMENT

References:

BALL, Stephen 'Education reform: a critical and post-structural approach' Buckingham, UK: Open University Press, 1994.

BECK, Ulrich, 'Risk society', Sage publications: London, UK, 1992.

BENTHAM, Jeremy, 'Utilitarianism', 1789.

BOURDIEU, Pierre, 'Outline of a theory of practice', Cambridge, UK: Cambridge University Press, 1977.

BOURDIEU, Pierre and Loic Wacquant, 'An invitation to reflexive sociology', Cambridge, UK: Polity Press, 1992.

BOURDIEU, Pierre, 'The state nobility elite schools in the field of power', Cambridge UK: Polity Press, 1996.

BOURDIEU, Pierre, 'The essence of neoliberalism', Le Monde Diplomatique, December 1998. (http://mondediplo.com/1998/12/08bourdieu).

BOURDIEU, Pierre and Loic Wacquant, 'New liberal speak: notes on the new planetary vulgate' Radical Philsophy, January/February 2001.

BOURDIEU, Pierre 'Firing back: Against the tyranny of the market' London: Verso Books, 2003.

CALDAS-COULTHARD, Carmen Rosa and Malcolm Coulthard, (eds) 'Texts and practices: readings in critical discourse analysis' London: Routledge, UK, 1996.

CHAMBERS, Robert 'Words, meaning and power in development' Lecture at the London School of Economics, Hong Kong Theatre, 4 p.m., 11 November 2001.

DILLON, Justin, James Hindson, Steve Gough, William Scott, and Kelly Teamey,. 'Mainstreaming environmental education in DFID programmes', Shrewsbury: Field Studies Council, 2001.

DILLON, Justin and Kelly Teamey 'Environmental education within Pakistan' London: King's College London, 2001.

CRUSH, Jonathan 'Power of development' London: Routledge, 1995.

ESCOBAR, Arturo 'Reflections on development: grassroots approaches and alternative politics in the Third World', Futures, June: 411–436, 1992b.

ESCOBAR, Arturo, 'Encountering development: the making and unmaking of the third world' Princeton: Princeton University Press, 1995.

ESCOBAR, Arturo 'Beyond the search for a paradigm? Post-development and beyond' Development, 43: 4, 2000.

ESTEVA, Gustavo 'Development' in Wolfgang Sachs, 'Development dictionary: a guide to knowledge as power' London: Zed books, 1999.

FAIRCLOUGH, Norman 'Discourse and social change' Cambridge: Polity Press, 1992a.

FAIRCLOUGH, Norman and Ruth Ruth Wodak, 'Critical discourse analysis' in Teun A. Van Dijk, ed., 'Discourse as Social Interaction' London: Sage. 258–284, 1997.

FAIRCLOUGH, Norman. and Louise Chouliaraki 'Discourse in late modernity: rethinking critical discourse analysis' Edinburgh: Edinburgh Press, 1999.

FAIRCLOUGH, Norman, 'Neo-liberalism as a focus for critical research on language' Globalisation research network: programmatic text. October 1999.

FAIRCLOUGH, Norman, 'Representations of change in neo-liberalism discourse: analysis of how processes of economic change are represented in a variety of texts', Posted to Language in the New Capitalism network 06/03/00, http://www.cddc.vt.edu/host/Inc/Incarchive.html (2000a).

FAIRCLOUGH, Norman, 'Language in the New Capitalism', Language in the New Capitalism network: paper archives and links: http://www.cddc.vt.edu/host/Inc/Incarchive.html (2000b).

FAIRCLOUGH, Norman, 'The dialectics of discourse', Textus XIV.2, pp. 231–242, 2001.

FAIRCLOUGH, Norman and Phil Graham, 'Marx as a critical discourse analyst: the genesis of a critical method and its relevance to the critique of global capital on Language and the New Capitalism'. website: http://www.cddc.vt.edu/host/Inc/Incarchive.html (2002).

FAIRCLOUGH, Norman, 'Analysing discourse: textual analysis for social research', London: Routledge 2003.

FEMIA, Joseph, 'Gramsci's political thought: Hegemony, consciousness and revolutionary process' Oxford: Clarendon Press, 1987.

FONTANA, Benedetto 'Hegemony and power: on the relations between Gramsci and Machiavelli' Minneapolis: University of Minnesota Press, 1993.

FOUCAULT, Michel, 'The archaeology of knowledge', New York: Tavistock Publications, 1972.

FOUCAULT, Michel, 'Discipline and punish: the birth of the prison', (A. M. Sheridan-Smith trans). Harmondsworth: Penguin, 1977.

FOUCAULT, Michel, 'Politics and the study of discourse' Ideology and Consciousness, 3, 7–26, 1978.

FOUCAULT, Michel, 'Power/Knowledge', in Colin Gordon, (ed.). 'Selected Interviews and Other Writings 1972 – 1977' Brighton: Harvester Press, 1980.

FOUCAULT, Michel, 'Disciplinary power and subjection', in Lukes, Steven (ed), 'Power' Oxford, p. 229–42, 1986.

FOWLER, Roger 'On critical linguistics', in Carmen Rosa Caldas-Coulthard, and Coulthard, Malcolm (eds). 'Texts and practices: readings in critical discourse analysis', London: Routledge, UK 3–14, 1996.

GRÜN, Marlo, 'An analysis of the discursive production of environmental education: terrorism, archaism and transcendentalism', Curriculum Studies, Vol. 3, No. 4, 1996.

JESSOP, Bob, 'The crisis of the national spatio-temporal fix and the ecological dominance of globalising capitalism', The International Journal of urban and Regional Research, Vol. 24, No. 2, 273–310, 2000.

LACLAU, Ernesto and Chantal Mouffe,, 'Hegemony and socialist strategies towards a radical democratic politics', London: Verso, 1985.

MERCHANT, Carolyn, 'Radical ecology', New York: Routledge, 1992.

PECK, Jamie and Adam Tickell, 'Neoliberalizing space' Antipode 380 – 404, 2002.

PECK, Jamie and Henry-Wai Yeung. 'Remaking the global economy: economic-geographical perspectives' London: Sage, 2003.

PEET, Richard and Elaine Hartwick, 'Theories of development', New York: Guildford Press, 1999.

PEET, Richard, 'Ideology, discourse, and the geography of hegemony: from socialist to neoliberal development in postapartheid South Africa' Antipode, 34, 54–84, 2002.

PHILIPS, Louise. and Marianne Jorgensen, 'Discourse analysis as theory and method' London: Sage, 2002.

PIETERSE, Nederveen 'Development theory: deconstructions/reconstructions' London: Sage, 2001.

PRAKASH, Madhu and Gustavo Esteva, 'Escaping education: living as learning within grassroots cultures' New York: Lang, 1998.

RAHNEMA, Majid and Victoria Bawtree, 'The post-development reader' London: Zed books, 1997.

RIST, Gilbert, 'History of development' London: Zed Books, 1997.

ROBINSON-PANT, Anne 'Development as discourse: what relevance to education?' Compare, 31, 3, 311 – 328, 2001.

ROBOTTOM, Ian. and Paul Hart, 'Research in environmental education: engaging the debate', Geelong, Australia: Deakin University Press, 1993.

SACHS, Wolfgang, 'The development dictionary: a guide to knowledge as power' London: Zed books, 1992b.

SACHS, Wolfgang, 'Planet dialectics – explorations in environment and development' London: Zed Books, 1999.

SAID, Edward, 'Orientalism' London: Routledge, 1978.

SAUVÉ, Lucie, 'Environmental education and sustainable development: a further appraisal', Canadian Journal of Environmental Education, Vol. 1 p. 7 – 33, 1996.

STEPNEY, Erin, 'Bourdieu on Bourdieu: reflexive sociology and the sociologist in society' Crossing Boundaries – an interdisciplinary journal, Vol. 1, No 3 - Fall 2003.

STUBBS, Michael, 'Grammar, text and ideology', Applied Linguistics, 15, 2: 201–23, 1994.

STUBBS, Michael, 'Whorf's children: critical comments on critical discourse analysis', In Wray, Alison & Ann Ryan, eds. 'Evolving Models of Language', Clevedon: Multilingual Matters pp. 100-16, 1997.

TEAMEY, Kelly, Justin Dillon, William Scott, and Steve Gough, 'Linking education, the environment and livelihoods', in Commonwealth Education Partnerships 2003, London: TSO, 2003.

The World Commission On Environment And Development, 'Our common future', Brundtland, Gro Harlem, Chair, 1987.

WEBER, Max, 'The methodology of the social sciences', Translated by E. Shils and H. Finch, New York: Free Press, 1949.

VAN DIJK, Teun, 'Critical discourse analysis', in Deborah Schriffin, Deborah Tannen, & Heidi Hamilton, (eds.), 'The Handbook of Discourse Analysis' (pp. 352–371) Oxford: Blackwell, 2001.

World Bank Group, 'Millennium Development Goals' website 2003. http://www.developmentgoals.org/index.html

World Bank, 'World Development Report 2004—draft outline' presented on the World Bank website for public commenting, 2003.

Notes:

1. When I observed the topic of this conference in the SDPI library during my stay in Pakistan in July, 2003 I was attracted to the theme being about knowledge production, consumption and legitimation in relation to policies in the South as it relates directly to the central questions embedded within my PhD research. The panel on 'Ir/ relevancy of social sciences in South Asia' seemed especially appealing as it presented an ideal opportunity to explore in more depth the issue of my own positioning as the 'outsider' researcher; to bridge the dilemma of not being linked to organic on-the-ground practices - of conducting analyses from 'outside' the actual context (here in the UK) to the context of Pakistan.

2. **Recommendations for implementing environmental education (through the 'ideal type') in Pakistan:**

Develop a better-documented and locally well-researched needs assessment—addressing health, education, environmental, social and economic issues. This might best cover all regions of Pakistan through local PRA methods.

Integrate work of different types from different development organizations.

Identify, document and disseminate good practice of environmental education that focuses upon needs and issues. Establish a research and knowledge database that is accessible. Creating an evaluation framework linking education, environment, health as a backbone for different agencies to refer to.

Develop a conceptual framework for professional development of all types of educators—formal and non-formal. Focusing on: Using the local environment within instruction and incorporating relevant local issues into instruction.

Find key people—politicians, academics, religious leaders, teachers, women (at every level), community leaders. Establish stronger links with the media—journalists—for better communication, outreach and action.

Establish a network of non-formal centres that are run by CBOs and NGOs, but are attached to schools to encourage more community involvement (parents, teachers, students).

Encourage more environmental input within literacy programmes. Expand the concept of literacy (literacies, literacy practices) to address the social, health and environmental issues within the community.

Identify and employ incentives for participation within different communities: Use of local and traditional knowledge—drama, medicine, environmental knowledge and economic opportunities—keeping profits within communities—local resources.

19

URBAN WOMEN REBEL:
VOICES OF DISSENT IN URDU POPULAR FICTION

*Kiran Ahmad**

ABSTRACT

The purpose of this paper is to highlight, 'alternative' stories, written predominantly by and for women that are published in Urdu popular digests. These particular narratives of dissent question socially constituted ideals for women, and deal with 'serious' issues such as the value of women's economic empowerment, preference for sons over daughters and child sexual abuse.

The paper does not claim that popular digests for women have become progressive and there is a 'revolution' of sorts taking place in them. Instead, it asserts that all the stories printed in these digests do not propagate socially constituted ideals, and that 'voices of dissent' are also present. Therefore, the conception of women's Urdu popular digests, as only catering to a demand for easy reading and reinforcing the gender status quo is not true.

This paper is divided into six sections. The first section gives a contextual background by portraying the significance of the topic. The second section illustrates the hierarchical distinction between literature and popular literature. The third examines two studies conducted on Urdu popular fiction for women. The fourth section presents a brief historical background of women's digests. The fifth section discusses the viewpoints of the editors of the two publications selected for this paper. The last section presents extracts from stories, which depict women's recognition of injustice and a questioning of socially constituted ideals.

Man is said to have language by nature. It is held that man, in distinction from plants and animals, is the living being capable of speech. This statement does not only mean that, along with other faculties, man also possesses the faculty of speech.[1] It means to say that only speech enables man (human) to be the living being he is as man (human).[2]

---

*Kiran N Ahmed presently works as a research associate at the Sustainable Developent Policy Institute. Her work focuses on popular fiction, violence against women and legal awareness.
Author's email: kiranahmed@sdpi.org.

Significance

These 'voices of dissent' are significant and worthy of analysis because:

First, popular digests are commercial ventures, so their printability depends on how well they sell. The fact that stories that present an alternate view are printed demonstrates that there is a demand for them, which in turn implies that the acceptability of alternate views is increasing. The market for Urdu digests written predominantly by and for women is huge. There are over a dozen monthly publications for women today: *Hoor, Kiran, Anchal, Khawateen Digest and Pakeeza* being some of the major ones. Circulation figures vary from 7,000 to as high as 1,30, 000. Publications of stories with alternative views in digests, which are mainstream and not specifically geared toward reform shows that narratives of dissent are being heard. In fact, the increase in the proportion of such stories indicates that there is a rising demand for such stories.

Second, fiction redefines boundaries and portrays socially unacceptable views of reality. It is a means of expression, which is relatively unfettered from socially constituted ideals. Ours is a conformist society, and fiction enables women to present views that are socially unacceptable.

The third and perhaps most important reason is that the voices of Pakistan's urban middle class rebels need to be privileged and magnified. This paper will show that the methods of analysis used by studies conducted on Urdu popular fiction only privilege the views of the majority. The voice of minority which rebels against socially constituted ideals is neither registered nor analyzed. The importance of registering alternate views stems from the fact that:

a) English has become, more or less, a global language. Urdu is not widely spoken or understood. The access 'gateway' that the rest of the world will therefore have to stories written by Pakistan's urban women is through secondary research in English, or their English translations. This leads to an added responsibility in bringing forth all the voices.
b) These stories go beyond socially constituted ideals. In bringing forth imagined or lived experiences of domestic violence, economic empowerment and other such issues present a more 'real' grasp of the life of a Pakistani urban middle class woman.

Fourth, language serves dual functions. It is both a 'tool for expression' as well as a grid through which we view reality. Its role as an expression of our thoughts and feelings is obvious enough. Its role as the grid or shaper of reality is much more complex. While it would not be possible to do justice to this notion in one or two lines, the idea does need to be presented here.

Basically, words shape our reality, for instance words like wise or fool divide reality into a binary concept, whereas the reality may be much more complex than this: a wise man can be unwise and a fool can be wise. Manipulation of the power of words by the state is common e.g. the war of 1857 is a 'mutiny' in British textbooks and a 'war of independence' in Pakistan's textbooks. In women's popular fiction too, there are certain subtle manipulations that can be gauged. One example is that of the word *majazee khuda* (second to God). This term has been used in a popular *hadith* (sayings of the Prophet (PBUH), which are not always authentic). It states that God revealed to Mohammad (PBUH) that if He were to allow a human being to prostrate before anyone aside from Allah, it would be for wives to prostrate before their husbands, hence husbands should be second to God for wives. In the August 1978 issue of *Pakeeza*, this was the title given for writing short stories on. All the three selected stories propagated this notion. The point here is that words shape our perception and the way we deal with reality. Language is important, and fiction, since it is an expression that entails use of language, is a powerful medium. It not only expresses the writer's imagination but also shapes the reader's perception of reality.

POPULAR LITERATURE

The power of literature/fiction is more or less accepted. However, there seems to be a hierarchy of sorts in this. Literature is, for the most part taken seriously, while popular literature is seen as being 'light' and frivolous.

For instance, Anwer Sajjad, a prominent Pakistani writer, sees the introduction of popular digests as a 'plug' for the vacuum created because of increasing greed for material wealth. He argues that after the 1958 Martial Law of Ayub Khan, subtle changes took place in our society. Through the introduction of the bonus voucher scheme, allotments, and prize bonds, people were directed towards material gains.

When people had a connection with literature they had a connection with their minds and spirits. In this vacuum where the relationship with the spiritual values of life was coming to an end, and a relationship with only a single value of earning wealth was being nurtured, it occurred to some shrewd individual that this emptiness could be filled in by stories which led the reader into the world of fantasies. The digests wiped out the important political and social issues and a wave of popularity spread itself from one end to the other. And according to Marx, this is supposed to be among the biggest of conspiracies, when the public is transformed into a passive consumer public, so that they should become incapable of thinking or taking any action.[3]

While I do not agree with his analysis, it at least carries some explanation for the perception of popular fiction as pandering to our desire for escapism.

Robert Brigg's work seems particularly relevant in understanding this hierarchical distinction between popular literature and literature. He draws on Lumby's analysis, who argues that the distinction between Literature, with its concern with worldly matters and popular culture as the satisfaction of a frivolous desire for mindless entertainment, is based on an older distinction between the public and the private spheres.

Public	Private
High culture	Popular Culture
Reason/Law	Desire
Politics	Morality
Work	Leisure
Seriousness	Frivolity

According to Lumby, this distinction is based on 'exclusivity', as in the Greek 'agora' or the Roman 'forum', where adult males could meet and discuss politics and philosophy. Women were excluded from such gatherings. The parallel institution we have in the East would again be the market place, where women go only if necessary, loitering is not favoured, while men have no such social pressure. These distinctions present a gender hierarchy where the public is seen primarily as the male domain, while the private attributed to the female one.

Lumby goes onto argue that the reading of popular literature in its contribution to the debate on the contemporary social situation can actually be seen as a feminist challenge to the public private distinction.[4]

STUDIES ON POPULAR DIGESTS FOR WOMEN

In Pakistan, in recent years, there have been two studies on popular fiction for women: one was led by Seema Pervez at the National Institute of Psychology-NIP, and the other by Tasneem Ahmar of Aks: a research, resource and publication center on women and media.[5]

The study carried out by NIP covered the period from 1975–1978 and was published in 1984. They selected five magazines for analysis: *Pakeeza Digest, Khawateen Digest, Akhbar-e-Jahan, Akhbar-e-Khawateen* and *Hoor.* Five issues were randomly chosen from each monthly and 10 issues were selected from each weekly. Thus a sample of 15 monthlies and 20 weeklies was taken from the issues of the five selected magazines.[6] A random sample of 80 stories was then selected and analyzed.

This study concluded that the image of the women characters was more or less the same in all the digests. The general image was of a girl who wants to be near to her significant others. She wants to be friendly and loyal, but has strong feelings of inferiority. She accepts her weakness and others' criticism. She is resigned to her fate and inspite of the strong desire to affiliate with people, she is hesitant in establishing relationships. She calls for help and wants to be protected and loved. The attitude of the 'press' towards her is merciful, protective and generous.

The analysis showed that the most popular central idea was that marriage or romance is the most important aspect of a woman's life. Fifty-one out of the 80 stories revolved around this basic idea. In a majority of the stories, the woman was portrayed as passive and fatalistic. Other people take decisions for her, if she ever does make them they must be in accord with social expectations. The female protagonist behaves in an emotional way, and failure in love destroys her whole life. At times she is forcefully deprived of her rights and sometimes she herself surrenders in the face of social injustice. She is the one who sacrifices when demanded by society and occasionally feels disgusted at her decision. She takes some steps to satisfy her ego, but most of the time they are based on irrational decisions.[7] This study does point out that there are stories that illustrate that reality is different from fantasy, and it is difficult for men to accept their wife's superiority. However this is not elaborated upon.

Tasneem Ahmar (1997) also presents the same findings. She too points out that 'serious issues' are sometimes discussed, but not elaborated upon.

> Much of the material in these magazines is written in an intensely emotional idiom. The style may well appeal to readers thirsty for pulp entertainment, but it also drives home a quintessentially conservative message. Whether deliberately or unintentionally, this literature strips women of their individual identity. They are shown to exist solely through their relationship with men, whether as wife, daughter, cook or mother.[7]...*although writers do occasionally discuss topics such as domestic violence and sexual harassment, most paint pretty pictures of female fantasy.*[8]

The methodology employed by the two analyses discusses only the majority viewpoints. One digest has on average 10–13 short stories. The ten stories that are frivolous get analyzed, while the three stories, that present an alternative view are sidelined in the conclusion of such studies. The 'voice of dissent' with its discussion of serious issues is drowned in the 'voice of majority'. The 'positive' stories are noticed but are not given any importance. These studies look *only* at what the 'majority' is saying. This amounts to reductionism and labeling. The message that comes across is that the portrayal of women in these digests is conservative and since these digests print what readers want to read, therefore urban middle class women want to see themselves in this manner.

The identification, recognition and resistance to injustice that comes across in the 'stories of dissent' are not brought forth. As a result, the idea of the urban middle class woman as being complacent with her role in life is reinforced.

Like many other travelers he (Kingblake) is more interested in remaking himself and the Orient, dead and dry – a mental mummy...[8] *than he is in seeing what there is to be seen.*

HISTORICAL BACKGROUND

Specialized periodicals for women came on the scene after the war of 1857 as a result of Sir Syed's reformist movement. Sir Syed published a journal, *Tehzeib-ul-Akhlaque*, aimed at improving the morale of Muslims. Its column writers stressed the need for educating women. In 1898, a weekly geared exclusively for women, called *Akhbar-e-Tehzeeb-e-Niswan* began to be published. Maulvi Mohammad Mumtaz was its founder and his wife, Mohammadi Begum, was its chief editor.[9] In 1908, Maulana Rashid ul Khairi brought out the first issue of *Ismat*. Syed Mumtaz Ali published another journal for women, *Shir e Madar*.[10] These journals catered to a very small section of the total population. In 1924 merely four out of thousand women were literate. Till the 1960s there was little change. Aside from the older more established ones, most magazines remained gender neutral, and would only have a small column or a section geared toward women readers.

With the passage of time the number of literate women increased and economic pressures led to an expansion in the number of working women. As a result, in the 1960s and the 1970s new digests began to be published. According to advertising expenditure data, the number of magazines published in Pakistan, increased from 214 in 1993 to 406 in 2000. The majority of these were in Urdu and were women's magazines.[11]

The two digests selected for this paper began to be published about 30 years ago. The first issue of *Khawateen Digest* was published in April 1973, and that of *Pakeeza* came out in April 1974. The format of both digests is more or less the same. There are 10–13 short stories, one or two episodinal novels, a section on beauty tips, one section titled 'diary' in which readers send verses from poems, or extracts from books, one section on psychological advice, one section on health advice, and one on show business news. *Pakeeza* also has a section on religious advice. In the 40 digests selected for this paper, I could not find a single short story or episodinal novel written by a man, all of them were by women. However, the possibility of men writing under pseudonyms cannot be ruled out. The writers write as a hobby, and are quite 'in touch' with the readers, who send questions about the writer's own life. In fact there seems to be a kind of intimacy, readers send in news about their family life, a brother's marriage, a niece's illness, and writers are willing to respond to questions about what they were given for *moonh dikhai* (gift given at marriage by the husband). Perhaps, the most astonishing aspect of these digests is the number of readers they have. *Pakeeza* has a readership of 70,000 and *Khawateen Digest* has a readership of 130,000.

VIEWS OF EDITORS

Pakeeza's editor, Anjum Ansar, has been working in this position for 16 years. She asserted that over the past five or six years the stories that are being submitted revolve around the problems one has to encounter *after* marriage. Previously, most of the stories were romantic and ended in marriage. Readers too seem to be appreciating these stories more, and seem to want more 'real life'. In response to a question on economic empowerment she had an interesting observation that six or seven years ago, mothers of prospective grooms would, in their letters, ask her to find them girls who are pretty and well versed in housework. The demand would be for a *'gharailoo'* (homely) girl, now however they ask for a working woman who would be able to contribute to the household expenses. With regard to media policy, she said that nothing had been given to them in print, and the changing regimes had little effect on their digests since they try to steer away from political matters. She added that the editors exercised censorship by removing lines they found obscene. Censorship also extends to stories or paragraphs that go against basic human rights such as rights of minorities. In this context, she also mentioned that she had readership amongst religious minorities in Pakistan, especially among the Hindus in interior Sindh. This is a credible claim since letters written by girls with Hindu sounding names get published. She also noted that over the years there has been an increasing interest in religion and spirituality. In response to which a regular advice column called 'roohani *mushwaray*' (spiritual advice) has been introduced, to give advice to women to help them with their problems. This section is specifically for Muslims and minorities are excluded.

Amtul Saboor has been working as the editor of *Khawateen Digest* for the past 25 years. She shared Anjum Ansar's view that changing political regimes had little formal impact since political issues were not covered. She emphasized that readers have a certain trust in these publications, so even advertisements have to be handled responsibly. She gave the example of an advertisement agency, which wanted them to print the ad of a certain facial cream. They were paying a hefty amount, but since the cream was relatively expensive, the staff took a stand and decided to withhold the ad till they had tried the cream themselves. The product did not live up to its promise and the ad was not printed.

Something that came across in conversations with both the editors was a defensive tone. Both stated that their task was to 'educate' young girls and they did whatever was in the girl's or women's best interest. One factor behind this could be the initial abuse and suspicion they had to face in their early days.[12] Another could be that they need to differentiate their publications from the other monthlies that have soft porn and violence, hence the insistence at decency. Yet another reason could be the 'Urdu medium-English medium' class divide we have in Pakistan. An 'English medium' asking questions about an Urdu publication usually raises suspicions of the publication being debunked.

Another interesting aspect was the 'flavour' each editor lent to her digest. As stated earlier, Anjum Ansar has started a column on spiritual advice. Though it does not list her name up front, she disclosed that she was the key person behind running it, and got this information from books published on *hadith*. Anjum Ansar considers religious knowledge to be important, and she tries to put in lessons wherever she can. She cited the example of a story, in which a mother is seeing off her two daughters who are using public transportation alone for the first time. Anjum Ansar added a line about the mother reciting *'ya hafeezo'*,[13] since this particular name of Allah is believed to protect one against accidents. Amtul Sabur, on the other hand, considers spiritual advice columns as a commercialization of religion, and strongly asserted that her publication did not have one. In terms of editorial changes she gave the example of a story in which the writer had shown the lead protagonist running into a *faqeer* (beggar/ spiritual wise man) who gives her advice. She removed this section, since it could have reinforced the idea of going to *faqeers* for spiritual advice, who more often than not, charge a fee for their services.

Perhaps, the very fact that voices of dissent still manage to 'get heard' despite editorial wariness at being termed anti status quo and the overall low key tilt of these digests, speaks volumes for the resilience and sheer relentlessness of our urban rebels.

VOICES OF DISSENT

I now present extracts from stories, which reflect a questioning of existing social norms. The extracts are relatively long. The aim is to reflect some sense of the 'tone' these stories have as well as to provide 'evidence' in support of my claim that there is an alternative 'world view' present in popular literature for women. The methodology for selection was fairly simple. I selected 40 stories from two publications, *Khawateen Digest* and *Pakeeza*, and went through each story. The ones that seemed 'dissenting' were then selected and quoted. Instead of what most seemed to say, the dissenting voices were selected and brought forth. These stories reflect a consciousness of injustice and resistance towards it.

> Feminist consciousness is the belief that personal problems result from unfair treatment because of one's group membership rather than from lack of personal effort or ability.[13]

PREFERENTIAL TREATMENT OF SONS

Story 1:
Context:
Rehmat Ali had internalized the social 'bias' of daughters being a burden and sons an asset. He brought up his children working on the assumption that his son would take care of him in old age and daughters would have to be married off and 'given' to someone else. His three daughters never received his attention. He was focused on his son, Saad, who was going to a very good school. He never forgot to attend his parent-teacher meeting, or check his progress. In case of the daughters however, he could not recall which grade each of them was in. When his eldest daughter, Samina stood first in her Matric exam, he was amazed to see her photograph in the newspaper. Her name 'Samina Rehmat Ali' made him realize the honour she had brought to his name. For a second he was ecstatic. However, that was only for a second. The thought that even though his daughter was talented, the benefit of this ability would be to some other family, not theirs, depressed him.

As years went by, his daughters started a tuition center and not only took care of their own expenses but also contributed to the household. The son on the other hand, was a spoilt brat, and left for Canada after taking the family's savings with him. Rehmat Ali had a heart attack, and woke up to find himself in the hospital.

> 'Saad', even after all that had happened he could only repeat this name.
> 'Who is Saad?' The doctor asked.

'My brother, he's in Canada, my father misses him very much.' A voice was telling the doctor, he could not tell if it was Samina, Sara or Maria.

'Your son is away, but you should be grateful to your daughters. It's because of your eldest daughter that you're alive today. You had a major heart attack but she managed to get you to the hospital very quickly.'

For the first time in his life, he brought up his trembling hand and stroked his daughter's head. He would have gladly slapped anyone, who claimed that daughters were a burden[14].

Story 2:
Context:
A woman had two daughters and a son named Nadeem. She gave preferential treatment to her son. Her son however ended up neglecting her in old age, while her daughters took care of her. One day her daughter -in -law accused her of stealing money and Nadeem failed to defend her.

'How could she say that, wasn't Nadeem Bhai there?'
'He was standing there when this happened.'
'What?'
Suddenly Rehma (the younger sister) started crying and told her sister what had happened.
'I had snatched morsels from your mouth, to feed him; this is why I'm being punished. Please forgive me God. I'd forgotten that everyone has his or her own place, and rights. Forgive me for not fulfilling your rights.' Amman was mumbling[15].

Story 3:
Context:
Najma's mother gave preferential treatment to her brother, Akhter. She had to help out in the kitchen while her brother was given time to study.

After a few days both took their exam. Najma stood first in her class, and showed the report card to her father. He was very happy. Her mother was happy too. However she also expressed her wish for her son to have the same kind of marks, since he was a boy and studying was very important for him.'

Najma got married, and had two children of her own, a boy and a girl. She was determined to change the way she was raised and tried her best to provide her daughter with the same opportunities her son had. Her husband passed away and she moved in with her parents. However she realized that her mother was repeating the same pattern, and giving preferential treatment to her grandson. She then decided to move out and go back to her husband's old house, even though it entailed difficulties for her.

'Najma, I'm very grateful for what you've done for us. Once Akhter comes back from England, life will become very easy for us.'
'Amman you still expect him to be obedient?'
'Yes, a bad son and a bad coin never go to waste.'

Akhter never turned up, and Najma supported her parents in their old age[16].

Only when women begin to identify unfair treatment of themselves as women can they begin to formulate a conscious reaction to these individual incidents and feelings.[17]

APPEASEMENT VS ASSERTION

Story 1:
Context:
A family was discussing their daughter's decision to not leave her husband and in-laws' house, despite their ill treatment.

> We were humiliated yesterday because of her refusal to come with us. It's not really her fault either. We ourselves teach our daughters to give preferential treatment to their in-laws, to consider them as their 'real' family. Her mother in laws' arrogance and cruelty is in part because of her own submissiveness. Why would the abuser stop if the abused does not even protest.[18]

Story 2:
Context:
Abeer was insecure because she came from a lower income group than her in-laws and did not have any family left to support her. Her solution was to appease and 'lie low'. However, she stayed unappreciated and more or less unhappy with her situation. A houseguest, Zaid, pointed out to her that her attitude was to be blamed for her unhappiness.

> Zaid: 'Learn to give some time and importance to yourself.'
> 'What do you mean?', Abeer paused between putting *parathas* in the hot pot. She could not understand what he was trying to say.
> 'What do you like to have for breakfast?', Instead of explaining, Zaid asked another question.
> 'Anything', she had never really done anything special in this regard, and would quickly eat whatever was available. The morning rush left little time for actually sitting down and having breakfast. She ate to fill her stomach since she needed energy to complete her daily tasks.
> 'Anything! You mean you don't like anything in particular, or rather you don't consider yourself important enough to have any definite likes and dislikes... an egg that someone didn't eat, toast that's been left, why should it be put in the dust bin, so you eat it. Am I right? This is the importance that you give to yourself.'
> 'But what does it matter?'
> 'It matters, it matters a great deal. Others will learn to give importance to us, only if we consider ourselves to be important. Last night you made cream coffee for Faizan, cold coffee for Sapna, black coffee for me—and what did you have?'[19]

Story 3:
Context:
A young artistic girl got married to a man who was physically and verbally abusive. Initially, she tried to resolve the situation.

> 'Tell your brother he needn't come here anymore, this is a house not a hotel.'
> Wiping her tears she consoled herself, everything will be okay. Soon after marriage everyone encounters such problems but with time we will both adjust. But then again knowing the kind of a person he is I'm the one who will have to adjust.

The following lines are from a fight she has when she tried to write poetry.

> 'Why can't you turn off the light? Are you trying to write a letter to some previous lover?'

'Is this all you can think of? I have the right to be in this house and to use its things; I'll keep the light on if I want to. Do whatever you want.'

'No, you do not have any rights over anything.' He started tearing up the pages she had written on. '*Shareef* (decent) women do not write such stuff.'

'No, you want to trample on my self-respect but I will not let you do that.'

'Remember I'm your husband.'

'I will accept whatever is reasonable, but this is unreasonable. Why are you so scared of my poetry? You're scared because if a woman wants to realize her capabilities, you push her within the four walls of your home portraying this as your manhood. You want to end her individuality, rust her capabilities and trample on her personality, because you fear that she would leave you behind.'

Eventually she left him and went back to her parents' house. Over there she encountered the social pressure of staying separated. Her husband then wrote her a letter asking her to come back. She decided to go back to him, thinking that it was her fault to have expected too much. Going back, however, proved to be a mistake as he got her to sign off all her dowry over to him, and divorced her.

She was prepared to sacrifice her individuality, her self and yet she had not gained anything. 'Why did I believe him, why did I come back? If I had not been here, he would not have been able to strip me of all I had left. This was my fate, but in this sinister drama who was the villain, the cruel man who had exploited and abused me in every possible way, or the two women (her mother-in-law and sister-in-law) who are silent at the treatment being meted out to another woman.'[20]

WOMEN STANDING UP FOR WOMEN

Story 1:
Context:
A man who had married again despite his first wife's resistance, decided to divorce his second wife.

Husband: 'You should be happy. I'm doing exactly what you wanted all along.'
First wife: 'This is not what I want, this is what you want. And I will not let you get away with this. You cannot tread on women's self respect as you please.'[21]

CHILD SEXUAL ABUSE

Story 1:
Context:
Her mother as a child, repeatedly told Seema that once she got married her husband would take care of her. Her father was an alcoholic and regularly beat up both his wife and daughter. After learning that his wife had tuberculosis, he considered killing her to be a better alternative than spending money on medicines. One night as he tried to kill his wife by hitting her with a heavy object, his 14 year-old daughter, killed him. She then ran off to her mother's cousin to confess and ask for help. He promised to help her and managed to convince everyone that the father had died accidentally. He increased his interaction with this family and promised the girl that he would send her sister to school, and pay for her mother's medical expenses if she agreed to have sexual relations with him.

Uncle: 'We could reach an agreement.'

Seema: 'Don't forget what I'm capable of. I've killed my own father.

Uncle: 'You fool, I'm not going to rape you. I won't force you into anything. I just want a deal. I'll bring you your mother's medicines and send your sister to school. On the other hand if you don't agree with me, this society as well as your own mother and sister will never forgive you and maybe you'll be hanged.'

Seema was trying to hold back her tears, there might have been a disabled day waiting for her outside but to her the night of sorrows seemed endless.[22]

Story 2:
Context:

A young girl was molested by her stepfather. She tried her best to not stay at home without her mother and other siblings. This was taken as a sign of her defiance, rather than as an expression of her fear. In any case, regardless of her mother's displeasure, she would always manage to avoid being with her stepfather. She not only successfully handled her stepfather, and discouraged his advances, but also made it clear to him that he did not intimidate her. One day he walked into her room, as she was asleep. She woke up and threatened to tell her mother. He in turn told her that she was powerless since she was scared of being divorced. Her mother overheard this conversation and tried to quickly arrange for her to be married off. She got married but never expected her husband to show any affection, or give her any importance. Things changed when her husband's cousin came to stay, and he began to openly flirt with her. A houseguest made her realize that appeasing was not going to get her anywhere; she had to assert herself. She started asserting herself and things changed for the better.[23]

ADULTERY

Context:

A woman with grown children, whose husband was settled in the United States, began a relationship with another man. The following lines are from the letter her friend wrote to her husband,

> Khalil Gibran asserts that in judging a woman who has been 'dishonest' to her husband, it's the husband's heart and soul that should first be judged.[24]

DOMESTIC VIOLENCE

Context:

Asifa got married to her cousin Sharjeel. Her mother-in-law and sister-in-law's behavior towards her was anything but ideal. Her husband too, started testing her limits, as he began abusing her physically at the slightest of excuses. The following extract is from an incident, where she wanted to attend her cousin and best friend's wedding. Her in-laws knew how badly she wanted to go, and deliberately decided to not attend the function before 10 p.m.

> 'What kind of a bargain is this? Even after giving everything, a woman still stays so cheap that she's not even able to get a little happiness in exchange. What kind of a selfish market is this of a man's world where a woman's sincerity, her hard work count for nothing. Sharjeel in marrying me, had gained a beautiful, faithful and sincere wife, but what had I gained? Why have I reduced myself to

this? Why do I let everyone in this house make a fool out of me? Even Sharjeel has gone to attend the ceremony, leaving me at home. I only need to tell my family about what's going on, and my in-laws will quickly straighten up. Why am I so cowardly?' All these thoughts were running through her mind, as Sharjeel barged in.

'Do you think you can intimidate me by bringing in our grandfather?' He pushed her up by her arm. 'Answer me. Have I stopped you from going to your cousin's house? Poor Asifa, can't even attend the wedding properly because she's stuck with a cruel man.'

He slapped her face.

'Your father calls me a cruel man.' He continued slapping her face, as she started screaming. Asifa was boiling with rage.

'Get away from me, you animal. You consider yourself brave because you can hit a woman.'

She ran into the bathroom and locked herself up. She only opened the door as she heard Sharjeel pleading for forgiveness.

She was a fool to have forgiven the cruelty and abuse inflicted on her; because of the repentance he had shown.[25]

WOMEN'S EARNING CAPACITY

Story 1:

Context:

A housewife was economically dependent on her husband, Ansar. She then began teaching and earned Rs 2000. Her husband borrowed it from her to contribute to the monthly 'committee', and told her that he would return it once he got back the money he had loaned to an office colleague. Guests arrived unexpectedly and she asked her husband to give it back so she could meet the new expenses incurred because of the guest's arrival.

> Husband: I've been working for eight years now, and have been giving you every single penny I earn. I don't gamble, I don't smoke and I don't drink. Whatever you cook, I've been eating willingly – you've brought in Rs 2000 for the first time, and are now trying to make me feel inferior.' He threw the money at her.
>
> Wife: (thinking to herself) '*Dadi* (paternal grandmother) you used to tell me that a man's income no matter how meager is blessed, and a woman's income even if it is made through honest means can not suffice. But you failed to tell me that the money a woman earns is so worthless that it can be thrown to the ground and spat on.'
>
> She picked up the currency and started weeping. 'Ansar, every time there has been even a small increase in your pay, I've expressed gratefulness. I've always held the money you gave me with respect, and I've always spent it as a sacred trust. I've spent hours worrying if even a penny has been wasted because of my or the children's negligence. I've always thought of your tired being every time I've spent it. This is the respect I've given to the money you earn—and you, you've thrown the money I earned. Isn't my hard work, hard work?' She kept questioning herself.[26]
>
> Feminist consciousness is developing a radically altered consciousness of our self and of others and of social reality...women have long lamented their condition but a lament pure and simple need not be an expression of feminist consciousness, as long as their situation is apprehended as natural inevitable and inescapable. Women's consciousness emerges only when there exists a genuine possibility for the partial or total liberation of women.[27]

Story 2:
Context:

Sara started her career as an assistant commissioner. She had her office during the day, she spent evenings with her friends, and at night she studied for her M. Phil exam. Her life was busy and happy. She then met Talha, who seemed to cherish her abilities, and she got married to him. Gradually her husband began to control her, and insisted that she leave her profession.

> Talha: 'I want to see you as a complete housewife.'
> Sara: 'So you want to see me as a *Naik Perveen* (Ms Piety), whose only concerns revolve around her house, what's to be cooked in that house and her children. True, there are many women in our society who spend their lives doing this, and this is valuable in its own way. But I'm not like that. If God has given me additional capabilities why shouldn't I put them to use. What's the point of spending so much time and effort in getting all these qualifications, if the only matter I'm supposed to use my mind for is what's to be cooked for dinner.'

Eventually she agreed, thinking that compromising would help in reducing their marital tensions. Instead, life became more difficult for her. Talha's complaints didn't stop, their focus became different as he began to find fault with everything she did around the house.

After four years of marriage the effort to please Talha, and become his ideal wife had left her exhausted, and she began to re examine the choices she had made.

> After marriage, housework and home should be important for a woman, but her own self should not be sacrificed either. Every woman has her own individuality and this individuality should continue. The house, husband and children should all be given attention, but a woman should also have her own identity. It's not enough to be recognized as someone's wife, or daughter or mother. 'Who was I before this marriage, and who have I become now. What did I get in return? I've tried everything eastern women are supposed to try to keep the sanctity of the house, but everything has failed, and I've been left with nothing.'
> 'I'm going to start work again. There is a school nearby that I'm going to start teaching at. I'm going to work no matter what.'
> 'The day you start work I'll leave you,' said Talha..
> This time his threat had no effect on her. 'The school is nearby and I can walk there easily,' she replied.
> Talha tried everything from threats to pleading to get her to change her mind, but this time she was determined.
> 'I have to work, for myself and for my children. If my spirit doesn't get any fresh air, it's going to die.'
> Sara had regained her own sense of importance as an individual, and she was confident that she would be able to assert herself.[28]

Story 3:
Context:

Saima was under psychological pressure because of her husband, Wasiq. Her educational qualifications were higher than her husband's qualifications, and he felt insecure because of this. Initially she tries to appease him and accepts all his decisions.

> Women try their utmost to make their marriages work, and men instead of appreciating this, do not even acknowledge this effort. Before marriage, girls are pampered and loved by their parents, but once they get married they have to put up with undue criticism. Husbands in their 'husbandness', deny them due respect, because their own egos are too frail to handle a woman. In trying to get along

with their husbands, women push their own intelligence, education and critical thinking to the background. In trying to make their husbands feel respected, women accept each decision without any criticism. However, this policy backfires. The husbands not only get into the habit of leaving out their wife from decision-making, but they also label her a 'fool', who has no understanding.

Saima then met another older woman who told her that going according to her husband's wishes was not going to get her anywhere. Women, who do this, get into the habit of sacrificing their own happiness for the sake of others. Husbands neither acknowledge nor appreciate those sacrifices. And the children too, who have seen their father degrading their mother, don't respect either parent.

Saima began to take time out for herself:

'What is this? Am I going to have to eat *daal chawal* (rice and lentils) for dinner?' shouted Wasiq.
'I'd gone for a hair cut,' she answered as if Wasiq's anger was of no consequence.
'Why isn't my tea here yet?'
'I was using a facial mask, have just taken it off. I'll make tea for you now if you'll take care of the baby,' she replied.
Wasiq lost his temper, and started his usual lecture about Saima's laziness and inefficiency. Saima stayed quiet, and then calmly nodded her head in agreement. 'You are right. I am not only lazy but also ill mannered.'
What could Wasiq say, everything he was planning on saying had already been said. Gradually, he began to see that his criticism had no effect on Saima now. She was no longer afraid of his temper tantrums.
One day she informed him that she has found a job for herself. Wasiq was shocked and tried to dissuade her.
'How will you work? Who will run the house?'
'But you say yourself, that it's the maid who runs the house, I don't do anything. So, the maid will continue to run the house,' said Saima,'
The day Saima received her first pay cheque, without asking Wasiq, she hired a young girl to help her out with her children. When he asked her about it, she replied that since her pay was going into the new maid's salary, so she didn't feel the need to ask him.

Eventually her husband realized that he could no longer intimidate her, while she led a happy and busy life.[30]

Conclusion

I have tried to show that there is a discussion of 'serious issues' and it has largely been ignored by the studies carried out on these digests. The next step would be to explore why there is this discussion. Why is it more acceptable to discuss issues of violence and class as familial struggles through stories? Is it simply the 'security' and possibility of creating an alternative reality offered by fiction writing, or is it something more complex. What are the other narratives of dissent and how are they different or similar to particular narrative? What are the readers' perceptions with regard to narratives of dissent, as well as 'typical' stories of romance?

Dissent by a minority, whether it is in the form of a protest against testing of nuclear weapons in a country where most of the population is celebrating this occasion, or a short story that speaks out against child sexual abuse, needs to be highlighted. This paper is an attempt at magnifying one particular narrative of dissent in Urdu popular fiction.

Way and weighing
Stile and saying
On a single walk are found

Go bear without halt
Question and default
On your single pathway bound[29]

APPENDIX

Digests that were included in this analysis:

Pakeeza June 1973
Pakeeza July 1973
Pakeeza August 1973
Pakeeza June 1974
Khawateen Digest November 1976
Pakeeza November 1976
Pakeeza December 1976
Pakeeza February 1977
Pakeeza June 1977
Khawateen Digest August 1977
Khawateen Digest August 1978
Pakeeza August 1978
Pakeeza November 1980
Khawateen Digest January 1984
Pakeeza June 1985
Khawateen Digest June 1985
Pakeeza August 1986
Pakeeza July 1987
Pakeeza June 1989
Khawateen Digest March 1999
Khawateen Digest July 1999
Khawateen Digest October 1997
Khawateen Digest June 2000
Khawateen Digest September 2000
Khawateen Digest December 2000
Khawateen Digest April 2001
Khawateen Digest November 2001
Khawateen Digest June 2002
Pakeeza June 2002
Khawateen Digest July 2002
Pakeeza July 2002
Khawateen Digest August 2002
Pakeeza February 2002
Khawateen Digest July 2002
Pakeeza August 2002
Pakeeza October 2002
Khawateen Digest November 2002
Pakeeza December 2002

Khawateen Digest February 2003
Pakeeza February 2003

References

Books:

HEIDEGGER, Martin, *Poetry Language Thought*, New York: Harper and Row Publishers, 1971.
SALIM, Ahmad, *Culture and Commitment*, Pakistan Committee for Cultural Development, UNESCO, 1989.
SAID, Edward, *Orientalism: Western conceptions of the Orient*, New York: reprinted by Penguin Group, 1995.

Research Reports:

Portrayal of Women in Media: An Evaluation of Gender Policies adopted by PTV during different Political Regimes, United Nations Development Program, November 2001.
Pervez, Seema, Portrayal of Women in Media, National Institute of Psychology, Monograph no. 8, 1984.
Changing Images: A National Study on Monitoring and Sensitization of the Print Media on the Portrayal of Women, Aks, 2002.

Articles:

Asdar, Kamran Ali, 'Digest Culture: Reading Pakistani Domesticity,' *Pakistan Perspectives*, Vol. 7, July – December 2002, pp. 77–88.
Ahmar, Tasneem, 'Pulp Fiction,' *The Herald,* December 1997, pp. 111–114.
Briggs, Robert, 'Reading Desires': *www.mcc.murdoch.edu.au/online/arts/h290/docs/desires.com*
Sarwar, Beena, 'Women in Pakistan: An overview,' *Changing Images: A National Study on Monitoring and Sensitization of the Print Media on the Portrayal of Women*, Aks.
Klatch, Rebecca E., 'The Formation of Feminist Consciousness Among Left and Right Wing Activists of the 1960s,' *Gender and Society,* Vol. 15, no. 6 December 2001.

Notes

1. Heidegger, Martin. 'Language: Poetry Language Thought', p. 189.
2. Writer's own Italics..
3. Salim, Ahmad, *Culture and Commitment*, p. 18.
4. Briggs, Robert 'Reading Desires': *www.mcc.murdoch.edu.au/online/arts/h290/docs/desires.com*.
5. For coverage of news relating to women see Aks publication, *Changing Images.*
6. See appendix 2 for a table on themes of the contents of short stories researched by NIP.
7. Pervex, Seema, NIP Monograph no. 8, pp. 50–51.
8. Writer's own Italics.
9. Ahmar, Tasneem, *The Herald*, December 1997, p. 113.
10. Ibid. p. 113.
11. Asdar, Kamran Ali, 'Digest Culture: Reading Pakistani Domesticity', *Pakistan Perspectives*, pp. 77–88, July-December 2002.
12. Ahmar, Tasneem, 'Pulp Fiction', *Herald*, p. 114.
13. Klein, Ethel quoted in Rebecca Klatch, 'The Formation of Feminist Consciousness Among Left and Right Wing Activists of the 1960s', *Gender and Society*, Vol. 15, December 2001, p. 795.
14. Rahat, Humera, 'Tuhfa', *Khawateen Digest*, Sept 2000, p. 156.
15. Ismail, Farzana, 'Harfe dua hai roshni', *Khawateen Digest*, July 2002, p. 196.
16. Naseem, Waheeda, 'Paraya Dhan', *Pakeeza*, June 1973, p. 84.
17. Klatch, Rebecca, 'The Formation of Feminist Consciousness among Left and Right wing Activists of the 1960s', *Gender and Society*, December 2001, p. 795.
18. Mumtaz, Zuhra, 'Shareek-e-Safar', *Khawateen Digest*, Nov. 2002, p. 222.

19. Amna, Naseem, 'Khud he dareecha kholain gay', *Khawateen Digest*, July 2000.
20. Aizaz, Iffat Gul 'Dard ka fasla', *Pakeeza,* August 1978.
21.
22. Hassan, Nadia, 'Raath', *Pakeeza*, October 2002, p. 63.
23. Amna, Naseem, 'Khud he dareecha kholaingay', *Khawateen Digest*, July 2002.
24. Nighat, Seema, 'Rozan', *Pakeeza*, August 2000, p. 184.
25. Mumtaz, Zuhra, 'Shareek-e-Safar', *Khawateen Digest,* August 2002, p .215
26. Iftikhar, Faiza, ' Sooraj key salthanath', *Khawateen Digest*, June 2002, pp. 178-180
27. Bartky, Sandra Lee, 1990, p. 14.
28. Chaudhary, Shazia, *Khawateen digest,* August 2002, p. 253.
29. Heideggar, Martin, *What is called Thinking?*

20
OWNING OUR STORIES

*Maniza Naqvi**

ABSTRACT

The paper locates our stories and imagines future story-telling in the context of boundaries, poverty, democracy, justice, peace, war, occupation, trade, corporations, development assistance and the international court of justice. The paper discusses the possibility of a world that would have a different context than the one we live in today. A place where the rights of defining past, present and future would belong to all of us and not just to a handful of the privileged. A different world where the terms of engagement that affect all our lives would be in a framework of cooperation not conflict. A world where the discussion on issues that affect us all would not be embedded in bombastic nationalism or hopeless religiousity, nor dismissive, disingenuous, reductionist, self-serving and bullying statements backed by military might for the sole purpose of profiteering, extraction of minerals, oil, arms sales, nor occupation and invasion, nor the destruction of the environment, and threats of endless war. A world where the discourse would be centered on a viewpoint of earth instead of real estate; cooperation instead of coercion and cooperatives instead of corporations.

*Maniza Naqvi is the author of two novels: Mass Transit and On Air both were published by Oxford University Press. Her forthcoming novel 'Stay with Me' will be published in May 2004.

ALL OUR STORIES:

Stories, I think do not reveal the truth, they do however expose untruths. A multitude of narratives, all versions of perceived reality prevent the rise and tyranny of a singular narrative. And in this way, through a multitude of stories, a balance is maintained and truth whether it exists or not is safeguarded by not being singled out. In receiving these narratives we are able to reason that all versions matter; all must be given consideration; that all opinions must be questioned and that all perceptions have validity. All truths are untruths all untruths are true. In the absence of a multitude of narratives, reason remains ruined.

I see reason ruined every day in newspapers, in images on TV channels and in the stacks of books, the so called literature of experts on all things Muslim, Pakistani and Middle Eastern. One of the greatest dangers facing the world today is the dangerous revival of a singular and value laden narrative of good and evil with its time released poison of hate. This view perceives the world in terms of fenced in real estate not earth and in terms of corporate interests not cooperation. These story-tellers with their narratives of antipathy are given credence by the powers that be. And they brand themselves as secular as they view the world through an optic of fear and control and weave their stories full of hate. Stories that justify the geographical, social and economic divisions in the world. Language is being used as a weapon with representations of people in dangerous ways.

Ignorance of each others stories leads us to assume that we know them. It allows us to maintain our perceptions of differences based on our own pre-conceived notions. When we do understand each others stories, we are transformed. We find that we don't know ourselves and we grow and gain.

Violence requires the other. Violence requires a lack of narrative of the other. It requires that the other remains silent or be articulated through a single voice.

Violence, its organization and place in our societies; its place within us; its control and rule over us; and our own stakes in its enterprise demands that no one speaks the truth without consequences. Whether, truths about an individual, a family, a community or a country, the only way left to speak it, write about it and be heard is to call it fiction.

Fiction is about imagination, it comes from what we are, it is a way of rescuing our pasts, our childhoods in a humane manner, to be able to shed light on and through the past into a better future. It allows for the formation of identity through art. It erases ethnicities and creates empathies.

I remember viewing a painting that had halted me in my tracks about a year ago. It was of a middle aged man, who looked very much like an uncle of mine: balding, overweight, clearly distraught and under stress, his hands wrung together, his eyes bloodshot and worried, seated on a wooden chair outdoors in winter, looking up as though at someone. The crumbling wall behind him through a gaping hole in it showed a gray city building in snow. The subject has been striped of his comfortable context and seemed isolated or being interrogated. The portrait had been commissioned by a wealthy, well-connected lawyer who upon seeing it, was so angry that he refused to accept it. He was insulted at the insinuation. The artist was Otto Dix, the subject of the portrait, was a wealthy Jewish lawyer, the city was Dresden, the year was 1921.[2] In 1921, amongst the other lone voices this artist had warned of the times to come given all the hatred in the literature of the day. And the victim had been insulted.

Edward Said has been vilified in the mainstream press which will condemn a man for taking on the cause of the dispossessed. Humanity is in repose, while apologists for cruelty and oppression roam free. And it seems that only one voice stands in their way, that of Noam Chomsky.

I wonder if the usage of the moon in so much of humankind's poetry and idea of love is because it is our way of observing ourselves. It gives us some distance from ourselves. It is our third eye our collective observer, the eye that we know looks upon us, the earth and its inhabitants and gives us a sense of oneness, a singular identity and therefore comfort. We allow ourselves through its vantage point a recognition of ourselves in a common identity without lines, without borders. Without all those divisions that are so unnatural to us and that seed and nurture hatred and fear and which have tragically now become as though our second skin, our nature.

The moon gives us the third eye, of us observing ourselves reminding us that we can be better than we are. Through its view we express our condition and are able to imagine what we can become. Through it we imagine past our present condition and see us as we really are. As we gaze upon the moon, we locate ourselves as grounded on earth, our relationship to earth. We rise up above the constraints of citizenship and nationality, these become insignificant as we recognize ourselves as inhabitants of earth. In gazing upon the moon, we betray nationality and citizenship and thus commit treason for a greater love.

From where I view the world, what do I see? Firstly, I see that there is no difference of feelings, emotions and values amongst people everywhere. Everywhere people want to send their kids to school, everywhere people want to be able to walk without fear in their streets and parks. Everywhere people want to be able to earn their livelihoods. Everywhere people do not want to receive handouts. Everywhere people want a fair hearing. Everywhere people want a fair and equitable justice system. I see a lot of people with common notions of kindness, peace, generosity, community. I see a lot of people who want to do the right thing and are searching for what that means. I see a lot of dedicated people who are asking the important questions and making the irrefutable case for changing the current trade regimes. I also see that the anti-globalization protest has been joined by parents and grand parents in growing numbers that coalesced in the anti war demonstrations. This growing number is asking the fundamental structural questions of why the world is organized the way it is. At my work place, I meet people who were willing to kill each other not too long ago, slowly moving back towards each other in peace. People who were willing to kill each other for separation and creating lines, are ignoring those borders that they helped create. I see that I cannot as a foreigner tell the difference between a Palestinian or an Israeli unless they are wearing a military uniform. The same holds for Serbs, Croats and Bosniaks, Pakistanis and Indians.

Everywhere I see boys at risk. Being pushed into violence, presumed guilty before they even know the definition of innocence. I see that I cannot tell the difference between the motivations of a young American soldier who joined the army to find a way out of poverty and a child in a *madrassa* (religious school) in Pakistan. I my view, I cannot see the reasons for closed borders and boundaries. My colleagues come from all the nations of the world, yet I find that we are one citizenship, that of the earth. It works for us, why can't it work for all?

Albert Camus considered writing the novel an act of rebellion. Because the novelist perceives and creates a different reality. But this rebellion, this powerful peaceful expression of questioning and expressing old and new truths is denied to more than half of Pakistan's population who are locked out of an education. They will never read a novel, let alone write one. They will never read or write. Meanwhile, others will take it upon themselves to describe and define Pakistan in their biased way. The way the world is organized today limits our stories, the terms and conditions that influence our abilities to access opportunities and articulate our aspirations and translate those into action truncate our streams of thoughts and so only a few selective stories get the opportunity to be widely read and only a few ever get written.

All our stories matter, all are valid. Isn't it time we did something about that? Our stories should speak about the possibilities of a different world where if there is evil it should be termed as that power that denies people, everyone access, equity, accountability and democracy. These are the themes of my two novels *Mass Transit* and *On Air*. My third novel *Stay with Me* is set in the context of a secret interrogation and incarceration.

These are without doubt challenging times for the entire world. It seems as though in Pakistan all of the difficulties imposed upon us and tolerated by us in the last fifty years and those with which we continue to struggle have become the way of the entire world. It is as though all that plagued us—now plagues the world. Pakistan's many realities have become the new world order. In this paper, I outline the thoughts that occupy my mind when I think of poverty, democracy, justice, peace and development in the context of war, occupation, trade, corporations, development assistance and the international court of justice. The implications of the way the world is chalked out today has a profound impact on our abilities to speak, to write, to be heard. South Asia has an enormous role to play in redefining our roles as story tellers.

The world is indeed shrinking, but not the way we wanted it to become smaller. Its not a global village the way we might have wanted it to be, that of cooperating harmonious integrated communities and cooperatives sharing common lands, objectives and values. It is not the world which would settle differences through arbitration. Its more like a feudal village with one powerful landlord while the rest are landless tenants: the *mazaras* and the *haris*.

The only way forward is through education. What impact would there be on our stories if there was 100 percent literacy and enrolment of children in school? Where everyone has enough to eat and where people are not indebted to others for the sake of being able to provide a meal for their families. What would be our stories if policy makers realized and acted upon the realization that the best and only homeland security and defence is education for the people. Here at home 24 million Pakistani children do not attend even primary school, they are lost into silence, unable to participate and connect with the world. Unable to access information. They comprise 17% of Pakistan's population; and 20% of the world's population of illiterates. Pakistan therefore has a large share of the world's illiterate population. 90 million Pakistanis cannot read or write. If we are interested in the defence of Pakistan, their education is our defence.

PERSPECTIVE OF A DIFFERENT PLACE/LOCATING OURSELVES:

I'll begin by outlining a world different from the one we are grid-locked in today. When we look at the images of earth taken from outer space we see our planet differently from the way it appears in maps. We see it without the lines that crisscross and divide it in the maps of the world.

The context of almost all of the world's policy arenas today is the protection and enforcement of these lines. The policy arena of today is trying to shift from this context as can be seen by the various debates and discussions on trade regimes but is for the most part guided by and indeed controlled by the need to justify these lines. Lines that keep people in and lines that keep people out. Bottom lines that keep most people out. Lines of exclusion. Lines that stop goods from being traded freely. Lines that stop the movement of people. A gridlock of lines. And in between these lines exist people. Angry people. People trapped by their circumstances. And it is these lines and their protection which has influenced and shaped the nature of political processes around the globe and spawned new lines. Refugee lines: Lines of desperate frightened people waiting to flee, waiting to return, waiting for work, for food, for water, for medicine at border crossings and boundaries. And there are the other lines of blindfolded men incarcerated without trials; protest lines, police lines, supply lines, headlines, frontlines.

People are angry, people are displaced, people are locked out, people despite the availability of tremendous information cannot take advantage of it, the gap between the rich and the poor continues to increase. The gap between the rich and the middle income is increasing.

Today these lines are the reasons why 10 million refugees seek refuge from war and hunger in the world. A total of 30 million people are displaced. There are people seeking jobs and a better life, fleeing war, violence and hunger and finding themselves incarcerated and subjected to further violence in the countries where they are fleeing too. We should discuss the possibility, the urgency now of a world where everyone would have a home, feel at home and the rights of the landless would be secure. A world in which no one would be displaced or homeless. Where people seeking homelands, safety, refuge and a better life would not be trapped at border crossings and locked up instead in concentration camps. Where militaries would not patrol borders and water ways, hunting down the poor who are seeking jobs. The world to the hunted is a place of barbed wire and barricades and secret camps.[3] Internment camps for illegal immigrants and whole populations living under occupation. We should discuss a world where secret camps, concentration camps called holding centers and off shore holding centers for refugees such as Baxter which replaced the notorious Wormarea would not exist.[4] A world where 3 million people would not be locked up in their own homeland in a virtual jail of barbed wire closures and would instead be free in a home land called Palestine. A world where extra judicial killings would cease to occur.

These lines are the reasons for why so-called democracy flourishes in one country while dictator after dictator rules another. We should discuss a world where stability would not be defined by the absence of political agitation and activism. A world where stability would not be defined by the presence of military forces or McDonald franchises, but instead by the diversity and cacophony of political discourse, the riot of voices and the rough and tumble of forward moving action for cooperation and creativity. We should discuss a world where political solutions are the first and the last solutions. A world where politics is democracy. We should discuss a world where people and their discourse are the safe guards and guardians of democracy, not military might.

These lines are very significant, in creating lies, myths and untruths about our human common bond. In creating conflict these lines are very significant. The enforcement of these lines, these 19th and 20th century borders influence culture, class and politics of the world and will continue to have a profound effect on democracy and peace in the 21st century.

SOUTH ASIA'S STORIES:

And today these lines, these border conflicts have the potential to end our planet. Pakistan and India are a case in point. The citizens of Pakistan and India bear the amazing responsibility and burden for the well being of our planet. More than 1.5 billion people or 1/6th of the world's population lives here. The world's largest democracy is here and one of its potentially great democracies in waiting, playing the part of the worst dictatorship is here too. The rapid changes that have occurred on the sub-continent, in the creation of states, changes in ideology, ideas and languages over centuries and in the last fifty-six years, make this region a breathtaking example of modernity. Yet approximately 40 per cent of the world's poverty sits here. Geography has been our selling point, and our curse. We sit in the heart of Asia, in fact to me, the very shape of the subcontinent resembles the shape of the heart.

One of the first English novels my mother gave me to read when I was a kid, was 'The Heart Divided' by Mumtaz Shahnawaz, one of the first Pakistani English novels, if not the first, to be published. English is a language that has come to belong to this gorgeous and variegated sub-continent where more than a hundred languages are spoken. It is our second language. And a significant number speak it. Combined with all the other factors and our ability to communicate between ourselves and the rest of the world in English, we, the people of South Asia will have a significant influence on shaping world opinion and in shaping the world's story. But first we must learn to rely on and respect each others opinions. There must be a reliance and respect between Indians and Pakistanis. Our strongest ally in the world forums can only be and should only be our neighbours.

Imagine what our stories would be if the sub-continent was a common economic space, a common cultural space not constrained by its borders. Think about the myths we would have to give up before we can do that. Imagine the influence we could have in changing the terms and conditions of interaction in the world. Fifty-six years ago, we were left divided as a result of confronting empire. Is there a chance now perhaps that we may join forces to confront it as it rears its ugly head again? Are we to write our story about the end of empire, or one about its short recess and continuation? Are we not to rise beyond that? In a world where power is defined by weapons, we must choose words. In a world where the use of weapons is justified by words and the word of the powerful is English, we must choose to win the battle for ourselves. In English therefore, we articulate and formulate the argument and counter argument, reorient opinion and the optic through which the world is viewed, and views us. It is in this second language of ours that we reach those who are disoriented, to reorient them to a story about ourselves told by us. We reorient ourselves as well. News about us, provided by us. Definitions of us, by us. Analysis of what we are and what we are not, by us. We must take back the space that has been taken from us. The language of imperialism? No longer. It belongs to us, it is ours. It allows us to articulate our story ourselves to an audience beyond ourselves, it shifts the balance of power if not in weapons then in words and that alone is the greatest fight and the greatest battle to be won.

Lets talk about a world where value-laden definitions cease to exist because of our influence. Where all things good are not considered as 'western' where secular does not mean European in its roots, where democracy does not have a definition embedded in the model followed by one country; where war is terrorism; and where the concept of progressive is not considered as 'western'. Where no definition is unique to just one country, race or religion. Where what holds true for one must hold true for all.

What are our definitions? Our human indicators show us as being socially and humanely rich. Our story is of strong families and our value for human relationships make us a people of peace, love and care. Our story is of social informal systems delivering on peace and equity. Our story is one of peace and social justice. Our story is one that values social equity and well being over financial dominance. Our story is of being socially and spiritually rich. Our story is of our investments in social and spiritual well being. Our story is of our people being socially and spiritually highly developed of placing a higher value on humanity. And this is borne out by indicators and statistics. There are more than 1.5 billion people living in South Asia and yet on a day to day basis the least amount of strife and violence occurs in South Asia compared to elsewhere. Industrialized countries have the highest amount of violence, strife and crime. The Subcontinent, both India and Pakistan are oft painted and represented to the world as violent and lawless. Much has been written about the most dangerous place on earth. Is that what we are? No doubt that with such a large population of over 1.5 billion people and population density we have our share of violence. But are the people, the ordinary citizens violent or lawless? More violent then elsewhere? That's what the stories seem to say in the news each day. Statistics interestingly enough say otherwise. Take for example Scandinavian countries, always held up as examples of the highest standards of living. Per 100,000 persons there are 13,000 incidents of crime. In Bangladesh per, 100,000 there are 89 incidents of crime. In India and Pakistan, per 100,000 the number is around 600. In the US per 100,000 the number is 4000. The US spends US$150 billion on its criminal justice system. There are 2 million people incarcerated in the US and this goes up to 6 million if you count everyone in the system in jail, in probation in half way houses and so on. That's 2.1 percent of the US population incarcerated. And 2 million people are employed in the industry of keeping people jailed. The prison industrial complex in the US is a significant industry. [5]

Truth, justice, human rights, idealism, passion, poetry, inspiration, the power of persuasion, the power of words, the defense of the human spirit. This was our story, this should be Our-story, it will be ours. The world refers to this way as secular, we call it *desi*. Our way. We protect the space required for freedom of speech, we can only do so if we are educated. We can lead in the world forums because we can speak English. If we want Urdu, Punjabi, Sindhi, Baluchi, Pushto, Dari, Bengali, Kashmiri and all the other languages to flourish freely and fearlessly, we must be educated. Only and only if we focus on a solid world class education for our children, can we have the most powerful defence. One, at once articulate and eloquent, that says that Pakistan and its people want to be understood by the world, want to engage the world and they want to do it on their own peaceful terms.

It is the justification of borders and lines on maps that concerns history and it will be rendering them irrelevant which will lead us to writing a different story, Our-story. These lines would become meaningless when we begin the collective story-telling of all the wrongs of the past, when we begin acknowledging and reconciling with our pasts. And the recording of all this will begin the cooperation and peace and the way forward. All of our collective stories, told in our voices by us at last.

Recently, while I was in Bosnia for work, a colleague's bad heart condition was explained to me using the metaphor of the entity lines dividing Bosnia. The metaphor resonated deeply with me. Divisions as illness, and the homeland as the heart. In July a Pakistani child went to have her heart repaired in India. Pakistan's Noor, protected by Indian doctors. Would this story have had any poignancy at all for us, if it had been England or the US that Noor had gone to for her medical treatment? I wonder. I don't think so. Because I think this story, of little Noor, is our story, in all its ironies, tragedies and joys and therefore it has the capacity to touch us deeply and indeed break our hearts. To quote from *On Air* 'If it doesn't have the capacity to break your heart, it can't be love.' Naz replies, 'Everyone wants a guarantee for the unbreakable'. The caller replies 'There's no way to do that.'. And Naz asks, 'So nothing ever gets broken?' And the caller reassures her, 'Divided, yes, parted, yes, separated, yes. But whole. All outcomes are predictable. Just solve for X where X=1. X being unity. Unity implies whole'.

The ability to speak in English or write it, should not be equated with modernity or moderation or secularism. That has been part of the problem. All definitions of us spewed out to us in English by others have been accepted as truths. To consider the ability to speak in English in that way would be a grave injustice to the diversity of languages and cultures of this land. We are a people of ideas and words and should be unwilling to be defined. We are as a region that is much stronger, more vibrant multi-dimensional, enriched, more resilient and English is our common denominator amongst ourselves in the entire region of over one hundred different languages, from Baluchi to Malyalam. English is one of our languages. Recently, I had the privilege to be on a panel of judges for awarding a literary prize to first manuscripts by young South Asian authors. These were authors originating from various regions of South Asia, from North South, from Bangladesh, India and Pakistan. The quality of writing and the range of topics assures me that the tradition of South Asian narrative is finding its own unique and powerful voice in English and as a result of being written in English, will have a more widespread audience within South Asia itself.

English. It is the language of today—of sciences, research, businesses and stock markets. The Russians, the French, the Germans, the Japanese, the Chinese concede to this. To enter into the international arena of any debate, to hold sway, to be a force of persuasion, requires that English be spoken and understood.

PAKISTAN'S STORIES:

Pakistan is running on the dedication, commitment, dynamism, and creativity, of its thoroughly modern citizens who are also aggressively and quite humorously, outwardly and upwardly mobile. Their stories are largely untold. They neither smoke designer cigarettes, nor drink European or American made liquour or recline on period or post modern furniture in their well air conditioned homes. They are farmers, engineers, factory workers, lawyers, trade unionists, home-makers, doctors, shopkeepers, students, day labourers, street vendors, architects, urban planners, masons, journalists, bankers, micro finance specialists, writers, painters, dancers, musicians, machinists, mechanics, dock workers, weavers, film makers, tailors, tanners, teachers, traders, taxi, truck and rickshaw drivers, carpenters, money lenders, brokers and hundreds of others. This is from where Pakistan's leadership is emerging. Completely comfortable in their identity and location. Home-grown, answerable to the residents in their neighbourhoods. Pakistan is organized and run by these leaders who are responsible for providing services and access to people in everything from jobs, to land, to finance, to water, to transport, to electricity. Pakistan is not being run by its government. The Government is strangling these leaders.

There is nothing anti-modern in Pakistan except those who will not give up power and their control over all of Pakistan's wealth. The vast majority of Pakistanis are modern though they would blush to admit it or at the very least be surprised to know it. Modernity is defined as that which breaks with the past and is new. A self conscious break with the past and a search for new ways of expression. [6] Pakistan by definition then is modern. Its only 56 years old. Those who live in Pakistan willingly or unwillingly broke with the past with the creation of Pakistan. For better or for worse. For the better part of these 56 years Pakistanis have been stopped on that natural course of moving forward, and have been forced to take the worst course of modernity. That is the story of the *mullahs*, monarchies and militaries who were developed during the cold war period all over the world.

Furthermore, almost 42% of Pakistan is now urban. Rural-urban migration has been intense. The context of cities, the terms of engagement required in city life, force people into new ways of thinking. City life is based on a mentality of modernity which breaks away from traditional ways of life. In fact for one purpose or the other the population of Pakistan has been in constant flux, in constant movement. Begin five thousand years ago or begin a hundred years ago the story is one of constant influx and outward movement. Begin only sixty years ago, from partition till present day, the migrations, immigrations and movement internally have been immense. Rural to urban, and then outward, look at the number of Pakistanis working overseas. Traveling back and forth from their places of work to their family homes in Pakistan. This change requires breaking from existing norms and traditions, adapting to new ways. This region is a mass of people constantly in transition. Constantly reinventing themselves. Thoroughly modern.

By modernity, I mean new and breaking from the past, this does not necessarily have a positive or negative meaning. The *hijab* in Pakistan is an indicator of modernity. As in my mother's generation the burqa symbolized modernity, because it indicated that a woman had to step out of her home, the hijab today too indicates a higher mobility of women. As long as it is a matter of choice, the hijab remains modern. The moment it is forced to be worn or taken off it becomes something quite different. Look around you, what a large number of hijabs one sees, in offices, on buses, on the streets, in schools, in colleges, at hospitals. Don't look at the head dress, count the heads. So many women, in the public space. A very different group that has had little access, is making its way into the forums of jobs and decision making. This is good!

The visibility of women in public spaces is higher than ever before. There are more women going to work, at schools, banks, hospitals, business offices and factories, then ever before. There are more women in parliament then ever before. Look at the number of women in the parliament in Peshawar. Incredible. All good things. The hijab in Pakistan is a westernization coming from France, Germany, Indonesia, Malaysia and Turkey it is a process—not a permanence. It has assured and eased women's mobility in the middle income groups and allows a culturally acceptable route to working in public spaces. As a fashion issue, it allows women coming from culturally conservative backgrounds a bridge for mobility, linking rural and urban sensibilities and east and west. And perhaps it allows women familiar with the west a way of experimenting and defining their melded identity. Who knows? The Human Development Report in July 2003 may offer up an economic explanation. It indicates that women in cities must work in order to make ends meet in household expenditures. The hijab perhaps allows urban women to work in a culturally acceptable way. As people adapt to working women there will be changes in what they consider as acceptable behavior. As long as this is a choice and not an imposition, it doesn't matter. No condition is static. South Asia is a crossroad, a land of rivers and a flow of people, it has no room for stasis. That is the way of South Asia, this is the way of Pakistan and its modernity.

Pakistan has grown much more than other low-income countries, but has failed to achieve social progress commensurate with its economic growth. While infant mortality and female illiteracy rates declined by 73 and 60 per cent, respectively, from 1960 to 1998. For countries that grew at about the same rate in Pakistan, the declines were of the order of 43 and 20 per cent, rrespectively.

Clearly, Pakistan is not the State of education, with 65 per cent men and 70 per cent of the women being illiterate. There are also significant gender gaps in both literacy and health status in Pakistan. While the male population completes an average of five years of schooling, the female population in Pakistan completes only two and a half years. The enrollment rate for boys is 77 percent as opposed to 60 percent for girls. 40 per cent of Pakistan is literate compared to 64 per cent for countries with similar per capita incomes. Why is that so? For starters, the State commits less than 3 per cent of GNP as its expenditure on education per year. The private sector is taking up where the State absconds from doing so. In Pakistan today, an estimated 23 per cent of primary enrollments and 17 per cent of secondary education enrollments are in private sector schools. These numbers exclude *madrassas*. The reality remains that the State has failed in its responsibility to its people.

In Pakistan, we have a dysfunctional and discriminating system of rule which is enabled and held together because of illiteracy. We must reverse the rule of illiteracy. Today, about 90 million of our fellow Pakistanis can't read at all. Today, 24.5 million Pakistani children don't go to school at all in Pakistan. Now. Today. Here is how much it costs to send a child to school in Pakistan per year: Six thousand rupees Rs 6,000. For those earning abroad, that's about US$100. One hundred dollars. Included in this are the costs of text books; a snack at school; clothes; cost of the teacher; class room maintenance; and transportation. These are costs which are a composite of costs put together from estimates by leading NGOs in the field of education in this country. US$100 to send a kid to school. The good news is that NGOs and the private sector have been fighting the good fight against illiteracy and making inroads and we can strengthen their hand.

Imagine that. To be able to open the world with knowledge for her and for him. Rs 6,000 per year, US$100 per year. We could do this, one child each. That's the cost of one cotton outfit at any boutique in Pakistan. That's the cost of air conditioning a room for one month. A cell phone bill per month. If you drive a car, that's about the cost of your petrol for two months. If you drive one of those SUVs probably that's the cost of petrol per month. The pair of gold earrings, you absolutely couldn't resist. Cigarettes? One night out on the town with a couple of friends. And if you're someone living and earning abroad, say in the USA, here's how much you probably spend on your de cafe mocca latte per day US$5. If you drink that every day, then for the amount of latte you drink you could have put 20 kids through school for a year in Pakistan! Can you imagine? If you give up one movie a month, you could put a kid through school in Pakistan. Give up two restaurant meals or one restaurant meal in a restaurant in London, or Dubai or Toronto, or DC or New York or San Francisco or LA or in Karachi or Lahore and you've got one kid in school for a year. Sending those 24 million kids to school is the responsibility of those of us who have an education.. Why? Simple. We've had an education, (and possibly at the cost of others not getting educated) and 24 million kids won't. All the resources of this country, were spent on us. Surely, its pay back time. This is a fight we can afford and win. This is a fight we cannot afford not to afford.

Look into the faces of girls and boys—especially the boys condemned to an education of memorizing lines that they do not understand. These creators, builders, healers, sportsmen, planners, savers, our hope, our future are all locked out of realizing their potential. Locked out of saving themselves and saving us. We owe it to them, we owe it to ourselves.

Almost 42 per cent of Pakistan is now urban, where the formal and informal private sector thrive in all sorts of things, from finance to fish and an education in English. While formal literacy rates, which are based on a measurement of government school enrollments, are very low, I would wager that the informal literacy rates are very high, thanks to the burgeoning private sector schools in the urban areas. And these numbers and trends, of private schools, of enrolments, of computer centers, of satellite dishes and TVs are growing every day. Good for them! Good for the country. Good for words, good for discourse. Good for business. Good for sales and circulations, say of an English novel.

OUR STORIES: A WORLD WITH A DIFFERENT CONTEXT:

As a writer, I believe in a world that can have a different context then the one we are living in today. I share with millions, with the majority of the world, a fervent desire for a world where fear and war are no longer the context. A different world, where war would be a thing of the past and it would be defined as terrorism.

I share with billions of people, a desire for a world where the terms of engagement that affect all our lives are in a framework of cooperation and not conflict. A world where every discussion on issues that affect us all would not be dismissive, disingenuous, reductionist, self-serving and bullying statements backed by military might for the sole purpose of profiteering, extraction of minerals, oil, arms sales, foisting bio-genetically modified foods on the world, or occupation and invasion, or the destruction of the environment, and threats of endless war. A world where the discourse is centered on a viewpoint of Earth instead of real estate; cooperation instead of coercion and cooperatives instead of corporations. A world in which definitions of words like occupation, repression, liberation, invasion, war, terrorism, resistance would reflect the context, condition and stories of the majority of the peoples of the world. We should talk of a world where one country could not unilaterally impose definitions that it does not abide by itself. Where one country because of its military might cannot expect compliance from the world when itself it usually finds no need to comply with the world. Where one power cannot demand that the world comply when it has vetoed most of what the world wants to comply with. Where one power cannot refuse to sign on to the leading human rights treaties, such as women's rights, children's rights, economic rights, social and cultural rights.

What impact would there be on our story if arms sales and defence budgets would not dwarf the resources spent on education or on saving and improving human lives and the environment? There is a powerful narrative in these numbers: Trade subsidies and tariffs that bar the import of agricultural goods into developed countries amount to US$300 billion dollars annually; The US defense budget is US$400 billion annually and the developed world spends a total of 600 billion on defense annually [7]; Total monthly cost of war in Iraq and Afghanistan is approximately US$100 billion. Total development assistance to developing countries is US$56 billion annually.

What impact would there be on our story if free trade and privatization were to be qualified and defined as to what these terms mean. A world where the discourse and actions for increasing trade and competition would mean that instead of lectures to low income countries on reform and privatization there would be a removal of trade subsidies and tariffs by the wealthiest countries who bar entry of goods from low income countries. A world where all countries could compete on an equal footing. Then the development assistance transfers of today would be meaningless because countries could trade and earn revenues far exceeding the current total development assistance. Trade subsidies that bar goods and services from the developing world into the developed world amounted to US$300 billion in agriculture subsidies in 2003. We know that 70 percent of the world's poorest rely on agriculture for their incomes. Total Development assistance over the past decade has been in the range of US$50-60 billion per year. If trade subsidies from OECD countries are removed, the gains for developing countries are enormous US$75 billion annually by 2015 in real income, and if developing countries remove subsidies as well, then the gains are US$120 billion per year. Far greater than the total development assistance. Its estimated that consumers in OECD and in developing countries stand to gain if subsidies are removed.[8] Then the question becomes, if consumers stand to gain, then who benefits from subsidies not being removed?

What impact would there be on our stories if our world was not controlled by entity superceding people's will and peoples politics. Corporations are that one entity that have no problems whatsoever creating lines and crossing them. The 21st Century Corporation has more rights, resources and mobility then any individual or State, functioning very much like the colonizers of the 18th and 19th century. Indeed the Corporation has the world's military might at its disposal. This entity is the only thing that can cross these lines, cross borders without hindrance, without questions. This is the only entity that is never an illegal immigrant, never has to wait till the cover of darkness to hurry across a border, or cross a river, never dies or drowns, or gets shot at or lives in fear. It is this entity, the corporation, that has redefined the map of the world. It maps the world according to its jurisdiction: according to its airwaves, networks, satellite frequencies, patents, copyrights, markets, distribution systems, its supply sources, supercede the lines recognized by Government's and States. Corporate entities and their cultures are at counter purposes with local political processes and development of democracy. Not only in the developing world but in the developed world as well.

What impact would there be on our stories if the world as a community of humans focused on social equity rather than a strident ideological focus on economic growth and privatization defined by stock market rises and job-less economic recoveries. Much has been written about the roots of terrorism lying in poverty. Why does the world insult the poor, why does it hate the poor so much? The facts are that much of the roots of the world's poverty lie in terrorism. The terrorism of centuries of empire, arbitrary drawing of borders, occupation, genocide, rape, loot, war and indiscriminate plundering of the world's wealth for the benefit of a few. That is terrorism. Past and present.

The world is poor because the rich will not share. We always focus on the US$1.0 per day scenario. How the poor do with so little. We should increase our questioning of why the rich are not satisfied with so much and continue to waste the world's finite resources. The per capita emissions of carbon dioxide in high income countries is 12.4 tonnes, while in the low income countries it is 1.0 tonne. The rich generate most of the world's pollution and the depletion of the environment and the poor bear the brunt of it since they are the most susceptible to the smallest changes in the climate, remember 70 percent of the poor rely on agriculture for their livelihoods.[9] The world's wealth is concentrated and embedded in the essentialness of discontent. And the rich everywhere, no matter what the country, seem to be a nationality apart, a nationality on to themselves. We should think of the implications of this and focus on all of this as well.

More than 50 countries of the world grew poorer over the last decade.[10] In a world of 6 billion people in which access to basic services such as water, shelter, education and health are constrained and limited; and in the case of health and water are diminishing; more than 90 percent of the wealth and resources of the earth are in the hands of less than 2 percent of the world's population, and even this is increasingly in the hands of entities called corporations. And this imbalance is based on the enforcement of these lines. And yet, while people cannot cross borders to seek jobs, there is little or no enforcement of checks or regulations on corporations crossing borders.

The following is a sobering story about the state of humanity[11]:

- There are 6 billion people on this planet. Of which 3 billion live on less than US$2 per day while, 1.2 billion live on less than a $1.0 a day. 46 million Pakistanis live below the poverty line and of this 25 million live on less than a dollar a day (less than the cost of a cup of tea each in a hotel in Islamabad).

- Eleven million children die each year of which 70% or 7.7 million die of communicable diseases
- Three million children die each year because of vaccine preventable diseases
- 113 million children are not in school. (Of these 24 million are in Pakistan)
- 1.5 billion people do not have access to drinking water
- 1.3 billion people don't have electricity
- 500,000 women die each year of pregnancy and child-birth related complications. (in Pakistan Maternal mortality remains high at 340 per 100,000 live births)
- 42 million people in the world are infected with HIV/AIDS. (80,000 people are HIV infected in Pakistan). Of these 39 million are in developing countries and 25 million are on the continent of Africa. 21 million have already died of AIDS since 1980. 17 million of them are Africans. Life expectancy in Africa is expected to drop to 30 years of age
- There are 13 million orphan children as a result of HIV/AIDS deaths. 12 million of them are in Africa
- The UNDP, HDR for Pakistan's reports that not only 65.1 percent of the extremely poor respondents were sick at the time of the survey but that they had on average suffered from their current sickness for the last 95 days. 30 million Pakistanis on average are sick for 95 days out of the year?

Of the world's population living in poverty, half live in South Asia. India has 40 per cent of the world's poor. In Pakistan, 33 per cent of population lives in poverty. And yet each on of their governments have focused on military spending and nuclear build up. They talk of war before they talk of life. This is criminal.

Poverty remains a serious concern in Pakistan. With a per capita gross national income (GNI) of US$440. According to the latest figures (for 1998–1999), as measured by Pakistan's poverty line, 33 percent of the population is poor's Pakistan and is at a crucial point in its development where it could either face social and economic disaster or make a comprehensive strategy that addresses the problems of the poor, according to the National Human Development Report 2003.[12]

We should talk about a world where a price is not attached to human life. Where a human life is not measured in dollars and cents, in rupees and paisas. A human being's life is at all costs the most valuable, any human being's life. We should talk about a world where we get rid of the term human capital and ensure that we do not see human beings as property. We are not capital. We are not property, we are not an input, we are not to be judged as useful or obsolete, productive or unproductive. We are not a line item in the category of productive assets.

We should think about a world with common institutions where all the nations would be involved and have an equal voice in the decisions which affect all of us and where there would be a strong General Assembly with one vote per country and without a coterie or club of veto powers.

We should talk of a world where food and medical assistance would be easily accessible to those in need, instead of rotting in warehouses because of inadequate or ruined distribution systems. Where children, all children would go to school, live in a safe environment and have access to health care. Where everyone would have access to resources including financial services.

We should talk about a world in which legitimacy of actions are judged by the rule of law. A world where the greatest ability to inflict violence does not have legitimacy. A world where might is not right. A world where technological supremacy, does not mean ultimate legitimacy over ethics, morality or principles. A world in which profit and technology do not trump humanity and democracy. We should talk about a world where governments should serve the people and not be replaced by the surveillance of people.

We should discuss the urgency for a world where everyone would be assured of justice, where there would be justice for all and no one would be above the law. A world where a strong International Criminal Court would prevail. Where truth and reconciliation would be the order of the day.

We should work towards and write about a world where our collective experience would be referred to as Our-story. Where the definitions and terms for the human condition are agreed upon by us all and are not laden with the value judgments of those in power. A world which would face up to this collective story and forgive and reconcile and where instead of debt relief there would be moral reparations for crimes against humanity. A world where borders would cease to matter and there would be a free flow of people.

In Pakistan, we need to recognize how far away we have moved from the ideals envisioned by Pakistan's founding leaders. The ideals for peaceful co-existence. We must move towards these ideals in unison for cooperative co-existence, respecting each others differences and recognizing that those difference are not greater than our commonality of being human beings. We have strayed dangerously far from the ideals. As Pakistanis, as good neighbours and good citizens, we need to understand and re- dedicate ourselves to common principals that range from co-operation, co-existence, common economic space, sharing of resources, justice and the safeguarding of everyone is institutions of faith and learning.

Ideals, no matter how lofty, which speak only through or adhere to a religious or racial identity will go horribly and terribly wrong because they begin to unravel the idealism of social justice in the logic of exclusivity of religion and race. This holds true for other countries as well.

The Reality

The world is locked in an embrace with death, hate and injustice. It is urgent now to end this process of hate and break the cycle by establishing the international court of criminal justice. Truth, reconciliation, punishment and forgiveness. We need to do this as a world community. We need to embrace forgiveness, sympathy and understanding. We need to embrace the very powerful notions of fragility and vulnerability. Our world is as fragile as are our limbs and emotions. How long can this fragile and intricately intertwined earth endure the ravages and disdains of business interests that cause the wastage of oil resources, dangerous fuel emissions, use of uranium depleted ammunitions, bombings, depletion of water resources and the destruction of forests, animal species, humans and erosion of our skies and our soil? How long will the world believe the myth that technology can fix everything, that technology can replace everything?

But the context of today is not one that embraces peace or mutually beneficial cooperation and understanding. Instead, the world and its citizens are locked in a very different and deadly embrace. And war-mongers are calling themselves peacemakers. Principals are being shunned for profit and personal gains. Predators roam the skies. And fear stalks the earth.

Whatever else one can say for September 11th, it is as though the hideous attack was embraced by all those wishing to control, rule, occupy, plunder, profit, beg and borrow. Every pundit and pontificator had an explanation for it. All of us had an explanation for it. Every greed and profit making motive on earth, whether it was for denying peoples' rights to land, or self determinations or putting into print deeply held notions and preposterous ideas of hate embraced it. And every greedy power hungry politician and businessman who could do so, embraced it for the purpose of swallowing up land, or aid, or guns, or power. Power and greed embraced it closest of all. All information has been reduced to the ridiculous. The population of the world has been reduced to being termed as a focus group. A media term, an advertising term, a marketing tool used by businesses.

And no one seemed to embrace or even allow for the thought that violence is a senseless act. Without reason. That violence occurs when reason fails. It seemed that this idea of treating murder as senseless could not be sold, there was no profit in it, and therefore, it was worthless.

And in all the causes and the reasons given, for 11 September no one can say with certainty which one was the real cause, because all are conjectures. But all this conjecturing and finger pointing spoke volumes about us our reality and the state of the world. All the provided reasons were centered around hate; religious fanaticism; revenge, poverty. And those who have embraced it most have done it for the insatiable need for fear, profit, greed, opportunism and war. In doing so we have in a way anesthetized ourselves from feeling anything.

With the vanishing of innocent people vanished the future of thousands upon thousands more, vanished a moment to feel our own vulnerability, vanished the opportunity to realize in this our collective fragility and our collective strength. The moon must have hid her face in pain, as we collectively gouged out our third eye.

And even the voices raised against war and retribution, seemed to be saying that war was wrong because it would spawn more terrorism. That the victims would rise to seek revenge. So in a way, many of the voices against war were not saying lets not harm them because they are human and like us but lets not harm them because they will harm us.

I wonder if we will ever have a world that is free of collective fear, profiteering, greed and war. Free of making a distinction between war and terrorism. Will we ever be a world free from the context of harming and harmed. A world free of prison complexes and security forces? Will we ever have a world whose context is justice, sympathy, mutual caring and understanding?

We should discuss the possibility of a world where the following definition of terrorism would apply: Violence by states, individuals or groups, directly or against unarmed civilians with the purpose of instigating fear, murder, coercion, repression, subjugation, resulting in psychological and physical injury including the deaths and displacement of civilian men, women and children. A definition is required for terrorism, if the world is to be spared the past and move peacefully, humanely and progressively forward.

We are now in the closing month of a horrific year for peace. And language is being used as weapon. Another year in which the message is clear. Might is right. All power to the violently powerful. All power to the violently wealthy. And yet most of us, refuse to accept this and are horrified and disgusted by it. And all the signs so far are that we'll continue to be horrified. The world is back to a blatant and open age of empire and occupation.

The world is a place of lines, barricades, and password like never before. Either you're in or you're out. That's the bad news. The good news is that 6 billion of us are out. And a very few people are in. There's a lot more of us. And you can't blame the kid wearing the military uniform of the invading forces in Iraq. Chances are he or she isn't even a citizen, or if they are, they're trying to make their way out of a ghetto or a Reservation through the opportunities for an education and income that the military provides them with. Look at their honest faces, their innocent bright eyed faces to see the truth of their circumstances and the choices they've had to make. Just like the faces of the children in the madrassas of Pakistan. Innocent, deprived, looking for a way out to a better life, thinking they're going places. They are all part of the 6 billion who are occupied.

I want to believe that the world is not uni-polar and that there are checks on this unquestionable might. I want to believe that there is the most powerful force of all the one that stands in the streets and avenues of the world to protest unchecked power. Millions of voices are not a focus group to be ignored and disdained.

The essence of democracy is in the asking of questions and the posing of questions. Democracy is essential for development and for a mutually sympathetic and kind world. Democracy is essential for social justice and equity.

And finally, we should discuss a world where the right to question is not conditional. There are no conditions for democracy, it is or it isn't. There is no need for lead up time, no bench marks. Democracy is a human right. The telling of one's own story and having it heard is a human right. This notion, that democracy requires some pre-conditions is false. We should discuss a world where this notion that historical, cultural, and political circumstances in certain parts of the world make some people or societies more able than others to be democratic, is deemed self serving for those in power who will not share it. A peaceful and democratic environment cannot exist without politics. In fact, in the absence of politics and debate, there can be no sustainable development.

If the world was such where there was democracy and accountability, what would be the stories we'd tell and in the absence of all this, what are the stories we continue to tell and who tells them?

Notes

1. Otto Dix, Dr. Fritz Glaser 1921, Viewed at the Neue Musuem in New York City April 2003.
2. Observor, June 15, 2003. (Observer June 15, 2003) Asylum-seekers arriving in Britain will be shipped to an 'offshore' camp in Croatia as part of a radical move to process all asylum claims outside European Union borders, The Croatian camp will hold up to 800 people. It has been built in at the village of Trstenik, 30 miles from Zagreb near the town of Dugo Selo. The £1 million centre, funded by the European Commission, will take refugees arriving at British ports and airports from the Balkans and eastern Europe. They would be immediately shipped to the 'transit processing centre', where their applications for asylum in Britain would be assessed. The Home Office confirmed last night that Britain hopes to get approval at the EU summit at Thessaloniki in Greece this week for a trial series of processing centres and 'zones of protection' for asylum seekers in conflict regions. Britain already has the support of the Netherlands, Belgium and Austria for the scheme The Observer has discovered, however, that building at the Trstenik camp, a disused army base, is already nearly finished. Its 13 former barrack blocks, each with 26 rooms, will detain around 60 asylum-seekers. At Tsrtenik a rusting watch tower dominates the one square-kilometre and a newly painted helicopter pad covers a concrete exercise yard. The base entrance is in the shadow of a nearby cement factory. A lone policeman confirmed that a truck in the camp car park was full of building materials 'because of this asylum business'. The website of the European Commission's delegation to Croatia confirms that contracts are being advertised to reinstall sewage, water systems and electricity at 'Trstenik asylum home'. The Observer has obtained a copy of a letter from Tony Blair to Greek Prime Minister Costas Simitis urging action on asylum at Thassaloniki. Attached to the letter are details of plans for Britain's vision of Europe's future asylum policy. The proposals have two main pillars. The first, of which the Croatian camp is the vanguard, are plans to set up a regional network of 'transit processing centres' outside the EU. Here asylum-seekers would lodge their claims and be detained while they are being processed. The camps will be placed in countries bordering the EU creating a 'buffer zone' from asylum seekers. Countries

likely to play host to such camps include Russia, Belarus, Romania, Bulgaria, Ukraine and Albania. Any asylum-seekers arriving in Britain and seeking to lodge a claim would no longer stay in Britain while their claims were processed. Instead they would be transferred out of the UK and into one of the camps. Britain wants the camps to be managed by the International Organisation for Migration with a screening system approved by the United Nations. High Commission for Refugees. Any applicants who are rejected will then be returned to their own countries. The second pillar of the policy is longer term and aims to create 'regional protection areas' in parts of the world which produce a lot of refugees and asylum-seekers, such as the Horn of Africa, Iraq and Afghanistan. These are likely to be less formal camps in countries like Kenya or Pakistan where eventually asylum claims could also be processed. However, critics have criticised the proposals as destroying the international framework for dealing with refugees set up by the 1951 Refugee Convention that has been a bedrock of international relations for more than half a century. Critics have warned that the policy will create a series of 'super Sangattes', a reference to the now closed asylum camp near Calais.

3. Observor April 27, 2003 Notorious Australian refugee camp shut The departure of its last six refugees may have passed almost unnoticed, but the closure of the notorious Woomera detention camp - synonymous with Australia's hardline immigration policy since opening in 1999 - marks a rite of passage for the country. The six refugees were moved to the Baxter camp outside the South Australian town of Port Augusta just before Easter. Billed as a more humanitarian camp, Baxter is described by detainees as being worse. In place of the razorwire is an electric fence, and compounds face inwards to prevent inmates from communicating with those outside or in other blocks. Last weekend 1,000 protesters were outside the gates of Baxter to reprise last Easter's Woomera protests during which several dozen inmates were sprung from behind the razorwire. There was a greater concern last week: two ramshackle boats were spotted travelling slowly down through Indonesia towards Australian waters, with 73 Vietnamese on board. One of the boats stopped in Borneo where, to Australian consternation, Indonesian authorities supplied the passengers with food, fuel and water. One boat has now given up close to Singapore, while the other is in the seas off eastern Java. An Australian welcome of two navy ships is waiting for the passengers, and will take them to offshore detention centres in Nauru and Papua New Guinea. Those centres are out of sight for Australians, and now the prefab accommodation blocks of Woomera, on the edge of the desert, are about to slide from the public conscience too. Three days after the centre closed, signs of the detainees' presence remain. A piece of packing cardboard has been decorated in Arabic script in marker-pen, and placed on top of an empty fishtank, with 'Thank you Australia' scribbled in one corner. In the indoor recreation rooms a map of Australia has been superimposed with the image of a shackled peacock. This is the first time journalists have been given unrestricted access to the camp. The management are jumpy: they become particularly keen for us to move on when we start working out the size of one room, which would have housed two detainees. With a small window and air-conditioner, it measures 8ft by 10ft. Three thousand people passed through Woomera. At its peak the centre was home to 1,500 people. Arif Ghaffari spent more than six months here from August 2001. Along with his parents Nader and Marzia and his brothers Asif, 11, and Atif, eight, the 13-year-old was an ethnic Hazara victimised by the Taliban in his Afghanistan home. 'At first I was so happy to arrive in Australia,' he said. 'They told us that we would be taken to Adelaide.' He only discovered what was happening when the bus stopped at the Woomera camp. From outside the windows, he could hear other Afghans complaining that there was no room for the new arrivals. As months passed, he found himself despairing of being released. 'I was getting scared. People were hanging themselves, they went on top of the kitchen block wanting to dive head first on to the ground. Every night the people who had been there years talked to us. They said: 'Are you crazy to come here? You are better to die in Afghanistan.'' Australia's Immigration Minister, Philip Ruddock, has become used to such cases, and is unmoved. 'If his claims warranted it he shouldn't have been in a boat trying to get to the front of the queue,' he said. The Government is satisfied that its refugee policy is working. Its aim was to stop unauthorised arrivals - boat people - and until last week's boats left Vietnam, no one had tried to get to Australia by sea since December 2001. Cross-party support now means the detention policy is seen as an invulnerable third rail of Australian politics: if you touch it, you die. Last year UN human rights committee chair Justice P.N. Bhagwati visited Woomera and described the regime as 'inhuman and degrading', possibly contravening UN conventions against torture, on the rights of the child, and civil and political rights. Australia dismissed the report as 'emotive'.

4. Mohan Gopal, Lead Legal Counsel, World Bank, draft strategy paper, 2003.
5. Webster's dictionary.
6. James Wolfensohn Speech in WB/IMF annual meetings Dubai in September 2003.
7. The World Bank Speech in Delhi by the former Chief economist Nick Stern (November 28, 2002) on making trade work for the poor, he set out this agenda for policy reforms that should be immediately undertaken by high income countries that would generate significant benefits for the people of the world.
8. HRD 2003.

9. HDR 2003.

10. World Bank 2003.

11. Business Recorder July 1, 2003 The HDI report of the UNDP of July 2003 warns that the extremely poor, defined as people with an annual income of less than Rs 15,350, have to spend Rs 18,497 a year on food, meaning they are obliged to borrow money so they can eat. In urban areas, the proportion of loans used to buy food is 56.8 percent in the case of the extremely poor, and 65.1 percent for the poor. Some alarming facts the report has highlighted are: inadequate credit availability pushes 50.8 percent of poor to borrow from landlord, enhancing its leverage on the poor and resultantly staying his tenets forever.Currently 57.4 percent poor work for landlord without wages. There are 52 percent urban poor engaged in micro enterprises with low profitability. This needs to be addressed by enhancing their profits. Moreover, average total households receipts of extremely poor are only 80 percent of their minimum food consumption requirement. A very elaborate analysis on the conditions of poor and available remedies was made in the report suggesting political and social framework to overcome crisis by an Islamic Pakistan as a modern, tolerant and democratic state. The report suggested that there should be realisation that poor cannot beleft to the free market forces, both at the inputs and output levels. Poverty occurs when the individuals in a fragmented community are locked ina nexus of power, which deprives the poor of their actual and potential income. There has been a difference between actual and potential income of the poor because of their deprivation from the tools to get the right price of their produce and right kind of public services. Local landlords, traders, creditors, disputes cause systemic loss to poor. Poor lose one-third of income due to absence of market access and no share in local government. The report also suggests to facilitate the building of autonomous organisations of the poor, particularly poor women, and establish institutionalised linkages with local governments.

21

Connecting North and South: The South Asian English Novel

*Muneeza Shamsie**

Abstract

This paper looks at the development of South Asian English novel, particularly in the twentieth century and its enormous success today. The discussion covers writers ranging from R.K. Narayan, Salman Rushdie and Michael Ondaatje, to Mohsin Hamid and Monica Ali. Their exploration of language, history and text has created new paradigms for English literature and a powerful voice across North and South.

*Muneeza Shamsie is editor of two pioneering anthologies on Pakistani English writing A Dragonfly In the Sun (OUP, 1997) and Leaving Home (OUP, 2001). She is now putting together a collection of stories in English by Pakistani women writers. She also contributes to Dawn, She and Newsline and www. LitEncyc.com

In the last two decades, English novels by writers of South Asian origin have dazzled the literary world. Their enormous success has provided South Asia with a powerful voice linking North and South. Their exploration of language, history and text has created new literary paradigms for the English novel.

The first English book by a South Asian writer, however, pre-dates the British Raj. This was the autobiographical *Travels of Sake Dean Mahomet* published in Cork in 1794. The author had served in the East India Company, sailed to Ireland, and later settled in England. He wrote *Travels* about his life and times in India to explain his country and—himself—to new European friends. He was reaching out to an Anglophone audience in a very specific way and creating an alternative narrative to mainstream British writing, to rectify existing stereotypes. He emulated the style of European travel writers and often identified with the European officers that he served in India, but he retained a consciousness of himself as an Indian. His book embodies the issues of narrative, language, history and text that South Asian writers in English, continue to tackle today.

In the nineteenth century, English became the language of government and the British introduced English as the medium of instruction in schools, to help the functionaries of the Raj. But Indians also acquired English to explain the Indian point of view to the British. English newspapers by Indians proliferated. They helped forge reformist and political movements in the country. An increasing number of South Asians also came into contact with English literature, which was dominated with narratives of empire, with images of 'natives' as half-naked sadhus, snake charmers, turbaned villains, suttee, and thugee.

During the British Raj, only two British authors, Kipling and Forster, wrote serious, major novels about India. Kipling's novel *Kim* (1901) upheld Empire while Forster's, *A Passage to India* (1924), questioned it. Even so, Forster's English and British characters could not find a meaningful friendship due to political and cultural differences. Thus Forster reinforced the imperial notion that East is East and West is West.

The South Asian English novel came into its own in the early twentieth century. By then English had became the language of political debate between the British Raj and the representatives of undivided India. Novelists such as Mulk Raj Anand, R K Narayan, Raja Rao, Ahmed Ali and GV Desani, were determined to forge their own voice in English, to provide a different view to British writers.

Narayan towered over the others. His first novel *Swami and Friends (1935)* introduced the imaginary town of Malgudi. This became the setting for many of his subtle, timeless, tales about small town life in India. The following extract from the *World of Nagaraj* (1990) embodies the economy and simplicity with which Narayan summarizes relationships and characters:

'Nagu! Nagu!' his mother called from the other side. 'The water is getting cold, come for your bath.' 'She still thinks I am ten years old, doesn't notice my age, that I'm past fifty.' She was frail and wasp-like and hobbled about the house with a staff in hand.
'Nagu. Nagu,' her thin voice plaintively continued on the other side of the door. He understood his wife's strategy. If she had come to call him, he would have snapped (he imagined), 'Don't disturb me now.' But mother's intrusion was different. He stirred himself mildly. 'I know when to bathe, Mother.'

Narayan's characters were rooted in Indian culture, yet their foibles and emotions were universal and he often wrote about conflicts between the old and new.

In 1940, the bilingual Ahmed Ali published his first novel, *Twilight in Delhi,* set against the 1911 Coronation Durbar, to provide an Indian view of the colonial encounter. He experimented with the English language to capture the sounds, nuances and rhythms of the sub-continent. He also wanted to go beyond this and convey the essence of Indo-Muslim culture, in which poetry plays a pivotal role – in conversation, in songs of celebration and of mourning. He used the English translation of these verses very effectively but he tried to incorporate the poetic images of Urdu and Persian literature too. This led to some rather awkward, stylized passages. But it is important to understand his linguistic strategy and to appreciate its courage and innovation: it was to be another forty one years before Salman Rushdie made a major linguistic breakthrough by successfully capturing the South Asian sound, in his pioneering novel *Midnight's Children* (1981).

Rushdie says he learnt 'a trick or two'[1] from G V Desani's novel *All About H. Hatterr* (1948). He says Desani's 'puzzling leaping prose' was 'the first genuine effort to go beyond the Englishness of the English language'. Rushdie describes Desani's Babu English as 'the semi-literate, half learned English of the bazaars'. which employed 'a unique phrasing and rhythm'. Rushdie's exploration of language went far, far beyond Desani. In *Midnight's Children,* he successfully broke down the normal rhythms of standard English, to incorporate the cadences of bilingual, South Asian English. He also created a 'dual' language, which captured the imagination of the wider English speaking world, by its originality, its sense of fun, but spoke more directly to South Asians, by appropriating familiar, un-English words or phrases and endowing them with literary space:

> Rashid, the rickshaw boy was seventeen and on his way home from the cinema. That morning he'd seen two men pushing a low trolley on which were mounted two enormous hand-painted posters, back-to-back, advertising the new film *Gai-Wallah,* starring Rashid's favorite actor Dev. *FRESH FROM FIFTY FIERCE WEEKS IN DELHI ! STRAIGHT FROM SIXTY-THREE SHARP-SHOOTER WEEKS IN BOMBAY!* The posters cried. *SECOND RIP-ROARIOUS YEAR!* The film was an eastern Western. Its hero, Dev, who was not slim, rode the range alone... As [Rashid] pedaled his rickshaw home he practiced some of the fancy riding he'd seen in the film, hanging down low on one side, freewheeling down a slight slope, using the rickshaw the way Gai-Wallah used his horse to conceal him from his enemies.

As part of the narrative, Rushdie also incorporated dialogue such as:

> Hanif booms, 'Yes, tickety boo! The boy is really ship shape! Come on phaelwan: a ride in my Packard, okay?'

Rushdie's linguistic strategy turned the key that opened the door for a host of others from Bapsi Sidhwa to Arundhati Roy. Newer writers are now absorbing and amalgamating other influences too: Kiran Desai's award winning first novel *Hullaballoo in the Guava Orchard (1998)* for example, combines aspects of both Rushdie and Narayan.

Literary narratives have influenced perceptions of empire, nationhood and the individual throughout history. In 1956, Khushwant Singh won America's Pulitzer Prize for his sparse but moving novel *Train to Pakistan,* about Independence and the Partition riots in a Punjab village. This was the first Partition novel by a South Asian English writer, to be published, though *The Heart Divided* by Mumtaz Shahnawaz (1957), set in Lahore and revolving around the Pakistan Movement, was probably the first to have been written. She died in 1948, leaving behind an unrevised first draft, published unedited by her family a decade later. In 1961, the ex-patriat Attia Hosain published *Sunlight on a Broken Column,* which describes the feudal, courtly culture of Lucknow and the polarization between the Congress and the

Muslim League, leading to Partition. The plot is held together by a young woman's struggle for self-determination.

In the newly independent countries of South Asia, there raged a huge debate about the validity of South Asians using English as a creative vehicle, because it had been the language of the colonial power. But the South Asian English novel had moved across continents into the diaspora already. In 1961, VS Naipaul in England published his fourth novel, *The House of Mr. Biswas,* based on the Hindu community in Trinidad, to which he belonged: it is a wonderful book, full of humour, lively observations and skilful prose.

In 2001, Naipaul won the Nobel Prize for Literature and is the only South Asian English novelist to do so. His citation included the words:

> He took a giant stride with *A House For Biswas*, one of those singular novels that seem to constitute their own complete universes, in this case a miniature India on the periphery of the British Empire, the scene of his father's circumscribed existence. In allowing peripheral figures their place in the momentousness of great literature, Naipaul reverses normal perspectives...'

Naipaul's recent work includes the *The Enigma of Arrival* (1987) and *Half A Life* (2001) about migration and the quest for self. However, the choice of Naipaul for the Nobel prize caused much controversy, due to his virulent right wing views, including the perception that material and intellectual impoverishment is endemic in post-colonial, third word societies.

Other writers such as Hanif Kureishi and Bharati Mukherjee have also drawn criticism for their harsh portrayal of South Asians, but Salman Rushdie remains the most controversial. He has lived in hiding since the *fatwa* against him, but Muslim anger over *Satanic Verses* (1988) demonstrates the connection between the electronic media, the written word, politics and culture. The fact that the debate has involved both North and South, with such intensity, has meant both polarization and discourse.

Meanwhile in 1967, expatriate, Zulfikar Ghose published *The Murder of Aziz Khan,* which describes the tussle between a small Punjab farmer and a group of industrialists. His was the first cohesive novel written in modern English by a writer of Pakistani origin. Ghose has written ten novels since, including a much-praised historical trilogy about Brazil, *The Incredible Brazilian* (1972–78). So by the late 1970s you have a South Asian, writing in English, living in London, then Texas, marrying a Brazilian and transposing the South Asian experience of empire, colonization, independence and martial law into another continent. The whole is held together by the narrator's elusive and mystical quest for a multi-cultural, multi-ethnic utopia. As a writer, Ghose defines himself through story telling and language: that trans-geographical space that an expatriate can truly call 'home.' He dislikes the notion of writers being pigeonholed into cultural categories and asserts that good literature is all that matters.

Ruth Prawer Jhabvala, is another author with a curious relationship of belonging-yet-not belonging to South Asia. Of Polish origin, she married an Indian, lived in India and made a major breakthrough with her sparse, tight prose and the manner in which her dialogues captured the nuances of Indian society and the Indian speech. Later, she won the 1978 Booker Prize for *Heat and Dust* in which two parallel narratives are set in modern and colonial India respectively. Her subversive, penetrating satire attacked Indian and British illusions about themselves and each other.

By then a new post-colonial generation had grown up and lived through the anti-Vietnam movement, the feminist revolution and the civil rights movement in America. In western academia post-colonial studies re-examining narratives of empire and patriarchy, began to proliferate. Furthermore, the presence of increasingly assertive migrant communities in the West, led a desire to understand different countries and cultures they had left behind. This too contributed to a greater awareness of new English literatures from the Commonwealth, which were forging new narratives, different to the Anglo-American norm. Across the Atlantic in multi-cultural America, black American, Jewish and feminist writers, along with other minority groups, were producing some of America's most exciting fiction. This in turn influenced and re-vitalized the novel in Britain. A new literary dialogue emerged. The interest in the South Asian English novel, which had been limited to a small, but faithful audience, entered mainstream English literature along with writing from Africa, the Caribbean, Canada and Australia. New Literary prizes and promotions also revealed that some of the best English writing was coming from Britain's erstwhile colonies. This sudden international success enabled more South Asian English writers to find international publishers, opened many doors and encouraged others to follow suit.

In 1977, Anita Desai won two major British awards for *Fire on The Mountain*. Her 1999 novel *Fasting, Feasting*, was her third to be short listed for the Booker Prize and compares the emotional strictures of India with the excess of America. Her exquisite prose and her vivid cameo portraits have earned her comparisons with Jane Austen. Meanwhile Nayantara Sahgal won the Sinclair Prize for *Rich Like Us* (1985), a critique of vested interests and Mrs. Gandhi's Emergency when dissent was silenced and so, corruption grew.

In 1980, Bapsi Sidhwa became the first Pakistani English writer, living in Pakistan, to receive international recognition since Ahmed Ali in 1940. The bawdy humor of Sidhwa's first novel *The Crow Eaters* (1980) was new to South Asian English fiction and she used the quirky, inaccurate English of her protagonist, Freddy Junglewalla, to increase the comedy. Sidhwa's third novel, *Ice-Candy Man* (1988) remains her most powerful and polished work. Narrated by an endearing, English speaking, Parsee child, this was the first to employ a narrative written in the cadences of Pakistani English, which enabled Sidhwa's narrator to happily switch from one language to another, the way that bilingual Pakistanis do. At the same time, she could act as interpreter for a wider Anglophone audience, without being self-conscious, clumsy or stylized:

> Godmother is already fitted into the bulging hammock of her easy chair and Slavesister squats on a low can stool facing the road. Their faces brighten as I scramble out of the pram and run towards them. Smiling like roguish children, softly clapping hands, they chant, '*Langer Deen! Paisey ke teen! Tamba mota, pag mahin!*' Freely translated. 'Lame Lenny! Three for a Penny! Fluffy pants and fine fanny!'

Ice Candy Man remains the only Pakistani English novel to describe and focus upon the Partition riots. Alongside Khushwant Singh's, *Train to Pakistan,* Chaman Nihal's *Azadi* (1975) and Shauna Singh Baldwin, *What the Body Remembers* (1999), Sidhwa's is one of the very few South Asian English novels to directly confront that traumatic bloodbath, which irrevocably changed and brutalized the region. Considering the importance and dramatic possibilities of Partition, there has been a rather limited response to it from South English novelists. One of the problems is that Hindus, Muslims and Sikhs were perpetrators and victims. Therefore, unlike the Holocaust victims, their moral stand, as individual communities has been eroded. This has led to a collective guilt, which South Asians find difficult to confront. In politics, it has led to rhetoric of 'the other', a distortion of history, accompanied by polemics and militiarization; in literature it has meant emasculation.

The handful of Partition novels by a younger generation, including *Looking Through Glass* by Mukul Kesavan (1995), *Shadow Lines* by Amitav Ghosh (1998) and *Salt and Saffron* by Kamila Shamsie (2000) weld the past and the present illuminate the other. Here the grandmother assumes the role of family historian.

A strong feminist consciousness is pivotal to the work of all South Asian women writers discussed here. In 1997, Arundati Roy won the Booker prize for *The God of Small Things* with its wonderful interplay of language, its chilling exploration of class, caste and gender. She sums up the powerlessness of a young divorced mother with the words:

> Within a few months of her return to her parent's home, Ammu quickly learned to recognise the ugly face of sympathy. Old female relations with incipient beards and several wobbling chins made overnight trips to Ayemenem to commiserate with her about her divorce. They squeezed her knee and gloated. She fought the urge to slap them.

Sara Suleri forged new directions with her elegant creative memoir *Meatless Days* (1989) divided into chapters according to metaphor. At the heart of it were the deaths of her sister and their Welsh-born mother, in road accidents. And it also looks at cultural intermingling:

> For my mother loved to look at us in race. I have watched her pick up an infant's foot—Irfan's, perhaps, or Tillat's—with an expression of curiously sealed wonder, as though her hand had never felt so full as when she held her infants' feet. They were Asiatic, happiest when allowed to be barefoot or to walk throughout the world with a leather thong between their toes—a moving thought, to Mamma. Sometimes when we ran into a room she would look at the fascination of race in each of us, darting like red foxes round her room. 'And to this,' her wonder said, 'to these, I am the vixen?'

Suleri now has a new book coming out *Boys Will Be Boys: A Daughters' Elegy* (2003) about her father, the journalist ZA Suleri,

In America, Bharati Mukherjee established her formidable literary reputation with her bleak portraits of the immigrant experience. She also wrote *The Holder of the World* (1993), set in the seventeenth century. She excavates the suppressed narratives of a colonizing, patriarchal, Anglo-American society and tells of two women who chose 'the unthinkable'. The mother, a young Puritan widow in New England, elopes with a Red Indian; the daughter, the wife of an English trader and pirate in India, finds happiness with an Indian Raja. So again, you have an unusual angle on history, a criss-crossing of oceans, cultures and stories.

By this time, the South Asian English novel was surging ahead and new writers were appearing every year and sweeping major literary prizes. The erudite Vikram Seth published his novel-in-verse *Golden Gate* commemorating San Francisco life. He went on to earn comparisons with Tolstoy and win the Commonwealth Writers Award for the grand and gargantuan *A Suitable Boy* (1993). Set in a fictitious town similar to Lucknow during the 1950's, it depicts a period of change from old to new. Vikram Chandra's wonderful epic *Red Earth and Pouring Rain (1995),* uses Hindu mythology and the concept of reincarnation, to enable his modern narrator to inhabit another century to re-interpret the turbulent life of James Skinner, the soldier son of an eighteenth century English adventurer and a Rajput princess. The concept of the great South Asian epic, lies at the heart of the Pakistani-born Adam Zameenzad's fourth novel, *Cyrus, Cyrus* (1990), a bawdy, ambitious work revolving around a man's search for dignity and salvation across four continents.

Today, some of South Asia's finest English writers live in other countries. This includes Amitav Ghosh in the United States and Rohinton Mistry in Canada, both award winning writers of extraordinary talent, grace and skill. Ghosh's third novel, *The Glass Palace* (2001)

looks at the movement of people between India, Burma and Malaya due to the imperatives of the British Raj. The whole is linked to Britain's commercial and political interests, which led to the use of Indian troops to quell rebellions and protect British interests in Burma and the Far East. Ultimately, it provides to a fascinating insight into Burma today and the factors, which created pro-Japanese, Indian National Army, during World War II.

Canada also boasts Sri Lankan Michael Ondaatje, one of the great contemporary English writers today[2]. His novel *The Skin of the Lion* (1987) describes the mass movement of European migrants into Toronto in the 1920's. He introduces the characters of Hana and Caravaggio, which he developed further in his famous sequel, *The English Patient* (1992) set in an abandoned Italian villa during World War II. Ondaatje explores issue of war, identity, language and race, through their stories and that of Kip, an army engineer of Sikh origin, and mysterious dying, burnt man, who seems English but is not. And there's exquisite writing, embedded with metaphors:

> Just fifty yards away, there had been no representation of them in the world, no sound or sight of them from the valley's eye as Hana's and Caravaggio's shadows glided across the walls and Kip sat comfortably encased in the alcove and the English patient sipped his wine and felt its spirit percolate through his unused body so it was quickly drunk, his voice bringing forth the whistle of a desert fox bringing forth a flutter of the English wood thrush he said was only found in Essex for it thrived in the vicinity of lavender and wormwood...

Ondaatje also pursued themes of history, antiquity and mythology in his next novel *Anil's Ghost* (2001) imbued with a rich Buddhist imagery and revolving around Sri Lanka's terrifying civil war.

Ondaatje has done much to encourage English creative writing in Sri Lanka and gave his Booker prize money to establish a prestigious literary prize there. One of the first winners was *Jam Fruit Tree* by Carl Muller (1993) about the Dutch burger community. Muller has been writing prolifically since. His work is notable for his experimentation with language to capture the Sri Lankan idiom, while Punyakante Wijenaike, another winner, has been writing English fiction. Sri Lanka has been through a process similar to India and Pakistan, where English non-fiction and journalism developed first, but Sri Lankan English fiction was considered an un-patriotic activity and did not receive the cognizance is deserved. In the diaspora, however, Sri Lankan writers made their presence felt, including Yasmine Gooneratne in Australia.

War and the derailment of society, is central to the work of several Sri Lankan English writers. The expatriate Romesh Gunesekara in Britain was short listed for the Booker prize for his poetic first novel *Reef* (1994), which reclaimed memories of Sri Lanka as a childhood paradise, slowly destroyed by increasing violence. His new novel Heaven's *Edge* (2003) is set in a beautiful, fictitious island, similar to Sri Lanka. War has reduced it, to a science fiction nightmare. The cause is lost, but the endemic violence remains: the choice is to kill or be killed. Recently, *July* by Karen Roberts (2001), also about the civil war, won the 2003 Dublin Impac Award. Shyam Selvadurai, the son of Tamil father and Singhalese mother, based his award winning first novel *Funny Boy* (1994), around the 1983 riots, which impelled his family's migration to Canada. His second novel *Cinnamon Gardens* (2002) looks at Sri Lanka during colonial rule, as Ceylon in the 1920's.

In other South Asian countries, young English language writers are also making their mark. In Australia, the Bangladeshi-born Adib Khan won a Commonwealth Writers Prize for his first novel. Now the Dhaka-born Monica Ali Briton, has taken the literary world by storm with *Brick Lane* (2003), which was recently short-listed for the 2003 Booker prize. Her riveting and poignant tale revolves around a young, Bangladeshi woman in Britain, who views Britain largely from the confines of her council flat in the east end of London, but finds self empowerment through courage and her own inner resources. Poverty, patriarchy, British racism and the change that overtakes the Muslim community after 9/11, glimpses of her impecunious sister in distant Bangladesh, are all woven into her quiet but riveting narrative which includes glimpses of her sister's struggle for survival and subsistence, in distant Bangladesh. There is a new young award winner from Nepal too, Samrat Upadhyay.

Over the years, the parameters of the South Asian English novel have been extended to successfully incorporate elements of South Asia's indigenous literature, music and dance. Gita Mehta's *River Sutra* (1994) weaves in Hindu myths, the poetry of Shankaracharya and Kabir, the *qawali* of Amir Khusro and the disciplines of the Indian ragas, to celebrate the antiquity and the composite culture of India. In Amit Chaudhuri's sparse novel, *Afternoon Raag* (1993*)*, the moods of classical Indian music are reflected in vagaries of the narrator's last days at Oxford. Chaudhri is notable for quiet understated prose, in marked contrast to the wordiness of so many other South Asian English writers.

In Pakistan, Kamila Shamsie has published three novels since 1998. Her third novel *Kartography* (2002), looks at issues of ethnicity, migration and belonging, in Karachi during the civil war of 1971, and the urban violence of the 1990's. The novel which has a greater emotional depth and range than her earlier work, was recently short listed for a major British award, but it is the linguistic strategy of her first two, which is of particular interest here.

Her first novel, *The City By The Sea* (1998), set in a fictitious Pakistani town, revolves around a privileged English-speaking boy Hassan. The nephew of a politician incarcerated by a military dictator, Hassan plays imaginary games in which he is knight—a very clear appropriation and indigenization of English literature and lore:

> At the gates of the Pink Mansion, though Sir Huss recalled that he was approaching alien soil, with its own rules. He cast off his knighthood and transformed himself into, Hassan, a commoner.

In her second novel, *Salt and Saffron* (2000) Shamsie incorporated elements of Indo-Muslim culture into her prose, employing a Ghalib couplet or the nuances of a *kathak* dance, as metaphor, and exploring the bilingual dimensions of an Urdu word or phrase. Thus, it became a reverse process: the appropriation of Urdu literature by an English narrative. Mohsin Hamid, the winner of a Betty Trask award, framed his powerful novel *Moth Smoke*, (2000), about drug and kalashnikov culture in Lahore, with an episode from Mughal history. More interestingly, the book's literary icon is the Urdu writer Saadat Hassan Manto and the central, metaphor of the moth and the flame was derived from oriental poetry.

Pakistan has a really exciting new crop of English language writers, including first novelists, Zeeba Sadiq, Musharraf Farooqi and Sorayya Y. Khan with much praised first novels. However the violence which has riven Pakistan since the 1980s, runs through the work of Shamsie and Hamid, as well as Nadeem Aslam, Uzma Aslam Khan and Maniza Naqvi.

Uzma Aslam Khan established herself with The *Story of Noble Rot* (2001) linking up the stories of a carpet manufacturer's wife with the mother of a boy working in a carpet factory. Her haunting second novel, *Trespassing* (2003), tells of a brutal murder, a forbidden love and an aspiring journalists discovery during the First Gulf War that freedom of expression has its limitations, in America. The novel is particularly remarkable for its descriptions of nature and its portrayal of a man displaced from his fishing village and caught up in the brutal underworld of Karachi. Meanwhile, Maniza Naqvi made a promising debut with *Mass Transit* (1998) which looks at a young woman's disillusionment and dislocation in the changing, fractured, overpopulated city of Karachi. She followed this up with *On Air* (2000) which mirrors society and a young woman's personal odyssey, through the calls she receives on the all-night, phone-in radio program, which she hosts. Maniza Naqvi's third novel is to be published shortly.

Inevitably perhaps, Britain is the heartland of South Asian English publishing. The Pakistani-born Tariq Ali has constantly asserted his universalism and challenged the history and rhetoric of the North, which marginalizes other cultures and civilisations. His historical novels, which are particularly strong on little known historical detail, include his 'Fall of Communism' trilogy, and his 'Islam Quintet' which has looked at the Fall of Granada, the Crusades and the Decline of the Ottoman Empire, so far. The British-born Hanif Kureishi, the son of a Pakistani father and an English mother, is one of the most powerful literary voices among British Asians today. An intelligent, ruthless and disturbing writer, he has received particular acclaim, including an Oscar nomination, for his plays, stories and novels dealing with the conflicts of British Asians and the exclusion, overt and covert, that they face. He claimed a Whitbread Award for his first novel *The Buddha of Suburbia* about an Asian boy growing up in Britain. His fourth novel *Intimacy* (1998) turned the whole issue of mixed marriages on its head. Kureishi shows clearly that Jay, a man of Asian origin and his wife Susan, are both Britons from a similar education and professional background and the break-up of their marriage has nothing to do with ethnicity.

By this time, an increasing number of South Asian English novelists, including Ali and Kureishi, had also found a niche as writers of film, stage, radio and television scripts, enabling them to reach out to huge audiences. In the 1980s, British Asian women realized the need to find a space for themselves in British publishing and formed a support group, The Asian Women Writers Collective, which launched several writing careers including that of the Pakistani born Rukhsana Ahmad. She was already a translator of Urdu feminist writing and she brought an awareness of this into her English fiction and plays. The talented Meera Syal's work as an actress and writer, includes scripts for the television series *Goodness Gracious Me* and the stage play *Bollywood Dreams*. She captured the imagination of the British public further with her novel *Anita and Me,* based on her childhood in England.

In Huddersfield, Nadeem Aslam won two first novel awards and was short listed for two more, for his poetic first novel, *Season of The Rainbirds* about bigotry, politics and mullahs in a small Pakistani town during the 1980's. His second about migration, *Maps for Lost Lovers* (2004) will be published shortly. This year Hari Kunzru's accomplished first novel *The Impressionist* won several awards. The book subverts and challenges Kipling, E M Forster—and Conrad's *Heart of Darkness*—as it follows the odyssey of a half Indian, half English boy across India, England and Africa.

Clearly, the narratives of English literature have come a long way over the last century and in today's global language, South Asian English writers have opened out windows for a wider, Anglophone audience, into a myriad of cultures and their complexity.

Selected Bibliography

AHMAD, Rukhsana, *The Hope Chest,* London: Virago, 1996.

ALI, Ahmed, *Twilight in Delhi,* London: Hogarth Press, 1940.

ALI, Monica, *Brick Lane*, London: Doubleday, 2003.

ALI, Tariq, *Redemption*, London: Chatto and Windus, 1990.

ALI, *Tariq, Fear of Mirrors,* London: Arcadia, 1999.

ALI, Tariq, *Shadows of the Pomegranate Tree,* London: Chatto & Windus, 1992. Tariq Ali, *The Book of Saladin,* London: Verso, 1998.

ALI, Tariq, *The Stone Woman*, London: Verso, 2001.

ANAND, Mulk Raj, *Untouchable,* London: Wishart Books Ltd, 1935.

ANAND, Mulk Raj, *The Coolie,* London: Wishart Books Ltd, 1936.

ASLAM, Nadeem, *Season of the Rainbirds,* London: Andre Deutsch, 1991.

ASLAM, Nadeem, *Maps for Lost Lovers*, London: Faber & Faber, 2004.

BALDWIN, Shauna Singh, *What the Body Remembers,* London: Doubleday, 1999.

CHANDER, Vikram, *Red Earth and Pouring Rain*, London, Faber & Faber, 1995.

CHAUDHURI, Amit, *Afternoon Raag,* London: William Heinemann, 1993.

DESANI, Gv, *All About H. Hatterr,* New York: Vintage 1985.

DESAI, Anita, *Fire on the Mountain,* London: Heinemann 1977.

DESAI, Anita, *Fasting, Feasting,* London: Chatto & Windus, 1999.

DESAI, Kiran, *Hullabaloo in the Guava Orchard*, New York: Atlantic Monthly Press, 1998.

FAROOQUI, Musharraf, *Salar Jang's Passion,* Chichester: Summersdale, 2002.

FISHER, Michael H., *The First Indian Author In English: Dean Mahomed (1759–1851) In India, Ireland and England*, New Delhi: Oxford University Press, 1996.

FORSTER, E M, *A Passage to India*, London: Edward Arnold Publishers, 1924.

ASLAM, Nadeem, *Season of the Rainbirds,* London: Andre Deutsch, 1991.

GHOSE, Zulfikar, *The Murder of Aziz Khan,* Karachi: OUP, 1998.

GHOSE, Zulfikar, *The Incredible Brazilian: The Native* London: Macmillan, 1972.

GHOSE, Zulfikar, *The Beautiful Empire,* London: Macmillan, 1975.

GHOSE, Zulfikar, *A Different World,* London: Macmillan 1978.

GHOSH, Amitav, *Shadow Lines*, New Delhi: Ravi Dayal Books, 1988.

GHOSH, *The Glass Palace,* London: HarperCollins, 2001.

HAMID, Mohsin, *Moth Smoke,* London: Granta, 2000.

GOONARATNE, Yasmine, *A Change of Skies.* Australia: Picador, 1991.

GOONARATNE, Yasmine, *The Pleasures of Conquest.* New Delhi: Penguin India, 1995.

GUNESEKERA, Romesh*, Reef,* London: Granta 1994.

GUNESEKERA, Romesh, *Heaven's Edge,* London: Bloomsbury, 2002.

HOSAIN, Attia, *Sunlight on A Broken Column,* London: Chatto & Windus, 1961.

JHABVALA, Ruth Prawer, *The Householder,* London, John Murray, 1960.

JHABVALA, Ruth Prawer, *Heat and Dust,* London: John Murray, 1975.

KESAVAN, Mukul, *Looking Through Glass,* New York: Farrar Strauss Giroux, 1995.

KHAN, Adib, *Seasonal Adjustments,* Australia: Allen & Unwin, 1994.

KHAN, Sorayya Y., *Noor,* Lahore: Alhmara, 2003.

KHAN, Uzma Aslam, *The Story of Noble Rot,* New Delhi: Penguin, 2001.

KHAN, *Trespassing,* London: HarperCollins, 2003.

KIPLING, Rudyard, *Kim,* New York: Tor Books, 1999.

KUREISHI, Hanif, *The Buddha of Surburbia,* London, Faber & Faber, 1990. Kureishi, *Black Album*, London: Faber & Faber, 1995.

KUREISHI, *Intimacy,* London: Faber & Faber, 1998.

MAHOMET, Sake Dean*, The Travels of Dean Mahomet, A Native of Patna in Bengal through Several Parts of India, while in the Service of the Honourable East India Company, written by himself in a Series of Letters to a Friend,* Cork, 1794.

MEHTA, Gita, *River Sutra,* London: William Heinemann, 1993.

MISTRY, Rohinton, *Family Matters,* London: Faber & Faber, 2002.

MUKHERJEE, Bharati, *The Holder of the World,* New York: Alfred Knopf, 1993.

MULLER, Carl, *Jam Fruit Tree,* New Delhi: Penguin, 1993.

NAIPAUL, V S, *A House for Mr. Biswas,* London: Andre Deutsch, 1961.

NAIPAUL, V S, *The Enigma of Arrival,* London:Viking, 1987.

NAIPAUL, V S, *Half a Life,* London: Viking 2001.

NAQVI, Maniza, *Mass Transit,* Karachi: Oxford University Press, 1998.

NAQVI, Maniza, *On Air,* Karachi: Oxford University Press, 2000.

NARAYAN, R K, *Swami and Friends,* Chicago: University of Chicago Press, 1980.

NARAYAN, R K, *A Tiger for Malgudi,* London: Heinemann 1983.

NARAYAN, R K, *The World of Nagaraj,* London: William Heinemann, 1990.

NIHAL, Chaman, *Azadi,* Boston: Houghton Mifflin,1975.

ONDAATJE, Michael, *The Skin of the Lion,* London: Secker & Warburg, 1987.

ONDAATJE, Michael, *The English Patient,* London: Bloomsbury, 1992.

ONDAATJE, Michael, *Anil's Ghost,* London: Bloomsbury, 2000.

RAO, Raja, *Kanthapura,* New Delhi: Oxford University Press, 1990.

RAO, Raja, *The Serpent and the Rope,* London: John Murray, 1959.

ROBERTS, Karen, *July,* London: Weidenfeld & Nicholson, 2001.

ROY, Arundhati, *The God of Small Things,* London: Flamingo, 1997.

RUSHDIE, Salman, *Midnight's Children,* London: Jonathan Cape, 1981.

SADIQ, Zeeba, *38 Bahadurabad,* London: Faber & Faber, 1996.

SAHGAL, Nayantara, *Rich like Us,* William Heinemann, 1985.

SCOTT, Paul, *The Raj Quartet: The Jewel In The Crown, The Day of the Scorpion, The Towers of Silence, A Division of Spoils,* London: William Heinemann, 1976.

SETH, Vikram, *The Golden Gate,* London: Faber & Faber, 1986; *A Suitable Boy,* London: Phoenix House, 1993.

SELVADURAI, Shyam, *Funny Boy,* London: Jonathan Cape, 1994; *Cinnamon Gardens,* Toronto: MccLelland & Stewart, 1998.

SHAMSIE, Kamila, *In the City by the Sea,* London: Granta 1998; New Delhi: Penguin, 1998.

SHAMSIE, Kamila, *Salt And Saffron,* London: Bloomsbury, 2000.

SHAMSIE, Kamila, *Kartography,* London: Bloomsbury, 2002.

SHAMSIE, Muneeza, *A Dragonfly in the Sun, an Anthology of Pakistani Writing In English,* Karachi: Oxford University Press, 1997.

SHAMSIE, Muneeza, *Leaving Home, Towards A New Millennium: A Collection of English Prose by Pakistani Writers,* Karachi: Oxford University Press, 2001.

SIDHWA, Bapsi, *The Crow Eaters,* London: Jonathan Cape, 1980.

SIDHWA, Bapsi, *Ice Candy Man,* London: William Heinemann 1998.

SHAHNAWAZ, Mumtaz, *The Heart Divided,* Lahore: Mumtaz Publications, 1957.

SINGH, Khushwant, *Train To Pakistan,* Karachi: Oxford University Press, 1998.

SYAL, Meera, *Anita And Me,* London: Flamingo, 1996.

SULERI, Sara, *Meatless Days,* Chicago: University of Chicago Press, 1989. (See also *Goodyear,* Suleri,S.).

UPHDYAY, Samrat, *Guru of Love,* Boston: Houghton Mifflin, 1993.

WIJENAIKE, Punyakante, *Giraya,* Colombo: Lake House Investments, 1971.

ZAMEENZZAD, Adam, *Cyrus, Cyrus,* London: Fourth Estate 1990.

Notes

1. Rushdie, Salman, 'Damme, This is the Oriental Scene For You,' *The New Yorker*, June 23 and 30, 1997.
2. The author wishes to thank Shyam Selvadurai and Dushyanthi Mendis for providing pointers on English language writing in Sri Lanka.

22

Freedom of Information in South Asia: Comparative Perspectives on Civil Society Initiative

*Mukhtar Ahmad Ali**

Abstract

Freedom of information is a pre-requisite for public accountability, strengthening of democratic institutions, citizens' empowerment and good governance. However, it is only recently that the countries of South Asia have started enacting laws to enable citizens to access information and records held by public bodies. In India, the right to information has been recognized through laws at the Union level as well as in many states. In Pakistan, the Freedom of Information Ordinance, promulgated in October 2002, is applicable only to the federal departments, while no province has as yet enacted any such legislation. The laws enacted so far for freedom of information in both India and Pakistan are very restrictive in scope and weak in implementation mechanisms but are significant in the sense that they mark the beginning of a shift away from the existing culture of secrecy in public departments. Other countries of South Asia have yet to respond to the increasing demands of civil society, corporate sector and international financial institutions for citizens' right to access information and records in the government, subject only to minimal exceptions relating to precisely defined considerations of national security and public interest.

*Mr Mukhtar Ahmad Ali is Executive Coordinator of Consumer Rights Commission of Pakistan (CRCP).

INTRODUCTION

Information has emerged as a defining characteristic of diverse societies in the contemporary world. Terms such as 'information age', 'information technologies', 'information societies', 'information economies', 'information asymmetries' or 'information gaps' are being increasingly used in academic and journalistic writings.

An information society seems in competition with an industrial society in terms of better understanding new technologies such as computers and Internet in the backdrop of socio-economic relations. Similarly, 'information-endowed' nations and communities are distinguished from the 'information-deprived' ones highlighting economic and developmental disparities. It is no co-incidence that information-rich societies are known for wealth generation and quality of life. Although disagreements do exist about the characteristics of 'information age' or 'information societies', it is widely recognized that 'wealth and power are increasingly being derived from the control—and production—of knowledge'.[1] Information and information-based activities are crucial to such knowledge production and control processes.

Political, economical and technological developments have geared up the process of information generation and now an unprecedented quantity of information is available in public circulation. Since mid-1980s, a wave of democratization swept the globe and opened up societies that were earlier under military dictatorships or under strict communist controls. In the economic domain, the predominance of the neo-liberal ideology and the consequent emphasis on market economy have created pressures in favour of transparency and greater information flows in certain sectors. Global business generally demands economic information to make informed investment decisions and many countries around the world have responded to such demands in selected ways. But most importantly, technological breakthroughs have revolutionized the traditional means of communications and made it difficult for states to control information flows. Thus the information that is available in the public domain today is simply unprecedented. This general condition, however, hides a number of asymmetries about access to information across various contexts.

A large number of people in developing countries have limited access to means such as print and electronic media whereby they could access authentic information. But the nature and authenticity of information that is made available to them through such channels is determined by the general situation of freedom of information in relation to government and corporate activity. It is also filtered at various levels in view of a variety of political, business or other considerations. Furthermore, the information made available through such channels may or may not be the most relevant to communities, interest groups and individual citizens. This necessitates that, in addition to the information made available through various channels, citizens have the right to access records and information held by the public bodies and corporate entities, which they find relevant to their lives. It is possible to have a situation wherein information about certain domestic activities and foreigners abounds, but citizens lack the most basic information essential for them to make informed choices and improve their quality of life.

In South Asia, generally with a common colonial legacy and different political trajectories, most of the time, governmental and corporate functions are performed in a culture of secrecy.[2] Although the situation has improved a bit and governments have begun to respond to the demands for openness and transparency in recent years, the region still has a long way to go to achieve the status of 'information-rich' or 'information-endowed'. However, India has made significant headway in information technology, and the reach-out and variety of print and electronic media in the entire region is growing at an unprecedented pace. Legal and institutional arrangements in different countries in the region remain colonial, which had been essentially designed to control information, and have failed to adjust with the changed circumstances and requirements of being independent and democratic states.

Against the background of common historical legacies of certain South Asian countries and the growing importance of information for development and economic growth in the contemporary world, it is important to analyze how civil societies across the region are engaging states on freedom of information and transparency. The nature of such engagements vary, and are explained by a range of factors that relate to different levels of economic development and political trajectories, and the diverse nature of civil society initiatives. The governments seem reluctant to be transparent; and whereever certain steps have been taken, these are essentially in response to either external pressures by the global business or international financial institutions, or to internal pressures by civil society. This paper makes an effort to look into the interplay of these pressures and how the same have impacted the public policies in the region, especially in India and Pakistan.

STATUS OF FREEDOM OF INFORMATION IN SOUTH ASIA

India, Pakistan and Bangladesh inherited certain laws that restrict and control information held by public bodies. The Official Secrets Act 1923 among them is so broad in its application that hardly any information or record escapes its cover.[3] This Act still remains in force in various South Asian countries and, despite repeated demands in recent years, it has not been repealed or amended in a substantial manner to allow greater transparency and access to information.

Other than the official Secrets Act 1923, laws that work against information disclosure and freedom of media in Pakistan include the Security of Pakistan Act 1952, the Maintenance of Public Order Ordinance 1960 and various sections of the Penal Code and the Code of Criminal Procedure. In addition to these, the Rule 18 of Government Servants (Conduct) Rules, 1964 states: 'No Government Servant shall, except in accordance with any special or general order of the Government, communicate directly or indirectly any official document or information to a Government Servant unauthorized to receive it, or to a non-official person, or to the press.'[4] Similarly, Articles 6 and 7 of the *Qanoon-i-Shahadat* Order (Law of Evidence), 1984[5] impose restrictions of disclosure of information. However, in the case of Ms. Benazir Bhutto vs. Federation of Pakistan,[6] the Supreme Court of Pakistan held that privileges claim under Article 6 and 7 of the *Qanoon-i-Shahadat* Order do not give absolute power to public officials to retain the documents or evidence at their will. Hence, the public interest is to be determined by the courts, and not by the public officials themselves.

In India, the Central Civil Service Rules, 1964 strengthen the Official Secrets Act 1923 by prohibiting government servants from giving out any document to anyone without authorization. In addition, Section 123 of the India Evidence Act 1872 does not allow evidence from unpublished official records without authorization by head of the relevant department. On the other hand, Section 124 of the Act reads: 'No public official shall be compelled to disclose communications made to him in official confidence, when he considers that public interest would suffer by disclosure'.[7]

In Sri Lanka, it is the Official Secrets Act No. 32 of 1955 that restricts disclosure of information and records held by public bodies.[8] Other laws that restrict information disclosure include Press Council Law No. 5 of 1973, Official Publications Ordinance No. 47 of 1946, Public Security Ordinance No. 25 of 1947 and Prevention of Terrorism Act No. 48 of 1979.[9]

These three countries had also inherited bureaucracies, management styles and organizational cultures, which exclude public participation, incidence of transparency and accountability to the people. These too have not been changed much over the last decades since independence and often work to actively or passively resist changes that are attempted or made for transparency and information disclosure. This explains why various interpretations through judicial decisions and sometimes even policy decisions have not been effectively implemented by the bureaucracies in different countries.

In Pakistan, for instance, government departments and ministries are required under rules to publish annual reports. However, in many cases, such reports are either not published or if they are published, they are in such a small quantity that most people hardly get to know about them. Their contents are often deceptive and lacking substance and aimed at hiding information instead of disclosing it. Their circulation is also generally restricted; and in many cases, most of the reports remain stacked in the store-rooms for years. As a matter of fact, these reports are prepared with the aim of just meeting the formal requirement under the rules and not really to promote transparency about the respective ministry or department.

Nevertheless, it is through judicial decisions and interpretations of various constitutional provisions that the right to information received constitutional justification in certain countries of South Asia. In India, for instance, the Supreme Court located the peoples' right to information within the ambit of their fundamental rights to life and liberty and freedom of speech and expression.[10] Similarly, the Supreme Court of Pakistan has ruled that the freedom of information is a pre-requisite for a fundamental right to freedom of speech and expression, which is enshrined in Article 19 of the Constitution.[11] Such judicial decisions and interpretations of constitutional provisions, however, have not led to legislative measures by relevant legislative bodies in India and Pakistan. Instead, such developments took place only when domestic political pressures built-up or when it became clear that lack of action would harm the economic interests of the country.

It was in India that, in view of advocacy efforts by certain civil society groups, the first right to information laws were enacted by the states of Tamilnadu and Goa in 1997. Other states that followed suit include Karnataka, Maharashtra, Delhi, Assam and Rajhistan. The Union of India passed the Freedom of Information Act in December 2002.[12] Pakistan is the only other country in South Asia that had promulgated the Freedom of Information Ordinance in October 2002. This, however, is applicable only to the federal subjects and does not cover the provincial subjects. No province in Pakistan has so far enacted any law to guarantee freedom of information.

Most of these laws suffer from serious flaws and inadequacies. In general, these exempt a large number of government records, exclude the private sector from their preview and are weak in providing efficient implementation mechanisms. These laws do not override the existing laws, which restrict their mandate. Nor has the Official Secrets Act 1923 been amended or repealed to allow greater freedom of information. However, these have widely been seen as positive developments and a significant break from the past culture of secrecy in which even the minimum access of citizens to official records was subject to official discretion. In fact, these laws introduce a cultural shift, whereby citizens can demand information, while relevant departments have to justify the denials if they opt for rejecting information requests.

NATURE OF CIVIL SOCIETY INITIATIVES AND THEIR IMPACT

As indicated above, different factors have contributed to the enactment of freedom of information laws in different countries. In UK, for instance, it was the change of government and the coming into power of the Labour Party that paved the way for the Freedom of Information Act 2001. In certain East Asian and East European countries, it has been closely linked with restoration of democratic systems. In the case of East Asian countries, additional pressures came from the global business for transparency and more economic information.[13]

In Pakistan, the demand for freedom of information and transparency in government departments basically emerged as a result of growing concern about corruption in late 1980s and 1990s. First such initiative was taken in 1990 when Professor Khurshid Ahmad, a Jamaat-i-Islami Senator, moved a private bill on freedom of information in the Senate. This, however, never attracted any serious attention of the house and was killed at the Senate's relevant standing committee level. Later in 1994, Malik Qasim, a leading politician and the then Chairperson Public Accounts Committee, also realized the importance of freedom of information and took steps to draft a freedom of information bill. This effort too failed because of bureaucratic resistance and the early dismissal of the government.

Another significant initiative was taken by Mr Fakhruddin G. Ibrahim, the law minister in the caretaker government in 1996–97. He drafted a Freedom of Information Ordinance. However, he resigned before the promulgation of the Ordinance by President Laghari in early 1997. It is widely believed that the original draft of Mr Ibrahim had been toned down after his resignation to restrict the scope of citizens' access to information. Even though it was a very weak law in a number of respects, it was allowed by the Nawaz Sharif government to lapse, as the Ordinance was never introduced in the form of a Bill in the Parliament, despite the fact that the government had declared accountability as its high priority agenda. Apparently, the Ordinance did not suit bureaucratic interests, while it was easier to just let it lapse in the absence of any significant awareness in the civil society or general public about its significance. Not surprisingly, the lapse of Freedom of Information Ordinance 1997 went almost totally unnoticed. Hardly was any protest or criticism reported on its lapse from any corner in the media.

The Consumers Rights Commission of Pakistan (CRCP) was the first civil society group that started demanding freedom of information from the year 2000 onward. In the course of its work for consumer protection, it had confronted serious information-related problems. The CRCP is convinced that freedom of information is a pre-requisite to protect consumers' rights. For instance, it had failed to access information held by certain public bodies such as Capital Development Authority (CDA) and Pakistan Council for Research in Water Resources (PCRWR) about the quality of drinking water in Islamabad. The CRCP later drafted a Model Freedom of Information Act in 2001 and got involved in sustained advocacy campaign for its enactment.

In the meanwhile, sensitivity about the problem of corruption had substantially increased against the background of worsening economic difficulties. The poor economic performance had also made the country substantially dependent on International Financial Institutions (IFIs) for development loans and balance of payment support. In 2001, the Asian Development Bank (ADB) included enactment of freedom of information law as one of its conditions for the release of loans. It is against this background that the current Freedom of Information Ordinance was promulgated by the military government in October 2002. Later, the National Accountability Bureau (NAB), while working on the anti-corruption strategy, realized the importance of freedom of information and became an advocate of a strong freedom of information regime in the government.

In short, the enactment of freedom of information in Pakistan can be attributed to a number of domestic and international pressures involving greater concern about corruption, advocacy by the CRCP and certain other civil society groups, and pressures by the IFIs. While the ADB conditionality might have played an important role in promulgating the Ordinance, it is the CRCP that has worked in a sustained manner since 2000 to create awareness and advocacy. Over the last year, it has also been engaged in efforts to get the Ordinance fully implemented through notification of Rules of Business and other steps by the government, especially in terms of improving record-keeping systems and staff training. Other civil society groups that have worked for freedom of information include Liberal Forum Pakistan, Centre for Civic Education (CCE) and Human Rights Commission of Pakistan (HRCP).

Unlike Pakistan, the first initiatives for freedom of information in India came from the grass-root movements. The Mazdoor Kisaan Shakti Sangathan (MKSS) emerged as a grass-roots movement in 1990 in Rajasthan to struggle for minimum wages and transparency in employment records and wage rolls.[14] Hence, the right to information and right to survival became united in its struggle. This movement had significant impact and forced the state government to take measures for increased transparency and access to information. A watershed development occurred in June-July 1997, when MKSS staged a 53-days long dharna in Jaipur, which forced the state government to issue a gazette notification whereby members of the public were entitled to a certified copy of official documents at the panchayat level at a nominal price. The MKSS was also a major driving force behind the formation of the National Campaign for People's Right to Information (NCPRI) in late 1990s.

As a result of grass-roots movements such as MKSS, freedom of information has become a significant issue in the political domain in India. In late 1990, the then Prime Minister, Mr V. P. Singh, appointed a cabinet committee to study means by which freedom of information could have been promoted. The committee, however, was dissolved on 27 August 1990 before it could issue a report. On 9 April 1990, the National Front government had also promised to amend the Official Secrets Act for greater transparency and access to information.[15] Although no concrete steps could be taken throughout 1990s, it was important to note that the issue was on the political agenda and, as time passed, it assumed higher priority in view of civil society pressures.

In 1997, the government set up a working group under the chairmanship of a consumer rights activist, Mr H. D. Shourie, to draft a bill for right to information. The draft bill prepared by the Working Group under Mr Shourie became a basis for another bill that was drafted in 2000 and presented in the Parliament. Later, this bill was debated upon in the cabinet and the two houses of the Parliament, and was finally enacted in December 2002. It has been a subject of intense debate at various forums in India, including the government. This is in sharp contrast to the situation in Pakistan where the drafting and promulgation of Freedom of Information Ordinance 2002 did not involve more than a few people in the government. As a result, there is greater awareness about the need of freedom of information in India than in Pakistan.

Conclusions

Citizens' access to information and records held by government bodies and corporate entities, subject to certain minimal exemptions, is crucial to achieve freedom of information and develop 'information-endowed' societies and economies. In the contemporary world, it is no coincidence that 'information-endowed' countries perform better in economic terms. It is essentially because information and knowledge have become substantial factors to explain growth, wealth and power.

The countries of South Asia, however, performed poorly in terms of freedom of information. The culture of secrecy is still predominant and legislative developments have failed to keep pace with requirements of building participatory, transparent and accountable systems of governance. Various kinds of pressures, however, have lately begun to make their impact in terms of pushing the governments to realize that greater transparency is required to meet the emerging challenges of governance and globalization.

The problem of corruption has witnessed unprecedented increase in the last two decades and it coincides with opening up of markets for foreign investors and products across the region. The inequalities, uncertainties and upheavals that the liberalization process causes are also seen as contributory factors to increased corruption in various societies. Civil societies and governments across the region are trying to confront this challenge of massive corruption. Their responses have varied between simple administrative and traditional types of legislative measures aimed at increasing punishments and strengthening anti-corruption departments to institutional reforms that are appropriate for the globalization context. It is widely realized that while it is important to strengthen traditional accountability and anti-corruption systems, greater transparency in public departments is essential for citizens to play an effective role and protect their rights against corrupt practices that hurt their lives and livelihood options.

More information and transparency is also needed in the private sector, which is fast growing in the face of states that are withdrawing from economic activities and provision of most public services. In such a context, it is important that governments not only play their regulatory roles effectively but also provide a transparent environment in which citizens could make informed choices. Conversely, private sector, especially the global business, also requires greater transparency and access to economic information to compete and make informed investment decisions.

Realizing the importance of freedom of information for good governance and global businesses, IFIs have also been pushing for it in member states. IFIs have not only themselves adopted information disclosure policies but have also included enactment of freedom of information laws in their conditionalities for loans. They, however, have been more influential in cases where member states were more dependent on borrowing from them.

Like others, South Asian countries have been influenced by all these factors, albeit to varying degrees, depending on specific domestic contexts. However, only India and Pakistan have so far enacted freedom of information laws. In India, significant grass-roots movements have emerged to demand access to information, and have fed into the political process to achieve enactment of suitable laws. This has been possible against the background of established democratic system in India, which allows greater spaces for engagement by civil society groups. Pakistan, on the other hand, did not witness any significant demand from the civil society in 1990s. Certain initiatives emerged from within the government with an aim of combating corruption but failed to gain ground in view of bureaucratic resistance and lack of active support from the civil society. Over the last few years, however, the situation has changed, as certain civil society groups such as the CRCP have begun to actively advocate for it.

Freedoms of information laws in both India and Pakistan have a number of common features. They include a lot of exemptions, exclude the private sector from their preview and are weak in providing implementation mechanisms. In addition, neither India nor Pakistan has repealed the Official Secrets Act 1923 to allow greater freedom of information. Old attitudes persist and bureaucracies are hugely resistant to change. The constituency for reform is still small and must grow and become more proactive to achieve more substantial and effective outcomes.

Notes

1. Coronel, Sheila S. (ed.), *Right to Know: Access to Information in Southeast Asia*, published jointly by the Philippine Centre for Investigative Journalism (PCIJ) and the Southeast Asian Press Alliance (SAPA), 2001.
2. In Pakistan, for instance, even the reports prepared by various official committees and commissions on corruption are treated as restricted and have been gathering dust in government offices without action. See Khan, Roedad, *Pakistan: Dream Gone Sour*, Karachi: Oxford University Press, 1997, p. 153.
3. See the Introduction of the 'Model Freedom of Information Act, 2001,' published by CRCP in 2001, p. 3.
4. *Government Servants (Conduct) Rules, 1964*, Islamabad, Pakistan.
5. Article 6 reads: 'No one is permitted to disclose official record relating to the affairs of the state unless authorized by the head of the department concerned, who shall give or withhold such information as he thinks fit'. On the other hand Article 7 provides that no public official can be compelled to disclose a communication 'when he considers that the public interest would suffer by disclosure.'
6. See NLR 1992 SCJ, p. 606.
7. *Global Trends on the Right to Information: A Survey of South Asia*, by Article 19, CHRI, CPA and HRCP, July 2001, p. 65.
8. Ibid, p. 132.
9. Ibid, pp. 132–134.
10. S.P. Gupta vs. Union of India 149 case.
11. Nawaz Sharif vs. President of Pakistan, PLD 1993 SC 473.
12. *Times of India*, 17 December 2002.
13. Note 1.
14. Bhatia, Bela and Dreze, Jean, '*Campaign in Rural India,*' Berlin: Transparency International, September 1998.
15. 'Freedom of Information and Expression in India,' *PUCL Bulletin*, April, 1991.

23

CORPORATE MEDIA AND THE ETHNIC PRESS: THE CASE OF THE URDU PRESS IN NEW YORK-POST 9/11

*Rehan Ansari**

ABSTRACT

The title of my paper refers very politely to the attacks on the civil liberties of Pakistani immigrants in New York by the US law enforcement authorities and non-reporting of the events by the US corporate media—the television networks, NBC, ABC, CBS, FOX, CNN, as well as the print media.

The crisis of 9/11 did not start on that day. It continues post 9/11, in Afghanistan, in Brooklyn and Queens, in Iraq, in Pakistan. There is a crisis in the media as well that is covering and not covering these events.

There are seven Urdu weeklies in the New York area, which began to follow stories of FBI/INS raids on Pakistani immigrants, detentions, deportations, the effect of the special registration law and the Patriot Act. In this article, I look at the Urdu press, covering these events in New York post 9/11, and how it responded to the crisis.

*Rehan Ansari, formerly Editor, Independent Press Association-New York, will teach media studies starting September 2004 at Beaconhouse National University, Lahore. He has also been a columnist for Mid-day (Mumbai) and The Hindustan Times.

We know well by now that the origins of the crisis that we are familiar with as '9/11' pre-date 11 September 2001. We also know that the crisis continues well after the 11 September 2001 in Afghanistan, Iraq and Pakistan. There has been some amount of discussion in all sorts of media in the US about the background, as well as the fallout of 9/11, not only in New York, Washington and London, but all across the world, especially in terms of what is called the 'War Against Terror'. What the mainstream US media has not discussed is the accumulating sense of unease and crisis within New York City, in areas like Brooklyn and Queens, where Pakistani immigrants, be they on Atlantic Avenue or in Jackson Heights, see themselves located squarely at the frontline of the skirmishes that mark the everyday domestic reality of what is called the 'War against Terror'.

Mainstream media in the US, be they the television networks—NBC, ABC, CBS, FOX, CNN—or the major newspapers, ignore the persistent assaults on the civil liberties of Pakistani immigrants in America, especially in New York. The New York Times, to be fair, does carry the odd report, but it does so in a way that reminds me of the way the Karachi Police (whom I often saw in action as I was growing up in Pakistan) would show up at the scene of a crime always late enough to ensure that nothing could be done, so much so that you got accustomed to presuming their complicity in the incidents that they were supposed to redress.

Since 9/11, I have been following and translating stories from seven weekly Urdu publications in New York for 'Voices That Must Be Heard', a weekly news service that puts out news compilations drawn from alternative news sources. There are almost 300 publications in New York City, including various kinds of papers and broadsheets put out by a diverse array of small, neighborhood, ethnic, community and the independent presses. 'Voices', a project of the Independent Press Association, chooses stories from precisely such non-corporate sources. The stories that I followed and translated were of FBI/INS raids on the homes, places of work, shops, offices and businesses of Pakistani immigrants, of detentions and deportations, and of the effect of the Special Registration Law and the Patriot Act on the Pakistani community in the city.

It would be accurate to say that prior to 9/11, the Pakistani Press in New York, which has names like Pakistan Post, Pakistan News, New York Awam (New York Masses) and Sada-e-Pakistan (Voice of Pakistan) (all Urdu) and the Muslims Weekly (English) are generally owned by men who have other businesses which tend to be tax consultancies, real-estate brokerage and travel agencies. The papers primarily serve as public relations fronts for these gentlemen who also position themselves as 'community leaders'. They carry reports of community events, social functions, festivals and entertainment galas. In the months that followed 9/11, however, it was this incredibly small, and often small-minded, press in New York that found itself at the forefront of having to report and highlight many issues of public interest, such as growing attacks on civil liberties, racial profiling, post war reconstruction, the effect of the crisis on the deeply interdependent nature of the world economy, capital and labor flows, migration and perceptions of 'America', both in this country and in others.

Whereas these papers had previously carried op-eds almost exclusively about politics in Pakistan[1], after 11 September, one saw a surge in local reporting reflecting on FBI/INS raids, the rights of detainees (both legal and illegal), the effect of the 'War Against Terror', the local economy of Coney Island, and a new interest in the cause of civil liberties activists who were from outside the community. There was also a very vital level of op-ed writing on American foreign policy and the globalization of the post 9/11 conflict.

The Pakistani press in New York became a crucial smoke detector for something burning in US society. Topics that are currently haunting discussions in the mainstream media, ranging from the US administration's assault on civil liberties to the subject of reconstruction in Iraq, first became visible in the Urdu press. A columnist wondered why the detainees in Guantanamo Bay didn't have rights that are available to anyone else in the territorial United States, which is essentially the question before the US Supreme Court today. Again it was in the New York Pakistani press that a writer asked a question concerning Afghanistan: 'So, when will reconstruction end?'

The following is a more detailed sense of the news that the papers carried.

Below is a selection of headlines and text translated from the New York Urdu papers post 9/11[2].

Authorities express surprise at the numbers of Pakistanis calling the INS on each other
M. R. Farrukh, Pakistan Post, 17 April 2002.

Ahmed Imtiaz is one of those hundreds of thousands of people who come to the United States dreaming about a happy and prosperous life. Before 11 September irrespective of his legal status, he was spending a quiet life earning an honorable living for his household.

Two months after 11 September he was picked up from his home in New Jersey. His apartment was raided by the FBI, the INS and a squad of Special Forces. At around 2:30 a.m. his wife, three kids and himself were awakened by a continuous ringing of the doorbell. When he got out and saw the officials, he panicked. He had previously never encountered a police officer at his door. The sight of the officers of three agencies belonging to the most powerful country in the world on his doorstep completely unnerved him. The officers took him to his bedroom and searched his home for two hours. He swore upon his innocence, pleaded with them. They arrested him.

Like hundreds of those arrested, Imtiaz was found to have no links with the atrocity of 11 September. Freed of terrorism charges he was transferred from FBI detention to the INS centre. There are people in the INS centre detained for seven months now, without charges, because the law allows that. Imtiaz found himself charged under immigration law. He was found to be in violation of a deportation order from five years ago. Imtiaz is now facing deportation. He has only a few more days in this county.

He has recently found out why he was arrested. A few years ago an argument with a friend over a trivial matter became an open sore between them. They stopped talking and Imtiaz forgot about the matter over time. Taking advantage of the post-11 September atmosphere, the former friend told the authorities that Imtiaz was engaged in suspicious activities. The authorities were on a war footing and acted so.

Who can the community of Pakistanis living illegally in the United States turn to?
M.R. Farrukh, Pakistan Post, 1 May 2002.

The White House, the Congress, and the army establishment in Pakistan are all projecting themselves as fighting the just war against terrorism. Meanwhile, it is the Pakistani community in the United States that is feeling persecuted, voiceless and abandoned. A few days ago, at a raid on a Pakistani family living in Queens, agents explained that the head of the household's name was somewhat similar to the name of a suspected terrorist! An officer present during the raid told the family that the authorities had every right to pursue any lead in the fight against terrorism.

Protest against detentions by New York TaxiWorkers Alliance, Coney Island Avenue Project, and 50 various organizations
Mohsin Zaheer, Sada-e-Pakistan, N Y, 19 June 2002.

The protest took place on June 15th on Coney Island Avenue, in Brooklyn, where high concentrations of people of Pakistani origin live. The crowd was large and diverse except that few Pakistanis attended. There were at most two dozen Pakistanis. Spokespeople from the Brooklyn Mela Committee,

Pak-American Merchant's Association and Makki Mosque were among those who refused to attend the march, saying that protests in their own neighbourhood bring greater risks of discrimination.

The victims of the War on Terrorism are Pakistanis living here, as the crackdown against illegal immigrants continues
Pakistan Post, 29 July 2002.

American officials are continuing their campaign against US-based Pakistanis, citizens of an important American ally in the War On Terrorism. More than 1,700 Pakistanis have been detained in this country on immigration charges; many have been deported.

The FBI and INS are focusing on Brooklyn, where Pakistanis live and their businesses are based. Authorities are knocking on Pakistanis' doors late at night, questioning the residents, searching their houses and arresting those they find to be undocumented immigrants. Some report that officials are seizing even legal documents of people they question.

The special relationship between America and Pakistan
Ifti Nasim, News Pakistan, 25 September 2002. (Ifti Nasim is a well-known humourist, Urdu poet and literary critic.)

In one of her poems, Sylvia Plath talks of a foot that was trapped in a black shoe for thirty years, poor and white, barely daring to breathe. That foot is Pakistan, which has suffered for thirty years in the black shoe of American-sponsored military dictatorships.

A Pakistani writes from an American jail
Azeem M. Mian, Pakistan Post, 9 October 2002.

A friend of the editors of Pakistan Post received a letter from Zubair Hanafi, which has been forwarded to me and I am including in this column. Zubair's address is the Brooklyn Detention Center. His prisoner number is 67898053. The letter bears an Aug. 15. postmark, meaning the letter has taken almost two months to get to me. Let us hope that Zubair is safe, either released in the United States or deported to Pakistan.

Few Pakistanis register on first day
News Pakistan, 22 January 2003.

On the first two days of registration, few Pakistanis have showed up: forty on the first day in New York (127 in the first two days); in Chicago, 70 appeared on the first day. An estimated 600,000 Pakistanis live in the United States, 200,000 in New York State alone. Most are undocumented, have incomplete legal status, or are under due process. If the registration requirements are enforced to the letter, an estimated 400,000 will be forced to leave the country.

Farewell United States! Is all hope now with Canada?
Pervaiz Ramay, Sada-e-Pakistan, NY, 12 February 2003.

Pakistanis fleeing the United States into Canada at the border at Niagara Falls are finding refuge at Viva Locasa, a church within US territory, just 15 minutes drive from the Canadian border. Most of the refugees are in terrible need since they left everything behind in their panicked flight.

Immediately following 9/11, the Urdu/Pakistani press in New York rose to the occasion. But where is the press now? How is it doing? Are they still sniffing in the wind for what is not yet apparent to anyone else? Or are these small community papers only good at the rapid, almost real-time dissemination of what a crisis feels like 'from the inside', only when the crisis is upon their heads? Further, have the intellectual and cultural horizons of the world that these papers present to their readers undergone any transformations? In terms of cultural reporting, before 9/11, there would be no writing in the op-ed pages of almost all the Urdu press that challenged mainstream, middle-class Pakistani Punjabi social mores. There was very little that one could see reflected about the transformations in a new immigrant community, or the awareness of a new generation of immigrants, or of second-generation Pakistani-Americans and their attitudes, and almost no new voices in the op-ed pages. In fact, more than one paper carried the prolific writings of a dead columnist. Maulana Maudoodi, a conservative intellectual and essayist and founder of the Jamaat-e-Islami in Pakistan, who in his lifetime wrote about everything under the sun—on marriage, death, cinema, literature, the economy, the upbringing of children, living in the west as a minority, and in the east as a majority, the separation of church and state—but who was, nonetheless, dead, was published with monotonous regularity in several of these papers. However, it needs to be pointed out that at least two papers—The Pakistan News (Urdu) and the Muslims Weekly (English)—are positioning themselves editorially, each in different but interesting ways, to the challenges of being interlocutors in post-9/11 New York.

I believe the creation and growth of these publications reflects the ways that 9/11 has forced members of the Pakistani-American community to redefine what it means to be Pakistani-American, as well as what it means to be a Muslim-American. The fact that the Muslims Weekly is an English language publication indicates an intention to move beyond the confines of a specifically Pakistani identity. It has an Israeli peace activist writing for it, which means that it is positioning itself in a different kind of role from what one is accustomed to seeing within the Muslim community in the United States. Its circulation jumped from 5,000 pre-9/11 to 25,000. Of its five paid staff, three are non-Muslim.

The Pakistan News, meanwhile, makes the effort of translating articles from the liberal English press in the United States into Urdu. Moreover, it is the first Urdu paper to give prominent column space to women (and not just in the 'Women's Pages'), to regularly publish an openly gay Urdu poet based in Chicago, and to foreground a generally liberal and progressive political/cultural agenda.

Barring exceptions like The Pakistan News (Urdu) and the Muslims Weekly (English), most Urdu/Pakistani publications in New York have not really evolved beyond the immediate need of reporting what affects the Pakistani community on a day-to-day basis. Furthermore, they are in a sense undergoing their own peculiar crisis of 'over-stimulation and under-statement', of exaggeration and exhaustion, and certainly of (self) censorship. They are not reporting on the alliances that are forming between activist and immigrant communities. The work of the New York Immigration Coalition, Asian American Legal Defense Fund, and the American Civil Liberties Union remains un-commented on, and un-analyzed. If at all it is reported, it is done so in the blandest way, by reproducing information from a press release. Nor is there any attempt to flesh out the personalities in these organizations and the issues that they concern themselves with. There was no analysis of the coalitions that made possible the Immigrant Workers Freedom Ride[3] in October 2003.

The Urdu/Pakistani press in New York did ask key questions, but has not been able to follow through on answering those questions. Severe resource constraints, which ensure that a journalist who writes for these publications never has the luxury to research and follow a story in order to write a well-rounded feature, or even keep to one beat, are certainly responsible for this state of affairs. But given the complex and challenging reality that the readers of these papers face, one hopes that at least some of the publications will find the wherewithal to evolve beyond their current limitations.

Notes

1. Mostly about the pros and cons of the Musharraf regime in Pakistan and the pronouncements from exile of the two civilian ex-Prime ministers—Nawaz Sharif and Benazir Bhutto.
2. For more information, and the full text of these articles see the archive of 'Voices That Must Be Heard'. (Voices), the weekly web-digest of the Independent Press Association, New York, at http://www.indypressny.org.
3. The Immigrant Workers Freedom Ride (a campaign to endorse and support the civil liberties of all immigrant workers in the United States) ended with a huge day-long celebration of America's Immigrants in New York's Flushing Meadows Park on October 2003. More than 125,00 labor activists and community supporters joined the nearly 1,000 immigrant workers who had traveled all over the US in an unprecedented effort to put immigration issues squarely on the national political agenda for 2004 and mobilize USA-wide support for changes in immigration policies. For more information, see http://www.ifwr.org Crisis/Media - Case Studies/157.

24

SOCIAL ORGANIZATION AND THE ROLE OF RELIGION IN THE NORTH-WEST FRONTIER TRIBAL AREAS, 1915–1935

*Sana Haroon**

ABSTRACT

This paper is aimed at determining the foundations of religious authority within the North-West Frontier 'tribal' society during the colonial period. Drawing on evidence from colonial administration records and hagiographic literature for the early twentieth century, this study considers the participation of mullahs in village society in the Tribal Areas.

The mullahs of the Tribal Areas created participatory and accessible 'spaces' within the Tribal Areas, and institutions of social arbitration and management of a regional community. Emerging 'public opinion' and this evidence of non-political solutions for inter-group dispute management, indicates the existence of a society that transcended the narrow definitions of genealogies and 'tribal' concerns.

Notions of civil society, emerging from a European experience, are clumsy in the South Asian historical and post-colonial context because it is impossible to equate definitions of state, society, and even modernity. The case of the Tribal Areas demonstrates that institutions of religion can be used to uncover a dynamic debate within Pakhtun 'tribal' society. Understanding the nature of social organization and change, as facilitated by the Pakhtun mullahs, makes it possible to define a public space, a political agenda, and a regional social formation emerging within the Tribal Areas.

---

*The author is presently completing her PhD at the School of Oriental and African Studies, University of London.

The eastern Pakhtun regions, demarcated as the Tribal Areas, a non-administered portion of the Indian north-west frontier, were the location for a series of armed mobilizations through the end of the nineteenth and the twentieth centuries, many of which were organized by a religious leadership. In 1897, an uprising in the Waziristan region led by the *Mullah* Powindah, targeted British communications lines and army outposts. Parties in Waziristan, the Khyber and Malakand mobilized in support of the Afghan Amirate during the Anglo-Afghan War of 1919, led by several *mullah*s of the region. In 1935, the Fakir of Ipi initiated a series of attacks on British concerns in Waziristan, and organized raids into the administered portion of the NWFP.

Because of the reactive, sporadic, and short lived nature of these mobilizations, religious organization and militancy in the Pakhtun regions has been understood as a purely ideological phenomenon. Scholarship on religion in the Pakhtun areas has caste the *mullah* as an insidious and retrogressive influence in Pakhtun society.[2] An overwhelming emphasis on the polemics of militant mobilizations led by religious elites has caste the practice of Islam in the Tribal Areas as the primary indicator of traditionalism and the mark of the 'tribal' Pakhtuns as a pre-modern society. Furthermore, Islam has been argued to be something 'imported' into an otherwise pragmatic society.[3]

I suggest instead, that in the absence of state-sponsored institutions, the cultivation of a public, religious practice became the grounds for an emerging political consciousness and political action. The *mullah*'s authority, the means by which he engaged and directed a regional social imperative, became the means for the mobilization of a series of responses, both within the Tribal Areas, and to the colonial government. Engaging participants across the region, outside the small clan groups that have been hitherto understood to constitute the population of the Tribal Areas—the *mullah*'s magnetism appears to be in his functionality rather than in his ideology—and the systems of informational exchange and dispute management that he enabled.

Using colonial and reformist religious literature to highlight the *mullah*'s functional role, it is possible to understand the *mullah* to be at the forefront of defining a public space, a political agenda, and a regional social formation. Far from being traditional, this was a modern paradigm. The *mullah*s of the Tribal Areas created participatory and accessible 'spaces' within the Tribal Areas, and institutions of social arbitration and management of a regional community. Emerging 'public opinion' and this evidence of non-political solutions for inter-group dispute management, indicates the existence of a society that transcended the narrow definitions of genealogies and 'tribal' concerns. While on, one hand this points to a new social formation, organizing outside the rigid structures of clan-tribe systems and political organization in India and Afghanistan, it is impossible to describe this as a conscious 'civil society'.

The emergence of civil society has been tied to the institutions of democracy, the rigors of state, and crucially, the notion of a citizenship – factors that can barely be identified within the colonial paradigm, let alone the non-administered Tribal Areas. Moreover, Andre Beteille argues in his study of 'Civil Society and its Institutions', that state and citizenship meet and mutually depend on the systems of internal arrangements—class, communities, and networks of interpersonal relations, but asserts that religion cannot be understood as such a mediator because its totalizing impulses erodes the autonomy and growth of the civil society.[4] The case of the Tribal Areas demonstrates, however, that institutions of religion became the platform for a dynamic debate within Pakhtun society.

Notions of civil society, emerging from a European experience, are clumsy in the South Asian historical and post-colonial context because it is impossible to equate definitions of state, society, and even modernity. Study of society within the Tribal Areas, that has presented tremendous obstacles to institutional and even national integration for Pakistan, cannot be constrained within these narrow theoretical paradigms and the fearful rejection of religious organization as inadmissible within the debate. A modern society was emerging in the early twentieth century Tribal Areas—one that contended with its institutional and political alienation from Afghanistan and India. Understanding the formation of this society, and the place of religion within it, takes precedence over the narrow confines of the debate over the constitution of the 'civil', and it is from this point that this study begins.

INTRODUCTION: THE SITUATION OF THE TRIBAL AREAS AND THE SOCIOLOGY OF THE TGRIBE

The North-West Frontier Tribal Areas were cut off from the Pakhtun ethnic continuum by the delimitation of the Durand Line in 1893, and cut off from the social and political institutions of greater India by the assigning of non-administered status between 1893 and 1897. Removed from both the sphere of Kabul's influence, and the educational system, emerging nationalist discourses, and participatory politics of administered India, the Tribal Areas existed in a state of social and political autonomy.

Until the separation of the Tribal Areas from Afghanistan at the end of the nineteenth century, Afghan officials at Kabul, Jalalabad, Khost and Lalpura had exercised some influence over the eastern Pakhtuns, and had held regional *jirga*s that included these communities. With Amir Abdur Rahman's (1883–1901) acceptance of the Durand Line and the principle of non-interference across the border, the eastern Pakhtuns were excluded from Afghan administrative systems.

On the other side, the judicial, policing, administrative and educational institutions of greater India were circumscribed within the borders of the Peshawar, Bannu, Kohat, Dera Ismail Khan and Hazara. The region, designated as 'tribal', was left to traditional systems of social management.

Colonial ethnographies determined that highly egalitarian tribe-clan groups created councils, *jirgas,* which dispensed justice within the community, subject to the informal social code of *pakhtunwali.* A *malik* or *khan,* whose title was generally hereditary, but whose position was dependent on the support and loyalty of members of the community, headed the tribe or clan, and the *jirga.* 'Traditional' social organization and management was left intact, and the colonial state only deputed a political agent, or in some cases, a resident, to the major tribal groupings, to maintain British defensive concerns in the region, and to manage treaties with the tribes.

'Tribal' *maliki* and *jirga* authority were existent institutions, but were limited, in part, by colonial valorization and reification of the 'tribal' structure, within a localized role. While the institutions of the *malik* and *jirga* were observable across the region, the authority of any single *jirga* was circumscribed within its own tribal unit. Some personalities, such as the *Nawabs* of Dir and the *Mianguls* of Swat, rulers of recognized 'states' within the frontier region, were recognized as having a proportionately greater weight and regional authority, but even this authority was circumscribed by the genealogies of the 'tribal' conglomerates that resided within and around state lands.

Fractured by the institutional alienation of the region, the genealogy of the eastern Pakhtun tribes was the primary feature in describing the regional village systems, access to resources, and political representations to the government of India. Major tribal groupings of *Yusufzais,*

Afridis, Shinwaris, Mohmands, Wazirs and *Mahsuds*, were subdivided on descent lines into clans and familial groups. An ethnographic map constituted the organizational schema of the Tribal Areas.

However, a closely interconnected group of religious elites overlay this otherwise ethnographically defined landscape. This *sharkh* or branch of the Naqshbandiyya-Mujaddidiyya *sufi silsila* of eastern Afghanistan, was the dominant religious influence in the region. *Mullahs* of this *sharkh* were deeply influenced by the revivalist Islam of Shah Wali Ullah, introduced by Sayyid Ahmed of Rai Bareilly in the 1830s, and developed under the influence of the north Indian *madrassa* Darul Ulum Deoband from 1890 onwards. Connections between *mullah*s within this *sharkh*, engendered by the fraternity of the *pirimuridi* line, or the chain of transmission of religious knowledge, made religious authority an integrated regional institution rather than just being a group of unconnected social elites.

LOCATING THE *MULLAH*: THE CLAN AND THE MOSQUE

Considering the foundations of religious authority in the frontier Tribal Areas counters a persistent bias in the study of Pakhtun social organization that has separated religion and 'real' Pakhtun culture into two separate domains. Religious functionaries have hitherto been considered at best secondary members of the 'clan'[5] whose membership in society and could be easily revoked. History of the region, rooted in colonial sources and analysis has described religious authority in the Tribal Areas as being opportunist seizures of power when traditional *maliki*[6] authority weakened. Yet the *mullahs* evidently had a real and undeniable connection with Pakhtun society and with the ethnographically defined 'tribe', in their facilitation of religious practice.

Religious authority was not something alien to and outside the clan system, but was deeply tied to it. Because human settlement in the Pakhtun region was organized by the genealogy of the tribe, village 'communities' corresponded to the clan-tribe system. Hence the *mullah*'s relationship with the practicing Muslim community was also a relationship with the clan-tribe system.

It was through the institution of the mosque and its attached *langarkhana* or alms house, that the Haji Turangzai, a religious authority from *Utmanzai* in the Charsadda district, came to the Non-Administered Territories, and began to forge a relationship with the independent Pakhtun clans. Similarly, the Mullah Chaknawar, originally from the Ningrahar region in eastern Afghanistan, created a relationship with the *Mohmands* and *Bajauris* through the institution of the mosque.

Paying for the running of the *langarkhana*, the alms house, and managing the upkeep and all necessary repairs and changes to the structure of the mosque, the *mullah*'s primary and indisputable function was to maintain and run the space within which religious ritual was performed. Moreover, he oversaw the practice of that ritual. The *mullah* led the congregational prayers once a week, offered a commentary on scripture and performed marriages and death rites. A religious sanctity underlay this role. The anthropology of human faith that granted the *mullah* a spiritual authority over society is beyond the ambit of this historical consideration of eastern Pakhtun organization, yet it undeniably defined something of the *mullah*'s social position.

A social importance was created by the *mullah*'s spiritual authority. As a commentator on religion, the *mullah* could accord sanctity, not only to the private and personal rituals of prayer, marriage and death, but also to the social and political rituals of human organization.

In a microcosmic enactment of the *dastarbandi* ceremonies of Afghanistan, in which the grand *pirs* of Kabul accorded divine sanction to the new *amir*, the village *mullah* sanctioned human authority, by representing the ultimate sovereignty of God over man.

A model of religious involvement in social and political community functions brought the village *mullah* into *maliki* and *jirga* management at the village-clan level. He would attend *jirgas*, read prayers before, and finally would approve the decisions of a *jirga* at the conclusion of a meeting. He was open to affect the decision making process and offer advice according to his assessment. The *mullah* could also himself initiate proceedings against an individual or suggest strategy towards other clans or the British by approaching the *malik* and clan *jirga*.

In return for the performance of his religious duties, the *mullah* was allowed to cultivate on lands parceled with the mosque, and to collect religious alms, *shukrana*, from the communities he served. Income derived from these two activities was the *mullah*'s to use as he pleased, towards the upkeep of the mosque, and the cultivation of his own influence and authority.

Hence, while the *mullah* was not a 'natural' member of the *jirga*, by virtue of not being a natural member of the clan, his connection to this society was not shallow or insubstantial. Once the *mullah* had accepted and been accepted at a mosque, he and his successors became deeply attached to the clan with which they were affiliated. Ghulam Nabi Chaknawari, son of the Mullah Chaknawar emphasized that his father considered himself a *mullah* of the Mohmands or *Khandan-e-Mohmand*.[7] By accepting a primary host that appreciated and responded to his religious authority, a *mullah* represented and acted on behalf of that clan. This 'primary' relationship generally handed down from *pir* to *murid*[8], connected certain lineages of *pirs* to particular clans both spiritually, and over time, familially.

A functional role brought the *mullah* into the clan-tribe system, not by genealogical descent, but by service to the religious congregation and to the *jirga*. It was the nature of this functionality—the inclusive spaces and institutions engendered by the *mullah*'s service to the clan—that both highlighted and nurtured an emerging society, connected by 'interests' and not by the narrow dictates of lineage.

THE MOSQUE AS A PUBLIC SPACE

Masjids had a very important role. This is where the Pakhtun culture and Islamic culture met.[9]

Host villages were expected to provide some quantity of food for the *langarkhana*, but making up a shortfall fell to the *mullah* whose prestige was gauged by the quality of his hosting.[10] The *mullah*'s primary role, as maintainer of the mosque, also gave him an authority over this functional, inclusive and vibrant arena of male village life in the Tribal Areas.[11] It was the nature of, rather than the ideological reasons for, religious practice, which made it a dynamic aspect of eastern Pakhtun social organization. Religion represented a 'public' space, whose nexus was the institution and the space of the mosque.[12] Daily and weekly communal prayers were performed at the mosque. Worshippers would remain to eat at the *langarkhana* and would meet visitors and exchange news in the *hujra*, a meeting space attached to the mosque. The mosque and its parts was a social space within the village.[13] Maintaining and making provisions for meals at the langarkhana, and maintaining the *hujra*, was the direct responsibility of the *mullah* of the mosque, the funds for which came out of his own budget.[14] As a social hub, the meaning of the space of the mosque cannot be confined to the performance of religious ritual, or some isolated notion of 'Islam'. The mosque was a 'public arena' within which opinion was being collectively formulated. A key function of this space in the Tribal Areas was simply 'gossip' or the exchange of information—an activity that was material and political in its concerns. It can be argued that this is a component of any 'collective' space. However in the case of the Tribal Areas, information was a commodity hard to come by. Mullahs were actively engaged in providing news, making opinion generation not an incidental, but an essential component of their authoritative role.

Frequent congregations of local male Pakhtun society met *travelers* and bearers of news in the *langarkhana*, made the mosque the central repository and dispensation point for news and organization. The mosque functioned as the central point on information dissemination in the Tribal Areas, which were otherwise cut off from reliable media access. Because few Pakhtun residents of the Tribal Areas could read and the region was virtually inaccessible by the combination of administrative segregation and its difficult terrain, little news penetrated the *sarhad*. Religious leadership was well placed to receive bearers of news through networks of *murids* and travelers who were sent or directed to them by colleagues in Afghanistan and India. The Mullah Powindah was said to run his own *dak* network between 'Faqirs of the Mahsud *aqwam*, the Raees of Khost, and the cities of Lahore and Peshawar' while Haji Turangzai's son maintained a more informal system of sending and receiving messages through travelers[15], ensuring reliable communications with colleagues. Other *mullah*s, including the Haji Turangzai, Mullah Chaknawar and Mullah Babra were part of *tablighi* networks, passing regularly from village to village within the Tribal Areas, the settled frontier and Afghanistan, and bringing news back with them to their host villages.[16]

Newspapers received from Afghanistan and India like the *Siraj ul Akhbar*, *Zamindar*, *Al Hilal*, *Pioneer* and *Soul*[17] would be read out in the mosque[18], and travelers would bring their stories there. It became the central reception point for outside communications. Information dissemination became the prime non-spiritual function of the mosque as newspapers with information on the progress of wars, the German expansion, the Bolshevik revolution and Afghan court politics were made available here. *Al Mujahid*, the newspaper of the Chamarkand colony, was distributed along these religious networks, carried out from Chamarkand by *Mujahidin*, and to religious affiliates in the Tribal Areas.

Carrying news into the Tribal Areas was a dangerous business. Anybody caught delivering letters to or carrying letters or newspapers from the Tribal Areas to British India or vice versa was under suspicion for aiding the anti-British movement there and subject to arrest[19]. Yet the demand for information in the Tribal Areas ensured that the clans received news of the war and its consequences, events and intrigue at the Afghan *darbar*, in British India and news from across the Frontier Tribal Areas.[20] Substantiated news was reported with the same authority as gossip and rumor. News of German advances was embellished with the declaration that the Turks were coming to liberate India, and that all of Germany had embraced Islam[21]. Reports of military successes and defeats, the progress of the Khilafat movement in India and activities of the nationalist movement were applauded by Tribal Areas anti-colonial activists.

As the administration in Peshawar made it more and more difficult for newspapers to get through, so as not to 'ignite' the sensibilities of the volatile frontier population, the value of information and the importance of the bearers of news only increased. When Mohammad Ali Kasuri led the prayers and gave a *waaz* [sermon] at the occasion of the eid prayers on his arrival in Chamarkand, he claimed that people came 'in great numbers, walking many miles' to hear him speak, because they knew he was going to bring 'news of the situation in India and with the war.'[22]

Illiteracy and the scarcity of written documents affected the process of communicating news and molding political opinion. Information, rather than being consumed individually and privately, was transmitted orally. Bayly suggests that this means of communication of information sped its dissemination and its effect, arguing that:

> It was the density and flexibility of indigenous routines of social communication which explains why north Indians were able to make such striking use of the printing press, the newspaper and public meeting ... in fact, [it will] help to explain why political leaders in a poor country with relatively low rate of general literacy should have been able to create a widely diffused and popular nationalist movement so early.[23]

When the religious congregation gathered, it received both spiritual and political tutoring. Christopher Bayly describes this as entering into a 'public debate' on a 'public religion', a congregational event that was intended to create consensus.[24] Through a 'routine of social communication', a religious congregation was also a political community. Its transformation took place within the domain of the mosque, and the form of religious practice. Moreover, it was sustained and enhanced primarily by the activities of religious practitioners. The practice of Islamic ritual provided a service that was almost impossible to replicate outside of its systems of exchange, communication and congregation.

Collective reception of information and the collective action or decisions that resulted from it occurred within the congregational domain of the mosque, linking religion inextricably to politics. Channeling outside information that impacted local opinion and decision-making, the mosque was at once a spiritual centre and a political vehicle. The *mullah* at the head, directly facilitating the import, interpretation, embellishment and consumption of information, conducted this process, and hence also became invested with an authority over the domain of information exchange.

The *mullah*'s socially interactive and authoritative function extended his pedagogic role to the discussion and representation of political issues. Because the religious congregation had political and information demands, the *mullah*, as leader of the congregation, was in a position to, and was encouraged to comment on issues of particular interest. Hence the *mullah* could use the traditional Friday sermon to comment on the content of news and its implications for the local population, and to push an agenda in relation to the Afghan and the British governments as well as local powers. As the mosque became a centre for the access of information, the very space of the mosque became an arena for the emergence of opinion.

INTER-GROUP ARBITRATION AND A TRANS-TRIBAL PARADIGM

Disparate social and political units occupying the 'Tribal Areas' were entirely politically independent of each other. Subsistence level agriculture at the village level made integrated markets unnecessary; and scattered, clan-based human settlements divided by harsh and difficult terrain left village level *jirgas* completely independent to govern as they wished. These polities were, at the same time, highly connected by the scarcity of resources such as land, water, roads, and the patronage structures of the Kabul court and British India.[25] Tensions between geographical proximity, yet social and governmental disparity, evince a complex system of inter-village and inter-tribal relationships, marked by intense competition between clans, even those of the same lineage, often turned bloody, sparking blood feuds that could go on for generations.

Neglecting to avenge the death of a kinsman was to lose face permanently, and to suggest to the world that the clan was easy prey. No participant in a feud could ever lay down his weapon when he was in the inferior position—such cowardice would have been an unacceptable and dangerous admission of weakness. This meant however that the cycle of violence between what were often neighbouring villages could potentially go on forever, bringing all commercial and productive activity to a halt until all male members of both kinship groups had been eliminated.

Anthropologists concerned with the Pakhtun regions have confronted the issue of political relationships across clan and tribal lines: the management of often vying interests between homogenous groups in the absence of a central and transcendental authority capable of asserting decisions and solutions over the different parties involved. Frederic Barth argues that in Swat there was a basic equilibrium between clans; inter-tribal antagonism meant that no one Khan would ever get too strong because an alliance of smaller Khans would appear who would oppose him.[26] Akbar Ahmed on the other hand argues that 'there was no natural tendency for rivalries between Khans and their parties to be checked and held in balance. Khans could, and when the opportunity allowed often did, drive out their opponents permanently.' Anthropological analysis of Pakhtun political relationships have mapped relationship-rivalry patterns of agnatic rivalry or *tarburwali*[27], to explain the struggles for power[28], both between individuals and clan units in an effort to establish an underlying cultural order of human and collective social action. These searches for primordial patterns of human conduct are limited, as they tend to dismiss social and political circumstances in asides. As a result, the role of the *mullah* as an inter-group diplomatic functionary, has been written out of the study of social relationships and politics in the Pakhtun Tribal Areas.

In the interests of progress and preservation of life, opposing parties would enter into brokered 'truces' to halt the feud without losing face. In the absence of any other trans-local authority, only the *mullah* was perfectly placed to arbitrate between antagonistic interest groups and affect such a truce. The history of inter-group rivalry in the early twentieth century Tribal Areas evidences the agency of different *mullah*s in resolving disputes and applying punishments.

Miyan Akber Shah, an anti colonial dissident who traveled through the Tribal Areas during the Khilafat period (1919–1923), described the violence of blood feuds and the agency of *mullah* in resolving them, in his autobiography. Akber Shah's entry into Doburjon in Bajaur was met with the chilling spectacle of streets empty of men. Here, it was said, men did not die natural deaths—they died by the bullet of an enemy. So terrible was the enmity that whenever fighting broke out, the Haji Sahib Turangzai would be summoned immediately to create a *tigah* or truce between the hostile parties, and until that time, the men would remain hidden in their houses to avoid being the next casualty.[29] The various groups involved were constrained to accept the *mullah's* every decision, and would enter into a pact to that effect before the *mullah* would even hear the case.[30] Then the case would be presented, the transgressor identified, and a suitable compensation for the wronged party decided.[31]

In situations where random and sporadic fighting was ongoing between two rival factions, the *mullah* had a slightly different role. Rather than just ascertaining blame and imposing a fine on the guilty party, he would broker a cease-fire. He would set terms of the cease-fire, mapping the boundaries between villages, and access to shared resources such as water. Finally, he would decide an amount of fine payable by either party breaking the peace. These cease fires had a limited life and had to be reviewed, renewed and patched up periodically, demanding a long term engagement and familiarity of the *mullah* with the situation.[32]

In this role, the *mullah* was not only the facilitator and pivot of inter-group and inter-personal relations in the Tribal Areas, but essential to the maintenance of normalcy. Mullah-led arbitration was a political mainstay throughout the frontier Tribal Areas. All major *mullah*s of the twentieth century frontier were documented as having spent significant amounts of their time traveling to the scene of a dispute, and offering a binding solution to the parties involved.[33] Haji Sahib Turangzai, along with the Mullah Sahib Chaknawar, Mullah Babra and Mullah Sayyid Akbar were some of the *mullah*s described as having brokered most truces in Mohmand, Bajaur and Khyber region.[34]

It was almost impossible for opposing factions to approach each other through any other means than *mullah*-led arbitration. Even the Halimzai Mohmands, who were part of the British 'assured' clans and had rejected the *mullahs'* political preponderance turned to the Babra Mullah to establish communication with the Malik Muhasil of the Kuda Khel clan to reach a truce.[35] Other forms of authority in the Tribal Areas were so unreliable, that when Mohmands from the Tribal Areas raided a village in the settled district of Utmanzai, the citizens of Utmanzai opened negotiations through the Haji Sahib Turangzai who secured the return of the looted sheep. Anti-British clans also turned to the Haji Sahib to bring British allowance holder 'assured' clans to account, having no access to the reparations system in effect through the Political Agencies because of their categorization as hostile clans.[36]

In what was a most dramatic recognition of *mullah* authority and the access it afforded, Colonel Bruce of the Indian army contacted Mullah Mahmud Akhunzada when Ajab Khan, an Afridi gang leader, abducted a British girl, Molly Ellis. Colonel Bruce asked the Mullah to arrange a meeting between British representatives and Ajab Khan who was a devotee of Mullah Mahmud, so that a settlement could be reached and the girl be released, unharmed. When the negotiations took place, they were conducted at Mullah Mahmud's residence.[37]

Religious intervention was solicited and accepted because of the *mullah*'s role on the basis of the *mullah*'s neutrality, rather than his ideological leanings. It was the very distinction between the tribal descent group and the functional role of the *mullah* that allowed him to perform this vital function as adjudicator. The tension between the *mullah*'s participation in and externality to the tribe-clan system created an authority that was able to, and required to, transcend the clan and its institutions of social management—the *jirga*.

Mullah-adjudication developed beyond the piecemeal interventions of any one *mullah* into a significant and an autonomous institution of social management in the region. Connections between members of this cadre, engendered by the institution of *pirimuridi*, the pedagogic chain of transmission of religious knowledge, created a unanimity amongst *mullah*s operating in the region.

PIRIMURIDI NETWORKS AND THE UNITY OF MULLAH-ORGANIZED DOMAIN WITHIN THE TRIBAL AREAS

The network of religious functionaries, the *pirimuridi* line, represented a public and integrated space for reparations and communications between otherwise competitive groups and individuals that had no institutionalized system of recourse to one another. The *mullah*s were deeply committed to maintaining unity within their cadre, making it possible for the institution of the *pirimuridi* line to transcend the close confines of the clan and tribal structure, while the individual *mullah* might be extremely invested within it.

The similarities of different *mullah*s' arbitration techniques and the coherence and unity of the *mullah* class is evidenced by the relationships between *mullah*s and the involvement of multiple *mullah*s in the same case, to reaffirm and bolster one another's authority. On one occasion, the Babra Mullah was unable to attend a large *jirga* meeting of Mohmands at Bagh.

He sent Haji Turangzai in his stead, carrying a letter bearing the seal of the Babra Mullah. The letter authorized the Haji to hear and decide the grievances of the Mohmand clans.[38]

Regular meetings of *mullah*s took place at Hadda, a village in Afghan Khost, historically important as it was the seat of authority of the Mullah Sahib Hadda (d. 1901), *pir* of many of the *mullah*s active in the Tribal Areas, and Chamarkand, important as a base of Sayyid Ahmed Bareilvi's resistance to the Sikhs in the 1820s and 1830s. Points of policy towards the British and social reform were discussed between *mullah*s at these meetings.[39] This organization meant that the *mullah*s were more than a group of loosely connected elites— rather a coherent and self aware leadership group whose internal cohesion was understood to be crucial to its success. Mutual support between the *mullah*s forbade appeal of decision to another religious authority.

Dissenters from within the *mullah* class were few, and were derided and marginalized quickly as in the case of the Shinwari Mullah, whose supporters' houses were burnt down on the orders of the Haji Turangzai.[40] Even the Nawab of Dir, who was seriously opposed to the Mujahidin movement and the Haji Turangzai-led *jihad*, was unable to affect the pro-Mujahidin sentiments and involvement of his most important *mullah*, the Shehzada of Rehankot.[41] So strong was impulse to maintain a unified front and prevent religion from becoming divided and less potent that the Haji of Turangzai even participated in the attack on Peshawar in 1927 organized by the Fakir of Alinagar, another *mullah* active based in the Mohmand area, despite his long standing disapproval of the scheme.[42]

The *mullah* cadre was deeply conscious of the importance of its internal cohesion, and presented and integrated an uniform system of policies and social order to the people of the Tribal Areas. Using the Hadda Mullah's shrine and Chamarkand as central organization point[43], the different *mullah*s involved in frontier affairs would meet regularly, as well as traveling to each other's villages and mosques and maintaining regular written contact.[44] Consulting one another on points of internal policy, the *mullah*s maintained a single face, promising to back up a weaker *mullah* through their own influence.[45]

When the Mullah Chaknawar threatened to start a campaign of house burnings when the Musa Khel *Jirga* refused to take his advice regarding British policy, he was promised complete moral support from Haji Sahib Turangzai, the Sandaki and Babra *mullah*s, amongst others. His colleagues promised to apply pressure on the Musa Khels and force them to come to an appropriate understanding with the Mullah Chaknawar.[46] If excommunicated by one *mullah*, an individual or clan was left entirely outside organized religion in the Tribal Areas, as other *mullah*s would uphold the decree.

Internal cohesion and clarity of purpose and solidarity within the *mullah* cadre made the networks of the *pirimuridi* line an effective system of dispute resolution. This was not just a neutral facility, however, Mullahs assumed the role of policing settlements, and maintained armed retinues, or *lashkars*, to assert this control over the Pakhtun communities.

THE *MULLAH'S LASHKAR*: THE MILITARISATION OF RELIGIOUS AUTHORITY

Diplomatic initiatives and social dictate by the *mullah* were strategically backed up by his *lashkar*, an army manned by both 'regulars'—the *shaikhs* or deputies and the *talibs* or students[47]—and irregulars, Pakhtun villagers participating in specific missions. Using the *lashkar* to demonstrate his popularity and generate enthusiasm for his decisions as well as using it to crush dissent and enforce punishments, the *mullah*'s *lashkar* was the backbone of his authority. The size of the *lashkar* was in part a measure of his strength and persuasive ability, and vice versa as a *mullah* with great renown would attract more fighting men. Haji Sahib Turangzai, the Mullah Chaknawar and the Babra Mullah were three of the most 'persuasive' authorities in this regard, with followings of at least forty men at any given time, going up to the thousands when they accommodated all the fighting men of various clans in a mission.

The *mullah* would convene a *lashkar* for three specific types of missions: to punish a political or moral transgressor; to enforce truces or exact penalty fines; or to attack a political adversary. The *mullah* would give the *ailans* of *jihad*[48], explained the nephew of the Babra Mullah, by sending:

> messengers on horses and designate a place where people should congregate. [This was] generally the *hujra* of a *qabila*. All the Baezai, Khwaezai, Safi and Qandhari would together designate a place where they should meet - in Nahaqqi or Safi or Qandhari or Ato Khel - something close [to the target] as a point of attack - then from there they would attack.'[49]

Leading the *lashkar* in an attack, the *mullah* would enter the transgressor's village and destroy his property.[50] Residents of his house were generally cleared out before it was set on fire, but members of the *lashkar* appropriated the transgressor's belongings as compensation for their efforts.[51] Other punishments included blackening the face of a social or political deviant,[52] or sitting him on a donkey and parading him through the village thereby humiliating him. Use of the *lashkar* could be subtler as well. A visitor to the region described an occasion when the Mullah Babra brought his men to the house of a truce breaker and remained there for two weeks until the dissenter agreed to a new settlement.[53] Custom required the 'host' to provide food and accommodations to his 'guests', the 'visit' almost bankrupting him.

These attacks were seldom intended to take or hold land or positions. They appear to have been a means of destabilizing adversaries in order to evince respect and consideration from them. They were also intended to, and effectively did, inscribe the potency of the Mullah's will on bystanders and participants.

MOBILIZING AN AGENDA: THE *MULLAHS* AND TRIBAL AREAS POLITICS

Collective performance of ritual activities, the *mullah*'s engagement in inter-group dispute management, and the mullah's own presence, backed up by his armed retinues, created a community that was subject to the authoritative and moral directives of the *mullah*. The concerns tabled by the mullahs were not necessarily ideological—rather the mullah drew on his functionality and authoritative presence to create and mobilize various political agendas within the Tribal Areas. Two of the most important of these mobilizations are discussed here—the Sandaki Mullah's mobilizations in opposition to the Nawab of Dir's territorial encroachments and taxation system in 1913–1915; and the Haji Turangzai and Mullah Sayyid Akbar's sidelining of British allowance holders amongst the Mohmands and Afridis. Both movements were more concerned with the creation of a regional consensus and unanimity than with the specific target.

Swat's politics were an important platform for early twentieth century religious organization. In 1908, the Khan of Dir, Nawab Aurangzeb Khan, whose father had been ousted by Umra Khan in 1895, but later returned to his throne, marched on Swat and annexed the northern territories of Nikpi Khel tribe in Swat.[54] The old Swat state had disintegrated, and the young Mianguls were incapable of organizing opposition to Dir.

In 1913, the Nawab of Dir began to demand taxes from the Nikpi Khel of western Swat. Mullah Sahib Sandaki immediately became involved in organizing a response to the territorial encroachments and increasing power of the Nawab.[55] Together with the still weak Mianguls, Mullah Sandaki led an attack on Dir, across the Swat River. Opposition to Dir began to grow under the influence of the Sandaki Mullah and his favored candidate for a new throne of Swat, Sayyid Jabbar Shah, descendant of Sayyid Akbar Shah, (a spiritual personality who had been amir of Swat from 1849-1857). The Sandaki Mullah organised the Nikpi Khel and other clans settled on the right bank of the river Swat against Dir, in support of Sayyid Jabbar Shah.

By 1914, the influence of Sayyid Jabbar Shah, promoted by the Sandaki Mullah, began to extend down towards Saidu and the Babuzai, threatening the Mianguls to the extent that they joined with the Nawab of Dir in opposition to Sayyid Jabbar Shah and the Sandaki Mullah.[56] The Mullah Sandaki and the Haji Sahib Turangzai together coordinated an opposition to the Mianguls of Swat again in 1915.[57] Soon after, Sayyid Abdul Jabbar Shah was discredited as being an Ahmedi, forcing the Sandaki Mullah to reach an uneasy truce with the Mianguls who were, meanwhile, gaining in power and influence under the Abdul Wudud Badshah. But the importance of the mullahs as representatives of tribal interests did not go unrecognized. The Sandaki Mullah received a gift of twenty thousand rupees for his military and diplomatic services from the clans of Swat a few years later.[58] Miangul Jahanzeb agreed that the Swat state had to strike a compact with this personality because of his popularity amongst the smaller khans.[59]

The Sandaki Mullah's efforts in Swat, alongside the Haji Turangzai and the Mullah Babra, demonstrated their great opposition to the accumulation of temporal power by any one group—whether clan, tribe or state. A system of ever shifting political alliances appeared to be directed at one end alone: maintaining a balance between the disparate groups that constituted the political map of the region.

The same agenda was upheld as the reason for religious mobilization against British allowance holders during this period. Pakhtun *mullahs* polarized the Tribal Areas into pro- and anti-British camps, advocating the attack and pillage of villages that were considered to have 'betrayed' the Pakhtun cause. In Mohmand, Malik Anmir's clan, the Gandab Halimzais and the Musa Khel were most affected by this policy, and was so violently and consistently targeted by the Haji Turangzai between 1915 and 1937, that a Gandao villager bitterly stated 'He was fighting his entire *jihad* against [Malik Anmir] because he and his people were jealous because [Malik Anmir] was very close to [Griffith, the Governor of the NWFP]'.[60]

British penetration into the frontier had increased tensions between clans and villages as individual maliks would reach terms and make commitments to the British without consulting other groups with vested interests in the issue. The Kuki Khels Afridis for example, protected the British interests in the Khyber pass, earning profits and gaining contracts for this job, but without sharing them with other clans who claimed equal proprietary rights over the road[61]. When the plan for the new Khyber railway was presented, 'unanimous opposition'[62] to the project was replaced by consent and commitment by several clans including the Qambar Khel[63]. This split in consensus was met with anger and hostility on the part of the remaining Khyber clans, and the Afridi clans attended a *jirga* of about six hundred people at Bagh, and asked the Mullah Sayyid Akbar to come forward to punish those intending to participate in construction the railway.[64] *Khutbas* or sermons at the Chaknawar Mullah's mosque scathingly referred to the 'iniquity of those working on the Khyber railway'[65].

The *mullah* took on the task of 'equalizing' disparities created by the colonial project. The *mullah* was the tool of punishment and chastisement of those clans that were seen to have betrayed the cause the majority. He isolated groups that were friendly to the British government and had participated in colonial road building schemes and the *khassadars*. He exerted pressure to re-establish social equilibrium, organizing opposition to clans that received allowances and support from the colonial government. Offering protection and support to clans that were individually weak, as Haji Sahib Turangzai did for the Safi Mohmands, *mullah*s could organize them collectively towards a larger cause.[66]

The *mullah's* authority to organize a political agenda was in a great part sanctioned and affirmed by participants in his mobilizations. This is best demonstrated in the Dir-Swat movement, where religious action could be read as an expression of social interests. The *mullah* elicited and represented a regional consensus. This consensus was couched in the notion of tribal 'autonomy' and preservation of the 'traditional' independence of the clan. Yet it is of crucial note that this effort reified the 'tribe', defending its autonomy and interests, to oppose the extension of any other form of trans-tribal authority. The mullah's efforts were aimed at maintaining an unchallenged control over the regional space of the Tribal Areas, as the only vehicle of dialogue and inter-group interaction in the region.

The very tribal condition and autonomy that led to the emergence of the *mullah* as a vehicle of social organization became the central political concern of the religious elite. While seemingly formidable, and the persistence of an age-old system of social organization, the notion of the tribe and the position of the mullah were emerging in the particular historical and administrative circumstances of the region.

CONCLUSION: RELIGIOUS LEADERSHIP IN 'NON-ADMINISTERED' SPACE

In the absence of an overarching political authority in the Tribal Areas, the *mullah*s occupied a governmental 'space', carrying out diplomatic functions and managing inter-group relationships on the one hand, and representing a 'national' interest and collective identity on the other. Assertions of *mullah*s' legitimacy and his effectiveness, while building on a local and individual relationship between spiritual guide and devotee, took place in the inter-group domain. Competition and camaraderie were moderated through the person of the *mullah* who suggested an immature, but functional relationship between the small group and the collective.

Mullah leadership was an efficient, coordinated and motivated form of social and political organization—one that was able to consolidate in the frontier Tribal Areas *because* there was no other form of inter-party organization or 'government'. Senator Ghulam Nabi Chaknawari, the son of the Chaknawar *mullah*, explained:

> In Afghanistan there was an existing *hakumat*. But in the *ilaqa-i ghair* [Tribal Areas], there were no police, no influence of state. It all went by the *riwaj* of the nation and the man and the *mullah*s. There were internal oppositions—enmities and friendships—but they all accepted the decision of the *mullah*.[67]

There was no institutionalized legal or political system in the frontier Tribal Areas, and it was this power vacuum that the *mullah*s were able to fill. Negotiating 'the *riwaj* [custom] of the nation, and the man, and the *mullah*s' religious leadership integrated social practices and political principles with the ability and will to adjudicate between competing parties.

The structure of the authority of the *mullah* in the Tribal Areas was not contained within or imparted by systems of government. Spaces engendered by religious practice and religious authority allowed institutions of social organization and consensus to emerge. Social practices and systems of organization within and without that space responded to its autonomy from colonial administration, emerging in part as a result of an entirely different system of 'civil' participation. Here, the religious authority did not operate within the structures and discourses of social governance in the administered districts. No codified and uniform law, no judiciary that was responsible to a word of 'law' rather than a community, and no policing of anti-social practices. No defined general social objectives, or alternate institutions capable of engendering them, existed in the Tribal Areas.

Religious leadership in the Tribal Areas was responding to the very state of statelessness presented by the frontier administrative structure. A discourse of anti-colonialism, the reification of the tribal system, and the militancy of religious activity was not emerging in spite of the state, but in its absence. The Tribal Areas were incorporated intact into the nation state of Pakistan in 1947, and the persistence of its non-administered status left the region institutionally underdeveloped. Institutionally neglected, tribe and religion continue to present the only two systems of social organization, and the region remains locked in a cycle of alienation, and the increasing concern with its own autonomy.

Bibliography

Primary Sources

1. *Books in Urdu*
Kasuri, Mohammad Ali, *Mushahidat-e-Kabul wa Yaghistan*, Lahore, 1953
Shah, Miyan Akber, *Azadi ki Talash*, Islamabad, Qaumi Idara Bara-e-Tahqiqi-e-Tarikh wa Shaqafat, 1989

2. *Official Records*
Special Branch Records, 1915–1930, Peshawar Archives, Pakistan.
DC Office Peshawar Files, 1915–1935, Peshawar Archives, Pakistan.
DC Office Special Reports and Files, Peshawar Archives, Pakistan.
NWFP Provincial Diaries 1915–1925, National Documentation Centre, Pakistan.
Political and Secret Annual Files 1919–1930, India Office Library, London.

3. *Government Publications*
Mahon, A H., and Lt A D G Ramsay, *Report on the Tribes of Dir, Swat and Bajour together with the Utman-Khel and Sam Ranizai*, Delhi, Superintendent Government Printing, 1901, Reprint Peshawar, Saeed Book Bank, 1981

Interviews
Ghulam Mohammad Din, Gandao, August 2002.
Senator Ghulam Nabi Chaknawari, Peshawar, February, August 2002.
Dr. Ahmed Yousuf, February 2002.

Secondary Sources
Ahmad, Makhdum Tasadduz, *Social Organization of Yusufzai Swat*, Lahore, 1962.
Ahmed, Akbar, *Pakhtun Economy and Society Traditional Structure and Economic Development in a Tribal Society*, London: Routledge, 1980.
Barth, Frederic, *Political Leadership Amongst Swat Pathans*, London: Athlone Press, 1965.
Bayly, Christopher, *Empire and Information*, Cambridge: Cambridge University Press, 1996.
Beattie, Hugh, *Tribe and State in Waziristan*, Unpublished Thesis SOAS, 1997.
Dupree, Louis 'Tribal Warfare in Afghanistan and Pakistan: A Reflection of the Segmentary Lineage System' *Islam in Tribal Societies*, Akbar Ahmed and David Hart (eds.) London, 1984.
Fox, Richard, *Lions of the Punjab*, London: University of California Press, 1985.
Freitag, Sandria, *Collective Action and Community: Public Arenas and the Emergence of Communalism in North India*, California: University of California Press, 1989.
Javed, Aziz, *Haji Sahib Turangzai*, Lahore: Idara-e-Tahqiq-o-Tasneef, 1981.

Lindholm, Cherry, 'The Swat Pakhtun Family As a Political Training Ground,' *Frontier Perspectives*, Charles Lindholm (ed.) Karachi: Oxford University Press, 1996.

Nichols, Robert, *Settling the Frontier: Land Law and Society in the Peshawar Valley 1500–1900,* Karachi: Oxford University Press, 2001.

Pinch, William, *Peasants and Monks in British India* California: University California Press, 1996.

Poullada, Roland, *Reform and Rebellion in Afghanistan 1919–1929*, Ithaca: Cornell University Press, 1973.

Reuter, Peter, 'Social Control in Illegal Markets,' *Towards a General Theory of Social Control*, Donald Black (ed.) London, 1984.

Warren Alan, *Waziristan: The Faqir of Ipi and the Indian Army; The North West Frontier revolt of 1936-37*, Karachi, Oxford University Press.

Yapp, Malcolm, 'Tribes and States in the Khyber',*Conflict of Tribe and State in Iran and Afghanistan*, Richard Tapper (ed.) London: Croom Helm, 1983.

Notes

1. Malcolm Yapp argues that the religious elite was trying to unite and 'manipulate' the divided Afridi and other Khyber clans after the 1840s. 'Tribes and States in the Khyber', in Richard Tapper ed. *Tribe and State in Iran and Afghanistan* (p. 186. R. O. Christensen speculates that religious mobilizations starting from 1897 and carrying on into the twentieth century were 'part of a millenarian movement invoking spiritual ideals in response to the forces of change that accompanied the advent of the British into tribal territory'. This sentiment, he argues, was provoked by the force of British colonial authority that had 'considerably weakened the traditional structure of secular authority amongst the clans, enabling religious leaders to place themselves, if only temporarily, at the head of a movement to re-assert tribal independence.' In introduction to 1981 reprint of Mahon, and Ramsay *Report on the Tribes of Dir, Swat and Bajour together with the Utman-Khel and Sam Ranizai*, (Peshawar, 1981) pp. 9–10. Alan Warren, in an attempt to uncover the nature of religious resistance considers an anti-colonial religious mobilization led by a religious functionary, the Fakir of Ipi, in Waziristan in 1935. Warren reads too closely and too literally into the Fakir's rhetoric of mobilization and armed opposition to conclude that 'the extent to which Islamic fundamentalism lay at the core of the Faqir of Ipi's motivations is only too apparent. He desired a status quo in which Muslims lived beyond the interference of western style administration directed by non Muslims.' Alan Warren *Waziristan: The Faqir of Ipi and the Indian Army; The North West Frontier revolt of 1936–37* (Karachi, 2000) p. 239.
2. Akbar Ahmed *Pakhtun Economy and Society.*
3. Andre Beteille, 'Civil Society and its Institutions', *Civil Society and Democracy* (Delhi, 2003) pp. 191–210.
4. The structure and categorization of the Pakhtun 'tribe' is irregular and indefinite across the region. This ambiguity, coupled with the colonial and pejorative implications of the word 'tribe' calls for a complete rethinking of the term. In this paper I have chosen to use the term 'clan' to refer to the village-based community.
5. The *malik* was the representative head of the clan who presided over the clan council or *jirga*.
6. Interview with Senator Ghulam Nabi Chaknawari Peshawar 3.2.2002. Khandan-e-Mohmand refers to the greater Mohmand 'tribe' made up of smaller clans. However this term is used loosely as the Mullah Chaknawar's did not have a relationship with all clans, or solely with clans, of the 'Mohmand' descent line.
7. Devotee of a *pir*.
8. Interview with Senator Ghulam Nabi Chaknawari, Peshawar, 3 February, 2002.
9. Aziz Javed notes that the abundance of the Haji Turangzai's *langar* was a point of prestige. Aziz *Haji Sahib Turangzai* p 46. Mohammad Ali Kasuri's very important account of his travels in the frontier Tribal Areas describes the food he was fed at the Haji Turangzai's langarkhana in Chamarkand in great detail and explains the importance of the *mullah's mehmandari*. *Mushahidat-e-Kabul-wa-Yaghistan* (Karachi, 1970?) p. 47. Also see Miyan Akbar Shah *Azadi Ki Talash* (Islamabad, 1989) p. 57.
10. Of these three congregational domains, only the mosque certainly existed in every village, as not every village or its *mullah* could afford to fund the langarkhana and a proper *hujra*.
11. This approach begins from the Sandria Freitag's study of the formation of the religious community in *Collective Action and Community: Public Arenas and the Emergence of Communalism in North India* (California, 1989).
12. Makhdum Tasadduz Ahmad explains that every Yousufzai village had a mosque, and every mosque had a *hujra*. His descriptions relate particularly to the Yousufzai of Swat, but hold true across Malakand and Mohmand. In *Social Organization of Yusufzai Swat.* (Lahore, 1962).

13. Aziz Javed describes the langarkhana as being an absolute prerequisite to the mobilization of and political authority over the Pakhtun peoples. He argues that in order to bring tribesmen together and to reach a political consensus amongst them, they had to be brought to one central location and housed and fed there. *Haji Sahib Turangzai*, p. 46.

14. 'Diary Book of Frontier Constabulary Mir Hamzah 1922/23' Special Branch Peshawar.

15. Hakim Mohammad Karim, the son of Haji Sahib Turangzai's Khalifa, Hakim Mohammad Abdul Ahad, states that much of Haji Turangzai's time was spent either going on '*doray*' (preaching missions) or receiving travelers on *doray* themselves. Interview with Aziz Javed, appendix to *Haji Sahib Turangzai*, p. 514.

16. Kasuri, *Mushahidat*, p. 53.

17. NWFP Provincial Diaries 1915–1917 note the dissemination of 'hostile propaganda' in mosques in the frontier.

18. Note on arrest of Shahzada Barkatulla's Messenger in 'Chamarkand Colony 1936' Mohmand Agency Records.

19. The *Sirajul Akhbar*, *Zamindar* and *Sarhad* were the most popular newspapers being sent to tribal areas.

20. NWFP Provincial Diaries 1914-1918.

21. Kasuri, *Mushahidat*, p. 48.

22. Christopher Bayly *Empire and Information* (Cambridge, 1996) p. 2.

23. Bayly, *Empire and Information*, p. 189.

24. Roland Poullada names women as another of these competition generating resources. 'here are elements in Pashtun tribal society which aggravate the natural tendency for men to fight over women. Women are a valuable commodity not only as cheap labor but also as bargaining counters in the interminable battle for family honor and status .. daughters are realized as potential assets to forward the interests of the family through strategic marriage alliances.' Roland Poullada, *Reform and Rebellion in Afghanistan 1919-1929* (Ithaca, 1973), p. 23.

25. Frederick Barth, *Political Anthropology of the Swat Pakhtuns*.

26. Louis Dupree 'Tribal Warfare in Afghanistan and Pakistan: A Reflection of the Segmentary Lineage System' In Akbar Ahmed and David Hart *Islam in Tribal Societies* (London, 1984).

27. Cherry Lindholm 'The Swat Pakhtun Family As a Political Training Ground' in Charles Lindholm *Frontier Perspectives* (Karachi, 1996).

28. Shah, *Azadi ki Talash*, p. 56.

29. Interview with Ghulam Nabi Chaknawari Peshawar, 8 February 2002.

30. The office of the Chief Commissioner NWFP reported Mullah Mahmud Akhunzada's involvement in brokering a truce and deciding the amount of blood money that had to be paid to the family of a murdered Aka Khel Afridi, NDC 885 NWFP Provincial Diaries 1916, Diary 4. Later he also brokered a truce between Kambar Khel and Malikdin Khel, NDC 884 for 1915, Diary 39.

31. Haji Sahib Turangzai, who brokered the cease-fire and truce between the Yousufzai and Qandahari Mohmands was expected to oversee its effectiveness and to re-establish the truce when it was broken. Political Diaries Mohmand, 1926, p. 55.

32. NWFP Provincial Diaries for the years 1915-1930 specifically note the diplomatic initiatives of Mullah Mahmud Akhunzada and Mullah Said Akbar amongst the Afridis, Mullah Fazal Din in Waziristan, the Babra Mullah, Mullah Chaknawar, Sandaki Mullah, and Haji Sahib Turangzai in Malakand Bajaur and Mohmand. Mentions are made of several lesser known *mullah*s, but these were invariably connected with the better known *mullah*s.

33. Political Diaries Mohmand 1923.

34. NWFP Provincial Diaries 1915, Diary 39; Political Diaries Mohmand 1924, 3 May 1924.

35. Interview with Naik Mohammad Ghazizuay, son of Ajab Khan Afridi, 10 August 2002. Copy of Letter from Colonel Bruce, in possession of Naik Mohammad Ghazizuay.

36. 'Confidential Mohmand Reports 1915-16'.

37. NWFP Provincial Diaries 1915-1937.

38. Khalil *Mujahidin Movement*, p 259.

39. Insubordination in Dir in Political and Secret Papers IOLC L/PS/10/929.

40. 'Haji of Turangzai's Activities' in DC Office Peshawar File 212 Bundle 11 of 1927.

41. The NWFP Provincial Diaries have repeated mentions of congregations of *mullah*s meeting at Hadda or at the Chamarkand base. Dr Ahmed Yousuf, grandson of the Babra Mullah states that the Babra Mullah was first introduced to the Hadda Mullah (who became his *murshid* or teacher) at the Chamarkand base. Interview with Dr Ahmed Yousuf, 14 February 2002.

42. Repeated mentions through NWFP Provincial Diaries and Mohmand Political Diaries 1915-1925.

43. Khyber Political Diaries 1923, Diary 26.5.23 - Mullah Sayyid Akber confers with the Tirah Mullahs on the treatment of British allowance holders.

44. Peshawar Archives Office of Chief Commissioner NWFP (hereafter CC NWFP) file PS 37/3 1927 FRP.

45. According to Saeed Maqsud Shah, grandson of Haji Turangzai and son of Saeed Fazl-e-Wudud Badshah Haji Sahib Turangzai was accompanied by forty men at all times, who would undertake *amr-bil ma'aruf* and *tableegh*

with him as well as forming a personal guard that protected him and carried out his instruction. Interview with Saeed Maqsud Shah, Ziarat Baba Sahib. 13.8.2002.

46. Dr Ahmed Yousuf; Senator Ghulam Nabi Chaknawari

47. Interview Ghulam Mohammad Din 13 August 2002.

48. This decision would be ratified by a tribal *jirga*. The *mullah* would rarely act without the sanction of a relevant *jirga* - to neglect this would be tantamount to a declaration of war.

49. Ghulam Mohammad Din stated that victory was declared in the battle of Gullo Sar Jang when Haji Turangzai's *lashkar* managed to kill four British officers and make off with ammunition and even clothes taken from the bodies of killed or wounded British soldiers. Even the battalion flag was taken and the rich material apportioned between the participant *malik*s.

50. NDC 884 NWFP Provincial Diaries 1915, Diary 1; The Babra Mullah threatens to blacken the faces of Burhan Khel Khassadars.

51. NWFP Provincial Diaries, 1915-1920.

52. Asif, *The Story of Swat*, p. 32.

53. NWFP Provincial Diaries 1915, Diary 9.

54. Asif, *The Story of Swat*, pp. 34-36.

55. NWFP Provincial Diaries 1915, Diary 12.

56. *Whos Who 1914*; Diary 16, 17 April 1915, NWFPPD 1915.

57. Barth, *The Last Wali of Swat*, p. 47.

58. Interview Ghulam Mohammad Din 13 August 2002.

59. Translation of Petition dated 30 December 1920, submitted to Political Agent Khyber by *jirga*s of Qambar Khel, Kamalai, Sepah and Aka Khel Afridis. 'Political and Secret Annual Files 1919–1920'.

60. Memo from Humphrys 1921 in 'Political and Secret Annual Files 1919–1922.'

61. Khyber Political Diaries in DC Office Peshawar 1921.

62. Khyber Political Diaries in DC Office Peshawar 1921 18 June 1921.

63. Khyber Political Diaries in DC Office Peshawar 1921 18 June 1921.

64. Political Diaries Mohmand 1925.

64. Interview with Senator Ghulam Nabi Chaknawari Peshawar 8 February 2002.

25

How Can Pakistan Reduce Infant and Child Mortality Rates? Lessons from other Developing Countries

*Dr. Shafqat Shehzad**

ABSTRACT

This paper explores the determinants of infant and child mortality using aggregate data from the sources of the World Bank for sixty-five developing countries. The objective is to identify the process through which certain developing countries have achieved enormous success in reducing mortality rates despite having lower per capita income than Pakistan. The cross-country comparison estimates various functional forms and tackles the problems of heteroscedasticity and endogeniety. A decomposition analysis shows the relative contribution of various factors responsible for Pakistan's higher than average infant and child mortality rates. The results show that substantial reductions in infant and child mortality rates can be achieved through advancements in female education. Although, there is a causal relationship between income and mortality, the significant impact of income becomes less important than female education when factors are decomposed.

Key words: Infant and child mortality, decomposition analysis, income and education.
JEL Classification: I12

INTRODUCTION AND PROBLEM STATEMENT

The World Development Report (1993, p. 34) examines that

> '...an initial index of child health is infant mortality rate and is taken to be a highly significant predictor of a country's economic performance. Over the past few decades, infant and child mortality fell everywhere in the world but the health outcome varied across countries and regions mainly because of income growth, improvements in medical technology/public health and spread of knowledge.'

Other empirical evidence suggests that the effects of the technological improvements in reducing mortality were most fruitful when accompanied by favorable public policies. While, most developing countries (e.g. Sri Lanka, Zimbabwe, China) managed to control high mortality rates, the situation in Pakistan remains neglected. In Pakistan, unlike many other developing countries, child health record is poor with unacceptably high infant and child mortality rates and this indeed does not represent a good health profile of the country. Pakistan experienced periods of rapid economic growth but was unable to translate this growth into compatible human development, (World Development Report, 1990, p. 180). The problem in Pakistan is confounded by low female literacy rate that is among the lowest in the selected sample of sixty-five developing countries. Although, high infant/child mortality is a result of many complex factors, at aggregate level, detailed evaluation of such factors is not possible due to lack of data availability. Also, the process of development is multi-dimensional and many development-related indicators turn out to be highly collinear. Hence, it is not possible to identify the effects of micro-level health measures across countries. Therefore, to find out major factors responsible for high infant and child mortality rates in Pakistan, the present study relies on aggregate data and explores major factors responsible for poor child health within and across countries.

DATA SOURCES AND DEFINITION OF VARIABLES

To carry out the cross-country comparison, following data sources have been used:

1. World Development Reports: Various published issues.
2. STARS Version 3.0 World Bank Data on Diskette 1995, a) Social Indicators of Development, and b) World Table 1995.
3. World Tables: Various published issues.
4. Human Development Reports: Various published issues.
5. African Development Indicators. United Nations Development Program, The World Bank. 1994–95 1991–92.

Definition of variables used in the models. All data relate to year 1990

Dependent variables
- Infant mortality = Infant mortality rate per thousand live births
- Under five mortality = Under-five mortality rate per thousand live births

Explanatory variables
- GNP = GNP per capita US$
- Adult literacy rate = Adult literacy rate
- Secondary education (total): Percentage of age groups enrolled in secondary education
- Primary education (female): Percentage of age group enrolled in primary education
- Primary education (male): Percentage of age group enrolled in primary education
- Number of doctors per thousand population

Instruments used in the 2SLS
- Urban population = Percentage of total population living in urban areas
- Age dependency ratio
- Education expenditure = Public expenditure on education as a per cent of GNP

Endogenous variable
- Number of doctors per thousand population

Table 2.1: List of Developing Countries in the Study (N = 65)

Algeria	Honduras	Peru
Bangladesh	India	Philippines
Benin	Indonesia	Rwanda
Bolivia	Iran	Senegal
Botswana	Jamaica	Sierra Leone
Burkina Faso	Jordan	Sri Lanka
Burundi	Kenya	Tanzania
Cameroon	Lao PDR	Thailand
Central African Rp.	Lesotho	Togo
Chad	Madagascar	Tunisia
China	Malawi	Turkey
Colombia	Malaysia	Uganda
Congo	Mali	Yemen PDR
Costa Rica	Mauritania	Zambia
Coate d' Ivorie	Morocco	Zimbabwe
Dominican Rp.	Mozambique	
Egypt	Namibia	
El Salvador	Nepal	
Ethiopia	Nicaragua	
Ecuador	Niger	
Gambia	Nigeria	
Ghana	Pakistan	
Guatemala	Panama	
Guinea	Papua New Guinea	
Guinea Bissau	Paraguay	

Source: Human Development Report (1993).

Table 2.2: Summary Descriptive of Selected Developing Countries (1990)

Variables	Mean	St. Dev	Minimum	Maximum	Number
Infant mortality	84.86	38.55	16.00 (Jamaica)	173.00 (Mozambique)	65
Under five mortality	134.82	70.65	20.00 (Jamaica)	297.00 (Mozambique)	65
GNP per capita	743.23	606.10	80.00 (Mozambique)	2490.00 (Iran)	65
Adult literacy rate	58.57	22.03	18.20 (Burkina Faso)	98.40 (Jamaica)	65
Female primary enrolment	76.05	29.85	17.00 (Mali)	129.00 (China)	58
Male primary enrolment	88.98	25.58	30.00 (Mali)	134.00 (Togo)	48
Secondary enrolment (total)	30.53	20.59	4.00 (Malawi)	82.00 (Egypt)	58
Doctors/1000 population	0.30	0.36	0.01 (Nigeria)	1.37 (China)	64
Age dependency ratio	0.86	0.13	0.50 (China)	1.10 (Kenya)	65
Education expenditure	4.25	2.00	1.10 Lao PDR	10.60 Zimbabwe	50
Urban population as per cent of total	36.10	16.42	6.00 (Burundi)	70.00 (Columbia)	63

Source: World Bank Data.

Table 2.3: Pakistan's Position Against the Average of Selected Countries

Variables	Mean	Pakistan's position	Difference from Mean[1]
Infant mortality	84.86	104	19.14
Under five mortality	134.82	158	23.18
GNP per ccapita	743.23	400	-343.23
Adult literacy rate	58.57	34.80	-23.77
Female primary enrolment	76.05	26.00	-50.05
Male primary enrolment	88.98	59.00	-29.98
Secondary enrolment (total)	30.53	22.00	-8.53
Doctors/1000 population	0.30	0.34	0.04
Education expenditure	4.25	3.40	-0.85
Urban population	36.10	332.00	-4.1

Source: World Bank Data.

Table 2.4: Ranks by GNP for Infant Mortality, Under 5 Mortality and Literacy Rates

Country	GNP(PC)	Rank	IMR	Rank	U5MR	Rank	Literacy	Rank
Mozambique	80	1	173	54	297	59	32.90	10
Tanzania	110	2	102	37	170	40	65.00	37
Ethiopia	120	3	130	46	220	50	66.00	39
Nepal	180	4	123	44	189	45	25.60	5
Chad	180	4	127	45	216	49	29.80	8
Guinea Bissau	180	4	146	51	246	55	36.50	14
Uganda	180	4	99	34	164	37	48.30	22
Malawi	200	5	144	50	253	56	47.00	20
Lao PDR	200	5	104	39	152	34	54.00	31
Bangladesh	210	6	114	40	180	42	35.30	13
Burundi	210	6	115	41	192	46	50.00	25
Madagascar	230	7	115	41	176	41	80.20	51
Sierra Leone	250	8	149	52	257	57	20.70	2
Mali	280	9	164	53	284	58	32.00	9
Nigeria	290	10	101	36	167	38	50.70	27
Niger	310	11	130	46	221	51	28.40	7
Rwanda	310	11	117	42	198	47	50.20	26
Burkina Faso	330	12	133	47	228	52	18.20	1
Gambia	340	13	138	48	238	54	27.20	6
Benin	360	14	88	29	147	32	23.40	3
India	360	14	94	32	142	31	48.20	21
Kenya	370	15	68	20	108	23	69.00	41
China	370	15	30	5	42	7	73.30	45
Cent. African Rp	390	16	100	35	169	39	37.70	15
Ghana	390	17	86	28	140	30	60.30	36
Pakistan	**400**	**18**	**104**	**39**	**158**	**35**	**34.80**	**12**
Togo	410	19	90	30	147	32	43.30	19
Zambia	420	20	76	30	122	31	72.80	42
Nicaragua	420	20	56	13	78	14	81.00	53
Guinea	440	21	140	49	237	53	24.00	4
Sri Lanka	470	22	26	4	35	6	88.40	60
Mauritania	500	23	122	43	214	48	34.00	11
Yemen Rp	540	24	114	40	187	44	38.60	17
Lesotho	540	24	95	33	129	28	78.00	48
Indonesia	560	25	71	23	97	21	81.60	54
Egypt	610	26	61	17	85	18	48.40	23
Bolivia	630	27	102	38	160	36	77.50	47
Honduras	640	28	63	19	84	17	73.10	44
Zimbabwe	650	29	61	18	87	19	66.90	40
Senegal	710	30	84	27	185	43	38.30	16
Philippines	730	31	43	9	69	13	89.70	61
Cote d' Ivoire	750	32	92	31	136	29	53.80	29
Dominican Rp	830	33	61	18	78	14	83.30	55
Papua new Guinea	850	34	56	14	80	15	52.00	28
Guatemala	910	35	54	12	94	20	55.10	33
Cameroon	960	36	90	30	148	33	54.10	32
Ecuador	960	36	60	16	83	16	85.80	57
Morocco	970	37	75	24	112	25	49.50	24

Congo	1000	38	69	21	110	24	86.60	34
El Salvador	1000	38	59	15	87	19	73.00	43
Peru	1020	39	82	26	116	26	85.10	56
Namibia	1080	40	102	38	167	38	40.00	18
Paraguay	1090	41	41	8	60	11	90.10	62
Colombia	1260	42	39	6	50	8	86.70	58
Jordan	1340	43	40	7	52	9	80.10	50
Thailand	1420	44	26	4	34	5	93.00	64
Tunisia	1450	45	48	11	62	12	65.30	38
Jamaica	1500	46	16	1	20	1	98.40	65
Turkey	1640	47	69	21	80	15	80.70	52
Panama	1900	48	22	3	31	4	88.10	59
Costa Rica	1900	48	18	2	22	2	92.80	63
Botswana	2230	49	63	19	85	18	73.60	46
Algeria	2330	50	68	20	98	22	87.40	35
Malaysia	2330	50	22	3	29	3	78.40	49
Iran	2490*	51	46	10	59	10	54.00	30

Source: World Bank Data. * Iran's GNP per capita shows last minute revision from GNP per capita
$2450 (See: World Development Report (1992)).

METHOD

While carrying out cross-country comparison, the very first problem relates to an appropriate representation of health status. Empirical studies show that at the macro-level, infant and child mortality rates represent the aggregate measures of the initial index of child health. To explore the effects of certain socio-economic and health-related factors on infant and child mortality rates, the following questions have been explored: 1) What is the role of education (especially that of females) in affecting health? 2) Does increase in income result in substantial decrease in mortality rates? 3) What is the process that determines good health status of children across countries? The study uses data from the World Bank for sixty five developing countries. The data represent trends and major differences across countries at a point in time but takes no measures to correct any prevailing differences.

Economic literature suggests that the relationship between infant/child mortality and per capita income may not be linear. For example, Hicks and Streeten (1979) examine that as income increases, the standard of living increases less and less steeply until it reaches an asymptotic limit. A Non-linear relationship capturing the asymptotic nature of these variables has also been estimated by Rodgers (1979). He used a number of different specifications for income variable (national income per head) including reciprocal, reciprocal quadratic and reciprocal logarithm. His results show that the income variable is a highly significant predictor of infant mortality. Kakwani (1993, p. 323) estimated various functional forms to see the relationship between infant mortality and GDP per capita. His estimation of functional forms gave peculiar results (the parameter a in the equation explaining infant mortality rate by means of logarithm of per capita GDP was negative and also there was a sharp discrepancy for maximum value of life expectancy for different functional forms. Because of these peculiar results, Kakwani dropped different functional forms and alternatively related an achievement index to the level of economic welfare. His results showed that economic welfare had a positive and highly significant effect on improving the living standards.

To estimate the relationship between infant/child mortality and income at the aggregate level, the present study estimates different functional forms as suggested by Rodgers (1979,

p. 348). To take care of the asymptotic nature of the health-related indicators, the following equations are estimated with the help of OLS.

$$CHs = \alpha + \beta (1/GNP) + error \qquad (a)$$
$$CHs = \alpha + \beta (1/GNP) + \beta_2 (1/GNP^{2)}) + error \qquad (b)$$
$$CHs = \alpha + \beta (1/\log GNP) + error \qquad (c)$$

To calculate the elasticity of infant and child mortality with respect to income, a double-log functional form has been estimated. The advantage of this functional form is that slope coefficients give the respective elasticity estimates. Anand and Ravallion (1993) obtain elasticity estimates of infant mortality with respect to GDP per capita and public health spending by using a double-log functional form. To find out the relative responsiveness of mortality rates with respect to per capita GNP, the following equations are estimated:

$$\text{Log } CHs = \alpha + \beta \text{ Log } (GNP) + error \qquad (d)$$

In functional form (d), the dependent variables are log of infant and child mortality rates. Two other variables (in log form) are added to equation d and these are literacy rate and medical facilities. The functional forms (a-c) postulate that infant and child mortality fall as GNP increases and the relationship is asymptotic in nature. In these specifications, the useful transformations of non-linear into linear function are (reciprocal) of GNP, GNP^2 and log of GNP. The advantage of double-log functional form as in (d) is that slope parameters present elasticity estimates and estimation by OLS result in unbiased estimates of bs. Besides exploring the specific income-mortality relationship, the impact of various other socio-economic variables is evaluated. This has been done by adding education and health-related variables in the bivariate regression models. The following models are estimated.[2]

$$CHs = \alpha + \beta_1 (1/GNP) + \beta_2 \text{ F\_prim} + \beta_3 \text{ M\_prim} + \beta_4 \text{ Sec\_tot} + \beta_5 \text{ Doc} + ei \qquad (e)$$
$$CHs = \alpha + \beta_1 (1/GNP) + \beta_2 (1/GNP2) + \beta_3 \text{ F\_prim} + \beta_4 \text{M\_prim} + \beta_5 \text{ Sec\_tot} + \beta_6 \text{ Doc} + ei \qquad (f)$$
$$CHs = \alpha + \beta_1 (1/\log GNP) + \beta_2 \text{ F\_prim} + \beta_3 \text{M\_prim} + \beta_4 \text{ Sec\_tot} + \beta_5 \text{ Doc} + ei \qquad (g)$$
$$\text{Log } CHs = \alpha + \beta_1 \log GNP + \beta_2 \text{ Log F\_prim} + \beta_3 \text{ Log M\_prim} + \beta_4 \text{ Log Sec\_tot} + \beta_5 \text{ Log Doc} + ei \qquad (h)$$

The method of ordinary least squares (OLS) assumes that the variance of the error term is constant for all values of the explanatory variables, e.g. $E(ui)^2 = \sigma^2 u$. This assumption ensures that each observation in the sample is equally reliable. However, for a cross-country comparison, this assumption seems doubtful. If violated, heteroscedasticity results in unbiased but inefficient (larger than minimum variance) estimates of standard errors and thus incorrect statistical tests and inference. To test for heteroscedasticity, the Goldfeld-Quandt (1965) test has been applied.[3] The test assumes that observations in a sample can be divided into two groups. Data are arranged from small to large values of the independent variable(s). As a second step, one-fifth of the central observations (c = central observations) are omitted and the remaining observations are divided into two groups of (N - c)/2 observations.[4] After omitting the central observations, separate OLS regressions are estimated for the first and last (N-c)/2 observations. The Goldfeld-Quandt test shows that the ratio of the error sum of squares (ESS) of the second to the first regression is significantly different from zero and the values are then referred to the F table with (N-c-2k)/2 degrees of freedom. Here N is the total number of observations, c is the number of omitted observations and k is the number of estimated parameters. Under the hypothesis of homoscedasticity, the disturbance variances shall be the same in the two groups and under the alternative; the disturbance variances shall differ significantly. The test statistic is $F(N_1-k, N_2-k) = ESS_2/ESS_1$. The sample values referred to in the F table show that a large value rejects the null hypothesis. Gujrati (1988, p. 334) examines that if there are more than one explanatory variables in the model, ranking of observations can be according to any one of the explanatory variables. OLS tests the hypotheses about the specific relationships between mortality and socio-economic variables.

To test the statistical significance of regression parameters, null hypothesis is 'the parameters of regression are equal to zero against the alternative that they are not equal to zero'. The study uses bivariate and multiple regression models to explore factors affecting infant and child mortality across developing countries. The goodness of fit in the models is represented by R^2.[5] In a multiple regression, inclusion of each additional independent variable is likely to increase residual sum of square (RSS) for the same $\sum yi^2$ that increases R^2. As each additional variable is added, there is a reduction in the degrees of freedom, see Gujrati (1988). For this reason the adjusted R^2 or $\overline{R^2}$ is calculated.[6] $\overline{R^2}$ is useful to compare regressions as it shows that increase in R^2 is not solely due to extra explanatory variables. The overall significance of the regression is tested by the ratio of explained to the unexplained variance as is given by the F distribution.[7] Judge et al. (1985, p. 864) show that R^2 and $\overline{R^2}$ do not include a consideration of the losses associated with choosing an incorrect model. Therefore, to avoid this problem, a criterion based on the mean squared errors is used. The test for examining the goodness of fit of the regression models is the Cp test as proposed by Mallows.[8] Judge et al examine that, 'Cp values with small bias tend to cluster where $Cp = K_1$. In using the Cp criterion, the recommended procedure is to obtain a Cp value where Cp is approximately equal to K_1. Cp values less than K_1 have a small prediction error'. The formula for calculating the Cp test has been reported below and SPSS Program calculates the value of the Cp test for bivariate and multiple regressions.

The application of least squares to a single equation assumes that explanatory variables are truly exogenous. Gujrati (1988, p. 75) shows that this means that there is one-way causation between the dependent variable and the explanatory variables. However, if this assumption of independence of explanatory variables is violated, e.g. $E(Xu) \pi 0$, then OLS may lead to biased and inconsistent estimates. Auster et al. (1969) estimate the relationship between mortality, medical care and environmental variables in a regression analysis across different states in the US. Their results show that health status and certain economic indicators may be determined simultaneously, therefore, the usual method of OLS may result in biased estimates of bs. To overcome the problem of simultaneity bias and correlated errors, they use two stage least squares method. A production function for medical services is specified in which medical services are produced with the help of inputs such as per capita number of physicians, paramedical staff, medical capital, drug expenditure, practising physicians and medical school.

Auster et al (1969) employ a number of instruments in the two stage least squares[9] and treat medical facilities as endogenously determined within the system.[10] Grossman (1972, p. 43) examines that the health production function may be subject to simultaneous equation bias because certain health inputs (e.g. medical-care) are correlated with the disturbance term.

To deal with the problem of endogeniety of health inputs, the study uses 2SLS, see illustrations in Gujrati (1988, pp. 603–620), Greene (1993, pp. 603–609), and Koutsoyiannis (1977, pp. 384–390). Two stage least squares involves application of OLS in two stages.[11]

In the first stage, the endogenous variable is regressed on the predetermined variables (the reduced form equation). In the second stage, predicted rather than actual values are used to estimate the structural equations of the model. The predicted values are obtained by substituting the observed values of exogenous variables in the reduced-form equations and are assumed to be uncorrelated with the error term. Thus, consistent 2SLS structural parameter estimates are obtained. The formulas for estimated coefficients in 2SLS and their standard errors are given below from the above-mentioned references: Let Z be the matrix of values of the instruments. Y is the dependent variable and X represents independent variables. The coefficients and variance-covariance matrix are stated as

$$b = [X/Z \ (Z/Z)^{-1} Z/X]^{-1} X/Z \ (Z'Z'^{-1} Z/Y$$
$$V(b) = S^2 \ [X/Z \ (Z/Z)^{-1} Z/X]^{-1}$$

If the number of instruments Z is equal to the number of explanatory variables X, the classical instrumental variable estimator results: $\beta = [Z/X]^{-1} Z/y$. This follows from formula for β because four innermost matrices cancel each other.

$$[X/Z \ (Z/Z)^{-1} Z/X]^{-1} = (Z/X)^{-1} (Z/Z) (X/Z)^{-1}$$

In 2SLS, the sum of squared residuals is obtained after projection onto the instruments and is called the projection matrix.

$$For \ e'P_z e, \ P_z = Z \ (Z/Z)^{-1} Z/$$

To test for specification error, Hausman Test (1978) has been applied. Hausman tests for measurement errors that occur if the variable assumed to be exogenous in the system is not uncorrelated with the structural disturbances. Greene (1993, pp. 287 & 619) examines that 'under the hypothesis of no measurement error, b (OLS) and b* (instrumental variable) are consistent estimators of b but least squares is efficient and IV estimator is inefficient.' If the hypothesis is false, only b* is consistent. The test examines the difference between b and b*. Under the hypothesis of no measurement error, plim (b - b*)=0, while if there is measurement error, plim will be non-zero.

$$HT = (b - b*)/[V - V*]^{-1} (b - b*) \sim c2 \ [k].$$

The Hausman test is then referred to the chi-squared distribution with number of degrees of freedom equal to the number of elements in β, and V, V* are the variances. However, some empirical studies, for instance Alderman and Garcia (1994, p. 504) show that 'Hausman test often lacks power and may be unable to indicate a significant difference when one exists'. The Hausman test uses instrumental variables for endogenous variables and is therefore sensitive to the choice of instruments.[12] Pritchett and Summers (1996, p. 854) describe a rule for good instruments: the correlation among the instruments should be low so that each instrument provides independent information. They show that the consistency of an IV estimate depends on zero correlation of IV with the error term even when $X/e \neq 0$. If instruments are perfectly correlated with X, this becomes impossible. To obtain powerful instruments for medical care, the present study uses a number of alternative variables that have low correlation with each other. However, at aggregate level, choice has been restricted by data availability.[13]
Before applying the 2SLS method, correlation coefficients have been obtained. Three variables have been chosen that appear to be appropriate candidates for instruments. These are education expenditure, urban population and age dependency ratio. The correlation between education expenditure and urban population is 0.138, for education expenditure and age dependency ratio is 0.079 and for urban population and age dependency is 0.353. Other variables having a high correlation with each other or low explanatory power were dropped.

EMPIRICAL ESTIMATES AND RESULTS

Results in table 4.1 show a significant negative impact of income on infant and child mortality. When a squared term is added to the linear model, infant and child mortality fall and the decline is asymptotic in nature. The results of model 3, table 4.1 need caution, as the intercept term for GNP per capita is negative.[14] A possible explanation could be the bounded nature of a dependent variable that needs be transformed. Also, this negative intercept term emerges only when the regressors are expressed in a reciprocal-log form. Thus, another specification has been estimated that is the double-log functional form. In all models, significance of overall regressions is shown by the value of F statistic that exceeds the table value at the 99 per cent level and hence implies a good model fit. The value of R-squared represents adequate variation in the infant and child mortality rates as explained by the estimated regression equation. Figures 4.1 and 4.2 graphically show the effect of income on infant and child mortality rates. With increase in income, infant and child mortality rates fall but fall less and less steeply, hence implying the asymptotic nature of the relationship. Therefore, it can be argued that income per capita is not the sole predictor of infant/child mortality rates, but certain other factors maybe important as well. The issue has addressed by adding total literacy rate and results are reported in tables 4.2 and 4.3. To explore if Pakistan is an outlier in the sample of sixty-five countries, Pakistan's dummy variable is included in the bivariate model. The results for infant and child mortality are given below:[15]

$$IMR = 54.779*** + 11660.476 \ (1/GNP)*** + 20.069 \ (\text{Pakistan})$$
$$(10.126) \ (7.337) \qquad\qquad (0.696)$$

$$R^2 = 0.466 \quad \bar{R}^2 = 0.449 \quad F = 27.138***$$

For the under-five mortality rate, the results are as follows:

$$U5MR = 79.946*** + 21339.730 \ (1/GNP)*** + 24.703 \ (\text{Pakistan})$$
$$(8.039) \ (7.304) \ (0.466)$$

$$R^2 = 0.463 \quad \bar{R}^2 = 0.446 \quad F = 26.771***$$

Results show that Pakistan is not an outlier in the sample of sixty-five developing countries. The same results appear when a squared term of GNP per capita is added. The results are substantiated by obtaining Cook's distance measure for Pakistan. Cook's measure shows how much the residuals of all countries will change if Pakistan were excluded from the calculations of regression coefficients. In two regressions, the value of Cook's distance measure for IMR for Pakistan is 0.00382 against the mean of 0.02. For child mortality, the Cook's distance measure for Pakistan is 0.0017 against the average of 0.06. The results therefore, suggest that although Pakistan is not an outlier, it is Pakistan's above-average infant and child mortality rates that are a cause of concern.

Table 4.2 and 4.3 gives estimates of literacy rate on mortality. The effect of literacy in affecting infant/child mortality is highly significant and negative. This means that literacy is an important factor in reducing infant/child mortality across countries. The spread of literacy is associated with enhanced understanding of health-related activities that can reduce mortality. The effect of income in reducing mortality works through ability to purchase more health-related services for children. Also, increase in income can reduce age-dependency burden of families and results in better health outcome. However, results need to be interpreted with caution as mortality may vary with the overall development of a country. For very low-income countries, increase in money income is associated with greater purchases of health and nutrition-related activities.

Table 4.1: Bivariate Regressions, Infant Mortality Rate (1990)

Variables	Model 1	Model 2	Model 3
Constant	55.096***	38.234***	-127.963***
	(10.263)	(5.437)	(5.391)
1/GNP per capita	11657.00***	23996.374***	–
	(7.365)	(6.176)	
1/(GNP per capita)^2	–	1273163.527***	–
		(3.428)	
1/Log GNP per capita	–	–	1316.694***
			(9.047)
R squared	0.462	0.548	0.565
Adjusted R squared	0.454	0.533	0.558
Cp	2.00	3.00	2.00
F value	54.238***	37.624***	81.846***
df	1	2	1
Number	65	65	65

Note: Figures in the parentheses are t values. *** represents significant at 99 per cent,** at 95 per cent.

Table 4.2: Bivariate Regressions: Under Five Mortality Rate (1990)

Variables	Model 1	Model 2	Model 3
Constant	80.337***	49.837***	-254.850***
	(8.158)	(3.879)	(5.852)
1/GNP per capita	21335.658***	43654.629***	–
	(7.348)	(6.109)	
1/(GNP per capita)^2	–	-2302879.258***	–
		(3.372)	–
1/Log GNP per capita	–	–	2410.764***
			(9.029)
R squared	0.461	0.544	0.564
Adjusted R squared	0.452	0.530	0.557
Cp	2.00	3.00	2.00
F value	53.996***	37.125***	81.530***
df	1	2	1
Number	65	65	65

Note: Figures in the parentheses are t values. *** represents significant at 99 per cent,** at 95 per cent.

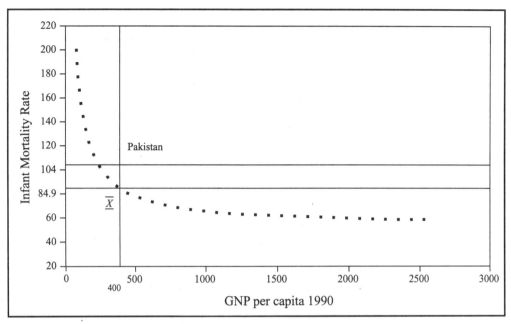

FIG. 4.1: EFFECT OF GNP PER CAPITA ON INFANT MORTALITY RATE (1990)

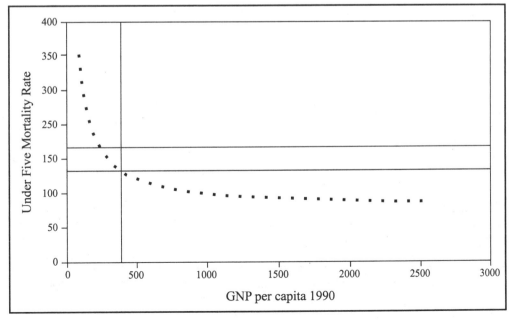

FIG. 4.2: EFFECT OF GNP PER CAPITA ON UNDER FIVE MORETALITY RATE (1990)

Table 4.3: Multiple Regression for Infant Mortality The Effect of Literacy

Variables	Model 1	Model 2	Model 3
Constant	127.286***	115.297***	3.376
	(14.050)	(10.239)	(0.139)
1/GNP per capita	786.035***	12534.764***	–
	(6.270)	(3.949)	
1/(GNP per capita)^2	–	-498353.515*	–
		(1.742)	
1/Log GNP per capita	–	–	842.343***
			(6.895)
Adult literacy rate	-1.046***	-0.0968***	-0.933***
	(8.698)	(7.650)	(7.646)
R squared	0.757	0.769	0.776
Adjusted R Squared	0.750	0.758	0.768
Cp	3.00	4.00	3.00
F value	97.086***	67.861***	107.786***
df	2	3	2
Number	65	65	65

Note: Figures in the parentheses are t values. *** represents significant at 99 per cent,** at 95 per cent & * significant at 90 per cent.

Table 4.4: Multiple Regression for Under Five Mortality: The Effect of Literacy

Variables	Model 1	Model 2	Model 3
Constant	218.410***	199.116***	-1.046
	(13.903)	(10.162)	(0.025)
1/GNPper capita	13166.580***	21452.434***	–
	(6.445)	(3.884)	
1/(GNP per capita)^2	–	-802000.767*	–
		(1.612)	
1/Log GNP per capita	–	–	1494.119***
			(7.040)
Adult literacy rate	-2.001***	-1.875***	-1.803***
	(9.594)	(8.516)	(8.506)
R squared	0.783	0.792	0.798
Adjusted R squared	0.776	0.781	0.792
Cp	3.00	4.00	3.00
F	112.033***	77.478***	123.118***
df	2	3	2
Number	65	65	65

Note: Figures in the parentheses are t values. *** represents significant at 99 per cent,** at 95 per cent & * significant at 90 per cent.

Whereas, for more developed countries, higher income is associated with greater economic opportunities that results in quality health. Anand and Ravallion (1993) explain two competing explanations of human development. The income-centred approach proposes investment in human capital, including health and education. The capabilities approach argues that even if the economic returns on investment in education and health care are zero, being healthy and literate should be taken as ends in themselves. Their results show a significant effect of income and public health expenditure in reducing infant mortality in Sri Lanka (1952–1981).

The present study estimates the relative magnitude of income, education and medical facilities across 65 developing countries. The estimates of double-log function estimated by OLS or infant and child mortality rates are given below.[16] For infant mortality rate, the effect of GNP is as follows:

log (IMR) = 7.372***   - 0.486 Log (GNP per capita)***
   (19.239)   (8.075)
$R^2 = 0.507$ $\overline{R}^2 = 0.499$ $F = 64.913$***

The effect of literacy rate and medical facilities is as follows:

Log (IMR) = 9.799*** - 0.319 Log (GNP)*** - 0.621 Log (Literacy)***
   (21.797)   (5.534) (5.630)
$R^2 = 0.674$ $\overline{R}^2 = 0.663$ $F = 64.122$***

Log (IMR) = 8.184*** - 0.277 Log (GNP)*** - 0.562 Log(Literacy)*** - 0.056 Log (Doctors)
   (13.666) (4.168) (4.799) (1.340)
$R^2 = 0.683$ $\overline{R}^2 = 0.667$ $F = 43.090$***

For the child mortality rates (1990), the following results have been obtained. Three equations are estimated as follows:

Log (U5MR) = 8.357*** - 0.576 Log (GNP)***
 (19.250) (8.425)
$R^2 = 0.529$ $\overline{R}^2 = 0.522$ $F = 70.978$***

Log (U5MR) = 10.096*** - 0.372 Log (GNP)*** - 0.757 Log (Literacy)***
   (23.011) (5.943) (6.311)
$R^2 = 0.713$ $\overline{R}^2 = 0.704$ $F = 77.725$***

Log(U5MR) = 9.159*** - 0.307 Log (GNP)***- 0.669Log(Literacy)*** - 0.086 Log (Doctors)**
                    (14.294) (4.315) (5.340) (1.925)
$R^2 = 0.729$ $\overline{R}^2 = 0.716$ $F = 54.068$***

Pritchett and Summers (1996) show that the long-run income elasticity of infant and child mortality lies between -0.2 and -0.4. Their results suggest that infant and child mortality can be attributed to poor economic performance in the developing countries. Anand and Ravallion (1993) collected data relating to Sri Lanka for infant mortality, public health spending and average income for the period 1952–81. They regressed a non-linear transformation of infant mortality rate over this period and showed that income had a significant negative effect on infant mortality rates and elasticity with respect to income was -0.79. This paper explores the effect of income per capita on infant and child mortality rates in Pakistan. To calculate elasticity estimates of infant and child mortality with respect to GNP per capita, a double-log functional form has been estimated. The results show that for sixty-five developing countries in 1990, elasticity with respect to income is -0.486 for infant mortality and -0.576 for under-five mortality. When literacy is added in the regressions, the effect of income remains significant at 99 per cent level but elasticity estimate declines from -0.486 to -0.319. For child mortality, the effect reduces to -0.372. The results, therefore, confirm that in developing countries, there is a quantitative significance of literacy and education in reducing infant and child mortality.

Table 4.5: Reciprocal linear estimates of infant mortality (1990)

Variables	OLS	2SLS
Constant	126.530***	130.807***
	(8.960)	(7.063)
Female enrolment (primary)	-0.650***	-0.546*
	(2.836)	(1.814)
Male enrolment	0.200	0.152
(primary)	(0.801)	(0.462)
Secondary enrolment	-0.541**	-0.499
(total)	(2.086)	(1.571)
Doctors/1000 population a	-18.731	-42.653**
	(1.517)	(2.102)
1/GNP per capita	4661.934***	3788.045**
	(2.988)	(2.073)
R^2	0.772	0.775
Adjusted R Squared	0.744	0.739
F value	27.470***	21.418***
Cp	6.00	–
Hausman statistic	–	2.142
Number	65	65
df	(5)	(5)

Table 4.6: Reciprocal Logarithm Estimates of Infant Mortality (1990)

Variables	OLS	2SLS
Constant	39.238***	55.337
	(1.152)	(1.305)
Female primary enrolment	-0.598***	-0.502*
	(2.656)	(1.722)
Male primary enrolment	0.168	0.125
	(0.689)	(0.395)
Secondary (total)	-0.453**	-0.444
	(1.753)	(1.423)
Doctors/1000 population a	-17.553	-38.349**
	(1.459)	(1.974)
1/Log GNP per capita	590.339***	505.727***
	(3.421)	(2.466)
R^2	0.783	0.789
Adjusted R Squared	0.757	0.755
F value	29.738***	23.278***
Cp	6.00	–
Hausman statistic	–	1.688
Number df	65 (5)	65(5)

Note: Figures in the parentheses are t values. *** represents significant at 99 per cent,** at 95 per cent and * significant at 90 per cent level. a:Endogenous variable

Table 4.7: Reciprocal Quadratic Estimates of Infant Mortality (1990)

Variables	OLS	2SLS
Constant	117.378***	123.387***
	(7.061)	(5.433)
Female primary enrolment	-0.612***	-0.529*
	(2.640)	(1.737)
Male primary enrolment	0.177	0.152
	(0.706)	(0.459)
Secondary (total)	-0.480**	-0.458
	(1.807)	(1.395)
Doctors/1000 population a	-18.130	-41.597**
	(1.468)	(2.101)
1/GNP per capita	8818.160**	6725.142
	(2.057)	(1.250)
1/(GNP per capita)^2	-364450.83	-244085.298
	(1.041)	(0.581)
R^2	0.777	0.779
Adjusted R Squared	0.744	0.735
F value	23.344***	17.674***
Cp	7.00	–
Hausman statistic	–	2.173
Number	65	65
df	(6)	(6)

Table 4.8: Double-Log Estimates of Infant Mortality (1990)

Variables	OLS	2SLS
Constant	6.064***	4.422***
	(5.350)	(2.737)
Log_Female primary	-0.664***	-0.992***
	(2.412)	(2.301)
Log_Male primary	0.574	0.816
	(1.406)	(1.435)
Log_Secondary (total)	-0.130	0.107
	(1.030)	(0.062)
Log_Doctors (per/1000 pop) a	-.0.101	-0.312***
	(1.649)	(2.706)
Log_GNP per capita	-0.209**	-0.088
	(2.198)	(0.660)
R^2	0.659	0.646
Adjusted R Squared	0.618	0.589
F value	15.908***	11.335***
Cp	6.00	–
Hausman statistic	–	4.125
Number	65	65
df	(5)	(5)

Note: Figures in the parentheses are t values. *** represents significant at 99 per cent,** at 95 per cent and * significant at 90 per cent level. a:Endogenous variable.

Table 4.9: Reciprocal Linear Estimates of Child Mortality (1990)

Variables	OLS	2SLS
Constant	225.526***	235.046***
	(9.549)	(7.716)
Female primary enrolment	-1.181***	-1.090**
	(3.081)	(2.201)
Male primary enrolment	0.234	0.243
	(0.559)	(0.448)
Secondary (total)	-1.064***	-1.082**
	(2.451)	(2.071)
Doctors/1000 population a	-29.962	-63.897*
	(1.450)	(1.914)
1/GNP per capita	7902.231***	6096.632**
	(3.028)	(2.028)
R^2	0.808	0.815
Adjusted R Squared	0.785	0.786
F value	34.707***	27.487***
Cp	6.00	–
Hausman statistic	–	1.693
Number	65	65
df	(5)	(5)

Note: Figures in the parentheses are t values. *** represents significant at 99 per cent,** at 95 per cent and * significant at 90 per cent level. a:Endogenous variable.

Table 4.10: Reciprocal Logarithm Estimates of Child Mortality (1990)

Variables	OLS	2SLS
Constant	79.159	114.176
	(1.387)	(1.630)
Female enrolment	-1.096***	-1.021**
(primary)	(2.904)	(2.117)
Male enrolment	0.181	0.200
(primary)	(0.442)	(0.381)
Secondary enrolment	-0.920**	-0.996*
(total)	(2.123)	(1.932)
Doctors/1000 population a	-27.995	-56.968*
	(1.389)	(1.775)
1/Log GNP per capita	992.041***	810.984**
	(3.431)	(2.395)
R^2	0.818	0.826
Adjusted R Squared	0.796	0.798
F value	36.934***	29.577***
Cp	6.00	–
Hausman statistic	–	1.267
Number	65	65
df	(5)	(5)

Note: Figures in the parentheses are t values. *** represents significant at 99 per cent,** at 95 per cent and * significant at 90 per cent. a:Endogenous variable.

Table 4.11: Reciprocal Quadratic Estimates of Child Mortality (1990)

Variables	OLS	2SLS
Constant	212.456***	226.125***
	(7.614)	(6.015)
Female enrolment	-1.127***	-1.067**
(primary)	(2.896)	(2.117)
Male enrolment	0.200	0.242
(primary)	(0.476)	(0.442)
Secondary enrolment	-0.977**	-1.025*
(total)	(2.190)	(1.887)
Doctors/1000 population a	-29.102	-63.678*
	(1.404)	(1.943)
1/GNP per capita	13837.781**	9583.907
	(1.923)	(1.076)
1/(GNP per capita)^2	-520476.456	-289777.957
	(0.885)	(0.417)
R^2	0.812	0.817
Adjusted R Squared	0.784	0.780
F	28.901***	22.381***
Cp	7.00	–
Hausman statistic	–	1.834
Number	65	65
df	(6)	(6)

Table 4.12: Double-Log Estimates of Child Mortality (1990)

Variables	OLS	2SLS
Constant	6.848***	5.102***
	(5.590)	(2.921)
Log_Female primary	-0.757***	-1.070***
	(2.546)	(2.470)
Log_Male primary	0.627	0.928
	(1.422)	(1.510)
Log_Secondary enrolment	-0.167	-0.026
	(1.219)	(0.140)
Log_Doctors per 1000 pop[a]	-0.126**	-0.342***
	(1.907)	(2.742)
Log_GNP per capita	-0.232***	-0.100
	(2.260)	(0.690)
R^2	0.703	0.684
Adjusted R Squared	0.667	0.633
F	19.458***	13.436***
Cp	6.00	–
Hausman statistic	–	3.577
Number	65	65
df	(5)	(5)

Note: Figures in the parentheses are t values. *** represents significant at 99 per cent,** at 95 per cent and * significant at 90 per cent level. a:Endogenous variable.

Table 4.13: Test for Heteroscedasticity Reciprocal-Linear Estimates of Infant Mortality

Variables	Regression 1	Regression 2
Constant	148.870***	-65.505
	(8.589)	(1.140)
Female enrolment	-0.794***	-1.902***
(primary)	(2.405)	(2.674)
Male enrolment	0.176	2.677***
(primary)	(0.521)	(3.441)
Secondary enrolment	-0.588	0.110
(total)	(1.050)	(0.188)
Doctors/1000 population	-8.658	-22.540
	(0.405)	(1.301)
1/GNP per capita	2595.029	35759.986
	(1.335)	(1.153)
R^2	0.766	0.744
Adjusted R Squared	0.676	0.627
ESS	4626.237	3075.526
F = (65-15-2(5))/2 df	0.664	-
Number &df	25 (5)	25(5)

Table 4.14: Test for Heteroscedasticity: Double-Log Estimates for Infant Mortality

Variables	Regression 1	Regression 2
Constant	6.821***	-7.653
	(5.405)	(1.669)
Log_Female primary)	-0.470*	-4.095***
	(1.800)	(3.009)
Log-Male primary	0.199	6.734***
	(0.561)	(3.600)
Log_Secondary total	-0.06	-0.301
	(0.624)	(0.622)
Log_Doctors/1000 population	-0.081	-0.173
	(1.242)	(0.938)
Log_GNP per capita	-0.215	-0.034
	(1.339)	(0.076)
R^2	0.663	0.729
Adjusted R Squared	0.534	0.606
ESS	0.901	1.543
F = (65-15-2(5))/2 df	1.712	–
Number & df	25(5)	25(5)

Note: Figures in the parentheses are t values. *** represents significant at 99 per cent,** at 95 per cent and * significant at 90 per cent.

Table 4.15: Test for Heteroscedasticity: Reciprocal-Linear Estimates of Child Mortality

Variables	Regression 1	Regression 2
Constant	265.298***	-113.638
	(8.765)	(1.176)
Female enrolment	-1.366***	-2.697***
(primary)	(2.371)	(2.256)
Male enrolment	0.138	3.936***
(primary)	(0.234)	(3.009)
Secondary enrolment	-1.274	0.139
(total)	(1.302)	(0.142)
Doctors/1000 population	-5.350	-41.017
	(0.143)	(1.408)
1/GNP per capita	4440.108	66225.633
	(1.308)	(1.270)
R^2	0.790	0.731
Adjusted R Squared	0.709	0.609
ESS	14107.216	8694.538
F = (65-15-2(5))/2 df	0.616	–
Number &df	25(5)	25(5)

Note: Figures in the parentheses are t values. *** represents significant at 99 per cent,** at 95 per cent and * significant at 90 per cent.

Table 4.16: Test for Heteroscedasticity: Double-Log Estimates of Child Mortality

Variables	Regression 1	Regression 2
Constant	7.507***	-7.405
	(5.675)	(1.481)
Female enrolment	-0.491*	-4.213***
(primary)	(1.793)	(2.838)
Male enrolment	0.172	6.987***
(primary)	(0.463)	(3.425)
Secondary enrolment	-0.094	-0.290
(total)	(0.803)	(0.549)
Doctors/1000 population	-0.103	-0.221
	(1.509)	(1.098)
Log_GNP per capita	-0.215	-0.125
	(1.277)	(0.255)
R^2	0.708	0.736
Adjusted R Squared	0.596	0.616
ESS	0.990	1.835
F = (65-15-2(5))/2 df	1.853	
Number & df	25(5)	25(5)

Note: Figures in the parentheses are t values. *** represents significant at 99 per cent,** at 95 per cent and * significant at 90 per cent.

The previous results show that the significant effect of medical facilities disappears when literacy is added as an explanatory variable. Thus, suggesting the possibility that education picks up the effect of medical facilities in case of infant mortality. The results in tables 4.5–6 show a significant positive impact of female education in reducing mortality but for male primary education, the effect is positive and insignificant.[17] The possible explanation can be multicollinearity with other education-related variables.

The effect of income on mortality turns out to be asymptotic in nature. This implies that after a certain point, increase in income adds less to its effect on mortality and education-related variables become more important. OLS estimates show a negative effect of medical facilities on mortality rates. When only this variable is included, the effect is significantly negative, but when other variables are added, the effect of medical facilities becomes insignificant. At aggregate level, endogeniety of medical facilities can cause this insignificant effect on mortality. To address this issue, a two-stage estimation procedure is adopted. Number of doctors is expected to be influenced by urban population, age dependency ratio and education expenditure. Therefore, they are used as instruments for doctors.[18]

$$Doctors = 0.739^{***} + 0.012 \, (U\_Pop)^{***} - 0.974 \, (Age\_Dep)^{***} - 0.009 \, (Ed\_Exp)$$
$$(2.499) \, (5.280) \quad (3.263) \, (0.565)$$
$$R^2 = 0.566 \quad \bar{R}^2 = 0.536 \quad F = 19.157^{***}$$

Besides these instruments, other variables used in the 2SLS equation are female primary, male primary, secondary total and GNP as instruments for themselves. Results show that the effect is now more negative and significant as compared to OLS estimates. The two stage least squares provides consistent estimates for the endogenous variable and the value of R^2 is also reasonable. Gujrati (1988, p. 606) shows that in a similar case, value of the endogenous variable is close to the actual value and is less likely to be correlated with the disturbance term. To further test for endogeniety and correlated errors, Hausman Test (1978) has been applied to all models 4.5–4.11. The value of test statistic is low in all models. However, the test does not reject at the 5per cent level that OLS and IV estimates are equal. Results therefore, need to interpreted with caution and may be attributed to weak instruments at the aggregate level. The results are therefore, inconclusive about confirming the hypothesis that 2SLS gives consistent estimates of the endogenous variable.

In cross-country comparison, heteroscedasticity can be another problem. To check this, two separate regressions are run for lower and higher values of GNP. Fifteen middle observations have been omitted to strengthen the explanatory power of the test. The ratio of the error sum of squares of the two regressions (ESS_2/ESS_1) is then tested to see if the ratio of the error sum of squares is significantly different from zero.[19] The F distribution is used for this test with $(N - c - 2K)/2$ degrees of freedom, where $N=65$, $c = 15$ and $K = $ *number of estimated parameters*. The results of Goldfeld-Quandt test are presented for four models.[20] The models test the critical assumption of the regression estimates that the disturbances (ui) have the same variance. If this assumption is not satisfied, unbiasedness and consistency of OLS estimators are not destroyed but estimators do possess minimum variance. The results show that in the present analysis, heteroscedasticity is not a serious problem.

DECOMPOSITION ANALYSIS

This section provides a decomposition analysis to identify the relative contribution of various factors that account for Pakistan's poor performance in child health. The selected indicators are infant and child mortality rates. Table 2.3 shows that in Pakistan, infant/child mortality rates are very high as compared to those prevailing in sixty-five developing countries. The positive difference from mean for infant mortality rate is 19.14 and for child mortality rate it is 23.18. Therefore, a decomposition of these factors is carried out and for bivariate regression of infant mortality can be written as follows:[21]

$$(Y_i - \overline{Y}) = \beta_i^* (X_i - \overline{X}) + \varepsilon_i$$
$$(19.14) = 11657.00 \ (1/400 - 1/743.23) + \varepsilon_i$$
$$(19.14) = 23996.374 \ (1/400 - 1/743.23) - 1273163.527 \ (1/400^2 - 1/743.23^2) + \varepsilon_i$$

For child mortality, this is written as

$$(Y_i - \overline{Y}) = \beta_i^* (X_i - \overline{X}) + \varepsilon_i$$
$$(23.18) = 21335.658 \ (1/400 - 1/743.23) + \varepsilon_i$$
$$(23.18) = 43654.629 \ (1/400 - 1/743.23) - 2302679.258 \ (1/400^2 - 1/743.23^2) + \varepsilon_i$$

A decomposition of bivariate regression analysis shows that income is highly associated with infant/child mortality. Pakistan's low income per capita ($400), as compared to ($743.23) contributes to explaining the positive difference from mean of the selected countries. The results show that the squared term for GNP turns out to be important factor in explaining mortality but is less so than GNP. For k variables, the equation for decomposition can be written as

$$(Y_i - \overline{Y}) = \beta_i^* (X1 - \overline{X}) + \beta 2^* (X2 - \overline{X}) + \beta_3^* (X3 - \overline{X}) + \ldots\ldots + \beta_k^* (Xk - \overline{X}) + \varepsilon_i$$

Table 5.1: Effect of Income on Infant Mortality

Infant mortality	1/GNP per capita	1/GNP^2
19.14	13458	–
19.14	27.704	-5.653

Table 5.2: Effect of Income on Child Mortality

Child mortality	1/GNP per capita	1/GNP^2
23.18	24.632	-
23.18	50.399	-10.225

Table 5.3: Decomposition of Factors on Infant Mortality

Infant Mortality	F_Primary	M_Primary	Secondary total	Doctors	1/GNP	1/GNP^2	1/log GNP
19.14	27.327	-4.557	4.256	-1.070	4.373	–	–
	19.14	26.476	-4.556	3.906	-1.663	7.764	-0.976	-
	19.4	25.125	-3.748	3.787	-1.534	–	–	7.910

Table 5.4: Decomposition of Factors on Child Mortality

Child Mortality	F_Primary	M_Primary	Secondary	Doctors	1/GNP	1/GNP^2	1/log GNP
23.18	55.554	-7.285	9.229	-2.556	7.285	–	–
23.18	53.403	-7.255	8.743	-2.547	11.064	-1.287	–
23.18	51.647	-5.996	8.496	-2.279	–	–	12.685

The first term tells how much of the difference between Y_i and $\overline{Y}$ is due to X_i being different from $\overline{X}$ and this is true for all other terms.[22] The results in tables 5.1 and 5.2 show how much of the positive difference between infant and child mortality rates is explained by male, female primary education secondary education (total), number of doctors/1000 population, GNP per capita, and GNP squared. The clear results are that it is Pakistan's very low female primary school enrolment that is mostly responsible for Pakistan's existing high mortality rates. This is shown by its relative magnitude of effect on infant and child mortality rates. The decomposition analysis enables us to derive what Pakistan's infant/child mortality rates would have been if it had female primary enrolment rate equal to the average of sixty-five countries. For calculations, see tables 2.3, 4.13 and 15 and the following method:

$$(Y_i - \overline{Y}) - \beta_I{}^*(X1 - \overline{X}) = \beta_I{}^*(X1 - \overline{X}) + \beta2^*(X2 - \overline{X}) + \beta_3{}^*(X3 - \overline{X}) + \ldots\ldots$$
$$+ \beta_k{}^*(Xk - \overline{X}) + \varepsilon i - \beta_I{}^*(X1 - \overline{X})$$

$19.14 - 27.327 = -8.187$

$Y_i - 84.86 = -8.187$

$Y_i = 84.86 - 8.187$

$IMR \text{ (Pakistan)} = 76.67$

Pakistan's IMR could have been 76.76 as contrast to 104 if Pakistan had a female primary enrolment rate equal to the average of other countries. The child mortality could have been

$23.18 - 55.555 = -32.375$

$Y_i - 134.82 = -32.375$

$U5MR \text{ (Pakistan)} = 102.44$

Other important factor is Pakistan's low level of GNP per capita but is less important than female education. The main factors responsible for Pakistan's poor child health are low female education and low GNP per capita that mostly explains the effect on infant and child mortality rates.

SUMMARY AND CONCLUSIONS

The study explores the determinants of infant and child mortality across countries in a production of health context. Theoretical background relating to health, Grossman (1972), explains that health is produced with the help of inputs: health inputs are converted into health outcome by some production technology. This study however, also includes the effect of income on child health: effect of income works through increased use of health and medical-care inputs that produce good health. Therefore, the inclusion of income variable suggests that the estimated relationship is hybrid in nature. The effect of education on infant and child mortality is expected to be negative because education increases health productivity. Results show a strong negative effect of female education on mortality rates across countries. The results support Grossman's efficiency hypothesis: more educated parents are able to produce better child health outcome as compared to the less educated. More educated parents are able to prevent deaths by using the available inputs more sensibly or may require fewer health inputs and time effort to produce a better health outcome. The results also support the Chicago-Columbia hypothesis: increase in education increases female productivity in child health production (Becker and Lewis, 1973). Results show a significant negative effect of female education on infant and child mortality rates. More educated mothers are better able to assimilate information on health-related issues that prevents infant and child mortality. The effect of income is also significantly negative. Increase in income results in an increase in purchasing power and parents tend to spend more on health and medical-care facilities. The Pennsylvania School, Behrman et al (1982), asserts that with increase in income, parents are able to invest more in child quality (health and education). Present results lend support to the hypothesis that with increase in income, more infant and child deaths can be prevented through increase in spending on health-related activities or better diet. In health production theory, Grossman (1972) examines that medical-care is an input in producing health. A greater use of medical-care results in better health output or reduced infant and child mortality. In a cross-country, it may be expected that medical facilities across countries are correlated with the disturbance term. However, test of endogeniety turns out to be inconclusive. The value of Hausman test is insignificant although, the effect of medical-facilities turns out to be more negative and significant in the 2SLS. The possible explanation can be the choice of weak instruments that is difficult to overcome due to lack of data availability.

The study presents estimates of elasticity for infant and child mortality rates with respect to income, education and medical facilities. Elasticity of infant mortality with respect to income is -0.486 and -0.576 for child mortality, thus suggesting a strong negative relationship between the two. The results are compatible with other studies, e.g. Anand and Ravallion (1993) and Pritchett and Summers (1996). The decomposition analysis identifies the relative contribution of various factors responsible for Pakistan's poor child health record. Results show that it is Pakistan's low female school enrolment rate that is mostly responsible for high infant and child mortality rates. Pakistan's mortality rates would have been far less if Pakistan had a female primary enrolment rate equal to the average rate prevailing in the selected developing countries. In Pakistan, high mortality rates root in low income, lack of health-care facilities and poor female education. The World Development Report (1993, p. 35) explains that success of public policies for improving child health depends a lot on education because better-educated individuals acquire and use new information more quickly. This acquisition of knowledge helps to explain large differences in child mortality by levels of mother's education in most developing countries. Similarly, traditional demographic transition theory, Bulatao and Lee (1983), found that sustained declines in infant and child mortality preceded the long-term declines in fertility. As child survival prospects increase, parents scale back fertility realising that fewer births are required to achieve a desired family size. This leads to parents' appreciation of the value of education and they tend to substitute quality for quantity of children. Thus, education directly contributes to lowering infant and child mortality because of parents' awareness of disease causation and prevention and increased utilisation of medical services when children are sick. This leads to better survival prospects or child quality in terms of improved health. Results show that if Pakistan plans to reduce mortality rates, the identified routes turn out to be better income, improved female education and health-care facilities. Improvements in health require that families become aware of disease causation (through increased education) and also have the means to act on that information (increased income). Therefore, in Pakistan, success in reducing mortality may depend on expansion of peoples' access to opportunities.

References

ALDERMAN, H; M. Garcia. (1994). 'Food security and health security: Explaining the levels of nutritional status in Pakistan'. *Economic Development and Cultural Change*, 42, No. 3, pp. 485–507.

ANAND, S; M. Ravallion. (1993). 'Human development in poor countries: On the role of private incomes and public services'. *Journal of Economic Perspective*, 7, pp. 133–150.

AUSTER, R., Leveson, I; D. Sarachek. (1969). 'The production of health: An exploratory study'. *The Journal of Human Resources*, 4, No. 4, pp. 411–436.

BARROW, M. (1988) O. Statistics For Economists. Accounting and Business Studies. Longman, London.

BECKER, G. S. and G.H. Lewis. (1973). 'On the interaction between the quantity and quality of children'. *Journal of Political Economy*, Vol. 81, pp. 279–288.

BEHRMAN, J. R; A. B. Deolalikar, (1988). Health and nutrition, In: H; Chenery, T.N Srinivasan, (Eds.), *Handbook of Development Economics*, Amsterdam, North Holland.

BEHRMAN, J. R. and R. Pollak and P. Taubman. (1982). 'Parental preferences and provision of progeny'. *Journal of Political Economy*, Vol. 90, pp. 52 T.N; 73.

BULATAO, R. A; R. L. Lee, (1983). 'Determinants of fertility in the developing countries'. Vol. 1& 2, New York Academic Press. Bureau of Statistics.

GOLDFELD, S; R. Quandt, (1965). 'Some tests for homoscedasticity'. *Journal of the American and Statistical Association*, 60, pp. 539–547.

GREENE, W. H. (1991). LIMDEP, *User's Manual And Reference Guide*. Econteric Software In. New York.

GREENE, W. H. (1993). *Econometric analysis*. (2nd Eds.), Pretence Hall, Englewood Cliffs, NJ.

GROSSMAN, M. (1972). 'The demand for health: A theoretical and empirical investigation'. New York: Columbia University Press, for NBER.

GUJRATI, D. (1988), *'Basic Econometrics*. McGraw-Hill Editions.

HAUSMAN, J. (1978), 'Specifications Tests in Econometrics,' *Econometrica*, 46, pp. 1251–1271.

HICKS, N., P. Streeten, (1979), 'Indicators of Development: The Search for a Basic needs Yardstick,' *World Development*, 7, pp. 567–580.

JUDGE, G.G., W.E Griffiths et al. (1985). 'The Theory and Practice of Econometrics,' *Wiley Series in Probability and Mathematical Statistics*.

KAKWANI, N. (1993), 'Performance in Living Standards: An International Comparison,' *Journal of Development Economics*, issue 41, pp. 307–336.

KOUTSOYIANNIS, A. (1977), *Theory of Econometrics*, second ed., ELBS.

PRITCHETT, L., L.H. Summers, (1996), 'Wealthier is Healthier,' *Journal of Human Resources*, Vol. 4, pp. 841–868.

RODGERS, G. B. (1979), 'Income and inequality as determinants of mortality: An international cross-section analysis,' *Population Studies*, Vol. 33, No. 2, pp. 343–51.

United Nations, Human Development Reports, Oxford University Press.

WAGSTAFF, A. (1986), 'The Demand for Health: Some New Empirical Evidence,' *Journal of Health Economics*, Vol. 5, pp. 195–233.

World Bank, *World Development Reports*, Oxford University Press.

World Bank (1995), *Social Indicators of Development*, Baltimore and London: John Hopkins University Press for the World Bank, pp. xiii, 409.

Notes

1. The values show the difference between Pakistan and mean of the selected countries calculated as ($Y_i - \bar{Y}$).

2. For details of variables, see appendix i.

3. Several other tests are available for testing heteroscedasticity. For details of methods for estimation and description, see: Greene (1993, pp. 392–407) and Gujrati (1988).

4. Gujrati (1988, p. 334) examines that central observations are omitted to sharpen the difference between small and large variance groups. In models having two variables, Monte Carlo experiments done by Goldfeld and Quandt suggest that c is about 8 if the sample is 30 and 16 for a sample of 60. Judge et al (1982) show that c = 4 if N =30 and c = 10 if N =60. The choice is however, arbitrary in practice.

5. The coefficient of determination, R2 is defined as the proportion of total variation in y explained by regression

   of y on x. R2 is unit free, $0 <= R^2 <= 1$. $R^2 = 1 - \dfrac{\sum ei^2}{\sum yi^2}$. Source, Barrow (1988, p. 206).

6. $\bar{R}^2 = 1 - (1 - R^2)\dfrac{n-1}{n-k}$, n number of observations, k= number of estimated parameters, source: Barrow (1988, p. 222).

7. $F_{k-1,\ n-k} = \dfrac{R^2/(k-1)}{(1-R^2)/(n-k)}$ If the calculated F ratio exceeds the table value of F at the specified level of significance and degrees of freedom, the hypothesis is accepted that regression parameters are not all zero and R^2 is different from zero, Source: Barrow (1988, p. 210).

8. For the Mallows Cp test, Cp is expressed in terms of F (k_2, T-k) random variable as

$$CP = \frac{(T - K_1)(1 - \bar{R}_1^2)}{1 - \bar{R}^2} + (2K_1 - T).$$ K_1 is number of variables in the equation considered as against the correct equation that has k variables, (Maddala, 1992, p. 498). For a regression, y = XB +e X=(TxK) matrix of constants of rank K. For further details, see Judge et al. (1985, p. 857).

9. The instruments used in the study include (per centage) of population more than 60 years old, birth rate, foreign born, health expenditure financed by health insurance, health expenditure in state and local government, rural population, population in areas of over one million, ratio of population of 1960 to 1950, total property income and labour force participation rate of females, source: Auster et al (1969, p. 417).

10. In a cross-country comparison, there is a possibility that certain other variables as GNP per capita and secondary enrolments may also be determined within the system. However, the emphasis of the study is on the issue of exploring the health-determining factors and not on how GNP and secondary school enrolments are determined. Also, the estimated models are single equations following Rodgers (1979). The proposed model is not a simultaneous equation model that explores the issue of endogeniety among other variables. Wheeler (1980) for example, estimated a simultaneous equation model of the relationships between life expectancy, GDP, adult literacy rate, calorie availability, population per doctor and nurse. He treated GDP, literacy and calorie intake as endogenous variables. The instruments used in the study were 1960 level of calorie availability, change in enrolment rates, and change in physical capital and labour input. His results showed poor fit of the models and imprecise estimates. The present study does not use simultaneous equation model for exploring the issue of endogeniety in GNP and female literacy rates. The main emphasis is to treat provision of medical facilities as endogenous as has been done in Auster et al. (1969).

11. For estimation procedures, see SPSS Manual and TSP User's Guide Version 4.3. Present study computes Hausman test with the help of TSP Program (1990). The test is pre-programmed in TSP. 2SLS estimates in SPSS and TSP are identical but SPSS does not calculate the Hausman test.

12. Koutsoyiannis (1977, pp. 270–272) show that 'in practice, the method of IV is difficult to apply because of the problem of finding appropriate instruments. There is always a degree of arbitrariness, which affects the estimates, and the choice affects the results. Therefore, the value of the Hausman Test is sensitive to the choice of instruments'.

13. The variables considered to potential instruments that have been tried are direct foreign investment, currency outside banks, total labour force, expenditure on basic social services, aid flow, export of goods and services, population growth rate and long term capital inflow. All these were dropped either because; 1) these were not strongly correlated with the endogenous variables; 2) highly correlated with each other; 3) highly correlated with the exogenous variables in the models.

14. The result is the same as that obtained in Kakwani (1993) where this specification gave the similar results.

15. Figures in parentheses are t values. *** represents significant at 99 per cent level.

16. Note: Figures in the parentheses are t values. *** represents significance of F value at 99 per cent. N=65.

17. The effect of male primary enrolment was negative when only this variable was added with GNP per capita variable.

18. The figures in the parentheses are t values. *** is significant at 99 per cent level.

19. The test for heteroscedasticity was carried out for all specifications results showed no presence of heteroscedasticity, hence the results are not reported.

20. For entire sample results, see tables 4.12-13 for infant mortality and 4.14-15 for child mortality.

21. For calculations, see table 4.1 for infant mortality and table 4.2 for child mortality.

22. For infant mortality see table 4.5-4.7 and for child mortality see tables 4.9 - 4.11.

26

FROM 'THINKING TOO MUCH' TO 'EXTINGUISHING OF THE HEART': THE CASE FOR QUALITATIVE RESEARCH IN SOCIAL AND HEALTH POLICY PLANNING

Dr Eaisha Tareen[*]

ABSTRACT

This paper highlights the need for more qualitative research in all social and health disciplines. Whether the issue under consideration is poverty or family planning, education or health, each can benefit from greater qualitative input, particularly in terms of bridging the research/policy gap. For any kind of sustainable development to be achieved, it is necessary to listen to and understand the narratives of the 'recipients' of the developmental policy.

I will first define the qualitative approach and differentiate it conceptually from the quantitative approach, with brief consideration of the philosophic underpinnings. The methodological and analytical differences of the approaches will also be outlined.

I use the area of mental health as a framework to illustrate the different approaches. I examine some recent quantitative studies on depression in women in Pakistan, particularly with regard to their conclusions and policy implications. I then discuss my own research on women in Lahore, which was a qualitative study of women's perception of social support and their experience of depression. This involved in-depth interviewing of women from different socio-economic backgrounds, who had been clinically diagnosed as being depressed.

Analysis of women's narratives reveals the importance of social and economic factors, as well as cultural norms and expectations in shaping the meaning, nature and experience of support in the context of specific relationships. It also reveals the women's complex and pluralistic conceptualisations of their experience of depression. Women's own explanation of their condition, primarily located in their interpersonal relationships and family concerns, linked by extension to wider social structures and institutions.

Comparison of the policy implications of this study with the previous ones shows how different research approaches to the same issue can have radically different practical implications. This research also raises the issue of the cross-cultural validity of the diagnostic category of depression.

---

[*]Dr Eaisha Tareen is a clinical psychologist based in Colchester, Essex. Her research interests lie primarily in the role of social, cultural and economic factors in mental health and illness. She has a particular interest in the experience and conceptualisation of depression in Pakistani women.

INTROCUTION

The paper addresses the problem of bridging the research/policy gap in the context of qualitative research in social and health policy planning. Whether the issue under consideration is poverty alleviation, family planning or the provision of health and educational services, for any kind of sustainable development to be achieved, it is crucial to listen to the views of the 'recipients' of the developmental policy. Prior even to the formulation of the aims and objectives of a policy, it is advantageous to determine the perspectives and attitudes of those whom the policy is geared towards. The current analysis aims to present the rationale for this. The paper outlines the qualitative approach to research and differentiates it conceptually from the quantitative tradition, giving a brief account of the philosophic underpinnings of both. The domain of mental health research is used as a framework to illustrate the different approaches. The study examines some recent quantitative studies on depression in Pakistan and then compares research on women in Lahore, through a qualitative study of social support and depression in Pakistani women. The implications of the quantitative/qualitative studies are compared to indicate how different research approaches to the same issue can have radically different policy implications.

QUALITATIVE *VERSUS* QUANTITATIVE APPROACH

Quantitative research is based on observations that are converted into discrete units that can be compared to other units by means of statistical analysis. While there may be variations of this, statistical analysis is a basic component of quantitative research. Qualitative research, however, examines people's words and actions in narrative or descriptive ways that represent the situation more closely as experienced by the participants (Maykut and Morehouse, 1994). While qualitative research places emphasis on understanding thorugh looking at people's words, actions and records, quantitative research looks past these words, actions and records to their mathematical significance. These surface differences between the two approaches reflect much deeper differences in philosophic assumptions. Qualitative research is based on a phenomenological position while quantitative research is based on a positivist position. Understanding of research is shaped by these two overarching perspectives—positivism and phenomenology. **Positivism** refers to objective inquiry based on measurable variables and provable propositions. Its focus is on explanation, prediction and proof. **Phenomenology**, on the other hand, aims to understand the *meaning* that events have for the people being researched. There are fundamental differences between the two approaches on questions related to ontology, epistemology, logic and teleology. It is beyond the scope of this paper to deal with these issues. It suffices to say that according to the positivist approach the knower can stand outside of what is to be known and hence true objectivity is possible. For the phenomenologist, the knower cannot be totally separate from what is known, hence the knower and known are interdependent. The ramifications of this are illustrated later. Similarly with regard to the role of values in understanding the world, the positivist holds that values can be suspended in order to understand, but the phenomenologist asserts that values mediate and shape what is understood. The positivist approach looks for causal relationships between events whereas the phenomenological approach holds that events shape each other and multidirectional relationships can be discovered (Lincoln and Guba, 1985).

The Qualitative Posture of 'Indwelling'

Indwelling refers to the posture taken by the qualitative researcher while engaging in research. To indwell means to exist within as an interactive spirit, force or principle. It literally means to live between, and within. Simply stated, it refers to being at one with the people being researched or understanding the person's point of view from an empathic rather than a sympathetic position. The qualitative researcher therefore attempts to gain an understanding of a person or situation that is meaningful for those involved in the research. A basic difference in qualitative and quantitative research relates to the methods and tools used in data collection and analysis. The traditional researcher aims for reliability and objectivity by means of standardised tests and statistical analysis. The qualitative researcher looks to **indwelling** as a posture and to the *human-as-instrument* for the collection and analysis of data (Maykut and Morehouse, 1994). A person, that is, a human-as-instrument, is the only instrument that is flexible enough to capture complexity; subtlety and constantly changing nature of human experience (Lincoln and Guba, 1985) Human beings are too complex to be studied by static uni-dimensional instruments used in traditional research. The human-as-instrument is responsive, adaptable, has knowledge-based experience and can assess the context of a situation. Moreover the human investigator can explore atypical or idiosyncratic responses in ways not possible for an instrument constructed in advance of a study.

RESEARCH IN MENTAL HEALTH

Most research in the area of mental health, being based on the biomedical paradigm, has focussed on and is aimed for objectivity and reliability. Individuals' personal accounts have generally been devalued as 'subjective' or 'biased'. This devaluation tends to be greater if the individuals are women and even greater if they are believed to be mentally ill (Miles, 1988). The concentration on diagnosis and classification of mental disorder and the devaluation of understanding of the 'disordered' in the mental health professions is the result of exclusive adherence to positivism (Ussher, 1992).

However, the objectivity of the scientific method is called into question in the case of psychiatric diagnosis. It has been claimed that all diagnosis is subjective as is evident from the lack of reliability between those doing the diagnosis (Busfield, 1996). Individuals and groups are not neutral variables; rather they are shaped by many forces: historical, social, cultural, economic and political. As these factors are generally ignored by the positivist framework, its assessment can only be partial (Ussher, 1992). It is the qualitative approach that allows access to the 'insider' view, of the individual who is suffering, and facilitates exploration of the contextual forces surrounding the individual.

Depression: Disease or Distress?

Within the extensive arena of mental health, the paper focuses on depression. There are a number of reasons for doing so. Firstly, there has been longstanding controversy over whether depression is a disease which strikes people or an understandable response to an unhappy situation (Grove and Andreason, 1992). The boundary between a 'normal' state of intense unhappiness and 'abnormal symptoms' is not at all well-defined. There may be similar cognitive changes, poor attention and concentration that may lead to impairment of memory, social impairment, work impairment, lack of interest and even biological dysfunction in both situations. However, in major depression, the quality of depressed mood is considered to be not simply a state of sadness, but to include feelings of hopelessness and helplessness. Secondly, whether conceptualised as illness or intense unhappiness, the fact remains that what is described as clinical depression is one of the most frequently diagnosed mental conditions. The statistics about depression clearly identify it as a major public health problem (Greenberg et al, 1993). Western studies indicate that about 6 per cent of the population meet the criteria for major depressive disorder or dysthmia at any time (Scott and Dickey, 2003). In the National Health Service in Britain, the cost of treating depression exceeds the cost of treating both hypertension and diabetes. However the direct health care costs are dwarfed by the indirect costs. Days lost from work owing to depression exceed all other disorders and the economic burden of family members and society is substantial (Broadhead et al, 1990 in Scott and Dickey, 2003). This may account for 60–85 per cent of the total cost of the illness and represents a significant proportion of the gross national product (World Health Organisation, 2001).

The World Bank publication of the global burden of disease (Murray and Lopez, 1996) highlighted the economic impact of depression. It indicated that by the year 2020, depression will be second only to heart disease in terms of worldwide disease burden. The report highlighted that investments in the improvement of health are essential for economic development. However, the assumption of universal validity of the diagnostic category of depression has been criticised. In a review of cross-cultural studies on depression, Marsella (1979, in Leff, 1992) noted that in Malaysia, Borneo, Africa and in many American Indians there were no concepts that represented depression as either a disease, symptom or syndrome. However, this did not preclude the existence of words or phrases that conveyed the experience of sadness. While acknowledging the universality of painful emotions relating to sorrow, the anthropologist Obeyeskere (1985) argues that it is illogical to assume that a constellation of symptoms reflecting this situation is a universal illness just because it is so regarded in western culture. These emotions are viewed in Buddhist culture as arising out of life conditions and inseparable from wider existential issues and are dealt with culturally without recourse to an illness model. Viewing them as illness, according to Fernando (1991) does not benefit the people concerned, rather it benefits imperialism, providing markets for Western products, such as antidepressants and 'experts', and fostering dependency on the West for advances in knowledge and promotion of research. Cross-cultural psychiatric studies of depression (and other mental disorders) have been criticised for their exaggeration of universals and de-emphasis of what is culturally particular (Kleinman, 1987). The assumption that Western diagnostic categories are themselves culture-free entities is viewed by Kleinman as a '**category fallacy**'[1], and is particularly applicable to 'dysthymia' (neurotic depression). This category:

> may hold coherence in the more affluent West, but it represents the medicalisation of social problems in much of the rest of the world (and perhaps the West as well), where severe economic, political and health constraints create endemic feelings of hopelessness and helplessness, where demoralisation and despair are responses to real conditions of chronic deprivation and persistent loss, where powerlessness is not a cognitive distortion but an accurate mapping of one's place in an oppressive social system, and where moral, religious and political configurations of such problems have coherence for the local population but psychiatric categories do not (1987: 452).

It is keeping this background in mind that research studies that have estimated the prevalence of depression in Pakistan will be reviewed. For effective policy planning and service development, it is necessary to gain information about the extent and nature of the problem or issue under consideration.

DEPRESSION IN PAKISTAN

Most of the studies have assessed the prevalence of depression alongside that of anxiety. A recent study, which focused solely on depression, comprised a survey of a general population sample in a Pakistani village (Hussain et al., 2000). Using a variety of questionnaires and schedules they found the prevalence of depression in men to be 25.5 per cent and in women to be 57.5 per cent. The authors suggest that the high prevalence of depressive disorder in Pakistan may be due to the high proportion of population who experience social adversity.

A study conducted at a medical centre in Gilgit in the northern areas of Pakistan, using the Hospital Anxiety and Depression Scale, found that 50 per cent of women attending the centre had anxiety and/or depression (Dodani et al., 2000). A community survey of mountain villages in Chitral, found (on 'conservative estimate') that 46 per cent of women and 15 per cent of men suffered from anxiety and depressive disorders (Mumford et al., 1996). Instruments used were the Bradford Somatic Inventory and psychiatric interviews. Another community survey by Mumford et al. (1997) in a village near Gujar Khan, estimated that 66 per cent of women and 25 per cent of men suffered from anxiety and depression. Again the Bradford Somatic Inventory, a questionnaire and psychiatric interviews were used as assessment tools. The authors concluded that there were high levels of emotional distress and psychiatric morbidity among women in rural areas of Pakistan. More recently the same survey method was used to investigate psychiatric disorders in an urban slum district of Rawalpindi (Mumford et al., 2000). On 'conservative estimates', 25 per cent of women and 10 per cent of men suffered from anxiety and depressive disorders. The authors concluded that levels of emotional distress and psychiatric morbidity in a poor district of Rawalpindi were less than half those in a nearby rural village, although rates in women were still double those in men. They offer the possible explanations that 'more healthy people migrate to the cities or that urban living is more conducive to good mental health in Pakistan'. I leave it to the readers to draw their own conclusions. This brings to mind a quote from an eminent professor in this field,

> ... 'all attempts to measure the prevalence of depressive illness are comparable to attempts to measure the prevalence of stupidity; the answer depends entirely on how stupidity or depression is defined in the first place'. (Kendell, 1988: 342)

The above-mentioned studies can broadly be categorised as based on quantitative research methods, using standardised instruments such as inventories, questionnaires and interview based schedules, all subject to elaborate statistical analysis. It is beyond the scope of this paper to discuss in detail the instruments used and the results and conclusions of individual studies. It suffices to say that they were all developed in a western context, using western concepts and categories, even though some have been translated and 'standardised' for the local population. The inappropriateness of translating psychological concepts derived in one culture for use in a different cultural setting has been discussed by many writers (e.g Obeyeskere, 1985).

Despite the apparently extraordinarily high rates of prevalence, limited attention was given to the reasons for this in the discussion section of the articles. A brief mention of emotional distress being 'negatively correlated with socio-economic variables in women' is all the reader gets, apart from a general mention of stress or disadvantage. The study by Husain et al. (2000) (which was the only one with some qualitative component) did give some breakdown of social adversity:

'multivariate analysis indicated that severe financial and housing difficulties, large number of children and low educational level were particularly closely associated with depression'

But what of the men and women who were the subjects of these studies? What about their thoughts, feelings, experiences, opinions? Where are they situated in the research? Are we to believe that such a large proportion of our population suffers from mental disorder because they scored high on questionnaires and rating scales, which many of them probably saw for the first time in their lives? And if there is such a high prevalence of mental disorder, why is it so? And what can be done about it? What implications does this data have for health policy planning? These are just a few of the many questions thrown out by these studies.

It is the phenomenological approach that facilitates attempts to answer some of these questions using qualitative methods of research. The qualitative researcher tries to gain an understanding of a person or a situation that is meaningful to those involved in the inquiry. He or she tries to experience the world in a similar way to the participants of the research. This understanding can be achieved through indwelling as described earlier. Indwelling requires the investment of sufficient time to learn the culture, test for misinformation introduced by distortion, either of self or of respondents, and to build trust (Maykut and Morehouse, 1994). Quantitative researchers assume that the world can be broken into simpler parts and therefore can be studied by less complex instruments. They assert that a standardised instrument, a pre-designed study, can assess human behaviour (and even emotions) because they view reality as quantifiable, as objective and as divisible into smaller and smaller parts without distorting the phenomenon being studied. The qualitative researcher, however, appreciates that human behaviour and human situations are too complex to be captured by a single instrument or observation. It is only the dynamic human instrument that can do so. He or she recognises the connection between the knower and the known and works with it rather than against it. A person or event can only be understood within the surrounding context or background. The goal of qualitative research is to discover patterns which emerge after close observation, careful documentation and detailed analysis of the research topic. It does not make sweeping generalisations, rather it offers contextual findings that are crucial for social and health policy planning.

Listening to Women's Words

A more recent study has been conducted by Tareen, (2000), that aims at listening to women's views on the nature and quality of social support available to them and its impact upon their experience of depression. The methodology adopted in the paper is qualitative in nature to have better access at a deeper and more meaningful level, to the 'insider' view, of the women who had been diagnosed as depressed. After all, what better way to understand the nature and role of social support in depression than to ask those who are considered to be depressed. However, during the field work, many more factors emerged as more important than relationship support and also questions of the very nature of the diagnostic entity of depression. The research was carried out in Lahore, the capital of the Punjab. Women were contacted through the psychiatric services. In order to reach women from diverse socio-economic backgrounds, psychiatric services from both the government and private sector were accessed. The criteria for inclusion in the study were that the women had been given a diagnosis of depression by a psychiatrist and that they were consulting a psychiatrist for a first or a new episode of depression. The twenty-nine women participants came from very varied socio-economic and educational backgrounds. In-depth interviews were conducted with them, using a semi-structured interview schedule. The following section provides findings in relation to women's experiences and views of their condition in order to illustrate the richness of information that can be gained using a qualitative approach.

Women's Experiences

The experience that was most frequently reported in describing their health was the emotion of sadness, udaasi. Many women viewed this as secondary to other experiences such as pain in some part of the body, or anger or inability to perform household duties normally. The head or the mind was the locus of many other experiences for the women apart from specific pain. These were expressed as 'a burden or load on the head', 'heaviness of the head', 'inability of the mind to work', 'numbness of the head' etc. A 'lack of mental peace' was also expressed, as was 'mental tension'.[2]

The Problem of 'Thinking Too Much'

'Thoughts' or 'thinking too much', ziyada sochna, were explicitly stated by some women as a cause for concern. Often the thoughts were perceived as a problem by other family members, such as husband or parents, rather than the women themselves. Women reported being told that their problems were due to 'thinking too much' and were advised 'not to think'. Saeeda[3] describes trying to explain to her father the difference between her thoughts and ordinary thoughts:

'I said Father, there is one [type of][4] thought that one thinks and it is gone, and there is one [type of] thought that causes me mental suffering.... There is one [type of] thought that becomes a sickness and causes suffering in my mind' (p. 17).[5] When questioned about the nature of their thoughts, some women just briefly described them as 'strange' or 'sad' thoughts, while others said they were about specific worries or conflicts that they had. Thoughts were a major focus in Habiba's presentation of her experience: 'Just thoughts. Too many thoughts come to my mind. Because of this my mind remains pareshan[6] [troubled] and I have headaches.' (p. 3).

She explains how she tries to make herself understand and accept her situation after marriage, but thinking about it makes her feel unwell and angry: 'I try to remain happy in this house, and I do remain happy, but sometimes circumstances are such that something may happen that may be disagreeable. That leads to a little pareshani. That makes me feel unwell. But then I [try to] make my heart understand that 'no, it doesn't matter, this is life and all this happens and this is God's will,' By saying this I reassure myself and after a little while my mind starts to get better, become normal and I feel normal. And if I let the same thing stay on my mind, keep thinking, keep thinking, then I start feeling very unwell. Because of that [I get] angry with the children, angry with my own condition, angry with everybody. And if I explain to my heart that 'no, it is this thing, this is life,' if I keep myself happy in this then

I start feeling better, I start becoming normal' (p. 4) Habiba talks of 'making the heart understand' and 'explaining to the heart', which then influences the mind. The intricate connection between the mind and the heart was also referred to by other women. Baby described her experience at her niece's wedding in the following terms: 'I was sitting there like a lost person. I sat there silently. A sadness... [the] mind heavy, [the] heart as if extinguished' (p. 3).

Other Experiences

Pareshani, which can be conceived of as an amalgam of distress, confusion and trouble, was a commonly experienced phenomenon. Another frequently expressed experience was *ghabrahat*. While this is generally translated as 'confusion' or 'bewilderment', in common parlance it has more emotional overtones. As expressed by the women, *ghabrahat* had connotations of restlessness, anxiety and an overall lack of peace and calm. Apart from pain other described physical experiences included muscle tension, weakness, dizziness, lack of sleep and appetite. The description of weakness was often accompanied by the expression, 'as if the body has no life in it'. Feelings of loneliness and tearfulness were expressed by some of the women. Anger was a less frequently expressed emotion, and was viewed as undesirable. Maqbool, for example, perceived her anger as needing 'treatment' as a lot of anger rose up or 'came' to her (p. 10). Feelings of being trapped were also expressed by a few women, while at least five clearly voiced the wish to escape from their present situation. According to Zainab: 'When there is that load on my mind, my heart is so confused, I feel such restlessness. Sometimes I go upstairs, sometimes down. Just like in a cage if you trap something then it flutters' (p. 7).

These descriptions of experiences are only possible when women are given the opportunity to express themselves in their own words. When asked to tick boxes on a questionnaire, with predetermined categories of 'headache', 'poor sleep' etc., women's words are eliminated, as is the context in which the 'symptom' occurs. It is this context which needs to be taken into account if any meaningful understanding of the women's condition is to be achieved.

Women's Views

This section briefly outlines women's own views regarding the causes of their condition or the factors contributing to it. These are mostly located in the interpersonal and family arena and comprise of matters related to immediate relatives. They are also linked, by extension, to broader social institutions and cultural norms and expectations regarding the roles and relationships of family members. The factors identified by the women can be broadly categorised as worries related to daughters and sons, family disputes and interpersonal problems, illness of relatives, death of a relative and physical illness. The primary worry of women with single daughters related to their marriages, which involved both the problem of finding suitable proposals and also financing the marriage. The following quote from Amina exemplifies these concerns: 'Seven daughters. It [the worry] is about their marriages, where [to whom] will they be. We search here and there. My husband is a heart patient. If anything happens to him—I think about him that if anything happens to him then what will happen. This worry mostly stays with me. There are so many girls. If anything happens to him then what will happen. Who will ask about us? What will happen? How will I do everything?'

(p. 7) Women who had sons were mainly concerned about their academic problems and employment issues. After issues related to sons and daughters, the next most frequently reported contributory factor was that of family disputes and interpersonal problems. For some the disputes were related to property or other financial matters, while for others, they comprised interpersonal conflicts or problems involving immediate relatives that they perceived as their own, as the whole family became involved. While many women voiced concerns about the health of relatives, some perceived the ill health of relatives, particularly the husband, to have a significant impact on their own condition. Serious or life-threatening illness of the husband, apart from constituting a threat of the loss of a significant other, also needs to be viewed in terms of its wider ramifications. A wife's identity is generally dependent upon her husband, as is her economic and material provision. Hence his serious illness implies a threat to her own identity, a threat to family life and family structure and standard of living, a threat to her status in the extended family and the society at large, and, consequently, a threat to self-esteem. The death of a close relative was also viewed as a causative factor. Although marital strain was reported by some women, a couple of the more articulate ones, regarded marital conflict as a specific cause of their condition. Aayesha, referring to her husband, said: 'He's the one who landed me in this situation' (p. 29) Similar feelings were expressed by Shamaila: 'This person is going to drive me mad' (p. 11).

Habiba viewed her feelings of sadness as being caused by the circumstances of her life, including a 'tight' financial situation. The nature of 'thoughts' that she had also troubled her and led to her feeling 'unwell'. However she attributed her overall condition to supernatural forces, as did her family. Although many women discussed the economic hardships they faced, they regarded them as cause for pareshani, rather than illness. While some described the difficulties they experienced in meeting household expenses, others focussed on pressures related to financing daughters' marriages. Zainab, for example, perceived her overall socio-economic situation as a source of sadness and worry: 'Look here, our financial circumstances are not so good, there are so many girls, two sons, five daughters. Then there are so many worries. I am ill also. One thinks what will happen to them after I have gone [died]. Of course God is the master of everybody, but one does think of such things.' (p. 11) Physical causes, either in terms of own physical illness or some external stimulus, were also viewed by some as contributory factors alongside others. Many women understood their condition in terms of multiple causative or contributory factors. Many other women differentiated the causes of sadness or depression from those of illness, which indicates that sadness was not perceived as illness.

Life Events and Chronic Difficulties

The importance of interpersonal, familial and other social factors, both in women's views and in their overall life situation is substantiated by the high prevalence of life events and chronic strains in the previous year. Almost all the women reported the occurrence of one or more adverse life events and/or the presence of long-term ongoing difficulties. All the events involved some kind of loss or threat of loss. The deaths of close relatives (mother, father, sister and brother) and of a friend comprised major losses due to the closeness of the women's relationship with them, and also constituted loss of a significant support figure. The illness of a close relative also connoted the threat of loss. In case of prolonged illness, it had become a chronic strain rather than a discrete event. For women who had suffered serious physical illness themselves, it had become a chronic problem. For some women life events and ongoing difficulties related to the marriages of daughters and sons. Although marriage is viewed as a positive event, it also connotes loss for the girl's family as she moves away to her new family. Problems related to arranging and financing daughters' marriages were major ongoing issues for some women as discussed earlier.

Although many women from the lower-middle socio-economic group mentioned various financial problems, approximately half experienced major economic difficulties, which in turn linked to other stresses, such as poor physical health, inadequate housing or even the inability to effectively fulfil the family's basic physical needs. Two women, a young separated woman and a widow, faced the severe social rejection and stigmatisation that are often experienced by women of little means living alone. Both were highly critical of society's harsh treatment of women, and deplored the 'petty-minded' and exploitative attitude of people towards women on their own. Two other women, a widow and a divorcee did not face similar difficulties because they had close male relatives with whom they lived and who provided economic support. Other long-term difficulties such as marital conflict and family disputes have been mentioned earlier.

Distressed or Depressed?

All the women participants of this research were experiencing significant emotional distress. For the majority this distress was clearly linked to their life situation, either to a major loss or other adverse life event or to chronic stresses and strains. In the case of a few the cause of their distress was less clear, in-depth inquiry revealing a generalised dissatisfaction with their life. For the first group the diagnosis of depression appeared to represent the medicalisation of life problems. They talked about themselves, their experiences, the issues and challenges they faced in a 'rational' manner, and did not appear to be 'mentally ill'. Their 'depression' appeared to be an understandable response to stresses in their social environment. The probability that others in a similar position would be likely to show similar responses and have similar experiences casts doubt on the validity of labelling them clinically depressed.

For the women themselves, depression as a category of mental illness held little relevance, apart from those who were educated and more familiar with western concepts. Women from rural and/or uneducated backgrounds were particularly likely to prefer alternate explanations of their condition, such as in terms of ailment or supernatural influences. While some rejected the possibility of their being ill, others in the face of medical expert advice conceded it, at the same time stating that they did not understand it. Although women themselves tried to explain their condition in terms of wider interpersonal and social factors, the experts tried to convince them that the problem was located in their mind. Many women were experiencing severe and prolonged emotional distress, and their condition may be termed depression, if this is viewed as an extension of distress, and assumptions of individual biological pathology are rejected. This research indicates that depression needs to be understood as a primarily social condition.

It is unfortunate that psychiatric classifications cover such a diversity of experiences, labelling them as 'symptoms' of mental illness. The problem is much greater in non-Western countries, where classificatory symptoms have been imported from the West but are used with little consideration of cultural variability and validity and limited checks on reliability. Very different conditions, therefore, may all be categorised as 'depression'. A condition that is primarily social needs to be clearly distinguished from one in which biological features predominate for effective management to be possible.

Implications of Different Research Approaches for Policy Planning

It is apparent that the different research approaches described in this paper will have varied implications for policy planning. Before looking at the wider implications it may be useful to consider micro-level implications, i.e. at the level of the mental health practitioner. The qualitative study highlights the necessity of listening to the personal accounts of those who are viewed as mentally ill. Clinicians need to listen closely to the words of those who sit before them and hear what they have to say, rather than simply recording various signs and symptoms and allocating a diagnosis, which can become a self-fulfilling entity. Listening to individuals' own words will also alert clinicians to the cultural diversity of conditions and, instead of dismissing them as cultural differences in presentation, will lead to a more critical attitude towards the use of concepts and categories derived from Western models and their unquestioned application in other cultures.

The quantitative researches that were described earlier indicate that a high proportion of the population is mentally ill. The policy implications of this could include extensive provision of psychiatric services all over the country. Psychiatric units in all district hospitals as well as local community psychiatric services would need to be established on an urgent basis. As psychotherapy is both time-consuming and expensive and cannot be provided to all, the need would arise for even more mass production of antidepressants and anxiolytic drugs. As the more commonly prescribed ones are very expensive and people would be unlikely to purchase them, they would have to be subsidised. There would still be great resistance on the part of the general public to take the drugs. The issue of side-effects can be side-stepped for now.

The members of the general public would first need to be convinced that such a high number of them are mentally ill. This would require extensive awareness campaigns involving the mass media and maybe door-to-door methods. Considering the stigma attached to mental illness, this will be an enormous task. One of the quantitative researches concludes that living in an urban slum may be more conducive to mental health than living in a rural village. This has very dramatic implications for policy planning. The whole rural economy may need to be overhauled and the rural structure of the society reconstituted to make way for urbanisation. As well-planned urban cities take time to develop, it may be possible to look at ways for the rapid development of urban slums, which are at least more conducive to mental health than rural villages. Economic and social implications will of course be enormous. Again, to gain acceptance within the general public, mass awareness campaigns will have to be devised. A few of the quantitative studies discussed the social difficulties associated with depression. Financial and housing difficulties were noted and a large number of children and low educational level were found to be associated with depression.

This of course implies raising the standard of living by providing adequate housing, as well as liasing with the population planning and education departments. The qualitative research too has its own set of implications. It underscores the need to assess support networks and examine family ties. If required, strategies may be collaboratively designed to improve support networks. If interpersonal problems are predominant, some form of interpersonal therapy involving relatives may be feasible. The question then arises as to who will do this. Considerations of time and cost are likely to preclude it being the psychiatrist. Whether, in Pakistani society, women would be at ease discussing interpersonal problems with a medical doctor, who is generally viewed as an authority figure, is another question. A non-medical practitioner might be more suitable to offer this or to provide support as well as help in finding solutions to practical problems. For instance, instead of being presented with a prescription for an expensive antidepressant to be taken thrice a day, a woman may be advised to meet her mother at least once a week (or whoever is her primary emotional support figure). This strategy may be more likely to have greater long-term benefits, as well as being more cost effective. Another possibility that could be explored is the formation of community support groups. These could provide women the opportunity to express themselves, develop new networks and/or facilitate the improvement of existing ones. They could also provide a forum through which they could jointly seek solutions to specific problems. The qualitative study highlights the need for mental health professionals to take into account the wider social and economic circumstances of people's lives. There needs to be greater linkage with other government agencies such as social welfare departments (which of course implies greater efficiency and effectiveness in the latter), as well as with voluntary organisations. At a macro-level, policies that work towards achieving a better standard of living need to be implemented. Government (and non-governmental) efforts towards poverty alleviation, family planning, provision of basic health and education services will all eventually contribute to a higher standard of living which in itself will have positive implications for mental health. Implementation of existing policies related to specific social practices that have detrimental social and economic consequences would be a significant contribution e.g. the practice of dowry and the expense incurred at the time of weddings. There also needs to be more in-depth research into the wider structural features of society that impact upon the experience of depression.

SUMMARY:

The contribution of qualitative research in this context is that it provides the opportunity for people to express their opinions about issues that concern them and allows in-depth investigation of a problem or issue. This is of vital importance in policy planning. It is only when the relevant information about an issue is available and the population towards which the policy is geared is consulted and their needs are determined, that an effective policy can be formulated. Quantitative research has its own role to play in this endeavour and its significance is not being denied in this paper. It simply needs to be rooted in the cultural context of the society or group being researched and culturally appropriate methods of investigation need to be devised. Both quantitative and qualitative approaches can be used to address different aspects of the same issue and thereby effectively complement each other. For the development of public policy, the voice of the public needs to be heard.

References

BUSFIELD, Joan, *Men, Women and Madness: Understanding Gender and Mental Disorder*, Macmillan Press Ltd., 1996.

DODANI, S. and R. Zuberi, 'Centre-based Prevalence of Anxiety and Depression in Women of the Northern Areas of Pakistan', *Journal of the Pakistan Medical Association*, 2000, 50(5), pp. 138–40.

FERNANDO, Suman, *Mental Health, Race and Culture*, London: Macmillan Education Ltd., 1991.

GREENBERG, P, L Stiglin, S. Finkelstein, et al, 'The Economic Burden of Depression in 1990,'*Journal of Clinical Psychiatry*, no. 54, 1993, pp. 405–418.

GROVE, William and Nancy Andreason, 'Concepts, Diagnosis and Classification,' *Handbook of Affective Disorders* (Second Edition), Eugene Paykel (ed), Churchill Livingstone, 1992.

HUSAIN, N., F. Creed, B. Tomenson, 'Depression and Social Stress in Pakistan,' *Psychological Medicine*, 30(2), 200, pp. 395–402.

KLEINMAN, Arthur, 'Anthropology and Psychiatry: the Role of Culture in Cross-cultural Research on Illness', *British Journal of Psychiatry*, no. 151, 1987, pp. 447–454.

LEFF, Julian, 'Transcultural Aspects,' *Handbook of Affective Disorders* (Second Edition), Eugene Paykel (ed), Churchill Livingstone, 1992.

LINCOLN, Y. and E. Guba, *Naturalistic Inquiry*, Beverley Hills, CA: Sage, 1985.

MAYKUT, Pamela and Richard Morehouse, *Beginning Qualitative Research: a Philosophic and Practical Guide*, London: The Falmer Press, 1994.

MILES, Agnes, *Women and Mental Illness: the Social Context of Neurosis*, Great Britain: Wheatsheaf Books Ltd., 1988.

MUMFORD, David, Fareed Minhas, Imtiaz Akhtar, Saeed Akhtar, Malik Mubbashar, 'Stress and Psychiatric Disorder in Urban Rawalpindi- Community Survey' *British Journal of Psychiatry*, no. 177, 2000, pp. 557–62.

MUMFORD, David, Khalid Saeed, Imtiaz Ahmed, Shazia Latif, Malik Mubbashar, 'Stress and Psychiatric Disorder in Rural Punjab- A Community Survey,' *British Journal of Psychiatry*, no. 170, 1997, pp. 473–8.

MURRAY, C. and A. Lopez, *The Global Burden of Disease*, Cambridge, MA: Harvard University Press, 1996; Jan Scott, and Barbara Dickey, 'Global Burden of Depression: the Intersection of Culture and Medicine,' *British Journal of Psychiatry*, no. 183, 2003, pp. 92–94.

OBEYESKERE, Gananath, 'Depression, Buddhism, and the Work of Culture in Sri Lanka,', *Culture and Depression*, Arthur Kleinman and Byron Good (eds), Berkeley: University of California Press, 1985.

SCOTT, Jan and Barbara Dickey, 'Global Burden of Depression: the Intersection of Culture and Medicine,' *British Journal of Psychiatry*, no. 183, 2003, pp. 92–94.

TAREEN, Eaisha, *The Perception of Social Support and the Experience of Depression in Pakistani Women*, (PhD thesis), London: British Library, 2000.

USSHER, Jane, 'Science Sexing Psychology: Positivistic Science and Gender bias in Clinical Psychology,', *Gender Issues in Clincal Psychology*, Jane Ussher and Patricia Nicholson (eds), London: Routledge, 1992.

World Health Organization, *The World Health Report 2001: Mental Health, New Understanding, New Hope*, Geneva: World Health Organization, 2001.

Notes

1. This refers to the reification of a nosological category developed for a particular cultural group that is then applied to members of another culture for whom it lacks coherence and validity.
2. Double quotation marks are used for direct quotes from the women.
3. Names in the text are pseudonyms chosen by the women themselves.
4. The text in square brackets refers to my explanation or clarification of what was said.
5. The page number is that of the transcript page.
6. Words that do not have exact English equivalents are kept as originals.

27

THE GLOBALIZATION OF REPRODUCTIVE HEALTH: A DERIVATIVE DISCOURSE?

*Mohan Rao**

ABSTRACT

This article briefly surveys the factors that shaped the emerging discourse of reproductive health, tracing the contradictions and ambiguities that surround this discourse, arguing that reproductive rights, reified, represents a marriage between multinational feminisms and international debt.

*Mohan Rao teaches at the Centre of Social Medicine and Community Health, Jawaharlal Nehru University, New Delhi. He is the author of Malthusian Arithmetic: From Population Control to Reproductive Health (Sage, forthcoming) and has edited Disinvesting in Health: The World Bank's Health Prescriptions (Sage, 2000).

INTRODUCTION

The last two decades of the twentieth century reverberated with intense debates about reproductive health and rights, and indeed wrongs. These debates embraced women's rights activists, public health workers, policy makers, donors and academics. One stream of argument sees all reference to reproductive rights—which it resolutely fights—as undermining the family and the community and is associated with the position of the Vatican, some Islamic countries and, more importantly, the Protestant fundamentalists increasingly setting the agenda in the USA. Another stream, at the opposite end of the ideological spectrum, argues that reproductive rights may perhaps represent population control by other means. Between the two are a range of institutions at the international level that have brought the agenda of reproductive health and rights center stage, in cluding the World Bank and the Population Council. Placing reproductive health and rights squarely on the world agenda was the International Conference on Population and Development (ICPD) held at Cairo in 1994.

The concept of reproductive rights has a long and tragic heritage, carrying a huge burden of preventable morbidity and mortality of infants and women, arising from lack of citizenship coupled with women's lack of rights over their bodies.

Various streams of thought, jostling uneasily with one another, congealed into the birth control movement in the nineteenth century gathering strength in the early twentieth century. The most prominent among them, the radical feminists and the socialists believed, and believed strongly, that it was women's right to control their own destinies, their own bodies. Access to birth control, then banned, was one element in their larger struggle for democratic rights. Socialist's ideas on birth control were also coloured by the feeling that the burden of repeated pregnancies was harmful to the health of working women; and by the belief that it was in the interests of capitalists—and not their own—to have an unlimited supply of cheap labour. Thus the first stirrings demanding free access to contraception arose in the ranks of the International Workers of the World (Gordon 1976).[1] Ultimately, the movement was taken over by the Neo Malthusians, whose concerns were radically different.

There were two prominent demands underlying the movement: legalization of access to contraceptives and to abortions. Unwanted births and maternal deaths in childbirth and in abortion, caused in William Farr's memorable phrase 'a deep dark and continuous stream of mortality' (Oakley 1984:32).[2]

The late nineteenth century saw the availability of what could be called modern contraceptives due to the invention of the vulcanization process. But what is also not frequently remembered is that legislation making abortions illegal was also a product of the nineteenth century in the first place (Doyal 1995)[3]. This is attributed partly to efforts at professionalisation of medicine: it was claimed that this move was necessary to reduce maternal mortality— although maternal mortality began to decline only in the twentieth century due mainly to improvements in standards of living. It was also partly due to Victorian prudery and the idea that a good bourgeoisie woman was an asexual being. In other words, that both sexuality, and unwanted pregnancies had to be criminalized.

It was within the wings of the Labour Party in the United Kingdom that the demands for legalization of contraception and abortion were enunciated with the formation of the Worker's Birth Control Group at the Annual Conference of Labour Women in 1924, although they met with fierce resistance from the men in the Labour Party[4]. In 1934, the Women's Cooperative Guild passed a resolution demanding de-criminalization of abortion and in 1936, the Abortion Law Reform Association was formed[5]. Stella Brown a socialist and feminist argued in *The Communist* in 1922:

Birth control for women is no less than workshop control and the determination of the conditions of labour for men...Birth control is women's crucial effort at self-determination and at control of her own person and her own environment (cited in Gupta, J.A. 2000: 1570).[6]

But all such 'liberatory' discourse suffered in the climate of the post First War reaction. Indeed the Soviet Union, which had initially passed far-reaching abortion laws making abortion more or less available on request, quickly rescinded these laws in the period. Along with England and France, the Soviet Union, reeling under the monumental loss of lives in the carnage of the war, was hesitant about undertaking measures that were anti-natalist. Indeed so pro-natalist, and gynaephobic, were the times that the first government report in the U.K on maternal mortality, deploring the huge loss of lives, observed that maternal lives needed to be saved as women produced children for the nation (Oakley 1984)[7]. As the world plunged into the Great Depression, the discourse that entered center stage was eugenics.

In the post Second War period, for a variety of reasons, chief among them Cold War concerns of a population 'bomb', it was population control that dominated thinking among influential international institutions and indeed the elites of the developing world. The availability of a range of contraceptives seemed axiomatically to guarantee that there was indeed a magic bullet for the 'population explosion'. But over the seventies, a range of groups came to critically examine both the strategies for population control and the assumptions on which they were based. It was evident that the various strategies of population control simply did not seem to be working. At the same time, the demographic catastrophe that had been forecast, simply did not arrive. Indeed, the projections on which they were based were seen to be deeply faulty.

Health care was an important agenda of what has been called the second wave of feminism. Not only did it spread across countries, but health came to be seen as deeply political, embedded in the structures of society and not merely a matter of scale and value- neutral technology. Women's groups in the West, now wary of the sexual revolution of the sixties brought about primarily by the Pill, wondered if this had indeed shaken the citadels of patriarchy. They were also deeply critical of the medicalization of women's health as the Boston Women's Health Collective's *Our Bodies Ourselves*[8] not only became a bestseller in the USA but in several other parts of the globe. Indeed this was nothing other than a call to arms for a profound reordering of relationship between the sexes and between the women and the medical industry. The hazards of new contraceptives became an important issue, brought to the fore in the West with the controversy over the Dalkon shield. Black women's groups, meanwhile, took up cudgels pointing to the deeply racist ideas underlying ideas of population control, and some among them accused white feminists of being color blind[9]. In the countries of the Third World, a range of women's groups and health groups trenchantly critiqued the family planning programs. The abuse of sterilization, and incentives that were offered to meet family planning targets, all came in for critique: they were profoundly anti-women, anti-poor and violative of human rights.

This movement became the cause of women coming increasingly on the agenda of development. There were also calls for rethinking the role of population policies in development. At the 1974 World Conference on Population at Bucharest, the First World countries that had gone in with the understanding that family planning programs were at the heart of development were shocked when many Third World countries insisted that 'development was the best contraceptive' even as they called for a new world economic order based on equity. There were equally strident calls for looking at the issue of development through the lens of gender as the role and position of women in the world came increasingly under scrutiny. Thus the UN declared a Decade of Women. At the same time, the first International Women and Health Meeting was held in Rome in 1977.

Reflecting these various pulls and pressures, at the end of decades of campaigning, in 1973, in the historic Roe versus Wade case, the US Supreme Court legalized abortion. However, this decision was soon under attack and as early as 1976 the Hyde Amendment prohibited Medicaid funding for abortion except in the case of rape or severe illnesses[10]. The issue of abortion has hung fire since.

The 1970s were exciting times in health development; indeed there was such a sense of optimism and hope that anything at all seemed possible as critiques of dominant models of health care found increasing resonance, leading to the historic declaration of Health For All through Primary Health Care (PHC) by 2000 AD at Alma Ata in 1978.

What defeated the hope and optimism of PHC was the onset of the 'decade of despair' (UNICEF 1989:2).[11] For this was precisely the period when, for a complex number of reasons, the long boom of the post-War golden age of capitalism ground to a profound crisis. This period was also marked by the rise of right-wing monetarist regimes in the USA and the UK, along with the domination in the belief in the mantras of what Hobsbawm describes as 'ultra-liberal economic theologians', whereby 'the ideological zeal of the old champions of individualism was now reinforced by the apparent failure of conventional economic policies' (Hobsbawm 1994: 409).[12] As the Keynesian world came increasingly under attack, that of actually existing socialism turned upside down. The collapse of the Berlin wall and the Soviet empire both provided more than metaphorical setting for a new phase of global capitalism, a phase that saw the shrinking of spaces that had opened up with the post-Second World War welfarist state—to labour, to Third World countries and the marginalized in general.

The remarkable similarities between Malthusian times and the 1990s have been widely noted. Both periods were characterized by a relentless drive to create free markets, 'not by chance nor as a result of spontaneous development, but as an artifact of power and statecraft. In nineteenth century England it was the outcome of the project of classical political economy; now it is a monetarist project, to create a global market society largely unconstrained by public action' (Wuyts 1998: 34).[13] Hartmann notes that population control discourses obtained a new lease of life, resurgence, in the 1990s as Cold War obsessions gave way to new definitions of security. The consensus in the corridors of the security establishment in the United States, is that population growth threatens international stability in the post-Cold War world. While it is acknowledged that economic growth and empowerment of women are necessary to reduce birth rates, vigorous family planning measures are the 'least costly' and 'most pragmatic' means for defusing the threat to international peace. 'The American interest is clear: we need to commit our leadership and resources to a multilateral effort to drastically expand family planning services' (Carnegie Endowment, cited in Hartmann 1993: 4).[14] At the same time the World Bank's thinking also underwent a shift from viewing poverty alleviation as the key to fertility decline to the view that population problems cannot wait for their solution on socio-economic development. Indeed, that population growth presented an obstacle to economic recovery and the 'necessity to succeed with the structural adjustment effort' (ibid: 4).[15]

As the structural adjustment program would cut the excesses in the economy, so too would the family planning program guarantee a correspondingly lean family. Indeed the reduction in state subsidies to welfare programs would increase the cost of supporting many children and thus persuade families to adopt family planning. 'Playing on images of excess and waste, the structural adjustment program and the family planning program would, in conjunction, streamline the social and economic corpus' of borrowing countries (Ali 2003:3).[16] This would require the constitution of new kinds of families within which the notion of individual choice is paramount, calling from a shift from structural development and social equity to behavioral modification and expanded contraceptive choice.

It is thus difficult not to separate the ICPD's call for reproductive rights from the context of the new global recession. Economists hesitated to use the word 'depression' to describe this phenomenon since it brought back painful memories of the 1930s, a period that had plunged the world into the horrors of fascism and the Second World War, but the 'recession' of the 1980s was similarly widespread and deep, with equally profound social consequences. The new world order that was crafted bore little resemblance to the new international economic order envisaged by the Third World at the time of Alma Ata but in a diametrically opposite direction, leading to a neo-liberal prescription of globalization, privatization and liberalization.

Thus the restructuring of Third World economies to ensure debt repayment began to drive economic policies, in the Latin American countries and Africa in the 1980s and in Asia in the 1990s.

These right wing economic policies, described variously as Reaganomics, Thatcherism, corporate globalization or monetarism, reflected an ideological commitment to unbridled market principles, ignoring the remarkable role that the state had played even in the advanced capitalist countries. One of the significant lessons of post-War economic growth had been the singular role that the state could play, and indeed needed to play, in capitalist countries to avoid recurrent periods of crisis due to falling demand. For instance, state involvement in public health had been considered critical, as state provision of public goods was also at the heart of the strategy to stabilize the economies and to increase productivity. In the new environment of the 80s, these Keynesian policies came under attack.

The new consensus shared a profoundly cynical view of the state, especially in developing countries, although neo-liberal free-market rhetoric often contrasted sharply with the actual practices of the Reagan and Thatcher governments in their own countries where the state was increasingly subsidizing the rich (Gershman and Irwin 2000)[17]. The diagnosis of the problems of poor countries was that the state played too great a role in the economy, preventing markets from acting efficiently, and breeding inefficient uncompetitive industries sheltering behind protectionist walls, thus distorting markets and prices.

Reducing the role of the state and increasing that of the market, irrespective of their social and indeed long-term economic costs, was thus at the center of this model of therapy. This was accompanied by the triumph of the ideology of individualism, competitive wealth seeking and unbridled consumerism among the rich. Along with the decrease of community values, this led to the undermining of public initiatives and institutions, especially those that served and protected the interests of the weak and the poor (Rao and Loewenson 2000)[18]. Economic growth, would trickle down to the less fortunate and thus result in overall development.

At the height of her economic and political power in the new uni-polar world, the United States found a way out of the impasse of falling rates of profit and increasing unemployment within her shores by opening up potential markets in the Third World countries. The debt situation became the vehicle for introducing these measures brought together under the rubric of the SAP. Future loans from international financial institutions and access to donor funds and markets became linked to accepting this broad package of macroeconomic policies.

Deflation, liberalization and privatization were applied in a uniform measure across Latin America and Africa in the 1980s. In the agricultural sector, this led to the reinforcement of colonial patterns of agricultural production, stimulating the growth of export-oriented crops at the cost of food crops. The problem at the heart of this pattern of production is that it reinforced the pre-existing international division of labour and was implemented at a time when the prices of primary commodities were the lowest in history. Indeed by 1989, prices for agricultural products were only 60 per cent of their 1970 levels (Hartmann 1995). Thus the more successful these countries were in increasing the volume of exports, in competition with other Third World countries exporting similar products, the less successful they were in raising foreign exchange to finance their imports. Thus many countries shifted back in time to being exporters of unprocessed raw materials and importers of manufactured goods, albeit with a sharp deterioration in terms of trade against developing countries.

In the industrial sector, where developing countries had been striving to break out of colonial patterns of dependent development, the withdrawal of state support plunged many enterprises into crisis. Such units were then allowed to close, or were privatized, or handed over to trans-national-corporations, typically with significant losses of employment (Sparr 1994).[19] Just as the state reduced its commitment to critical sectors such as education and health, so also the flow of capital across borders in search of labour, raw materials and markets, indeed the frenetic search for quick profits, typically weakened the state. Further, over this period, capital across the globe was increasingly concentrated in fewer and fewer hands with an implosion of mergers and acquisitions.

Together, these policies and processes increased indebtedness, increased the rate of exploitation of wageworkers across the globe, and shifted wealth from productive to speculative sectors. The policies also led to the increase of casual, poorly paid and insecure forms of employment. Fund cuts in education and health also meant that already weak and under-funded systems of health, education and food security collapsed. Together they increased levels of poverty in already poor countries even as a few people became richer and the middle and upper classes obtained access to manufactured products hitherto available only in the rich countries.

Gershman and Irwin note that the involvement of the World Bank and the IMF in molding the policies of countries in Latin America, Africa and parts of Asia expanded dramatically in the 1980s: by the end of 1991, 75 countries had received structural adjustment loans worth more than the equivalent of 41 billion dollars (Gershman and Irwin, 2000).[20] At the same time, the debt of the developing countries soared from 658 billion dollars in 1980, to 1,375 billion dollars in 1988, to 1,945 billion dollars in 1994 (Report of the Independent Commission on Population and Quality of Life 1996).[21]

Increasingly, critiques of these policies came to be voiced even in influential circles. The UNICEF initiated a striking series of studies that indicated that the costs of structural adjustment had been disproportionately borne by the poor, in particular by women and children (Cornia, Jolly and Stewart 1988)[22]. What was called for was adjustment, but with a human face, in the shape of safety nets for those rendered vulnerable by the programs of structural adjustment.

One important consequence has been commonly described as the feminization of poverty as females increasingly had to strive to hold families together in various ways in the face of increasing pressures, chief among them increasing poverty and insecurity. In many countries, more women entered the labour force but at lower wages and with inferior working conditions than those for men. Simultaneously, the extent of unpaid labour in households, performed largely by women, increased as public provision of basic goods and services declined. Young children, especially girls, were increasingly withdrawn from school to join the vast and grossly underpaid informal labour market or to assist in running the household. The involvement of children and adolescents in crime and delinquency increased under these circumstances. Rising food prices, along with cuts in subsidies for the poor, meant that an increasing proportion of families with precarious resources were pushed under the poverty line, affecting women and girl children disproportionately. It is not surprising that studies indicate that morbidity levels increased even as poor people were increasingly unable to access health institutions, which under the reform measures, typically introduced fees for services. Given increasing levels of under nutrition, it is not surprising that infant and child mortality rates, which had hitherto shown a secular decline, either stagnated or in the case of some countries, actually increased.

The Bank did, in the face of these challenges, make some changes as poverty reduction again figured on their agenda. These took three forms: a prescription for labour intensive growth; investing in the poor *via* the development of human capital—chiefly investments in health and education; and finally, the promotion of safety nets and targeted social programs. In other words, there is an implicit recognition that specific programs are necessary to protect the poor from the consequences of structural adjustment and that growth by itself does not reduce the problem of poverty. But this re-thinking was seriously limited. The Commonwealth Secretariat for instance observed:

> ...any benefits women may have attained from compensatory measures have been only incidental. They have not prevented devastating setbacks in crucial areas such as maternal and child health services, basic education and training, childcare, and the provision of credit, extension and other support services to help women as producers (Commonwealth Secretariat 1989: 8).[23]

More significantly, between 1990 and 1993, sub-Saharan Africa alone transferred 13.4 billion dollars annually to its creditors, substantially more than it spent on education and health combined. From 1987 to 1993, the net transfer of resources from Africa to the IMF was 38 billion dollars (Gershman and Irwin 2000).[24]

Increasing inequalities in income, in health, and so on, were also distressingly apparent in other countries that had followed similar economic trajectories. Indeed they were also increasingly visible among the poor even in the developed countries. In a number of the developed industrial countries, mortality differentials increased sharply in parallel with widening disparities in socio-economic status (Davey Smith and Egger 1993).[25] Significant reversals in health status were also observed in the newly independent states of Eastern Europe (WHO 1998).[26] Sharp declines in life expectancy have also been recorded in countries of the former Soviet Union, involving 'a health crisis of unforeseen proportions in the Russian Federation' (Evans, T, Whitehead, M., Diderichson, F, Bhuiya, A and Wirth, Meg (Ed.) 2001: 3).[27] Of great importance to the concept of reproductive health is data from Russia that indicates that class disadvantage preceded and took a greater toll than gender disadvantage (Shkolnikov, V.M, M.G Field and E.V. Andreev, 2001).[28] In China, the economic changes, along with the 'one child per family' norm, since officially abandoned, have accentuated the gender discrimination and thus the problem of 'missing girls'. Significantly, China too embarked upon a RCH approach just when conditions were getting worse for women in China. Poignantly, as in countries like India, medical expenditure is emerging as a leading cause of the impoverishment of families as the health system collapsed.

But the promise of GDP growth under SAP proved to be elusive. About a 100 countries, it was evident, had undergone economic decline. Per capita income in these countries was lower than it was earlier. In Africa, the average household consumes 20 per cent less than it did 25 years ago. Many SAP- implementing countries fell from their initial debt into a debt trap, wherein they had to take increasing loans merely to pay back the interest on their initial loans. Since they now received less for the products they exported, they were forced to undertake repeated devaluations and thus not only paid more for their imports but also for their debt repayment. They were thus caught in a vicious circle of low capital, borrowing, devaluation and less capital.

It is not surprising that these two decades have often been described as lost decades. Structural adjustment programs did not reduce debts, cut down levels of poverty or return countries to a path of growth. The external debt stock of developing countries increased from 616 billion in 1980 to an estimated \$2.2 trillion at the end of 1997. Yet at the same time, the flow of resources to rich countries actually increased, as indeed they were designed to. In 1960, the poorest 20 per cent of the global population received 2.3 per cent of the global income. By 1991, their share had sunk to 1.4 per cent. Today, the poorest 20 per cent receive only 1.1 per cent of global income. The ratio of income of the wealthiest 20 per cent of the people to that of the poorest 20 per cent was 30 to 1 in 1960. By 1995, that ratio stood at 82 to 1. This is based on distribution between rich and poor countries, but when the maldistribution of income within countries is taken into account, the richest 20 per cent of the world's people in 1990 got at least 150 times more than the poorest 20 per cent (UNDP 1992).[29] The 20 per cent of the world's people who live in the highest income countries account for 86 per cent of the global consumption; the poorest 20 per cent, only 1.3 per cent. In other words, while the world had grown incomparably richer, the wealth generated had been distributed remarkable unequally. It is thus not surprising that critics have argued that 'globalization is really about the expansion of TNC activities to the developing world on TNC's terms' (Raghavan, C. 1996: 13)[30], and that 'globalization is proceeding largely for the benefit of the dynamic and powerful countries' (UNDP 1997).[31] It can also perhaps be described as a neo-colonial marriage between metropolitan financial interests and metropolitan industrial interests (Patnaik, P. 1999).[32] In this context, does reproductive health represent a marriage between international capital and bourgeoisie feminisms?

While it is in the context of both the retreat from PHA and the increasing marginalization of poor countries and their poor population that we must locate the discourse on reproductive rights, there were also other factors, other discourses that came into play. Debates on population refined some themes, sharpening them, while others were unabashedly and crudely racist. One related scarcity, security and war and the second, the now famous IPAT equation, refined ideas attributing environmental degradation to population growth, while Maurice King was unabashed in his genocidal views on withholding health care in poor countries.

In the anti-women, anti-poor environment of the period, and partly as a consequence, there occurred the rise of virulent 'fundamentalisms' in various religions, Hindu, Muslim and Christian. These are clearly political projects seeking to mobilize discontent and anger with the deeply divided world, a world wherein modernity has failed to deliver, where hopelessness with the state of things led to the immense appeal of these atavistic forces seeking to recreate a golden period of innocence and plenty that never existed. Thus Christian fundamentalism, that is dictatorship of the holy minority, finds its natural place in the neo-liberalism of the New Right today: the withdrawal into the family and the 'community', undermining the autonomy of women and reinforcing that of patriarchy (Eisenstein 1982).[33] There has been in a sense a complete about-turn in the politics of these groups; earlier, suspicious of Others and the Government, they retreated into their communities and churches. Today, however, they have found a new stridency as they increasingly utilize corporate funding to influence politics and have come to command the Presidency of the United States. Although the huge health and indeed financial costs of limiting women's access to abortion are unambiguously clear, across the world there has been a phenomenal growth of the anti-abortion movement, aiming to bring back restrictive laws limiting, or criminalizing, abortion. They are nowhere as strong as in the US, where not only has funding for abortion been withdrawn in many States, but doctors and nurses performing abortions have been shot at and clinics fire-bombed or vandalized. Federal funding for abortions is prohibited, affecting in particular, poor women of color and other ethnic minorities (Jacobson 1990).[34] The politics of fetal rights, indeed of privileging the rights of the fetus over that of the mother, reached its absurd limits when a Californian court in 1986 ordered the arrest of a woman on charges of medical neglect of her fetus (Doyal 1995).[35] The new globalization also means that there is a globalization of the right-to-life campaigners. Indeed it was the influence of this movement over Republican policies that saw the Reagan government enacting the global gag rule, and at the 1984 World Population Conference at Mexico City, announce that population growth was a 'neutral' phenomenon even as the government cut funds to family planning programs providing or promoting abortion services.

The availability of new technologies—of so-called gene therapy and IVF, of the specter of human cloning—raises a host of issues of morality and ethics that has added to the fulminant strength of the right-to-lifers. Their strident stands are derived apparently by Biblical injunctions and not the more quotidian and secular concerns of what these technologies imply for the rights of mothers, of the poor and indeed, the diseased or disabled. It is also not surprising that there is a new lease of life provided by such currents to discredited ideas of eugenics as authors increasingly do not feel ashamed to argue for instance that intelligence is inherited and indeed racially determined (Herrnstein and Murray 1994).[36] This is of course also related to attacks on the welfare state initiated by Margaret Thatcher by blaming the poor for their poverty. Rose notes, for instance, that neo-liberalism provides the perfect niche for biology-as-destiny arguments in garbled pseudo-sciences (Rose 2001).[37] As in Malthusian discourse, what Thatcher was doing was arguing that the poor had no moral right to claims on the state.

Not accidentally, the new 'plague', AIDS, also provided an impetus to the focus on reproduction. The onset of the AIDS pandemic came as a profound shock to the developed world that believed that infectious diseases were a thing of the past in their societies. As Rosenberg remarks:

> (AIDS reminds us), we have not freed ourselves from the constraints and indeterminacy of living in a web of biological relationships—not all of which we can control or predict. Viruses, like bacteria, have for countless millennia shared our planet and our bodies (Rosenberg 1992:287).[38]

Its initial association primarily with gays and drug addicts seemed to suggest that it was a disease of the dregs of society, reinforcing existing prejudices of class and sexuality. But when the enormous costs of the disease to society, its seeming ability to cross barriers of class, and its mutability came to the fore, efforts were on to take stock of the disease and to control its spread in the general population. Since not very much was known about the epidemiology of the disease, one primary method of prevention was obviously sexual continence and the use of condoms. But when the association of AIDS with other reproductive infections became apparent—evidence strongly suggests the facilitating role of genital ulcerative diseases (chancroid, syphilis, or herpes) in HIV-1 transmission (de Schryver and Meheus 1990)[39]—it was evident that the ambit of intervention had to be broadened to reproductive health as a whole. Thus the impetus for improved management and control of STIs, and the resultant shift in focus from special treatment centres, was primarily due to the advent of HIV infection and AIDS (Chen et al 1991).[40]

The World Bank was, over this period, increasingly setting the agenda for health. World Bank lending in the health sector is thus larger than the entire budget of the WHO. Within the health sector, and especially following the publication of the influential 1993 Report *Investing in Health* (World Bank 1993)[41], the Bank's policies of health sector reforms have meant redefining public spending in health to an essential package of clinical services, phasing out public subsidies especially for tertiary care. It also urges governments to foster competition and diversity in supply of health services. One hallmark of these reforms has been the concept of fee for services. Critics have argued that these policies have been a clarion call for privatization and a more 'cost-effective' version of selective PHC. In the process, public health is dismembered, diseases are divested from their socio-economic context, concentrating on specific technology dependent programs and thus sounding the death knell to concepts of PHC (Qadeer 1999).[42] In other words, as the prospects for HFA receded, we saw again the dominance of the magic bullet approach to public health technology, accompanying what Renaud resonantly described as eliminating society from disease, whereby disease occurrence is ascribed to individual proclivities and failures (Renaud: 1975).[43] As we witness increasing privatization of health care, along with cuts in state spending on health, we see the reversal to technologically driven vertical programs. Thus while a holistic vision of public health has been eclipsed, the chicken of technological determinism and methodological individualism has come home to roost with a vengeance.

Implementing these have meant that it is assumed that macro-economic policies that have eroded the previous gains in health somehow cease to matter. In other words, an increasingly biological notion of the determinants of ill health and disease in populations, turning public health on its head. Given the overwhelming influence of the Bank on health and population policies of borrowing countries, it is not surprising when the Bank made a 'paradigm shift' to reproductive health, borrowing countries were quick to follow. Thus while the onslaught of the Right provided the impetus for feminists in the West to highlight the critical importance of reproductive rights at the ICPD, it was also brought to centre stage by the concerns of the population control lobby and the World Bank to infuse a new lease of life into family faltering family planning programs.

There was then, a coming together of seemingly opposed groups in crafting the 'Cairo consensus'. On the one hand was the population control establishment, composed of a wide array of actors ranging from the World Bank and Population Council to a number of NGOs, nation states, health personnel and academics (Bandarage 1997).[44] This group apparently realized that the demographic goal of reducing fertility could not be attained without taking into account women's ability to make decisions regarding reproduction and fertility. In other words, even for purely instrumental reasons, there had to be a change in approach to the population issue. On the other hand were the women's rights activists, feminist academics and some health activists. Many of them undoubtedly brought to the forefront First World feminist concerns; others had indeed campaigned against coercive population control programs and policies in the Third World. They were united in opposition to fundamentalist groups from the USA and from conservative Islamic countries and the Vatican (Petchesky and Judd 1998).[45] It is important thus to remember, as Ravindran points out that the demands for reproductive rights and health did not originate in Cairo, and was not an idea formulated by the population control agencies or other international agencies that supported them (Ravindran 1998).[46] Nevertheless, it is as the Cairo consensus that they cast their influential shadow.

The Cairo consensus was indeed a significant, if modest, step forward. It meant a break from the past in various manners. It signaled a move away from demographically driven population policies that 'attribute poverty and environmental degradation to women's high fertility, and, in turn, women's high fertility to an absence of information and methods' (R Petchesky 1998: 2).[47] It also challenged the 'moral arsenal' of Christian, Hindu or Islamic fundamentalists to curtail rights of women in the name of tradition or culture, often fraudulent and concocted. It further meant, a redefining of the population field that had neglected sexuality and gender roles, focusing instead largely on outcomes such as contraceptive efficacy or declines in birth rates or more recently, reproductive infections (Dixon-Mueller 1993).[48] Above all it provided a fillip—and sanction from international covenant—to health groups fighting coercive population programs in a number of countries. It was now possible for these groups to argue that these programs violated international covenants that the government itself was signatory to.

But was this merely a 'semantic revolution' (Correa 2000: 7)?[49] Is feminist rhetoric being used by international population agencies to legitimize and gloss over narrow instrumentalist concerns (Correa and Petchesky 1994)?[50] Was it merely a 'Western' concept, lent credence by the undoubted economic and political power of the West and therefore to be rejected?

It is true that reproductive health and rights cannot have a universal, trans-historical meaning, or indeed relevance, in a world differentiated by nationality, class, ethnicity, religion, race and so on (Bandarage 1997).[51] Women's ability to make reproductive decisions is mediated by multiple and complex processes by which class, caste, religion, the family, in short, the institutions of patriarchy, interact with and are acted upon by the state and international structures. That is to say, there is a need to integrate the politics of the body into a larger framework that emphasizes the transformation of the state, social, demographic and economic development policies (Petchesky, R 1998).[52]

Thus women's control over their bodies, over reproduction is an issue of power, both between the sexes and among various layers of society. Differentiation among women also has a profound implication for the ability to exercise such control. A range of practices, laws, values and institutions provide the hegemonic basis for patriarchy. The challenge of reproductive rights is thus about challenging both the ideology and practices which allow others to control women's bodies. Correa and Petchesky thus argue that notions of power and rights to resources are intrinsically imbricated in the discourse on reproductive health. Thus the struggle for reproductive health is nothing less than the 'democratic transformation of societies to abolish gender, class, racial and ethnic injustice' (Correa and Petchesky 1994: 107).[53] In other words, reproductive health is an important part of a broader conceptualization of rights, of the good world. As Petchesky puts it:

> As part of collective feminist efforts to reclaim property in our bodies, we must redefine all essential health care and services...we must reconnect our self-ownership to our right to common resources. Of course, in a world where the language of social need and common property is rapidly disappearing in the universal babel of the market (which so easily co-opts the idea of individual choice), this would almost mean turning the world upside down. The language of reproductive freedom is still burdened with 300 years of the dominant Euro-American model of dichotomisation between self and community, body and society. But language has as much resilience and power to transform as do the social movements that deploy it and the politics that re-invent it (Petchesky 1995: 406).[54]

Is reproductive health actually about turning the world upside down? Or is claiming too much for the concept, important though it is? Is it a case of spinning a strong argument from insubstantial threads? Can the concept carry the burden of transforming the world? Turning the world upside down was of course what the struggles of workers, the dispossessed, sought to do in past times when 'liberte, fraternite and egalite' were cries echoing across borders. But in a world of liberalization, privatization and globalization, a world in which workers were up against a wall, increasing joining the ranks of the surplus population, could a call to arms for reproductive rights help them storm the metaphorical Bastille? Finally, is there a profound confusion between cause and consequence? How then does one justify the position of the Government of Eritrea at Cairo?

The Government of Eritrea issued a statement that was astonishing in scope, revealing a vision that is rare for the times and throwing the gauntlet back to the West and indeed those rallying for reproductive rights. It was not arguing that reproductive rights were not an important goal, nor was it arguing that this goal was not desirable, nor unattainable. Nevertheless, its position was that given existing conditions, there were prior claims to justice, to equity, and to rights that obtained moral and political precedence. It thus warrants quoting, even if at length:

> In the case of Africa in particular, it is debatable whether reduced population growth will mitigate its marginalization in the world economic order and accelerate its development. Africa enjoys, on the whole, considerable comparative advantages in terms of territorial expanse and natural endowments. Its population density—even taking into account current rates of fertility—is and will remain low in relative terms for the foreseeable future. The appalling poverty and deprivation that stalk the continent are not certainly due to overpopulation and they will not be eradicated if family planning were to be introduced through attractive palliatives and public education programs. The scourge of ethnic conflicts, massive internal and external population displacement and widespread deprivation will not be healed by the most prudent and comprehensive demographic policy.

In the event, what is required is a much bolder and holistic approach that addresses and tackles the real causes of underdevelopment existing imbalances in the terms of international trade must be adjusted to promote rapid and sustainable development in the countries that are lagging behind and in which the economic gap is widening. Furthermore, it is a matter of historical reality that population stabilization is likely to be achieved as a byproduct of rather than an antecedent to overall development. The various programs associated with family planning, and especially the social safety nets for the elderly, public education programs for adolescents, empowerment of women, etc. cannot be implemented on a sustainable basis from external funding. Internal development would be essential and indeed a prerequisite for an undertaking of this scale. In brief, the answer does not lie in a compartmentalized and piecemeal approach but on a comprehensive and innovative approach to the crucial issue of development in the Third World. (Government of Eritrea: 1994 cited in Hartmann).[55]

But as in the case of PHC, even the RHC proposed at the ICPD was waiting to be reshaped. Arguing that the vision of a good social and economic policy and a just population policy, despite being desirable is not pragmatic, Jain and Bruce of the Population Council suggest a transitional strategy that they name the '1994 strategy'. This 'focuses primarily on fertility reduction', 'paying attention to those aspects of reproductive health that interact directly with the avoidance of unwanted fertility' (Jain and Bruce 1994: 195).[56] RHC, in this view, was limited to safe abortions, treatment of pre-existing conditions, such as RTIs—in order to make particular contraceptive methods acceptable, and the treatment of contraceptive side effects. Was this, then, what all the storm and thunder of reproductive rights was about? Making contraceptives more acceptable? For of course, there was a new generation of contraceptives—injectables, implants and so on, waiting for the cornucopia of the markets of Third World women's bodies.

There was of course, no original sin committed at Cairo when liberal feminists, predominantly from the West, went into alliance with the Neo-Malthusian population control establishment. Indeed it was precisely this relationship that had spawned the global population control movement in the 1950s. However, during the intervening years, there had been a critical distancing. The fact that a section of feminists, referred to by Hodgson and Watkins as reproductive health feminists, were now willing to be fellow travelers with the World Bank, along with the population control establishment, however was entirely new (Hodgson and Watkins 1997).[57] Was this a marriage of multinational-feminisms with international debt? It has been argued by other feminists that there can be no such thing as a 'feminist population policy', that the Cairo consensus merely replaced population control with 'population stabilization', that it paid little attention to neo-liberal macro-economic forces profoundly shaping the health of women worldwide, and particularly in the developing countries and, finally, that the price paid for the consensus was too high (WGNRR forthcoming)[58].

Critics also argued that in the agenda of rights of the ICPD, reproductive choice refers to the plethora of contraceptive devices that a 'free' woman is supposed to be 'empowered' to choose from. In other words, that what is being attempted is to create a 'rational', utility maximizing consumer in the contraceptive market place produced by the reproductive technology industry of the West. It has been noted that in the era of reproductive technologies, the concept of choice is reduced to consumption that fosters a private enterprise in women's bodies (Raymond 1996).[59] Thus as feminist discourse is co-opted by development jargon, reproductive rights become divested of rights to food, employment, water, health care and security of children's lives.

As if in answer to these questions, the World Bank produced a policy document *India's Family Welfare Programme: Towards a Reproductive and Child Health Approach* (Measham and Heaver 1995).[60] Having paid obeisance to the concept of reproductive health, and the transformation to India's family planning program this would harbinger, the Bank argues:

> The new consensus recognizes that an important goal of reproductive health programs should be to reduce unwanted fertility safely, thereby responding to the needs of individuals for high quality services, as well as to *demographic objectives*. (Emphasis added The World Bank 1995: 38).

Thus is a mountain of hope and optimism transformed into a lowly molehill. The very heart of the idea of reproductive health mooted by feminists—that there be no over-riding demographic goals—is torn out in this avatar of reproductive health.

It has been noted that the new reincarnation of old concerns with population control under the rubric of reproductive rights does not camouflage the essential concerns of both the World Bank and private funding agencies from the West. This is evident from the financial allocations envisaged at ICPD: 10.2 billion dollars on family planning, 5 billion dollars on reproductive health and 1.3 billion dollars on HIV/AIDS and other STD by the year 2000 (Bandarage: 1997).[61]

A fascinating study of the discourse of reproductive rights in India, noted that although there was recognition and commitment, at the policy level to a 'paradigm shift' this was envisaged through the lens of the ongoing marketization and reforms of the health sector. Based on a study of documents and field interviews, Kurian concluded:

> Even as this discourse of universal reproductive health was accepted, the discussion of the basic feminist concepts that founded the discourse of reproductive health—such as rights, choices and empowerment—was transformed to suit the fundamental tenets of neo-liberalism ... reproductive ability becomes a currency of the market... since for a majority of people, this linking of the private and public actually limits their access to health. (Kurian 2003: 237).[62]

Kurian argues that the blurring of the lines between 'client' rights and citizens rights, leads to a re-statement of women as bearers of reproduction with the state's curtailment of its role as an agent of equity and social justice. When overwhelming evidence around the globe indicates that neo-liberalism has fundamentally added to the burdens borne by women, what the policy seeks to do is to transfer social responsibility of reproduction—shared by the state, the family and the market—primarily to the family i.e. women, and the market.

> It is clear that the current moment of restructuring can be viewed as a concerted discursive and political struggle around the very meaning of the public and private. The proponents of globalization seek radically to shrink the public—the realm of political negotiation—and at the same time, expand and reassert the autonomy of the private sector and the private sphere (Brodie cited in Kurian 2003:221).[63]

Thus the doctrine of the day turned the feminists' slogan that the personal is political on its head. It is therefore not surprising that expressions of disquiet, dismay and indeed anger were soon forthcoming. In response to the Indian government's country paper at the Fourth World Conference of Women at Beijing in 1995, seven all-India women's organizations prepared an alternative document wherein the ICPD came in for stringent criticism:

> The slogan of sisterhood needs to be placed in the contemporary international situation when the so-called developed First World, led by the USA, wants to impose its agenda on the rest of the world in the name of globalization...the direct impact was seen in the recent Conference at Cairo ...where the agendas of the G-7 group were pushed through and issues concerning Third World women were left unaddressed. For instance in Cairo the issue of abortion dominated the proceedings. The representatives of million of Third World women in Cairo hoped, while supporting the struggles of Western women for their right to abortion, at least some attention would be paid to their experience. Instead they did not get the support of women representing the First World.
> We strongly believe that where the inequality of nations is increasing, where the development of the First World is in direct proportion to the underdevelopment and exploitation of the Third World, the slogan of sisterhood would mean to protect the interests of poor women in the Third World and to strengthen the global struggle against new forms of colonialism *(Towards Beijing: Crucial Issues of Concern*: 1995:36)[64].

Arguing that issues of development of poor countries in the new global order received short shrift at the ICPD, it was also argued that the ICPD did not take adequate note of processes that governed health in Third World countries, which, in the current global scenario were working fundamentally against the interest of the Third World. The alternative document notes that: 'women's health should not be subordinated to population goals nor restricted to reproductive matters' *(Towards Beijing: Crucial Issues of Concern*: 1995:33).[65]

Further, the agenda, which marginalized issues of equity and development of developing countries, equally marginalized other important health concerns of these countries. Even as the health implications of larger macro-economic changes were proving extremely deleterious to women's health, the focus on reproductive health seemed seriously misplaced. As Qadeer noted, 'The ICPD converted women's health into issues of safe abortion and reproductive rights alone; it marginalized issues of comprehensive Primary Health Care and social security', both of which are under attack in the new world order (Qadeer: 1995: 117)[66]. It also recalls that the scandal of chemical sterilization of women in India with quinacrine was carried out under the rhetoric of both choice and reproductive rights till the Supreme Court issued a ban on it (Rao 1998).[67]

Krishnaraj notes that the establishment now adduces the argument that given certain enabling conditions—primarily education and health, it is assumed that there is an automatic improvement in women's autonomy, this in turn leading to lower fertility. This appears not only pragmatic, commonsensical, but also eminently pro-woman. However, these processes are neither simple nor linear. The issue of course, as the famous case of Kerala shows us, is that fertility reduction can indeed take place without other conditions—that would in fact 'empower' women—ever changing (Krishnaraj 1998).[68] Thus while women's autonomy may help reduce fertility, reduction in fertility does not necessarily imply any improvement in women's power or status. Indicators such as the sexual division of labour, access to resources, control over incomes or indeed even access to education and income, may well remain unchanged, despite control over reproduction. In a society where the unit of production is still the family/household, where practices of marriage and birth are family-ordained, where women's lives are deeply embedded in community, reproductive rights are also difficult to translate operationally. For instance, in India, women's rights to property are deeply curtailed by personal laws defined by religion. While Hindu fundamentalists point to the anti-women nature of Islamic personal laws, which they would want altered, the Hindu personal laws are also anti-women[69]. Changing these is simply not on the agenda in India, with the right wing holding political power.

International funding has meant that a plethora of NGOs have moved into research on reproductive health, giving the issue a sense of urgency and priority perhaps not warranted otherwise. Examining data on mortality among women, Qadeer argues that the reproductive health approach is epidemiologically seriously misplaced. The largest chunk of deaths occurs in the pre-reproductive age group. Deaths due to causes associated with reproduction constitute 2.1 to 2.9 per cent of all female deaths. In all age groups within the reproductive years, communicable diseases constitute the highest proportion of deaths, more than three times than due to causes associated with reproduction. What is more worrying is that there is a rising trend of deaths due to communicable diseases among women in the reproductive age group. As the all-India Survey of Causes of Death (Rural) for the year 1992 reveals, among the causes of maternal deaths, anemia and puerperal sepsis together account for the largest proportion of deaths, 31 per cent, followed by bleeding of pregnancy and puerperium—largely due to anemia—which accounts for 25.6 per cent of deaths (GOI 1992)[70]. While deaths due to anemia in pregnancy is appallingly high, it is nevertheless the case that the proportion of women who are dying due to anemia and who are not pregnant, is several times higher than the proportion of women who are dying pregnant and anemic. Further, that although deaths among pregnant women with anemia have somewhat declined, deaths among women with anemia, who are not pregnant, shows a rising trend. This points to the serious limitation of concentrating on women only when they are pregnant. Further, given that the levels of under-nutrition in the population are so extraordinarily high, given too that the proportion of the population below the recommended daily allowance of calories has been estimated to have increased from 65.8 per cent in 1987–88 to 70 per cent in 1993–94 (Panchamukhi 2000)[71], it is not surprising to find this reflected in a rising prevalence of deaths due to anemia. In other words, given the overall health situation among women, dominated by communicable diseases, anemia and under-nutrition, to concentrate on reproductive health is to utterly miss the woods for the trees.

It has been argued that the focus on reproductive mortality has been seriously misplaced since women in reproductive ages suffer huge, and unquantified, morbidities. Reference is then usually made to some studies that have been very influential (Bang et al 1989).[72] It is however, not legitimate methodologically to utilize morbidity data to the exclusion of mortality. To state that reproductive morbidities is high, even though it may be true, is to misstate epidemiological priorities since they pertain to surviving populations, which elide morbidities that have already taken a toll (Rao 2000).[73]

A review of studies on reproductive morbidities notes the astonishingly wide variation in the study findings in the country and concludes that much of this could be due to widely varying sampling designs and diagnostic procedures. The review also points to selection bias, variable reference periods, as well as lack of standardization in clinical definitions and criteria for RTIs. The review concludes that there are low levels of correspondence between the frequently used modes of identifying RTIs and the difficulties thus in obtaining a valid and reliable idea of the prevalence of the problem of reproductive morbidity (Mamdani 1999).[74] What constitutes reproductive morbidity is further confounded by the absurd inclusion of nutrition in the domain of reproductive health (Jeejabhoy and Rao 1995).[75] By the same logic, ignoring the fundamentals of what constitutes a cause, the Bhopal gas disaster can also be termed a reproductive health issue since it had manifest reproductive consequences.

This is not of course to argue that reproductive health is a non-issue, but simply to put it in a public health perspective. For public health is above all, concerned with the total population, and any claim can only be relational. Perhaps what has occurred is that anxious to get on to the reproductive health bandwagon, far too many people claimed far too much for the concept. But what is equally clear is that ICPD represents, a retreat from the vision of HFA: under the rhetoric of reproductive rights, the rights of the vast majority of women to access resources, the most basic determinant of health, are being denied. Born of a marriage of multi-national feminisms and international debt, reproductive rights, reified, fits in well with the neo-liberal agenda of the day.

Notes

1. Gordon, Linda, *Women's Body, Women's Right*, Harmondsworth: Penguin, 1976.
2. Oakley, Ann, *The Captured Womb: A History of Medical Care of Pregnant Women*, Oxford: Basil Blackwell, 1986.
3. Doyal, Lesley, *What Makes Women Sick: Gender and the Political Economy of Health*, London Macmillan, 1995.
4. Pat Barker's novel *The Eye in the Door* captures, in an aside, quite brilliantly the liberatory effects of employment and wages among women, and how their spouses in the Labour movements, watched with dismay, if not anger, the new shape this gave to their marriages and families. Would they want to go to the pubs with their mates, asked a disgruntled husband, himself returning from a pub with his mates!
5. Note 2.
6. Cited in Gupta, Jyotsna Agnihotri, *New Reproductive Technologies, Women's Health and Autonomy: Freedom or Dependency?* New Delhi: Sage, 2000.
7. Oaklay, Ann, 1984, op cit.
8. Boston Women's Health Book Collective, *Our Bodies Ourselves*, New York. Simon and Schuster, 1971.
9. Marsha J. Tyson Darling notes that racism and sexism were both institutionalized in the 'science' of eugenics: Marsha J.Tyson Darling, 'The State Friend or Foe: Distributive Justice Issues and African American Women,' Silliman and King (ed), 1999, op. cit.
10. Doyal, Lesley, 1995, op. cit.
11. Unicef, *The State of the World's Children, 1989*, New York: OUP.
12. Hobsbawm, E.J., *Age of Extremes*, Delhi: Viking, 1994.
13. Wuyts, Marc, 'Malthus, Then and Now: The Novelty of Old Ideas on Population and Economy,' Dies Natalis Address, Institute of Social Studies, The Hague, 1998.
14. Hartmann, Betsy, *'Old Maps and New Terrain: The Politics of Women, Population and Environment in the 1990s,'* Madras: International Conference: Reinforcing Reproductive Rights, WGNRR, 1993.
15. Ibid.
16. Ali, Kamran Asdar, 'Myths, Lies and Impotence: Structural Adjustment and Male Voice in Egypt,' *American Ethnologist* (forthcoming).

17. Gershman, John and Irwin, Alec, op. cit.
18. Rao, Mohan and Loewenson, Rene, 'The Political Economy of the Assault on Health,' *Background Papers*, Dhaka: People's Health Assembly, 2000.
19. Sparr, Pamela, 'What is Structural Adjustment?' *Mortgaging Women's Lives: Feminist Critiques of Structural Adjustment*, London: Zed Books, 1994.
20. Gershman, J and A, Irwin, 2000, op. cit.
21. *Caring for the Future: A Radical Agenda for Positive Change*, Report of the Independent Commission on Population and Quality of Life, New York: OUP, 1996.
22. Cornia, G.A., Jolly, R. and Stewart, F.(eds), *Adjustment with a Human Face: Country Case Studies*, Oxford: Clarendon Press, 1988.
23. Commonwealth Secretariat, *Engendering Adjustment for the 1990s*, London, 1989.
24. Gershman, J. and Irwin, A., 2000, op. cit.
25. Davey-Smith, G and Egger, M.M., 'Socio-Economic Differentials in Wealth and Health', *British Medical Journal*, Vol. 307, 30 October 1993.
26. World Health Organisation, *World Health Report 1998: Life in the 21st Century; A Vision for All*, Geneva, 1998.
27. Evans, T, Whitehead, M., Diderichson, F, Bhuiya, A and Wirth, Meg (eds.), *Challenging Inequities in Health: From Ethics to Action*, New York: OUP, 2001.
28. Shkolnikov, V.M, Fielkd, Mark G. and Andreev, Evgueniy M, 'Russia: Socioeconomic Dimensions of the Gender Gap in Mortality,' Timothy Evans *et al* (ed), op cit. 2001.
29. United Nations Development Program, *Human Development Report 1992*, New York: OUP, 1992.
30. Raghavan, C., 'What is Globalization?' *Third World Resurgence*, Vol. 74, 1996.
31. United Nations Development Program, *Human Development Report 1997*, New York: OUP, 1997.
32. Patnaik, Prabhat, 'The Political Economy of Structural Adjustment: A Note,' *Disinvesting in Health: The World Bank's Prescriptions for Health*, M.Rao (ed.),New Delhi: Sage,1999
33. Eisenstein, Z., 'The Sexual Politics of the New Right: Understanding the Crisis of Liberalism for the 1980s', *Signs*, Vol. 7, 1982, pp. 567–588.
34. Jacobson, J., '*The Global Politics of Abortion*,' Worldwatch Paper 97, 1990.
35. Doyal, Lesley, 1995, op. cit.
36. Herrnstein, R. and Murray, C., *The Bell Curve: Intelligence and Class Structure in American Life*, New York: Free Press, 1994.
37. Rose, Hilary, 'Colonising the Social Sciences,' *Alas Poor Darwin: Arguments Against Evolutionary Psychology*,?' Hilary Rose and Steven Rose (eds), London: Vintage, 2001.
38. Rosenberg, Charles E., 'What is an Epidemic? AIDS in Historical Perspective,' *Explaining Epidemics and Other Studies in the History of Medicine*, C.E.Rosenberg (ed.) Cambridge: CUP, 1992.
39. De Schryver, A. and Meheus, A., 'Epidemiology of Sexually Transmitted Diseases: The Global Picture,' *WHO Bulletin*, Vol. 68, no.5, 1990.
40. Chen, L.C, Sepulveda, A. Segal, S.J., 'Introduction: An Overview of *AIDS* and Women's Health,' *AIDS and Women's Reproductive Health*, L.C.Chen, A.Sepulveda and S.J.Segal (eds), New York: Plenum Press, 1991.
41. World Bank, *World Development Report 1993: Investing in Health*, Washington D.C.: World Bank, 1993.
42. Qadeer, Imrana, 'The World Development Report 1993: The Brave New World of Primary Health Care,' *Disinvesting in Health: The World Bank's Prescriptions for Health*, Mohan Rao (ed), New Delhi: Sage, 1999.
43. Renaud M., 'On the Structural Constraints to State Intervention in Health,' *International Journal of Health Services*, Vol. 5, no. 4, 1975.
44. Bandarage, A., *Women, Population and Global Crisis: A Political Economic Analysis*, London: Zed Books, 1997.
45. Petchesky, Rosalind P. and JUDD, Karen, 'Introduction,' *Negotiating Reproductive Rights: Women's Perspectives Across Countries and Cultures*, Petchesky R.P. and Judd, K. (eds.), London: Zed Books, 1988
46. Ravindran, Sundari, 'Reclaiming the Reproductive Rights Agenda: A Feminist Perspective,' *The Place of Reproductive Health in India's Primary Health Care*, Mohan Rao (eds.), New Delhi: CSMCH, 1998
47. Note 45.
48. Dixon-Mueller, R., 'The Sexuality Connection in Reproductive Health,' *Studies in Family Planning*, Vol. 24, No. 5, 1993.
49. Correa, Sonia, '*Weighing Up Cairo: Evidence from Women in the South*,' Fiji: *DAWN*, 2000.
50. Correa and Petchesky, 'Reproductive and Sexual Rights: A Feminist Perspective', *Population Policies Reconsidered*, (eds.), Sen, G, Germain, A, and Chen, L.C. op. cit., 1994.
51. Bandarage, A., 1997, op. cit.
52. Petchesky, R., in Petchesky and Judd (eds), op. cit., 1998.

53. Note 50.
54. Petchesky, 'The Body as Property: A Feminist Re-vision,' *Conceiving the New World Order: The Global Politics of Reproduction*, Faye D.Ginsberg and Rayna Rapp (eds.), Berkley: University of California Press, 1995.
55. Hartmann, Betsy, op. cit. 1992, p. 152.
56. JAIN, Anrudh and Judith Bruce, 'A Reproductive Health Approach to the Objectives and Assessment of Family Planning Programs,' *Population Policies Reconsidered*, Sen, G. et al., 1994.
57. Hodgson, Dennis and Watkins, Susan Cots, 'Feminists and Neo-Malthusians: Past and Present Alliances', *Population and Development Review*, Vol. 23 (3), 1997.
58. Women's Global Network For Reproductive Rights, 'The ICPD and After,' Amsterdam (forthcoming)
59. Raymond, J.G., 'Connecting Reproductive and Sexual Liberalism' *Radically Speaking: Feminism Reclaimed*, D. Bell, and R. Klein, (eds.), London: Zed Books, 1996, cited in Rupsa Mallik, 'Pre-Natal Victimization of the Female Life World,' unpublished MA Dissertation, The Hague: Institute of Social Studies, 1999.
60. Measham, Anthony R. and Heaver, Richard A., *India's Family Welfare Programme: Towards a Reproductive and Child Health Approach,* Washington DC: The World Bank, 1995.
61. Bandarage, Asoka, *Women, Population and Global Crisis: A Political Economic Analysis*, London: Zed Books, 1997.
62. Kurian, Rachel, *Marketising Reproductive Rights,* New Delhi: Kali for Women, (forthcoming).
63. Brodie, J., 'Shifting the Boundaries: Gender and the Politics of Restructuring,' *The Strategic Silence: Gender and Economic Policy*, I. Bakker (ed.), London: Zed Books.
64. 'Towards Beijing: Crucial Issues of Concern,' *Lokayan Bulletin*, Vol. 12, nos. 1–2, 1995.
65. Ibid.
66. Qadeer, Imrana, 'Women and Health: A Third World Perspective,' *Lokayan Bulletin*, Vol. 12, nos. 1–2, 1995
67. Rao, Mohan, 'Quinacrine Sterilisation Trials: A Scientific Scandal,'*Economic and Political Weekly*, Vol. XXIII, no. 13, 28 March 1998.
68. Krishnaraj, Maithreyi, 'A Gender Critique of Economic Theories of Population' *Gender, Population and Development*, Krishnaraj, Maithreyi, Ratna M. Sudarshan, and Abusaleh Shariff, (eds.), New Delhi: OUP, 1998.
69.. AGNES, Flavia, 'Redefining the Agenda of the Women's Movement within a Secular Framework,' *Women and the Hindu Right: A Collection of Essays*, Urvashi Butalia and Tanika Sarkar (eds.), New Delhi: Kali for Women, 1996.
70. Government Of India, Ministry of Home Affairs, Office of the Registrar General, *Survey of Causes of Death (Rural), India, 1992*, New Delhi.
71. Panchamukhi, P.R., 'Social Impact of Economic Reforms in India: A Critical Appraisal,' *Economic and Political Weekly*, Vol. XXXV, no. 10, 2000.
72. Bang R. A., et al., 'High Prevalence of Gynaecological Diseases in Rural Indian Women,' *Lancet*, Vol. 1, 1989.
73. Rao, 'Family Planning Programme: Paradigm Shift in Strategy?' *Economic and Political Weekly*, Vol. XXXV, No. 49, 2000.
74. Mamdani, Masuma, 'Management of Reproductive Tract Infections in Women: Lessons from the Field,' *Implementing a Reproductive Health Agenda in India: The Beginning*, New Delhi: Population Council, 1999.
75. Jeejabhoy, Shireen J. and Rao, Saumya Rama, 'Unsafe Motherhood: A Review of Reproductive Health,' *Women's Health in India: Risk and Vulnerability*, Bombay: OUP, 1995.

28
GENDER AND DEVELOPMENT (GAD) IN SOUTH ASIA: NEW POLICY AND STRATEGIC OPTIONS

*Dr W. G. Somaratne**

ABSTRACT

This paper analyzes the issues involved in mainstreaming gender and development in South Asia. A comparative analysis of GAD issues in South Asia shows that gender inequality retards economic growth. The disparities between men and women in sharing power and resources; gender biases in rights and entitlements; and conventional religious taboos and myths on gender hinder achieving true economic growth and reduce the well-being of men, women and children in the region. New policy and strategic options including complementary economic and other micro policies, operational options and programs are also suggested for reducing gender inequality and improving the economic development in South Asia.

*Research Fellow, SAARC Human Resource Development Centre (SHRDC), Park Road, Chak Shehzad, Islamabad, Pakistan; (Email: wgsomaratne@hotmail.com).

INTROCUTION

The worldwide demand for food is expected to double within the next thirty years. Industrial output and energy are expected to triple worldwide and increase six fold in developing countries (Parikh, 1998). From 1900 to 2000, world population grew from 1.6 billion to 6.1 billion (United Nations, 2001). With heavy population pressure, changing demand of goods and services and an alarmingly high level of environmental degradation, achieving the objective of sustainable development will be a major challenge for developing countries in the next decade.

South Asia (SA) has 23 per cent of the world's population and 43 per cent of the world's poor (see Table 1). SA is not just the poorest region in the world, it is also the most illiterate, the most malnourished, the most militarized and the least gender-sensitive region (Stiglitz, 1998). Despite its rich bio-diversity, the per capita availability of natural resources such as land, water, and forests is fairly limited. Environmental degradation such as air pollution and land degradation is alarmingly high. The high rate of population growth (ranging from 3.1 per cent in Bhutan to 2.6 per cent in Pakistan during 1995–2000) and low genuine savings rate have resulted in negative growth in per capita real wealth in Bangladesh, India, Nepal and Pakistan (Shah, 2003). Negative growth in per capita wealth is likely to have significant impacts on the development of human capital, especially women. The urgency of achieving gender equality and women's empowerment can be gauged from the fact they have been identified as one of the three millennium development goals developed by the United Nations General Assembly (ADB, 2003).

In most South Asian countries, the structure of agriculture has been changing from labour intensive and subsistence level to large scale and capital intensive. The structure of industrial sector has also been modified from inward-looking or import substitution industrialization (ISI) to outward-looking or export orientation. In this context, sectoral composition of the South Asian economies has been changed from agriculture to higher concentration of industrial and service sectors including trade in service sectors. At the same time international policy environment has also been modernized in line with 'globalisation'[2] and MDGs to encourage international market integration by removing barriers in trade, foreign direct investment and transfer of technology (including information technology).

With these changes in the policy environment, in future, agriculture, industries and services sectors will be far more integrated and intensified. However, given the rapid rate of environmental degradation and gender inequalities sustainable development will be a major challenge in South Asia.

The objective of this paper is to discuss issues involved in mainstreaming gender and development; to conduct a comparative analysis of gender and development in South Asia and suggest new policy and strategic operational options to improve gender equality and economic growth in the South Asian region.

This paper has three sections. Section one presents a comparative analysis of gender mainstreaming in South Asia including gender related issues in development. Section two presents policy and strategic-operational options and mechanisms for empowering women and enhancing economic development in South Asia. The third section comprises of concluding remarks.

Table 1: Selected Indicators of Economic Development and Environmental Change in South Asia

Indicators	Nepal	Sri Lanka	Bangla-desh	Pakistan	India	Maldi-ves	Bhu-tan	South Asia
Population (Millions) (2001)	23.6	19.6	133.4	141.5	1033.4	0.27	2.1	1379.8 (23)
Annual Population Growth Rate (per cent) 1995–2000)	2.7	1.1	1.6	2.6	1.7	1.9	3.1	1.8
Density of population (2001)	165	304	1025	183	348	–	–	289
GNP per capita (US$ –2001)	250	830	370	420	460	2107		450
Rate of GDP Growth (per cent) (1999–2000)	6.5	6.0	5.9	4.4	3.9	4.8	7.0	4.2
Real GDP Per capita (PPP US $) –2001	1310	3180	1610	1890	2840	4798	1833	2730
Population below the National Poverty Line (per cent)	**42.0**	**25.0**	**35.6**	**34.0**	**35.0**	–	–	**43.5**
Growth in per capita real wealth (1970–93)	-2.6	–	-2.4	-1.7	-0.5	–	–	–
Gross domestic savings (per cent of GDP)–2000	16	17	18	12	21	–	–	20
Under–5 mortality rate per 1000 (2000)	100	19	82	110	96	80	100	95
Adult Literacy Rate (per cent of people – age15 and above) (2000)	59.6	94.4	52.3	57.5	68.4	96.6	58	66
Agriculture productivity (Agr. Value added per agri. Worker) 1995 US$ (1998–2000)	188	753	296	630	397	–	–	401
Per cent Change in Forest and Wood Land	–	17.9	-13.4	19.7	-0.7	–	–	–
Per capita Agri. Land (ha)	0.61	0.33	0.10	0.54	0.29	–	–	–

—   Not Available
The figure in the parenthesis is total South Asian population as a per centage of world population;
Sources: Little Green Data Book, 2001, World Bank; World Development Report (2000/2001); Attacking Poverty, 2001, World Bank; World Bank Economic Review, 1999; World Resource Institute, 1994; UNDP (2003).

GENDER MAINSTREAMING IN SOUTH ASIA

Gender[3] mainstreaming means that 'women and men have equitable access to and benefit from society's resources, opportunities and rewards and have an equal participation in influencing what is valued and in shaping directions and decisions' (Gibb, 2001). Strategies to promote understanding of the 'why' of gender mainstreaming often include demonstrating gender issues in apparently 'gender neutral' policies and programs. Gender mainstreaming involves full participation of women in all aspects of life, and addresses access issues to increasing women's participation in the spheres of development where they are weakly represented. The religious or cultural traditions that define and justify the distinct roles and expected behaviors of males and females are strongly cherished and socially enforced. In some countries, there are groups, which seek to impose more stringent divisions between males and females than currently exist, while feminist movements seek to reduce or eradicate these divisions. A woman in South Asia is usually unwanted before birth; disadvantaged as a baby girl; has a childhood of drudgery and is denied education; married and isolated as a girl;

in poor health and uncared for in pregnancy; and is threatened by violence throughout her life. So it is hardly a surprise that most women in South Asia are not in a position to overcome problems in economic, social and political fronts.

In South Asia, governments have adopted various economic and social strategies to achieve the goal of gender equality and sustainable development. Investment liberalization and regionalization of trade, in particular, opened employment opportunities for women in labour intensive agricultural and other industries. Though increased access for women in paid employment in export-oriented industries was opened, the quality of that employment was often questioned. As the Human Development Centre's report (2000) points out, the human costs of poor governance, regional economic non-cooperation and military confrontation are heavier on women of the region. Moreover, women bear the brunt of the lost lives as a result of disease, hunger, civil and military strife and poverty. Women and girls in South Asia face further discrimination in access to health, education, and employment.

Gender and Development Issues in the South Asian Region: Comparative Analysis

Recognition of the status of women and promotion of their potential roles in development are no longer seen only as issues of human rights or social justice. Investment in women is now also recognized as being crucial for achieving sustainable development. Economic analyses recognize that a low level of education and training, poor health and nutritional status, and limited access to limited resources not only depress women's quality of life, but also limit productivity and hinder economic efficiency and growth (ADB, 2003). It is necessary to promote and improve the status of women for reasons of equity and social justice but it also makes economic sense and is an effective development practice.

Table 2: Gender Disparities Profile in the South Asian Region

Country	Life Expectancy at Birth (2000)		Adult Literacy Rate (%) (2000)		Gross Enrollment Rate – Primary School (1995–1999)		Share of Earned Income
	Female (Years) (1998)	As a % oF Male	Female	Male	Female	As a % of Male	Female as a a % of Male
India	63.9	102	45.4	68.4	71	83	34
Pakistan	62.6	99	27.9	57.5	62	70	26
Bangladesh	58.2	100	29.9	52.3	70	97	30
Nepal	57.2	99	24.0	59.6	63	74	50
Sri Lanka	75.4	108	88.6	94.4	100	98	55
Bhutan	62.0	104	30.0	58.0	12	76	48
Maldives	68.0	98	96.8	96.6	98	98	55
South Asia	63.2	102	42.3	66.0	70	–	33
Developing Countries	–	105	64.5	80.3	–	90	–

\#   Weighted Average
Source: Mahbub ul Haq Human Development Centre, (2000).
         Mahbub ul Haq Human Development Centre, (2003).

Women must be promoted by paying greater attention to their needs, concerns and contributions in order to achieve targets of economic growth and poverty reduction. It is also important for human development including population planning, sound management of natural resources and environmental governance[4]. Public policies and investments that promote the development of women can generate economic dividends in terms of higher economic growth; improved productivity; reduced cost of health and safety nets; low fertility, and infant and maternal morbidity and mortality rates; and increased life expectancy. Increased investment in women further produces a healthier, better-educated, literate and flexible workforce.

Most countries in South Asia are undergoing rapid economic and social change through dynamic changes in the national and international policy environment. Impediments to women's participation in the development process undermine the true and potential contribution of almost half of the population. This in turn creates economic loss for the region. Opening up of opportunities for women, especially in education and income generating activities with reduction in population growth, improved health and education of children, easing pressures on environment and improved nutrition status, poverty reduction and sustainable development, indicate that under investment in women is an uneconomic proposition (Word Bank, 1994). It creates detrimental economic and social effects in the countries, if women are marginalised in the development process. In most countries, development programs that include measures to expand women's participation and economic opportunities and increase their incomes, or promote improvements in education and health result in greater economic efficiency and decreased levels of poverty.

Table 3: Gender Disparities Profile in the South Asian Region (Cont'd)

Country	Female Population (2000)		Economic Activity Rate (2000) (Age 15+)	Female Professional and Technical Workers	Gender Development Index (GDI)	Gender Empowerment Measure (GEM)
	Number (Millions)	As a % of Male	Female % of Male	As a % of Total	(2000)	(2000)
India	491	94	50	—	0.560	0.24
Pakistan	66	92	42	26	0.468	0.176
Bangladesh	63	95	76	35	0.468	0.223
Nepal	12	100	66	—	0.470	—
Sri Lanka	9.5	102	55	49	0.737	0.274
Bhutan	1.05	98	65	—	0.444	—
Maldives	0.14	93	80	40	0.739	0.361
South Asia	643	94	52	3	0.542	0.228
Developing Countries	2395	97	67	—	0.634	—

\#   Weighted Average
Source: 'Human Development in South Asia – 2000', Mahbub ul Haq Human Development Centre, (2000).
    'Human Development in South Asia – 2002', Mahbub ul Haq Human Development Centre, (2003).

In all countries in South Asia, except Sri Lanka, women still lack access to education, decent health care, safe drinking water, family planning services, decision making at both the household and community level, employment and income generating opportunities, information and resources (Table 2 and 3). Women continue to suffer from inferior or conventional economic, social and legal status, poor health, illiteracy; long hours of arduous work and the burden of multiple roles—house wife, house maid, caretaker, and child bearer.

Women and the Economy in South Asia

South Asia, with GNP per capita at US$460, is home to nearly 50 per cent of the world's poor living on less than $1 a day. Since 1990 the region has experienced rapid GDP growth, averaging 5.5 per cent a year, which has helped to reduce the consumption poverty rate substantially: India has reduced its poverty rate by 5-10 per cent since 1990; most other countries registered a significant reduction in poverty over the period, except for Pakistan where poverty has stagnated at around 33 per cent – using national poverty lines (World Bank, 2002).

Table 4: Economic Profile of South Asian Economies and Related Human Development Indicators

Country	GNP capita (US$) (2000)	GDP per Growth Rate (%) (1999-2000)	Real GDP capita Growth (%) (1999-2000)	Human Per Capita (PPP) (US$) (2001)	Gender Development Index (HDI) # (2001)	Development Index (GDI)
India	450	3.9	2.0	2840	0.590	0.560
Pakistan	440	4.4	1.9	1890	0.499	0.468
Bangladesh	370	5.9	4.1	1610	0.502	0.468
Nepal	240	6.5	3.9	1310	0.499	0.470
Sri Lanka	850	6.0	4.3	3180	0.730	0.737
Bhutan	590	7.0	3.9	1833	0.511	0.444
Maldives	1960	4.8	2.3	4798	0.751	0.739
South Asia	444 (460) *	4.2 (5.5) $	2.3	2730	0.582	0.542
Developing Countries	1230	5.4	3.9	3850	0.655	0.634

* Figure in the parenthesis is the GNP per capita for South Asia, 2002;
$ Figure in the parenthesis is the economic growth rate in South Asia for the year 2002;
Source: 'Human Development in South Asia – 2000', Mahbub ul Haq Human Development Centre, (2001).
'Human Development in South Asia – 2002', Mahbub ul Haq Human Development Centre, (2003).
Human Development Index – 2003, UNDP (2003).

Looking beyond consumption poverty at other indicators of social progress, the region has had encouraging success in some areas: for example, mortality in children under five has reduced substantially since 1990 (from 129 to 99, per 1,000), especially in Bangladesh (144 to 77, per 1,000) and appreciable gains have also been achieved in total enrolments and completion rates (ibid). Further, between 1970–1993, adult female literacy rates rose from 17 to 35 per cent in South Asia; female primary school enrolments rose between 1960 and 1992 from 39 to 80 per cent in the SA region (ADB, 2002). At the same time, challenges remain in key areas such as gender balance in education and health outcomes, child malnutrition, and maternal mortality: nearly half of all children under the age of five are malnourished and youth illiteracy is high—23 per cent for males and 39 per cent for females. The resurgence of tuberculosis and the threat of HIV/AIDS are also a cause for concern in the region. Considering the Human Development Index (HDI), in 2002, Maldives maintained the highest HDI in

South Asia, surpassing the HDI in Sri Lanka. All other countries in the region maintained slightly improved HDI in the year 2002 (Table 4).

While sustained growth would be necessary for poverty reduction, concomitant improvement in institutional service delivery mechanisms and targeted policy mechanisms will also be essential for achieving progress in gender equity, poverty alleviation and other areas in social development in the region. In South Asia, between 1970 and 2000, women participation in the labour force increased remarkably by improving gender equity in the development process. Bangladesh has shown a remarkable improvement in absorbing women's labour force into the development process during the last thirty years (Table 5).

Table 5: Women as Per centage of Total Labour Force in Selected South Asian Economies

Country	1970	1980	1990	1995	2000
Bangladesh	5.4	43.0	40.7	42.2	42.0
India	29.4	33.8	31.2	32.1	32.0
Nepal	39.3	39.4	40.3	40.5	41.0
Pakistan	9.0	23.4	26.1	28.5	29.0
Sri Lanka	25.0	27.0	34.6	35.7	37.0
Bhutan (1994)	—	—	—	32	—
Maldives (1994)	—	—	—	22	—
South Asia	**21.6**	**33.3**	**34.6**	**35.8**	**33**
Developing Countries	—	—	—	—	40

Source: Asian Development Bank (2003).

\#   'Human Development in South Asia – 2002', Mahbub ul Haq Human Development Centre, (2003).

Table 6: Employment in South Asia by Major Sectors (1995–2001) (per cent)

Country	Gender Status	Agriculture	Industry	Services
Pakistan	Female	66	10	23
	Male	41	20	39
Bangladesh	Female	78	8	11
	Male	54	11	34
Sri Lanka	Female	49	**22**	**27**
	Male	38	23	37
India (1994)	Female	78	10.9	11.1
	Male	58.3	16.5	25.2
Nepal (1996)	Female	93.7	1.4	4.5
	Male	78.9	4.9	13.2
South Asia	**Female**	**15**	**2**	**4**
	Male	**10**	**3**	**8**

\#   For each country male figures are per centages of male labour force and female figures are per centage of female labour force

Source: 'Human Development in South Asia – 2000', Mahbub ul Haq Human Development Centre, (2000).

'Human Development in South Asia – 2002', Mahbub ul Haq Human Development Centre, (2003).

In spite of the above achievements much still has to be done in South Asia to reduce gender gaps. As shown in Table 6, female labour use was dominant in the agricultural sector in most

South Asian countries, compared to industries and service sectors. However in Sri Lanka,[1] both male and female labour forces are almost equally involved in all three sectors. In most countries in the region, technological change in agriculture has replaced female labour force. For instance, manual weeding done by female labourers has been replaced by spraying chemicals by men. Further women's participation in formal industrial sectors, such as the garment industry is rising. For instance in Sri Lanka the per centage of female participation in three Export Processing Zones (EPZ) was about 74 per cent; 82 per cent; and 90 per cent respectively (Atapattu, 2000).

Globalization and its impact on Women

Although globalization opens up opportunities, South Asian women may not be in a position to access them. As stated by Mahbub ul Haq Centre (Human Development Report, 2000), 'the new markets, tools and rules of this global era have failed to alleviate the poverty of most of South Asia's women'. Only urban, educated, relatively affluent women are able to take advantage of the increased opportunities for work that come with the influx of foreign multi national and trans-national corporations. The average earned income share of women in South Asia is 24.7 per cent, far below the developing country average of 32.4 per cent. Therefore, state intervention directly through investment or through partnerships with private sector is necessary for improving women's acess to the opportunities created by globalization.

Female Education Issues in South Asia

Denial of women's right to education is the most serious discrimination. Education is probably the only vehicle that can break the vicious circle of poverty. Although significant investment has been made to improve the status of education in South Asia, vast gaps still remain between educational achievement in men and women and girls and boys. As shown in Table 7, more than half of South Asian adult illiterates are women; more than two-thirds of South Asian out-of primary school children are girls; nearly two-fifths of girls enroled in primary school drop out before grade five; and female vocational education enrolment rate is also low.

Considering the above facts, it is obvious that, women in SA are more vulnerable in terms of getting economic, social and political benefits. Education empowers women to take control of their lives. Education is the key to overcoming oppressive customs, religious taboos and myths and traditions that have negated the needs of women. Provision of education for females will generate benefits for women in particular and society in general by reducing child and maternal mortality and fertility; and improving family health. State intervention for a targeted approach with strategies for compulsory primary education is essential. This can be done by building partnerships with NGOs and other private sector organizations to increase investment in education.

Table 7: Status of Female Education in South Asia

Status of Primary Enrollment ratio– Net (1997)	India	Pakistan	Bangla- desh	Nepal	Sri Lanka	Bhut- an	Mal- dives	SOUTH ASIA
Girls	71	62	70	63	100	12	98	70
Boys	83	71	80	93	100	14	96	81
Total	77	67	75	78	100	13	97	76
Secondary enrolment ratio— Net (1997)								
Girls	48	17	16	40	79	2	49	41
Boys	71	33	27	68	73	7	49	61
Total	60	25	22	55	76	5	49	51
Literacy rate (%) 2000								
Female	45.4	27.9	29.9	24	88.6	30	96.8	42.3
Male	68.4	57.5	52.3	59.6	94.4	58	966.66	66
Total	57	43	41	42	92	47	97	54
Drop-out rate (%) 1994								
Girls	41	56	33	48	1	16	6	41
Boys	35	46	31	48	2	19	9	35
Female teachers (as a % of total primary teachers) 1997–98	36	35	31	22	96	30	94	37
Public Expenditure on Education (As a % of GDP) 1995–97	3.2	2.7	2.2	3.2	3.4	4.1	6.4	3.2

Source: 'Human Development in South Asia – 2000', Mahbub ul Haq Human Development Centre, (2000).
'Human Development in South Asia – 2002', Mahbub ul Haq Human Development Centre, (2003).

Female Health Issues in South Asia

The manifestation of gender discrimination ranges from preferential treatment of boys in provision of food and health care, to rape, dowry and death. An estimated 208,000 women die annually due to pregnancy and birth-related complications. A large majority of girls become mothers before the age of 20. A majority of South Asian women are chronically ill because of malnutrition, lack of adequate health care, and frequent child bearing, About 60 per cent of women in their child bearing years in South Asia are under weight and stunted due to inadequate nutrition during their own childhood (UNFPA, 1998). Infant mortality rates are comparatively high in Nepal, Bangladesh and Pakistan compared to other countries in the region. In Maldives 51 per cent and in India 18 per cent more girls die, before their fifth birthday, than their male counter parts (Table 8). Poverty is the major contributory factor to the ill health and malnutrition of women in SA. The tradition of sequential feeding—male first then to female, is practiced in some communities in South Asia. Such a tradition takes a heavy toll on the health of young girls and women.

Table 8: Under – 5 Mortality Rates in South Asia

Country	Male	Female	Ratio: (Female/Male)
Bangladesh	106	116	1.09
Bhutan	98	94	0.96
India	82	97	1.18
Maldives	53	80	1.51
Nepal	110	124	1.13
Pakistan	108	104	0.96
Sri Lanka	22	20	0.91
SOUTH ASIA	**86.9**	**99**	**1.14**

Source: UNFPA – 1999;

Table 9: Health Profile in South Asia—2000

Characteristics	India	Pakistan	Bangla-desh	Nepal	Sri Lanka	Bhutan	Mal-dives	South Asia	Develop Countries
Population with access to (2000)									
Safe water (per cent)	88	88	97	81	83	—	—	89	79
Sanitation (per cent)	31	61	53	27	83	—	—	37	52
Population per doctor (1992-95)	2083	1923	5555	20000	4348	5000	5263	2273	1282
Maternal Mortality ratio (per 100,000 live births) (1985-99)	540	340	350	540	60	380	350	492	—
Public Expenditure on Health (as per cent of GDP) (1995–99)	0.8	0.7	1.7	1.3	1.7	3.2	3.7	0.9	2.5

Source: 'Human Development in South Asia – 2002', Mahbub ul Haq Human Development Centre, (2003);

In South Asia, it is necessary to increase investment on provision of health facilities at least proportionate to the rate of GDP growth in each country. Provision of health facilities should be improved by building partnerships with the private sector, targeting the poor, children, and women separately rather than a generic type of investment on health. It will generally improve the health status of women and girls in the long run. It is necessary to avoid the expenditure phobia of health expenses and shift to consider health expenditure as a long-term cost of investment for improvement of future workforce in the country.

Issues in Gender and Governance in South Asia

Although South Asia has had several women heads of state, women in South Asia have the lowest rates of participation in the structures of governance. For example, in South Asia5 :

- Women occupy only 7 per cent of the parliamentary seats
- Only 9 per cent of cabinet ministers are women
- Only 6 per cent of positions in the judiciary are held by women
- Only 9 per cent of civil servants are women
- Only 20 per cent members of local government are women

Table 10: Women in Parliament and Female Professionals and technical Workers in South Asia

Country	Per centage Share of Parliamentary Members			Female Professional and Technical Workers (as per cent of total) (1991–2000)
	Single or Lower House	Upper House or Senate	Total (Both Houses)	
Bangladesh	12.4	—	12.4	35
India	8.8	8.5	8.7	—
Nepal	5.4	15	7.5	—
Maldives	6.3	—	6.3	40
Sri Lanka	4.9	—	4.9	49
Pakistan	2.8	2.3	2.6	26
Bhutan	2.0	—	2.0	—
SOUTH ASIA (unweighted)	**7.4**	**7.5**	**7.3**	**3**
World	13.3	10.6	12.8	
Nordic Countries	38.3	—	38.3	
Sub-Saharan Africa	11.6	13.2	11.8	
East Asia	9.5	13.0	10.1	

Source: Human Development in South Asia – 2000', Mahabub ul Haq Human Development Centre, (2000).
      Human Development in South Asia – 2002', Mahabub ul Haq Human Development Centre, (2003).

Decision - making in all domains has traditionally been done by males in SA. However, over the past two decades South Asian women's involvement in decision-making processes has increased. As indicated in Table 10 below, the South Asian women's share in the decision making process of legislature is somewhat lower than the world figures of women contribution in parliamentary representation. In public administration, Sri Lankan women contribute about one half of the workforce in professional and technical fields compared to other countries in SA. Women's empowerment in South Asia should be strengthened by mainstreaming women's concerns in development by decentralizing power from the centre to the regions. Civil society, NGOs, community organizations and political parties should make efforts to empower women in the decision making process. A minimum quota for women members in parliament should be ensured by enacting laws and devising constitutional provisions in each country in South Asia.

New Policy and Strategic Options in Improving Gender Equity and Development in South Asia

Gender equality is an issue of development effectiveness, not just a matter of political correctness or kindness to women. New empirical evidence demonstrates that when women and men are relatively equal, economies tend to grow faster. The poor move more quickly out of poverty and the well-being of men, women and children is enhanced (World Bank, 2002). So, policy guidance and the need for new strategies arises from the evidence that gender plays a decisive role in determining economic growth, poverty reduction and effectiveness of development strategies. The integration of mainstreaming gender into the decision making process of development in SA is necessary to avoid gender-related barriers and other impediments in the poverty reduction and sustainable development process. Further, sound policies and programmes for integration of gender concerns into main stream decision making process can also assist to improve both gender equality and economic development as 'win-win' solutions. The following policy and operational options are suggested to formulate gender-sensitive polices and gender-focused programmes to improve women status and productivity in South Asia.

Political Will: A Necessary Pre-Condition for Pro-Women Development

Poverty and the political economy in developing countries have a close link. In SA, political power and wealth go hand in hand. Small-scale peasants including women have no way to break the vicious circle of poverty. If the strong political economy is there, they have the ability to distort policy environment in gender and development. If such political economy exists, poor men and women have no way to build accumulated capital, and use improved technology and other skilled manpower to enhance productivity and income levels.

The South Asian governments should intervene in the following specific areas to facilitate gender equality:

- Formulate gender-sensitive policies and programmes for economic and social development
- Modify regulatory and legal frameworks that prevent women from participating in economic development
- Build institutional capabilities for implementing programmes for advancing women's status and monitoring and evaluation of such gender-focussed programmes
- Strengthen the sex-disaggregated database for gender analysis
- Prepare periodic multi-sectoral Country Specific Gender Assessment (CGAs) that analyze the gender dimensions of development across sectors and identify-gender responsive actions important for poverty reduction, economic growth, human-well being; and development effectiveness
- Mobilize resources for addressing gender disparities

Implementing Sound Policy Options: Conceptual Shifts

In the SA region, implementing gender-neutral policy framework requires conceptual shifts to gain 'win-win' solutions by maintaining gender equality and improving economic development. To maintain sustainable partnerships with all stakeholders in gender mainstreaming and gain benefits for women, it is necessary to build goodwill, commitment to experimentation, leadership, fine-tuning solutions and institution building. Conceptual shifts for creating gender equality are as follows:

- Empowering poor women as actors in identifying their problems and seeking their own solutions
- Engaging poor women as partners in the process, not as beneficiaries and using people-centered frameworks for planning and implementation
- Building partnerships with private sector organizations through incentives to mobilize resources rather than expecting all resources from the state
- Granting real rights and ownerships of assets for the poor women (e.g. land rights) for further improvement and investment and not just a 'sense of ownership'

Creating Employment Opportunities and Higher Incomes for Women and Their Families

Educated and healthy women can engage in productive activities, find employment opportunities in the formal sector, and earn higher incomes for their sustenance. Investments in targeted female education and health projects tend to increase abilities and thereby employment in enterprises. So a good option is to open up targeted labour-intensive, micro enterprises by employing women (e.g. Cut-flower and foliage industry in Sri Lanka). The state should provide financial and technical support directly, or by building partnerships with private sector organizations. Further, the state should facilitate providing market information on products, and product standards. Training of women for producing standard (quality assured products) products is necessary. Partner organizations should be encouraged to integrate into regional and international niche markets. The investment will increase the country's total economic output, as well as creating opportunities for women thereby gaining gender equality.

Protection and Expansion of Women's Asset (or Capital) Base

While income and consumption are important, building asset base (i.e. capital) for the poor women in rural areas in South Asia is very important to achieve one twin objectives of opening access to assets for women and alleviating poverty through increased productivity of labour. The building of assets among women includes investment on:

- Human capital (especially girls' and women's skills, knowledge, beliefs, attitudes, labour ability and good health)
- Natural capital (using forests, water, land, fish and minerals for women)
- Social capital (relationships of trust and reciprocity, groups, networks, and customary law among women groups for empowerment)
- Physical capital (basic infrastructure to access markets for women and girls)
- Financial capital (monetary resources—savings and access to credit for women and girls)

Protection of current assets of the women is possible through designing an insurance scheme for poor women in the SA region. Cash payments, in-kind payments, or public works employment during the drought, major crop failure or natural disaster can provide for subsistence needs for women while reducing the need to over-exploit natural resources. Regular program can also be designed to encourage poor women to work on environmental improvement projects or crisis program to provide pro-women safety nets.

Improving Female Education to Gain Access to Resources

The governments in South Asia should target primary education as a 'Social Vaccination' to create social immunity for female children who are a prime target within the MDGs of universal primary education. School dropouts in primary schools and child labour have a positive correlation in South Asia. The government should devise education policies and program for compulsory primary education, with provision of free school textbooks and uniforms, removing the school fees at least up to the secondary level, and provision of necessary infra-structural facilities. But, it should be phased out initially at the primary education level with compulsory provisions and at the second stage, it can be expanded up to the secondary level. (e.g. Free education policy in Sri Lanka from primary to the post graduate level, provision of free textbooks and school uniforms for primary and secondary levels). Further, the government should reserve the quota of 20 per cent of placements in private schools for under privileged girls. India has already implemented this policy measure. The objective of offering education for poor females is to strengthen their abilities to access resources and reduce gender inequality in the South Asian region. Further, improving education means strengthening awareness of women to improve their own and family health status including infant mortality, family planning and family nutrition. Primary education—'social vaccination' indirectly assists in improving gender equality among women by creating a base for solving most social and economic problems faced by them.

Improvement of the Quality of Good Governance with Gender Equality

A growing body of literature suggests that gender equality in rights and resources leads to a reduction in corruption and better governance. Although the correlation between gender and corruption may reflect the exclusion of women from positions of power and thus from the opportunity to engage in corrupt practices, evidence from micro level studies is consistent with the country level correlation (World Bank, 2002).

Reallocation of Investments Through Private-State Partnerships

Target-oriented investment towards poor women for improving resource base and opening access to natural resources should be encouraged. For this purpose, incentive packages should be formulated to attract private sector investments and technology by building private-state partnerships for pro-women enterprises (e.g. production of palmyrah leave-boxes for packing tea with Stassen Exports (Pvt) Ltd. and cut-flower projects in Sri Lanka).

Community-Based Actions for Sharing of Resources

Developing effective community-based institutions for collective management of resources is a key element in designing programs to aid gender equality in each country in the region. Collective management is a viable option, which can reduce the cost of maintaining state-owned institutional mechanisms particularly for sustainable management of common property resources (CPR) through creating access for CPR for poor women. It will allow poor women to better-tailor designs depending on their needs. It is advisable to encourage women-community participation for alleviation of poverty and reduction of environmental degradation, by strengthening the bargaining power of women-users. Through such women-based community approaches, all stakeholders of CPR can become partners in the process for maintaining gender equality, alleviating poverty and improving environmental management.

Granting Environmental Entitlements with Co-Management of Natural Resources for Poor-Women

'Environmental entitlements' can be created for poor-women to use natural resources in a sustainable way through community participation. Such as rights to the forests for firewood; water rights to landless people including women; and rights to lands for landless women. Further, the government, through a regulatory role, can strengthen local user organizations, provide technical assistance and mediate to avoid conflicting claims on the resource (e.g. Joint Forest Management program in India, the government owns land but the state provides technology to maintain forestry; poor-women can get benefits of firewood and when it matures, income will be shared with the community. It may lead to achieve win-win solutions by reducing poverty, protecting the environment and maintaining gender equity. Co-management can include setting up a citizen oversight board to monitor the performance in pro-poor women development projects.

Co-Investment with Poor-Women

The state should design targeted pro-women development programs which involve co-investment with local women and farmer's organizations. The state can mobilize long-term capital and technology for pro-poor women projects, such as soil conservation or improvement, and micro-watershed improvement projects. The state has the options for co-investment through matching funds and establishing revolving funds, by providing necessary seed capital. As Ambler (1999) pointed out, provision of funds for better water supply, sanitation and energy services through rural electrification programs can assist in reducing health associated effects of poor, including women and girls—indoor cooking smoke and poor hygiene and illiteracy with poor lighting through co-investment with rural women user communities.

CONCLUDING REMARKS

Gender inequality retards economic growth and poverty reduction. Gender-based division of labour, disparities between males and females in sharing power and resources; gender biases in rights and entitlements; and conventional and religious taboos and myths act to hinder achieving true economic growth. It has led to gender inequalities and contributed to increasing the level of poverty in South Asia. These findings make it clear that the only way to address gender inequality issues is by introducing multi-dimensional approaches to fight against poverty in South Asia.

Gender issues are also central to the commitments made by most South Asian nations with the Millennium Development Goals (MDGs) including the goal of gender equality and empowerment of women and the Fourth World Conference on Women in Beijing in 1995. The incorporation of gender issues in mainstream development policies and actions needs to be sensitive to the specific conditions in each country in South Asia. Most countries in SA have already tried to integrate gender equality issues into their policy framework, particularly in the education and health sectors.

Though each country in South Asia has liberalized their economic policy environment at various degrees, mainstreaming gender perception has not been given the due prominence in policy arena. Liberalization with a human face integrates mainstreaming gender perspectives with complementary sectoral and micro level policies, programs and operational options. The complementary policies and operational devices suggested to integrate mainstreaming gender and development perspectives are: improved employment opportunities and higher incomes for women and their families; improving female education to gain access to resources; protection and expansion of the asset (or capital) base of the women; improvement of the quality of good governance with gender equality; re-allocation of pro-women investments through private-state partnerships; community-based actions for sharing of resources for women; granting environmental entitlements with co-management of natural resources for poor-women; and co-investment with poor-women. Through these policy mechanisms, it is expected to strengthen the abilities of women in the economy; expand enrollment of girls in schools; improve women's health; increase women's participation in the labour force; intensify women's options in agriculture; and provide capital or assets to women. Understanding the gender and development issues, formulating right policies and strategic operational options, implementing program through right institutional mechanisms are necessary to improve gender equality, which is a paradigm shift in the right direction to achieve the MDGs in South Asia.

References

ADB (2003), 'Policy on Gender and Development,' Manila, Philippines: Asian Development Bank.

AMBLER, John (1999), '*Attacking Poverty While Improving the Environment: Toward Win-Win Policy Options,*' Paper presented for the Forum of Ministers Meeting as part of the UNDP-EC Poverty and Environment Initiative, New York, USA: Social Science Research Council.

ADB (2002), *Population and Human Resource Trends and Challenges*, Manila, Philippines: Asian Development Bank.

ATAPATTU, Danny (2000), '*Women and the Economy of Sri Lanka,*' Islamabad: Mahbub-ul-Haq Human Development Centre.

GIBB ET AL., Heather (2001), *Gender Mainstreaming: Good Practices from the Asia Pacific Region*, Ottawa, Canada: The North South Institute.

MAHBUB ul Haq Human Development Centre (2000), *Human Development in South Asia – 2000*, Karachi, Pakistan: Oxford University Press.

MAHBUB ul Haq Human Development Centre (2003), *Human Development in South Asia 2002*: Agriculture and Rural Development, Karachi: Oxford University Press.

PARIKH, Kirit S. (1998), '*Poverty and Environment: Turning the Poor into Agents of Environmental Regeneration,*' WP1, Working Paper Series, Geneva: UNDP.

SHAH, Amita (2003), 'Development and Environment: Towards a South Asian Perspective,' Sandee Newsletter, issue 7, no. 1, Nepal: Sandee, August 2003.

SOMARATNE, W.G. (2002), 'Globalization and the Sri Lankan Agriculture: Challenges and Opportunities,' *Sri Lankan Agriculture for the Next Decade: Challenges and Opportunities*, W.G. Somaratne (ed.), Colombo, Sri Lanka: Hector Kobbekaduwa Agrarian Research and Training Institute.

STIGLITZ, Joseph (1998), 'Development: East Asian Model Still OK for South Asia,' Lecture compiled by Feizal Samath, Colombo, Sri Lanka.

UNDP (2003), *Human Development Report*, New York: Oxford University Press.

Unescap (2003), *What is Good Governance?* Bangkok, Thailand: UNESCAP *(http://www.unescap.org/huset/gg/governance.htm)*.

UNFPA, (1998), *The State of the World Population*, New York: Unfpa.

United Nations (2001), *Road Map towards the implementation of the United Nations Millennium Declaration: Report of the Secretary General*, New York: United Nations.

United Nations (2001a), *World Population Monitoring 2001*, Population, Environment and Development, New York: UN.

World Bank (1992), *World Development Report-1992—Development and the Environment*, Washington DC: The World Bank.

World Bank (1994), 'Enhancing Women's Participation in Economic Development': A World Bank Policy Paper, Washington D.C: World Bank.

World Bank (2001), *World Development Report-2001 – Attacking Poverty*, Washington DC: The World Bank

World Bank (2002), *Millennium Development Goals: South Asia,* Washington D.C: World Bank (http://www.developmentgoals.com).

World Bank, (2002a), *Integrating Gender into World Bank Work: A Strategy for Action*, Washington D.C.: The World Bank.

Notes

1. Research Fellow, SAARC Human Resource Development Centre (SHRDC), Park Road, Chak Shehzad, Islamabad, Pakistan; (Email: wgsomaratne@hotmail.com).
2. The globalization means *'boundaryless trade and information' or 'integration of the world economy through trade, investment and the global movement of capital'*. The objective of globalization is to improve international market integration through removing barriers in trade, foreign direct investment, transfer of technology, and information (Somaratne, 2002).
3. The term gender refers to *'culturally based expectations of the roles and behaviors of males and females'* (United Nations, 2001). The term distinguishes the socially constructed from the biologically determined aspects of being male and female. Unlike biology of sex, gender roles and behaviors can change historically some times relatively quickly, even if aspects of these roles originated in the biological differences between the sexes.
4. Governance is defined as 'the process of decision-making and the process by which decisions are implemented' (UNESCAP, 2003). Governance can be used in several contexts such as corporate governance, international governance, national governance and local governance.
5. Mahbub ul Haq Human Developent Centre report 2000.

ANNEXURE

6th Sustainable Development Conference

Sustainable Development:
Bridging the Research/Policy Gaps in Southern Contexts
December 11 – December 13, 2003

Organized by the

Sustainable Development Policy Institute (SDPI)
Islamabad, Pakistan

Venue for Opening Plenary/Sessions/Closing Plenary
Holiday Inn, G-6, Islamabad

Sustainable Development conference Series: A Background

SDPI's Sustainable Development Conference series is another dimension of outreach to the general public as well as policy makers where emphasis is placed on emerging sustainable development issues in Pakistan. It is an important channel of policy advice where each session of the conference is followed by a panel discussion consisting of representatives from the government, community representatives, NGOs, and donor agencies.

First SDC
The first SDC, titled *The Green Economics Conference*, was organized by SDPI in 1995. This Conference focused on the interaction between economics and the environment, and included research papers on trade, fiscal policy, EIAs, green accounting, forestry, energy, industry and the urban environment.

Second SDC
The second SDC, in 1996, addressed the broad theme of sustainable development including pollution abatement, resource management, conservation of biodiversity, the transfer and use of technology, trade and environment, human development and poverty alleviation, and social capital and governance. The conference was successful in highlighting key issues facing the country and bringing out the latest thinking and analysis to identify solutions.

Third SDC
The theme of the third conference was *A Dialogue on Environment and Natural Resource Conservation*. The Conference, held in 1998, focussed on stimulating a dialogue on practical policy options for key environmental challenges facing Pakistan. The two broad thematic areas of Urban Environment and Natural Resources concentrated on urban pollution, water resource management, deforestation and sustainable agriculture with presentations by experts from within Pakistan and the South Asian region.

Fourth SDC

The Fourth Sustainable Development Conference titled 'Discourse on Human Security' was organised in collaboration with RCSS, ActionAid, IPRI and SNPO in 2000. It focused on the changes and improvement in government policies and practice with regard to human security. The conference was designed to raise awareness of senior policy makers, key federal and provincial government officials and civil society groups like the media and NGOs on security issues. The immediate feedback from government, NGOs and media was extremely encouraging.

Fifth SDC

The fifth conference titled Sustainable Development and Southern Realities: Past and Future in South Asia critically re-examined the conceptualization and implementation of sustainable development in its multiple dimensions: economic, political, social, and moral. The conference scrutinized and consolidated some of the ideas presented at the World Summit on Sustainable Development in Johannesburg, and resituated debates in the South Asian context.

Thursday, December11, 2003	Day one
Opening Plenary	9:30 am – 11:00 am

Welcome and Introduction
Dr. Saba Gul Khattak
Executive Director, SDPI, Pakistan

Opening Address
Mr. Shamsul Mulk
Chairman, Board of Governors, SDPI, Pakistan

Inaugural Address and Book Launch by the Chief Guest
Mr. Shaukat Aziz
Federal Minister for Finance

TEA	11:00 am – 11:30 am

Thursday, December 11, 2003	Day one

Concurrent Session A-1	11:30 am – 1:15 pm

State, Violence and Migration
Chair: Armin Hasemann, Director FES

Speaker	Title
Chandrika Parmar (India)	Indo Pak Partition: Community and Violence
Ahmad Salim (SDPI, Pakistan)	Partition of India: The case of Sindh
Rukhsana Qamber (Pakistan)	Implications of immigration on Pakistani identities
Ritu Menon (India)	Doing peace: Women resist daily battle in South Asia
Imtiaz Ahmad (Bangladesh)	Comments
Discussion	

LUNCH	1:15 pm – 2:00 pm

Concurrent Session B-1   11:30 am – 1:15 pm

Mass Media and the National Press
Chair: Dr Mehdi Hassan, Pakistan

Speaker	Title
Rehan Ansari (USA)	Corporate Media and the Ethnic Press—the Case of Urdu Press in New York - post 9/11
Ayesha Haroon (Pakistan)	Media, Policy, Advocacy
Shafqat Munir (SDPI, Pakistan)	Freedom of Information: The Right to Know
Mr Mukhtar Ahmad Ali (Pakistan)	Freedom of information in South Asia: Comparative perspectives on civil society initiative
Shujauddin, APP (Pakistan) and Sameea Jamil, Kinnaird College (Pakistan)	Comments

Discussion

LUNCH	1:15 pm – 2:00 pm

Concurrent Session C-1   11:30 am – 1:15 pm

Governance and Decentralization/Devolution: Democracy in South Asia
Chair: Haroon Sharif, DFID, Islamabad

Speaker	Title
Foqia Sadiq Khan (SDPI, Pakistan)	A Benchmark Study on Law-and-Order and the Dispensation of Justice in the Context of Power Devolution
Farrukh Moriani (Pakistan)	Issues in Devolution: A Case Study of Sindh
Dr. Abid Q. Suleri and Ali Rind (SDPI, Pakistan)	Manchar Lake: Case Study
Arshad Bhatti, British Council, (Pakistan)	Comments

Discussion

LUNCH	1:15 pm – 2:00 pm

Thursday, December 11, 2003 — Day one

Concurrent Session A-2 — 2:00 pm – 3:45 pm
Education and Identity
Chair: Dr Tariq Rahman, QAU, Islamabad

Speaker	Title
Ahmad Salim (SDPI, Pakistan)	1971: Historical Falsehoods in our Textbooks
Rubina Saigol (Pakistan)	Between the Sacred and the Secular: History Teaching and Identity Formation in India and Pakistan
Tahir Kamran (Pakistan)	The problematic of identity in educational discourse of Pakistan: A historical perspective
Ajmal Kamal (Pakistan)	Censorship in Pakistani Urdu Textbooks
Yamima Mitha (Pakistan)	Comments

Discussion

TEA	3:45 pm – 4:15 pm

Concurrent Session B-2 (Panel I) — 2:00 pm – 3:45 pm
IR/Relevance of Social Sciences in South Asia
Chair: Dr. Masuma Hasan, Member SDPI Board of Governors and Former Cabinet Secretary, GoP

Speaker	Title
Itty Abraham (USA)	Policy Intellectuals and Public Intellectuals
Shaheen Sardar Ali (UK)	Social Sciences and the Academe: The Achilles heel of postcolonial societies?
Faisal Bari (Pakistan)	Social Sciences Research and Education in Pakistan: Relevant/ Irrelevant
Dr Talat Mahmood (Germany)	The Knowledge Production Function and R and D Spillovers
S. Akbar Zaidi, Economist	Comments

Discussion

TEA	3:45 pm – 4:15 pm

Concurrent Session C-2   **2:00 pm – 3:45 pm**

Globalization and WTO: Post Ministerial Debriefing Session
Chair: Mr. Onder Yucer (Resident Representative UNDP)

Speaker	Title
Ratnakar Adhikari (Nepal)	Rhetoric and inclusiveness: Frustrating tales of LDCs' accession to WTO
Pradeep Mehta (India)	Singapore Issues: Way forward for Developing Countries
Tahir Hussain (Islamabad)	Fair Trade after Cancun: Agriculture Remains the Test Case
Dr Abid Q. Suleri (SDPI, Pakistan)	Implementation Issues: UR to Cancun
Qasim Niaz, Joint Secretary, WTO Wing, Ministry of Commerce, (Pakistan)	Comments
Discussion	

TEA   3:45 pm – 4:15 pm

Thursday, December 11, 2003   **Day one**

Concurrent Session A-3   **4:15 pm – 6:00 pm**

Education and Medium of Instruction
Chair: Fakhr Zaman, Chairman World Punjabi Congress, Lahore

Speaker	Title
Shahid Siddiqui (Pakistan)	English as Medium of Instruction
Ali Ahmed Rind (SDPI, Pakistan)	Sindhi as Medium of Instruction
Dr. Ahsan Wagah (Pakistan)	Language Development in Pakistan – Forced Ignorance of the Root Language
Wahid Baksh Buzdar	Regional Languages and the Medium of Instruction
Shafqat Tanvir Mirza (Pakistan)	Education and medium of instruction
Dr Sarfaraz Khan (Pakistan)	Pashto as Medium of Instruction in NWFP: Facts and Politics
Yamima Mitha (Pakistan)	Comments
Discussion	

Concurrent Session B-3 (Panel II)

4:15 pm – 6:00 pm

IR/Relevance of Social Sciences in South Asia
Chair: Dr Najma Najam, Vice Chancellor, FJWU, Rawalpindi

Speaker	Title
Dr (Ms) Iftikhar Hasan (Pakistan)	Research in Social Sciences Regarding Gender Equity – Its Impact on Policy Making Bodies
Kelly Teamey (UK)	Bridging the Ideal and the Real in Social Sciences: the case for Applying Critical Discourse Analysis in examining Environmental Education Practices in Development Context of Pakistan
Dr Nighat Saeed Khan (Pakistan)	Physician Heal Thyself: Social Science and Humanity Academe in Pakistan
S Akbar Zaidi (Economist)	Comments
	Discussion

Concurrent Session C-3

4:15 pm – 6:00 pm

Peace and Security in Nuclearized South Asia
Chair: Karamat Ali, PILER, Karachi

Speaker	Title
Haider Nizamani (Canada)	People's Perceptions of Nuclear Security
Pervez Hoodbhoy (Pakistan)	Where is India-Pakistan Nuclear Race Heading?
Ayesha Siddiqa Agha (Pakistan)	From Defense to Development
Lt. Gen (Ret.) Kamal Mateenuddin (Pakistan)	Comments
	Discussion

Friday, December 12, 2003

Day Two

Concurrent Session A-1 (Panel I)

9:00 am – 10:45 am

National Environmental Quality Standards (NEQS)
Implementation in Pakistan for Industrial Pollution Control
Chair: Dr Parvez Hassan, Chairman NEQS Implementation Committee, Pakistan

Speaker	Title
Mohammad Atif (Pakistan)	Hurdles in Implementation and Achievement of NEQS in Leather Sector
Azher Uddin Khan (Pakistan)	Past, Present and Future of NEQS Implementation in Pakistan
Irfan S Alrai (Pakistan)	Environmental Quality Standards and its Application in Developing Countries
Dr. Noman Qadir (Pakistan)	Comments
	Discussion

TEA	10:45 am – 11:15 am

Concurrent Session B-1 Panel I   9:00 am – 10:45 am

Alternative Realities: The Voice and Role of Fiction Writers
Chair: Muneeza Shamsie, Writer and Critic

Speaker	Title
Arshad H Bhatti (Pakistan)	Literature and Development
Kiran Nazir Ahmad, (SDPI, Pakistan)	Voice of Dissent in Urdu Popular Fiction
Maniza Naqvi (Novelist, Pakistan)	Owning our Stories
Uzma Aslam Khan (Novelist, Pakistan)	Comments
Discussion	

TEA	10:45 am – 11:15 am

Concurrent Session C-1   9:00 am – 10:45 am

Farmers Rights Program: Impact of Globalization on Lives and Livelihoods of the HKH Communities
Chair: Dr Wajid Pirzada, Director PARC, Islamabad

Speaker	Title
Gopichand Sedhain (Nepal)	Case Study from Nepal
Avanthi Weerasinghe (Sri Lanka)	Case Study from Sri Lanka
Rizwana Syeda (Bangladesh)	Case Study from Bangladesh
Dr. Abid Q. Suleri/Qasim Shah (SDPI, Pakistan)	Case Study from Pakistan
Mita Dutta (India)	Intellectual Property Rights and Access to Seed: A Case Study of Himalayan Region in India
Ratnakar Adhikari (Nepal)	Comments
Discussion	

TEA	10:45 am – 11:15 am

Friday, December 12, 2003   Day Two

Concurrent Session A-2 (Panel II)   11:15 am – 1:00 pm

National Environment Quality Standards (NEQS)
Implementation in South Asian Region for Industrial Pollution Control
Chair: Maj (R.) Tahir Iqbal, Minister of Environment

Speaker	Title
Mahmood A Khwaja (SDPI, Pakistan)	Regulating Industrial Pollution Control Through Effective Collaboration of Policy Makers, Universities, Research and Development Organizations and Industry
Rita Pandey (India)	Industrial pollution control in India: Issues in design and enforcement of regulation
Ram Charitra Sah (Nepal)	Compliance Monitoring of Industrial Effluent Standard in Nepal
Saiful Islam (Bangladesh)	Environmental Protection and Pollution Control in Industrial Development as a Requirement for Sustainable Development in Developing Countries: Evidence from Bangladesh
Engg. Asif Shujah Khan (DG Pak EPA, Pakistan)	Comments
Discussion	
LUNCH	1:00 pm – 2:30 pm

Concurrent Session B-2 Panel II   11:15 am – 1:00 pm

Alternative Realities: The Voice and Role of Fiction Writers
Chair: Maniza Naqvi, Novelist

Speaker	Title
Uzma Aslam Khan (Novelist, Pakistan)	Improvisation
Muneeza Shamsie (Writer and Critic)	Connecting North and South: The South Asian English Novel
Kiran Nazir Ahmad (SDPI, Pakistan)	Comments
Discussion	
LUNCH	1:00 pm – 2:30 pm

Concurrent Session C-2   11:15 am– 1:00 pm

Labour Policy in South Asia

Chair: Khwaja Ejaz Sarwar, Secretary Labour, Ministry of Labour and Manpower, Pakistan

Speaker	Title
Karamat Ali (Pakistan)	Labor Policy in Pakistan
Shirin Naher (Bangladesh)	Role of Labor Policy and its Impact on Women Workers: An agenda for Dialogue in Bangladesh
Halina Ward (IISD, UK)	Comments
Discussion	

LUNCH	1:00 pm – 2:30 pm

Friday, December 12, 2003   Day Two

Concurrent Session A-3   2:30 pm – 3:45 pm

Resource Rights and Sustainable Livelihoods

Chair: Mr. Bashir A. Wani, IG Forests Ministry of Environment

Speaker	Title
Adil Najam (USA)	Broadening the security debate: Human and environmental dimensions
Dr Shaheen Rafi Khan and Shahbaz Bokhari (SDPI, Pakistan)	Resource rights and sustainable livelihoods: A case study of Pakistan's Dir-Kohistan forests
Mehmood Cheema (Pakistan)	Mitigating Insecurity: Experience of ERNP-Dir Kohistan Sub-Project
Kimberly Vilar (Argentina)	The role of the action researcher in bridging the gap between research production and policy making: thoughts on IIED-AL¥s recent experiences in local urban upgrading research processes
Fahd Ali and Dr Shaheen Rafi Khan (SDPI, Pakistan)	The Potential Impact of TBT and SPS Measures on Pakistan's Fisheries
Sana Ullah Khan, Dir-Kohistan ERNP, (Pakistan)	Comments
Discussion	

TEA	3:45 pm – 4:15 pm

Concurrent Session B-3   2:30 pm – 3:45 pm

Child Labour and the Informal Economy: Issues and Solutions Organizer
Chair: Johannes Lokollo, Country Director, ILO, Pakistan

Speaker	Title
Shahbaz Bokhari (SDPI, Pakistan)	A Rapid Assessment of Scavengers in Pakistan
Shyma Salgado (Sri Lanka)	The National Approach to Eliminate the Worst Forms of child Labour - the Sri Lanka Experience
M Saifullah Chaudhry (Pakistan)	Worst Forms of Child Labour: A situation analysis of Six Hazardous Sectors
Tracey Rizvi (Pakistan)	Legal Aspects of Child Labour in Pakistan
Zulfiqar Ali Gondal (Pakistan)	Comments
Discussion	

TEA	3:45 pm – 4:15 pm

Concurrent Session C-3   2:30 pm – 3:45 pm

Population, Health and Poverty
Chair: Dr. Majeed Rajput (Chief, National Health Policy, Ministry of Health)

Speaker	Title
Dr W G Somaratne (Sri Lanka)	Gender and Development (GAD) in South Asia: New policies and strategic options
Dr Eaisha Tareen (UK)	From "Thinking too much" to "Extinguishing of the heart" — the case for Qualitative Research in Social and Health Policy Planning
Dr Mohan Rao (India)	The Globalization of Reproductive Rights: A Derivative Discourse?
Prof. Dr. Mehtab Karim (Dept. of Community Health Sciences, AKU)	Comments
Discussion	

TEA	3:45 pm – 4:15 pm

Friday, December 12, 2003 ·   Day Two

Concurrent Session A-4   4:15 pm – 6:00 pm

Natural Resource Management
Chair: Shamsul Mulk, Chairman Board of Governors, SDPI

Speaker	Title
Nazir Mehmud, (Pakistan) (confirmation awaited)	Fresh Water Cotton Initiative
Dr. Waqar Jehangir (Pakistan)	Water Resources Management for Sustainable Agricultural Productivity: Issues and Challenges
Babar Shahbaz (SDPI, Pakistan)	Forest Reform Process: Impact of Newly Created Institutions on Livelihood Assets in NWFP
Urs Geiser (Switzerland)	The urgency of (not necessary) policy-oriented research—The example of power devolution and natural resource management in the North West Pakistan
Faisal Shaheen (SDPI, Pakistan)	Agriculture—from public good to private asset Consequences of policy inaction in rural Pakistan
Dr Ghulam Akbar, WWF (Pakistan)	Comments
Discussion	

Concurrent Session B-4   4:15 pm – 6:00 pm

Women Workers and the Changing Labour Markets
Chair: Ch Manzoor Ahmad, MNA

Speaker	Title
Dr Ely Ercelawn (Pakistan)	Women at Work in Bondage: Unfree Labour in Pakistan
Mashuda Khatun Shefali (Bangladesh)	Women Workers in MFA to ATC Era: Empowerment Under Threat
Gloria DeSilva (Sri Lanka)	Development—at what price for women?
Dr. Rehana Siddiqui (Pakistan)	Comments
Discussion	

Concurrent Session C-4   **4:15 pm – 6:00 pm**

Population, Environment and Development
Chair: Dr. Mushtaq A. Khan (CRPRID)

Speaker	Title
Shaheen Attiqur Rehman (Pakistan)	Gender: Impact of Quality Education & Early Childhood Education
Dr Shafqat Shehzad (SDPI, Pakistan)	How can Pakistan reduce infant and child mortality rates? Lessons from other developing countries
Abdul Qadir Rafiq (Pakistan)	Poverty-Environment Nexus in the Context of Institutional Framework in Pakistan
Ali Abbas Qazilbash and Mohsin Babbar (SDPI, Pakistan)	Factors associated with Increased Suicides among Pakistani Youth: a case study of 366 attempted suicides in Sindh
Shahnaz Wazir Ali, Executive Director PCP, (Pakistan)	Comments
Discussion	

Saturday, December 13, 2003   **Day Three**

Concurrent Session A-1   **9:00 am – 10:45 am**

Women, Security and Peace
Chair: Ms. Socorro Reyes, UNDP, Islamabad

Speaker	Title
Swarna Rajagopalan (India)	Research, policy, reality: Women, security, South Asia
Gloria DeSilva (Sri Lanka)	Can women be peace builders?
Rita Thapa (Nepal)	Women in Conflict – Will Their Backs Hold?
Huma Ahmad-Ghosh (USA)	Deconstructing the Human Rights Discourse: Relevance for Afghan Women

TEA	10:45 am – 11:15 am

Concurrent Session B-1   9:00am – 10:45 am

Trade and Sustainable Development
Chair: Sartaj Aziz, Former Finance Minister (To be confirmed)

Speaker	Title
Adil Najam (USA)	Towards a Proactive Agenda for the South
David Boyer (Canada)	Capacity Building for Trade and Sustainable Development: Emerging Lessons from the Trade Knowledge Network
Shaheen Rafi Khan (SDPI, Pakistan)	Regional initiatives required to implement the agreements on Technical Barriers to Trade (TBT)
Annie Dufey (Chile)	Protection and liberalization of goods and services under the WTO
Faisal Shaheen (SDPI, Pakistan)	Market and state policy interventions to promote sustainable development
Halina Ward (UK)	Trade and Investment Linkages with Corporate Social Responsibility
Sartaj Aziz, Former Finance Minister	Comments
Discussion	
TEA	10:45 am– 11:15 am

Concurrent Session C-1   9:00 am – 10:45 am

Civil Society and Advocacy
Chair: Urs Geiser, University of Zurich, Switzerland

Speaker	Title
Sana Haroon (UK)	Social organization and the role of religion in the North - West Frontier Tribal Areas, 1915 – 1935
Arshad Bhatti (Pakistan)	Rethinking Activism, Redesigning Advocacy
Tariq Banuri (USA)	Civic Entrepreneurship
Discussion	
TEA	10:45 am – 11:15 am

Saturday, December 13, 2003	Day Three

Concurrent Session A-2	11:15 am – 1:00 pm

Refugees Issues
Chair: Philip Karani, UNHCR

Speaker	Title
Saba Khattak (SDPI, Pakistan)	Comparing Afghan Refugees and Local Population: What is to be Done?
Imtiaz Ahmad (Bangladesh)	State and Statelessness in South Asia: A Contribution to the Critique of State and Nationality
Sikandar Mehdi (Pakistan)	Pakistan and Afghan Refugees: Politics of Possession and Dispossession
Philip Karani (UNHCR)	Comments
Discussion	

LUNCH	1:00 pm – 2:00 pm

Concurrent Session B-2	11:15 pm – 1:00 pm

Food Security
Chair: German Valdiviya, Country Rep. WFP, Pakistan

Speaker	Title
Subhashini Ali (India)	Food Insecurity and its Consequences: Some Indian Experiences
Dr Abid Q. Suleri (SDPI, Pakistan)	Food Security Analysis in Pakistan
Minnie Matthew (India)	Food Security Situation: A Case Study of India
Wajid Pirzada, Chief Technical Officer, PARC (Pakistan)	Comments
Discussion	

LUNCH	1:00 pm – 2:00 pm

Concurrent Session C-2   **11:15 am – 1:00 pm**

Role of Media in Advocating Population Issues
Chair: Saleem Gul Sheikh (PEMRA)

Speaker	Title
Naseer Memon (Pakistan)	Sindhi Media - Environment and Development Coverage
Asmat Ullah (SDPI, Pakistan)	Structural-Functional Role Taxonomy of Media and Sustainable Development Campaigns
Zafarullah (Pakistan)	Coverage to Communication: Disseminating Vital Messages
Dr Syed Abdul Siraj, Chairperson Dept. of Mass Communication, AIOU, (Pakistan)	Comments

Discussion

LUNCH	1:00 pm – 2:00 pm

Saturday, December 13, 2003   **Day Three**

Concurrent Session A-3   **2:00 pm – 3:45 pm**

Forced Migration and Human Trafficking
Chair: Tariq Ali Bokhari, Ministry of Women Development:

Speaker	Title
Prof. Ishrat Shamim (Bangladesh)	Trafficking of women and children: Changing scenario and policy implications in South Asia
Salma Ali (Bangladesh)	Forced Migration and Human Trafficking
Ayesha Aftab (Pakistan)	Labour Migration and Trafficking of Women: An Insight into the Socio-Economic Implications
Dr Farhat Sheikh, TAF (Pakistan)	Comments

Discussion

TEA	3:45 pm – 4:15 pm

Concurrent Session B-3   2:00 pm– 3:45 pm

Gender (In) Justice

Chair: Dr Faqir Hussain, Secretary, Law and Justice Commission of Pakistan

Speaker	Title
Nausheen Ahmad (Pakistan)	Hudood: Still a Controversial Issue?
Anjana Raza (Pakistan)	The Mask of Honour
Subhashini Ali (India)	Honour Killings
Shaheen Sardar Ali, UK	Comments
Discussion	
TEA	3:45 pm – 4:15 pm

Concurrent Session C-3   2:00 pm – 3:45 pm

Energy Pricing in Deregulated and Liberalized Environment

Chair: Mirza Hamid Hassan, Former Secretary Water and Power

Speaker	Title
Fahd Ali (SDPI, Pakistan)	Pricing electricity from a fossil fuel power plan
Girish Sant, Prayas (India)	Electricity Pricing in India – Past and Present
Mohammad Shabbir	Energy Pricing of IPPs in Pakistan
Hussain A Babur (Pakistan)	Pricing in the De-regulated Electricity Sector – Envisaged Framework for Pakistan
Mazhar Qureshi, Hagler-Bailly (Pakistan)	Comments
Discussion	
TEA	3:45 pm – 4:15 pm

Concluding Plenary   4:15 pm – 5:30 pm

Concluding Address

Ms Shaheen Sardar Ali

Professor of Law, University of Warwick, UK; former Minister for Health, NWFP; and former Chairperson for the National Commission on the Status of Women

Mr. Tariq Banuri

Stockholm Environment Institute-Boston, USA/ePoor Organization, Pakistan

Former Executive Director, SDPI

Word of Thanks

Dr. Saba Gul Khattak

Executive Director, SDPI

TEA

Mailing Address: PO Box 2342, Islamabad, Pakistan
Telephone: ++(92-51) 2277146, 2278134, 2278136, 2270674-6 *Fax:* ++(92-51) 2278135
Street Address: #3, UN Boulevard, Diplomatic Enclave –1, G-5, Islamabad URL: www.sdpi.org
e-mail: main@sdpi.org
SDPI is an independent, non-profit research institute on sustainable development